PENGUIN BOOKS

PEOPLE OF GOD

Penny Lernoux, who was a practicing Catholic, reported from Latin America for two decades in such publications as *The Nation* and *Harper's*, and is the Latin American Affairs correspondent for the *National Catholic Reporter*. Author of *Cry of the People* and *In Banks We Trust*, she received numerous awards, both for her journalism and for her books, including the Sidney Hillman Foundation Book Award for *Cry of the People*. Penny Lernoux died in 1989.

PEOPLE OF GOD

THE STRUGGLE
FOR WORLD CATHOLICISM

✛   ✛   ✛

PENNY LERNOUX

PENGUIN BOOKS

PENGUIN BOOKS
Published by the Penguin Group
Viking Penguin, a division of Penguin Books USA Inc.,
40 West 23rd Street, New York, New York 10010, U.S.A.
Penguin Books Ltd, 27 Wrights Lane,
London W8 5TZ, England
Penguin Books Australia Ltd, Ringwood,
Victoria, Australia
Penguin Books Canada Ltd, 2801 John Street,
Markham, Ontario, Canada L3R 1B4
Penguin Books (N.Z.) Ltd, 182–190 Wairau Road,
Auckland 10, New Zealand

Penguin Books Ltd, Registered Offices:
Harmondsworth, Middlesex, England

First published in the United States of America by
Viking Penguin, a division of Penguin Books USA Inc., 1989
Published in Penguin Books 1990

1   3   5   7   9   10   8   6   4   2

LIBRARY OF CONGRESS CATALOGING IN PUBLICATION DATA
Lernoux, Penny, 1940–1989
People of God: the struggle for world Catholicism/Penny
Lernoux.
p.   cm.
Reprint. Originally published: New York: Viking, 1989.
Includes bibliographical references.
ISBN 0 14 00.9816 X
1. Christianity and politics—History—20th century.
2. Christianity and social problems—Catholic Church—History—20th
century.   3. Catholic Church—Doctrines—History—20th century.
4. Catholic Church—History—1965–   I. Title.
[BX1793.L47   1990]
282′.09′048—dc20   89–29750

Printed in the United States of America
Set in Times Roman

To a man of God—
prince of the church and
servant of the people

When you say law, I say God.
When you say peace, justice, love, I say God.
When you say God, I say liberty, justice, peace.

—DOM PEDRO CASALDÁLIGA
Bishop of São Felix, the Brazilian Amazon

ACKNOWLEDGMENTS

FIRST ACKNOWLEDGMENT MUST GO to an anonymous religious leader who encouraged me to write this book. He believes that Catholics should know more about what is happening in the church and that they should protest against Rome's authoritarian actions. I am also grateful to Tom Fox and Dawn Gibeau, the editors of the *National Catholic Reporter*, for their insights, friendship, and support.

Special thanks must go to Helen Lichtenstein, who worked untiringly on the research; to Viking editor Gerald Howard, who shaped the manuscript, and Robert Hatch, for editing; and to my family, who were so supportive throughout the work. I am also indebted to Alfred Giannantonio, who helped me complete the European research.

I am grateful to Ethel M. Gintoft, executive editor of the Milwaukee *Catholic Herald*; Father Gene Pocernich in Milwaukee; the Reverend William Wipfler of the National Council of Churches; Deborah Huntington, a Methodist writer; journalist June Erlick; Jim Wallis, editor of *Sojourners* magazine; Thomas Quigley of the U.S. Catholic Conference's Office of International Justice and Peace; the theologians Matthew Lamb and Johann Baptist Metz; Tim Harvey and Audrey Stone, who worked with me on the Latin American research; Rosa Alayza at the Centro Bartolomé de las Casas in Lima; David Molineaux, editor of *Latinamerica Press*; the Italian writer Giancarlo Zízola; and Santiago Fernández Ardanaz and Pedro Miguel Lamet of the Spanish Catholic magazine *Vida Nueva*. Thanks are also due to the Data Center in California; the Center of Concern in Washington, D.C.; Maryknoll's Justice and Peace Office; the Public Affairs Office of the Seattle archdiocese; and the IDOC documentation center in Rome.

I also owe a large debt to the many people who spoke frankly to me about the subjects in this book. They include lay people, priests, nuns, and bishops; Protestant leaders; academics; journalists; and politicians. These anonymous sources provided information and insights which form the backbone of this book.

CONTENTS

PEOPLE OF GOD

INTRODUCTION

NEARLY TWENTY-FIVE YEARS after the Second Vatican Council, or Vatican II, the Catholic Church has changed radically in many parts of the world. No longer identified with the rich and powerful, it has become a force for democracy, justice, and peace. The reforms spawned by Vatican II have not gone unchallenged, however. Since 1978, when John Paul II became pope, a counterreformation, known as the Restoration, has been in progress. Were it to succeed, Catholicism would revert to the narrowness and authoritarianism of the pre–Vatican II church.

As a Catholic observer who has lived in the Third World for nearly thirty years, I have followed developments in the church, at times in despair but mostly with optimism. The hope that a new church of the poor has given to the impoverished masses of Latin America is, in my opinion, the most significant political development in the region in recent decades. That church has also given me new faith. I thus share the pain inflicted on the church of the poor by a Eurocentric Vatican unable to perceive the needs and gifts of other cultures. I also believe that many of the commands issued by Rome have little or nothing to do with spirituality but reflect a worldly desire to retain power.

The following account of the politics of Catholicism was written in response to the urgings of Latin American, U.S., and European Catholic leaders, who felt it important to record the extent of the Vatican crackdown, along with the attempts to resist the Restoration by continuing reforms begun by Vatican II. At stake are two different visions of faith: the church of Caesar, powerful and rich, and the church of Christ—loving, poor, and spiritually rich.

PART I

ROME

CHAPTER 1

✠

THE WAY
OF THE CROSS

IN THE MISTY HIGHLANDS of northwestern Guatemala there thrives a strange and wondrous church. Most of its members are illiterate Indian peasants who earn a subsistence living from farming the grudging hillsides and by weaving palm hats. Once a week they gather to celebrate the Word of God—sometimes in hidden forest glades, depending on the extent of military persecution. In these simple ceremonies the Indians share their feelings about a reading from the Bible, reflecting on what it means to be a Christian in the midst of extreme poverty and repression. They also remember their martyrs—the children who were burned alive, the pregnant women who were bayoneted, whole families that were tortured to death by the army because a Bible was found, buried beneath the dirt floor of a hut.

Every village in this region of El Quiché has a bloody story to tell. During an eight-year reign of terror that did not begin to subside until a civilian president took office in 1986, thousands of Indians were killed or relocated to concentration camps. By the army's own count, it destroyed 440 Indian villages, some dating to pre-Columbian times. Persecution against the Catholic Church was so ferocious that not a single priest or nun remained in the Quiché diocese. All the chapels were closed, and convents were occupied by troops. In order to celebrate Communion, undercover catechists traveled hours on foot, carrying consecrated Hosts hidden among ears of corn or in baskets of beans or tortillas. Anyone caught with such "subversive material" could expect a slow death by torture. Yet the people kept faith.

Typical of Quiché's "church of the catacombs" were the five catechists of Santa Cruz El Quiché—Lucas, Justo, Angel, Domingo, and Juan—who gave their lives for their people; their moving testimony was recorded by a Spanish priest, Father Fernando Bermúdez, who worked with Quiché's underground church until death threats forced him to flee to Mexico.[1] One day in 1982, Santa Cruz, a small market town north of Chichicastenango, was taken over by the army. The villagers were assembled and told that the catechists were "subversives" whom their relatives must kill that very night. Otherwise, the army would raze Santa Cruz and neighboring villages.

The army then withdrew, and the villagers discussed the brutal choice, unanimously concluding that "we won't do it." The catechists were loved and valued for their religious work and for the instruction they had given to promote cooperatives. But such consciousness-raising was subversive in the military's view because it helped to awaken the Indian masses, a majority of Guatemala's population. Teaching Indians to read and write could be punished by death, as demonstrated by the murders of fifteen priests and a nun who were involved in literacy and leadership training programs for the Indians. The Bible was, of all books, the most subversive because it taught that everyone was equal in the sight of God—hence the ferocious persecution of catechists.

The villagers had refused to do the deed, but the five catechists insisted that they must: "It is better for us to die than for thousands to die."[2] At 4:00 A.M. a weeping procession, led by the catechists, arrived at the cemetery. Graves were dug, the people formed a circle around the kneeling men, and relatives of the five drew their machetes. Many could not watch the scene; some fainted as the blades fell, and the executioners' tears mingled with the blood of the catechists. The bodies were wrapped in plastic and buried. The villagers returned home in silence.

Next day the army captain in charge of the area was informed that his orders had been carried out. Another source of subversion had been eliminated. Or had it? Forcing the catechists' relatives to kill them was part of an army policy aimed at alienating Indian recruits from their village origins by demeaning their race, religion, and traditions. But it failed to work in Santa Cruz or elsewhere in Quiché because the people honored such martyrdom. "We remember them with holy reverence," said a witness to the catechists' deaths, "because it is thanks to them that we are alive today." Life, explained a young Guatemalan, is meaningless "unless you give it away."

In such a community of faith people fear not death, but infidelity—to one another and to their beliefs. They daily live the drama of Christ on the cross, yet they are convinced of the possibility of change because their struggle itself is a sign of resurrection. The people of Quiché's church really do believe in the Bible, particularly the command to so love one another that they are prepared to die for their communities. Though as poor and backward as the fishermen in Jesus' Galilee, they possess what many in more developed societies lack—a sense that there is a moral way of life, just as the early Christians were known as the people of "The Way." In that respect Quiché's church is not unusual in Latin America, where many such communities have sprung up in the past two decades. But in most First World settings it can only seem strange to give one's life for a religious belief.

Nevertheless, it was such a way of living faith that originally projected the Christian message, not only through actual martyrdom but in the way Christ's followers behaved. They "stood out like a sore thumb," in the words of religious scholar Michael Green,[3] because they lived their beliefs. As the Greek philosopher Aristides* described it to the Roman emperor Hadrian,

> They love one another. They never fail to help widows; they save orphans from those who would hurt them. If they have something, they give freely to the man who has nothing; if they see a stranger, they take him home, and are happy, as though he were a real brother. They don't consider themselves brothers in the usual sense, but brothers instead through the Spirit, in God.[4]

It was a love that led the churches in second-century Rome to feed 20,000 of the city's poor, not as a political strategy but as a way of following the Word. Wealth was voluntarily shared in response to Christ's call to renounce riches. Although "this unscientific primitive communism . . . was certainly not good financing," in the disapproving words of an American church historian,[5] it proved an enormously successful means of evangelization. Some joined the new religion to take advantage of such charity, and there were cases of fraud. But they were the exceptions in a church which, in its time, was unique in its unrestricted charity and compassion.

The vision was soon blurred, however, by the politics of the Roman Empire, which corrupted the church with the temptations of money and power. While the early church obviously needed a structure to survive, it made a fundamental mistake in the fourth century by adopting the Romans' legalistic hierarchy, the principal beneficiary of which was a clerical class that had not existed in the early church, a federation of

---

* Saint Aristides was the author of an early Christian apology presented to the emperor to protest anti-Christian slanders and persecutions.

small communities. After the Emperor Constantine officially recognized Christianity in 313, the state bestowed money and privilege on its leaders. Some of the clerics became extraordinarily rich, and election battles over wealthy sees not infrequently became violent; in 366 the struggle for the bishopric of Rome ended in mass murder. Although a segment of the church attempted to remain loyal to its original Christian ideals, money and power prevailed.

Throughout the Middle Ages there were periodic attempts to return to primitive Christian purity—for example, the sporadic appearance of rebellious religious orders and the religion-inspired uprisings of impoverished serfs. But their efforts were thwarted by a church-state alliance that used the Gospel for the imperial ambitions of popes and monarchs. "When the Western world accepted Christianity, Caesar conquered; and the received text of Western theology was edited by his lawyers," wrote the philosopher Alfred North Whitehead. "The brief Galilean vision of humility flickered throughout the ages, uncertainly. The deep idolatry of the fashioning of God in the image of the Egyptian, Persian, and Roman imperial rulers was retained. The church gave unto God the attributes which belonged exclusively to Caesar."[6]

Two Visions

Although Caesar's church remains a world power, a remarkable change has occurred in Catholicism since the 1960s. Throughout the Third World and in some parts of the First, believers are beginning to recapture a "Galilean vision" in which love, not power, is the key force. The principal reasons for this development are the Second Vatican Council, or Vatican II, of the early 1960s and the emergence of new political and religious challenges from the Third World.

Vatican II not only recognized that the Catholic Church is in and of this world; it also laid the groundwork for reforms that, if pursued, could revive the structure and style of the early church through greater pluralism and a respect for cultural diversity. The timing of the council was also crucial because it coincided with a historic shift in Catholicism from a West European institution to a world church. Embracing two-thirds of the globe's Christians and four-fifths of humanity, the Third World has become the dominant force in Catholicism, itself the world's largest religion. As pointed out by Catholic and Protestant theologians, the Third World's poverty is a crucial factor in this dominance. Poverty, as anyone who has suffered it can attest, is dehumanizing; at the same time, the poor have a gift recognized by Christ, who chose to proselytize among them. U.S. religious orders call it a "theology of letting go"—of being able to let go of material possessions and secular power for the good of the community and for Christ.[7] Unlike the small upper and middle classes in Latin America, the poor willingly share the little they have, as in Quiché, where peasant families often pool their rations of beans and corn. The poor would certainly welcome greater material benefits—enough to eat, a house with running water and electricity, a school for their children, and adequate medical facilities. But for the most part they have not developed the upper class's exaggerated acquisitiveness, or its desperate fear of losing its acquisitions.

While the Third World poor have little in the way of material goods, they have something that the First World has lost in the technological race—a sense of community. Although industrialization has uprooted millions from their traditional ways of life, communal relations are still strong in Latin America, Africa, and Asia because of deep loyalties to the extended family, which is the nucleus of community. Solidarity in Christ was the backbone of the early church, and it is this that gives such communities as Santa Cruz El Quiché a Galilean vision. "The Third World will continue to confront the First with what it really means to be a Christian," said Giancarlo Zízola, a popular Italian Catholic writer. "And this will enrich our faith."[8]

The need for such enrichment is attested to by countless surveys in the United States that show widespread dissatisfaction with the country's moral drift. Despite the continuing religiosity of a majority of the American people, a deep rift has developed between religious values and secular behavior. Large numbers of people feel alienated in a society that places more importance on material gain than on the personal relationships that once defined and gave meaning to life in a community. Tolerance and freedom—the trademarks of American liberalism—are "not enough for human beings to live by," argues social historian Walter Russell Mead. "Liberalism itself is incapable of providing new identities and ties to replace those which are lost; it leaves a society composed of lonely, isolated individuals. The resulting alienation and despair can end up being profoundly subversive of the tolerance and freedom created by liberalism. People turn, individually and en masse, to religious cults, revivals or to virtually any ideology that offers the prospect of positive values."[9]

In the 1980s, when many Americans found an answer to such alienation in fundamentalist religion, others experienced a radical recreation of faith through witness in the community, an example being the Sanctuary movement—itself a response to suffering refugees from Guatemala and El Salvador. While many churches were torn between these two quite different visions of faith, the impact on the Catholic Church was particularly significant, not only because of its numerical strength—with 53 million believers it is the largest church in the United States—but also because of the considerable political power wielded by the Vatican.

Under the influence of Vatican II and sister churches in the Third World, particularly in Latin America, the U.S. bishops had begun to take a more prophetic stance, challenging the Reagan administration on such issues as its Central American policy, nuclear warfare, and economic policy, and encouraging greater pluralism in the church. But just when these initiatives were beginning to bear fruit, Pope John Paul II intervened in an attempt to force the U.S. church back into the pre–Vatican II mold of an authoritarian institution that demanded unquestioning obedience to Rome's commands. The pope also insisted that Catholic government officials adhere to church teachings, even when these would negate civil laws. The attempted rollback, part of a worldwide attack on increasingly independent churches, strengthened President Reagan's hand by undercutting the most outspoken American bishops, particularly in regard to the arms buildup, and by providing support for his policies in Central America and elsewhere. When William Wilson, Reagan's first ambassador to the Vatican, claimed that "a parallelism in viewpoints" existed between Washington and Rome, he wasn't exaggerating: John Paul made much the same claim to a group of cardinals during a meeting in Rome for the preparation of the 1985 synod to review Vatican II.[10]

While Washington can inflict enormous material damage on other countries, the Vatican is capable of even worse harm in areas where Catholicism is the dominant religion, such as Latin America. Arms and money can wear down resistance, but not destroy it if the impoverished masses believe that God is on their side—the essential message of liberation theology. But Rome can damage, even destroy, the religious leaders who have given the people a new faith in themselves.

A Global Phenomenon

The "Roman winter" is part of a worldwide resurgence of religious fundamentalism. In the United States, fundamentalism is often associated with the movement of born-again Christians who believe in the inerrancy of the Bible and the doctrine of creationism, but it is not limited to the United States or to certain Protestant churches. It is a recurrent phenomenon in history, particularly in times of cultural stress when traditional values are challenged by political, economic, and social changes. The violent upheavals in Iran make evident the explosive potential of religious fundamentalism—as do the bombings of abortion clinics in the United States. Regardless of theological differences, religious fundamentalists share certain characteristics, such as a reverence for authority and a fear of secularization—or "secular humanism," as the Vatican and U.S. evangelicals call it. They also insist that they alone possess the truth, and they usually align themselves with the political right. In the United States they have been called the New Right to distinguish them from traditional forms of political and religious conservativism.

Among the New Right's activists are fundamentalist Catholics who yearn for an "old-time religion," found today chiefly in the Polish pope's homeland, and who have made common cause with Reagan's evangelical supporters and the Roman Curia in the attack on liberal Catholic leaders. But that they are pushing against the tide is shown by numerous surveys revealing a desire for greater liberalization, particularly in the areas of sexual behavior and lay participation in church administration.

The "Restoration," as John Paul's supporters call the return to Roman law and order, parallels a renewed assertiveness by the largely reactionary Curia—the church's Roman court and central government. Like most bureaucracies, the Curia aims to maintain its power, which was weakened by the papacies of John XXIII and Paul VI. John Paul's Vatican longs for the past; the pope wishes to restore an authoritarian church model based on that of the Middle Ages, when the state and its institutions were uniformly Catholic and there was a patriarchal ordering of the sexes. As the pope told a Polish audience in 1979, "To deserve the name at all, a civilization must be a Christian [read Catholic] civilization." The pope, being politically astute, appeals to modern concerns in his speeches on human rights, social justice, and religious liberty, but the Vatican's failure to live up to his brave words has robbed them of substance. As the 1971 Roman synod recognized, "Anyone who ventures to speak to people about justice must first be just in their eyes. Hence, we must undertake an examination of the modes of acting . . . found within the church itself."[11]

The critical issue, recognized by both papal supporters and critics, is the unfinished business of Vatican II. Not a few church historians believe that the council was convened in the nick of time. By letting the cork out of the bottle, John XXIII reduced the explosive tensions in the church over authority and power. Vatican II did not resolve basic questions about power-sharing among the bishops, pluralism among churches of diverse cultures, or the role of the laity or women. But it did point the way, and that in itself was an emormous contribution, given the Vatican's traditional rigidity. The church was moving gingerly along this new path when John Paul appeared and ordered it to retreat. Vatican II had been misinterpreted, asserted Cardinal Joseph Ratzinger, head of the Vatican's Congregation for the Doctrine of the Faith, a latter-day version of the Inquisition, and any who thought otherwise should leave. Local churches soon felt the lash. Some, like the Dutch church, were seriously wounded, but others, including the Latin Americans and the Americans, fought back, each in their own way. So there was a standoff of sorts.

But not for long. While the Vatican was mulling over new tactics to deal with the rebellious Third World churches, they were immersing themselves in the reality of their peoples, joining in popular uprisings and producing new theologies that challenged Roman hegemony, not least because Rome produced nothing itself. Ratzinger believed that pluralism threatened the church, but that, said the French Dominican Marie-Dominique Chenu, one of the theological stars of Vatican II, was "utter nonsense." "Uniformity is a caricature of unity. Unity implies diversity. Today pluralism is necessary for theology and for pastoral work. I think the new churches of the Third World should have autonomy."[12]

Pluralism—or diversity in unity—is the unfinished business of Vatican II. The authoritarianism of the Catholic Church derives from its secular history, not from its roots in the early Christian communities. They attracted followers not by ordering them, like Ratzinger, to toe the line, but by a persuasive message of love. Bishop Kenneth E. Untener of Saginaw, Michigan, said he worried about the "prevailing wind [of] corporate severity" because it reflected a return to the unforgiving, narrow-mindedness of Caesar's church. As an example, he cited John's Gospel account of Jesus forgiving an adulteress, a story that was missing, he said, from early Greek manuscripts because the church "hushed it up," lest Jesus appear to have been soft on sin. "The more severe the church became in its discipline—and this happened very early—the more difficult it became to tell a story like this about Jesus."[13]

"Back to an apostolic church!" has been the call since the 1200s to return to a collegial or pluralistic church. It cannot be silenced by h handed discipline. Moreover, world communications and scholarship advanced to the point where it is no longer possible to deny that R has usurped many powers belonging to the bishops and that it has those powers for a highly questionable ecclesiastical *Realpolitik*. T John Paul chose to protect the Vatican Bank's American director, Ar bishop Paul Marcinkus, despite his dealings with Italian wheeler-dealer connected to the Sicilian mafia, only adds to the widespread impression that the Vatican is more concerned with self-preservation than with the loving message of Christ. Similarly, Rome's close identification with the Reagan administration's policies, particularly in Latin America, has cost it considerable credibility in the world's most populous Catholic continent. The churches need to "demythologize" the Vatican and the papacy, said Bishop Thomas J. Gumbleton of Detroit. "It is a human instrument that can do evil just like any other human instrument."[14]

Many church analysts believe that progress toward a Christ-centered church—toward the vision of Galilee—will continue, but at a slower pace for the duration of John Paul's reign. In some countries a reversal may occur through the ongoing appointment of conservative bishops, yet there is an inevitability in the forward march, just as there was at the end of the Middle Ages when the invention of printing enabled people to read the Bible—previously held to be the prerogative of the clergy. The use of the vernacular in the Mass and the growing literacy of Third World peoples have had an irrevocable effect on millions of Catholics who have rediscovered Jesus. Attempts to drag them back to a doctrinaire, ritualistic, but spiritually empty church will not work, warn theologians and lay leaders, but only encourage secular disaffection and conversion to the fundamentalist churches.[15]

The tragedy of John Paul is that, with all his many gifts, he has lacked the one most needed at a time when the church is changing from a European to a world institution—the ability to listen. "The trouble is that the Pope places much more of a priority on how the church should be organized," said Otto Maduro, a prominent Venezuelan Catholic writer. "If he put more emphasis on the society he wants, or even on the way the church should move to bring about the society he wants, he would probably understand that the church has to change. Not even thinking in terms of liberation theology; just thinking in terms of a moderate, liberal, democratic capitalist outlook, the church would have to change along the lines of Vatican II." The Italian writer, Giancarlo Zizola, was yet more vere: "The pretension to reduce all that is human to Christianity, all Christianity to the Catholic Church and the whole church to a 'Polish model' suggests to even the most impartial viewers that the church is determined at any cost to make one of the worst mistakes in its history, by ignoring the spiritual needs of society, abandoning post-modern man to his solitude and denying the possibility of helping the future of humanity through the message of the Gospel—a church, in sum, that runs the danger of fulfilling Ratzinger's fear of being reduced to a sect."[16]

A Crossroads

The following chapters of this book describe the politics of this divided church and their impact on politics in the First and Third Worlds, particularly the United States and Latin America. They also show how the opposing visions of faith affect social values. In El Quiché, for example, where faith is daily lived in community, people are prepared to give their most precious gift—their lives—for their brothers and sisters, whereas in the United States, said layman John A. McDermott, many Catholics go to church for worship, family, or tradition, but do not yet see in the church "an organizing principle for their whole lives."[17] Yet that the seeds are there is shown by the increasing number of Jesus-centered Catholics and by the spontaneous development of such ecumenical movements as Sanctuary, which came into being not because of directives from the religious higher-ups but because of the religious convictions of a radical community of believers, Republicans and Democrats, Catholics, Protestants, and Jews. No one in Sanctuary has been tortured or killed for such beliefs, in contrast to the suffering of the underground church communities in Guatemala, but some have been put on trial and gone to jail. In the American context that takes guts, but guts—the courage to be different for Jesus' sake—was what the early Christian church was about. Through such courageous witness do people call their communities to the transcendental values that offer hope of a better world.

CHAPTER 2
✠
THE REAWAKENING

IN THE EARLY CHRISTIAN ART of the catacombs Jesus Christ was portrayed as a beardless, kindly looking, and youthful shepherd—a leader who encouraged love and earned confidence. But with the rise of the church of Constantine in the fourth century his image changed to a rigid iconographic emperor, bearded and of stern mien, who inspired awe and commanded obedience. Although later artists depicted Christ in many different styles, the early images bespeak the millennial duality of a church divided between humility and power. While the Christ of the New Testament was a man of the people who spurned secular power and riches, through the ages his message has often been confused by its identification with the political and social institutions of the time. Under the Emperor Constantine, for example, Christian theology was adapted to suit the Roman Empire's imperial ideology: "One God, one Logos, one emperor, one empire," in the words of the Constantinian court bishop, Eusebius of Caesarea. Church and state thus became indistinguishable and would remain so until the Enlightenment in the eighteenth century. The Protestant Reformation, though it challenged papal rule, did not attack church-state alliances, since many of the new churches depended on the protection of the European princes, who in turn used Christianity as a means of expanding their secular power.

Throughout Christianity's history there have been calls to return to a Christ-centered church. Even Saint Augustine, the prophet of the imperial church, worried about the corrupting effects of worldly power on Christianity. From the 300s onward, church councils were held in almost every century to reform a corrupt clergy and an absolutist papacy, but while some practices changed or were abolished, many church leaders continued to act like the Pharisees whom Jesus scorned: "These people honor me with their lips, but their hearts are far from me." Efforts at renewal drove the institutional church deeper into its shell, inevitably making the major periods in Catholic history, such as the Counter-Reformation and the Counter-Enlightenment, times of reaction. Along

the way scholars and saints were rejected, even martyred, by the institution, and the original ideal of the papacy as an office of service and
testament was distorted by an imperial Roman court of worldly office
seekers.

During the fifteenth century, when the Renaissance was in flower,
the bishops tried to challenge papal power at councils held in the cities
of Constance and Basel which established the supremacy of the body of
bishops over the pope and laid the groundwork for a more equitable
sharing of power. But the initiative failed, largely because of the allegiance
of the temporal powers to Rome. The papacy, in turn, became more
beholden to the European aristocracy, particularly after the Protestant
revolt. In contrast to the Middle Ages, when the church dominated the
state, powerful monarchies, particularly in Spain and France, gained control over local churches through a system of patronage that gave the
crown the right to appoint bishops and collect tithes. A variation of the
system still functions in some countries, particularly in Latin America,
through a concordat, or treaty, with the Vatican that bestows official
favor on Catholicism, extending even to the teaching of that religion in
public schools. Until recently the quid pro quo was government approval
of bishops' appointments.

The consequences for modern Catholicism of centuries of authoritarianism were twofold. One was the juridical primacy of the papacy over
the bishops, which culminated in the First Vatican Council in 1869. Vatican I declared the pope infallible in matters of faith and reversed the
tradition of local election of bishops by centralizing such power in the
Vatican. By the twentieth century Roman power was juridically absolute,
even though it did not correspond to the original apostolic vision. Absolute power encouraged popes to behave like absolute monarchs, although in fact their secular power was limited by that of the nation-states.
Not until the advent of John XXIII in 1958 did the church begin to
recapture the earlier ideal of papal power as a charismatic service that
owed its ultimate legitimacy not to secular tradition or theological interpretations but to the testament of Christ and the Twelve Apostles. Pope
John caught the world's imagination because, like Christ, he wanted to
"guard the sheep" with unselfish love.[1] Catholics and non-Catholics were
inspired by his message because he represented the spirit of the Gospels,
not the entrenched and worldly interests of the Vatican.

A second consequence of authoritarianism was the failure of the
church to serve as society's conscience. Cynical alliances were made with

temporal powers in order to preserve the church's privileges, a recent example being the Catholic Church's record in Nazi Germany. Although Catholicism was not the only Christian church to engage in such politics, for most of its history it served as a bulwark *against* social and political change, including democracy and a respect for human rights. While the reforms brought about by Vatican II have helped to overcome the idea that God is directly involved in politics through his personal representative in the papacy, some reactionaries, particularly in the Roman Curia, cling to the old order of "integralism," which denies the separation of church and state.

The belief in the "perfect society" of a political-religious Christendom stems from the Middle Ages when the church was the guardian of civil and religious institutions. By the time of the Renaissance, however, believers, particularly in the educated classes, had begun to resist a clerical caste. Erasmus, one of the great Christian humanists of the period, argued for a more Christ-centered church, one more concerned with community and values than with splitting theological hairs. "You will not be damned if you do not know whether the Spirit proceeding from the Father and the Son had one or two beginnings," he said, "but you will not escape damnation if you do not cultivate the fruits of the spirit: love, joy, peace, patience, kindness, goodness, long-suffering, mercy, faith, modesty, continence and chastity."[2] Erasmus—like the post–Vatican II church—did not believe that clerics had an authoritative answer to all of life's questions. And he wanted to restore the papacy's moral authority by depoliticizing it. But since political authority was the bedrock of church power, whereby a clerical class placed itself above ordinary men and women, his ideas were anathema in Rome. Protestant dissidents, while sharing Erasmus's desire for moral reform, insisted on imposing their own uniformity and institutions, and they, too, parted company with the liberal churchman. The Renaissance vision of a common spiritual heritage in Christ flickered and died, leaving an unbridgeable gap between Catholic and Protestant Europe.

Many religious wars later, when Europe was exhausted from fighting, Erasmus's ideas emerged again through the influence of some of the leading scholars of the Enlightenment, including the English philosopher John Locke and the French writers Blaise Pascal and Voltaire. Locke argued for the need for truth, or the test of reason, in religion. He did not deny God's existence but believed, like Erasmus, that Christianity had been cluttered by questionable dogmas, and he urged a return to essential Christian beliefs. His political outlook also influenced his religious opinions. Religion was a voluntary association, he argued, and governments should not force believers to accept a particular church, since the "care of each man's salvation belongs only to himself." Religious authoritarianism would decline, he believed, if members were allowed to have a say in the churches' direction and the emphasis were changed from dogma to moral practice.

While Locke's rational, utilitarian Christianity appealed to an emerging capitalist society, it posed the risk of reducing religion to secular ethics or a mechanical Christianity that ignored the mystery and emotion of religion. Pascal, while he also supported reason and opposed the corrupt authoritarianism of the papacy, believed in a mystical faith that could provide a true understanding of the universe and its meaning to humanity. He argued that reason, being human, could not supply all the answers and hence could not replace the belief in God. "We come to know truth," he said, "not only by reason, but still more so through our hearts." An austere scholar who lived like a monk, Pascal did not subscribe to the generally optimistic outlook of the Enlightenment, which emphasized the liberation of humanity from ignorance, tyranny, and superstition by means of science and reason. Future generations, he warned, were as likely to act as irrationally as those in the past.

Voltaire brought English ideas on philosophy and science to France. His disdain for organized religion—"If God did not exist, he would have to be invented"—led to a lifelong dedication to justice for victims of religious persecution. Although he believed that Christianity was necessary for social cohesion, he hated the Catholic Church's arbitrariness. His feelings were shared by the masses, who were ground down by court and clergy. The ostentation of some of the French religious orders—costly meals on silver plates, splendid horses and carriages, and frequent card parties and concerts—was a source of continuing scandal. "There were more coffee-pots and tea-sets, snuff boxes and knick-knacks on their tables than books of theology," said one observer of a local monastery.[3] When the French Revolution occurred, clerics as well as aristocrats were sent to the guillotine.

The revolution in France, England's earlier revolt against the papacy, and the influence of the Enlightenment put an end to the concept of Christendom as a total society and gave rise to the modern secular state. The division was formally sealed in 1795 when the separation of church and state was decreed in France. Contrary to the doomsayers, the Catholic

Church gained renewed vigor from the revolutionary fallout, which weakened its traditional patrons in Europe. Even the nonbelieving Napoleon came to reconcile himself to the papacy, in part to persuade his skeptical European peers that he believed in God but also because of his discovery that Catholicism was a useful means of social control. Napoleon's conviction that belief in an afterlife helped the poor to accept their unequal lot was the cynical side of Pascal's mystical vision: However scandalous the behavior of church representatives, Christianity continued to offer hope and a spiritual salve for suffering. Though bloodied and distorted, the memory of Christ survived.

Modern integralists see an unbroken line from the Renaissance and the Reformation to the Enlightenment, culminating in the French Revolution and twentieth-century communism. The fall of Christendom is thus attributed to the accumulated evils of liberalism. But the theory is full of historic holes, not least because it assumes that one development automatically triggered another and that all were caused by man's sinful rejection of Mother Church. Nor is it clear, as the integralists claim, that events in France were disastrous for the church (the trend toward a separation of church and state was evident elsewhere in any case). The Revolution helped sweep away institutions that had a negative effect on the church, including the hated Inquisition, and hastened the end of the ecclesiastical princedoms in Germany, which had stood between the Catholic masses and the papacy. Though originally opposed by Rome, the wars of independence in Latin America, which were inspired by the French Revolution and encouraged by French occupation of Spain, opened up that vast region to direct penetration by the Vatican. Local churches, which previously had been pawns of the Spanish crown, reported directly to Rome, although there were frequent instances of interference by the republican governments in the selection of prelates and the establishment of local church policy. By the time of the First Vatican Council, in the late 1860s, the church had regained international power, which was reflected in the decree of an infallible papacy.

While the First World War and the Depression changed society dramatically, a succession of popes still looked firmly backward to the integralist ideal of a Christendom united under Rome. War and other evils, they said, had been inflicted on a world that had denied a Catholic rule. Although twentieth-century popes occasionally acknowledged the world's direction, such as in relatively progressive statements on economics, they took the aristocracy's attitude toward the lower classes. A classless society was unnatural, they believed, and class violence was godless communism and satanic. The Vatican not only allied itself with politically reactionary groups but in some countries, such as France and Italy, actively promoted them. American democracy was an aberration, they believed, because of the divorce of church and state, and Catholics should "prefer to associate with Catholics," thus avoiding liberal contamination. Anything that smacked of liberalism, from the Renaissance to modern Catholic scholarship, was treated as an atheistic conspiracy. Under Pius X, in the early 1900s, persecution of Catholic historians and other scholars was so intense that the entire church reverberated with fear.

During the reign of Pius XII (1939–58) the arrogance of the Vatican reached its apex, reflected in its religious absolutism and the law of the imperial church. An Italian aristocrat, Pius was totally autocratic and utterly confident of the papacy's God-given rights. Like his predecessors, he longed for a return to the Middle Ages when "men had a clear consciousness of . . . what was allowable and what was forbidden." He was unable to see that the church had contributed to the shaping of society, with all its evils, or that his failure to denounce Nazism had played into Hitler's hands.

The 1950s, when Rome was simultaneously engaged in the Cold War and in a struggle against postwar religious liberalism, was a painful time for many Catholics. American Catholics, better educated and more affluent than their immigrant forebears, rebelled against Rome's absolutism, particularly its sexual taboos. Many also objected to the church's intellectual narrowness—the Index of forbidden books, the banning of slightly progressive Catholic publications, and attacks on such films as The Moon Is Blue, which in hindsight seem only mildly irreverent. Religious practice was often mechanical, with emphasis on parroted catechisms and a ritualistic devotion to saints and relics. Questioning was discouraged, and Catholics either submitted to the church's rule or left— which many did. Author Richard Gilman, describing an unctuous and overbearing priest whose only solutions to his marital problems were "platitudes and rote advice," captures the smug authoritarianism of the period.[4] Like so many others, Gilman drifted away from an institution that preferred admonition to compassion.

In Europe the revulsion against a right-wing papacy cost the church most of the working class, while youth rebelled against Catholicism's sexual and intellectual strictures. In the Third World the impoverished masses continued to observe the rituals of a fatalistic religion, never understanding the hope of the Resurrection. Bishops and priests adhered to the old patterns, through political alliances with the upper classes. Yet the walls of Rome were beginning to give a little, thanks to the then little-known struggles of European theologians and the weight of world opinion.

Aggiornamento

When John XXIII announced his intention to convoke the Second Vatican Council a mere three months after assuming the papacy, the Roman Curia was stunned. The elderly Italian had been chosen in 1958 as a transitional figurehead between papacies and was not expected to make waves. Instead, he boldly confronted the church with *aggiornamento*—a "bringing up-to-date."

Throughout the council (1962–65) bishops spoke of the unexpected presence of the "Holy Spirit," which had helped to turn the church toward the world—though in fact the world had been clamoring at the church's doors for decades. Church scholars, particularly in Europe, had waged a guerrilla war against the Vatican since the early 1900s, and by the start of the 1960s many bishops privately agreed that things had to change. John's great gift to the church was his ability to read the signs of the times. A historian with a strong background in pastoral work, he had been on the blacklist of Pius X for his suspected liberal tendencies, and it was not until after World War II and the death of the autocratic Pius XII that he was able to place his humanistic mark on the church. Unlike his predecessors, John believed that the church not only could not afford to continue in "holy isolation," but that it had been guilty itself of temporal errors. Being a human institution, it was capable of human failings, one of which was its refusal to join the world in its search for a more just social, political, and economic order. John did not want the council to revert to the usual theological nitpicking, since basic questions of faith were not at issue. He was concerned primarily about "the way faith is presented"—the same concern that had been expressed through the centuries in the call to return to a Christ-centered church. Like earlier reformers, he felt the best way to recapture that vision was through service and love, not authoritarianism, and he expressed that belief by his support for a sharing of authority with the bishops and for democracy in civil society.

The Curia did its best to forestall the council and, when that failed, to sabotage it by writing council documents that reaffirmed the power of the imperial church. But though unable to stop the sniping, John set the tone of the meeting in his opening speech, when he exhorted the bishops to cease being prophets of doom and to offer the world the medicine of mercy. He also made the council genuinely ecumenical by inviting other churches to send observers. Perhaps most important, John encouraged the bishops to reach back into church history, to the councils at Constance and Basel in the fifteenth century and to the early church, and thereby reestablish the principle of shared authority with all the church's members. These ideas were expressed in the biblical phrase "People of God"—a community of believers moving forward with humanity in the search for a better world, all sharing in the responsibilities delegated by Christ. Although many aspects of the council have since been forgotten, "People of God" has become part of the Catholic vocabulary.

The council's achievements were extraordinary. Bishops were given greater liberty, the laity more participation in the church. Latin was replaced by the vernacular, and respect for religious freedom and cultural diversity was a key issue in the council documents. The council also stressed Catholicism's special concern for the poor and committed the church to a dialogue with the world and other religions.

The two great documents of Vatican II were the *Dogmatic Constitution on the Church* and the *Pastoral Constitution on the Church in the Modern World,* although the texts on the bishops and religious freedom were also important in prying open the Vatican gates. The writing of the *Dogmatic Constitution* demonstrated the opposing forces at work within the institution and the new understanding of the church's role that emerged from dialogue within the council. The original text, which had been prepared by the Curia, was rejected as triumphalistic, outdated, polemical, and too juridical. Council debates led to new drafts that were more biblical, historical, and pastoral in tone. Thanks to Pope John's intervention, attempts by the curialists to use procedural devices to derail the process were defeated. The final text, approved by the overwhelming majority of the 2,156 delegates, bears the clear mark of *aggiornamento.*[5]

As in other Vatican II documents, the emphasis in the *Dogmatic Constitution* is on service, not authoritarianism, the principal values being witness, ministry, and fellowship. "Christ Jesus," said the document, "though he was by nature God, emptied himself, taking the nature of a slave, and 'being rich, he became poor' for our sakes. Thus, although the church needs human resources to carry out her mission, she is not set up to seek earthly glory, but to proclaim humility and self-sacrifice, even by her own example."

While the *Dogmatic Constitution* deals primarily with how the church sees itself, the *Church in the Modern World,* as its name implies, is a pastoral reflection on relations with the world. Had it been left to the Curia, the document would never have been written. But the bishops felt a need to break out of "holy isolation" by addressing questions of importance to humanity, including economic and social life, political pluralism, human rights, and world peace. The council admitted that the church did not have "the solution to particular problems" but expressed its desire to work with all those of goodwill, including other religions and nonbelievers. While repeatedly expressing a desire to serve humanity, the council said that the church did not want "privileges offered by civil authority" and was prepared to renounce even legitimate rights when their use might "cast doubt on the sincerity of her witness." In other words, there was to be no return to a medieval Christendom.

The roughest battles were over a sharing of power among the papacy, bishops, and laity, and over the bishops' demand for an overhaul of the authoritarian, Italian-dominated Curia. Although the council reaffirmed the papacy's special role as the "rock of unity" of faith and fellowship, it partially restored the power balance by reasserting the importance of the bishops as a body—what is known as "collegiality." The council spoke frequently of a church government in which bishops and the pope worked together, in contrast to centralized Roman rule. It also gave strong encouragement to local bishops' conferences, which were described as "nearly indispensable," and established an advisory council, or synod, of bishops that was to meet at regular intervals and, it was hoped, might evolve into a permanent parliament with legislative functions.

Lay Catholics also received recognition as belonging to the "common priesthood of the faithful," which, while differing from the hierarchical priesthood, was nevertheless an integral part of "the priesthood of Christ." In cases where ordained priests were not available, said the council documents, lay Christians could provide valuable services, including "sacred services." Bishops and priests should encourage lay participation in the church and accept positive criticism.

While Vatican II weakened Roman rule and the clerical class, it was by no means a death blow. Paul VI, who succeeded John when the council was still in progress, supported the liberal majority on most issues, and he subsequently reorganized the Curia to give it a more international cast. But in several key matters, including birth control and the naming of bishops, he followed the established Roman pattern of denying change. Despite the urging of his own advisory commission against a denunciation of artificial contraception, as well as the warnings of the council fathers that a "no" would lead to a new "Galileo affair," Paul felt compelled to uphold the church's existing stand on the issue. *Humanae Vitae,* his encyclical on the subject, alienated large sectors of moderate and progressive Catholic opinion. On the other side of the spectrum, conservative Catholics complained loudly about the change from a Latin to a vernacular Mass. Some blamed the backlash on a crisis of leadership, charging Paul with weakness. But with hindsight—and the succession to the papacy of a Polish absolutist—Paul's willingness to balance different pressures through compromise has come to be seen as a virtue, and one that is sorely missed.

A Roman Spring

Despite ongoing skirmishes between local churches and the Vatican, the council provided substantial support for Catholic renewal. Liturgical reform, greater emphasis on the Bible, and increased lay participation in church life gave real meaning to the "People of God." National churches showed a greater willingness to listen to the laity, and pluralism in the church and in society was encouraged. Paul VI continued the spirit of *aggiornamento* in such writings as *On the Development of Peoples* (*Populorum Progressio*) and his letter *Octogesima Adveniens,* which placed the church on the side of the weak, particularly the Third World poor. His statements also underlined the church's break with the past by insisting that, because of the poverty and discrimination suffered by a majority of the world's people, the church "cannot plead for the status quo." He also rejected Catholic identification with any political party or ideology, since there could be no direct tie between a "political option and the Gospel." The Roman synods of bishops in 1971 and 1974 continued these themes by urging transformation of unjust economic and political systems and by committing the church to a respect for freedom of expression and other human rights in the church itself.

Although the Americans and the Latin Americans had not played an important role at Vatican II,* their churches were among those most

---

* One of the jokes at the time of Vatican II was that the American bishops had so little understanding of collegiality that when the subject first came up, Boston's Cardinal Richard Cushing was reported to have told the pope, "Let me know where you want this college, and I'll build it." (*National Catholic Reporter,* October 9, 1987)

immediately affected. The council's support for bishops' conferences energized the American conference, which became increasingly outspoken on international as well as domestic issues of moral concern. Consultation with the laity gradually became customary in the preparation of episcopal pronouncements, drawing Catholic society into a debate on their country's role in the world. Changes in Catholic education, church administration, and rituals encouraged greater interest in the Bible and a more Christ-centered church, at the same time that priests and nuns became increasingly involved in issues of justice and peace. Efforts were made to reach out to those in the Catholic community who had been hurt or confused by the church's earlier authoritarianism. Tolerance for other religions as well as for dissent against church teachings on birth control became the order of the day. In contrast to the church of Pius XII, when much energy was expended on admonitions against eating meat on Friday or the sins that would land a person in purgatory, the post–Vatican II church in the United States was primarily concerned with charity, justice, and community.

The council's impact on Latin America was even more dramatic. A traditionally reactionary institution wedded to the upper classes, the Latin American church had begun to change in the 1950s, particularly in Brazil, Chile, and Peru, where more liberal prelates were disturbed by the marked inequalities in their societies. Under their influence and that of Vatican II the Latin American bishops shifted their allegiance to the poor at a historic hemisphere meeting in 1968 in the Colombian city of Medellín. Taking their cue from Paul VI, who traveled to Bogotá to open the meeting, they urged a transformation of Latin American society through long-delayed reforms, including land and income redistribution and greater participation by the masses in political life. The bishops denounced the "institutionalized violence" of oligarchic rule as a social sin and urged the formation of popular movements that would promote the political and spiritual liberation of the poor, as well as greater self-reliance. The church's preferential option for the poor,* which was recon-

---

* A "preferential option for the poor" does not exclude the middle or upper classes but means that those most in physical need are given special attention by the church, not only through its charitable works but also through its public pronouncements as, for example, on just wages or land redistribution. While such an option clearly has political and economic implications, it is also based on the Old Testament's mandates to help the needy and on Christ's own life, which was dedicated to proselytism among the poor.

firmed eleven years later at a similar meeting in Puebla, Mexico, brought
on decades of martyrdom for the church in Latin America, including the
imprisonment, torture, and assassination of more than a thousand bishops, priests, and nuns. Yet it also occasioned an intellectual and spiritual
flowering within the Third World's largest Catholic Church. Among the
most important results were the development of liberation theology, with
its emphasis on the emancipation of the poor and oppressed; the growth
of educational techniques that used the Bible for consciousness-raising;
and the appearance of tens of thousands of "base communities" of poor
people who sought to change society through Christian witness.

The reformist spirit of Vatican II was also felt in other Third World
countries, where hierarchy and laity, encouraged by the new emphasis
on local leadership, began to develop their own theological responses,
rituals more in keeping with local customs, and community organizations
that often gave the poor their first genuine experience of democracy. Like
the Latin Americans, the African and Asian churches supported social
reforms and in some countries were in the forefront of struggles against
dictatorships.

A Spirit

The "spirit of Vatican II," as it came to be known, pointed to a more
pluralistic, lay-oriented church, and in many places, particularly in the
Third World, the "spirit" prevailed, despite attempts by the Curia and
John Paul II to restore papal domination. But the optimism that had
characterized the Catholic leadership in the 1960s was gradually replaced
by a pragmatic realization that further changes would come slowly and
that the reformists would have to fight to maintain advances already
gained.

The main obstacle to change was, and still is, the institutional machinery. The council fathers had expected that the synods instituted by
Vatican II would eventually share in papal decisions and that national
bishops' conferences would play a significantly larger role in the church,
the Curia a less pervasive one. But no mechanism was established to give
juridical weight to such reforms or to return the election of bishops and
other powers to local churches. The centralized bureaucracy had proved
to be a strong counterforce to change even during the papacies of John
and Paul. Under John Paul II it regained much of its lost influence. By
the time of the synod on the laity in 1987, for example, synods had become

little more than papal rubber stamps, national bishops' conferences were under attack, and pluralism was a forbidden word—at least in Rome. Yet elsewhere the seeds of Vatican II continued to bear fruit. All roads did not lead to Rome, local churches discovered, because Catholicism in the crucial decades after Vatican II had become a global institution and its needs and hopes outweighed the interests of a European bureaucracy or the inertia of tradition.

As John XXIII had said, the important thing was the way faith was expressed. The Vatican might cause local bishops considerable anguish, but down at the base believers continued to develop their vision of a "People of God," regardless of Roman politics. An explosion of faith was occurring around the globe because people had rediscovered the memory of Jesus, and that was something they were unlikely to forfeit.

CHAPTER 3

✝

THE CATHOLIC COUNTERREFORMATION

IN JANUARY 1979, when the Catholic Church was still in a state of shock over the untimely death of Pope John Paul I, his tall, white-haired Polish successor arrived in Mexico to open the third hemisphere conference of bishops. The meeting offered the world its first opportunity to take the measure of John Paul II, and thousands of journalists flocked to Mexico to cover the event. A pope in Catholic Latin America automatically draws crowds, but John Paul was a star in his own right. The Mexican peasants saw in his commanding presence a literal incarnation of God, while even the most skeptical were charmed by his graciousness and willingness to join with the crowds in singing, clapping, and dancing. Skier, poet, and intellectual, this virile man with ruddy cheeks and a ready smile seemed destined to make a mark on the world.

The question was, what kind of mark? Although the answer should have been plain even in those early days of John Paul's papacy, few, if any, saw it. The signals were confusing and open to different interpretations; and the problem was compounded because many of the pope's speeches were couched in Vaticanese, the baroque and often obscure language of the Roman Curia. Thus John Paul was reported to have condemned the Latin Americans' liberation theology, though he had not. He was hailed as their champion by church progressives because of his outspoken defense of human rights, while conservatives claimed him as one of their own when he admonished priests and nuns to stay out of politics and to obey their bishops. Their responsibility was different, he said, explaining that the church should be a "teacher of the truth. . . . Not a human and rational truth, but the truth that comes from God, the truth that brings with it the principle of the authentic liberation of man."[1]

John Paul's seemingly contradictory message was to be repeated in dozens of other countries during his ceaseless travels around the globe. Seven years later in Colombia, for example, he would say much the same things about the needs of the poor for a just wage, sufficient land, and other basic rights while again cautioning against the political and social activism of priests and nuns in helping the poor to secure such rights. "Contradictory, generalized and revolutionary" were how a local columnist described John Paul's twenty-eight speeches in Colombia. The same words had been used at the time of his Mexican sojourn. In journalistic circles the pope became known as the "Wojtyla Enigma"; there was even a book with that title.

As John Paul settled into his reign, however, the contradictions began to resolve themselves. Pope watchers agreed that he was progressive on economic issues and a strong defender of human rights, but conservative on religious matters. While true, the description was too simple for so complex a man. How, for example, did one reconcile his championship of the rights of humanity with his denial of the rights of the members of his own church? For John Paul there was no inconsistency in such a stand, and he maintained it before and after becoming pope, most notably at the Second Vatican Council, which he attended while archbishop of Krakow. As noted by the French theologian Marie-Dominique Chenu, one of the theological stars of Vatican II, the record of the proceedings in the council committee responsible for the key document, *Dogmatic Constitution on the Church,* showed that Archbishop Wojtyla had opposed a definition of the church as the "People of God." Wojtyla envisioned not a church of the people but a "perfect society" in which laity worked under the direction of priests and bishops to achieve the "truth" of a life lived in faith. Though such a society had never been "perfect," Wojtyla believed that by striving for personal salvation, single-minded Catholics could join forces to achieve the "authentic liberation of man" from hunger, violence, and other social and political injustices. The problem with such a definition was that it was outdated in much of the world. It also harked back to the "prototype of the church as an absolute monarchy," said Chenu.[2] Nevertheless, that prototype had worked to the advantage of both the church and the people in Poland, and it was only within a Polish framework that the papal enigma could be understood.

Polish nationalism has been identified with Roman Catholicism since the tenth century, when the Polish ruler Miezko converted to Christianity on his marriage to a Bohemian princess. Rome's favor not only protected Poland from German ambitions but also made Catholicism a symbol of national unity (it was through papal fiat that Poland became a sovereign state in 1024). The outpost of Christianity on the eastern boundaries of

Central Europe, Polish society retained a sense of itself as the Catholic bridge between East and West. (Among the tourist sights in Warsaw is a stone that marks the exact geographical center of Europe.) At the height of its glory in the 1500s, Poland, in union with Lithuania, was the largest state in Europe. But by the late 1600s it had become a pawn in the interminable struggles for power among Russia, Prussia, and Austria. Because of the constant upheavals, the Enlightenment had little impact on Polish institutions, including the church. Indeed, Poland did not officially exist in the latter part of the eighteenth century, having been repeatedly partitioned by the major powers. Although Thaddeus Kosciusko, the champion of Polish independence in the period, was influenced by the French and American revolutions, the dominant factor in the unsuccessful uprising led by Kosciusko in 1794 was nationalism.

In 1920, when Wojtyla was born, the Poles drove the Russians from the gates of Warsaw, and the following year the country became a republic. Independence was brief. In 1939 Hitler invaded Poland, precipitating World War II. Some 6 million Poles were killed during the war, and 2.5 million were deported to Germany for forced labor. All but 100,000 of the prewar population of 3.1 million Jews were exterminated. After the war the foreign masters changed, and instead of fascism, Poland became subject to communism. Through all these travails Catholic Poles clung to their faith. The people rebuilt the hundreds of churches destroyed in World War II, and new recruits appeared to replace the 3,000 priests who had died.

Among them was Karol Wojtyla. Born into a modest family of deep religious convictions, he lost his mother at the age of nine and, four years later, his only brother. Despite the personal tragedies and the terrible years of the war, when he worked as a laborer in a stone quarry and in a chemical factory, he never lost his zest for life or determination to do what he thought right. In obedience to the latter he joined an underground group that smuggled Jews out of the ghetto. And it was for the sake of his people—the need to "express the meaning given to man and the world by their relationship with God"—that he became a priest.[3]

The priest in postwar Poland was product and promoter of the cultural forces that nourished nationalistic yearnings—just as, in a different cultural context, the priest in Chile helped to keep democracy alive during the long winter of General Pinochet. Pilgrimages, processions, and other religious events had not only spiritual significance but were also a form of political protest. Alone of Poland's institutions—and of Chile's—the church was able to withstand the state's persecution, providing a protective umbrella for other groups, including workers and intellectuals. Thus the Polish church thrived and flowered, experiencing a major renewal. Such, too, was the experience of the persecuted churches in Brazil and the Philippines. But Poland was different in several crucial respects. Its totalitarian state had been imposed by a foreign power, not an internal force. The identification of Catholicism with nationalism was almost as old as the Polish people. And the church had survived and flourished in the midst of persecution because it was an absolute monarchy, ruled from the top by the cardinal primate and his fellow bishops. Unlike the South American churches, which developed an internal democracy in response to external dictatorship, the Polish hierarchy demanded and got absolute loyalty from its troops. The loyalty may have been pro forma in some respects—abortion and divorce rates were surprisingly high—but the church was undoubtedly the principal mediating force in Polish society, whether for labor unions, peasant farmers, or university students. It did not need its own political party because it had the political allegiance of a majority of the people. Thus it was the church—or, more exactly, John Paul—that encouraged the emergence of the Solidarity labor protest movement and the church that helped avert a bloodbath when Solidarity was crushed in December 1981. Indicative of the church's power, police officals were unable to disperse the crowds from outside John Paul's private quarters when he visited Poland in 1983. A priest had to be asked to intervene. Within minutes of his order to leave, the crowd had melted away.[4]

In some ways, therefore, Poland represented the "perfect society" of the Eurocentric church that had existed before World War II. Everyone knew his or her place, in society and in the church. Baptisms, vocations, attendance at Mass, and the other yardsticks of Catholic allegiance were among the highest in Europe, and a united church could speak not only for the particular needs of a clerical caste but for the broader interests of the country's 36.5 million Poles. Nowhere else in the Catholic world did the church command such power. "For the Pope and those who think as he does," said one Vatican analyst, "Eastern Europe is where the old-time religion has been preserved—ironically, thanks to communism."[5]

It was this church that formed Wojtyla's zealous commitment, theological orthodoxy, and belief in absolute obedience and absolute power. A man of great compassion, he understood the sufferings of the Poles and of the other peoples who lived under Soviet imperialism, but democracy was an alien experience. In Polish terms the concept of a "People of God"—or a more democratic church that accepted diversity as a sign of unity—was suicidal, for it was only by speaking with a single voice that the church in Poland had survived. "There is not, and cannot be, any difference of opinion in the Polish church," explained Father Adam Boniecki, who worked under Wojtyla when he was archbishop of Krakow.[6]

As pope, Wojtyla yearned toward the "Christendom" of the Middle Ages, of a Europe—a world—united not by a single government but by a single faith. Modern Poland was a type of Christendom, albeit an uncertain one because temporal power rested with the Soviet Union. Notwithstanding, many Poles, the pope included, believed their society was peculiarly suited to serve as Europe's mediator because it was both Slavic (Eastern) and "Latin" (Western). "Is not the Holy Spirit disposed to see that this Polish Pope, this Slav Pope, should at this very moment reveal the spiritual unity of Christian Europe?" John Paul asked suggestively during a visit to the tomb of a Czech saint who had helped convert the Baltic peoples.[7]

Out of personal belief and because of his country's own need, John Paul preached unceasingly about human rights, which became one of the great rallying cries of his papacy. But the first right was always the right of religion or, more precisely, Catholicism, and if other rights had to be postponed, such as labor or voting rights, that price had to be paid. In Poland this was perhaps understandable since the church had become the political means to all other rights. But in nations with a different historical experience the unbroken line between human rights and an authoritarian, conservative church was not readily understood. If John Paul favored social justice, went the reasoning, he must favor political democracy, and if he supported democracy in the larger society, why would he oppose it in his own church? But as he showed in speeches and in encyclicals, the pope was highly suspicious of pluralistic societies, particularly capitalist ones, which were seen as cruel, decadent, and materialistic.[8] They were better than Marxist ones only because they respected religious freedom in principle, if not always in fact, and there was an outside chance of converting them. But they were not John Paul's idea of Christendom. However important to Catholicism, the Third World was still an appendage of the First, in the pope's opinion, and thus the battles played on the Southern stage were only reflections of the ideological struggles in the North. Nicaragua was to him the mirror of Poland at the end of World War II when the country still had a mixed economy and some freedoms. The pope was certain how it would end.[9]

"He is a good man," said his former housekeeper in Poland, dismissing any "enigma."[10] And that he is: He cares not for material possessions, is extraordinarily spiritual, loves children and the poor, tirelessly serves the church, and has frequently risked his life by visiting countries with hostile governments and/or peoples. Yet, like anyone else, he is a product of his environment. Wojtyla traveled as a student priest and later as a prelate, but the only place where he lived outside Poland for any period of time was Rome, and Rome, as many priests and nuns who have resided there admit, instills an ingrown, often cynical view of the world that has little bearing on reality. John Paul came to Rome with his Polish cultural baggage—and a coterie that was inevitably dubbed the "Polish mafia"—and assumed the trappings of the Roman papacy. But for all his efforts to be an Italian bishop to his Roman subjects and a multilingual leader of a universal church, he could no more become an Italian than he could understand what it meant to be an American, an Indonesian, or a Brazilian. Therein lies the great tragedy of his papacy: In trying to mold Catholicism to an authoritarian Polish model, the pope has unleashed a counterreformation just when the church of Vatican II is poised for a leap ahead to a faith commitment equal to the challenge of the third millennium.

A Conclave

Not all the cardinals who supported Archbishop Wojtyla's papal candidacy understood the importance of the Polish factor. When they gathered in Rome in 1978 to choose a successor to John Paul I, they were still shaken by the unexpected death of the gentle Albino Luciani, who had reigned for only thirty-three days. The leading candidates among the Italians were pre– and post–Vatican II cardinals respectively, neither of them with the pastoral experience needed to minister to ordinary Catholics and neither able to get a majority of the conclave's votes. The cardinals therefore began to cast about for a non-Italian pope. The decision to look outside Italy was unusual but not unprecedented, since in its earlier years the church had at times been ruled by non-Italians, the most recent being the Dutch Adrian VI in the sixteenth century. Wojtyla, who had received some votes at the conclave that elected John Paul I, quickly became the front-runner because he possessed the two qualifications the cardinals thought most important—pastoral experience and good health. After Luciani's sudden death the custom of electing older men no longer seemed so wise, and Wojtyla, at a youthful fifty-eight, promised a long and vigorous papacy. The Pole was charming and profoundly spiritual; he spoke several languages, if haltingly, and had had experience in public affairs as a leader in the Polish church's often difficult negotiations with the state. That he represented a militant church in a Marxist nation was an asset to the hard-line anticommunists, particularly the West Germans. The liberal swing vote, led by Vienna's Cardinal Franz-Josef König, also backed Wojtyla's candidacy, less because of his anticommunism than the mistaken belief that because he had participated in Vatican II he would continue its reforms.

Many cardinals had become acquainted with the future pope during the Vatican Council or on visits to Poland, and he impressed them as an energetic young prelate deeply concerned with the rights of his people. He was that, of course, but in the special context of Poland. To the outsider, Wojtyla seemed a liberal, particularly by comparison with Poland's intransigent primate, Cardinal Stefan Wyszynski, who had seen no need for Vatican II and wanted no part of its reforms. But the younger Pole's acceptance of the council's mandate was never more than superficial. While he could readily accept ritual changes, such as a vernacular Mass, on major issues such as a more democratic church he was almost as reactionary as Wyszynski. Wojtyla's attitude toward the council's *Dogmatic Constitution on the Church* should have been a clue to the direction of his future papacy, but few cardinals knew about or could recall what had occurred in the subcommission responsible for that text. After all, thirteen years had passed, and only those who had read the notes of the proceedings would have known that Wojtyla had argued against the document and in favor of maintaining a hierarchical church.

There were other signs, however, such as his opposition to reforms proposed by church leaders at synods in Rome. At one such meeting Wojtyla put forth the view that the collegiality of bishops did not mean that they were the pope's equals, though such was the definition under church law, but rather loyal troops whose duty was to rally round the papacy. At the 1971 synod he joined with the Germans to lobby against a semantic change in church language from "ministerial priesthood" to "priestly ministry," because they feared that a "priestly ministry" could jeopardize the priest's ecclesiastical monopoly, permitting others to assume such functions as preaching and teaching catechism. The dangers down that road frightened these churchmen even more—married priests and women priests. The aim of Vatican II had been to broaden church responsibilities, but in Wojtyla's opinion a ministry "from below" would destroy the distinctions between the laity and a clerical class. He also reinterpreted—some said misinterpreted—the synod's position on the struggle for justice, which it had described as a "constitutive dimension of the preaching of the Gospel." In other words, the struggle for justice was an integral part of faith and not something that could be separated out by an ivory-tower religion. Wojtyla, on the contrary, gave the struggle for justice no special significance, seeing it as only one among several aspects of faith, others being more important.[11]

Perhaps only a minority of the electors understood the kind of pope they were choosing, as John Paul himself suggested when he later remarked that the "eminent cardinals" did not realize "what sort of man I am." If the others were misled, so was much of the rest of the world during the first years of his papacy. Yet Wojtyla had made a clear statement of his position by visiting the Roman tomb of Monsignor José María Escrivá de Balaguer at the time of the funeral of John Paul I. Escrivá had founded the lay movement Opus Dei, a right-wing Catholic group that gained ascendancy in Franco's Spain. As archbishop of Krakow, Wojtyla had visited Opus Dei centers in Europe, and a collection of his speeches at these gatherings had been published by Opus Dei and sent to the Vatican Secretary of State. "The Work," as Opus is popularly known, is heartily disliked by many bishops for its secretiveness, intrigue, and right-wing tendencies, and John Paul's predecessors had kept it at arm's length. But on becoming pope, he elevated Opus Dei to a worldwide prelature, giving it the status of a major religious order. The knowledge of Wojtyla's close identification with "the Work" might have given some cardinals pause, but few of them knew of the connection until after he had become pope.

A Fundamentalist Message

The profile of the papal enigma only gradually grew clearer, for John Paul was indeed a complex being. At one minute a jovial man was seen kissing a baby, or fraternizing with the poor; in the next, a stern disciplinarian was ordering his priests to shape up fast. In fact, it was no contradiction, for the two images formed the complementary parts of a populist integralist.

To the world John Paul offered the smiling face of the populist. Though an intellectual, he did not share the intellectual's disdain for the masses, knowing from his own experience in Poland that the ordinary person often harbors a deep reservoir of religiosity. Popular religiosity—veneration of the Virgin Mary, adulation of individual saints, enthusiasm for religious processions—is an important feature of Catholicism in Poland as well as in Ireland and Latin America. It also recalls the religious grandeur of Europe's past—the soaring cathedrals, monasteries, religious art, and music. John Paul, who thinks in terms of peoples—not nation-states—is deeply supportive of the populism that enables a people to express political, economic, or social aspirations through religious gestures and symbols. As the guardians of Catholic symbols, priests possess the cultural means to speak as the collective voice of the people. John Paul often used that power when confronting the state in Poland. His speeches, particularly during his travels, have expressed the same desire to act as mediator for the hopes of the common people. Ideologies, said the pope, are corrupt—one has only to look at the injustices in communist and capitalist societies to realize that something is terribly wrong. But Roman Catholicism offers an incorruptible truth: Obey and be saved.

Like Protestant fundamentalism, John Paul's Catholicism has a clear set of rules and it is the responsibility of priests to make sure they are obeyed. Hence the face John Paul presents to his priests is often stony. There is to be no slacking off, no admission of weakness either within the clerical class or toward the laity. John Paul has strong opinions about how a Catholic civilization should function, and those who dare to disagree quickly feel his anger. As one shaken Third World cardinal told it, the pope refused to listen to his plea that the situation in his country was not as painted by right-wing extremists. " 'I'm telling you,' thundered the Pope, 'to fix the complaints.' "[12]

The civilization he envisions is essentially integralist—a throwback to the "perfect society" of an earlier European Christendom when the church was both the mediating force in secular society and the only source of spiritual salvation. Integralism responds to the religious fundamentalism in Polish Catholicism and the yearnings in other parts of Europe, particularly in France, Italy, and Spain, for a return to the old religious certitudes. Opus Dei and its Italian counterpart, Communion and Liberation, represent one type of integralism, Polish Catholicism's "absolute monarchy" another. But for those who do not live in Poland or are not European integralists, the message is often confusing. This is particularly so in the Third World, which John Paul frequently visits. Millions of people turn out to see him, but often the only memory they retain is of a gesture—the pope donning a poncho in Ecuador or wearing a tribal headdress in Africa. The ideals he enunciates are grand, but everybody knows you can't eat ideals. The crowds come away from the stadiums and public squares convinced that, despite John Paul's wonderful show, nothing will change. Populists are a familiar political breed in the Third World, and when John Paul speaks of a new Christendom—a "civilization of love"—people shrug. Even in Latin America, which experienced a Christendom of sorts during the colonial period, the majority of the people now have no inkling of its meaning.

Having told the poor multitudes of their rights and responsibilities, John Paul then lines up his bishops, priests, and nuns to lecture them about authority, obedience, theology, even dress. The tensions in this duality occasionally show, particularly when the pope is tired—the pace of his trips exhausts members of his entourage who are half his age. Although he demonstrates in his presence and gestures that he genuinely loves the people, he is also in a hurry to assemble his church for the march to the third millennium. Close up, and with no television cameras in attendance, he sometimes displays the impatience of a general on the eve of a major engagement, as occurred in Brazil on his visit there in 1980.

Salvador da Bahia is the cultural heartland of Brazil, the birthplace of its most imaginative art, literature, cuisine, and Afro-Brazilian cults. But in one respect it is unexceptional: Like every other Latin American city, it is ringed by slums. Among them is a *favela* built on the edge of a swamp where the people pay homage to the Virgin Mary by baking her image in bread. When it became known that John Paul would visit the slum's church the people baked for him a small bread Virgin. Obviously in a hurry—John Paul's daily schedules on such trips usually included half a dozen speeches and visits to different organizations—the pope came bounding up the hill to the slum chapel, intent only on giving his blessing, saying a few words, and leaving for his next appointment. But the woman who had been chosen by the *favela* as its representative insisted on giving the pope the bread Virgin. Perhaps no one had told him of its importance, but John Paul took one look at it, flicked his finger in dismissal, and rushed back down the hillside. He looked like a man pursued, with clenched teeth and frozen smile—who wouldn't with such an exhausting schedule? Still, there was a sense of disappointment on that muddy hill. The people—including the woman with the bread Virgin—felt blessed because "He" had actually come to them, but it had been like a flash of light and just as incomprehensible.

Human Rights in the Church

The most democratic church in the Catholic world, Brazilian Catholicism was among the first to suffer disciplinary measures under John Paul's Restoration. The Curia objected to the Brazilians' liturgy, theology, and base communities—that is, to just about everything that made the South American church so effective. Nor did it like the bishops' tendency to deal directly with other Catholic churches in the region, such as the Nicaraguans, or with the Portuguese-speaking Africans. But because the Brazilian hierarchy was united in defense of its model of church, the Curia could not bring the bishops to heel. While individual bishops, cardinals, and theologians were harassed, Rome found that Brazil's church had advanced too far for the reforms brought about by Vatican II to be undone.

Although Peru was the intellectual birthplace of liberation theology, the Brazilians led Latin America in applying it to pastoral work with the Christian base communities. Blessed with visionary bishops and theologians, the Brazilian church was also out front on the most important issues in the Third World, especially democracy, hunger, and the foreign debt. Consequently, it was among the first to sound the alarm about the papal crackdown, which it correctly saw as a serious challenge to Vatican II.

John Paul and his curial advisers were not so rash as to make a frontal attack on that most important event in Catholicism of this century, but their actions belied their words of support for Vatican II. When they spoke positively of the council, they were not referring to its progressive influence but to the "true council" that was simply an extension of the past. Throughout Vatican II the Curia and like-minded bishops had fought to insert passages that upheld the traditional authoritarianism of the church, and it was these inserts that John Paul's papacy interpreted as representative of the council's intent. That this was patently not so, those present at the council could attest. Nor had it been the intention of Pope John XXIII, who convened Vatican II, or his successor, Paul VI, both of whom had held the Curia at bay. But as Pope Pius XI once observed, "Only a Pope may undo what a Pope may do."

While there was widespread muttering against the retrenchment, it fell to Brazil's most gifted theologian, Leonardo Boff, to attack the controversy publicly by accusing Rome of acting like a "ruling class." In his explosive book, *Church: Charism & Power*, Boff argued that the fundamental issue facing Catholicism in the 1980s was human rights in the church. "The church recognizes the unfathomable dignity of the human person and so can be the conscience of the world with respect to human rights," he wrote. "But proclamation alone is not enough. The church will only be heard if it gives witness by its practices, if it is the first to respect and promote human rights within its own reality. Otherwise, one would be right to criticize a church that sees the speck in the eye of another while ignoring the beam in its own."[13]

As if to prove the accuracy of Boff's warning, the Vatican's Congregation for the Doctrine of the Faith brought the Brazilian to trial and sentenced him to a year of silence. Although Boff's punishment became a *cause célèbre*, it was only one of dozens of occasions when the increasingly powerful Curia penalized dissenters. By the fall of 1986 anxiety had spread throughout the institution. Representatives of religious orders in Rome, for example, spoke repeatedly of the atmosphere of fear and of how people were "keeping their heads down" in the hope that they would not attract the Curia's attention. "These guys play hard ball," said an American priest who worked with the Curia. "They are cruel."[14]

They are also building their careers. "If they do their work, they automatically go up the ladder," explained an insider of the promotion system in the Curia. "They become a monsignor, then under secretary of a congregation [equivalent to a ministry], archbishop, and perhaps cardinal. Their world is completely encapsulated, which is one reason why they do not understand the church's problem with women. They do not work with women since most of the lay jobs are handled by men. The women's job is housekeeping. John Paul thinks that natural since most Polish nuns are housekeepers and women are kept in their place in the Eastern countries."[15]

A retort to this sort of comment, made by members of the Curia so frequently that it became a cliché, is that the Roman Catholic Church has been around for 2,000 years. Despite the waves of protest that from time to time break against Peter's rock, they are convinced that it will stand for another two millennia. Their dismissal of the popular bornagain Protestant churches in Latin America is typical: Eventually, they said, the people will tire of these novelties and return to the Catholic Church, as they always have. There is no need for change or to become alarmed. On the contrary, *romanitas*—the highly prized sense of identification that comes to those who labor long in the Vatican's vineyard—demands calmness, historical perspective, and not a little cynicism. It is also imbued with a sense of timelessness and the delicious decadence of

Rome itself. Every corner of the city reveals an ancient fountain or church that had been constructed long before the New World was even known. The inhabitants of São Paulo, Managua, or New York may believe they live at the center of the world, but the Romans know better.

For those who toe the Vatican line the prizes are often rich—a job that is not too demanding, ecclesiastical titles and important friends, and a way of life that in some cases rivals that of princes. For example, *Civiltà Cattolica*, the Jesuit-run Vatican organ, is housed in a Roman palazzo with magnificent gardens, marble floors, hand-carved ceilings, and priceless murals. Nothing to disturb the mind there. But then there is a price for such a life: Vatican censorship of the publication is accepted as normal, even as desirable. If there is a shade of cynicism in the overwhelming luxury, well, that is the way of Rome. At one time, there had been a debt on the journal's palace, but it was paid off when an enterprising Jesuit discovered that the construction of a neighboring hotel had killed an ancient palm tree in *Civiltà's* gardens. The Jesuits sued the hotel, which paid a sum equal to the debt, and everyone lived happily ever after. Or almost everyone—the enterprising Jesuit was sacked for talking out of turn about papal integralism and for suggesting that the Vatican be a bit more understanding of the Nicaraguan revolution.

"It's difficult to live in Rome and not lose your faith," admitted a U.S. priest, echoing the feelings of other foreign religious who deplore Roman worldliness. Some, particularly the Americans, were so unhappy that they counted the days till they could leave. Yet all admitted that Boff was right in believing that the struggle had to be waged in Rome. "Religious people in other parts of the world have not understood the need to focus on human rights in the church," said the representative in Rome of a major U.S. women's religious order. "Those in missionary work in particular are so busy trying to deal with society's hurts that they don't realize that these rights are the key to all others. It's much easier to challenge secular authority than Mother Church. At the same time, there is a failure to perceive the connection between religious rights and the social message to change society and its structures. Yet these rights are crucial to pluralism, dialogue, and decentralized rule. What happens to the Christian base communities in Latin America, for example, when church leadership is taken over by a new group of bishops appointed by this papacy? They can change the teaching orientation, make things difficult for progressive religious and lay leaders, end theological debate, alter the whole thrust of the church. We see the same things happening in the United States. Boff is right: The foremost issue for Catholicism's future is human rights in the church."[16]

It is a measure of this danger that advocates in Rome for the Sandinista government believed that Managua's religious differences with the Vatican could prove more damaging in the long run than the military conflict with the *contras*. "The Vatican has a lot to lose in Nicaragua by encouraging a schism between the pro-Sandinista and anti-Sandinista churches," said one high-level observer. "But the crisis with the Vatican is also dangerous for the Sandinistas. The *contras* are a spent military force, but the dispute with the church could go on causing the government serious harm to its image. By having priests in the government, the Sandinistas have shown other countries that Christian-Marxist dialogue is possible. On the other hand, the conflict with the Nicaraguan hierarchy and the Vatican has given the revolution's enemies ammunition to attack the Sandinistas as anti-Catholic."[17]

Nor is the conflict limited to Nicaragua. "John Paul's insistence that the universal church adopt his own cultural and religious perspective has upset the evolution of the churches in other countries," claimed a Latin American ambassador to the Vatican. At a time when local churches are seeking new approaches to political and economic challenges, he said, John Paul's papacy is trying to force them back into conformity with a centralized institution whose authoritarian, anticommunist leadership would allow them no say in their countries' development. "John Paul is involved in politics in Poland, but the Curia frowns on Cardinal Sin doing the same thing in the Philippines. The Vatican wants to run everyone's foreign policy. This could prove more dangerous than Reagan's East-West military strategy because it tends to Christianize political confrontations, particularly in the Third World. Actually the pope is not that much different from Reagan: He wants Catholics to follow his anticommunist line which in the Third World usually means support for right-wing regimes, as in the Philippines."[18]

The problem, said a West German church official with experience in the developing nations, is that Rome "doesn't listen to others, particularly in the United States and the Third World. This insensitivity has been compounded by John Paul's cultural outlook. The Vatican does not understand non-European cultures and cannot put itself in the shoes of people in other countries."[19]

Nor for that matter can the Germans. Despite historical antagonisms between Germans and Poles, their postwar bishops are in complete accord in a hatred of communism and on the need for a recentralization of the church under European leadership. Authoritarians for the most part, the German bishops saw a different side of World War II from that experienced by Wojtyla. Despite the horrors of the Third Reich, the German hierarchy went along with Adolf Hitler, partly in the interest of self-survival but also because of a concordat that Hitler signed with the church, giving it a government-guaranteed income and a status equivalent to a state within a state. The postwar bishops grew up in that period of fateful compromise, and some retain neofascist yearnings, as expressed in their support for Opus Dei. John Paul's integralist vision accords with the Germans' political outlook for both religious and ideological reasons. In religious terms integralism harks back to the Christendom of the Middle Ages when church and state were inseparable, but it was also the seed of the fascist corporate state, which was based in theory on the medieval estates and guilds. Instead of political parties, different sectors of society (i.e., capital, labor, farmers, and professionals) were supposed to be represented by modern versions of the guilds, although in practice only the capitalists and the landowning classes benefited from the fascist corporative states of Hitler and Mussolini. Such a system held considerable appeal for the Catholic Church, which had lost much of its earlier power through the rise of labor movements and new political parties espousing socialism and democratic egalitarianism. The forerunners of fascism in France, Germany, and Austria, playing on middle- and upper-class fears of political domination by the masses, portrayed themselves as the champions of law and order, Christian morality, and private property. These fears were shared by Catholic leaders who, when the older order of the aristocracy gave way, tended to align themselves with the new integralists.

Thanks to the concordat with Hitler (which continued after the war), the German church has not shared the fate of other European churches, which have to depend on the voluntary offerings of a dwindling Catholic membership. While only a minority of German Catholics practice their faith, all are forced to pay a religious tithe as part of their taxes. Thus the German hierarchy has no financial need to coddle the Catholic masses, which perhaps explains the attitude of Cardinal Joseph Ratzinger, head of the Vatican's Congregation for the Doctrine of the Faith, and other German bishops who think numbers less important than absolute obedience. So long as the money continues to flow, they can afford to ignore statistics that show a church in decline.

Money is also a major source of the Germans' power in Rome. After the United States the richest church in the Catholic world, the Germans know how to use their financial muscle, in contrast to the American bishops, who obediently produce millions of dollars for the Holy See without asking for an accounting or an occasional favor in return. The German church has its own aid agencies, Adveniat and Misereor, which exercise considerable influence among Third World churches, particularly in Latin America. A German cardinal, Joseph Höffner of Cologne, oversaw Vatican finances until his death in 1987.

Höffner and Ratzinger were the big guns in the German hierarchy. For example, Ratzinger, who had had a long and bitter personal feud with the liberal German theologian Hans Küng, supported Höffner's condemnation of the latter, which resulted in the church's suspension of Küng's license to teach Catholic theology. Ratzinger also blocked the appointment of German theologian Johann Baptist Metz to the chair of fundamental theology at the University of Munich. Unlike Küng, who invariably comes out fighting, Metz is a gentle man who has tried to avoid conflicts. Nevertheless, he was punished because his "political theology" had inspired the Latin Americans' liberation theology. "I protest," wrote a furious Karl Rahner of Metz's shabby treatment. But Rahner, though one of the greatest German theologians in this century, made no impression on Ratzinger, for Rahner was also on the hit list.[20]

Meanwhile, Cardinal Höffner tried to whip the U.S. and Brazilian bishops into line. Like the White House, the German hierarchy was much exercised by the American bishops' pastoral letter on nuclear warfare, which questioned the Reagan administration's arms buildup. In 1982, when the document was still being drafted, Höffner wrote sharply to the then president of the National Conference of Catholic Bishops, Archbishop John Roach. Höffner virtually accused the Americans of selling out to the Russians because they were disturbed by Washington's unwillingness to renounce the first use of nuclear weapons and by the inability of mutual deterrence to end the arms race. He also claimed that the U.S. bishops would demoralize the German forces in NATO if they declared that the use of nuclear arms was immoral. While Höffner was berating the bishops, a stream of U.S. government officials, including Secretary of State George Shultz and Vice President George Bush, complained to the pope about the bishops' peace stance. Ratzinger then persuaded John Paul to schedule a meeting in Rome between the American and German bishops for the purpose of settling their differences.[21]

Höffner arrived at this meeting with guns blazing: The Americans, he said, were provoking a dangerous schism in the church; they were playing the Soviets' game, and they would destabilize Europe, especially Germany, which was on the eve of an election. Didn't they realize that they were interfering with Germany's autonomy? While the Americans could have made a parallel charge against Höffner, papal pressure forced them to pacify the Germans by softening their stand on nuclear deterrence. Certain that the U.S. bishops would reword their pastoral letter in accordance with German demands, Höffner emerged from the meeting with a smug smile: "On the basic points," he told reporters, "there are no differences."[22]

Threatened with a showdown, the Catholic leadership of one of the most powerful countries in the world bowed to German-Polish foreign policy. Perhaps because the Brazilian bishops knew better the ways of the Vatican, or perhaps because they were more courageous, they were better than the Americans at defending their beliefs. Höffner descended on São Paulo to carry out an investigation of the archdiocese's theological faculty, and Cardinal Paulo Evaristo Arns received him with open arms, saying his people had nothing to hide. Höffner poked about for signs of Marxist theology and then, apparently finding none, announced to the Brazilian press that São Paulo's program for seminarians was a model for the world. Since São Paulo is the theological training center for much of Brazil, Höffner's endorsement was important. No sooner had he returned to Europe, however, than he wrote a violent condemnation of the theological faculty, deeply wounding Arns, who saw it as a personal attack on his administration.[23] The report might have led to reprisals had it not been for a frank dialogue between the Brazilian bishops and the pope in 1986, when Boff's punishment, the Höffner report, and other unpleasant incidents were discussed. Although the meeting cleared the air, and the Brazilians' determined unity encouraged the pope to be more flexible in dealing with the Third World's most powerful hierarchy, harassment of Boff, Arns, and others continued. At one point, for example, the Vatican threatened to close the São Paulo theological faculty if Arns did not send some priests to study in Rome. The Curia clearly aimed to Romanize Arn's priests, but the cardinal could also play the game: Figuring there was safety in numbers, he sent eight instead of the required two.

Papal Troops

Wishing to think the best of John Paul, bishops who suffered under his papacy dismissed the harsh actions as the work of the Curia or over-

zealous loyalists. "Sometimes I think his message is deliberately misinterpreted by the Curia," said an Italian bishop whom the Vatican had
punished. He cited as an example a papal speech in support of Communion and Liberation (CL), the Italian version of Opus Dei, which was
immediately seized upon by the Curia's followers in the Italian hierarchy
as evidence that only CL could serve as a model for the laity. "But John
Paul did not say it had to be the sole model," argued the bishop, "but
only that he preferred it."[24]

Other bishops suggested that John Paul's frequent travels inevitably
meant that many administrative decisions were left to the Curia. But even
had he spent more time in Rome, the situation would have been much
the same, for the Curia traditionally handles day-to-day affairs. Further-
more, the pope on several occasions went out of his way to emphasize
his confidence in the Curia, as when, at general audiences in Rome and
on his trips, he warned local bishops of the need to cooperate with the
Vatican's government.[25] Theoretically the Curia is supposed to serve as
a two-way bridge between bishops and pope, but in practice communications flowed in only one direction, from papacy to bishops. The extent
to which John Paul knew of and approved specific decisions taken by the
Curia was open to question, but it was generally agreed that "John Paul
sets the policy, and the rest follow," as an official of the Curia described
the process. "Almost every order starts with the words, 'The Holy Father
wants . . . ,'" said an American priest in Rome. But some of the things
the pope was purported to want sounded more like the petty desires of
individual Curia members.

Students of Vatican intrigue said that a major communications problem had arisen because John Paul usually received information from only
one group of people, often the most reactionary. "Even the most open
person can become closed if the only information he gets is always fil-
tered," remarked one informed observer. No friend of the Curia, he
nevertheless admitted that most of the letters received by the Vatican
consisted of hostile comment. "The only thing the Curia knows is the
negative side of the church, and they get frightened. They think the most
terrible things are going on when in reality many of the complaints are
exaggerated gossip or outright lies."[26]

Nevertheless, John Paul had chosen his informants, and they presumably reflected his thinking. John Paul had handpicked the inquisitorial
German, Cardinal Ratzinger, for the most important post in the Curia.
The bishops he relied on for information from other countries were often
unrepresentative and unpopular authoritarians, notably Colombian Car-

dinal Alfonso López Trujillo, who was so disliked by his own priests and nuns that they had twice attempted to obtain a Vatican investigation of his archdiocese. The favors John Paul bestowed on Opus Dei and Communion and Liberation also indicated his outlook. Strong on discipline and blindly loyal to the pope, these movements exhibited the same religious zeal and obedience as did Poland's militant Catholics. But John Paul's fondness for them was not shared by the Spanish or Italian bishops. The Spanish hierarchy tried in vain to dissuade him from elevating Opus Dei to a religious prelature. Opus Dei took a dubious hand in Spanish finance and politics, while also acting in competition with the bishops, and the Spanish hierarchy thought it had sound reasons for its opposition. The pope did not listen. Nor did he listen to the Italian bishops' complaints against Communion and Liberation. Like the Spaniards, the Italians wanted to distance themselves from an earlier identification with a political party—in their case, the Christian Democrats. Communion and Liberation, on the other hand, had gained a foothold in the right wing of that party and was determined to drag the rest of the Italian church back into the ideological melee. Despite the bishops' protests John Paul gave Communion and Liberation his support, in part because it shared similarities with Catholic fundamentalist movements in Poland.[27]

Papal Politics

The most irksome—and confusing—aspect of such favoritism was the double standard it invoked. John Paul saw nothing wrong with Communion and Liberation's partisan political activities, even though the movement was headed by priests, whereas any priest or nun associated with the opposite side of the Italian political spectrum could expect serious trouble, possibly even expulsion. "It's okay to be involved in politics," explained an Italian theologian, "so long as you're against communism."[28]

Cultural conditioning also marked John Paul's attitude toward activist priests and nuns like the Chileans. He sensed a faintly Marxist odor about people who were fighting a strongly anticommunist government. At the same time, the Polish church, as the primary opposition in that country, was "up to its neck in politics," said a South American bishop. So how could the pope simultaneously play politics in Poland and tell priests in other countries to stay out of politics? On one level there was no inconsistency. No priest or nun, regardless of the government's ideology, was allowed to hold public office, the theory being that partisanship prevented them from speaking to and for all Catholics. Although some individuals suffered, among them Democratic congressman Robert Drinan of Massachusetts, a Jesuit priest, the ban was generally accepted. But many religious and bishops parted company with John Paul on the extension of the ban to all political activity. As anyone could see, the pope and the Polish bishops were themselves deeply immersed in politics, including the moral and financial support of Solidarity, negotiations with the government for greater freedoms, and the establishment of a fund financed by Western countries to save Poland's small farmers from collectivism. There was also the matter of a clandestine Polish church that served the needs of Catholics in Lithuania, the Ukraine, and other parts of Russia, as well as the aggressive militancy of younger members of the Polish clergy, one of whom, Jerzy Popieluszko, was murdered by the Polish police in 1984 because of his pro-Solidarity activities.[29] Granted, there was nothing partisan about such activities since they did not imply support for a political party. It could also be argued that Polish bishops and priests had a legitimate religious role to play on the broader political stage as the conscience of their people. But if such was the case in Poland, why was it not equally true in other countries?

Nevertheless, the pope constantly inveighed against clerical engagement in politics, particularly in the Third World. At his meeting with the Brazilian bishops in 1986, for example, he insisted that they should not assume the role of politicians, economists, intellectuals, or labor leaders. In Latin America, where "the opportunity for the church to count in the everyday lives of its members is unequaled anywhere else in the world," the clergy "receive wordy dissertations and warnings about 'excesses' " from the Vatican, wrote A. Roy Megarry, publisher of Toronto's *Globe and Mail*. "If the church is to be really relevant, it must be (as it always has been) involved in social affairs. If it is to be effectively involved in social affairs, it will inevitably be involved in politics." If the pope were really sincere in wanting social reforms in Latin America and elsewhere, said Megarry, he could not deny to churches in those countries the same role assumed by the church in Poland. Yet that is exactly what happened. Cardinal Jaime Sin, for example, lost favor with the pope because he supported the opposition that ousted Philippine dictator Ferdinand Marcos. That Sin had played a positive role in promoting the return to democracy was irrelevant. "The Vatican does not want church figures to publicly show a preference for one person or group in a country," explained a high-ranking Vatican official.[30]

Yet Archbishop Bruno Torpigliani, the papal nuncio in the Philippines, was just as guilty as the cardinal of publicly identifying with a particular group, only Torpigliani supported the Marcos family. A close friend of the dictator's politically powerful wife, Imelda, Torpigliani appeared on local television with Marcos's defense minister during the exhibition of a "confessed" leftist priest who had been tortured by the military and was later killed in suspicious circumstances. Sin said Torpigliani was Marcos's pipeline to the Vatican. "The first lady runs to the nuncio and tells him what she wants, he calls Rome and passes it along as his own suggestion, and then he would come here to tell me what to do," complained the cardinal, adding that the nuncio "is too much." Sin said that Torpigliani called Rome almost daily to complain to Cardinal Casaroli, the Vatican secretary of state, who in turn tried to influence Sin in a more diplomatic way. But neither prelate made any impression on Sin, which led to a coldness in relations with the pope, who showed his disapproval of the Filipino by failing to invite him to the 1985 synod on Vatican II.[31]

As Cardinal Sin later admitted, the Filipino church took a big risk in supporting the nonviolent resistance that brought Marcos down, when the Vatican wanted to play it safe. But after millions of Filipinos took to the streets in support of Corazon Aquino, the pope had no choice but to follow the Philippine bishops' lead. John Paul was clearly relieved when Marcos departed peacefully without involving the church further, but unlike other chiefs of state, he expressed no gratification at the outcome, limiting his remarks to a pro forma statement about his affection for the Filipinos. Sources in the Curia said that in the months leading up to Marcos's downfall, Casaroli, on the pope's instructions, had warned Sin that he was setting a bad example for other bishops by becoming too deeply immersed in politics. Once the peaceful revolution was over, Sin was called to Rome for private criticism by the pope.[32]

Sin's supporters in Rome confirmed that his reception at the Vatican was unpleasant. "He was treated like dirt," said one. "But he reacted. Who were they to stand judgment on him?, he wanted to know. He had all the backing of his own bishops and people, and he said they [the Vatican] were not going to treat him that way." That the Vatican did not treat him more harshly—unpleasant words were, after all, only words— was due to several factors. The most important was that Sin and the other bishops had a good cause. From a moral viewpoint, to have done nothing would have made the bishops "a party to the destruction of our people," said the Philippine bishops, in a reference to Marcos's rigging of presidential elections. "We would be jointly guilty with the perpetrators of the wrong we want righted." At the same time, the bishops felt that, given the size of the communist insurgency in the Philippines, the alternatives were a "continued dictatorship from the right or an eventual dictatorship from the left," said Father Bienvenido Nebres, the Jesuit provincial superior in the Philippines and an adviser to Aquino. The bishops "simply had to get involved and do something." Sin's supporters said that the cardinal believed the people had nowhere to turn but the church, although they admitted that the bishops had also acted to stem the growing defection to the left of disillusioned priests and nuns. The specter of a divided church and a Marxist government in the Philippines persuaded the Vatican to abstain from a public upbraiding of Sin, who, while given no hero's reception in Rome, at least did not suffer the ostracism of priests who joined the Sandinista government.[33]

A similar regard for the status quo was evident in the Vatican's policy toward South Africa. Thus in early 1987, when 8,000 people, including 2,000 children, were in detention because of their opposition to the racist regime, the papal nuncio, Belgian archbishop Jan Mees, gave the South African bishops a stern lecture about meddling in politics. Quoting a papal injunction, Mees said the church should stay out of politics, meaning that it should cease its denunciations of apartheid. South African president Pieter Botha had made the same point during an earlier meeting with the bishops in Pretoria, and Mees said that the pope wished to encourage more such "dialogue" between church and state.[34]

Apartheid supporters declared themselves "extremely pleased" with Mees's lecture to the bishops, but the latter were outraged. Denis Hurley, the outspoken archbishop of Durban and at the time president of the Southern African Catholic Bishops' Conference, demanded and got an apology of sorts from Mees and the Vatican—not about the substance of Mees's statement but about the criticism it had stirred up against the bishops in the government-controlled media. While Hurley felt "sure the Holy Father is with us in our stand against this unjust system of apartheid," the Vatican declined to provide a clear statement of such support. Similarly, the Curia's initial response to Hurley's report that Father Smangaliso Mkhatshwa, secretary general of the bishops' conference, had been brutally tortured while in detention was, according to informed church sources in Rome, that the Vatican could not take Hurley's word for it and that he was probably exaggerating. Ten days later, when there could be no doubt that Mkhatshwa had been tortured because the South African supreme court admitted as much, Rome sent a cable of protest.[35]

The South African government could also discredit the bishops by pointing to funding from the Vatican Bank as a sign of papal support. From September 1982 through mid-1985, for example, the Vatican Bank participated in eight bond issues totaling $251.9 million for three South African government entities—the city of Johannesburg, the Department of Posts and Telecommunications, and the South African Transport Services. The bonds were "irrevocably and unconditionally guaranteed by the Republic of South Africa." No U.S. institution was involved in the bond issues, the U.S. banks having decided not to underwrite additional South African financing because of protests in the United States against apartheid. The Vatican Bank, under no such constraints, joined the scheme through its subsidiary, the Banco di Roma per la Svizzera. Internal correspondence between the Curia and the Banco di Roma's board of directors showed that neither thought there was anything morally wrong with the bond participation, since the sums involved were "modest amounts."[36]

Papal Encyclicals

As in politics, John Paul's major writings reveal his Polish character. The first of his encyclicals, *Redemptor Hominis* (*The Redeemer of Man*), which was to set the tone of his papacy, emphasized the importance of Catholic truth as the path to salvation. Its strong support for religious freedom reflected John Paul's concern for the churches in the socialist bloc. Another theme that was to be repeated in subsequent messages was the idea of a third way, between collectivism and individualism, whereby people acted together in "solidarity"—a word he used repeatedly and that would become the name of the Polish labor movement. *Redemptor* also signaled the coming storm over Vatican II by warning that the church should be "more resistant with respect to . . . various novelties." Later the pope would say that Vatican II had caused "confusion and divisions" among the world's Catholics and that the "Christian fabric should be remade."[37]

Laborem Exercens (*On Human Work*), his third and best-known encyclical, was even more specifically addressed to its intended audience. As observed by one student of the pope's works, *Laborem* "acquires lustre only when read as a message to Solidarity: It acquires universal value only when 'Polandized.' "[38] Completed in 1981, four months after John Paul was wounded by a would-be assassin, *Laborem* was written in honor of both the ninetieth anniversary of *Rerum Novarum*, Leo XIII's encyclical on labor, and as a framework for Solidarity's development in Poland. At the time, Solidarity was engaged in an intricate minuet with the government, and *Laborem* offered sound practical advice by warning that unions "do not have the character of political parties struggling for power" and should not "have too close links with them." In the Polish context this meant that Solidarity should not push the government too hard or attempt to set itself up as the political opposition. Within days of *Laborem*'s appearance the Polish bishops published the encyclical's section on politics, urging Solidarity "to return to the negotiating table."[39]

The encyclical's treatment of women also revealed John Paul's Polish concerns. He spoke of their role as mothers, emphasizing that they should not have to neglect the care of their children to work outside the home. He did not say that women should not take jobs, but rather that mothers should not be forced to do so. As pointed out by Peter Hebblethwaite, a Vatican writer, Polish women slaved in factories where working conditions were comparable to the nineteenth century—this in addition to caring for their homes and families. Although John Paul's objections could be applied to many countries, including the United States, they clearly served the cause of Polish women.[40]

Vatican II had encouraged local churches to develop their own responses to different realities. In his letter *Octogesima Adveniens* Paul VI had acknowledged that "in view of the varied situations in the world, it is difficult to give one teaching to cover them all or to offer a solution which has universal value." Instead of specific suggestions, he offered critical/prophetic values which individual churches were to apply in their particular societies. John Paul, on the contrary, wished to homogenize church teaching on social questions so that there would be a Roman Catholic formula for every eventuality, much as the Vatican formulated—or tried to formulate—a foreign policy for all national churches.[41]

Nevertheless, local churches found that they could read what they wanted into John Paul's encyclicals, and this was especially so of *Laborem Exercens*, which had considerable impact in the United States and the Third World. Its insistence on the priority of labor over capital and its plea for democracy in the workplace made a strong impression on workers the world over. John Paul left no doubt that he supported unions, profit-sharing, employee stock-option plans, a guaranteed minimum wage, and restraint on the part of management in demanding wage concessions. No union leader could have said it better than John Paul: "The labor movement, to which the church and Christians have given an original and diverse contribution, claims its rightful role of responsibility for the construction of a new world order. Human work is a key, probably the essential key, to the whole social question if we really try to see that question from the point of view of man's good."[42]

Yet *Laborem,* like other papal works on the rights of humanity, suffered from a fatal flaw: While recognizing that all human beings were fundamentally equal, the pope refused to apply that principle in his own institution. "The church's treatment of large segments of its own membership (women, 'meddlesome' theologians, the Latin American church, resigned priests, married men who wish ordination and probably many more) seems on the face of it to belie the sincerity of the commitment," observed religion scholar Paul Lakeland. Unlike some critics of John Paul, Brazilian theologian Leonardo Boff did not blame the pope for this situation or pin the problem on the Polish factor. The gap between the church's social messages and its actual practice had, he thought, been so persistent that the explanation must be sought in its very structure. As an example, he cited the church's seemingly contradictory position on revolution—against the Mexican upheaval in the 1920s and in favor of Franco's forces during the Spanish Civil War. Both events centered on violent conflicts between social classes and caused enormous bloodshed, but the church, which traditionally opposed violent class warfare, changed its position according to its own interests: The Mexican revolutionaries were anticlerical; the Franquistas, proclerical. "Whatever the interpretation," said Boff, "first in one direction and then in another, it always points to the same effort: to strengthen the survival of the institution so that the Gospel may be made present in the world." Unfortunately that entirely proper religious goal was habitually pursued through the imposition of power—not persuasion—the Gospel serving as a weapon of coercion, as in the excommunication of clerics who supported Mexico's independence from Spain. The institutional church was so concerned with maintaining power, said Boff, that it had come to hold authority as the highest truth, whereas Christ had based his message on weakness and powerlessness: Those who followed him did so not from obedience to authority but in response to his persuasive message of love. Vatican II had recognized the need for conversion within the church, but even then it had been in personal rather than structural terms. "If conversion does not reach the institution of the church," Boff insisted, "then we cannot speak of Gospel conversion."[43]

The Crackdown

As Boff said, John Paul is a man of "clear conscience and impeccable personal character." That he is set in his ways does not detract from his essential goodness, but it does make it difficult for equally good men and women to get a hearing. "John Paul wants to ignore certain realities," said a European theologian. "For example, one-quarter of the marriages in Rome and one-third in Milan are not performed in the Catholic Church. Fifteen days before the vote on abortion in Italy he came out with a statement saying that anyone who supported abortion would be excommunicated ipso facto. Nevertheless, nearly two-thirds of the voters approved abortion. Surely this says something about what the people think about the church's position on sexual issues."[44]

An American priest with long experience in Rome agreed that the pope sometimes dealt with illusions. "His near assassination was a shock to him," said the priest. "His attitude was, Why would anyone want to kill me? He couldn't understand that there might be people who did not agree with him." The pope's trips abroad, he added, tend to reinforce this view. "He gets these enormous turnouts which he believes are proof that people think he is doing the right thing. And he is a man who does want to please. He only sees the real feelings of resentment occasionally, as on his trips to Holland and France."[45] (The visit to Holland provoked massive antipapal demonstrations, and the crowds in France were distressingly small.)

Yet unlike Cardinal Ratzinger, who was prepared to accept a "leaner" church that was totally subservient, John Paul was sufficiently a politician to realize the importance of consensus. When forced to face the possibility of serious division, he was capable of compromise. Thus when the united Brazilian bishops made clear their unhappiness over the Curia's persecution, John Paul paid attention. He may not have agreed with the Brazilians that there was nothing wrong with liberation theology, but he accepted their premise that the Brazilian church's work with the poor was an essential aspect of evangelization. Vatican sources reported that the arrival in Rome of petitions carrying 2 million signatures from Brazilian Catholics opposed to Leonardo Boff's punishment was also a factor in the pope's more conciliatory attitude. Such showdowns are rare, however, because local churches are still in awe of Rome or not sufficiently united, or because they prefer the more diplomatic solution of simply ignoring the Vatican's edicts (the Asian tactic). Surrounded by like-minded advisers, John Paul believes he is widely liked and that he is doing the right thing in reasserting discipline, although most polls show substantial opposition to his stands on sexual and theological matters.

John Paul hardly ever mentions his warm-hearted Italian predecessor, John XXIII, who was the architect of Vatican II. Instead, he singles out for praise Pope Pius X, who reigned at the turn of the century. Pius believed himself a jovial, pastoral pope, and he did enjoy considerable popularity among Italy's poorer classes. But he was also a most intolerant leader who tried to enforce church adherence to outdated practices. Under Pius the Index of books forbidden to Catholics expanded significantly, and publishers, editors, and authors were routinely excommunicated. Seminaries were closed, and those that remained open were closely scrutinized. Pius was convinced that "modernism," or a religious consideration of contemporary thought and science, was the "synthesis of all heresies." Hence all clergy and seminary teachers were forced to take an oath against modernism that was not abolished until Vatican II. To ensure that his orders were obeyed, he created an ecclesiastical spy ring, Sodalitium Pianium, that spread its net across Europe and to the United States. Sodalitium was not disbanded until 1921 when its head, Monsignor Umberto Benigni, became a spy for Mussolini. Among Sodalitium's targets was the future John XXIII. Although Pius X was canonized by Pope Pius XII, the beatification process was delayed four years because Vatican lawyers doubted that Pius had really practiced the virtues of love and prudence.[46]

There is something of the same fear of modernism in John Paul's faith. Citing Saint Augustine, he affirmed that "faithful ignorance is better than temerarious knowledge." He also asserted, somewhat incoherently, that true faith "serves as a yardstick to determine whether philosophies are in conformity with it or not." His belief that the church should not be contaminated by the world emerges perhaps most clearly in his insistence that priests and nuns should look and act differently from the laity. He is a stickler for proper religious dress, constantly urging priests to be proud of the symbolism of their clothes. He is equally stern about the importance of adhering to religious vows, particularly celibacy. Indeed, the first major instance of discipline under John Paul's papacy arose from requests for laicization by priests who wished to leave the priesthood, usually in order to marry. Although hundreds abandon the priesthood each year, John Paul has no mind to make it easy for them. The already lengthy process has been dragged out even further, the aim being to discourage apostasy. There is no evidence that it has that effect. As in other matters, the pope's unforgiving attitude reflects Polish feelings. "Public opinion treats very badly a priest who leaves the ministry," observed Father Adam Boniecki, who worked in the Krakow diocese before becoming the editor of the Polish edition of the Vatican newspaper, *L'Osservatore Romano*. "Nobody publicly proclaims a departure. Rather, it is concealed, as though it were something shameful."[47]

John Paul also takes a tough line with the laity. Because of the church's ban on divorce, Catholics have sought a loophole in church law that allows annulment of a marriage. Traditionally the church had sanctioned annulments only for "sexual incapacity," although exceptions were made for wealthy individuals, particularly those from the European aristocracy. After Vatican II, however, the procedures became more flexible, and by the 1980s the overwhelming majority of the requests (45,000 out of 46,000 in 1987) were granted for "mental incompatibility." John Paul thought the situation disgraceful; he demanded that ecclesiastical judges tighten up on procedures and cease providing a type of "Catholic divorce." He also promised that during his papacy there would be no concessions toward civil divorce, artificial birth control, or abortion. As he warned Americans on his trips to the United States in 1979 and 1987, there could be no dissent on such questions.[48]

The pope has proved equally intransigent against the assumption by the laity of any priestly functions, such as preaching, distribution of communion during Mass, or other "intrusions" on the clerical monopoly of the sacraments. Nor will he countenance any discussion of women ministers. Theologians who raise such questions can expect prompt discipline by the Congregation for the Doctrine of the Faith. Rome acts as though its members were "dumb sheep," complained U.S. theologian Charles Curran, one of numerous scholars to be so treated.[49]

The extent to which the pope is prepared to go in order to enforce discipline emerged in the unhappy experience of the Dutch church, which had been the most liberal in Europe when John Paul ascended Peter's throne. The drama played out in Holland was unusual in that it affected the entire church, but for that reason it served as a precedent for actions against other national churches.

All the factors, and quite a few of the actors, that would become familiar in John Paul's worldwide crackdown were present in January 1980, when the pope convened an extraordinary synod of the Dutch bishops. Appropriately, it was held in the "Hall of the Broken Heads," where at one time the Vatican had kept decapitated statues. Ostensibly the discussions were about the dissension within the Dutch church between a majority of progessive bishops and a minority of conservatives, but the real issue was the exceptionally democratic state of Dutch Catholicism. More than any other European church, the Dutch had put Vatican II into practice by easing the distinction between the laity and the clergy. Lay people, particularly women, helped prepare the liturgy and taught catechism and Scripture classes. During Mass they gave Bible readings and helped distribute communion. Priests and nuns were organized into democratic councils that made recommendations to the bishops, and most of the bishops followed a common pastoral plan. The Dutch church was also extremely active on justice and peace issues, leading protests against the installation of U.S. missiles in Europe and against dictators in the Third World. Though diffuse and sometimes anarchic, this style of Catholicism proved a resounding success in Holland's highly secularized society, and by the time of the 1980 synod, it had overtaken the Protestants to become the largest church in the country.

Conservative Dutch Catholics had never approved of such goings-on, and the Curia shared their opinion, but not until John Paul took command did heads begin to roll. Even before the synod, the Congregation for the Doctrine of the Faith had called the Dutch bishops' chief theological adviser to account, and when the bishops met in Rome, they were told they would be exposed to "the ministry of authority," an infelicitous expression coined by the synod's secretary, Father Joseph Lescrauwaet, who would later be appointed a Dutch bishop. The meeting, attended by John Paul and his top adherents in the Curia, was stacked against the Dutch, who made a brave fight but conceded defeat at the end of the second week. Everything that the Dutch church had achieved since Vatican II was to be wiped from the slate. To assure their submission the bishops were solemnly made to sign a set of forty-six propositions on the altar of the Sistine Chapel. John Paul then lit a candle in front of the altar, as a symbol of the bishops' communion with him, but the flame flickered and died.[50]

The propositions reasserted the traditional authority of bishops over priests and priests over laity, one clause reading, for example, that "neither bishops nor priests are the delegates of the faithful." Lay men and women were forbidden to prepare the liturgy or to teach catechism and Scriptures. Priests were to toe the line and hold their tongues, their councils being "incompatible with church structures." The Curia was to have the last word on liturgy and pastoral planning, supervision that effectively placed the Dutch church under Roman tutelage. The Dutch reacted with dismay, sorrow, and defiance, but the Vatican seemed not to notice. Having humiliated the country's Catholic leadership, the Curia then began adding bishops to the original group of seven. All were curial yes-men of Lescrauwaet's stripe. In a break from established practice, they were named without consultation with the acting bishops or even with Holland's Cardinal Johannes Willebrands. Their appointments caused massive protests throughout the country, and opinion polls showed that only 53 percent of Dutch Catholics felt confidence in their bishops, compared to 88 percent prior to the fateful synod.[51]

Among the most tragic results of the crackdown was the death of Bishop Theodorus Zwartkruis, a popular prelate who was among the most progressive in the hierarchy. Known to all as "Teddy," he was shocked by the appointment of Lescrauwaet and another equally right-wing Dutchman as his auxiliary bishops. "Who can you trust anymore?" was his pained reaction to this imposition. After writing a sorrowful letter to his congregation, he suffered a cerebral hemorrhage. His final words as he was taken away in an ambulance: "The last two weeks have been the hardest in my life."[52]

The reaction among Dutch Catholics was formidable. When one of the auxiliary bishops started to give the pope's blessing at Zwartkruis's funeral, the people angrily abandoned the cathedral. Rome's "administrative violence . . . caused Bishop Zwartkruis grave if not insupportable tensions," charged the Dutch weekly, *Elsevier's Magazine*. "At the very least there is an indirect link between Rome's conduct and the unexpected death of the bishop. The Vatican has not only humiliated Dutch Catholics in every possible way but also ignored, in the most incredible manner, society's own respect for the rights of local churches."[53]

The "administrative violence" engendered a growing indifference to the Roman Catholic Church, and in some cases to revulsion against it. John Paul felt the heat of the disapproval during his visit to Holland in 1985, when he was met with savage demonstrations. Police had to shoot over the crowds to force them to disperse, and some protesters were injured in the melees. A bomb was found at a site where the pope was to appear; hostile posters went up everywhere. "Move over, John Paul," said one. "You're hiding Jesus." "Welcome" speeches by Dutch Catholics were equally chilling. "How can we have any credibility in the preaching of the Gospel of liberation when it is being proclaimed with a pointed finger instead of an extended hand?" the president of a local missionary council challenged the pope. The hostility and the lack of cheering crowds obviously made an impression on John Paul, who tried to reassure the Dutch that he understood their feelings. But it was too late to repair the damage. On the one hand was a people who believed they had been deeply humiliated; on the other, a pope convinced that what he had seen in Holland was proof of the "disorders and divisions" caused by Vatican II.[54]

The Third World

If the Dutch affair marked the end of John Paul's honeymoon with the Europeans, his trip to Central America was the turning point for him in the Third World. Since more than half the world's 900 million Catholics are to be found in the developing countries, those areas hold the church's future. Unlike much of Europe, where Catholicism is in decline, the Third World churches are vibrant and growing. Latin America leads the way, with the largest number of Catholics and the most advanced indigenous theologies and lay movements. It was also the setting, in Nicaragua, for the first revolution in which Marxists and Catholics joined forces to overthrow a U.S.-backed dictator. John Paul's visit to Central America in 1983 therefore attracted more than usual interest. His attitude toward the Sandinista government in Nicaragua would indicate to both Washington and the supporters of liberation theology as to where the Vatican stood on the issue of Christian-Marxist dialogue. He was also expected to express disapproval toward the bloody military allies of the United States in the region. The trip itself was hazardous because much of Central America was in a state of war, and there was always the possibility that an extremist would try to kill the pope. Vatican security was particularly concerned about Guatemala, where General José Efraín Ríos Montt, a born-again dictator, was massacring Catholics, and El Salvador, where a right-wing death squad had murdered San Salvador's Archbishop Oscar Romero.

The high point—or, as it turned out, the low point—of the eight-day swing through eight countries was Nicaragua. John Paul was extremely unhappy with the situation there, and throughout the year before his visit relations between Managua and the Holy See had been tense. Influenced by Colombian Cardinal López Trujillo, who led the right wing of the Latin American church, the pope in August 1982 wrote a diatribe against Nicaragua's pro-Sandinista church, accusing it of causing a schism. Then, in October, John Paul met with General Vernon Walters (Ret.), a former deputy director of the CIA and later a roving ambassador for President Reagan. A hard-line Catholic with contacts in the extreme right of the European and Latin American churches, Walters discussed with the pope the situation in Nicaragua. Soon thereafter, John Paul demanded that the four priests in the Sandinista government resign their posts.

Although much was made of the coincidence in timing between Walters's visit and the papal order, John Paul's hostility was aroused less by Washington's desires than by the threat Nicaragua posed to his plans for a Catholic Restoration. The pro-Sandinista church, better known as the "popular church," had emerged "from below" and was thus anathema to a pope bent on reestablishing a top-down hierarchy. The attacks upon Managua's then archbishop Miguel Obando y Bravo, viewed by many Nicaraguans as Reagan's lackey, merely confirmed for the pope the heretical schism of the "popular church." And in this instance authority was a major issue for political as well as structural reasons. John Paul's experience in Poland had shown him that the church could survive and thrive despite a Marxist government so long as it represented nationalistic aspirations. But in Nicaragua nationalism is identified with Sandinismo —which embodies gut feelings about patriotism and cultural pride and is symbolized by the country's national hero, Augusto César Sandino, who waged a guerrilla war against an occupying U.S. Marine force earlier in this century.

Catholics, especially poor ones, had played an important role in the 1979 revolution that toppled Anastasio Somoza, and the appointment of priests to head important government offices, including the foreign, education, and culture ministries, was a recognition of that contribution. But the presence of priests in government was highly dangerous, in the pope's opinion, because it symbolized the fusion of Catholicism with Nicaraguan left-wing nationalism. Unlike Poland's docile Catholics, the Nicaraguan popular church was not willing to take orders from Rome; it produced instead its own theological interpretations in support of the revolution. These were received with sympathy by many churches in Latin America which admired the revolution because of its commitment to the poor. Both the Sandinistas and the Vatican understood the stakes: If Nicaragua could demonstrate to the rest of Latin America that Christian-Marxist cooperation made Rome superfluous, the Vatican might lose its hold on the most populous Catholic region in the world. As noted by the Irish political writer Conor Cruise O'Brien in a shrewd analysis of the pope's plight, Catholic Sandinismo was potentially a latter-day version of the split caused in European Catholicism by the Protestant Reformation.[55]

Negotiations leading up to John Paul's visit to Nicaragua were therefore extremely complex. At one point he announced that he would not come if the priests did not quit the government, but the Sandinistas flatly refused to be coerced. As one high-ranking Nicaraguan official admitted, having the priests in government was one of the Sandinistas' trump cards, and they would leave only when the Vatican was prepared to give something equally important in return, namely religious as well as diplomatic recognition of the revolution. Having lost that round, the Vatican was asked by the Sandinistas to provide assurances that the pope would not use his visit to Nicaragua to solicit support for the *contras* or Obando y Bravo. According to Nicaraguan officials, the Curia promised there would be no polemics in the pope's speeches, but almost from the moment he stepped off the plane in Managua John Paul stirred up a storm.

Since every gesture and word could be misinterpreted in so charged an atmosphere, it had been agreed that the then three-man junta would come forward to greet the pope at the airport instead of the usual lineup of cabinet ministers because the latter included priests. Nevertheless, the cabinet was massed in the background to receive a collective salute from the pope. Everything seemed to be going according to plan until one overenthusiastic official, apparently not realizing the sensitive protocol, stepped forward to greet the pope. John Paul then had to continue down the line—and there, kneeling in front of him, was Father Ernesto Cardenal, the white-haired minister of culture. When Cardenal tried to kiss the pope's ring, John Paul yanked his hand away and, wagging a finger of admonition at the priest, said, "You must regularize your situation with the church."[56]

The scene showing Cardenal in tears was televised nationwide, causing anger everywhere. Cardenal was not only a hero of the revolution but also the most famous living poet of a country where poets are held in the highest esteem. For many the pope's rebuke signified the humiliation of the revolution as well as a beloved priest. But if John Paul had given Cardenal his blessing, it would have been hailed as symbolic approval of the fusion of Christianity and Marxism. (Cardenal also happened to be the best-known Nicaraguan proponent of that synthesis.) However, few observers of the airport drama understood the dilemma. To the uninformed viewer John Paul looked angry—which he may well have been—but such was his habitual pose during tiring ceremonies with government officials. While listening to long welcoming speeches, the pope often held his jaw in his hand as if he had a toothache and crossed his arms over his chest in what might have seemed a belligerent gesture.

Tempers were already frayed, therefore, by the time John Paul appeared at Managua's main plaza for the principal event of the visit—an open-air Mass attended by upwards of 700,000 people, the largest crowd in Nicaraguan memory. Many Nicaraguans had hoped for some word of comfort for the teenage sons and daughters they had lost in combat with the *contras* (a funeral for seventeen young casualties had been held the day before in the same plaza). Others expected him to say something encouraging about their hard-won revolution against the Somoza dictatorship. In vain. Instead of soothing words, a fiery John Paul lit into the popular church, warning the people of their obligation to obey their bishops, though for many Nicaraguans the bishops appeared to be allied with the *contra* opposition. The unity of the church was endangered, he said, by "unacceptable ideological commitments, temporal options and concepts of the church [i.e., the popular church] which are contrary to the true one." The authoritarian tone, and repeated references to "the bishops," set the crowd on edge, and soon there were shouts, then chants: "We want peace!" "People's power!" Accustomed to obedient crowds, John Paul was outraged. "*¡Silencio!*" he roared. But the crowd would not be silent: "We want a prayer for our martyrs!" Again, "*¡Silencio!*"[57]

Daniel Ortega, then head of the junta and later the elected president of Nicaragua, tried to make amends with a plea for understanding as the pope was returning to his plane. But John Paul was in no mood for excuses. He was "very sad and very angry," and now convinced that all the terrible things Obando y Bravo had said about the Sandinistas were true. On his return to Rome he ordered Cardinal Ratzinger to prepare a cautionary analysis of liberation theology which, when published the following year, turned out to be a diatribe against the popular church in Nicaragua. In April 1985, a little more than two years after his fateful visit to Nicaragua, he made Obando Central America's only cardinal. Fearful that his church would be swallowed up by the revolution, John

Paul had not known how to play a mediating role, although that was exactly what was needed for Nicaragua's deeply divided church. As in Holland, many Nicaraguans retained bitter memories of the papal visit, and some said they would never forgive the pope for his performance at the gigantic open-air Mass. Still, it is hard to imagine how else he could have behaved, given his Polish background and his fears for the church.

Around the World

Although the Central American tour was more politically charged than most of John Paul's visits to the Third World, it revealed certain characteristics that were common to his travels.* The most important, in the opinion of religious analysts, was that he "didn't listen." Instead of using such trips (which consumed 15 percent of his time) to dialogue with local church leaders, John Paul lectured them on the need for greater discipline. Written in Rome, his talks often reflected the negative opinions of the Curia and did not address the complex realities of individual churches. John Paul, complained bishops, theologians, and lay leaders, came to lay down Roman law and to reinforce centralized power through pageants to the papacy. Although local churches had to assume the costs of such visits, which were sometimes inordinately expensive, the pontiff's hosts were often treated as mere propmen—they were expected to be present at the papal spectacles but not to open their mouths, save to praise John Paul.

The principal motif in such pageants was a grandiose procession and Mass, sometimes with sets worthy of Cecil B. deMille. On his visit to Caracas in 1985, the main event was an outdoor Mass held atop a towering, flower-strewn pyramid. For the sweating masses gathered below, the pope was a barely perceptible figure among all the props. As elsewhere on such trips, a crowd of vendors hawked scarves, hats, T-shirts, pictures, figures, ashtrays, and balloons, all displaying the papal effigy, in addition to the usual collection of rosaries and candles. The vendors were poor people looking to make a buck, whereas well-to-do operators had been exploiting the papal image for weeks before his arrival through commercials on television and radio and in newspapers and magazines. Con-

* John Paul visited 65 nations in the first seven years of his papacy. On his 32 journeys he covered 310,292 miles and gave 1,128 official speeches. (*L'Osservatore Romano*, January 19, 1987)

sumers were urged to buy a new wardrobe in honor of John Paul's visit, and a television and car as well.

As an amateur actor in his youth and a lifelong lover of theater, John Paul relishes spectacles (he engaged movie director Franco Zeffirelli to organize some of his solemn sessions at St. Peter's basilica).[58] The people also enjoy the show, and turn out by the millions to see him. But since nothing ever comes of the promises and exhortations, return engagements are not notably successful. On his second trip to the Dominican Republic, for instance, the crowd was significantly smaller than it had been on his first visit. Similarly, only one-quarter of the horde that flocked to see him on his first visit to Zaire was on hand when he returned in 1985. Television ratings for his visit to Colombia in 1986 were low—on average, only 12.8 percent of the country's viewers watched the transmissions, although for many people TV was their only way to see the pope.[59] The crowds were still respectable, but there was no novelty, since Paul VI had previously visited the country in 1968. The novelty also wore off for the world press, and the throngs of reporters that accompanied his first trips gradually diminished. In a 1986 poll that asked U.S. Catholic editors to list the top religious stories of that year, John Paul's travels were relegated to ninth place; as a newsmaker, he trailed Seattle's Archbishop Raymond Hunthausen and theologian Charles Curran, both of whom had been attacked by the Vatican.[60]

For the crowds the papal presence was a talisman of sorts—the people kept the papal ashtrays and scarves as mementos, however crass, of his visit. But they also yearned for something more—a small improvement in their lives. The pope could not wish away misery, but local churches could provide organizational support to help the people improve their conditions. Unfortunately much of such work was frowned upon by the Vatican because it had indigenous political or cultural overtones. Just as the Latin Americans' liberation theology was denounced as a political threat to a centralized Roman administration, African cultural traditions were rejected as dangerous to the purity of the European faith. Giancarlo Zízola, an Italian expert on Vatican affairs, argued that in contrast to the Apostle Paul, who did not attempt to attach any cultural model to the Christian message, John Paul's journeys were aimed at establishing cultural hegemony under the papacy. John Paul himself made the same point when urging Third World peoples, particularly the Africans, to avoid the dangers of "inculturation" by maintaining unity with and through the pope.[61] The stubborn hostility of the Curia to indigenous forms of Ca-

tholicism and the humiliation of Third World religious leaders gradually
began to sink into the collective conscience. Disenchantment also increased because the papal visits had no perceptible effect, save for their
cost to already poor churches. "The Pope doesn't listen and so he doesn't
understand the real needs of the people," said an Italian missionary with
long experience in Zaire. "People become disillusioned. That's why so
few turned out for his second visit."[62] "The church is not going to stem
the loss of the faithful, particularly the young, by popularizing the pleasant
and telegenic face of the Pope," agreed the French church historian André
Mandouze. "So many hands outstretched, so many children embraced,
so much money spent. So many promises made and rights proclaimed in
terms that are as generous as they are generalized and so many express
prohibitions that are as precise as they are unworkable. I would prefer
a real communion of people with the right to discuss and respond—a
different kind of encounter than that with ancestral authority."[63]

But John Paul did not see it that way. "He believes that only he can
save the world," explained a Vatican journalist. As an example, he cited
the pope's response to journalists' queries as to whether it was politic to
go to Protestant England when it was at war with Catholic Argentina
over the Falkland Islands. "I am the Pope!" John Paul responded, as if
amazed by the question. "I must go where I'm needed," he said, poking
one journalist to add emphasis. "The group's impression," said the journalist, "was that the Pope thought only he could do anything."[64]

From Washington with Love

In fact, there were some things that only a pope could do, as the
Reagan administration well knew. For example, at Washington's suggestion the Vatican undertook to mediate a territorial dispute between
Chile and Argentina over the Beagle Channel. The hostility between the
two military regimes was serious enough to cause talk of war, but the
State Department under Carter had no influence with Argentina because
of its criticism of human rights violations, and still less under Reagan,
when his administration sided with Britain in the Falklands War. Chile
was similarly unapproachable because the U.S. Congress had cut off
military aid. The Vatican, however, persuaded the two sides to negotiate
by promising papal visits if agreement were reached. (Both governments
were eager to receive John Paul's blessing after the unpleasant things
Paul VI had said about them.) John Paul was unable to patch up differ-

ences between Argentina and Britain, but his negotiators resolved the Beagle Channel dispute, and in the spring of 1987 he set out for the Southern Cone to fulfill his promise to Chile and Argentina. Unfortunately for the Argentine generals, they were not around to bask in the pope's radiance, having been replaced by a civilian government, but Chile's wily Pinochet got his reward despite widespread opposition from local Catholics, who thought it disgraceful that the pope should accept an invitation from one of the worst violators of human rights in South America. The Vatican achieved two goals—the resolution of a territorial dispute between Catholic states and the establishment of its credentials as a mediator in international conflicts. Not since Leo XIII in the nineteenth century had Rome served as an international arbitrator, and John Paul was clearly determined to reassert that role as part of his Restoration of papal power and a uniformly Catholic world.

His services as go-between were also important in the three-sided game in progress among Poland, the Soviet Union, and the United States. Seeing a fellow conservative in the papacy, President Reagan seized every opportunity to praise the pope and his brave followers in Poland. Washington strongly supported Solidarity, and when it was outlawed in 1981, the U.S. government imposed economic sanctions on Poland. While the Reagan administration claimed the decision reflected its concern for human rights, European political analysts, including skeptical members of the Vatican Secretariat of State, observed that U.S. interests were served by encouraging any local challenge to Soviet hegemony. Washington also supported the pope's attempts to gain more space for the church in Poland and elsewhere in the socialist bloc, again not from solicitude for religious rights but because such efforts were bound to incommode the Soviets. Although Reagan tried to woo the pope into a "sacred alliance" against Moscow, through direct telephone calls to John Paul and during a meeting of the two leaders in mid-1982, Cardinal Casaroli, the savvy Vatican secretary of state, succeeded in preventing an American embrace.[65]

Moscow, for its part, viewed the Polish pope with considerable apprehension, since he wielded enormous power in its most obstreperous satellite and had shown that he could cause Catholic unrest elsewhere in the empire, as in the Ukraine. Stalin had sneered at Catholicism's importance—"How many divisions has the pope?"—but his successors in the Kremlin were much less inclined to dismiss John Paul. Gradually, therefore, a tenuous relationship developed between Rome and Moscow, based on a pragmatic trade-off of political favors for religious ones. On the issue of U.S. economic sanctions against Poland, for example, the pope supported an agreement between Poland's strongman Wojciech Jaruzelski and Cardinal Josef Glemp to work for their elimination. In February 1987, a month after a "historic" meeting between Jaruzelski and the pope to discuss such problems, President Reagan lifted the sanctions. Although some political prisoners had been released, the situation in Poland hardly warranted Reagan's claim that "the light of liberty shines in Poland." The change in policy therefore had to be attributed to other factors, including pressures by the pope.[66]

Washington could afford the gesture, and if it made the pope happy, so much the better, since his hostility toward the Sandinistas was a help to Washington. Although John Paul had his own religious reasons for opposing the Sandinista revolution, Rome and Washington agreed on several vital areas. One was that Nicaragua was setting a bad example for the rest of Latin America. Not only had the Nicaraguans thrown off the gringos' yoke; they were also refusing to take orders from Rome. The specter of religion-fueled rebellion worried both power centers, which saw liberation theology as the wedge for Marxist revolution. In fact, most of the region's liberation theologies were not Marxist, but having always dismissed Latin America as a cultural backwater, neither Washington nor Rome was inclined to waste time trying to distinguish one variety of theology from another. One had only to look at Nicaragua, said officials of the State Department and the Curia, to know what could happen elsewhere in Latin America. Consequently, Nicaragua's "popular church" became synonymous with liberation theology, despite the objections of Gustavo Gutiérrez, the Peruvian father of liberation theology, and other leading theologians.

John Paul's feelings about communism were fed by the German bishops, who, even before Wojtyla's ascension, had been fulminating against the "socialist" tendencies of some churches in South America. The Germans preferred right-wing governments that were strongly anticommunist and procapitalist, even though such regimes frequently persecuted local Catholic churches. Unable to understand that capitalism had produced one standard of living in Germany but quite another in Latin America, they were horrified when some South American bishops, most notably the Peruvian and Brazilian hierarchies, denounced the voraciousness of foreign capitalism. Liberation theology and the Christian base communities were blamed for such radicalism, although the communities were only seeking the same basic rights that were taken for granted in Germany. The German-Polish alliance in the Vatican interpreted protests against right-wing regimes and their foreign multinational allies as proof of Marxist tendencies among the churches. Washington could not have agreed more. So this became a second area of agreement, not only in Latin America but in other parts of the Third World, such as the Philippines, where both Washington and Rome supported the Marcos dictatorship to the bitter end. "The Vatican's viewpoint," said an American bishop, "is essentially compatible with Reagan's outlook." Nobel laureate Gabriel García Márquez agreed. John Paul had a "certain mindset" that blocked his understanding of situations that did not fit into the East-West mold, he said after a private audience with the pope.[67]

Highly placed church officials confirmed that it was sometimes difficult to "get through" to John Paul. According to one cardinal present at a meeting to prepare for the 1985 synod, John Paul opened the discussion by telling Chicago's Cardinal Joseph Bernardin that he did not understand why the U.S. hierarchy was sending bishops to visit Cuba and Nicaragua or why the bishops did not "support your own president's policies in Central America." After hearing this salvo, said the prelate, Cardinal Sin, who was then deeply involved in the rising opposition to Ferdinand Marcos, rolled up his eyes as if to say, "Now we have to run our churches to please Reagan." The discussion ended, said the cardinal, after Bernardin made a reasoned reply, explaining the U.S. bishops' position against the *contra* war. No more was heard on the subject for the rest of the meetings.[68]

During the same period John Paul met with Senator Robert Dole (R.-Kan.), who visited the pontiff on behalf of President Reagan to obtain the pope's views on Central America. Dole gave the pope a letter from Reagan outlining Washington's strategy on Nicaragua; a second letter from the President on the same subject was delivered by the U.S. Embassy in Rome. Because of a Vatican "gaffe," as a Curia official called it, Rome's response to the two letters on Nicaragua was "It's good"—possibly because Reagan had emphasized a diplomatic solution without mentioning the threat of military reprisals. In any case, Reagan interpreted the message as providing papal support for his Central American policies—a support that apparently did exist in view of John Paul's challenge to Bernardin. But the President spoiled things by blurting out that message to participants at a State Department conference on religion. They immediately relayed it to the press, prompting a Vatican denial that the pope had given any endorsement of a "concrete plan" for Central America.[69]

The denial, made by the Vatican's ambassador to Washington, Archbishop Pio Laghi, could be interpreted in light of Laghi's subsequent statements in which he admitted a "parallelism in viewpoints" of the Vatican and Washington but insisted that there were no specific arrangements between Reagan and the pope. William Wilson, Reagan's first ambassador to the Vatican, used Laghi's very words to describe such common concerns as liberation theology, Nicaragua, Poland, the Middle East, and U.S.-Soviet tensions—subjects he had an opportunity to discuss with the pope and other high-ranking Vatican officials.

Much of the Curia's information comes from like-minded hard-liners in other countries, and these bishops are often sympathetic to, or members of, the wealthy elites that dominate business and politics. Such was the case in Brazil, where European multinationals, including Germany's Volkswagen, were locked in a struggle with progressive bishops over land ownership in the Amazon. From Germany came complaints by important lay leaders, government officials, and bishops; in Brazil, similar charges were made by conservative Brazilian churchmen, who had important sponsors in the Curia, such as Cardinal Agnelo Rossi, the Brazilian dean of the College of Cardinals. The complaints did not deal with the real issue (i.e., that a given multinational was in trouble with a bishop for its treatment of impoverished peasants), but implied that the bishop was a Marxist sympathizer, involved in politics and/or poisoning the minds of the faithful with theological and liturgical innovations. The underlying boast of such groups was that, unlike their opponents, they were loyal to the pope.

Critics of this sort had been around in the United States prior to the 1980s, but when Reagan came to power they were aided by quasi-government religious organizations which had their own lines to the Vatican. The Institute on Religion and Democracy, for example, had access to the Holy See through its most prominent Catholic member, social critic Michael Novak. The institute was an early champion of Archbishop Obando y Bravo, and it cultivated Nicaraguan defectors who had an entrée to the Vatican, such as Humberto Belli, a protégé of Obando who worked in a Vatican secretariat and later became an important anti-Sandinista propagandist in the United States. These private and semi-private groups continually fed information into the Vatican from Central America and the United States at the same time that U.S. officials in Rome were providing their appraisals of people and events. The flow of information became livelier and more direct after the United States reestablished relations with the Vatican in 1984, thereby opening official channels of communication. How much of it the Curia swallowed was impossible to say—Vatican officials claimed to distrust all such intelligence.[70] But since the pope had no sympathy for the Sandinistas, it could be assumed that they listened, using any allegations that advanced the Vatican's own particular interests.

U.S. officials have maintained a close relationship with the Curia since World War II when the CIA's predecessor, the Office of Strategic Services (OSS), worked with the Vatican. After the war the CIA created a special unit to tap into the Vatican's rich lode of information, and it cooperated with the Curia in helping Nazi criminals find refuge, primarily in Latin America. (See Chapter 10.) During the crucial 1948 elections in Italy, when the Communist Party seemed likely to win power, the CIA worked closely with Vatican agencies to secure the victory of the Christian Democrats. State Department documents showed continuing CIA interest in Vatican affairs in the 1960s and 1970s, including reports revealing U.S. pressure on Paul VI to support President Nguyen Van Thieu in South Vietnam. The thrust of the reports was that the pope was an important ally who had the means to influence world affairs.[71]

The extent to which the CIA cooperated with John Paul's papacy in providing information was unknown, but one ambassador to the Vatican with long experience in Rome was convinced that the CIA supplied the Curia with background data on diplomats accredited to the Vatican, particularly those representing leftist governments, such as Nicaragua.[72] The FBI's spying on Archbishop Raymond Hunthausen at least suggested links to subsequent Vatican disciplining of the Seattle prelate. Using the Freedom of Information Act, the *National Catholic Reporter* obtained FBI documentation that showed the agency had been keeping files on Hunthausen and Detroit's Auxiliary Bishop Thomas Gumbleton because of their antiwar activities. The FBI withheld six pages of information on Hunthausen on the ground that the material had originated at another unnamed agency, possibly U.S. Naval Intelligence, which had also kept files on Hunthausen, or the CIA. Although the Gumbleton files dealt with his campaigns against the Vietnam War and racial inequalities during the late 1960s and early 1970s, the Hunthausen documents showed that he had been an object of surveillance through 1983—the same period when the American bishops were preparing their controversial peace pastoral on nuclear war. Representative Don Edwards (D.-Calif.), chairman of the House Judiciary Subcommittee on Civil and Constitutional Rights, told the *Reporter* that the investigation of the bishops "fits right into" a pattern of harassment of critics of the administration's foreign policy, citing nearly sixty cases of suspicious break-ins of offices belonging to groups opposed to Washington's Central American policy, including churches.[73]

Since the FBI sometimes shares information with the CIA, it is not impossible that the data on Hunthausen was passed on to the Vatican. Hunthausen had been particularly outspoken in his opposition to the arms race, and he and Gumbleton had played key roles in persuading the U.S. bishops to write the letter on nuclear warfare. A stream of important U.S. officials had visited the Vatican in the same period, including President Reagan, Vice President Bush, Secretary of State Shultz, Defense Secretary Weinberger, and General Walters, all of whom may have complained about the bishops' peace stance, although William A. Wilson, Reagan's first ambassador to the Vatican, insisted that they did not mention the letter. Meanwhile, the German bishops, led by Cardinal Höffner, had denounced the American bishops for their position on nuclear deterrence. After Höffner's meetings with the French bishops, they, too, joined the chorus. Back in the United States, Republican activist Paul Weyrich and his New Right followers among Catholic fundamentalists, including the archconservative weekly *The Wanderer,* flooded the Vatican with criticisms of Hunthausen. As in Brazil, where tensions between the local church and the papacy were basically about politics, the attack on Hunthausen was not direct, allegations about religious sins serving as a smokescreen for the real attack. Hunthausen needed to be disciplined, it was said, because there was too much democracy in his archdiocese and he had sanctioned all manner of liturgical innovations. But since many other dioceses in the United States were guilty of the same practices, there was no convincing reason for Hunthausen to be singled out except for his antiwar activism.

Archbishop Pio Laghi, Rome's ambassador to Washington, later confirmed that Hunthausen's refusal to pay taxes for defense and his protests against nuclear weapons had been the subject of many of the complaints. Nevertheless, he insisted that "at no time did the Holy See pursue with Archbishop Hunthausen the criticisms it received." Discussions, he said, were solely about doctrinal and pastoral matters, and Hunthausen agreed that it was so. Still, there is more than one way to skin a cat. By punishing Hunthausen, Rome sent a warning to the U.S. bishops to pay more attention to spiritual matters and less to political ones, and at the same time gave some of its most important allies, especially in Germany and the United States, symbolic support in the controversy over the arms race. The pope made a similar point on his visit to the United States in 1987 by ignoring the bishops' letter on nuclear warfare despite its ongoing importance. Edward L. Rowny, White House adviser on arms control, could thus state that the Reagan administration's defense policies were "in harmony" with the pope's criteria but not with some positions adopted by the U.S. bishops.[74]

Archbishop Laghi was formerly apostolic delegate to the United States before his elevation to pro-nuncio, or ambassador, in 1984, while William Wilson had been one of Reagan's California buddies and his financial adviser, then graduated from personal envoy to ambassador to the Vatican. Laghi was much the smoother of the two. A charming if ambitious career diplomat, he had served as papal nuncio in Nicaragua, India, and Palestine. He was posted to Argentina in the 1970s during the height of the military terror, and that was probably his most difficult assignment. Although individual Argentines remembered him with gratitude for risking his life to help them, he was criticized for failing to speak out against the atrocities. His public speeches also revealed ambivalence. In 1976, in the early months of the military regime, he gave a speech to the army in which he cited the church's just-war theory to sanction the military's campaign against dissent. He then blessed the troops. Of course it was not the nuncio's job to supplant the Argentine bishops in denunciation of human rights violations—a task most of them refused. On the other hand, said Emilio F. Mignone, an Argentine Catholic writer and human rights activist, Laghi displayed considerable cynicism in his public embrace of the junta. According to Mignone, Laghi played tennis regularly with Admiral Emilio Massera, among the most bloodthirsty of the military leaders, and, said Mignone, he admitted giving communion to a general he knew to be involved in the massacre of five Irish-Argentine priests and seminarians—this at the funeral Mass for the slain priests. Old acquaintances in Rome also discerned a certain cynicism, or *romanitas,* in Laghi, whom they described as "conservative because he is ambitious for his career." Although Laghi disclaimed such ambitions, he was mentioned in Vatican circles as a candidate to replace Casaroli as secretary of state.[75]

The go-between for John Paul and Reagan, and for the Curia and American bishops, Laghi had a sensitive job. He tried to keep a low profile but was frequently in the news because of Rome's disciplinary measures against American Catholic leaders, most notably Archbishop

Hunthausen. Laghi, who was called upon to apply the punishment, was furious when Hunthausen went public with the matter. It made him look bad, and his defense had the same self-serving tone that he had used in Argentina to dismiss Mignone and other supplicants who wanted him to speak out against mass torture and murder. It wasn't his fault, he complained to *The New York Times,* if Americans had a "Watergate complex" about Rome's desire to handle its affairs "behind the door."[76]

For all his discretion Laghi could not hide the fact that by the end of 1987 he had been instrumental in the appointment of nearly 100 U.S. bishops and twelve of the country's thirty-three archbishops. A good many were Curia yes-men, and while their number was not sufficient to tip the balance in the 405-member bishops' conference, the trend was ominous for moderate and progressive sectors in the U.S. church. Catholic traditionalists shared the Reagan administration's optimism that, with time, the new bishops would stem the liberal trend, much as it was hoped that Reagan's Supreme Court appointments would slow down an activist court.

In Rome Bill Wilson made a splash of sorts by his business and political contacts, including those with Libyan leader Colonel Muammar al-Qaddafi. A well-to-do Californian with interests in oil, real estate, and the stock exchange, Wilson was among a small group of businessmen who in the 1960s had urged Reagan to go into politics. He advised Reagan on his personal finances, negotiating the $500,000 purchase of Reagan's ranch near Santa Barbara and leading the fund-raising drive in California for his 1980 presidential bid. A member of Reagan's "kitchen cabinet," Wilson was appointed presidential envoy to Rome in 1981. Vatican insiders said the appointment was primarily a "feather in the cap" of a man who was less interested in diplomacy than in business. Wilson had converted to Catholicism as a young man and was a member of the powerful Knights of Malta, an international organization comprising a *Who's Who* of the Catholic right. His personal friendship with Reagan and self-described conservatism—he thought Vatican II had been a disaster—were apparently the major considerations in his appointment.[77]

When he was not traveling on business affairs, the tall, distinguished-looking Californian got on well with the Curia, particularly Archbishop Paul Marcinkus, the American-born head of the scandal-ridden Vatican Bank, who secured offices for Wilson in prime Vatican property near the papal apartments. Wilson returned the favor by writing to then attorney general William French Smith on Marcinkus's behalf, for which he received a rap on the knuckles from senior Justice Department officials.

They feared that Wilson might involve Smith in an Italian government investigation of Marcinkus's links to Michele Sindona, a convicted financial embezzler who had worked closely with the Vatican Bank.[78]

Wilson was valued primarily for his intimacy with Reagan, but it did not hurt that he agreed with the Curia about Poland, Nicaragua, and the dangers of Marxism in Latin America. (Wilson, who was fluent in Spanish, had a ranch in Mexico and business interests in Chile.) According to Wilson, he never "heard any adverse comment [on aid to the *contras*], so I have to assume they are in favor of it. But that's one of those cases where you have to read the tea leaves. They have to be very careful about that. They have the problem with the troops working out of Honduras, another country; the problems with the Miskito Indians. The Vatican is concerned about the welfare of all these people, so they have to be careful."[79]

Over a period of years Wilson's usefulness was eroded by a lack of diplomacy. He caused several flaps in addition to the Marcinkus incident, one of them coming after his claim that Rome supported the Reagan administration's position on El Salvador—which may have been true but was hardly diplomatic. Another uproar greeted charges in a Roman newspaper that he had given the Curia a hit list of "subversive" priests and nuns in Central America, urging that they be relieved of their duties. Wilson denied the charge, although he did admit that he would be pleased if the Catholic Church exercised in Central America the "stabilizing" influence it exerted in Poland.[80]

His last caper—an unauthorized visit to Qaddafi—led to his resignation in 1986. The Reagan administration had held Qaddafi responsible for terrorist attacks on the Rome and Vienna airports, and Americans and U.S. companies had been told to sever ties with Libya. Nevertheless, Wilson held talks with Qaddafi's representatives in Libya shortly after the airport outrages. He defended the propriety of his visit and denied reports of business dealings on behalf of the Pennzoil Company, of which he had been a board director, but Secretary of State Shultz was angered by the trip at a time when Washington was trying to isolate Qaddafi. It did not seem to bother Reagan, who, when Wilson resigned, expressed "deep appreciation" for his friend's work at the Vatican. Indeed, some Washington analysts thought there was more to the matter than a tiff with the State Department, which had not only known of Wilson's business trips but allowed him to keep his seat on Pennzoil's board until the Libyan scandal broke. According to sources in Washington and Rome, Wilson had been communicating with Libya "over a period of time," and when matters turned nasty after the airport attacks, he reportedly asked the prime minister of Malta, Karmenu Mifsud Bonnici, to relay to Libyan officials information designed to defuse the situation. Wilson had insisted when he was appointed to the Vatican that he had been given blanket authority by then national security adviser William Clark, another member of the California clique, to undertake missions at his own discretion, and it was later charged, during congressional hearings, that Clark and his successor, Robert McFarlane, had approved Wilson's secret talks with Qaddafi. While Clark and McFarlane denied the allegations, the affair suggested that Wilson may have maintained "back-channel communications" with the White House that bypassed the State Department. That such channels were in place became public knowledge when the Iran-*contra* scandal broke in 1986.[81]

Two Leaders

The "parallelism" between Reagan's Washington and John Paul's Vatican also reflected certain similarities in the two men. While the Curia looked on Reagan as a "cowboy" and privately disdained his crude power plays,[82] the pope shared with Reagan a mental fixity that made him equally stubborn. Just as Reagan was convinced that tax cuts would reduce the budget deficit, John Paul refused to be dissuaded from his conviction that a Polish hierarchical model best served the universal church. In their dealings with other countries, both revealed a parochial view of the world's diverse history and cultures. Although John Paul was better educated and a much deeper thinker, his political vision was stuck in the Cold War fifties, which were also the formative period for Reagan's politics. Thus neither man could understand the nationalistic yearnings of the Third World, which were inevitably attributed to Marxist influence. Skilled showmen, they were at ease with crowds and television cameras, and in the early years of their administrations were known as the "Great Communicators." But with time their messages came to have a hollow ring, and people ceased listening.

Like the Reagan administration, John Paul's papacy was weakened by scandal, particularly the goings-on at the Vatican Bank. Yet no one questioned the strength of his personal integrity, which set him apart from nearly all other world leaders. Still, as Catholic writer Colman McCarthy observed, more than inner goodness is needed for a pastor trying to claim the world's moral leadership.[83] By insisting on sterile dogmatisms and exhorting obedience, John Paul repeatedly lost opportunities to advance his cause. As John XXIII knew, modern society is not persuaded by authoritarianism but by compassion, service, and a willingness to listen.

PART II

LATIN AMERICA

CHAPTER 4

✝

LIBERATION THEOLOGY: ROME VERSUS LATIN AMERICA

WHILE THE STRUGGLE for world Catholicism has taken many different forms, such as disputes over religious dress or the use of local cultural symbols in Catholic rituals, the most important battles have been over theology. In contrast to Catholics in Europe and the United States, who tend to dismiss theology as an esoteric subject of interest only to religious scholars, people in the Third World have developed their own theological responses, an example being Latin America's Christian base communities, which regularly meet to reflect on the meaning of faith in the midst of poverty and repression. The people do not use complicated words—most are barely literate—but as attested by priests and nuns who work with the communities, their observations are often profound because they live their theology through solidarity, charity, and self-sacrifice. Theology is not an ivory-tower science but the practical application of faith, and as such it can challenge the secular and religious authorities on many issues, from agrarian reform to birth control and lay ministers. Just because the Vatican says that something is so does not mean it is God-given—that it is right—since many of its fiats are questionable on historical grounds, such as a papal monopoly on bishops' appointments, as well as on Christian ones. Theology can therefore become a highly subversive influence, by questioning the religious rationale for Roman power.

As the guardians of the faith, theologians have always been closely watched by Rome for any deviation, although there have been times, as during Vatican II, when their questioning was welcomed because it helped develop new understandings of faith. But during John Paul's counterreformation theologians were again scrutinized for possible "heresy" by the Congregation for the Doctrine of the Faith, which became the most feared office in the Vatican: Its decrees could—and did—destroy not only individual careers but also entire churches, as occurred in Holland, where the Congregation imposed its reactionary rule.

Until John Paul's papacy the Congregation carried on its affairs in relative secrecy. Most people knew there had been an institution called the Inquisition, but it was widely assumed that trials of heretics had ended with the Enlightenment. In fact, the Holy Office of the Congregation of the Universal Inquisition, as it was then called, continued to be active, but its persecution of theologians and other dissenters was an in-house affair rarely mentioned in public. The idea that the chief inquisitor would agree to a newspaper interview was unthinkable, and it was equally unlikely that a popular publication would see anything newsworthy in an obscure office of the Vatican. But in the 1980s, when Catholicism became front-page political news, the Restoration's "theological bunker" attracted considerable interest. Cardinal Joseph Ratzinger, the Congregation's white-haired prefect, became the subject of a best-seller on theology,[1] and he appeared frequently on the covers of mass-circulation periodicals, including *The New York Times Magazine* and *Newsweek*.

The interest in Ratzinger was not misplaced. Known in Vatican circles as "the pope's man," his power within the Curia was equaled only by that of Cardinal Casaroli, the secretary of state. As the Vatican's chief disciplinarian, his job was to enforce a worldwide crackdown on dissident bishops, theologians, priests, and nuns. The cardinal remained cool in the face of the controversies he aroused, rarely displaying anything but a courtly courtesy. His phlegmatic temperament matched the slow turnings of the Congregation's bureaucracy, but it also reflected a loyal servant's sense of security: None of his decisions was made without the approval of the pope, who used Ratzinger as a lightning rod to deflect criticism from himself. "If Ratzinger didn't exist, the pope would find someone just like him," commented an Italian theologian.[2]

Like American neoconservatives, Ratzinger underwent a mid-age conversion from progressive to conservative. He had been theological adviser to Cologne's Cardinal Joseph Frings at Vatican II, and Frings had received a standing ovation from his fellow prelates at the council after he denounced Ratzinger's future office as an institution "whose methods and behavior do not conform to the modern era and are a source of scandal to the world."[3]

The son of a Bavarian policeman, Ratzinger grew up in Nazi Germany and as a teenager was conscripted into the army of the Third Reich. He later said that his Catholic faith helped immunize him against Nazism.

In 1946, convinced that his country required a "Christian rebirth" as well as material reconstruction, he entered a German seminary. An aesthete with a high regard for polished manners and literary elegance, he was more interested in intellectual pursuits than in the mundane matters of parish life, and after ordination he chose to become a theology professor. Ratzinger honed his faith on Saint Augustine's vision of the church as a holy mystery in opposition to the world. Augustine's pessimism also influenced him, contributing to his later rejection of the "scandalous optimism" of Vatican II.

Cardinal Frings early recognized Ratzinger's brilliance, appointing him his theological adviser when he was only thirty-five. Despite his independence from Rome, Cardinal Frings headed the conservative wing of the German church, which was to be an important factor in Ratzinger's development. Frings's opposite was the late Cardinal Julius Döpfner, archbishop of Munich, who was counseled by the great Jesuit theologian Karl Rahner. During Vatican II Ratzinger formed part of the theological vanguard led by Rahner although even then he revealed a pessimism in regard to the sinful world. Still, he remained a liberal influence in German Catholic circles for most of the 1960s, contributing to the development of such future theologians as Brazil's Leonardo Boff, who was his student. The same man who would later discipline Boff for challenging church structures could then write: "The meaning of prophecy is not so much in predicting the future as in the prophetic protest against the self-righteousness of the institution, a self-righteousness which substitutes ritual for morality and the ceremonial for conversion. . . . God, throughout history, has not been on the side of the institution but on that of the suffering and persecuted."[4]

Ratzinger began to change in the late 1960s when student protests threw German universities into turmoil. He was teaching then at the ecumenical University of Tübingen, and the students' radical shift to the left disturbed him. He also suffered in repeated confrontations with his more liberal colleague Hans Küng. Küng wanted the church to move forward with the reforms begun at Vatican II, whereas Ratzinger, more prudent and less visionary, hung back. The sharp-tongued Küng lost no opportunity to ridicule Ratzinger in front of the students, comparing Ratzinger's half-empty classes with his own overcrowded ones. "If you want to be a cardinal in Germany today," Küng taunted him, "you have to start practicing early." Increasingly isolated, Ratzinger abandoned Tübingen to return to his native Bavaria. He later recalled that at the faculty farewell party he was again made the butt of the liberals' sarcasm when a colleague presented him with his book, *Farewell to the Devil,* on the outdatedness of a literal Satan. Ratzinger believed in the devil's existence, and the author poked fun at him in the dedication: "To my dear colleague Professor Joseph Ratzinger, to whom I find it harder to say farewell than to the devil."[5]

As Ratzinger himself admitted, he had a thick skin, and if he was hurt by such barbs, he did not show it. In any case, he would have the satisfaction of seeing Küng disciplined by the Congregation for the Doctrine of the Faith in 1979, two years before he became its prefect. By that time he was the cardinal of Munich, one of the most important sees in Europe. The liberal theologians who had been in power under Cardinal Döpfner lost ascendancy as Ratzinger, in combination with Cologne's Cardinal Höffner, began to reassert control. In 1980 the German bishops withdrew Küng's license to teach Catholic theology.

Ratzinger's critics claimed that he changed when he became a cardinal because he was more interested in power than in upholding his earlier beliefs, but Ratzinger insisted that the turning point had been his confrontation with the students at Tübingen. He said he had been appalled by the hypocrisy and "psycho-terror" of the left and that this had made him alter his opinion about Marxism, which he previously had thought an acceptable starting point for discussion. "I think that in those years I learned where discussion must stop because it is turning into a lie."[6]

Like his American neoconservative counterparts, who went from one extreme to another, Ratzinger never seemed to doubt the rightness of his position at any given time. "From the very beginning," he told *The New York Times'* Rome correspondent, E. J. Dionne, Jr., "I had a big need to communicate. I wasn't able to keep for myself the knowledge which seemed to be so important to me."[7] There is no doubt that he communicated—he wrote numerous books and theological treatises. He also maintained contact with the right-wing Italian lay movement, Communion and Liberation, and, through the German hierarchy's Third World aid agencies, with Colombia's then archbishop Alfonso López Trujillo, leader of the right wing of the Latin American church. A crucial meeting occurred at the bishops' synod in 1977 when Ratzinger became acquainted with Poland's Wojtyla. They shared common feelings about Marxism and the need to restore order in the church after the "excesses" of Vatican II. Each was impressed by the other's religious orthodoxy, intellectual capacities, and ability to communicate. So in 1981, when John

Paul was reorganizing the Curia, it seemed natural that he should call on his friend for the most difficult assignment at the Vatican.

Although Rome's modern-day Inquisition no longer employs the rack and the stake, the Congregation for the Doctrine of the Faith is nonetheless feared because of the damage it can do to careers and, especially, to prophetic work on behalf of ordinary Catholics. The task of the prefect has never been popular, since it is his duty to guard the orthodoxy of Catholicism. Over the centuries that job has been tainted by excesses and scandal; in the late 1900s some viewed it as an anachronism. Much depended on how the office was used—as a yardstick to measure and uphold Christian revelation or as a club to beat back new ideas: In many cases, the charge of heresy was simply an excuse to destroy dissent against established structures. As prefect, Ratzinger followed in the tradition of the office, showing no mercy and expecting no complaint, while also exhibiting two unusual characteristics. One was his intellectual training, which placed him among the best qualified theologians to head the Congregation in this century. The other was his willingness to share his opinions. Careful never to talk about the political intrigue that buffeted his office, he did occasionally consent to speak to the press about his theological concerns, sometimes with astonishing candor. Such statements usually drew howls of rage from moderates and progressives who were furious at his negative interpretation of Vatican II and his preoccupation with European culture, to the exclusion of all others. Still, consciously or not, Ratzinger did the liberals a favor by explaining the aims of John Paul's papacy, thereby alerting church leaders to what was afoot.

His first major foray into the public arena was a long interview with an Italian journalist, Vittorio Messori, that was later published in book form as *The Ratzinger Report*. The interview caused a sensation because Ratzinger asserted that the "Restoration" of discipline was "altogether desirable and, for that matter, is already in operation in the church." The need for what he called "right thinking" reflected his view that a corrupt world had tainted the church. The post–Vatican II years had been "decidedly unfavorable for the Catholic Church" because it had entered into dialogue with society instead of holding itself apart from "a progressive process of decadence." New ideas in the church had been "misleading," "disastrous," "catastrophic." The laity did not respect the right of priests to run their lives, women were ignoring their most important functions as virgins and mothers, and people no longer believed in the devil. In the United States the church had surrendered to a society where "money and consumption appear to be the measure of everything." Third World churches were obsessed by political liberation. Where would it all end?[8]

Church leaders were amazed by the outburst, which they described as "breathtaking in its superficiality." Contrary to Ratzinger's alarmist and lurid diagnosis, Vatican II had been "a visible work of the Holy Spirit," declared Austria's Cardinal Franz König. "The emphasis on a 'Restoration' reveals a nostalgia for the past . . . when the church viewed society as bad in itself." Catholicism did not collapse after Vatican II, agreed Nicolas Lash, a theology professor at Cambridge University, but just "the particular citadel that we once erected." So why was Ratzinger so alarmed about a more mature relationship based on dialogue between church and world? Hans Küng, who knew his foe of old, had an answer: "Ratzinger is afraid. And just like Fyodor Dostoyevski's Grand Inquisitor, he fears nothing more than freedom."[9]

Although Ratzinger could not deny the documents of Vatican II, which had far greater weight in church teaching than his statements to an Italian journalist, he insisted that the "spirit of optimism" that brought about liturgical, theological, and pastoral reforms had been misinterpreted. He wanted to retreat to security, in effect to resurrect the fortress church that had existed prior to Vatican II. His idea of "positive" religious groups in an otherwise decadent world was Communion and Liberation and other such militant movements that were totally subservient to the hierarchy and upheld the integralist belief that society and its laws should reflect church teaching in every detail. What it meant, said U.S. theologian Daniel Maguire, was that thirteenth-century minds would have authority over twentieth-century ones. Underlying Ratzinger's campaign was the implication that all who did not accept his, i.e., the pope's, viewpoint were guilty of rebellion against the moral teachings of the hierarchy. But if anyone was guilty of subversion, it was Ratzinger, who ignored the teachings of the church's fathers, as incorporated in the most important documents of Vatican II, such as *Dogmatic Constitution on the Church;* the encyclicals of Paul VI; and such statements of the bishops at their synods as *Justice in the World.* Of course anybody could interpret a section of a document—it was the spirit of renewal of Vatican II that counted. And in that regard the bishops stood by the council at their 1985 synod when they reconfirmed the church's commitment to Vatican II.[10]

Still, as Dionne remarked, Ratzinger remained the "reference point" for the ongoing struggle in the church: To be for or against Ratzinger was to define one's religious outlook. Those who shared his fears agreed with his pessimistic vision of a "minority in opposition to the rest of the world." They were, in the words of a German bishop, "hiding in a cave as the heathen hordes pass by." Their world was a daunting place, inhabited by Satan, who could appear in all sorts of guises, including that of theologians. Christians who hoped for a sunlit church where the world could find acceptance, harmony, and communion were not welcome in the "cave" because they were a disruptive and tainted element that would not promise absolute obedience. Better that they should leave, said an official of Ratzinger's Congregation, because those who remained would be that much stronger in their faith.[11]

The Return of the Inquisition

An energetic man despite his frail appearance, Ratzinger began cracking the whip immediately upon taking office. Cases that had become stuck in the Congregation bureaucracy were speeded up, a new code of canon (church) law was promulgated, and the word went out to priests, nuns, and bishops that they had better toe the line. A stickler for details, Ratzinger insisted on legalistic rituals in which every "t" had to be crossed and every "i" dotted. Although some cases involved relatively straightforward questions of church doctrine, others were so tenuous that the only apparent motivation for disciplinary action was the rebellious attitude of the victim. "Ratzinger," said a Rome-based U.S. theologian, "demands obedience. Theologians are not to think creatively but only to teach the magisterium, or church doctrine."[12]

The difficulty arose principally in gray areas that were not defined as divine revelation but as provisional and reformable theories. The provisional part of the Catholic map covers a huge area. That Rome could make mistakes was illustrated by John Paul's rehabilitation of Galileo nearly three centuries and a half after his condemnation by the Inquisition. In 1979 the pope recognized Galileo's contribution to science, conceding that Rome "cannot conceal that he suffered greatly at the hands of churchmen and church bodies."[13] Galileo was among the countless victims of an institution that persecuted Christians for daring to challenge manmade truths. Ratzinger himself admitted that certain beliefs that were held to be absolute even as late as the 1950s were actually no more than "a theological hypothesis," a case in point being the existence of an intermediate "limbo" where unbaptized children were supposed to go when they died.[14] Yet on the basis of some disputed hypothesis he was prepared to punish priests, bishops, even entire hierarchies, as in the conflict with Peru's bishops over liberation theology. Hans Küng thought Ratzinger was power-mad: "*La vérité catholique—c'est moi!*"[15] But Ratzinger saw himself as a loyal servant who loved his church, and that was undoubtedly true—his love or loyalty was not in question but the kind of church he served. As Dionne pointed out, critics felt that the cardinal's religious convictions merely sanctified the worldly power of the Vatican hierarchy, whereas Vatican II had upheld a communal and democratic church of the "People of God."[16]

Had there been more dialogue and less arm-twisting by Ratzinger's Congregation, feelings might not have become so bitter, but the cardinal insisted on total capitulation. On the face of it the punishments may have seemed relatively mild—revocation of a church license to teach Catholic theology, removal of the church's imprimatur (approval) from a theologian's books, and, in the most severe cases, a period of silencing. Nevertheless, the impact was considerable: A heretofore honored member of the club was thrown out on the street. He would no longer have access to the official church network, including Catholic universities, unless his local bishop was sufficiently courageous to defy Rome (few were). The fruits of years of work with local Catholic groups could wither and die since the bishop could no longer provide protection and was likely to be reluctant even to be seen in the presence of the pariah. The damage was particularly serious in the Third World, where Catholic movements of poor people were just beginning to emerge and still needed the theologians' support to provide intellectual justification for a non-European approach to faith.

Yet in the end these battles were no more than contests for a particular piece of turf. In the larger war the unwieldly and outdated Vatican machine could only slow down the final outcome, not change it. Ratzinger's opponents were determined and intelligent; instead of a rehash of medievalism, they offered exciting new ideas. Every move that the Vatican makes is instantly reported around the world so that, even had Ratzinger wanted to keep a low profile, he could not have avoided the press. The tighter the cardinal turned the screws, the louder the screams, until the whole Catholic world rocked with the scandal. People who had never heard of Hans Küng or Leonardo Boff bought their books because of the Vatican crackdown, and what had been a focus of "heresy" in one country soon spread to others. The man behind it all had not stopped the spread of rebellion but aided it.

The first to be punished under John Paul's papacy was a French Dominican, Jacques Pohier, who got into trouble because he raised questions about Christ's resurrection. Pohier lost his license to teach Catholic theology and was prohibited from giving public lectures. The Dominican's case attracted little attention since his work was not well known outside theological circles, but there was a tremendous outcry over the next victims—Küng and Belgian theologian Edward Schillebeeckx, who had a wide following among Catholics and Protestants. Küng's theological sins were considerable in the opinion of the Congregation, perhaps the most serious being his questioning of papal infallibility. Although the Swiss theologian had been an adviser to the German bishops at Vatican II, he had become a thorn in the hierarchy's side by the late 1960s, engaging in an on-again, off-again tussle with the Congregation for the Doctrine of the Faith. He was regarded as particularly dangerous because he did not mince words about the church's oppressive structures, and he refused to be put down. When the Congregation demanded his presence in Rome for questioning, Küng refused to go without a guarantee of the right to elementary due process—an unheard-of request. He was sentenced in absentia for "contempt" of church doctrine and stripped of his license to teach Catholic theology.

Schillebeeckx was also called to Rome for questioning, a move that produced a flood of protest letters from irate Europeans. The Congregation thought his writings had a Protestant taint, particularly his suggestion that in certain circumstances a Christian community without priests could choose the ministers it needed, men or women, married or not. A professor at a Dutch university, Schillebeeckx served as theological adviser to Holland's progressive bishops. Cardinal Willebrands, then the Dutch primate, defended Schillebeeckx at the Vatican, not only because he respected the Belgian scholar's work but also because the accusations effectively put the entire Dutch church on trial. That Holland's church was in the dock with Schillebeeckx was borne out by the fateful synod in 1980 which led to the restructuring of Dutch Catholicism. (See Chapter 3, pp. 55–58.)

Unlike Küng, Schillebeeckx went to Rome for his interrogation and perhaps for that reason was let off with no more than a slap on the wrist. Unrepentant, he continued to turn out controversial books and was again criticized by the Congregation in 1986 for his refusal to recant. Meanwhile, three Latin American liberation theologians were placed under investigation—Peru's Gustavo Gutiérrez, considered the father of liberation theology; El Salvador's Jon Sobrino; and Brazil's Leonardo Boff. Of the three only Boff was interrogated in Rome and punished, but it was a near thing for Gutiérrez as well. In the United States moral theologian Charles Curran suffered Küng's fate by losing his right to teach at Washington's Catholic University. How many others were on Ratzinger's hit list was unknown, but no one doubted the existence of dozens of dossiers.

Nor did Ratzinger limit his activities to investigations of theologians. Among other destabilizing measures, he sabotaged discussions between Catholic and Episcopal theologians, and by 1986 Protestant leaders were saying that the "cordial coexistence" between Rome and Protestant churches that had existed after Vatican II had become a "dead letter." Even the High Episcopalians, who were closest to Catholic rites and beliefs and were prepared to accept the principle of papal primacy, said they were no longer so certain they wanted to cooperate with the Catholic Church. "We need more time to think before taking the risk of a Cardinal Joseph Ratzinger operating in our midst," their leaders said.[17]

The cardinal also issued a flurry of documents on church doctrine, some of which attacked the positions of theologians in other countries as, for instance, a study of sexual morality commissioned by the Catholic Theological Society of America. He called bishops' conferences to account—for example, his censure of a catechism approved by the French hierarchy—as well as individual bishops like Seattle's Raymond Hunthausen. He censored books, wrote books, and also had time to plan papal strategy for the bishops' synods in Rome. Only the pope surpassed his energy. Yet much of it seemed futile or divisive. Undoubtedly a chill had entered the church body. "And let no one doubt that this crackdown is worldwide and deadly serious," warned a South American cardinal. Protest made no impression on the steely Ratzinger—"I don't see any convincing reason why Rome should do this," fumed Austrian Cardinal König of the disciplinary measures against theologians.[18] At the same time the Vatican could not force dissenters to recant. Unlike the Inquisition, the Congregation could not call on an army to enforce its decrees. The extent to which Catholics accepted or rejected its teachings depended on how persuasive it was—and most people are not persuaded by threats. Saint Augustine had once said, "Rome has spoken; the case is concluded." But in the 1980s the response was "That's Rome's opinion."

New Winds in Latin America and the United States

Of Ratzinger's many battles none was so politically important to the church and the rest of the world as the struggle over liberation theology. The new theology not only threatened Rome's control over Catholic Latin America; strains had also passed to Africa and Asia, where local theologians developed their own versions. Moreover, the Catholic Church in the United States had been infected by the social activism of the Latin Americans. During the 1970s, when liberation theology gained a wide audience in Latin America, returning missionaries promoted it in the United States. Under the influence of Vatican II and the martyrdom of sister churches in Latin America, the U.S. bishops had criticized human rights abuses in the South American dictatorships. But it was only in 1980 that the American church began to display a hitherto unknown militancy in its relations with the U.S. government because of the murders in El Salvador of Archbishop Oscar Romero and four female American missionaries. Romero was admired in Catholic circles in the United States because of his work on behalf of the poor and his support for democracy—key elements in liberation theology. His assassination shocked the U.S. bishops, who took up Romero's call for an end to U.S. military aid to the Salvadoran junta. The subsequent rape and murder of three American nuns and a lay worker by Salvadoran soldiers sharply increased U.S. Catholic opposition, particularly after the incoming Reagan administration tried to dismiss the killings as an accident—Secretary of State Alexander Haig's story was that the women, presumably after being raped, were killed while running a roadblock. The more Haig and other officials tried to whitewash the junta, the angrier grew public reaction, particularly among Catholics. Five months into Reagan's term, congressional mail was running 600 to 1 against military aid to El Salvador.[19]

The dispute over El Salvador was the opening salvo in a series of confrontations between the bishops and the White House over Central America, the arms buildup, and the economy. Reagan's supporters blamed "Marxist" liberation theology for religious opposition to U.S. policies in Central America, some Pentagon officials even going so far as to claim that "bishops and churchmen have been extremely unhelpful in trying to deal with the realities of the [communist] threat down in Latin America."[20] Liberation theology was also singled out for unfavorable notice in the document *A New Inter-American Policy for the Eighties,*

written in 1980 by Reagan's advisers on Latin America, including Roger
Fontaine, who became his Central America adviser on the National Security Council, and Lewis Tambs, who served as U.S. ambassador to
Costa Rica until he was forced to resign because of his involvement in
the Iran-*contra* scandal. Popularly known as the "Santa Fe Document"
for the city in which it was written, *A New Inter-American Policy* served
as a charter for the Reagan administration's Latin American policies.
Several of its proposals were adopted, including an attack on liberation
theology, which was held responsible for the church's criticism of "productive capitalism" in Latin America.[21]

Although liberation theology responds to Latin American needs and
cannot easily be transplanted to the First World, it reflects the same
independent spirit that has come to characterize the post–Vatican II
church in the United States. The desire for a more lay-oriented and Christ-
centered church that emerges from liberation theology is also obvious in
the United States, as shown by numerous polls and the trend toward
greater lay participation in the running of local churches. While the challenges from the United States and Latin America are different, the bottom
line is a greater respect for pluralism in the church. But this Rome has
refused to accept.

The Reagan administration supported the papacy's get-tough policy
with local churches, not because Washington cared in the least who was
appointed a bishop or how religious rites were conducted but because
the American bishops comprised an influential opposition group in the
United States, and a strongly anticapitalist liberation theology challenged
U.S. hegemony in Latin America. While the U.S. bishops might sway a
segment of public opinion, the threat in Latin America was more serious
because liberation theology imbued political struggles with a religious
fervor in a region where Catholicism had historically provided the ultimate
stamp of political approval. Since the time of the Spanish Conquest, the
Catholic Church had bestowed God's blessing on the civil powers, not
only through church rituals honoring the appointment of a governor or,
later, the assumption of power by a military dictator, but through a
proselytism that taught the masses to accept their miserable lot. It was
God's will, the bishops had preached, that a few should be rich while the
majority remained impoverished. The church-state alliance endured until
Vatican II, when the winds of change burst upon the church. In Latin
America, where the Catholic Church is one of the three institutional
powers, along with the military and the landowning and industrial elites,

the impact was akin to a hurricane: In less than a decade the church shifted its institutional allegiance from rich to poor, gave birth to liberation theology, and undertook the organization of thousands of grassroots Christian base communities that would give the poor greater participation in their church and society and lead to the emergence of a new, more militant faith.

The church's new message that God was on the side of the poor had a far greater impact on the poverty-stricken masses than the theories of Marx and Lenin, whose work and even names were unknown to the majority. Whereas Catholicism had previously encouraged fatalism, the post–Vatican II church taught the poor that they were equal in the sight of God and that they should take history into their own hands by seeking political and economic changes. It was not God's will that their children died of malnutrition but the result of sinful man-made structures, the bishops said. Suffering, which had traditionally been endured in the expectation of a better life in the hereafter, gained a different symbolism when identified with the hope of Christ's death and resurrection: It suggested that a community of believers could overcome their wretched conditions by working together for the common good and a better future. Members of the base communities became agents for change; although many were killed by repressive regimes, their blood gave impetus to the movement. The church of El Quiché in Guatemala, for example, continued to grow in its religious commitment to a more just society not despite, but because of, the martyrdom of so many of its catechists. (See Chapter 1, pp. 5–7.)

In the first decade after Vatican II the Latin American church served as a catalyst for change in secular society by encouraging the formation of base communities which would become the seeds for other intermediate organizations of poor people, such as labor unions and peasant federations. But by the second decade the process of democratization had affected the church itself, which in several countries, notably Brazil, became more pluralistic in its internal organization. Liberation theology, which began as an intellectual reflection on the sufferings of the people, gradually changed to a theology of the people in which the experiences of the base communities were the principal reference point.

Ironically, the push for greater egalitarianism could not have occurred without the institutional protection of the church, which was the only power able to withstand military persecution. Political parties, labor unions, student movements, and a free press were ruthlessly repressed in the 1970s and early 1980s but never completely destroyed because of the intervention of the church, which provided a protective umbrella under which they could regroup and rebuild. Even Chile's General Pinochet, the most bloodthirsty of Latin America's modern dictators, was unwilling to break completely with the church. Whether they believed in God or not, the region's leaders were unwilling to renounce centuries of tradition that had made the church the moral guardian of society. To deny the church was to deny their own authority, yet at the same time that authority was being subverted from within by the church. A political awakening was occurring in Latin America that endangered the economic interests of the upper classes and their allies in the United States, but, try as they might, they could not contain the religious-inspired rebellion. No matter how many priests and nuns were murdered, or how often the bishops were threatened, the seeds of popular democracy continued to spread. Only Rome could make any impact on a Catholic rebellion, and it therefore fell to Cardinal Ratzinger to deal with a major source of the problem—the Latin American theologians.

The Attack

Ratzinger seemed well equipped to lead the battle. He was an eminent theologian who had trained one of liberation theology's best-known proponents, Leonardo Boff, had the absolute confidence of the pope and the support of the right wing of the Latin American church, and could be relied upon not to be swayed by people's feelings in the matter. But the cardinal also suffered a crippling handicap: He knew nothing about Latin America.

With a Eurocentric view of the world, Ratzinger was incapable of grasping the originality of Latin American theology as a specific response to a social location. Like all people, theologians are a product of their environment. Most work in intellectual centers is removed from the strivings and hardships of ordinary people, and this is reflected in the often esoteric quality of their writings. The first generation of liberation theologians was trained in such environments, primarily in Germany, France, and Belgium, but on their return to Latin America they found the real world in the slums and rural villages. So they put away their books in French and German and began to learn a new theology based on the experience of the impoverished masses. This was no academic exercise but an awakening that came from actually living with the poor—being exposed to the hunger, smells, noises, and sickness that constitute the daily struggle for survival in an overcrowded Third World slum.

Although the Latin Americans were the first to identify their theology with the poor, the universal church had been moving toward such an option since the 1960s, when Vatican II proved the key event by redefining the church as a community of believers—the "People of God," or "*Pueblo de Dios*"—and *pueblo* has always been understood as the masses, the poor. Primarily a European event, Vatican II nevertheless deeply impressed the Latin American bishops who attended the council and the pioneer liberation theologians. The latter were influenced by German theologian Johann Baptist Metz, himself a student of Karl Rahner, one of the great theologians of Vatican II. But even Metz's "political theology," which used faith as a measure of the political economy, seemed too European in a Third World setting. Back in Lima, Gustavo Gutiérrez began to compare his reality with what he had learned in middle-class Europe, and found that the two worlds were as remote from each other as different planets. His analysis of the causes of poverty and injustice in Latin America would have added little to the debate—the statistics of misery were well known—had he written as a social scientist, but Gutiérrez was a priest who felt passionately about the suffering he experienced in Lima's slums. He therefore focused on the religious dimensions of the issue, producing a new understanding of faith, truth, and grace from the perspective of the Latin American poor.

Looking at Peru's history, which was typical of Latin America's tragedy, he rejected the trickle-down theory of development that the United States had tried to sell the Latin Americans through the Alliance for Progress. It hadn't worked and wouldn't work, Gutiérrez concluded, because the majority would continue in bondage to the rich. The only answer was economic and political liberation from a neocolonial relationship with the United States and Europe and from internal structures of oppression. The basis for his analysis of liberation was not Marxist revolution but the Exodus and Christ's Good News to the poor of freedom from oppression. Therein lay its originality, for in the framework of Catholic Latin America the God of the Exodus and the Christ of the poor were much more radical than the unintelligible dialectics of Marxist intellectuals.

Gutiérrez also reinterpreted classic doctrines of sin to include the sins of societies as, for example, U.S. behavior toward Latin America and that of the Peruvian oligarchy toward the country's peasants. It was not enough to seek liberation from personal sin, he argued, since faith also meant a commitment to work for social justice. Conversion demanded society's transformation, not just a change of heart.

The call to change unjust structures was clearly political, but, claimed Gutiérrez and other liberation theologians, the Latin American church had always been political. Originally it had been the proselytizing arm of the Spanish empire, the Inquisition being its CIA. It took Spain's part in the wars of independence and afterwards allied itself with the most reactionary elements among the Latin American elites. Liberation theologians wanted the church to change sides; neutrality was impossible, they said, because of the church's historic influence in Latin America: Silence was also a political statement in support of the status quo.

Although it was not yet known as liberation theology, Gutiérrez's work provided the framework for discussions at the bishops' hemisphere meeting in Medellín in 1968. Many of his theories were adopted, including a preferential option for the poor and a denunciation of unjust structures of social sin, or what the bishops called "institutionalized violence." Implicit in their declaration was a recognition of the futility of elections and other trappings of a formal democracy that would not alter the desperate poverty of the people. Therefore the church had to help the poor organize themselves to challenge and overcome existing structures.

Though it was not put so bluntly, Medellín also acknowledged the inability of the church's traditional social teachings to deal with Latin America's desperate situation. Many of the bishops had earlier been enthusiastic about the reformist potential of the Christian Democrats, a church-linked political movement that upheld such teachings, at least in theory. But the failure of President Eduardo Frei's mild reforms in Chile (and the subsequent election of Socialist Salvador Allende and his overthrow by the military in 1973) as well as the lackluster performance of Frei's Christian Democratic counterparts in Venezuela suggested that a more radical approach was needed—hence the church's endorsement of liberation theology at Medellín.

While only a minority of the bishops at Medellín understood the full implications of the documents they signed, the military and upper classes were quick to get the point: Their traditional ally had betrayed them. During the first years after Medellín, hostilities were limited to a few skirmishes, but by 1973 the church was at war with the state in many parts of Latin America. The more priests and nuns were persecuted, the angrier became the bishops, who also suffered repression because of their outspoken criticism. By the end of the 1970s, when more than 850 priests and nuns had been martyred, the minority of bishops who had been committed to upholding the needs of the poor had become the majority. At the bishops' hemisphere meeting in Puebla, Mexico, in 1979, when John Paul made his first major public appearance, the bishops reconfirmed their historic decision at Medellín to ally themselves with the poor, despite opposition from the Curia and a minority of right-wingers in the Latin American church.

In the months leading up to the Puebla meeting Colombia's then archbishop Alfonso López Trujillo did his best to stack the assembly with his own men in order to persuade the delegates to adopt an alternative to liberation theology—a so-called third way between communism and capitalism that was based on the church's social doctrine and was essentially a Christian Democratic model. López was secretary general of the bishops' service organization, the Latin American Episcopal Conference (CELAM), which had been responsible for Medellín, and during the 1970s he systematically purged CELAM's institutions of any influence from the liberation theologians. Since CELAM was also in charge of organizing the Puebla meeting, he was in a strong position to impose his agenda. But López underestimated two important factors. One was the determination of the progressive Brazilian bishops, the most numerous in Latin America, and particularly Cardinal Aloisio Lorscheider, who as president of CELAM set the tone for the meeting. The second was reality. In the decade between Medellín and Puebla the poor had become poorer and military repression had caused the deaths of tens of thousands of people. Symbolic of the tragedy was San Salvador's Archbishop Romero, who pleaded with the bishops at Puebla to give him some sign of support to prevent the destruction of his church and his own murder. The voice of Romero, who was killed the following year, was like a cry from the people, and the bishops responded by signing a statement in support of Romero and by reconfirming Medellín and hence liberation theology.

John Paul's feelings about the events at Puebla, though known, were not understood. For example, when the document written by the bishops at Puebla was edited in Rome, certain passages were changed in a subtle but significant way. It was widely assumed at the time that the changes had been the work of López Trujillo, but the pope undoubtedly approved. As a cardinal, he had questioned liberation theology's emphasis on a "horizontal" church, meaning that it was too democratic.[22] He was also concerned about Marxist influence on the theology's analysis of Latin

America's political economy. From John Paul's viewpoint any concessions to Marxist theory inevitably lead to communist totalitarianism. But while this may have been true in Eastern Europe, it is questionable when applied to most strains of liberation theology. For one thing, there are several variants of Marxist doctrine, including Leninism and Stalinism (i.e., the dictatorship of the party) that have no relationship to liberation theology. For another, the charge of "Marxist analysis" is extremely vague, lending itself to a confusion of three quite different things: Marxism is variously defined as a materialistic philosophy of history, a strategy of class warfare, and a study of capitalism as an economic system. That the majority of liberation theologians use the last alternative while rejecting the others is lost on Rome, which cannot understand how strongly such study appeals to a people who have suffered colonialism and a robber-baron style of capitalism. Nor can the Vatican comprehend that class warfare has been going on in Latin America since the Spaniards enslaved the Indians. Such "institutionalized" war, in the words of the Medellín documents, is directed by the rich against the poor. To say that this is not so is to deny history.

As in Poland, there are in many parts of Latin America no political alternatives to religious opposition. Whatever arguments may be offered against the Latin American church's role in leading the struggle for the poor, the fact is that it is the last and only source of justice for the poor. Political parties, labor unions, intellectual movements, the press, every means of achieving structural change have been tried and failed. Only the church has withstood the repression and remained loyal to the poor.

As observed by Phillip Berryman, a popular American religious writer, liberation theology was the herald of a larger movement "of the excluded—women, non-whites, the poor—onto the stage of history."[23] Just as women are asserting a new role in First World societies, Third World peoples seek their own cultural and political identification. No matter what Rome and Washington believe, it is impossible to hold back the tide. The imperial powers, Russia included, face a cultural explosion that promises to fragment spheres of influence, making the imposition of a single political, economic, or religious model more difficult. Ratzinger rushed about, trying to prevent cracks in the Roman fortress, but there were too many, and more appeared all the time. Many believed it a good thing. Raymond Panikkar, an Indian theologian, spoke of the fissures as the "grace of Babel." "We are not pluralists if we are all integrated into the same vision of the world. We are pluralists if we accept that none of us possesses the philosophical stone, the key to the secret of the world, access to the center of the universe, if such exists. Our human frailty should cure us of unreal and messianic dreams of new world empires even if they are announced with a great fanfare of trumpets for liberty, God and truth. These are truly positive symbols, but we do not possess them in their totality or have a monopoly over them."[24]

Although John Paul was as concerned as Ratzinger about Catholic fragmentation, he did not share the German's take-it-or-leave-it attitude. Whereas Ratzinger did not care how much havoc he caused among local churches so long as order was restored, John Paul worried about the loss of large numbers of dissident Catholics. For example, he told a South American cardinal that he feared liberation theology might cause a schism in Latin America and he would not allow that to happen.[25] So he used a carrot nearly as often as a stick in confrontations with the Latin Americans, perhaps sensing that a direct attack on liberation theology would alienate the tens of thousands of base communities that formed the most vibrant part of the Latin American church. While Ratzinger played the policeman, the pope attempted a more subtle approach, by appropriating the language of liberation theology in his own social teachings. Although John Paul's conception of liberation differed substantially from that of the liberation theologians, the tactic had the advantage of preventing an open break with Rome.

Nevertheless, the breach existed. "In countries where great poverty exists," said an Indian Jesuit, "the church will simply cease to be relevant if it is not committed to social and political justice. And that frequently means political involvement."[26] Such involvement was sanctioned in Eastern Europe, but Ratzinger opposed it in countries that respected religious liberty, at least theoretically, even if their governments persecuted church people. His reasons were as much political as religious: The option for the poor meant a commitment to religious as well as economic and political justice. In contrast to the cardinal's hierarchical Christendom, the symbol of authority in the church of the poor was service, not power. Ecclesiastical institutions, said Leonardo Boff, "must be like the chalice, serving the precious wine of the Spirit but not substituting for it." But Ratzinger's church tried to substitute for it, by claiming all the truth for itself because truth was power. Boff was not brought to trial by Ratzinger for any Marxist heresy, any more than the real cause of Galileo's inquisition had been his scientific teachings. They were persecuted because they were political agitators against papal omniscience.

The appeal of liberation theology in Latin America lies in its integration of religious and political liberation: If religion previously served as a repressive political tool, it can also be used as a means of political liberation. In other cultures it is not always easy to find such a perfect match of religion with politics, but in Latin America Catholicism is the cultural starting point for everything else, the one element that unites peoples with different languages and historical experiences. Latin Americans do not have to change their basic religious beliefs—their culture—to achieve liberation, but only their perspective.

That outlook is not Roman. As observed by Harvard theologian Harvey Cox, the demographic center of Christianity "is rapidly shifting to the black, brown, yellow, poor southern hemisphere. This means that our millennium-long habit of thinking of Christianity as being somehow centered in Europe with branch offices around the world is dying. It will not be that way anymore, and, frankly put, many of the churches in the Third World think of this movement as a great liberation out of a kind of incubator of centuries in which they had to become little Europeans in order to become Christians."[27]

The "de-Northification of the Gospel," as Cox put it, led to constant clashes with Rome by bishops who objected to the legislation of religious norms for totally different societies. The Brazilians were particularly unpopular with the Curia, but some of the Asians and Africans could be just as difficult on questions of politics and culture, such as indigenous liturgies and married priests.

Matters came to a head in March 1983, when Ratzinger sent ten critical observations about Gutiérrez's work to the Peruvian Bishops Conference, asking them to issue a statement on—in actuality to condemn—the Peruvian's writings. The timing could not have been worse, or better, depending on one's viewpoint, since the Peruvians had to deal with the problem in the wake of John Paul's disastrous visit to Nicaragua, during which he had strongly questioned the "popular church." The liberal leadership in the Peruvian church had made a commitment to social justice and was actively involved in organizing the poor. Cardinal Juan Landázuri, the archbishop of Lima and primate of Peru, had been co-president of the Medellín conference, and he served as Gutiérrez's protector against conservative bishops who shared Ratzinger's views. Because the bishops themselves were divided, Ratzinger could not be certain of a condemnation. Nor did it help the cardinal's cause when thousands of angry Catholics wrote the Peruvian bishops to protest against Gutiérrez's treatment. Among the writers was the German theologian Karl Rahner, whose prestige in Latin America far outweighed that of Ratzinger.

Still, the Curia could always count on a loyal claque to applaud Rome's battles for the faith in the interests of its own economic and political ambitions. The Latin American loyalists included wealthy businessmen and politicians who owned important newspapers, magazines, and radio and television stations. The media helped fan the conflict with the Vatican by publishing sensationalist accounts of developments in the church—"The Vatican condemns liberation theology," was a typical example of the exaggerated headlines and stories that constantly appeared in Lima on the subject. In a specific case, such as the Gutiérrez controversy, the tactic normally is to leak news from Rome in order to scare the local bishops. Thus in early 1984, when the Peruvian bishops were meeting to discuss Gutiérrez's situation, the right-wing Lima magazine *Oiga* published for the first time the "text" of a private talk Ratzinger was reported to have given to the pope and other high-ranking officials on the "fundamental danger" to the faith posed by liberation theology.* But while the story caused a sensation, it failed to persuade the liberal bishops to oppose Gutiérrez. In April, a year after Ratzinger had issued his original demand and four major assemblies had been held on the subject, the bishops were still deadlocked, unable to make a pronouncement. Two different reviews of Gutiérrez's writings—one critical, the other approving—were therefore sent to Rome to let Ratzinger deal with the problem he had created. The bishops' failure to condemn Gutiérrez did not sit well with the local oligarchy or the Curia. The Lima daily *La Prensa,* which had ties to the right-wing Opus Dei movement, blasted Landázuri for supporting Gutiérrez. It also published a cartoon that became famous in Peru in which the cardinal was shown blessing three snarling wolves that were supposed to be "Marxists" infiltrating the church.[28]

Meanwhile, at the Vatican Ratzinger was digesting not one but two defeats. A month before the Peruvians' final assembly on the subject, he had called a summit meeting in Bogotá on liberation theology, hoping to get a condemnation from the Latin American bishops since the Peruvians

---

* *Oiga* frequently attacked the progressive sector of the Peruvian church, sometimes inventing mischievous fantasies, such as a story claiming that Gutiérrez intended to run for president on the ticket of the Izquierda Unida, a left-wing coalition. The article was picked up by other right-wing publications, including the so-called Catholic Agency of Information, which, contrary to its title, had nothing to do with the Peruvian church.

did not seem up to it. But the majority of the delegates said they had no theological problems and wanted nothing to do with condemnations. Several complained privately that Ratzinger came across as a supercilious German who thought he could tell the "colonies" how to behave. The cardinal was so taken up with doctrinal red tape, said one bishop, that he failed to understand that the Latin American churches had other, more pressing matters to worry about, such as "millions of starving people."[29]

But Ratzinger was persistent. In the next five months he sent a letter to Leonardo Boff accusing him of serious deviations and demanding that he appear for an interrogation at the Vatican, published a harsh thirty-five-page criticism of liberation theology, and called the Peruvian bishops to Rome to settle the Gutiérrez case to his liking. The Vatican also issued an ultimatum to the priests in the Sandinista government to resign their posts or leave the priesthood.

Ratzinger's widely publicized "Instruction" on liberation theology apparently was meant as a backdrop for the Boff interrogation and the Peruvian assembly in the fall of 1984, but events did not work out as he had anticipated. The cardinal seized the initiative at the opening of the two-week meeting with the Peruvians by presenting them with a draft document described as "coarse and violent" in its denunciations of liberation theology. Under a section called "Erroneous Opinions," for example, was a series of propositions lifted from Gutiérrez's work that Ratzinger wanted condemned wholesale. But since the propositions formed the framework for the Peruvian church's social work, any denunciation would have meant a condemnation of the bishops themselves. Unlike the Dutch bishops, who had been forced to sign their own death warrants at a similar meeting in Rome in 1980, a majority of the Peruvians refused to accept the document. Other tactics were then attempted, including attacks against Cardinal Landázuri's pastoral programs with the poor, but this, too, backfired when the cardinal's indignant supporters turned on the Curia, accusing Rome of trying to impose a centralized, authoritarian rule. In the heat of the battle Javier Ariz Huarte, auxiliary bishop of Lima and president of the bishops' doctrinal commission, suffered a heart attack.[30]

Landázuri arrived on the first plane from Lima. A genial bear of a man who had led the Peruvian church for thirty-two years, he was famous for his diplomatic skills. Much was at stake in the confrontation with Ratzinger, for if the German succeeded in getting a condemnation of

Gutiérrez and thus of Landázuri, years of work with the impoverished base communities could be destroyed. The Peruvian wasted no time in seeing the pope. He emerged all smiles from the meeting, which should have been a warning to Ratzinger. Although John Paul shared Ratzinger's feelings about liberation theology, he could not afford to ignore a cardinal of the stature of Landázuri, who was widely respected in the Latin American church. Ratzinger was therefore left to fend for himself and lost every round to Landázuri. When he tried to get himself elected chairman of the meeting, the Peruvian insisted on a point of order: It would not be an official meeting of the Peruvian hierarchy unless Landázuri was in charge. Ratzinger retaliated by insisting on including officials from the Congregation for the Doctrine of the Faith at the meeting and reintroducing his draft document condemning Gutiérrez. To avoid further acrimony, he said, the bishops should give their secret votes on the document to the Congregation's representatives, who would tally the results. But this caused outrage even among the conservatives, who joined with the other bishops in unanimously rejecting the proposal. Incensed by the criticism of Congregation officials, Ratzinger demanded that the bishops accept his interpretation of liberation theology. Tempers at this point were so raw that an explosion was imminent. Instead, John Paul appeared to calm the waters, reading the bishops a speech about the "People of God," the terrible afflictions suffered by the poor in Peru, and the church's determination to continue its preferential option for the poor. Not a word was said about condemning liberation theology.[31]

When the bishops returned to work, they quickly agreed on a compromise document that, while taking note of Ratzinger's "Instruction" on liberation theology, did not condemn the theology or Gutiérrez. On the contrary, the bishops expressed appreciation for the work of "those who practice liberation theology," noting that it had been the means to a new commitment to the poor, a resurgence of religious vocations, and a "spiritual deepening." They also reiterated a call for "the right application of distributive justice and the establishment of institutions and structures that truly incarnate it." Goodwill was not enough to change unjust structures, they said, because the poor needed to be united and organized to achieve bargaining power. The bishops' sole disciplinary measure, if it could be called that, was to urge Peruvian theologians to evaluate their own work.[32]

The document was hardly what Ratzinger had had in mind when he began the laborious process. Instead of yes-men, the cardinal had come up against bishops who felt passionately about the church of the poor. They were not fighting over minor doctrinal questions but life-and-death issues that affected millions of impoverished Peruvians. "A church born of the blood of martyrs cannot be held back by a document," said Gutiérrez, in explaining why a man so brilliant as Cardinal Ratzinger had lost the battle.[33]

Although there were other ways of bringing the Latin Americans to heel—and these would soon be applied—Ratzinger consistently suffered defeat in the intellectual arena because he could not emerge from his ivory tower. Believing himself culturally superior, he repeatedly set himself up for a fall. His arguments against liberation theology were easily challenged by the Latin Americans because they knew what it meant to live an option for the poor, whereas Ratzinger thought poor Latin Americans stupid and easily misled. To him, what the church needed were competent academics to tell the people what to do, not a "popularized" liberation theology in base communities incapable of "discernment" or "critical judgment." The Latin American poor were actually better off with their old religious fatalism. "The defense of orthodoxy," explained the cardinal, "[was] really the defense of the poor, saving them pain and illusions which contain no realistic prospect even of material liberation."[34]

His "Instruction" on liberation theology revealed a similar mindset. Although the first part of the document dealt with the reality of poverty and oppression in Latin America, the second section on the unorthodoxies of liberation theology was a caricature of that theology, revealing the prejudices of a middle-class German obsessed by communism (it turned out that he had not written the first part, which was later tacked onto the second). In a divided Germany this was understandable, but in Latin America Marxism was a preoccupation of the small middle class. None of the liberation theologians had written a work in support of Marxist class warfare, nor had any provided a rationale for killing. The "oppressor" was not a target to be killed but a human being to be won over through forgiveness and reconciliation. Liberation theology did not support armed revolution—which, as in the Vatican's own teachings, was considered a last resort—but active nonviolence because revolution destroyed the social "ecology" of society. "We do not favor violent methods that advocate certain ideologies like Marxism," insisted Bishop Ivo Lorscheiter, then president of the progressive National Conference of Brazilian Bishops and an advocate of liberation theology.[35]

In a penetrating analysis of Ratzinger's "Instruction," Uruguayan

Jesuit Juan Luis Segundo argued that the cardinal had set everyone off on a phantom chase after Marxist theologians when in reality the real issue was Vatican II. At the heart of Ratzinger's argument was the old demand for a separation of the religious from the secular, the church from the world, that had been rejected by the Second Vatican Council. Ratzinger had focused on liberation theology's denunciation of unjust social structures in the belief that people who sought to change structures would inevitably be caught up in Marxist class warfare. The church should stay out of such struggles—reject the world—to concentrate on its spiritual message of individual salvation. Quite apart from the fact that liberation theologians rejected class violence as a means of changing structures, Ratzinger's theory denied a crucial point—that structures inflicted far greater misery on generations of human beings than individual acts of sinfulness. "The worst type of sin, in fact the only 'mortal sin' which has enslaved man for the greater part of his history, is the institutionalized sin," wrote African liberation theologian Laurenti Magesa. "Under the institution, vice appears to be, or is actually turned into, virtue. Apathy toward evil is thus engendered; recognition of sin becomes totally effaced; sinful institutions become absolutized, almost idolized, and sin becomes absolutely moral. . . . Recognition of sin, and therefore repentance for sin, is made practically impossible when sin is idolized as an institution."[36]

Liberation theologians did not argue against personal conversion, but they believed that the struggle for justice was also a "constitutive dimension" of faith, in the words of the 1971 synod of bishops. Ratzinger, said Segundo, did not want to understand the full implications of Vatican II and subsequent teachings by the bishops on the alliance between church and society in the search for a better world. In closing Vatican II, he recalled, Pope Paul VI had asked rhetorically whether the council might have "deviated" by accepting modern culture. "Deviated, no; turned, yes," the pope immediately replied, underlining the "intimate union . . . between human and temporal values and . . . spiritual, religious and eternal values."[37]

In trying to resist the integration of politics and religion in Latin America, said Segundo, Rome was primarily concerned about the loss of power—the change from an ecclesiastical hierarchy to a more democratic institution in which the people revered and obeyed their pastors because of their courage, humility, and vision, not because it was foreordained by Rome. Such was the reason for the extraordinary popularity of Brazil's bishops and for the hostility against the Nicaraguan bishops.

"In the eyes of Vatican diplomacy," argued Segundo, "Nicaragua—and potentially Brazil—[is] the most dangerous country, the central religious element used to define such dangers being the existence of a strong popular church."[38]

When all the smoke had cleared and the last words had been said on Ratzinger's "Instruction," the consensus was that it had not changed any of the essentials of the debate but had at least clarified the stakes. Liberation theologians claimed that Ratzinger had given the theology official recognition by accepting "liberation" as a valid religious point of reference. Opponents of liberation theology had a field day in quoting Ratzinger's denunciations in the press. But the sounds from these battles were not heard in the everyday din of life in the slums and villages, where priests and nuns worked as usual with the base communities. San Salvador's Archbishop Arturo Rivera y Damas put his finger on it: The discussions between Rome and the liberation theologians, he said, "in no way affect or change our commitment to the poor."[39]

Boff's Inquisition

Thanks to the outcry against the Ratzinger document, including sharp criticism by Cardinal Casaroli, the Vatican's secretary of state, Rome issued a second, less dictatorial and more hopeful document on liberation theology in the spring of 1986. "Instruction on Christian Freedom and Liberation" recognized that the concerns of the liberation theologians must be central to the church's work. The desire for liberty and liberation was "among the principal signs of the times of the modern world and rooted in Christian heritage," it said. Oppressed peoples had a "perfectly legitimate" right to seek a change in structures and institutions when they used "morally licit means." Those suggested included reforms and passive resistance, which in the Latin American context meant active nonviolence, but the "Instruction" also accepted armed struggle "as a last resort to put an end to an obvious and prolonged tyranny which is gravely damaging the fundamental rights of individuals and the common good."[40]

The optimistic Gutiérrez thought the document marked "the end of an era" and that the discussion on liberation theology was "closed."[41] But other analysts believed his conclusions premature because, when examined carefully, the second "Instruction" was seen to be a rephrasing of the first in more subtle language. While there were no blasts against Marxist analysis, the document repeated earlier warnings against theological "adulterations" and the intervention of priests and nuns in the "political construction and organization of social life." Central to the document was the primacy of personal liberation from individual sin in any attempt to change social structures. As pointed out by Salvadoran theologian Jon Sobrino, the document recognized the importance of both the spiritual and social need for liberation but "unquestionably subordinate[d] the second to the first." Neither instruction understood that "the theology of liberation is trying to make a new synthesis between the two." Thus the second document emphasized the spiritual values of poverty; an option for the poor meant the bestowing of charity, not justice. Nor could the option exclude anyone, since there were other forms of poverty besides material want, such as a lack of spirituality. Practically speaking, this meant that religious who gave up teaching in middle-class high schools to work among the Latin American poor had misinterpreted the option, as John Paul told Salvadoran priests and nuns on a visit to their country. What the document seemed to be saying, noted one observer, was that "orthodoxy—getting the ideas straight—is more important than orthopraxy—doing the right thing."[42]

The second "Instruction" also made it clear that the only reliable liberation theologian was the pope. Thus the document restated his frequent warning to theologians to carry on their work "in the light of the experience of the church herself. It pertains to the pastors of the church, in communion with the successor of Peter, to discern its [the experience's] authenticity."[43] Ratzinger had said much the same thing in his writings and interviews; John Paul merely changed the tone.

He used the same tone in his meetings with the Brazilian bishops on the eve of the document's publication. Brazil had become a major headache for the Vatican because of Ratzinger's insistence on disciplining Boff, who was enormously popular in Brazil and had the backing of some of the church's most powerful figures, including São Paulo's Cardinal Paulo Evaristo Arns and Fortaleza's Cardinal Aloisio Lorscheider.* If Gutiérrez is the intellectual father of liberation theology, Boff is the leading proponent of its pastoral application among impoverished Latin Americans. Boff's work also reflects the deep commitment of the Brazilian bishops to social and religious justice. By putting the theologian in

---

* Because of a heart condition, Lorscheider had discouraged his papal candidacy in the conclave that elected John Paul II. He had received Cardinal Wojtyla's vote in the election won by John Paul I.

the dock, Rome in effect accused the Third World's most powerful church of heresy.

Unlike Gutiérrez's case, the issue was quite simple: Boff wanted a more democratic church that responded to the needs of the poor. His argument was that, once the Emperor Constantine had domesticized Christianity as the state religion, the church had become more concerned with the dynamics of power than with the original message of the Gospels. Boff did not advocate a break with Rome but sought a reform from within, so that authority would be identified with service, as in the early Christian church.

Boff's work was not as well known in international circles as were Gutiérrez's writings, and it seemed unlikely that Ratzinger would have turned on his former student had he not been encouraged by the dissidents in the Brazilian church, who did not like its progressive direction. Chief among these were Cardinal Agnelo Rossi, who worked in the Curia; Cardinal Eugenio de Araujo Sales, the archbishop of Rio de Janeiro; and the German-Brazilian theologian Bonaventura Kloppenburg, who became a bitter foe of liberation theology under the influence of Colombian Archbishop López Trujillo. López was furious over the results of the Puebla meeting, and according to Brazilian sources, he had sworn to "do in" the National Conference of Brazilian Bishops as well as Boff.[44] His group had connections to the Vatican through friends in the Curia like Rossi, and López himself frequently saw the pope. He was one of the few Latin Americans on the consultative board of the Congregation for the Doctrine of the Faith (another was the archbishop of Brasilia, José Freire Falcão, an Opus Dei sympathizer).

In Rio, Cardinal Araujo Sales kept up a continuous barrage against liberation theology with the help of the Brazilian establishment's publications, particularly O Globo and Jornal do Brasil. Like López Trujillo, he was much feared by the priests and nuns who worked in the archdiocese because of his fierce temper and authoritarian ways. Unable to persuade the doctrinal commission of the Brazilian bishops' conference to move against the liberation theologians, he set up his own inquisition, the first target of which was Boff's book, Church: Charism & Power. He also fired Boff's brother Clodovis and another well-known liberation theologian from their teaching posts at two Catholic universities in Rio. He tried to force four other priests to resign because they had criticized his silencing of a colleague, Father Francisco de Roncha Guimaraes, who had been forbidden to teach or write. In the midst of his battle with the cardinal

Guimaraes died of a heart attack. At the funeral Mass for their friend the four priests spoke of his "passion and death," which infuriated Araujo Sales, who demanded but did not get their resignations.[45]

Boff believed that the cardinal took his condemnations of *Church: Charism & Power* to Rome, where he had the ear of the Curia. Knowing that the Congregation for the Doctrine of the Faith had a dossier on Boff, the Brazilian bishops asked Ratzinger to let them conduct their own investigation of the theologian, but since the commission was headed by Cardinal Lorscheider, a friend of Boff and a fellow Franciscan, Ratzinger refused. He claimed that, because Boff's works had been translated, the case had become international and could be dealt with only by Rome, although Gutiérrez, who was better known, had been judged by his own bishops. In May 1984, Ratzinger sent Boff a six-page letter of criticisms which centered on the Brazilian's challenge to the hierarchical structure of the church. He also summoned Boff to Rome for a "colloquy," a euphemism for an interrogation.[46]

Already angry about the Vatican's refusal to recognize the principle of shared authority in the matter of the interrogation, the Brazilian bishops were further annoyed by a negative report by Cologne's Cardinal Höffner on the São Paulo archdiocese's theological faculty. (See Chapter 3, p. 44.) The Höffner inquiry appeared to be linked to the Boff investigation because Cardinal Arns, who is also a Franciscan, had been Boff's spiritual director and was strongly identified with his work. A graduate of the Sorbonne who speaks seven languages fluently, the short, bespectacled prelate is known as a fighter. He holds a special place in Brazilian hearts for his fearless opposition to the twenty-one-year military regime that ended in 1985 (Arns received so many death threats during the dictatorship that he lost count). Although Casaroli thought highly of him, he was not popular with other members of the Curia because of his refusal to knuckle under, and for some time he was on the pope's blacklist thanks to unfavorable reports from the conservative Latin American bishops. John Paul may also have been taken aback by Arns's tough stance during his visit to São Paulo in 1980 when Brazil was still under military rule. At the end of the visit the local army commander offered to fly the pontiff to his next destination in a military helicopter. As the pope paused, a soft but insistent voice interjected. "If you go with the army," the cardinal advised, "you go alone." John Paul went with Arns.

As observed by Archbishop Helder Cámara, long the prophet of the Brazilian church, Rome seldom seems to hear about "the good that is done in the name of the theology of liberation."[47] But matters soon changed after Ratzinger's summons of Boff to Rome, which set off an avalanche of tens of thousands of letters from angry Brazilians. As Boff remarked, it was quite clear that he had not been called to Rome "merely because of a book. This is also a wholesale judgment against our church, which is concerned with the rejected, the miserable and the poor of our society." Agreed an influential Brazilian church leader: "Rome is jealous of the vibrancy of our church, dislikes our theology because it is not European, and is fearful of our numbers. This is a conflict over power, period."[48]

Gentle and soft-spoken, Boff managed to put a brave face on his ordeal in Rome largely because of the support of Cardinals Arns and Lorscheider, who announced that they intended to accompany him to Rome—an unprecedented act that made serious trouble for Ratzinger. For one thing, the supportive presence of the leaders of the Brazilian church left the cardinal with no basis for his claim that a dissident "popular church" was in conflict with the hierarchy. For another, Lorscheider was a brilliant theologian and debater who had gotten the better of Ratzinger in previous encounters. Worst of all, the Brazilians' defiance had made the "colloquy" an international news event that was bound to turn the first interrogation of a non-European theologian into a major scandal.

Ratzinger sought to downplay the drama by preventing the Brazilian cardinals from accompanying Boff to the Congregation's offices, but the feisty Cardinal Arns said that if they were turned away, he would tell the whole world that Boff's book hadn't told the half of it, that the Curia was even worse than he had said. Ratzinger backed down, although he still insisted on inquisitorial protocol. Boff, who was staying at the Franciscans' house in Rome, thought he would drive to the appointment in one of the Franciscans' cars, but Ratzinger insisted that he come and go in a car provided by the Curia. The incident over the car was the one moment when he felt really bad, Boff recalled, because the enormity of a "trial" suddenly dawned on him. But he quickly recovered his native Brazilian humor. "When one of Ratzinger's secretaries arrived with another theologian, I asked them if they were going to handcuff me," he later told *Der Spiegel*. "One of them said, 'If you like, Father, yes.' Nobody could go with me. [The Brazilian cardinals had to make their own way to the Vatican and wait until after Boff's private conversation with Ratzinger to join the colloquy.]

"Once inside the palace they rushed me along a labyrinth of corridors so I couldn't be seen by the press and especially by . . . the Brazilian television people, who had managed to get in. Suddenly I found myself in front of a door with an iron grate, and so I asked my companions, 'Is this the torture chamber?' 'For God's sake, Father, of course not!' one of them answered."[49]

Boff kept up his good humor once inside the small interrogation room—the "room of the knights of the round table," as he called it—saluting Ratzinger with a smart, "*Grüss Gott, Herr Kardinal.*" A cordial Ratzinger told Boff to read his responses to his charges, then questioned him politely about their differences. Afterwards there was a coffee break and banter, and it was then that the knives emerged:

"A cassock suits you very well, Father Boff," said Ratzinger, "and it also offers proof to the world of who you are."

"But it's not easy to wear in Brazil because of the heat," responded Boff.

"But that's how people recognize your devotion and patience, and they will say: He is paying for the sins of this world."

"Of course we need proofs of spiritualism, but they don't come from a cassock but from the heart, and it is the heart that should be well worn."

"But one doesn't see the heart, and something has to be seen, doesn't it?"

"Yes, but it could be that the cassock is a symbol of power. When I wear it on a bus, people feel they have to get up and give me their seats. We should be the servants of the people."[50]

After they were joined by Cardinals Arns and Lorscheider, the interrogation became an informal chat about Brazil. Met by cheering crowds on their departure from the Congregation, the Brazilians were convinced that the worst was over and that the most Boff could expect was a slap on the wrist. Arns gave the "V" sign for victory to the crowd of journalists, which infuriated Ratzinger, whose temper may already have been frayed by the circus outside the Congregation for the Doctrine of the Faith. In addition to the shouting throng of journalists and well-wishers, vendors were doing a brisk trade in Boff's forbidden book.

However suave during the interrogation, Ratzinger had not intended to let Boff off the hook, and in May 1985 he imposed an indefinite period of silence on the theologian for promoting "revolutionary utopianism foreign to the church." Boff was not allowed to write, teach, edit any publication, or speak in public. Deeply hurt by the unexpected harshness of the punishment, Boff nevertheless accepted it, saying he would rather "walk with the church than walk alone" with his theology. But he could not help asking the Franciscans' Minister General John Vaughn, "Does this mean, then, that I am all alone now?" "No," replied Vaughn, "the whole church is with you!"[51]

So it was. From being a little-known South American theologian, Boff became a best-selling author throughout Europe and especially in Ratzinger's own country, Germany. In Brazil his offending book sold more than 50,000 copies. Boff's dispute with Rome made him a celebrity among the poor he had championed, reported Adriano Hipólito, bishop of the huge Rio slum of Nova Iguaçu. "These are humble people," said Hipólito. "Before, they did not know who Leonardo Boff was and they didn't know or care much about liberation theology. Now, everyone knows."[52]

A priest in São Paulo described a similar experience. Returning from a meeting late at night, he stopped at a small grocery store for a beer. Joining the conversation of the three other men at the counter, he found to his amazement that they were discussing liberation theology. None were churchgoers or belonged to a Christian base community, but they were genuinely interested in all the fuss that had been caused by Boff's punishment. "Imagine people wanting to talk about theology over a beer at eleven at night," said the priest. "If Ratzinger wanted to propagate liberation theology, he sure did a good job."

An Easter Present

Tensions between Rome and Brazil continued to mount throughout 1985. Petitions and letters from all over the world poured into the Vatican protesting Boff's treatment, and in Brazil the National Movement of Human Rights published a book, *Roma Locuta,* that provided all the documentary background to the controversy, including correspondence between Boff and Ratzinger.[53] The angry cardinal had the book banned, but it was a best-seller nonetheless. As pointed out by the leaders of the Human Rights Movement, the Brazilian church had been their only protector during the military dictatorship, and the least they could do was protest when the human rights of a Brazilian theologian were being violated by the Vatican. By the beginning of 1986 matters had reached such a state that the pope found it prudent to tape a video message to Brazilian Catholics in an attempt to blunt their criticism of him. But the message, which dealt with poverty and hunger, made little impression. It was then that Cardinal Casaroli, the practiced diplomat, stepped in.

A moderate who could see more than one point of view, the secretary of state had heard repeatedly from the Brazilians about the behavior of the Curia, and it was his belief that the solution was to bring the two sides together to talk out their differences in the presence of John Paul. In March 1986 an extraordinary summit took place in Rome in which the Brazilian bishops were given an opportunity to explain their side of the story—their reality of oppression and poverty—to the Vatican's bureaucrats. Apparently aware that he had been hearing only the conservatives' version, John Paul opened the meeting with a talk in which he stressed his impartiality. In order to restore unity among the Brazilian bishops, he said, they needed to engage in "an adult dialogue between persons, Christians and pastors. I am sure that you will not take my words amiss if I say to you that one step in the direction of communion with the episcopal conference is worth more than ten steps taken with the risk of damaging or even shattering communion." Since the overwhelming majority of the episcopal conference was united behind liberation theology and Boff, the warning was understood to be directed at the dissidents, primarily Rio's Cardinal Araujo Sales. Indeed, the cardinal admitted that he was in the minority and that "the minority is getting smaller all the time."[54]

The meeting was unusual in that the Brazilians had the opportunity not only to reply to their dissident compatriots in the pope's presence but also to assess the Curia's performance. According to those present, discussions were "hard." At one point, for example, Cardinal Bernardin Gantin, the conservative prefect of the Vatican's Congregation for Bishops, complained of the failure of Bishop Ivo Lorscheiter to respond to his queries. A towering, no-nonsense Brazilian who was the president of the National Conference of Brazilian Bishops, Lorscheiter replied that he had sent the answering letters and had personally checked with Gantin's office that they were on file. "I think you should spend more time in your office," he advised Gantin. With all eyes on him, including the cold stare of the pope, Gantin began to stutter. No more was heard about unanswered letters.[55]

At another meeting to discuss religious publications John Paul approved a series of books on liberation theology that the Brazilians wanted to publish despite Ratzinger's objection that Boff was among the editors. When talk turned to a second series, on biblical commentaries, Araujo

Sales immediately started to complain about how dangerous the books would be. But Ratzinger apparently had had enough of the infighting. "I am talking," he snapped at Araujo Sales, "and would be grateful if you do not interrupt. I've already agreed to the series."[56]

The Brazilians were also given an opportunity to preview the second "Instruction" on liberation theology, as they had requested. At breakfasts and dinners with the pope, talks on liberation theology were wide-ranging and productive. In a relaxed moment after one dinner John Paul leaned back, with his hands behind his head, and began to muse on the possibilities of rethinking theology in terms of the ethics of liberation. Archbishop Lucas Moreira Neves, then secretary to Cardinal Gantin and among the Brazilian hard-liners in the Curia, interrupted the promising monologue to complain that it was really too bad that the Brazilian church had so many good authors and editors and a sizable readership and that they were making money (on their books) whereas the Vatican was not. But why, replied the Brazilian cardinals, did Moreira Neves not say "our" theologians since they belonged to the entire church?[57]

Although the Brazilians came away from the meeting with the conviction that they had not changed any hearts in the Curia, John Paul showed himself more politically sensitive to the challenges faced by men like Arns, Lorscheider, and Lorscheiter. As evidence that he could be persuaded to be more flexible, the Vatican announced the end of Boff's "penitential silence" during Easter Week. Boff's joy at the unexpected "Easter present" was equaled only by that of the bishops, who received an extraordinary message from the pope the following week. In his letter John Paul told them that their church was an example to the world because "you and your longtime collaborators in pastoral service bear the witness of extraordinary closeness to your people, solidarity with their joys and sorrows and readiness to educate them in the faith . . . but also readiness to help in their needs and to share their afflictions and efforts." He said that he was convinced that "liberation theology is not only opportune but is useful and necessary. The poor of this continent are the first to feel the urgent need for this Gospel of radical and integral liberation." The theology should of course be developed within the context of the church's social doctrine, he observed, but who better to take charge of this "delicate task" than the Brazilian bishops? It was to them, he said, that he was assigning the role of harbingers of liberation theology in the universal church.[58]

The message—which was read to a meeting of the bishops in São

Paulo by a subdued Cardinal Gantin—brought spontaneous applause and a chorus of alleluias. "First one, then dozens more, and in moments, more than 300 bishops were singing," said one of those present. "If you could only see the happiness of these bishops who have struggled so long to explain to the Holy Father what they are doing. It is as if ten years were added to their lives."[59]

The Return of the Enforcer

In an institution that has endured nearly 2,000 years, wars are not settled in a few days, even at a summit meeting with the pope. While John Paul had offered the Brazilians an olive branch, that did not mean the Curia felt obliged to cease its guerrilla skirmishes over liberation theology. Thus despite his Easter amnesty Boff found that the Curia was continuing to "closely examine everything I write and say in public, analyzing it in detail."[60] The Vatican also demanded and got the resignations of the entire editorial board of the Franciscans' Brazilian publishing house, Editora Vozes. Although no reasons were given for the drastic action, Vozes was Boff's publisher. It had also published *Roma Locuta,* the book by the Human Rights Movement that had been banned by Rome. A worldwide crackdown on religious publishing houses had been going on for several months, and Vozes, with its popular works on psychology and sociology, would probably have been a target in any case. The change in directors made little difference in policy, however, since the replacements were drawn from Brazilian Franciscans, most of whom shared Boff's point of view.

The crisis at Vozes came on top of the controversy with Rome about the publication in Brazil of a fifty-four-volume series on liberation theology. Designed to assist pastoral agents, religious, and bishops, the collection represented the work of more than 100 Latin American theologians. But Ratzinger succeeded in blocking it despite John Paul's verbal approval during his meetings with the Brazilian bishops. As pointed out by Boff, Ratzinger's position was at variance with canon law because local bishops and religious superiors were responsible for giving approval (imprimatur) for such publications. All the books had imprimaturs, yet Ratzinger refused to budge. The cardinal's intransigence, said Boff, made the region's liberation theologians feel they had again been singled out for humiliation. Meanwhile, Cardinal Araujo Sales returned to the attack, sending Rome a denunciation of another book by Boff, *La Iglesia se hizo pueblo,* published in 1987. The book, which described the commitment of the Brazilian bishops to the poor, was "dangerous and unorthodox," in the cardinal's opinion.[61]

And the wars continued. In mid-1988 Dom Pedro Casaldáliga, the outspoken bishop of the Brazilian Amazon, was called on the carpet by Cardinals Ratzinger and Gantin for his "unorthodox" criticism of Ratzinger's negative analysis of liberation theology and for other alleged sins—for example, Ratzinger objected to Casaldáliga's description of San Salvador's murdered archbishop Romero as a martyr because he had not been canonized by the Vatican. Following secret interrogations by the cardinals in Rome, Casaldáliga was told to sign a prohibition on his writings, speeches, and interviews that would have effectively silenced him. When he refused, he was warned that he would receive a communication from Ratzinger. Three months later, Casaldáliga received a letter on official stationery from the papal nunciature in Brasilia containing a silence order that he was told to sign. But since the document had no date, signatures, or seals from Ratzinger's and Gantin's congregations, the feisty bishop claimed it did not constitute a legal document. He also challenged the cardinals' accusations as having no theological or pastoral basis under canon law.

Although many Brazilian bishops were shocked by the gag order, the conservatives were delighted. Casaldáliga had gotten what he deserved, said Cardinal Araujo Sales, adding that he would have to knuckle under. But the bishop, who is internationally known for his impassioned poetry and courageous stance on behalf of the Amazon's impoverished peasants and Indians, was not about to go quietly, and within a week of the announcement of his punishment many sectors of the Brazilian church were up in arms: The Casaldáliga affair promised to be just as problematic for the Vatican as had been Boff's silencing.

The situation in Peru was equally tense. Insisting that the bishops fulfill an earlier promise to produce a manual of dos and don'ts on liberation theology, Ratzinger showed up in Lima to make sure the work was in progress. Although he made no condemnations of either the theology or individual theologians, the visit was seen as ominous. Unlike Brazil, where a majority of the bishops supported liberation theology, the Peruvian church was more evenly divided. Cardinal Landázuri had held the post-Medellín church together by force of his personality and diplomatic skills, but he was approaching the mandatory retirement age of seventy-five. In the early 1970s Peru had taken the lead in putting the

Medellín documents into effect, startling the Latin American and European bishops with an endorsement of socialism. In the decade between Medellín and Puebla religious vocations shot up, and many of the young priests and nuns went to work in slums or impoverished villages. But after John Paul's election a cold wind began to blow over the Andes. Most of the bishops appointed were conservative, and by 1985 all of Peru's archdioceses were controlled by Ratzinger supporters save for Lima, where the aging Landázuri held firm. Even there Gutiérrez's followers could not be sure of complete support because during the cardinal's absences his conservative auxiliary bishop, Alberto Brazzini, tried to bring the liberation theologians to heel. Yet despite the ongoing skirmishes, the seeds planted by liberation theology continued to bear fruit through the gradual democratization of society.

CHAPTER 5
✝
RELIGIOUS EMPOWERMENT: THE RISE OF POPULAR MOVEMENTS

ALTHOUGH ROME MAY CLAIM the last word on liberation theology, the case is by no means concluded. After two decades of church-supported grass-roots organizing, the Latin American poor are too "liberated" in the practice of their faith to return to the old ways. The momentum that began in the 1960s has acquired a dynamic of its own, and as San Salvador's Archbishop Rivera y Damas observed, the church of the poor will continue on its own path regardless of ecclesiastical power struggles.

In Lima, for example, church support for grass-roots organizations in the *pueblos jóvenes* (or "young towns," a euphemism for the slums) has helped spawn a huge network of neighborhood organizations that have given the poor their first taste of local democracy. In the sprawling slum of Villa El Salvador, for instance, the 400,000 inhabitants elect their own mayor and municipal council, both of which constantly pressure the city government for improvements. Mobilized block by block, the inhabitants have established neighborhood groups for everything from road construction to government-subsidized milk programs for children. Despite economic hardships Salvador's poor carry on with determination, as shown by the improvements in the older part of the slum, where homes with brick and cement walls have replaced those made of reeds. Even the poorest sections boast trees in spite of the scarcity of water in the surrounding desert. The women, who lug cans of water from a distant well, first use the water for cooking, then recycle it for washing. Whatever remains of the dirty liquid is thrown on the saplings, which miraculously thrive in the sterile desert.

The same determination is evident in Lima's tuberculosis victims, who have become a recognized political force in the slums by organizing to demand their rights. Because of the extreme poverty in Lima's overcrowded slums, malnutrition, tuberculosis, and typhoid have risen sharply, but the city's public hospitals are woefully underequipped to deal with the problem. The TB victims lobby the city authorities for such basic items as film for the few X-ray machines that exist, but the primary reason for their organization is to give its members a shared sense of hope and courage. Their symbol is the tree of life.

The Peruvian church has played a major role in encouraging such groups through its support for Christian base communities, which grew out of liberation theology's advocacy of a more just society and which frequently were the first blocks in new social structures at the neighborhood or village level. The communities' success in Peru—as in other Latin American countries—derives from several factors. One is that they fill a need by giving the laity responsibility for pastoral work in areas with a shortage of priests. The base community not only deals with this problem but also offers an imaginative alternative to the cumbersome parish structure, which typically encompasses large numbers of people from different classes and with different goals and interests. Most people do not relate to a parish organization, and thus the local church is no more than a "supermarket for the sacraments," in the words of the liberation theologians. The communities, in contrast, are small—usually fifteen to twenty families per group—and are composed of people from the same village or neighborhood slum. The overwhelming majority are poor, and many are strengthened by the communitarian traditions of the Peruvian poor.

Although the Peruvian church has attempted to attract members of the middle and upper classes to such communities, few have joined the movement because of class prejudices and the indifference of affluent Peruvians to social injustice. For the poor, on the other hand, the communities serve as the motor for social change and, in the slums, as a means of bringing together impoverished rural migrants from different parts of the country. "Alone, life is hard, but in a group things begin to get easier," explained a member of a base community in a Lima slum.

Though small, the groups are like mustard seeds, spreading to the next street or village, crisscrossing the country. In a nation in which the poor have never had a voice, the growth in a relatively short time of a national movement of poor Peruvians is politically and socially significant. Through their promotion of other popular groups, from street theaters to labor unions, the communities have also shown how faith can be the leaven in society. As one European observer of the communities said, they give "real meaning to the Lord's words, 'For where two or three meet in my name, I shall be there with them.' "

Usually the communities begin through the work of evangelizing teams of priests and nuns and/or laity, sometimes from existing communities, who encourage the people to gather in small groups for Bible study and to celebrate the sacraments. Unlike the hierarchy of traditional parishes, the priest does not function as the "boss," but rather as an "animator" of the group who stresses the intrinsic worth, courage, and ability of the poor despite their lack of professional qualifications, including literacy. When church leaders show that they are genuinely interested in hearing the opinions of the poor, they give the latter a sense of confidence—a belief that they do matter—that is crucial in the conversion from religious fatalism to a new, more mature faith.

Vatican II encouraged the communities by sanctioning Catholic rituals in the local vernacular. The use of Spanish, Portuguese, and such Indian languages as Quechua in the celebration of the sacraments sparked new interest in the Bible, which is the chief instrument for reflection at community meetings. Instead of the classical theological approach, in which truth is deduced from a set of established and unchangeable beliefs (usually by a member of the church hierarchy), community members use liberation theology's methodology of "see, judge, act," by first studying their historical reality and then using Bible readings to reflect on it. Reflection leads to action, such as the decision to organize a community nutrition program for infants or to join a labor union. Whereas traditional theology engenders fatalism, because nothing can be done to alter an immutable order, liberation theology encourages change. Religious awareness is reinforced by celebrations in which the people express their popular traditions, such as dancing the liturgy, in contrast to the church's earlier disdain for such "popular religiosity." Unlike the traditional parish Mass, which is often cold and remote, community celebrations are joyful events, with much clapping, singing, and embracing.

The communities have also benefited from their spontaneity. There is no single founder, constitution, set of rules, or timetable for the communities' formation. Most go through a slow consciousness-raising process that takes several years or sometimes a decade, depending on the political and social awareness of the members. Each community has developed different priorities, although the emphasis is always religious. Because there is no clerical caste to direct them, the communities take responsibility for themselves, apportioning religious and social work among their members, such as catechism classes or soup kitchens, according to ability and the will of the majority.

For poor people the communities often offer the first genuine experience of democracy at the local level. Fundamental to the experience is the freedom to think, speak, decide, and create. In discovering their own worth, the poor frequently move on to a new level of awareness that leads them to participate in neighborhood associations, such as the milk program in Salvador, and, eventually, to become part of larger movements, such as labor unions and political parties. Religious empowerment thus encourages democratization of everyday life.

Rosa María, the mother of five, is typical of the Lima poor who have benefited from membership in a base community. Although she originally joined the group for religious reasons, contact with other women in similarly impoverished straits gave her needed peer support. Bible-reading discussions, in which the community reflected on the Gospels' meaning in their daily lives, helped the group understand the causes of common problems, such as hunger and unemployment, and encouraged them to do something about their plight. Through such contacts Rosa María and five other women organized a neighborhood soup kitchen that serves cheap, nourishing meals. The restaurant, which operates out of a dirt-floor shack, provides a service to the community and gives the women a small income. Although the work is hard—the women must rise at dawn to buy vegetables and soup bones at a distant market—and the growing cost of food is a constant problem, Rosa María and the others take pride in their achievement. "It may not seem much, but we try our best," she said, smiling through her broken teeth. "Just taste how good our soup is!"

The values stressed in the base community, particularly love of neighbor, reinforce the traditional community values of Lima's overwhelmingly Indian slum population. The Indians, having abandoned their ancestral villages in the hope of a better life in the city, found a cruel, alien world in Lima, where even the Spanish language was foreign to them. Many were unable to find steady work, and because they wore peasant dress, spoke Quechua, and were unfamiliar with the city's ways, they were often mistreated. The one element that was not strange was Catholicism. In the same period that the *pueblos jóvenes* were expanding across Lima's gray hills, priests and nuns, under the influence of liberation theology, began moving into the slums. Often it was they who helped the newcomers, by showing them how to get an appointment at a public hospital, for example, and by encouraging them to form neighborhood groups to deal with common problems. Although the church could not alter Peru's economic and political structures, it gave the poor hope by accompanying them in their suffering.

Like the base communities, Lima's neighborhood associations are less concerned with national politics than with such immediate issues as running water, health facilities, schools, and roads. Nevertheless, they provide lessons in rudimentary democracy through the election of boards and councils that represent families on each street and through a variety of complementary activities, such as neighborhood newspapers and drama clubs, which also contribute to political awareness. Some of the most active lay leaders have become involved in local politics through election to municipal office or have taken an important role in the development of labor unions. Thus a political constituency has gradually emerged in the slums. It is Christian and democratic and supports the left-wing coalition, United Left, the second largest political force in Peru after the centrist American Popular Revolutionary Alliance (APRA) of the middle and lower middle classes. The slum movements also serve as a counterweight to the right-wing military and their allies in the upper classes, as well as to the viciousness of the Maoist Sendero Luminoso ("Shining Path") guerrillas, who in their attacks on the peasantry have proven as merciless as the Red Guards. Although the urban poor confront enormous problems, including unemployment, disease, and hunger, they are beginning to learn the basics of democracy—a historic change in a traditionally feudal nation. The example of the base communities, where all members are equal, has played a crucial part in that change. More important than the mechanics, however, is the newfound knowledge that, as Rosa María said, "God is on the side of the poor."[1]

Today millions of poor Latin Americans belong to base communities. The extent of their social activism varies from country to country, according to the attitudes of the local bishops and the political awareness of the poor. In countries with conservative hierarchies, such as Colombia, the communities are dominated by the bishops in a top-down relationship that makes them just another parish activity, although even in Colombia a parallel movement of independent base communities is thriving. In nations with progressive bishops, the relationship is more democratic, bishops and religious acting as advocates for the communities without dominating them.

The awareness and leadership skills provided by the communities have changed the thinking of a whole generation of poor Latin Americans, encouraging them to found labor movements and to engage in a political struggle for change. Politics is not understood as a partisan response, however, but as a means to fulfill the Gospel imperative for peace and justice. The pressures for democracy increased political awareness in Peru, hastened the end of a twenty-one-year military regime in Brazil, and contributed to the Sandinista revolution in Nicaragua and the downfall of the Duvalier dictatorship in Haiti. Another result has been the growth of church influence in the political arena, particularly in countries where it is the only voice that can speak above ideological divisions, as in El Salvador and Chile.

Sociologists, political scientists, and theologians see parallels between this awakening and the political and economic changes brought about by Protestantism. Like the historical model of the Protestant church, the base communities are small, congregational, and self-managed, and all members are equal. Or as an American student of the movement commented, they are "what we were about before we got into the business of immense suburban church congregations or millions of viewers of the electronic church."[2] Political scientist Daniel Levine, a specialist in politics and religion in Latin America, pointed out that congregationalism enabled the Protestants to establish a mutually reinforcing relationship between their religious ideas and an emerging capitalism through the fusion of "religion with daily life." Base communities also give their members the means to express religious commitment in daily life through solidarity and group structures. The heightened awareness of community members and a new, biblical framework for common action have undercut the established order, bringing a different dimension to politics that Levine predicts will be "explosive."[3]

Brazil

While Peru first pointed the way, through the ground-breaking work of Gustavo Gutiérrez and other liberation theologians, Brazil has provided the leadership for a new model of church that challenges both the state and Rome. In contrast to other churches, such as that in Chile, where a majority of the bishops favor pluralism in society but *not* in their own institution, many of the Brazilian bishops share Leonardo Boff's democratic vision of a church of the poor in which service, not power, is the distinguishing characteristic.

Brazil's church was not always thus. As elsewhere in Latin America, the institution was until recently concerned with the needs of the upper and middle classes. Politically and theologically conservative, it seemed an unlikely candidate to become the Third World's most progressive Catholic church, yet in the space of only two generations the Brazilians took the lead in pastoral, theological, and liturgical innovations.

Like other churches in the region, the Brazilians were strongly influenced by Vatican II, but they had the advantage of having embarked on such reforms a decade before the council occurred. Thus Vatican II represented a confirmation of their policies rather than a new direction. Church historians agree that the catalyst for the changes in Brazil was a short, frail-looking priest with enormous vision—Dom Helder Cámara. Although Archbishop Cámara later became internationally famous for his resistance to Brazil's twenty-one-year military dictatorship, his poetry, and his prophetic denunciations of the Third World's bondage to the First, his greatest contribution was the formation of the National Conference of Brazilian Bishops (CNBB) in 1952 at a time when bishops' conferences were unusual (not until Vatican II did they receive official sanction) and the Brazilian church lacked a unified voice to speak to the political and economic challenges facing the country. The CNBB subsequently became the principal motor for social change in Brazil, and indeed all Latin America, through its leadership role at the bishops' hemisphere conferences in Medellín in 1968 and Puebla in 1979, when the region's church made a preferential option for the poor. It also supported the growth of Christian base communities, which today number more than 4 million members in Brazil.

Born in Brazil's impoverished Northeast, Dom Helder had firsthand experience of the most poverty-stricken, feudal region in the country, and during the 1950s, when he was involved in national education programs, he supported attempts by reformist governments to achieve a modicum of social justice. The charismatic Brazilian was popular with two successive papal nuncios to Brazil, including the liberal Dom Armando Lombardi, who virtually reshaped the Brazilian hierarchy through appointments of progressive bishops. Thanks to the nuncios' influence, the Vatican supported Cámara's initiative to establish the CNBB, and for twelve years he ran the conference as its secretary general.

The CNBB played a key role in persuading the hierarchy to promote national and regional organizations of the laity concerned with social justice, such as the Movement for Grassroots Education (MEB) in the Northeast. Founded as a Christian alternative to communist peasant leagues, the MEB developed over a thousand church-sponsored radio schools that brought poor people together in literacy circles in which they critically examined the region's poverty, malnutrition, and illiteracy. As in Peru, the basic tools were the Bible and the consciousness-raising techniques of Brazilian educational philosopher Paulo Freire, which made the people aware of their rights and responsibilities. Meanwhile, in Barra do Piraí, near Rio de Janeiro, Agnelo Rossi, then a bishop, had begun experimentation with "popular catechists" to baptize, aid the sick and dying, and act as coordinators of small communities without priests. Although Rossi's idea was a narrow one—he saw the coordinators as a way to strengthen the church's presence among the poorer classes in areas where Protestant churches were active—the communities soon developed a momentum of their own by adopting the consciousness-raising techniques of the MEB.

These seeds of the base community movement spread rapidly, greatly increasing the Brazilian church's influence in society but also changing the church itself, so that it gradually became the "People of God" described by Vatican II. Ironically, the base communities received a substantial boost from Brazil's right-wing military, which outlawed political parties, student and labor groups, peasant leagues, and other democratic organizations following the 1964 coup. The only institution able to withstand the repression was the Catholic Church, although such progressive church leaders as Dom Helder had a hard time of it—one of his closest advisers was assassinated by a paramilitary group, and the archbishop was repeatedly threatened. For nine years, between 1968 and 1977, Cámara was blacklisted by the Brazilian press and banned from radio and television. Several of his most important projects, including the Movement for Grassroots Education, were destroyed, and Cámara lost his influence in the CNBB because of a conservative backlash in the hierarchy that paralleled the military crackdown.

Nevertheless, the bishops protected the base communities because of their ties to the institutional church. In areas where popular movements were destroyed by the military regime the communities became surrogates for democracy, enjoying a boom in membership. By the end of the 1960s, moreover, a growing number of bishops had become disenchanted with the regime because of its brutal repression. Dom Helder, they said, had been right to take a strong stand against the dictatorship. "The harshness and cruelty of the socio-economic conditions caused the church to align itself with the people," explained Dom Luís Fernandes, the bishop of Petrópolis.

The more the church protested, the more its leaders were persecuted; by the mid-1970s church and state were virtually at war. Yet even during the worst period of persecution, when priests were being murdered and bishops threatened, the generals were unable to cow the CNBB. Thus the churches—and particularly the base communities—became the only place in society in which the people could express themselves.

Contrary to expectations that the bishops' social activism would become less urgent after the military's departure in 1985, it soon became apparent that the Brazilian poor would get nothing from the government bureaucracy without the church's help. Lacking strong democratic institutions or broad-based reformist political parties, Brazil experienced only cosmetic changes under a civilian government that pandered to the same economic groups that flourished during the military regime. Corruption was as widespread as ever, and police brutality, particularly in rural areas, continued unchecked. Consequently church leaders felt they could not withdraw from the struggle for social justice.

Because of its influence, commitment, and a network of base communities with millions of members, the church was a formidable political opponent. And although skirmishes continued between the bishops and the Curia, the pope loyally backed the former in a showdown with the government over the Brazilian church's first priority—agrarian reform.

"Sem Terra"

Even with 140 million people, the giant country has more than enough land to go around—in theory. In fact, millions of poor Brazilians have been forced off their small farms since the advent of agribusiness in the 1950s. The process accelerated during the military dictatorship, which opened up the Amazon to foreign and local speculators who cleared more than 100 million acres of jungle to create enormous ranches, some the size of countries. The Amazon had always served as a last frontier for landless peasants, but by the end of the 1970s even that huge reserve had been appropriated by the wealthy business and military elites. Today 12 million peasants are without land, according to church statistics, whereas 5,000 wealthy Brazilians control half the arable acreage. Although more than one billion acres could be farmed, only 500 million are productive, most of the remainder being held for speculative purposes by businessmen and bankers.

The lack of land has driven millions of peasants to the cities, swelling the slums and contributing to a socially explosive situation. Disease and mortality rates have increased, crime has proliferated, and food riots are not uncommon. Two-thirds of the people are malnourished and one-third are illiterate. According to the United Nations, 10 million Brazilian children suffer mental defects because of undernourishment. Brazilian statistical agencies calculate that approximately 70 million people live in absolute poverty, even though Brazil boasts the world's eighth largest economy.[4]

The Brazilian church looked to Tancredo Neves to change this situation. A centrist politician, Neves was elected president on a platform that included agrarian reform as a major plank, but Neves died just before he was due to take office in 1985. José Sarney, his successor and a wealthy landowner, proved less than enthusiastic about Neves's promises. Although he announced that the government would redistribute 100 million acres of uncultivated land to 1.2 million families by 1990, the plan soon encountered opposition from the large landowners, who formed private armies to fight the reform under the aegis of the Rural Democratic Union (UDR). The UDR also spent lavishly to elect its own representatives to congress and to hobble the government's agrarian reform institute, which was eventually abolished. Under pressure from the UDR Sarney emasculated the reform, and by the end of 1986 only 9,000 families had received land, whereas 12,000 families were driven from their farms in the same period. "The plan appears to be little more than a poor 'excuse' for a meaningful reform, and will exacerbate the feeling of injustice and lead to increased violence," predicted the respected Brazilian Institute of Social and Economic Analysis (IBASE).[5]

As during the dictatorship, the bishops became the standard bearers of agrarian reform. Their Pastoral Commission for Land already had agents in place throughout the country to provide legal and moral support for peasant federations, and in 1986, at the urging of the base communities, the bishops officially blessed peaceful land invasions by a nationwide movement of the landless known as "Sem Terra." By 1987 more than fifty camps, containing thousands of landless peasants, had been established on the periphery of unfarmed estates in an attempt to pressure the government to expropriate. Meanwhile, the CNBB underscored its support for agrarian reform by urging all bishops to turn over their rural landholdings to the peasants, which many did.[6]

Sarney attempted to undercut the bishops' opposition by taking his case to the pope in July 1986, but John Paul upheld the bishops' position. He repeated his support a few months later, during a visit to Rome by Bishop Ivo Lorscheiter, then president of the CNBB, telling Lorscheiter that "the church must make sure that the agrarian reform in Brazil is not a failure."[7]

Neither the government nor the UDR was pleased with these statements. Sarney complained of "the involvement of the church in an ever-growing number of organizations and activities, infiltration of political movements and the growing politicization of religious education—with agrarian reform topping the agenda." The church wanted to "ride the government" on agrarian reform, said Justice Minister Paulo Brossard. The UDR, for its part, claimed that while it had "the greatest respect for the Pope when he speaks about God, his comments on the need for courageous land reform show that he is completely out of touch with the social-economic reality of Brazil."[8]

In fact, the pope was well aware of Brazilian reality, having received extensive dossiers on the agrarian situation from the CNBB, including details of the church's persecution by the government and the large landowners. "We are living as in the worst days of the dictatorship, when anyone defending the interests of the workers was liable to be persecuted and defamed," said Lorscheiter. "Once again we hear that old refrain the generals used, that the priest's place is in the sacristy and the worker's in the factory, that priests who help the needy are subversives."[9]

Lorscheiter was not exaggerating. In 1986 the large landowners declared war on the church, with the tacit support of government officials. A death list of 106 people was drawn up, including seven bishops, twenty-one priests, and seven sisters. Although church leaders sought government protection, local authorities ignored their pleas. As a result, five religious were killed and one seriously injured between 1985 and 1987. Early in 1987 Bishop Marcelo Pinto Carvalheira, who headed the diocese of Guarabira in the violent Northeast, narrowly escaped death when gunmen shot up a peasant meeting where he was present and the main target of the assault. In February a bomb was thrown into the patio of the home of Cardinal Lorscheider, archbishop of Fortaleza—the second bombing of his residence in less than a year. Indicative of the escalating land war that raged across the Northeast and the Amazon was the rise in the number of peasants murdered: The average for such killings in 1984 was one every three days; in 1986 it was one a day. In the first five months of 1986 alone there were 2,244 land conflicts, according to the church's Land Commission.[10]

The bishops blamed the violence on the UDR and the lack of government concern for what one priest called a "Wild West without sheriffs." Church sources said that three of Sarney's cabinet ministers supported the UDR. It is an indication of the depth of antichurch feeling in government circles that some officials talked of expelling foreign bishops. The government also refused entry visas for thirty foreign priests. "I am not going to say that this is an obvious case of ideological discrimination," said Bishop Lorscheiter. "But it does seem very strange that the requests for entry which receive the stamp 'rejected as unsuitable' are precisely those of priests slated for dioceses headed by so-called progressive bishops."[11]

The UDR was well financed by more than 10,000 large landowners who generated revenue through cattle auctions. The money was used to support the campaigns of friendly legislators and for space in major magazines and newspapers, such as the news magazine *Veja,* which were controlled by the business elites and sympathetic to the landowners' cause. The UDR also had the support of Tradition, Family and Property (TFP), an ultraright Catholic sect that had worked with the CIA to achieve the overthrow of the reformist President João Goulart in 1964 and that specialized in terrorist tactics. According to the UDR and the TFP, agrarian reform was "communist," and any peasants occupying land would be "repelled with lead."[12]

Much of the UDR's power resided in its private armies composed of former members of the military and police who were left jobless at the end of the military regime (one such company of hired gunmen was known as "The Solution"). According to a report by the Brazilian Institute of Social and Economic Analysis, the police in some regions "connived" with UDR landowners, even though it was "public knowledge that priests, church agents, laymen and members of rural trade unions who support or appear to support agrarian reform have received death threats from . . . the UDR or its sympathizers." Nor did the government disguise its sympathies. After a priest who had been threatened by the UDR was murdered, Justice Minister Brossard blamed not the UDR but the church. Meanwhile, the federal police chief warned the bishops that they could expect police intervention if they did not control the peasants.

Church authorities, he said, should also "talk with their priests and pray." Retorted Cardinal Avelar Brandão Vilela, the centrist archbishop of São Salvador de Bahia, "The church does not have the obligation to follow the recommendations of the police."[13]

Although the bishops staunchly stood by the peasants, no one believed there would be a quick or easy solution to the land conflict. "The wealthy landowners can do anything and get away with it, even murder," said a U.S. missionary. But then life was cheap in the backlands of Brazil—on an average, forty-five dollars a head. Few professional killers got rich on the business, but it was a living. Detailed accounts, including the names of the alleged murderers, were published annually by the church's Land Commission. But rarely was any judicial action taken, because the murders often occurred with the complicity of local judges and police officers.

An exception was the killing in 1985 of Father Ezechiele Ramin, an Italian missionary who died on the border of the Amazon states of Rondonia and Mato Grosso. The authorities apprehended three of the assassins and put out a warrant for the arrest of the majordomo of a local ranch. Since Ramin had tried to resolve a conflict between landowners and peasants, he was viewed as part of "a leftist plot against private property," in the words of a local general. He was returning from a meeting with the peasants when his Jeep was set upon by six men. A peasant leader accompanying the missionary was injured but managed to escape into the bush. A single bullet would have sufficed to kill Ramin, but the *pistoleiros,* as if driven by rage, shot him twenty times in a fusillade that destroyed the Jeep. Yet none had had dealings with the priest; his killing was routine.

Father Josimo Moraes Tavares, a Brazilian priest, met a similar end the following year in the frontier town of Imperatriz in the northern state of Maranhão. Tavares had received repeated death threats because of his work with the church's Land Commission, but local authorities refused to provide police protection. A month before his murder the UDR published a letter in a local newspaper threatening him with death. Some 150 members of the UDR were meeting in Imperatriz on the day Tavares was shot down by a hired gunman. The assassin, who was caught in a neighboring state in possession of an army-issued revolver, admitted that he had received $30,000 from two landowners to kill the priest and that he had earlier been paid $15,000 by two other ranchers for a failed attack on Tavares. Despite such evidence Justice Minister Brossard refused to blame the landowners, claiming that "foreign priests" were responsible for the violence by encouraging land invasions.[14]

But the church refused to be intimidated by killings and threats. Following the murders of Tavares and a leader of the local peasants' union, Maranhão's eleven bishops published a communiqué excommunicating the state governor, the secretary of justice and public security, and the local heads of the UDR. "These individuals," said the bishops, "must account to the people for land grabbing, for the impunity with which farm workers have been murdered, for the small towns destroyed and for countless arbitrary violations of the law and of human rights. They raise themselves as the vestiges of authoritarianism against the farm workers, against the agrarian reform, against the church and against democracy."[15]

A month before his death Tavares had offered his last testament to the peasants: "I am pledged to the struggle for the cause of the poor, defenseless laborers, an oppressed people in the jaws of the giant landowners. If I do not speak out, who will defend them? I am not held back by fear. What value has my life, in the light of the deaths of so many farm workers who have been killed, assaulted and expelled from their lands?"[16]

Democracy

The church's work on behalf of social justice "can affront many interests," admitted Bishop Lorscheiter, but it had an obligation to "speak like the prophets"—not as the voice of any political party but on behalf of the common good, which was "another way of engaging in politics."[17] Brazil's political and economic elites did not see the difference. They argued that the church was involved in issues—including agrarian reform, a new constitution, voting, and party platforms—that were the business of politicians. But religious leaders insisted that the church was trying to teach the Brazilian poor the elements of democracy, not directing them to vote for a specific party, as had been the Catholic Church's earlier practice. "The great task ahead of us is to become an organized people," explained Dom Mauro Morelli, bishop of two sprawling urbanizations in northeastern Rio de Janeiro. "Our challenge is not to overthrow the government; it's to help people to stand up and become aware and struggle for a new society."[18]

The instrument chosen by the Brazilian church to achieve that end was the Christian base community. While many popular organizations existed at the time of the coup, for the most part they depended on the patronage of the political elites and were only marginally successful in extracting benefits from the state. Under the military most of them, and especially the labor unions, were repressed or co-opted. The base communities filled the gap, creating and reactivating neighborhood groups under the church's protection, but with a radically different approach. Instead of being appendages of local politicians, the new organizations became independent pressure groups—a Brazilian variation of the New England town meeting. Their strength depended on the large number of poor people attracted to such groups and on an organizational network that integrated thousands of neighborhood associations.

The phenomenal growth of the communities reflected the strength of the CNBB, which made them a national priority. The best organized and largest bishops' conference in Latin America, the CNBB not only has a vast network of church institutions, such as schools, clubs, and publications, but has also created national pastoral commissions to deal with human rights, land rights, slum dwellers, workers, Indians, blacks, abandoned children, and prisoners. The commissions work on both regional and local levels, interacting with civil associations that address the same problems, such as peasant federations and labor unions, and using thousands of pastoral agents to carry their messages to the base communities. For example, the Pastoral Commission for Human Rights is subdivided into local networks that include civil organizations, such as lawyers' and journalists' groups and neighborhood associations, as well as the base communities. It not only defends prisoners from physical abuse and torture and obtains for them legal defense; it also campaigns for better housing, schools, health facilities, and decent wages, since these, too, are human rights. No other Brazilian institution, including the military, has such a far-ranging system of interrelated groups.

Hard though they tried, the generals could not stop the spread of these cells of democracy, and by the time they left office in 1985 there were an estimated 80,000 communities with more than 4 million members. In addition, thousands of neighborhood groups had sprung up in the cities through the influence of the communities, which transmitted the experience of collective and democratic leadership to the larger social movements. "It is not an exaggeration . . . to state that these widespread social movements would not have been possible without the support and active engagement of Catholic agents and lay people through the networks of the CNBB," said Maria Helena Moreira Alves, a founder of the Brazilian Workers Party, itself an example of such movements.[19]

As shown by the growth of neighborhood movements, the communities also had an important multiplier effect. In one sense, their influence reflected the institutional power of the bishops. On the other hand, a dynamic was at work within the communities that made them different from traditional lay movements because they changed the church itself. By taking up the cause of the people, the Brazilian church evolved into a new kind of church, adopting the same democratic style that it encouraged in civil society. Although the base communities were originally intended to convert the poor, in the end the poor converted the church as well.

As observed by Cardinal Arns, archbishop of São Paulo, Brazilians tend to follow individuals rather than parties. The example of individual bishops has therefore been particularly important in helping the poor overcome their fear of authority and feelings of inferiority grounded in a culture of poverty. For example, Dom Pedro Casaldáliga, the poet-bishop of the Amazon, is so poor that his peasant parishioners had to buy him a pair of shoes for the pope's visit in 1980. A small, seemingly fragile Spaniard who is famous for talking back to the military, Casaldáliga is revered by the peasants throughout the Amazon backlands. To see this man and other bishops line up at an old water trough outside a jungle hut to brush their teeth in the morning is to gain some measure of the nature of the Brazilian church's leaders. Though they could live in palaces, they have deliberately forsaken wealth to give their resources to the cause of the poor.

Cardinal Lorscheider, the ruddy-faced archbishop of Fortaleza and a papal candidate in the 1978 conclaves, is another of these shirtsleeve pastors, a man who refuses to build new churches in slums where his people cannot even roof their shanties. Like Casaldáliga, he is undeterred by threats: His residence was twice bombed and he has a long history of run-ins with the local military. Lorscheider proved equally courageous in trying to persuade Rome that Latin America's needs differed from those of middle-class Europe. "Vatican II had an optimistic view of the world," he said. "But we have discovered an underworld where discrimination and dependence prevail. This institutionalized disrespect of the people is contrary to humanity and to the very principles of Vatican II."[20]

The power of such men is considerable. When Cardinal Arns convokes a meeting at the cathedral, tens of thousands of people show up.

Leader of the world's largest archdiocese, the short, soft-spoken prelate is a national hero because of his opposition to the previous military regime and his championship of the rights of workers. For six years he oversaw a highly dangerous clandestine operation by church lawyers to photocopy government transcripts of the testimony of political prisoners tortured by the military regime. More than a million pages were hidden in archdiocesan buildings where the work was compiled under the supervision of Jaime Wright, a Presbyterian minister whose brother was tortured to death by the army. In 1985, after the military had left office, the archdiocese published *Brasil: Nunca Mais* (*Never Again*) as a testament for those who had suffered and died during two decades of dictatorship.[21]

Many priests who work with poor communities place their hopes in a Christian form of socialism whereby the majority can participate in the country's political and economic life. But such a democracy would demand a radical change in structures that would be bitterly fought by the Brazilian elites and their allies in Europe and the United States. Indeed, the threat of a mild agrarian reform and the proposed nationalization of a U.S. mining company were among the chief reasons for the U.S.-supported military coup against President Goulart in 1964. Although the base communities have increased the political awareness of a new generation of poor Brazilians, the outlook, said the bishops, is for a "long, hard struggle."[22]

Meanwhile, the Brazilian church has not only helped to deepen the faith commitment of millions of poor Brazilians—the original goal of the base communities—but has also achieved an influence unparalleled in its history. Before the coup, two-thirds of the Catholic university students polled in Rio de Janeiro called themselves "atheist" because the church "is on the side of an order that is unjust and antipeople." In 1978 three-quarters of the students declared themselves "believers" because the church had become the voice of the voiceless. An additional 15 percent said they "believed in the Brazilian church but not in religion."[23] Slum dwellers expressed similar feelings. "In '78, seeing that the church was helping the people, I began to participate again," said a lapsed Catholic who was active in a popular movement. "It wasn't that I stayed away from the church for all those years, but rather the church that stayed away from the people." Three decades ago the Brazilian church was seen as an institution that "didn't need the poor." Today it is trusted as the one organization that "will not betray the poor in pursuit of its own self-interests," said a woman leader of the base communities in São Paulo.[24]

"Neurotics for Orthodoxy"

Such influence was an important factor in the Vatican's more guarded approach to dealings with the Brazilians, particularly after the rows over liberation theology and meddling by the Curia. (See Chapter 4, pp. 104–113.) With 374 bishops the Brazilian church held a significant place in world Catholicism (only the United States and Italy had that many bishops). Nor could Rome ignore the weight of the world's largest Catholic community. Following the Brazilians' summit meeting with the pope in 1986, a public truce was established, although the Curia continued to snipe at the Brazilians in private meetings and communications.

The Curia did not like the base communities because they were agents of democratization within the church and challenged Brazil's political and economic authorities. According to some in the Vatican, the Brazilian church's concern with the poor made it "sectarian" because it paid insufficient attention to the needs of the middle and upper classes. Others charged that the base communities were "communist cells."[25]

Nor did Rome approve of such Brazilian "inculturations" as the use of native music and themes in the liturgy. The Vatican banned an Afro-Brazilian Mass written by Bishop Casaldáliga and the poet Pedro Tíerra, and set to the music of the black pop singer Milton Nascimento. The Mass, which celebrated the memory of runaway slaves and reflected Brazil's black roots, was judged too political and too racial. Similarly, the papal nuncio, Archbishop Carlo Furno, took umbrage at the inclusion in a São Paulo liturgy of the name of a political prisoner murdered by the military regime, on the ground that litanies could name only canonical saints.[26]

Acting like a schoolmaster, Furno did not endear himself to the bishops—at one point he demanded a list of all the courses given on liberation theology under the bishops' auspices over a seven-year period, including the names of hundreds of participants. "The papal nunciatures are not expressions of the Gospel," said Bishop Morelli. "They're the long arm the Vatican uses to control everything. These 'neurotics for orthodoxy' have been trying to change the Brazilian church's direction."[27]

The "administrative center," as some liberation theologians called Rome, also kept up pressure to conform to theological orthodoxy. In early 1987 agitation again started up against Leonardo Boff because of his writings, and the following year Rome attempted to silence Bishop Casaldáliga, in part because of his support for liberation theology but also because of a trip to Nicaragua. After Casaldáliga took to Managua a message of solidarity from twenty-three bishops for Foreign Minister Miguel D'Escoto, a Maryknoll priest who was then on a hunger strike to protest the *contra* war, the Brazilian bishops' conference got an earful from the Vatican about disloyalty. Casaldáliga did not help matters by questioning the usefulness of *ad limina* visits, the obligatory visit to the Vatican which bishops are supposed to make every five years. "What kind of bishop is this who prefers to visit a country opposed to the church of Rome rather than embrace the Pope?" wondered a shocked member of the Curia. "A 10-minute encounter with the Pope every five years is just a formality," responded Casaldáliga. "He already has enough problems to preoccupy him, and I don't see how we can have a meaningful conversation in so short a time."[28]

Father Ricardo Resende, Casaldáliga's colleague in the Amazon, shared the widespread opinion in the Brazilian church that Rome's views were irrelevant to their daily struggle on behalf of the poor. Resende, who made his first visit to the Vatican in 1985, five years after his ordination in the Amazon, was bitterly disappointed by the display of opulence. His dismay appeared to be widely shared, to judge by a Latin American saying: "Rome is a city of great faith because so many go there and leave their faith behind."[29]

In the Vatican's view, however, the Brazilians were potentially in schism—which was true if schism meant a rejection of Roman hegemony. Like Catholic dissidents everywhere, the Brazilians refused to take Cardinal Ratzinger's advice that they leave the institution, insisting that it was their church, too. Indeed, some Brazilians argued that Rome was in schism by refusing to recognize the principle of power-sharing that guided the early church. In time, the Vatican's ultimate weapon—the appointment of bishops—could take a toll of Brazil's activist church. On the other hand, the reality of poverty and injustice often has a radicalizing effect on orthodox churchmen. Such was the case with Archbishop Cámara, who supported a neofascist political party in his youth but became an outspoken defender of human rights when confronted with the cruel poverty of Brazil's slums. Similarly, Resende's Irish bishop, Patrick Hanrahan, was considered a stuffy conservative who pandered to the urban middle classes until he was assigned to the embattled Amazon. Within a week of his arrival he had a run-in with the local military over squatters' rights. The situation, he discovered, was not unlike the terrible experiences suffered earlier by his own countrymen. By the end of his first year in the Amazon Hanrahan had become as outspoken and determined as Resende.[30]

Although individual bishops could, and did, cause the Vatican trouble, undoubtedly the most challenging aspect in the situation was the message that the Brazilian model sent to the rest of the Catholic world. The Brazilian church had not only accepted Vatican II's reforms but continued the path toward a more pluralistic, Christ-centered church. John XXIII and Paul VI had encouraged such reforms in the belief that, by addressing humanity's problems, the church would become a more vital presence in the world. Brazil's church was proof that they had been right. As shown by opinion polls, it was the most respected institution in the country. All the groups that in Europe traditionally eschewed the church—labor unions, university students, intellectuals—felt a debt of gratitude to the Brazilian church for providing the only democratic space during the long years of the dictatorship and to the bishops in particular for repeatedly risking their lives in confrontations with the military. The church's continued support for democracy in the Sarney years, especially its position on agrarian reform, gave it the most influential voice among the poor. Although it faced numerous challenges, from the extreme left and right and from the new evangelical churches that had invaded the country, Brazilian Catholicism thrived on adversity. No matter what the hour of a Mass or rosary, the churches were jammed. Baptisms and religious vocations shot up, and each year thousands of Brazilians joined the growing base community movement. Once an aging dinosaur, the Brazilian Catholic Church had gained a dynamism that made it one of the most powerful organizations in the country. That power was not based on the traditional Roman formula of money and influence among the upper classes, however, but reflected the church's identification, both in society and its internal organization, with the majority of Brazilians—the poor and powerless. Such, too, had been the basis of the power of Christ.

Chile

"In Orwell's famous novel, *1984,* a small minority, with the aid of technology, was able to control the overwhelming majority," said Bishop Carlos Camus, in describing life beneath the boot of a megalomaniac dictator. One of hundreds of Chilean priests to suffer persecution under General Augusto Pinochet, Camus clung to his faith despite the Orwellian signs around him. That he was not optimistic about Chile's future was shown by a controversial pastoral letter he published in 1987. Entitled "Journey Toward Suicide," it predicted that, since "dialogue no longer seems possible, the only road that is left is violence and national suicide."[31]

Worse for Camus than any suffering personally inflicted on him was the arrest and torture of his eighteen-year-old niece. The girl was detained in March 1987 after her sister's identity card was allegedly found at the scene of an explosion caused by leftist terrorists. When the police could not find the sister, they took the girl as a hostage, using what Camus described as "Nazi methods." The experience so marked the girl, said her uncle, that she felt like a vegetable. "She is a very young girl, just out of high school, and was very affected. They kept her blindfolded and forced her to keep her arms up. They said they were torturing her mother in the next cell and that they were going to rape her that night, and all the time the torturer, who was a woman, kept saying insulting things about me, the cardinal [Santiago's Cardinal Juan Francisco Fresno] and the church."[32]

The girl was among the lucky ones. She was released after three days because of the scandal Camus was creating on the eve of the pope's visit to Chile. Although she carried psychological scars, she was alive and had not been disfigured by a cross burned or cut into her face or chest, a common punishment suffered by Chileans arrested because of their work with the church or because they were relatives of a priest or bishop.[33]

Was the girl's sister involved with leftist terrorists? The bishop couldn't believe it. She was a "little rebellious, like all youth today, [but] incapable of killing a bird." Yet that anything could happen in a country so polarized was shown by the violent scene at an open-air Mass conducted by the pope in Santiago two weeks later. Some 700 people were injured in the melee that accompanied a "Mass of Reconciliation" when young toughs from the slums began throwing rocks and sticks. Priests who recognized some of the rock-throwers said they did not belong to any political group but were members of gangs of jobless youths who roamed the Santiago slums and took advantage of any occasion to express their hatred of a government that denied them food, education, and the possibility of jobs. "We regret the violence," said Chilean liberation theologian Ronaldo Muñoz, "but it's an expression of the drama Chile is living. Those kids wanted to be recognized, and the only way they could be noticed was by using extreme aggression. It's a scandal, but not so big a scandal. For us, the scandal is that the Pope speaks to us against violence while he is protected by these violent people," the police and other armed forces. "Young people don't believe him when he is protected by the same guns that hurt them."[34]

But what was the pope to do? If he openly confronted the Pinochet government with its sins, he would provoke more persecution of the church and give ammunition to the left. If he blessed the dictatorship—and he gave a blessing of sorts in a balcony appearance where he was accompanied by the dictator—he would disillusion the majority of Chileans. So he tried to walk a fine neutral line. On his flight to Chile John Paul had said that such dictatorships were "transitory," a statement that many seized upon as an omen of Pinochet's downfall, in a hoped-for replay of events in Haiti and the Philippines where the church had played a key role in the overthrow of unpopular dictators. But as the pope pointed out, "I am not the evangelizer of democracy; I am the evangelizer of the Gospel."[35] He had no magic wand to whisk away Pinochet, nor could he restore democracy in a land so fearful and divided.

Few people who lived outside Chile could understand how the Pinochet regime had survived so long when it was so widely hated. The pope had said that the Chilean bishops should follow the example of the Philippine church,[36] so why had they not encouraged a rebellion? These were among the questions asked at the time of the pope's visit—one of the few occasions after the 1973 coup when the international press focused on Chile. Camus knew the reason—fear, not just of physical violence by the military but also of what might replace Pinochet.

Disarray

Unlike Brazil, where the mass of the people follow no particular ideology, Chilean society is the most politicized in South America. Rich or poor, urban or rural, most of the country's 12 million people have an ideological position. In the 1960s, when Chile's political tragedy began, the population was spread fairly evenly across the spectrum from right to left, and polls in the 1980s showed that the distribution remained unchanged. The Christian Democrats, who stood in the center, tried to achieve a national consensus during the presidency of Eduardo Frei in the late 1960s, but Frei was unable to deliver on promised reforms, and the way was paved for the election of the Socialist, Salvador Allende. His attempts to change economic structures to favor the poor provoked furious opposition from the Chilean right and the U.S. government, which backed General Pinochet's coup in September 1973.

The Christian Democrats and their fellow travelers in the church hierarchy initially welcomed the coup, in the mistaken belief that, once the military had cleansed the government of leftist influence, it would restore power to them. But it soon became evident that the military hated the Christian Democrats as much as it did the socialists and communists and that its idea of government was unmitigated terror. Between 5,000 and 30,000 people died in the weeks after the coup, according to Amnesty International. But repression did not end with the first bloodletting; it continued year after year, until Chile came to resemble Orwell's fictional world. Hundreds of men and women were "disappeared" each year, victims of such paramilitary squads as the Anti-Communist Chilean Action. Between 1973 and 1986 more than 151,000 Chileans suffered detention for political reasons. Often they were caught in dawn raids when army troops with blackened faces invaded the slums. The troops cut off electricity and telephone lines and went from house to house rounding up all males between the ages of fifteen and sixty, often shooting at random. "It is barbarous, exactly the same as what went on in the Warsaw Ghetto," said the Christian Democratic leader Gabriel Valdés.[37]

Political activists, union organizers, leaders of popular organizations, and church workers were among those singled out for attack. Although torture was illegal, Amnesty International and the Chilean church reported its routine use, the most common methods being beatings, electric shock, burnings with cigarettes, rape, and intense psychological torture in which tape recordings of relatives' voices, or children crying, were often used. Amnesty also reported that the torturers employed specially designed equipment and that their "techniques are so sophisticated that it points to their having been trained in the practice."[38]

The effect of such brutality was to disorient the political parties, which had had no experience of institutionalized terror. The Chileans rightly prided themselves on a long tradition of civilized behavior in politics, and the idea of torturing one's opponent to death was unthinkable. The Chilean Communist Party, for example, followed the Italian communists' example of engaging in dialogue and upholding democratic institutions. And Allende's Socialist administration scrupulously respected pluralistic debate, as shown by the wide spectrum of opinions expressed in the legislature and the media. Although the Christian Democrats could have participated in a U.S.-supported plot to defraud him of the presidency, they, too, played by the rules.

Instead of encouraging unity, the unprecedented repression increased divisions within and between the parties. Many political leaders were forced to flee the country, and tentative attempts at cohesion repeatedly failed. While the right wing of the Christian Democrats was prepared to make a political deal with the right, and the left wing with the left, the center remained immobilized. In contrast to the Philippines, there was no individual and no set of goals to unite the parties, although most wanted Pinochet to go. A 1986 poll showed that the only two people who could have attracted a national following were Allende and Frei, both dead.[39] Meanwhile, the army, which was the dominant military force in Chile, continued to back Pinochet, partly because he pampered its officers and men but mostly because it feared the resurgence of a leftist government and a civilian backlash against the military's many crimes, as had occurred in Argentina. After events in Haiti and the Philippines, the Reagan administration also decided it was time for Pinochet to go. But like the Christian Democrats, the Chilean bishops, and anti-Pinochet elements in the military, Washington hesitated, fearing that a united opposition would inevitably lead to a deal with the left. While the politicians dithered, Pinochet consolidated plans to stay in power until the end of the century. The left began to lose hope of a negotiated solution, and that encouraged the emergence of a guerrilla movement that almost managed to assassinate Pinochet in the fall of 1986.

The Pinochet regime "has not fallen because there still is no unity among the political forces," explained Bishop Tomás González, the pastor of Punta Arenas and a member of the progressive wing of the hierarchy, in the spring of 1987. "Nor has it lost all international support, and for a long time it received very strong support. It has not fallen because it is based on violence and a growing fear. And this is the first experience of such terror for Chileans—a traumatic experience. We always said, 'We're like England or Switzerland; we're never going to suffer a dictatorship.' We did not understand that we had a Prussian military structure or that the United States was exporting a Doctrine of National Security that encouraged the intervention of the military in national affairs. If we ever return to democracy, the first thing we must do is humanize the military. Anything that a captain says is the law; if it's a general, it's divine law. Pinochet is the messiah."[40]

González was not far off the mark in his description of Pinochet, who compared himself to "the best Roman emperors." Born in the fishing port of Valparaiso in 1915, he worked his way up through the ranks of the military to become commander of the Sixth Army. Believing he could trust him, Allende appointed him commander-in-chief, a fatal error that might have been avoided had Allende read some of Pinochet's writings on the so-called Doctrine of National Security, which holds that the West is at permanent war with communism and which has served as a geopolitical manifesto for dictatorships in Latin America. Like many of his military counterparts, Pinochet developed a strong distaste for politicians, particularly the left and the Christian Democrats, and this later showed in his refusal to have any dealings with the political center. The longer he stayed in power, the more indispensable he believed himself. "It is me or the communists," he told supporters. "It is me or chaos." "He is a man who needs to find a daily enemy in order to subsist," said a critic. "Without them, he wouldn't know who he is."[41]

Pinochet's justification for staying in power was that he was the savior of the "fatherland." Although his term in office was supposed to end in 1989, he had ambitions to continue as president through 1997. Under the rules of a 1980 constitution drawn up by the military, Chileans were to vote in a plebiscite in 1988 on a presidential candidate chosen by the four-man junta, which naturally turned out to be Pinochet. Although most of the political parties demanded that the plebiscite be changed to free elections, the government went ahead with its plan to give Chileans the limited alternative of a yes-no vote on their candidate. While still divided on ideological grounds, fourteen parties ranging the political spectrum united to campaign for a no vote, and in October 1988 Pinochet was defeated by an 11 percent margin. The no vote meant that the regime would have to hold presidential and congressional elections in December 1989 and that Pinochet would step down from the presidency the following March. But the political opening would remain under military control because the heads of the armed forces were empowered to retain their posts until 1993, including Pinochet, the commander-in-chief of the 57,000-man army. No one doubted that the military would continue to dominate the political arena, as Pinochet himself warned following his defeat. That he had risked so much on an election was a measure of Pinochet's supreme self-confidence—neither he nor his followers had expected to lose. At the same time, he had the legal means to retain ultimate power, regardless of who was elected president, and the military could always claim reasons of national security to interrupt the constitutional process.

Equally problematic was the position of the left, which was proscribed from participating in politics by the 1980 constitution. The military also made it clear that it would not countenance another Allende. Yet the socialists and communists commanded upwards of 40 percent of the electorate, mostly poor Chileans. Exclusion of so large a sector from national life could only produce more violence. After sixty years of following a nonviolent policy by seeking change through elections, the Communist Party concluded that the only option under Pinochet was armed resistance. "We may have committed errors," said a party leader, "but one is at least not the error of illusion."

The political parties' minuet, now to the left, now to the right, obscured the real issue—economics. As Bishop González observed, Chileans for a long time believed themselves more European than Latin American because of their high literacy rate and long tradition of democracy, but beneath the surface of political sophistication were the same class differences that divided other Latin American nations. A small elite controlled industry, finance, and most of the land. A fairly sizable middle class (for Latin America) identified its interests with those of the elite, although it was willing occasionally to allow the poor a few crumbs. The poor—rural laborers, copper miners, and slum dwellers—believed that Allende would give them a chance for a decent life. But while he initiated a sweeping agrarian reform and attempted to redistribute income, Allende had three strikes against him. One was the hatred of the upper classes, which fought his reforms tooth and nail. The second was the hostility of the Nixon administration, which cut off aid and damaged Chilean trade, and of the U.S.-owned copper companies, which had for long dominated the country's exports. The third was the impatience of Allende's own Socialists, a violent wing of which tried to push the government faster than it was politically feasible to move. Later allegations that Allende destroyed the economy do not take into account the fact that many of the country's economic problems were created by the United States and by upper-class sabotage. The poor did fare better under Allende, despite economic difficulties, and the rich resented it.[42]

A Divided Church

Divisions among the political parties caused Chileans to look to the Catholic Church for a solution. But the church, while widely respected for its defense of human rights, was as split as the parties. Some of the differences could be attributed to the same class lines that divided lay society, only in the church's case they were concerned less with economics than with power. Whereas the hierarchy had traditionally ruled the church as a top-down institution, a more democratic and prophetic church model was emerging in the base communities, as in the Brazilian church. A majority of the bishops feared this development; it reinforced their chronic concern about Marxism, for the model usually emerged in poor sectors, where the left was strong. Then, too, Cardinal Fresno's leadership tended to be more cautious than that of his predecessor, Cardinal Raul Silva, who retired in 1983. Silva was so outspoken in opposition to the government that he became known as the "red bishop," whereas Fresno repeatedly held out an olive branch to Pinochet, only to be crudely spurned. Like Washington, the Vatican wanted to ensure continuing influence in a post-Pinochet Chile—hence Fresno's encouragement of a dialogue to speed the dictator's departure under "controlled" circumstances which would exclude the left. But the tactic suffered from the same weaknesses as Washington's plan: Pinochet refused to go, and the exclusion of the left from Fresno's "National Accord" robbed it of crucial support.

"Don Pancho," as Fresno preferred to be called, was handpicked by the pope to replace Cardinal Silva, apparently because of his pastoral experience. But that experience, in a quiet seaside town on the northern coast of Chile, hardly prepared him for the political intrigue of Santiago. The cardinal's friends said that if he had had his way, Fresno would not have been in the center of a political imbroglio between government and church. But he was a loyal follower of the pope, and the pope, according to Vatican sources, wanted the Chilean church to "mediate" between the military and the centrist opposition. It seemed no coincidence that Fresno's search for a political solution began in 1985 when he was appointed cardinal. Since Chile already had one cardinal, and two red hats were unusual for so small a bishops' conference, church analysts assumed that the pope hoped the added prestige would help Fresno to deal with Pinochet and the political opposition.[43]

However much Fresno and other bishops may have wished to normalize relations with the government, Pinochet made it impossible for them to do so by his harsh repression of the people and unceasing persecution of the church. A 1986 poll of the bishops showed that even the most conservative of them opposed Pinochet—a conclusion confirmed by a series of hard-hitting pastoral letters from the bishops' conference denouncing torture, arbitrary arrest, the judicial system, censorship, corruption, increasing poverty, and other government sins. Fresno himself reviled "the systematic violation of human rights as a form of idolatry of political power" and threatened to excommunicate the minister of the interior.[44]

Pinochet responded by charging that the church was trying to set itself up as "a new political party." He also warned that "all those who go around defending human rights and such things [would] be expelled from the country or imprisoned." They were not empty threats. More than 400 foreign priests were expelled in the first thirteen years of the dictatorship, and several priests were killed. Some bishops also received death threats because of their defense of human rights. Dozens of churches were set on fire, bombed, or defaced by paramilitary groups working with the knowledge and approval of the government. The Santiago archdiocese also reported that Chileans arrested by the security forces were warned to stay away from Christian groups, the aim being "to disrupt [the church's] pastoral work," said Cardinal Fresno.[45]

Repression was inevitable because the churches were the only institutions not under military control that were allowed to function after the coup, and therefore became the sanctuary of the persecuted. Pinochet might have closed the churches as well, but one of the alleged motives for the coup had been the preservation of Christian values. The regime also felt a need for religious legitimization, if only symbolic, as through the traditional independence day Mass in the Santiago cathedral that is always attended by the president and his cabinet.

In the beginning of Pinochet's regime, all the religious groups had banded together in an ecumenical effort, the Committee of Cooperation for Peace, to help the victims of repression by providing legal services and technical and financial aid to the poor. Between 1973 and 1975 the Committee initiated legal actions on behalf of 7,000 people in Santiago alone. But in 1975 the Committee was disbanded under government pressure. Although Protestant churches and Jewish synagogues carried on independently, it fell to the Catholic Church to form a national human rights organization, the Vicariate of Solidarity. Since Catholicism is the religion of 80 percent of Chileans, including Pinochet, the bishops were in a stronger position to contest the government than were the Protestants, who account for only 15 percent of the population. To their credit, the bishops took on the responsibility, even though it cost the church the allegiance of the upper class and led to severe harassment. Tens of thousands of Chileans will remember that when the Catholic Church gave them its protection it never asked for an account of their political past. To receive assistance it was enough to be in need.

In the first decade of its existence the Vicariate dealt with 298,577 cases of human rights violations. Although its lawyers could do little about a government-controlled judiciary that refused to process proven crimes, they were able to locate and obtain the release of some imprisoned Chileans. The Vicariate's records were also an important source of information on human rights abuses for such international organizations as Amnesty International. Its doctors and social workers were active in a church network of soup kitchens, health centers, and other popular organizations that were often the only recourse of the poor. But the staff paid a heavy price for its commitment: One was killed, and ten served prison terms. Monsignor Ignacio Gutiérrez, the Spanish Jesuit who headed the Vicariate, was banned in 1984 from returning to Chile; the executive secretary, Enrique Palet, frequently received death threats. His house was splashed with blood, and a guard was wounded. Palet also received a box containing a pig's head with a bullet between the eyes.[46]

Bishops and priests associated with the poorer sectors suffered frequent attack. In mid-1985 the cathedral and home of the archbishop of Concepción were painted with abusive slogans after Archbishop José Manuel Santos denounced the beating of one of his priests by a paramilitary squad. The following April a paramilitary group fire-bombed the home of Sergio Contreras, bishop of Temuco and secretary-general of the bishops' conference. The day before the attack, Contreras had protested the military occupation of Temuco's cathedral during a visit to the city by Pinochet. In August Bishop Miguel Caviedes of Osorno narrowly escaped injury when a rifle bullet, fired from outside his home, passed inches above his head and through the wall of his study. Caviedes's crime was that he had supported Cardinal Fresno's public exhortation to the country's supreme court that it act in the case of a youth who had been burned to death by an army patrol. In March 1987, on the eve of John Paul's visit, Bishop Camus of Linares received death threats because he admitted that he was "frankly in opposition" to the Pinochet regime. Among the threats was a pamphlet that said, "Camus, if you continue playing politics in the church, you are going to meet St. Peter."[47]

Priests were routinely beaten and jailed. Father Liam Holahan, an Irish missionary priest working in a Santiago shantytown, was severely beaten by riot police after the funeral of a victim of the repression. Holahan said he was handcuffed and hauled into a bus where policemen bloodied his head with a truncheon and stamped on him. "When I said I was a priest, the repression got worse. They called me a communist and insulted the church and the bishops." At the police station, he said, the police took turns beating and kicking him for two hours, at one point threatening to crucify him.[48]

Father Dennis O'Mara, a native of Chicago, belonged to the Sebastián Acevedo Movement Against Torture, a nonviolent group that organized sit-ins and demonstrations. On one such occasion, when O'Mara tried to aid a sixty-five-year-old priest who was being beaten by a police officer, he was beaten and arrested himself. He was expelled from the country for distributing Christmas cards that contained a plea for peace and an end to torture. Instead of being expelled, Chilean priests were imprisoned. For example, Father Renato Hevia, director of the Jesuit monthly *Mensaje,* was jailed in December 1985 on charges of "jeopardizing the country's internal security" because his magazine had criticized the state of siege.

The church also had its martyrs. Among them was a middle-aged French missionary, Father André Jarlan, who is venerated as a saint by the inhabitants of the Santiago shantytown of La Victoria, much as Archbishop Romero is by the poor in El Salvador. Jarlan worked with the young people in the slum, attempting to discourage drug addiction and alcoholism, which had increased with poverty. (Three-fifths of shantytown youths were jobless.) "When I talked to him, I felt like a person of value," said a twenty-five-year-old ex–drug addict, who credited Jarlan with changing his life. "He listened. He didn't scold. He encouraged." In September 1984, during one of the military sweeps through La Victoria, a youth was killed and dozens more wounded. The streets were filled with tear gas, and Jarlan went to his room to pray. He was reading Psalm 130, traditionally used in funeral Masses, when a stray bullet from a policeman's submachine gun passed through the wall of his room and killed him instantly. Jarlan's friend and superior, Father Pierre Dubois, found him slumped over his desk. News of his death spread rapidly, and angry voices shouted for justice. The police had cut off La Victoria's electricity, and Dubois, fearful of more violence, pleaded for calm. The people quieted, then began to set burning candles in front of the parish house and throughout the muddy streets, until the whole slum was ablaze with light.[49]

For the slum inhabitants Jarlan is their unofficial patron saint. The children call him their *"amiguito"* ("little friend"), and his photo hangs in many slum homes. Dubois and his other French companions kept Jarlan's room as a shrine, the Bible open to Psalms 129 and 130, the blood stains still on his desk, and a sign outside that said "Welcome."

In honor of the first anniversary of his death the parishioners sent up a thousand balloons, each carrying his photograph. One cluster of white balloons rose higher than the others, colliding with a police helicopter overhead, in what was regarded as a sign of hope.[50]

Because Jarlan had become a symbol of resistance, it was necessary to desecrate his memory. In 1986, after a guerrilla group tried to assassinate Pinochet, the security forces struck out blindly, arresting and killing at random. Dubois, who had worked for twenty-eight years with the Chilean poor, was expelled from the country, along with two other French priests who had worked in La Victoria. The police sacked Jarlan's room, destroying the shrine. The small parish house and the chapel were riddled with bullets, and part of the chapel was left in ruins. Two U.S. priests, Maryknollers Thomas Henehan and Terrence Cambias, who also worked in a slum, were arrested at the same time, in addition to a Chilean priest, Father Jorge Orellana, and two Peruvian lay workers. The latter were deported.[51]

The bishops described such persecution as a "culture of death." But hope, like La Victoria's white balloons, continued to rise. One sign was the growth of dialogue in the Christian base communities. In contrast to the Allende years, when the communities were rent with dissension between his supporters and critics, repression brought people together. Although the leaders of the political parties could not overcome their differences, down at the base people achieved a mutual respect that cut across party lines. The left and the church also benefited from the experience. Many of those who volunteered for the most dangerous jobs with church groups, such as lawyers defending political prisoners, came from the left, and their courage gained them the respect of bishops and religious who worked with the poor. At the same time, the church's willingness to suffer repression for the sake of human rights impressed the left. Indicative of changed attitudes was the sharp increase in Mass attendance in Santiago from 20 percent of the Catholic population before the 1973 coup to 43 percent in the post-coup years. Vocations also multiplied, as did the membership of the base communities, which were estimated to have upwards of 100,000 members by 1980.[52]

While the church's defense of human rights made its religious message credible to the working class, its outreach to the poor raised problems within the hierarchy. As in Brazil, the communities began to associate faith with the struggle for social justice—the goal of liberation theology. As surrogates for democracy, they became advocates for more participation by the laity in decision-making within the church. Such developments were welcomed by a majority of the Brazilian bishops, but in Chile the majority feared politicization of the base communities and the demand for greater autonomy within the church. Conflict in the church "is not between clergy and laity nor between the poor and the hierarchy, but between different models of the church," said Chilean theologian Muñoz. "Among the poor you can find very conservative people who expect authoritarian leadership. And you can find bishops very near the poor, supporting the church's prophetic mission."[53]

The fear of politicization reflected the church's experience during the Allende years when a group of priests and lay leaders known as Christians for Socialism embraced the government. Some made support for Allende a condition of membership in the base communities, many of which were split along party lines. As in post-revolutionary Nicaragua, the bishops opposed attempts to forge a Christian-Marxist dialogue on the ground that a sectarian approach would divide the church. They also believed that the movement's public criticisms of the hierarchy threatened its authority. In fact, the bishops themselves had taken a partisan position in support of President Frei's election and were clearly identified with the Christian Democrats (just as Managua's Cardinal Miguel Obando y Bravo was associated with a Nicaraguan version of the party).[54]

Christians for Socialism disbanded after the coup, leaving the church's relationship to politics unresolved. Under Cardinal Fresno's direction the hierarchy became deeply involved in politics through its negotiations with party leaders, yet it objected to the growing social commitment of the base communities. Studies of the Chilean church by Brian Smith, a U.S. expert on the subject, showed that 60 percent of the bishops opposed the consciousness-raising methods that made the Brazilian base communities so dynamic while 70 percent thought that important church decisions should be left to the hierarchy. Only one-third wanted a more democratic style of church community. In contrast, 70 percent of the priests, nuns, and lay leaders sought more democracy in the church, and 40 percent favored Brazilian-style base communities. More than half the nuns and two-thirds of the laity believed that decisions should be reached by consensus. The position of the base communities, Smith concluded, was quite different from that of most bishops and more akin to that of Christians for Socialism. The conflict between a hierarchical model and a communitarian one remained latent because of the many other problems imposed by the repressive dictatorship, but once Chile returned to democracy, said Smith, there would be more pressure for greater democracy in the church.[55]

The communities also complained that the church leadership "is more concerned with calculated diplomacy than prophetic attitudes demanded by the [political] situation." "The feeling is that the hierarchy, the church as an institution, is not standing with us in this situation," explained a priest who worked with the slum poor. "Instead of raising their voice against abuses that cause such great suffering, they're cutting political deals with the higher-ups."

In fact, the hierarchy was split between the center-right, which wanted to maintain a dialogue with the government in order to help mediate the political crisis, and a progressive wing that believed it was more important to maintain good relations with the people. Pinochet did not help the former with his repressive tactics, which forced the bishops' conference to follow the progressives' lead in denouncing human rights abuses and protecting the Vicariate of Solidarity. But Chilean priests and nuns believed the Fresno church wanted to reduce its visibility in that controversial area.[56]

Fresno's attempts at rapprochement with the Pinochet regime also divided the church. A supporter of the 1973 coup, Fresno was a government favorite to succeed Cardinal Silva in Santiago. ("Our prayers have been answered," announced Pinochet's wife on learning of his appointment.) While no one doubted the cardinal's good intentions, his wealthy upbringing made him more at ease with the elites than in the shantytowns, where he was unpopular because of his rare visits and his perceived attempts to make deals with Pinochet. (Fresno was known among the poor as "*Frenos*," Spanish for "brakes.") While some church analysts believed his caution helped him in his role as a peacemaker, others felt he allowed himself to be used by the government. For example, on Christmas Eve 1985 the cardinal went to the presidential palace with a gift for the dictator and to talk about "reconciliation." Instead of a dialogue, Fresno was subjected to a twenty-minute lecture by Pinochet about his meddling in politics. The president then handed him a huge, gift-wrapped box, threw open the doors of the conference room, and embraced him in the presence of reporters and television cameras convoked for the occasion. Sources close to Fresno said that he was "disconcerted and depressed" by the incident.[57]

Indicative of the cardinal's caution, he declined to receive U.S. Senator Edward Kennedy in 1986 for fear that he would be associated with an important critic of the Pinochet regime. Equally telling was his refusal that year to suspend the traditional Te Deum ceremony in the cathedral to honor Chile's independence day in September despite widespread government repression. The independence day Te Deum is the high point in the religious-political calendar of most Latin American countries, and its celebration in the presence of president and cabinet signifies the church's respect for the government. Although Fresno's vicars argued strongly against holding the ceremony, he went ahead with it on the ground that the tradition should not be "altered on account of political contingencies, which are passing." Fresno made matters worse by disinviting to the Te Deum leaders of the political opposition, including Gabriel Valdés, then president of the Christian Democrats.[58]

Although some bishops refused to attend the ceremony, the impression given by Fresno's action was that the church was eager to maintain good relations with the government, said Muñoz. The feeling among the poor "is that our shepherds marched into the plaza arm in arm with the wolves that are scattering and destroying the flock." That opinion was vividly expressed a few months later when the pope visited a shantytown in Fresno's company. Although the cardinal maintained a prudent silence, the mere mention of his name brought hissing jeers.[59]

Two weeks after the Te Deum, Fresno was again at the presidential palace to accept a gold medal from Pinochet on the anniversary of his appointment as a cardinal. He used the event to repeat his earlier proposal of a dialogue between the government and the opposition, but as usual Pinochet turned a deaf ear. Like the earlier Christmas meeting, Fresno's acceptance of the medal was designed to aid quiet diplomacy, but quite a few Chileans thought the cardinal was being manipulated.

However hapless many perceived him to be, Fresno had the backing of the then papal nuncio, Bishop Angelo Sodano, who made known his feelings by taking a highly visible place at a televised gathering of government sympathizers to promote Pinochet's election campaign. Pinochet strongly attacked the church during his speech, which occurred at the same time that the three French priests from La Victoria were being put on a plane for Europe. When he returned to Rome in 1988, following his promotion to Vatican secretary for public affairs, the Chilean regime awarded Sodano the "Grand Cross of the Order of Merit" for his "skill and brilliance" in diplomacy.

Sodano was influential in the appointment of several conservative bishops, and they shared his attitude toward the government. For example, Bishop Antonio Moreno, who was named vicar of the northern zone of Santiago, forbade priests and nuns from participating in peaceful protests against the dictatorship, including public prayers. Another Sodano appointee, Bishop Jorge Medina, gained fame as a signatory of the "Declaration of the Andes," a manifesto against liberation theology and the church of the poor. Yet another appointment, Bishop Pablo Lizama, had previously been a police chaplain. Indicative of Rome's support for the conservatives' rapprochement with the government was a Vatican investigation of a seminary in southern Chile that was accused of allowing its students to participate in protests against the regime. Students and faculty were warned that the Vatican would not tolerate such activities.

Nevertheless, a minority of bishops continued to speak out against human rights abuses and to defend the people; they included Bishops Camus and González and Jorge Hourton, the auxiliary bishop of Santiago. As observed by Muñoz, the church's voice "is the only one that can be expected to be taken seriously by the government," provided that "it sounds consistent." But as Bishop González pointed out, it was not consistent. He told the story of a general whom he had excommunicated for authorizing the use of torture. " 'But I'm a Catholic, and I go to Mass, to communion,' the general complained to me. Those are problems for your conscience, I told him. Anyone who tortures another or knows that a person is being tortured offends God. I met him again some time later, and he told me, 'I'm not worried anymore because the military chaplain told me not to concern myself and that you're crazy.' "[60]

Studies of religious influence in the armed forces showed that when officers could not obtain such comfort from their chaplain or bishop, they left Catholicism for churches that did offer support. The principal beneficiaries were the U.S.-sponsored evangelical churches, which had attracted 15,000 members from the armed forces by 1986. Many were affiliated with the U.S.-based World Association of Christian Military. According to the studies, military converts were often "zealous proselytizers, anti-Catholic, anticommunist and anti-Marxist" who believed in the divine origin of authority and projected this belief onto the hierarchical command of the armed forces and the government. God was the "Super Warrior"; the Virgin Mary, the "Virgin General." Evil was the political opposition.[61]

Some bishops, such as Pablo Lizama, the former police chaplain, bemoaned the loss of members of the military because of the church's defense of human rights.[62] Others expressed concern about their diminished authority among the elites who ran the economy and the government. A few worried about the people. Unlike the Brazilian church, which believed that genuine democracy had to be built from the bottom up, the Chilean church wasted its prestige by trying to reestablish a formal "democracy" governed by the Christian Democrats in alliance with the military. But such a democracy would not resolve the political and economic tensions that had led to the coup in the first place. As Father Damián Acuña Jarpa, a Chilean priest who had worked with all sectors of society, noted: "The church is not going to be strengthened by all this because it is involving itself in affairs that are not its business. It is like trying to end a fight between a married couple: The only one who loses is the mediator."[63]

A Papal Visit

John Paul's trip to Chile in the spring of 1987 generated enormous—and unrealistic—expectations on the part of the Chilean church, the people, and the Pinochet regime. Every papal word and gesture was scrutinized, yet the outcome was not unexpected—a plea for reconciliation and a reiteration of support for Fresno's church and the bishops' role in attempting to mediate a political solution. While he spent forty minutes in a private meeting with Pinochet, and said a private prayer with the general and his wife, he also thanked the Vicariate of Solidarity for its "devotion on behalf of human rights," listened to the complaints of the shantytown poor, and met briefly with the political opposition, including the socialists and communists as well as the Christian Democrats. He saw the violence at his open-air "Mass of Reconciliation."[64]

But the substance of the papal message was a familiar theme that had been repeated in many other countries, democracies as well as dictatorships. While John Paul spoke eloquently of the importance of not remaining "indifferent in the face of injustice," he warned the Chileans to avoid being "seduced by violence and the thousands of reasons that seem to justify it." He also lectured the base communities about sticking to religion and avoiding "the temptation to identify with parties or political positions," particularly "extraneous ideologies," meaning Marxism.[65]

Despite such warnings, the pope remained optimistic about Chile's future. On his flight to Santiago he told journalists that the Pinochet dictatorship was a "transitory" phenomenon, whereas the situation in

Poland was "much more demanding and difficult" because the Polish dictatorship was supported by the Soviet Union. While true, the statement ignored two critical issues in the Chilean dilemma. One was the lack of unity in the Chilean church. "The Pope once told me that 'in Poland all the bishops are united against the dictatorship,' " said Bishop Camus. "But I pointed out that unity is easy when the dictator is an atheist, but it's not so easy when the dictator is a Catholic." The second was the belief that there was a quick fix, in the form of a church-sponsored political transition to democracy. According to *New York Times* correspondent Roberto Suro, "Vatican officials believe Chile can be salvaged without creating an opening for the left, as has been done elsewhere on the continent in the last ten years." But nowhere else on the continent was there such a large leftist political force. Unlike the situation in Argentina or Brazil, the Chilean socialists and communists were established parties with a long history of participation in their country's political life and undeniably large followings in the working class. (The Chilean communists formed the largest Communist Party in the Western world outside Italy.) To believe that "reconciliation" was possible in Chile without giving a voice to the left was as unrealistic as the Vatican's wish that the Italian Communists would disappear.[66] Moreover, church mediation suffered serious weaknesses, including Pinochet's refusal to negotiate and the hierarchy's close identification with the partisan interests of the Christian Democrats. Had the bishops assumed a more daring role, by inviting all the country's parties to a dialogue, and had they shown their commitment to democracy by encouraging it in their own institution, the church might have played a larger role in Chilean politics. But Fresno chose to follow Rome's lead, thus forfeiting the influence that the Brazilian bishops had gained by taking an independent path.

While the churches in both countries have earned the regard of their peoples by their defense of human rights, the Brazilian church will have the greater impact in the long run because it has shown more concern for democracy than for institutional power. Only a minority of the Chilean bishops understand what the Brazilians have long known—that if the church is really serious about democracy, it must promote a "democracy of everyday life" in the church itself. However important a cardinal's mediation in political affairs, the church's greatest legacy to the future is education. By itself, the Brazilian church cannot end poverty and injustice. But by encouraging the growth of popular movements through the democratic example of base communities, it is sowing the seeds of inevitable change.

CHAPTER 6

✠

RELIGIOUS WARS IN LATIN AMERICA: THE "SECTS"

IRONICALLY, the Vatican's refusal to countenance a more pluralistic, lay-oriented church has contributed to the growth of U.S.-sponsored Protestant fundamentalist churches in Latin America. As Archbishop Cámara observed, Rome is unable to comprehend "the good that is done in the name of the theology of liberation," particularly the base communities. Yet the communities are the best hope to counter the spread of generally anti-Catholic, born-again churches. Although the socially activist communities are the political opposites of the fundamentalists, they offer many of the same things that attract the poor to the latter, including a more personalized religious environment, solidarity, and a sense of equality. Surveys by Catholic institutions showed that wherever base communities flourished, fundamentalist churches were unlikely to gain recruits. But because Rome feared the loss of its institutional power to a democratic base, it discouraged the growth of the communities. Encapsulated in its own small world, the Curia could not see that it was aiding Catholicism's avowed enemies in the fundamentalist churches by opposing a lay-directed renewal.

Catholics and mainline Protestants in Latin America call the fundamentalist evangelical churches *sectas*, or sects, to distinguish them from older Protestant denominations and later arrivals like the Mormons and Jehovah's Witnesses. But the term also carries a pejorative meaning, suggesting that the sects are not really churches but groups of people who follow strange practices and ideas. In fact, many of the sects are bona fide religious institutions, an example being the Pentecostals, the fastest growing of the new churches. Catholic leaders blame American money and missionaries for the fundamentalists' phenomenal success, when the principal cause lies in the failure of their own institution. The Catholic

Church's own studies show the seriousness of the challenge: Every hour 400 Latin Americans convert to the Pentecostals or other fundamentalists. One-eighth of the region's 481 million people belong to Protestant sects, and in some countries, such as Guatemala, it is estimated that half the population will switch churches by the end of the century. Not since the mass baptisms of Latin American Indians by the conquering Spanish in the sixteenth century has Latin America witnessed a religious conversion of such magnitude.[1]

The challenge clearly worried the Vatican. "The springtime of the sects could also be the winter of the Catholic Church," warned Brazilian Archbishop Lucas Moreira Neves, then secretary of the Vatican's Congregation of Bishops, in 1985. According to a study by the Brazilian Institute of Geography and Statistics that same year, nearly 10 percent of the country's 140 million people belonged to 4,077 sects, many of them single congregations, the majority Pentecostal. Most were active in areas where the Catholic Church was understaffed and/or where there were few base communities, as in Rio de Janeiro, where the conservative Cardinal Araujo Sales held sway. The primary reason for their success, according to studies by Catholic scholars, was the deterioration of social and economic conditions.[2]

Not until 1979, at the bishops' hemisphere conference in Puebla, Mexico, did the Catholic hierarchy attempt a serious analysis of the phenomenon. Unlike Catholic extremists who blamed Washington for some deep fundamentalist plot, the bishops admitted that the church was largely at fault. "If the church does not revitalize the religion of the Latin American people," they warned, "a vacuum will develop that will be occupied by the sects." In the years following the meeting, the Latin American bishops repeatedly urged Rome to tackle the issue, and in 1986 the Vatican published a document on the subject that was surprisingly self-critical. While agreeing with the Brazilians and other Latin American bishops that the sects were supported by "powerful ideological forces as well as economic and political interests [in the United States]," the document upheld the Puebla assessment that the new churches were fulfilling "needs and aspirations which are seemingly not being met in the mainline churches. The church is often seen simply as an institution, perhaps because it gives too much importance to structures and not enough to drawing people to God in Christ."[3]

Supposedly the most Catholic nation in South America, Colombia provides a good example of the challenge. Despite the hierarchy's claim that the Colombian church is a "model for the world," because of its doctrinal purity and loyalty to the pope, many Colombians are estranged by the bishops' identification with the country's upper-class elites and often uninspiring religious ceremonies. Priests at Bogotá's huge central cathedral are lucky if fifty Catholics show up for Sunday Mass. Surveys by Colombian pollsters showed that 71 percent of the people did not attend Mass and that the majority of those who did were older than fifty. Such statistics, said the editor of a local Catholic magazine, reveal "a church that is faithful to the Vatican but not to the people."[4]

Despite the Colombian government's close identification with Catholicism and its harassment of sects in some rural areas, Pentecostals, evangelicals, and other such newcomers have made rapid inroads. "Fifteen years ago," said an evangelical pastor in Bogotá, "it would have been difficult to find people who would admit to being evangelical. Now you find evangelicals everywhere." Because they are more common, they are more accepted, particularly in the cities.

The change in attitude is part of the breakdown throughout Latin America of a rural system of social and economic patronage. Since the 1950s, millions of peasants have left their villages because of guerrilla and military violence or to seek a better life in the cities, changing the balance of Latin America's population from rural to urban. Uprooted from families and religious traditions, living in slums and at the mercy of criminals and sometimes official predators, the urban poor are a fertile seedbed for evangelical proselytism. "In a society in permanent and progressive disintegration many peasants and slum inhabitants need religion as a refuge in order to deal with fear, threats, repression, hunger and death," explained a report on the subject by Pro Mundi Vita, a Belgian-based Catholic think tank. But too often the Catholic Church ignored such needs, said Pro Mundi Vita, because it lacked clergy, money, and imagination.[5] The sects had the wit to build on the people's yearning for religious symbols, or "popular religiosity," as a means of protest against social, political, and economic conditions.

Protest usually means turning off the worldly din. The fatalism in popular Catholicism, which encourages prayer to saints for miraculous cures or for protection, is easily transferred to an all-powerful Jesus. Many sects are also premillennialist, believing in Christ's imminent return and thus encouraging passivity in the face of social injustice. "I've got nothing in this world but a mansion in the next," boasted a popular evangelical song, summing up the attraction of a religion that promises, even for the most downtrodden, a personal relation with and equality before God. "What man needs," declared a Pentecostal leader in Brazil, "is contact with God."[6]

In Pentecostal churches contact means dancing, popular songs, and such physical gestures as raising arms to heaven. By contrast, the traditional Catholic liturgy often seems remote; and community relations, so important to the impoverished urban newcomer, are frequently nonexistent. In many parishes there is only one priest to serve 10,000 faithful. Priests, unlike evangelical pastors, are expected to spend long years on theological study, an experience that often alienates them culturally from their people, whereas evangelical recruits are urged to go out and proclaim their conversion, on buses, streetcorners, and in parks, to attract more faithful to the cause. Poor Latin Americans are also impressed by the emphasis on strict morality and the resulting change in social habits that transforms the neighborhood bum into an upright community leader. "Once a man surrenders his life to Jesus," proclaimed Argentine evangelist Luis Palau, "he finds he can stop drinking and chasing women."[7]

Because of the sects' political conservativism and their emphasis on passive acceptance of authority, they are popular with right-wing military regimes, particularly in those countries where the military is under attack from the Catholic Church. In Chile, for example, where General Pinochet welcomed such groups, more than 10 percent of the population converted to fundamentalist and Pentecostal churches, including members of the armed forces. It wasn't hard to see why Pinochet preferred them to the Catholics. While the bishops were forever complaining about torture and illegal detention, the fundamentalists were often the regime's strongest defenders. During a visit to Santiago in early 1987, U.S. televangelist Jimmy Swaggart promised Pinochet he would "tell the world that Chile is a free country." He also congratulated the dictator for having expelled the devil (i.e., the left) in the bloody 1973 coup.[8]

Central America

Tensions were particularly severe in Central America because the religious war coincided with a shooting one. On the one hand were U.S. and Central American Catholics who opposed Washington's policies in the region; on the other, fundamentalists who supported them. Thus the competition for souls had strong political overtones. Complicating the picture was the position of the Vatican, which agreed with Washington's assessment of the Sandinistas and liberation theology but opposed U.S. warmongering as counterproductive and harmful to the church's interests. Nor was Rome happy about the spread of fundamentalist churches, many of which were connected to U.S. religious leaders associated with the Republicans and strongly supportive of the *contra* war.

The fundamentalist surge in Central America was led by such televangelists as Swaggart and Pat Robertson, who backed the *contras* and allied themselves with right-wing governments. They preached a God-is-an-American religion in which any challenge to U.S. hegemony was dismissed as the work of the devil. "You can make a strong case for saying the American way is synonymous with Christianity," claimed William Murray, a U.S. evangelical who supported the fundamentalists' *contra* aid operations.[9]

Robertson, who apparently believed he had a special mission to save Central America, was active throughout the region. His "700 Club" show, heavily weighted with anticommunist rhetoric, was beamed in Spanish to the region. He also made substantial donations to pro-U.S. forces in Central America, regularly visited the area, and invited friendly dictators to appear on his program. Most of his broadcasting about Central America was designed to buttress U.S. policy, as, for example, a series on El Salvador which claimed that reports of right-wing violence were exaggerated. Robertson told viewers that he had dined with the "conservative" Roberto D'Aubuisson and found him a "very nice fellow"—this though D'Aubuisson had been involved in the murder of Archbishop Romero, according to the Salvadoran government.[10] Robertson also made regular pleas for U.S. military aid to El Salvador, announcing at one point that the Cubans were about to invade the country. Thanks to donations from concerned viewers, Robertson's organization was able in 1985 to send $20 million in "humanitarian" aid to the regimes in Guatemala and El Salvador and to *contra* "refugees" in Honduras.[11]

Among his more controversial ventures in Central America was a much-publicized association with the Pentecostal general who had become dictator of Guatemala following a coup in 1982. General José Efraín Ríos Montt had converted to the Christian Church of the Word, known as the Iglesia Verbo in Guatemala, and, on becoming president, he appointed two church elders as top deputies and asked the church to serve as "spiritual adviser" to his government. Soon after taking power, Ríos Montt began capitalizing on Iglesia Verbo's ties to U.S. fundamentalists, particularly Robertson.

The Iglesia Verbo is an offshoot of Gospel Outreach, a California-based evangelical missionary group which, like other U.S. fundamentalist churches, arrived in Guatemala after a devastating earthquake in 1976. The missionaries combined relief work with evangelization and made many converts, including members of the Guatemalan military. Deprived of U.S. military aid because of Guatemala's record of human rights violations, Ríos Montt's government immediately became friendly with Robertson, who was seen as a promising fund-raiser for the more than $1 billion the general hoped to get from U.S. fundamentalists. The tele-preacher obtained the first interview with Ríos Montt after the coup, which was aired on his "700 Club," and made frequent appeals for prayers and financial support for the regime. Washington applauded such charity, and three months after the coup representatives of the U.S. government, including then presidential counselor Edwin Meese, attended a strategy meeting on Guatemala that would be a dress rehearsal for a private network to fund the Nicaraguan *contras*. Also at the meeting were Robertson, Jerry Falwell, and Francisco Bianchi, who was Ríos Montt's top aide and an Iglesia Verbo elder. Part of the scheme was to improve Guatemala's image in the United States by portraying the general as a deeply religious man struggling to save his country from communism. Robertson was especially helpful, telling his TV audience that the general was "a great guy" and "impeccably honest." "He is putting down wrongdoers and punishing those who are evildoers. . . . Let it be an example of what God can do when His people are in charge."[12]

On another occasion, during an interview with Ríos Montt's pastor, Robertson told viewers that "we should urge that the U.S. State Department send 'mercy helicopters' [to Guatemala]. . . . If Guatemala goes communist, then Mexico goes communist, and then you've got the whole border of the United States filled up with Russian agents." According to Robertson, Ríos Montt represented a "median" way between repressive oligarchy and communism—"a better way, the kingdom of Jesus Christ." The broadcast triggered a flood of letters to the White House demanding the restoration of U.S. military aid to Guatemala.[13]

Ríos Montt's government also received aid from U.S. churches through the efforts of Gospel Outreach, which organized a shipment of grain, clothing, drugs, and building materials, as well as 500,000 Spanish-language Bibles. Part of what Outreach called International Love Lift, the shipment was worth approximately $1 million—a pittance compared to Ríos Montt's expectations but, as it turned out, the only major contribution. During a State Department briefing for Robertson and other fundamentalist leaders in July 1982, department officials had expressed support for a convoy of "a thousand" trucks from all over the country to carry supplies from the churches for a second shipment, the idea being that the convoy "might be the vehicle that could get U.S. recognition for the Montt government," in the words of a State Department official. But the idea never materialized. Robertson later backed off from any major financial commitment, saying only that he hoped to send a small team of medical and agricultural experts and perhaps $350,000. Nevertheless, the input from U.S. fundamentalist churches proved important to Riós Montt's "Beans and Bullets" rural pacification program, a euphemism for Indian concentration camps patterned on the "strategic hamlets" in Vietnam.[14]

A semifeudal society in which the predominantly Indian population is treated like serfs, Guatemala in 1954 had been on the verge of establishing some modest reforms under a democratically elected government when President Jacobo Arbenz was overthrown in a CIA-sponsored coup.[15] For the next thirty years the country was run by a succession of military dictators, who killed tens of thousands of inoffensive civilians, making Guatemala the worst human rights violator in the hemisphere. Bands of guerrillas periodically sprang up, but they were soon wiped out by the military's scorched-earth policy, which also took a tragic toll of Indian communities. Ríos Montt, who had begun his administration with a speech about the need for love, was supposed to stop the bloodletting, but within four months of taking power his government had killed 2,600 people, according to Amnesty International. Amnesty also reported widespread torture and "large-scale extrajudicial execution of non-combatant civilians in the countryside." Approximately 50,000 Indians were relocated to Ríos Montt's "model villages," while upwards of 100,000 fled their ancestral homes. Ríos Montt's religious supporters said it was necessary to massacre the Indians because the "Indians are demon-possessed. They are communists." During the general's year-and-a-half reign more than 15,000 people were murdered, including Catholic priests and hundreds of catechists, among them the five catechists of Santa Cruz El Quiché. (See Chapter 1, pp. 5–6.) This was the government that Robertson hailed as "an example of what God can do when His people are in charge."[16]

While Catholics were being slaughtered, missionaries from Gospel Outreach and other U.S. fundamentalist churches received the army's blessing to supply the destitute Indians in the model villages with food, medicine, and clothing. A Gospel Outreach team leader reported that the aid program served as a "wedge for further evangelical activity." At a time when Catholic catechists were prohibited on pain of death from holding meetings, fundamentalist preachers routinely received military permits. Such was the religious repression at one point that Pentecostal military officers detained Guatemalans at checkpoints when they admitted to being Catholics. Fundamentalist preaching became increasingly anti-Catholic because the Catholic Church, which had denounced human rights abuses, was seen as the military's enemy. Catholic bishops were routinely insulted, and some received death threats, including Ríos Montt's own brother, Bishop Mario Enrique Ríos Montt, who was forced to flee the country. Evangelical pastors who did not subscribe to the dictator's fundamentalist creed were also persecuted. Twelve were assassinated, sixty-nine kidnapped, and forty-five "disappeared." In addition, eighty-eight evangelical churches were destroyed, and fifty more occupied by the army. When the general was finally overthrown in August 1983, his fellow army officers gave as one reason for ousting him the abuse of the principle of separation of church and state by a "fanatic and aggressive religious group."[17]

Nevertheless, Ríos Montt's legacy lived on. During his period in office there was a significant increase in conversions to fundamentalist churches, particularly the Pentecostals, and by the time he was overthrown more than one-quarter of the Guatemalans had become converts. Already unhappy about the invasion of its traditional territory by Protestant groups, the Catholic Church expressed deep resentment over its persecution by a "born-again" general in league with U.S. fundamentalist missionaries. But the Pentecostals remained unrepentant, many agreeing with Jimmy Swaggart that Catholicism was a "false cult" and the "doctrine of devils."

Robertson's financial aid to the *contras* was of a piece with his support for Ríos Montt's murderous regime. Among the largest private donors to the *contra* cause, Robertson's Christian Broadcasting Network (CBN) raised millions of dollars for food, medicine, clothing, vehicles, and other aid for so-called Nicaraguan refugees who also happened to be *contras* or Miskito Indians drawn into the *contra* struggle. Although Robertson tried at first to pretend that CBN contributions were not meant for the counterrevolutionaries, his organization did not deny that the supplies were being shipped through intermediary groups with close ties to the

Reagan administration or that they were being sent to the war-torn Nicaraguan-Honduran border, where the *contras* were headquartered. In contrast, such politically neutral refugee aid groups as the United Nations High Commission on Refugees purposely located their Honduran relief camps at least thirty-three miles from the border to avoid involvement with the hostilities. That CBN's refugees were indeed *contras* was confirmed by Mario Calero, the brother of *contra* leader Adolfo Calero, who said that the counterrevolutionaries were an army of refugees. "Some of the refugees are freedom fighters," he said, adding that he considered himself one of them. This humanitarian aid served two purposes: It freed other funds for the purchase of military hardware, and it was enlistment bait for the Miskitos, thousands of whom had crossed the border after periodic clashes with the Sandinistas. Hungry and penniless, the Indians often had no choice but to join the *contras,* although they hated them at least as much as they did the Sandinistas. "It's clear that the border relief programs are not designed to meet the long- or short-term interests of the Miskitos, but rather are designed for political purposes as a conduit of aid to the *contras,*" a relief official told *Sojourners* magazine.[18]

Robertson never hid his feelings in the matter. He frequently likened the *contras* to freedom fighters, and when Congress balked at providing more aid in 1985, he went on television to denounce the "craven submission of our leaders and Congress to the demands of communism [which] makes you sick to your stomach." Robertson also visited a *contra* training camp in Honduras to preach his fundamentalist gospel and distribute good cheer. "I think God is in favor of liberty and justice and He is against oppression," he told the troops, comparing the *contra* struggle to the American Revolution. "If we can do something to help these men fight for freedom, I think it is perfectly in God's plan." The visit, which was later shown on U.S. television, shocked some religious leaders, since God's self-appointed envoy seemed to be saying that the *contras* had God's blessing. Richmond's Bishop Walter Sullivan, who was among the most outspoken Catholic opponents of U.S. aid to the *contras,* was so outraged that he publicly criticized Robertson, saying "I cannot imagine Jesus reviewing troops." Robertson furiously replied that he had not been reviewing troops and that, if Sullivan didn't watch his words, he might be in trouble for "libel and slander."[19]

When faced with challenges from the evangelicals, Robertson had a way of sliding around the issue. One of his toughest critics was the liberal evangelical magazine *Sojourners,* which published an exposé of CBN's relations with the private *contra* funding network and cited CBN's frequent refusal to answer questions. Although it was known that CBN had contributed millions of dollars for humanitarian aid to Central America and that $3 million had gone to a *contra*-related organization, the Nicaraguan Patriotic Association, Robertson refused to address the subject directly, saying only that "the fact is that communists [his description of the Sandinistas] make people suffer. If that makes it [CBN aid] political, then, I'm sorry, we're still going to help them." But why, wondered *Sojourners,* had CBN become concerned about Central American refugees only after Congress had refused to continue funding the *contras*? And "why is CBN working with groups whose efforts are aiding the *contras* and thereby making possible the further killing, torture and general abuse of Nicaraguan civilians?"[20]

Sojourners and its editor, Jim Wallis, are highly respected in certain sectors of the evangelical community. Therefore, instead of snapping at Wallis as he had at Sullivan, Robertson took the more conciliatory approach of writing to say that "most of the reports which allege . . . [CBN] aid to the Freedom Fighters of Nicaragua are not true." Less than a year later, however, he told a meeting of religious broadcasters in Washington that he was supplying "chaplains" and Bibles to the Honduran-based *contras,* thus admitting a direct link to the *contras.* As Wallis observed, most of the secular press missed the religious implication of Robertson's aid to the *contras.* "They didn't think it was any big deal, since a lot of other right-wing political organizations were doing the same thing. But religious people were outraged that they [Robertson's organization] were doing this in the name of God and that many churches had been unknowingly involved through their connections to CBN. Christian support for terrorism, whether it be from the Right or the Left, is simply wrong. To allow political ideology to overshadow human needs and fundamental issues of life and death is to go seriously astray. And to use the plight of innocent refugees, who have already suffered so much, to cloak political motivations is to compound the offense."[21]

"Satanic" Catholicism

While the mainline Protestants and liberal evangelicals worked toward an ecumenical understanding with local Catholic leaders, the sects often preached a hatred of Catholicism as satanic. A letter from the head of one such group in Guatemala, for example, spoke of doing "battle in the heavenlies" against the pope and his priests so that God would "arise and scatter [Guatemala's] enemies and establish her upon the rock that is Jesus Christ."[22] The tone of fundamentalist and Pentecostal radio programs, which blanketed Central America, was similarly aggressive, and some of their films were not only anticommunist but also anti-Catholic. Swaggart, whose televised shows were so perfectly dubbed in Spanish that some thought him Hispanic, took frequent swipes at Catholics.

With U.S.-sponsored sects claiming that the pope was the "Beast" of the Apocalypse and with millions of dollars pouring into the area from televangelists like Robertson and Swaggart, local bishops could hardly be blamed for suspecting a plot. The bishops had not forgotten Nelson Rockefeller's description of their church as an untrustworthy ally, following a tour of Latin America for President Nixon. Many were familiar with similar slurs from members of the Reagan transition team in the "Santa Fe Document." (See Chapter 4, pp. 89–90.) Guatemala's Bishop Ríos Montt, for one, was convinced that the spread of the sects was part of a larger U.S. political design, because the phenomenon, which began in the 1970s, coincided with changing perceptions of Latin American Catholicism in Washington. "The Catholic Church south of Texas is regarded as too large, too strong," he told *The New York Times*. "Because we cannot be confronted or fought directly, we must be weakened and divided."[23]

In fact, the fundamentalist explosion in Central America was due primarily to the violent upheaval in the region. As elsewhere in Latin America, the people sought solace in religion, and the sects were more than willing to provide it. Military persecution of socially activist sectors of the Catholic Church also created a religious vacuum in places like Guatemala. However, in Nicaragua, where progressive church groups were encouraged, harassment of the sects by the Sandinista government actually contributed to their growth.

Most local Catholic churches were dirt-poor, understaffed, and in no position to match the gifts of food, clothing, and other handouts financed by the sects' U.S. sponsors and which poor Latin Americans said were a definite incentive to convert.[24] Nor could they afford a vast communications network to market their gospel. Swaggart alone spent $15 million a year on his overseas missions, including a private school system in El Salvador that educated more than 13,000 children and a similarly large operation in Honduras, where nearly 20 percent of the population was evangelical.[25] Progressive Catholic leaders claimed that the televangelists' campaigns were debasing because of the "use of fear and guilt to prepare clients for the 'marketing' of religious products." "Such methods, apart from their lack of respect for the person as the subject of his or her own destiny, generally fail to bring about a lasting transformation or conversion," argued liberation theologian Pablo Richard. "Consequently, those who follow the sects often show little perseverance and normally fall into political or religious indifference." Agreed a Catholic priest, "If people hear of better miracles somewhere else, they switch churches. If they can't obey the order to stop smoking or drinking or dancing, they drop out."[26] They also tended to splinter, into dozens of subgroups and sub-subgroups, to the point where many sects were composed of a single pastor and a dozen families who celebrated their particular faith in the pastor's small living room.

Although some fundamentalists eschewed political involvement, even voting, because of the stress on the hereafter and the imminent Second Coming of Christ, the evangelicals as a group represented a politically conservative force, much as they did in the United States. The agenda varied according to the country. In Brazil, for example, evangelical congressmen worked to ensure that a new constitution placed Brazil "under the protection of God" but not the Catholic Church. In Central America the evangelicals followed an anti-Sandinista line that portrayed the U.S. role in the region as a power for good. Evangelicals were also convinced that they could turn the masses against liberation theology. "I can see where liberation theology would be attractive to an oppressed person," said one evangelical pastor. "But it's attracting people only because we evangelicals haven't done our job in the past."[27]

Catholic pastors made much the same comment about the challenge from the evangelicals. While many were convinced that the answer to the fundamentalists lay in the base community, only a minority of bishops strongly pushed the communities' development because of the Vatican's frequently voiced concern that they were too democratic and liable to become involved in social and political issues. The Curia was also suspicious of the communities because they were a popular expression of liberation theology. "Unfortunately," said Pro Mundi Vita of the Vatican's attitude, "the church's efforts have been directed more toward preserving discipline, order and doctrinal purity than the great work and challenge of being evangelical."[28]

PART III

THE
UNITED STATES

CHAPTER 7
✠
THE "AMERICANISTS"

WHILE THE TURBULENT LATIN AMERICANS frequently cause the Vatican headaches, European theologians say that Rome is more concerned about dissent in the U.S. church.[1] Latin America has the numbers—it is the most populous part of the Catholic world—as well as martyrs and a theology that challenges Roman hegemony. But the U.S. bishops lead the largest church in one of the two superpowers. The Americans are also rich, and Rome respects money and power.

U.S. Catholicism has historically posed a challenge to the Vatican because of its pluralistic tendencies and the insistence on a respect for the separation of church and state, which runs counter to the European integralist belief in a church-dominated society. At the end of the last century, for example, progressive American church leaders scandalized Rome by suggesting that the U.S. experience might serve as a model for the universal church. While the idea was enthusiastically taken up in France, the challenge was squashed by the papacy. Like Latin America, the U.S. church did not throw off its European straitjacket until after Vatican II, although signs of change were evident during the council when the U.S. bishops, encouraged by the work of the American Jesuit John Courtney Murray, lobbied successfully for a declaration in favor of religious liberty.

Although the Latin American church took the lead in the decade after Vatican II by adopting liberation theology and a preferential option for the poor, the U.S. church also underwent substantial changes. Some, such as a newfound concern for social justice, could be partly attributed to the influence of the Latin Americans, particularly the example of such martyrs as El Salvador's Archbishop Romero. Ordinary Catholics were most affected by the changes in rituals, such as the shift from a Latin to an English Mass, but other, less obvious changes proved equally significant, including a more democratic style of government within the church and the appointment of progressive bishops through the influence of Rome's then apostolic delegate to the United States, the liberal Belgian prelate Jean Jadot. These bishops welcomed the reforms brought about by Vatican II, helping to change the U.S. church into a more pluralistic institution in which new ideas and ways of doing things were encouraged. The hierarchy also challenged Washington over Central America and the arms buildup; justice and peace became its mandate. It was an amazing change from the fortress church of the 1950s when the idea of a bishop joining an antigovernment peace demonstration would have been unthinkable.

Although Paul VI caused widespread anguish among American Catholics by refusing to countenance artificial birth control, in most respects his papacy encouraged a more liberal direction in the U.S. church. But matters changed radically after John Paul II became pope. As in Latin America, Rome attempted to reassert a conservative influence through disciplinary measures against liberal prelates and theologians, a flurry of authoritarian decrees (mostly on sexual morals), and the appointment of papal yes-men. In an earlier period, when the U.S. church was less secure in its position in the United States and the prospects of a more pluralistic church were nonexistent, the bishops would undoubtedly have knuckled under. But after Vatican II bishops, religious, and laity changed irrevocably. The postconciliar generation of bishops displayed a confidence in the church's place in American society—with 53 million believers Catholicism is the largest church in the United States. The dialogue and openness that had characterized Vatican II suited the American way of doing things, and once the shock of such changes as an English Mass wore off, many Catholics welcomed the renewal. Moreover, by the time John Paul ascended Peter's throne a new generation of Catholics had become accustomed to a Vatican II church. They might honor the man, but they did not like John Paul's finger-wagging—hence the refusal to accept his message. Bishops and theologians fought back, and papal infallibility—the keystone of Vatican power—came under increasing attack. The Americans, Rome discovered, were just as unruly as the Latin Americans.

U.S. Democracy
versus Roman Catholicism

Given the freewheeling culture in which the American church developed, it is surprising that there were not more conflicts with Rome prior to Vatican II. Although tensions occasionally arose over the more pluralistic tendencies in U.S. Catholicism, Rome was able to put down rebellions because the church was still a European-dominated institution and most European church leaders upheld an authoritarian papacy. Moreover, so long as the Americans did not directly attack papal power or try to propagate their ideas in Europe, they were able to slide around the question of democracy. The Vatican generally supported those bishops who argued for an American church instead of a German- or Polish-style church in the United States. During the nineteenth century bitter feuds erupted between the Irish-American bishops, who urged greater Americanization, and the Germans and Poles, who wanted to protect a European faith against American influences. The Irish view prevailed after Rome refused to take the latter's side. In contrast, the Americanizers lost a key battle with Rome at the turn of the century when they tried to promote a U.S. model for the universal church that respected religious pluralism and a separation of church and state.

The ideas of the "Americanists" coincided with a larger movement in Europe, known as modernism, that aimed to bring the Catholic Church into step with the modern world through a renewal similar to that which occurred at Vatican II. Unlike the classicists, who dominated Rome, the modernists did not believe the church was a "perfect society" immune to change. On the contrary, they shared the conviction of earlier religious reformers that the post-Constantine church had fashioned itself in the image of secular power and that many religious practices had changed with historical exigencies. And indeed the church so defined itself: Its model of itself was the institution, a "view that defines the church primarily in terms of its visible structures, especially the rights and power of its officers," as one church historian said.[2]

Although Rome was primarily concerned with the challenge from European modernists, the "Americanists" were singled out for censure by Pope Leo XIII after their liberal ideas spread in 1897 to France, then in the throes of a power struggle between republicans and monarchists, the latter supported by Rome. In addition to the French controversy and the threat to papal power posed by Americanism and theological modernism, the Americans challenged a European power in the Spanish-American War, which broke out in the spring of 1898. The war, which was supported by the U.S. church, was seen in Europe as proof that the Americans had become a political as well as a theological threat. In 1899 Leo issued a letter, *Testem Benevolentiae,* which called the U.S. church to order, by denying the idea that it could be "different from that which is in the rest of the world." Leo also insisted that the American church would be better off if it "enjoyed the favor of the laws and the patronage of public authority"—that is, if the country were a Catholic state. While conservatives within the U.S. church were pleased with the letter, most progressives kept a prudent silence, and the dispute soon died. Since the controversy had primarily been among intellectuals, the average American Catholic was unaffected by the letter—many did not even know of its existence. Yet the charge of Americanism would continue to haunt the U.S. church.[3] After Pius X became pope in 1903, the Vatican began a worldwide crackdown on modernism, including strains in the United States. Such liberal Catholic magazines as *The New York Review* were forced to cease publication; dozens of books were put on the forbidden Index; seminaries were cleansed of any modern taint, including secular newspapers; and U.S. scholars identified with the movement saw their careers ruined. The experience left permanent scars. Intellectuals became cautious, and an incipient native theology was repressed before it could flower. Not until the 1960s and 1970s, in the aftermath of Vatican II, would U.S. theology regain its earlier vigor.

Cross and Flag

Although Roman Catholicism altered little in the intervening half century, the U.S. church underwent a major change, from a poor immigrant church to an upwardly mobile institution, symbolic of which was the Catholic exodus to the suburbs. For decades the U.S. church had preached the virtues of education and hard work as a means to success in America, and by the 1950s the immigrants' children and grandchildren were beginning to realize that dream. But a price was paid in the process: Lost in the super-patriotism of the postwar church was a distinctiveness—a standing apart from the prevailing materialism—that was so important to religion's spiritual appeal and that had glimmered here and there in the American church's earlier history. Priests and bishops embarked on massive building programs, ostentation being the symbol of American success. Few questioned Senator Joseph McCarthy's political witch-hunts, not only because pro-Americanism was synonymous with anticommunism but because Pope Pius XII was himself a Cold Warrior.

Although the Curia continued to distrust Americanism, the United States became the Vatican's chief ally in countering communism in Europe. Catholic schoolchildren in the United States took up collections for such embattled prelates as Hungary's Cardinal Jozsef Mindszenty, and Washington provided millions of dollars to help the Holy See's political crusade against the Italian Communists. (See Chapter 10, p. 289.) The decade was remarkable not only for its anticommunist rhetoric but for the unprecedented harmony between the American church and Rome.

Cardinal Francis J. Spellman, New York City's "Powerhouse," symbolized the period. Authoritarian and remote—he rarely preached in St. Patrick's Cathedral—he wielded enormous influence in Rome and Washington. Spellman was a stern disciplinarian who frequently inveighed against lax morals; he also played political hardball to obtain his ends. His consuming passion was the communist threat, as shown by his first magazine article after his appointment as cardinal, "Communism Is Un-American." He was a strong supporter of Senator McCarthy, also a Catholic, and refused to condemn his Red-baiting tactics—a position shared by many other bishops as well as 40 percent of the nation's Catholics.[4]

Nurtured on a religious-political culture that identified communism as anti-American and anti-Catholic, U.S. Catholics were less willing than the Protestants to denounce McCarthy, even after his televised hearings revealed the style of the man. For the same reason, they were natural recruits for the fledgling Central Intelligence Agency (CIA). Similarly, U.S. Catholic missionaries in some Third World countries, particularly Latin America, routinely collaborated with the American embassy in the belief that they were helping to fight godless communism.[5] Although the Spellman era ended with the election of the two Johns to the presidency and the papacy, the Cold War alliances endured, as shown by the many Catholics in the U.S. intelligence establishment and the ongoing cooperation between the CIA and the Curia. (See Chapter 3, pp. 69–70, and Chapter 10, pp. 287–89.) In the 1980s, when the pendulum swung to the conservatives, they provided the underpinnings for the Vatican's friendly relationship with the Reagan administration.

Like Pius XII, John Paul is virulently anticommunist, although he is not pro-American, as shown by his critical writings on capitalism. His alliance with Washington is tactical and does not imply a regard for U.S. democracy. John Paul shares with the Curia a suspicion of political and religious pluralism, believing in the integralist vision of a society dominated by Roman Catholicism. Nevertheless, he aided Washington by disciplining bishops who were outspokenly critical of the Reagan administration and by emphasizing individual piety at the expense of social justice, thereby undercutting the social activism of the U.S. hierarchy. As during his visit to Nicaragua, his trips to the United States seemed to emphasize one word only—"No!" Unable to grasp the historical reasons for the Sandinista revolution, he was equally impervious to the importance of pluralism in U.S. culture. His refusal to countenance dissent, in addition to his fierce anticommunism, proved a boon to the Reagan administration in its battles with the U.S. bishops. While Washington could not silence its critics in the hierarchy, Rome had the means, if not to shut them up, at least to cause them pause. Bishops began to look over their shoulders for fear that Rome was watching, and fear made them more cautious.

Opposing Visions

As in previous conflicts with the Vatican, such as the "Americanist" episode, relations between Rome and the U.S. church were complicated by a vocal papist lobby in the United States. Its members objected strongly to the Vatican II model of church and to the bishops' criticisms of the Reagan administration. They bombarded the Vatican with denunciations, persuading the already suspicious Curia of scandalous goings-on in U.S. dioceses. They also served as point men for Washington's confrontations with the bishops over Central America, the arms buildup, and the economy. Most belonged to the New Right, a conservative political alliance of fundamentalist Catholics and Protestants, or the neoconservatives, a highly visible group of former liberals led by such Reaganites as Jeane Kirkpatrick. Ranged against them were an equally outspoken if larger group of progressive Catholics who were active in justice and peace movements and who wanted to continue the reforms begun by Vatican II.

Although the liberals' voice had been drowned out by the antimodernist campaign, World War II, and the Spellman church, it was never entirely silenced. Dorothy Day and Peter Maurin, who in the 1930s inspired the formation of the pacifist Catholic Worker communities that foreshadowed the peace groups of the 1980s, consistently spoke of the need to share with the poor, of the possibilities of active nonviolence, and of genuine personal involvement. But it was not until the eighties, when Day was dead, that American Catholics began seriously to address the issues of war. Coincidentally, Day had entitled her autobiography *The Long Loneliness*.

The willingness of Catholics to take on such controversial questions was also due to the religious coming of age symbolized by the election of John F. Kennedy. Many Catholics had previously risen high in business and politics, even to cabinet posts, but Kennedy's presidency marked a turning point, a time of pride for American Catholics, though one of caution, too. Kennedy's brother-in-law, Sargent Shriver, recalled that when candidates for Kennedy's cabinet were being selected, "it was almost axiomatic that we wouldn't pick a Catholic because of the fear that Kennedy would be accused of creating a Catholic cabal."[6]

Shriver's contention that Catholics had "gone from have-nots to haves" in the decades after Kennedy's death was borne out by the figures on rising affluence. While there were no data to challenge his tongue-in-cheek comment that "half the bank presidents in this country are Catholics," undoubtedly a good number of those in executive suites belonged to that faith. Prosperity may have given Catholics a greater sense of security in dealing with WASPs on Wall Street, but this does not explain the more activist social stance of the church, since wealthy Catholics are no different from other well-heeled individuals in their opposition to social change.

Instead, there was the dizzying series of events that drew Catholics into a religious and political maelstrom, starting with the civil rights movement led by the Reverend Martin Luther King, Jr., in the 1950s and early 1960s, in which many Catholics participated, bishops included. King's campaign coincided with two other crucial developments, Vatican II and the Vietnam War. Vatican II had sought to understand the "signs of the times" by encouraging believers to reflect critically on the pressing questions of their era, chief among them justice and peace. It also gave local bishops a liberty and responsibility unknown since the early church to speak out on such issues. However, at the conclusion of the Council in 1965 most American Catholics still hesitated to apply such radical thinking to the Vietnam War. There were exceptions, like the Jesuit Daniel Berrigan and his brother Philip, a Josephite priest, who engaged in dramatic acts of civil disobedience in protest against the war. But by and large the antiwar sentiment of the sixties that erupted on college campuses and in the counterculture was not shared by American Catholics, and those who joined the protests tended to be followers, not leaders. The majority of Catholics went along with the enthusiasm, confusion, and eventual disillusion that characterized the populace at large. The bishops did not make an unequivocal plea for an end to hostilities in Vietnam until 1971, by which time almost no one supported the war.

On the heels of Vietnam came the bloody CIA-supported military coup in Chile, Watergate and President Nixon's resignation, and the landmark decision by the Supreme Court declaring abortion legal. Of these events only the last posed a significant challenge to the American bishops because it forced them to think seriously about the moral implications of life and death. From such reflection they would inevitably draw conclusions about the nuclear threat, for how, they asked, could they condemn abortion without also condemning the possible destruction of humanity?

Discussion of the connections between such issues—or what Chicago's Cardinal Joseph Bernardin called the "seamless garment" of Christian response—remained tentative during the Carter years, largely because of the President's peacemaking efforts and his concern for human rights in the developing countries, however confused and unsuccessful such policies may have been. But the advent of Ronald Reagan quickly changed matters, not because of his political alliances or economic conservatism but because of Latin America.

Unlike Vietnam, which is remote and predominantly Buddhist, Latin America is next door and overwhelmingly Catholic. Many American missionaries have worked in the area, and a number of U.S. bishops have visited or even served there. The assassination of El Salvador's Archbishop Romero in 1980, followed a few months later by the murders of the four American religious women, galvanized American Catholics as nothing before had done—not Vietnam or Chile, Watergate or the hostage crisis in Iran. From the start of 1981, when Reagan renewed military aid to the Salvadoran government, the Catholic leadership, and ever larger numbers of priests, nuns, and lay people, turned hostile to Washington's Central American policies. By 1982, when the administration's support for the *contra* war against the Nicaraguan government had become generally known, relations between church and state were the most tense of this century.

Central America, which was chosen by Secretary of State Haig as the Reagan administration's first test of power in the East-West confrontation, also became the rallying point for the New Right and the neoconservatives. Like the Roman Curia, they blamed liberation theology and a "popular church" for religious agitation in Central America—one of the New Right's Catholic stars, Republican Senator Jeremiah Denton, actually held hearings on the subject.

Although Jerry Falwell and Pat Robertson were the most prominent religious advocates of Reagan's Central American policies, Paul Weyrich, a founder of the New Right, and the ultraconservative Catholic weekly, *The Wanderer,* were more effective in undercutting the U.S. bishops by encouraging American Catholics to complain to Rome. An Eastern Rite Catholic who had left the Roman community because of Vatican II, Weyrich was influential in furthering Falwell's career—he was credited with coining the phrase "Moral Majority." He also helped found the Heritage Foundation with the financial aid of Joseph Coors, the arch-conservative head of the Coors brewery. Heritage, which was the first and most influential of the New Right think tanks, was followed by various other Weyrich lobbies, including the Washington-based Free Congress Research and Education Foundation, which campaigned for the New Right's religious and political agenda. Among the latter's spinoffs was the Catholic Center, which was organized to generate "significant nega-tive publicity for the bishops" and make them "squeal and scream in anguish."[7]

The center's "truth squads" worked hard to focus adverse attention on such critics as Seattle's Archbishop Raymond Hunthausen, who sup-ported the Sanctuary movement and opposed Washington's arms policies. To teach Catholics how to turn the screws, Weyrich's center organized a series of workshops in Seattle and other cities where progressive bishops presided over the churches. A main source of likely participants was said to be the subscription list of the Minnesota-based *Wanderer,* which had a circulation of 40,000 and was eagerly read in the Vatican for its "ex-posés" of liberal American prelates. Leading the workshops was a Cuban exile priest, Father Enrique Rueda, often present at White House brief-ings on Central America and director of a weekly program on the government-financed Radio Martí, which transmitted anti-Castro prop-aganda to Cuba.[8] Rueda had made himself popular in New Right circles by damning liberation theology as Marxist and by suggesting that any group associated with it, such as the Maryknoll missionaries and the Brazilian bishops, were "an integral part of the subversive movement" led by the Soviet Union.[9]

Rueda's stated aim was to make "troublemakers" of the workshop participants so that they would circulate petitions, write letters to the Vatican, publish newspaper advertisements, discourage church donations, and otherwise harass targeted bishops. Although he claimed that "the Vatican is telling us to do this," the inspiration more likely came from Washington, given the close connections of Rueda and Weyrich to the

Reagan administration and to their mutual friend Joseph Coors, the financial backer of Rueda's workshops and one of President Reagan's personal advisers.[10]

Weyrich, who prided himself on being a shrewd "political mechanic," was the chief strategist. He stressed the importance of "labeling the opposition, putting them in a box and telling others that the opposition is composed of people who do not follow the Pope."[11] The tactic paid off because John Paul's papacy was "constitutionally disposed," in the words of an American Jesuit with long experience in Rome, to believe such smears. The Weyrich-*Wanderer* network, complained an archbishop from the Midwest, "has been setting Rome's agenda for the U.S. church."[12]

Other agenda setters included the Catholic members of the Washington-based, neoconservative Institute on Religion and Democracy (IRD), particularly the writer Michael Novak and Jesuit James Schall, who were sharp critics of the liberal trend in the U.S. church. Unlike the New Right, the neoconservatives were only marginally interested in such domestic issues as abortion and school prayer, their major concern being foreign policy, particularly defense, relations with the Soviet Union, and the wars in Central America. Although they thought of themselves as "progressives," they were actually a throwback to the Cold War fifties, before the "optimistic pragmatism and social engineering of Kennedy liberals," to use Novak's words.[13]

As admitted by Lutheran pastor Richard John Neuhaus, one of the IRD's founders, the Institute had "a specific political agenda," at the top of which were liberation theology and Central America.[14] Dubbed "the official seminary of the Reagan administration" by liberal religious leaders, the IRD from its inception in 1981 worked closely with the State Department, providing speakers for briefings and turning out articles and papers on El Salvador and Nicaragua. It also launched a smear campaign against the mainline Protestant leadership and established a controversial intelligence newsletter aimed at governments and corporations under attack by labor unions and church activists.

The IRD's *pièce de résistance* was a 1985 conference on religious freedom cosponsored by the State Department. The event was believed to be the first-ever occasion in which the department joined with individual religious groups to hold a public forum on the subject, and to judge by the adverse reactions, it was probably the last. Held at the State Department, the meeting was partially financed by the government, which provided nearly $45,000 to bring speakers to Washington. Neither the

Catholic nor the mainline Protestant churches were invited to be sponsors, though together they represented the largest number of believers in the United States. "We couldn't exactly offer the entire world a hand in sponsoring it," was the explanation of an IRD spokesperson.[15]

It was easy to see why. Used as a platform by President Reagan to denounce the Sandinistas for threatening to send church leaders to "relocation camps" and for "fire-bombing" a synagogue (both charges being false), the conference quickly turned into a mudslinging attack on the mainline churches because of their criticisms of the Reagan government. When church and state join to address problems of religious liberty "and then use the occasion and the setting (a conference room of the State Department) . . . to castigate other religious groups who are not even present, the question of religious freedom in America becomes a high agenda item," complained United Methodist Bishop Leroy Hodapp.[16]

The Vatican, on the other hand, shared the IRD's opinion that the U.S. Catholic Conference and the Protestants' National Council of Churches had taken an excessively liberal position on Central America. Novak, who was read by Cardinal Ratzinger, the Vatican's chief hatchet man, and whose writings were promoted by the right-wing Italian Catholic movement Communion and Liberation, expressed the feelings of many in the Curia when he denounced liberation theology. Equally influential were the conservative American cardinals—New York City's John J. O'Connor and Boston's Bernard Law—who formed part of the same coterie as Novak and Jesuit Schall. O'Connor was opposed to dialogue with the Sandinistas, and he questioned his fellow bishops' criticism of U.S. military aid to El Salvador, one of his arguments being that bishops should not "pit their knowledge against knowledge professed by our own State Department."[17] Such opinions were reinforced by a procession of high-ranking U.S. officials to the Vatican for interviews with the pope. How much they influenced John Paul was open to question, but after his visit to Central America in 1983, it was clear that he did not share the U.S. bishops' assessment of the situation—as shown by his challenge to Cardinal Bernardin over the U.S. church's failure to support Reagan's policies in the area. See Chapter 3, p. 67.

The Bishops' Challenge

Despite Vatican disapproval and the lobbying of such groups as Weyrich's Catholic Center and the IRD, the U.S. bishops' conference held firm in its criticism of U.S. policies in Central America. The bishops were encouraged to take a tough line by American missionaries working in El Salvador and by Arturo Rivera y Damas, Romero's close friend and his successor as archbishop of San Salvador. In April 1981, Rivera y Damas wrote Vice President George Bush that "the 'right' in our country believes you do support them. . . . The provision of military assistance at this moment in our country's history simply strengthens the military and increases the attitude of arrogance among them."[18]

Such reports by people who daily lived the tragedy of El Salvador confirmed the bishops' belief that the situation was not understood by the State Department. Both Secretary of State Haig and Jeane Kirkpatrick, Reagan's chief adviser on Latin America, were Catholics of the Spellman school who saw the world as divided between East and West; consequently their arguments failed to impress the post–Vatican II Catholic leadership. Invitations to the White House for personal briefings by President Reagan were no more successful: The President's guests were charmed and charming, but they refused to budge on their position that U.S. policies in Central America were immoral. This unexpected intransigence frustrated the administration, which showed its impatience by claiming that the bishops were the chief impediment to a military strike against communists in the Caribbean basin—meaning the opponents of the Salvadoran government, the Sandinistas, the Cubans, and anyone else who challenged U.S. hegemony. So great was government concern, *Soujourners* magazine reported, that a high-ranking general, in a bombastic speech to military leaders at the National War College, had stated that "the greatest challenge to all that we do now comes from within the churches."[19] Instead of balking the church, however, such rhetoric focused media attention on the bishops' statements, giving them a wider audience than they might otherwise have gained.

By encouraging the church to take up issues of justice and peace, Vatican II had helped a new generation of American bishops to shed Spellman's "my country, right or wrong" mindset. Thus they were not disposed to believe everything the White House told them—fortunately, in view of the series of scandals in 1981 about a faked "white paper" on El Salvador and such U.S.-backed pseudo-reforms as a land-distribution project based on the "peasant-pacification program" in Vietnam. Intelligent, articulate men for the most part, the bishops responded to the challenge in El Salvador as any smart executive would, by getting their own firsthand reports through frequent visits to the country and interviews

with a broad spectrum of Salvadoran society. Having no East-West premise to blind them, they came to conclusions also reached by U.S. historians, political scientists, and sociologists. The Salvadoran conflict, they
said, was not due to Soviet intervention, but to "internal conditions of
poverty and the denial of fundamental human rights. We believe that any
perception of Central America's problems, stated primarily in terms of
global security, military response, the transfer of weapons and the preservation of a society that has not promoted the participation of a majority
of the people, is gravely mistaken."[20]

The Salvadoran experience proved important for the bishops in several ways. It deepened their awareness of the Third World and encouraged
them to look at problems from a North-South perspective. Their willingness to take a stand that was unpopular on the political right contributed
to a maturing process that would prompt the bishops to examine other
areas of concern to society, including nuclear war and the economy. The
dialogue that led to their conclusions on El Salvador was equally important, since it became the principal teaching tool of the bishops' conference.
As remarked by Bishop James Malone, the conference's future president,
the American church had begun to teach "not simply through a finished
product, but through the process that led us to [a] finished document.
Teaching is, after all, not a unilateral activity. Teaching and learning are
mutually conditional."[21]

One of the things the popular organizations had taught the Latin
American bishops was the importance of listening—especially to the victims. The knowledge acquired by consulting the poor changed the bishops'
assumptions about themselves, their society, and their faith. Something
similar happened to U.S. religious leaders, missionaries, and lay people
who, after contact with the Salvadoran poor, began to rethink their faith
and its relationship to society. The needless poverty and the mindless
violence made them question their own lifestyles: Why were they so
privileged in material goods yet so lacking in the spiritual riches of the
Salvadoran poor? How was U.S. national security being served by arming
a murderous dictatorship that massacred its people? What did U.S. involvement in El Salvador say about American values, and about the
churches' teaching of values? Just raising such questions was a new experience for many. Each door opened onto the next, as had been the
case in Latin America.

On average, 1,000 Catholic missionaries return to the United States
each year, for leave or reassignment. They form the core for a new type

of work, known as "reverse mission," that developed in the early 1980s. Although traditional missionary appeals for prayers and money continued, the emphasis shifted from good works to reforming public opinion about the U.S. role in the Third World. Reverse mission was a way to get Americans to hear what the poor were saying, particularly in Central America. It was also a way to stimulate Americans to ask tough questions about what it meant to be a Christian in one of the world's wealthiest, most powerful nations. The missionaries spoke of their experiences to churches, schools, civic groups—to anyone who would listen. With first-hand information, with photographs and documents, reverse missionaries put many countries on the amorphous map of Christian consciences, rousing in Catholic parishes an unprecedented interest in Third World affairs. "People are interested in knowing what we see and how we interpret it, and they're compassionate about trying to understand it," said a Catholic missionary.[22]

One result of reverse mission was that thousands of Americans who had never considered themselves "activists" joined organizations, staffed picket lines, and circulated petitions to protest U.S. policies in El Salvador. The experience of Representative Thomas Downey, a New York Democrat from a heavily Catholic district, was typical of the "astonishing" impact. One day Downey received a visit from several Maryknoll nuns, who had just returned from Central America and were unhappy about the U.S. military buildup there. Downey suggested they take their message to his constituents, and they did just that. For months afterwards, he recalled, people visited his New York office to discuss Central America. "I'd ask them how they heard about it, and they'd say, 'Well, this nun came to talk . . .' "[23]

Although government officials tried to dismiss such "do-gooders" as naive, people listened to their message, in part because it was based on personal experience but also because it offered an alternative to the administration's cynical *Realpolitik*. Indicative of such feelings was the public outcry that defeated Reagan's nomination of Ernest Lefever, an apologist for the South African government, to be assistant secretary of state for human rights. "Whether naive or not, many Americans believe that U.S. foreign policy ought not to contradict deeply held moral principles—at least not too blatantly," observed foreign policy expert Richard E. Feinberg.[24]

In November 1981, when Reagan was signing the secret National Security Decision Directive 17 approving support for the *contra* war, the bishops issued yet another denunciation of U.S. policies in Central America. As they recognized, the conflagration was no longer limited to El Salvador but was spreading throughout Central America.

Supposedly secret, most of the United States' bellicose moves in the area soon became public because of ferreting reporters, leaks by disaffected government officials or plain stupidity—such as a CIA manual for the *contras* that gave instruction in dirty tricks. Like later embarrassments over arms shipments to Iran, support for the *contra* war assumed that Washington could carry out highly sensitive—not to say illegal—activities without detection, or that at the very least it could talk its way out of trouble. Journalists might be gulled for a time, but few were disposed in the 1980s to ignore an important news event, in contrast to the unspoken cooperation that had made it possible twenty-five years earlier for the CIA to carry on a secret war in Laos without much ado. That government officials did not foresee the considerable public reaction to discovery of their actions was a measure of their isolation and arrogance. However, for the more pessimistic observer, such as foreign analyst Richard Barnet, it also proved that "political leaders [could] secure the approval—or at least the passive acquiescence—of large majorities of citizens by appealing to the worst within us."[25] Certainly that was the appeal of the U.S. invasion of Grenada in 1983, which was applauded by the American public presumably because it was a quick, though not particularly efficient, operation against an easy target and not one of those guerrilla wars that drag on for years.

Not everyone was numb to the duplicity of the Reagan administration, however. The protests from church groups grew louder, and loudest of all was the Catholic Church. As a major pressure group with an impact on public opinion, the Catholic leadership could not be ignored. The problem, as Reagan officials saw it, was that you couldn't talk turkey to the bishops, who, unlike congressional critics, were immune to presidential demands that they shut up. Diplomacy had been tried repeatedly. At one point Haig, whose brother was a Jesuit priest, marshaled some high-ranking Catholics in the government, including Kirkpatrick and James Buckley, under secretary for security affairs, to jawbone a five-man delegation led by Archbishop James Hickey, head of the church in Washington, D.C., about El Salvador. It didn't work, and two days later Father Bryan Hehir, the foreign policy expert of the U.S. Catholic Conference and a member of Hickey's delegation, was telling Congress that the only solution to the Salvadoran conflict was to stop arms shipments and encourage talks between the government and the guerrillas. The Salvadoran bishops, he said, feared that more arms would only make more of them martyrs.

That kind of talk was hard to deal with, particularly when it came from an obviously sincere man of God. And it got worse as the *contra* war expanded, with a stream of Catholic leaders appearing on Capitol Hill, talking to important committees, buttonholing politicians, and generally raising hell. "Taking on the churches is really tough," complained Langhorne Motley, then assistant secretary of state for inter-American affairs, when in the spring of 1985 the House of Representatives, thanks largely to church lobbying, was about to vote down Reagan's request for military aid to the *contras*. Motley's replacement, Elliot Abrams, agreed: "The battle over Central America is a battle for the high moral ground, but it is much harder for us to win that battle when a lot of church groups are opposing us and saying we don't have it."

Hickey, for example, told Henry Kissinger's bipartisan presidential commission on Central America that the *contra* war was "unwise, unjustified and destructive." U.S. policy, he said, "neglects the root causes of the problems, strengthens the extremists of both right and left, relies on military force rather than diplomatic creativity and applies human rights standards only selectively." The U.S. bishops wanted Washington to cease supporting the *contras*, to engage in talks with the Sandinista government, and to resume aid to Nicaragua. They urged the United States to deemphasize military aid in Central America and to concentrate on economic and social reform. "The first requirement for future U.S. policy," said Hickey, "is to change the basic thrust of present policy and stop the drift toward a regional war in Central America."[26]

Coming from Hickey, this advice could not be dismissed as the ravings of the Catholic fringe. Politically moderate and theologically conservative, he nevertheless was an outspoken critic of the *contra* war because he had seen the results of U.S. militarism in El Salvador, where two of the murdered churchwomen had been working under his sponsorship when he headed the Cleveland church. If a centrist bishop like Hickey felt so strongly about the situation, maybe there was something in the church's complaints. Such was the conclusion of at least some members of Congress, who were persuaded against the *contra* war by the testimony of Catholic leaders.

The bishops also opposed as "provocative" the U.S. arms buildup in Honduras. In testimony before Senate and House committees their

representatives said that Washington's use of Honduras as a springboard
for the *contra* war "threaten[ed] the precarious peace" in Honduras while
increasing tensions throughout the region. But Defense Under Secretary
Fred C. Ikle scoffed at the idea that the Reagan administration would
use Honduran military facilities for anything but housing. "Let me emphasize," he said, "that these contingency facilities in Honduras are no
American bases but Honduran facilities to which we would have access.
Nor are they a precursor to a permanent U.S. military presence in the
region."[27] That was not the impression in Honduras, however. According
to *New York Times* reporter James LeMoyne, U.S. officials had admitted
that the situation might require a permanent U.S. presence. "We don't
want to be here forever," a U.S. military official told LeMoyne. "But it
could just turn out that, like South Korea, when all this is over, we remain
here."[28] (That such had been the intent was revealed in September 1988,
when the Honduran government sought congressional approval for permanent U.S. military bases.)

The U.S.-built facilities certainly suggested more than temporary
housing. They included nine combat airfields, two radar stations, roads,
tank traps, fuel storage areas, and air intelligence installations. Some
1,200 American troops were stationed on a revolving basis at or near the
Palmerola air base. In addition, more than 40,000 U.S. troops underwent
training in mock invasions of Nicaragua between 1983 and mid-1986.[29]
The bill to U.S. taxpayers for these activities was at least $100 million.

The consequences of this buildup were as clear to U.S. Ambassador
John Ferch as they were to the U.S. bishops. In mid-1986 Ferch was
removed from his post as ambassador to Honduras because of his misgivings about the military policy. "I always thought we meant what we
said," Ferch explained. "We wanted pressures [on the Sandinistas] so we
could negotiate. I'm beginning to think I accepted something that wasn't
true." He was dismissed, said Ferch, "because they [the Reagan admin-
istration] want somebody down there to be strong enough and proconsul
enough that no Honduran government is going to object to anything."[30]

The constant need to defend Central American policies from such
criticism had a wearing effect on administration spokesmen, who showed
their exasperation by resorting to the old tactic of smearing critics as
leftists. Opinion polls did not improve their tempers: Surveys showed a
steady increase of opposition to U.S. militarism in Central America, from
two-thirds at the start of Reagan's administration to an overwhelming
majority by the time of his second term. More than four-fifths of those

polled said they opposed a U.S. invasion of Nicaragua. Political analysts believed that such strong domestic opposition was primarily responsible for staying Reagan's hand.

As in Latin America, where the bishops had refused to halt their criticism of the military despite government blandishments and threats, the Reagan administration retaliated with the claim that the American bishops were playing politics. Assistant Secretary of State Motley denounced "religious persons [who] use the credibility they enjoy to market their personal, philosophical and political beliefs." According to Motley, it was "time to take politics out of the pulpit and the pulpit out of politics." Kirkpatrick and Vice President Bush also questioned the motives of church activists.[31]

But church leaders insisted that such politics had always been a religious mission. In pointing to the injustices and violence caused by Washington's warmongering in Central America, U.S. bishops were not saying that a particular party or political leader was wrong but that the policy was wrong. "Christians in the United States cannot ignore the cause of peace and justice in Central America," said Maryknoll Father Leo Sommer. "Our past policies have contributed to the present injustice by [encouraging] flagrant human rights abuses of 'friendly' dictators and military regimes. Christians cannot condone, much less materially support, violent movements attempting to hold back inevitable fundamental change in favor of a more just society. The application of our founding fathers' principle of freedom and justice for all will do more to counteract communist influence in the area than bombs and bullets."[32]

The basic issue, as Sommer pointed out, was not whether churches should be involved in politics but on which side the churches stood. Christians who opposed political and economic domination, Sommer argued, had to expect "the same kind of opposition met by Archbishop Helder Cámara of Brazil who said he was called a Christian when he fed the hungry but a communist when he questioned the reason for hunger."[33] Motley illustrated the archbishop's point when he charged that, by questioning Washington's policies in Central America, some U.S. churches had allowed themselves to be used "as window dressing" by Marxists.

Despite such rhetoric the U.S. bishops remained hostile to Reagan's Central American policies. In November 1987, during their annual conference, they again criticized the White House for failing to seek a diplomatic solution to the Central American wars, which they said had cost more than 150,000 lives, displaced nearly 2 million more, and caused hundreds of millions of dollars in damages. Washington was too preoccupied with Nicaragua, the bishops said, and had thus failed to perceive that "poverty, burdensome foreign debts and militarism plague the region. The issues of geopolitics which have so dominated the U.S. public discourse on Central America in recent years should be taken up directly with the principal sources of U.S. concern, the Soviet Union and Cuba. . . . We should not use Central American lives as pawns in a superpower struggle."

Like the Central American bishops, the U.S. hierarchy wanted Washington to support the peace process begun by the region's governments in 1987, but the White House would have none of it. The negotiations were "fatally flawed," according to Reagan, because they did not contain adequate guarantees that the Soviet Union and Cuba would stop supporting Nicaragua. On the eve of the December 1987 summit between Reagan and Soviet leader Mikhail Gorbachev, both admitted that Nicaragua had become an impediment to better relations. Gorbachev thought it ridiculous to claim that "the security of the United States is being threatened by the Sandinista regime," but Reagan insisted that Nicaragua was "one of the greatest obstacles" to cooperation with the Soviets. Nicaragua was therefore one of the subjects of talks between the two leaders in Washington. U.S. and Soviet officials said that Gorbachev proposed "reciprocal Soviet and American pledges to refrain from deliveries of weapons" to Central America. However, spokesmen for the Reagan administration said the White House was not interested in the offer and that it would not abandon its friends in the region.[34]

War and Peace

Although Reagan's Catholic supporters failed to persuade the Catholic hierarchy to accept Washington's viewpoint on Central America, they could claim some success in encouraging Rome to force the bishops to desist from a denunciation of nuclear deterrence. Concern about the arms race had been building for some time, but it was not until 1980, at a meeting of the bishops in Washington a few days after Reagan's election, that it crystallized into a determination to raise national consciousness about the nuclear threat. Philadelphia's conservative cardinal, John Krol, a close associate of John Paul II, had the previous year underlined the problem in testimony before the Senate Foreign Relations Committee. "Deterrence," he had said, "can be tolerated as a lesser evil than use, as long as serious negotiations are pursued, aimed at phasing out nuclear deterrence. If the pursuit of that goal is forsaken, the moral attitude of the Catholic Church would almost certainly have to shift to one of un-compromising condemnation of both use and possession of nuclear weapons."[35]

Already unhappy about U.S. policies in Central America, the bishops foresaw more dangers in Reagan's stubborn resistance to serious peace negotiations. Bishop Thomas Gumbleton, who was president of the U.S. chapter of the international Catholic peace group, Pax Christi, succeeded in getting an hour of discussion on the question added to the meeting's agenda. Forty-five bishops were members of Pax Christi, and several expressed their worries during the time allowed for debate. It might have ended there had only the Pax Christi group been concerned, but the sustained applause that greeted the discussion showed that a majority of the bishops believed it was time to take a stand.

Despite calls from popes, cardinals, and bishops for arms reduction by the major powers, successive U.S. governments had continued to stock the country's nuclear arsenal. The Soviets obviously had nothing to lose by ignoring the Catholic Church, but it was a different matter in the United States. Government officials therefore began to express concern over what the bishops might say on the subject. The administration was not worried about a statement as to the dangers of nuclear war, since yet another assertion of the obvious only meant that more weapons were needed to keep the peace. But the situation might turn awkward if the bishops were to say that the policy of deterrence was itself immoral because deterrence assumed a willingness to use arms—even in a first strike—that could destroy the world. A charge of that sort would lead inevitably to a call for nuclear arms reduction when the administration was committed to a buildup.

Following the pattern of consultation on Central American issues, a five-man committee was established to write a pastoral letter on the sub-ject under the leadership of then Archbishop Joseph Bernardin, former president of the bishops' conference. It broadened the teaching-listening experience by sponsoring two years of hearings and discussions on the arms buildup. Dialogue with different sectors within the church and with the wider society led to a national debate, often heated, that encouraged thousands of people to take the nuclear question seriously. Some bishops even distributed copies of drafts of the pastoral letter for comment by local groups, much as the Latin American bishops invited the Christian base communities to discuss important documents. The letter went through three drafts, each stage eliciting further debate and refinement, thus strengthening the final document and building support for its acceptance.

Government officials were among the many people asked for their opinions. Those approached included Secretary Haig, Defense Secretary Caspar Weinberger, and Eugene V. Rostow, director of the Arms Control and Disarmament Agency. But while the views of the administration were given a respectful hearing, they did not prevail. By the fall of 1982, when the second draft was published, it was clear that the bishops were about to identify nuclear deterrence as a "key element" in a "sinful situation."[36] Washington would therefore have to use its big guns. National Security Adviser William Clark, a former seminarian known in government circles as "Mr. Catholic," was commissioned to send the bishops a sharp critique of their draft, and General Vernon Walters, a right-wing Catholic who later became Reagan's ambassador to the United Nations, was dispatched to Rome to present the government's case to the pope.[37]

Meanwhile, Reagan's Catholic supporters hurriedly formed various committees composed of prominent right-wing writers, politicians, and church people to debunk the peace pastoral. The most important was the Weyrich-*Wanderer* network, which flooded Rome with letters of complaint. "I don't believe in bishops engaging in this sort of thing," said Weyrich of the discussion on nuclear war. "I will stop when they stop."[38]

Weyrich's "truth squads" worked hard to focus adverse attention on such peace bishops as Seattle's Archbishop Hunthausen, who had helped galvanize the bishops to write the letter on nuclear warfare. *The Wanderer* published no fewer than fifteen articles critical of Hunthausen in one year, all of which were sent to the Roman Curia, courtesy of the newspaper, which weekly airmailed two dozen free copies to the Vatican. A. J. Matt, Jr., editor and sole proprietor of *The Wanderer*, dismissed Hunthausen as "just off the wall. He's one of the many pacifists in the American hierarchy."[39] The paper's ally, Catholics United for the Faith (CUF), shared his view. (A fundamentalist wing of the U.S. Catholic Church, CUF specialized in sending to the Vatican damaging letters about American prelates it deemed objectionable.) Meanwhile, a group calling itself "Catholics United against Marxist Theology" ran newspaper ads urging Seattle Catholics to protest against Hunthausen by reducing church donations (Sunday collections actually increased). The group's spokesman, Danny L. Barrett, a Boeing Company employee, told the Seattle

Post-Intelligencer that its aim was to create a national network of opposition to Hunthausen that would send complaints to the Vatican. As noted by Rembert Weakland, the archbishop of Milwaukee and himself a right-wing target, such "slander" and "injustice" did not contribute to a "dialogue based on mutual trust and respect" but was aimed at "politiciz[ing] the church" through "dubious moral means."[40]

Events at the end of 1983 strengthened the impression that the Vatican was "constitutionally disposed" to believe such scandal. In an unusual move, the Vatican ordered an investigation of Hunthausen's conduct of archdiocesan affairs. Bishop Walter Sullivan, head of the Richmond, Virginia, diocese and, like Hunthausen, a highly vocal critic of the nuclear buildup, was also investigated. Hunthausen was later stripped of most of his powers. Many American Catholics, including bishops, were convinced that the archbishop's punishment did not reflect religious failings but was a warning to the U.S. hierarchy to cease its political activism.

While Weyrich's followers were gunning for Hunthausen, another group, the American Catholic Committee, rushed out a book, *Justice and War in the Nuclear Age,* which depicted the bishops as utopians, maybe even leftists, for failing to perceive that the only issue worth considering was the Russians' incalculable wickedness.[41] Founded in 1982 to deal with "the misinterpretation of Catholic teachings"—meaning misinterpretation by the bishops—the committee was headed by Philip F. Lawler, an official of the conservative Heritage Foundation, which had been founded by Weyrich with Coors money. Backup was provided by Robert R. Reilly, who had also worked for the Heritage Foundation before being appointed to the U.S. Information Agency to develop private-sector programs, such as a conference sponsored by the Catholic Committee that led to *Justice and War.* Among the committee's star attractions was John O'Connor, New York's future cardinal.

O'Connor was a member of the committee responsible for drafting the pastoral letter. As a naval chaplain, he had written extensively about the just-war theories of Saint Augustine, which the Catholic Church had traditionally used to rationalize war. He had friends in high military places, among them Defense Secretary Weinberger, with whom he corresponded about the pastoral letter. Claiming that he was backed by a "silent majority,"[42] O'Connor attempted to tone down the letter. He regretted the "preoccupation with the fear of nuclear warfare," and thought that chemical warfare might not be immoral, if the weapons were nonlethal. He also supported the Reagan administration's theory of limited nuclear wars, although American scientists had repeatedly pointed out that, with nuclear weapons, escalation to total war would be inevitable. He insisted that deterrence "worked," adding that "nuclear weapons may be with us until the end of time."[43]

O'Connor tried various tactics to get his views adopted, including a rewrite of the draft letter's section on deterrence and more than 100 other amendments to the document, all of which were eventually rejected. His only significant victory—changing the wording in the second draft from a "halt" to a "curb on" nuclear testing—proved ephemeral when the bishops' conference, voting on the final draft, insisted overwhelmingly that "halt" be restored. As Catholic writer Jim Castelli noted, the issue did not hang on a small semantic difference but meant "the difference between a freeze and a chill."[44]

O'Connor's objections were easily overridden, but the bishops found it more difficult to resist suggestions from the Vatican. John Paul had frequently spoken out against the nuclear arms buildup, but he had not gone so far as to condemn deterrence. Nor had he ever proposed unilateral nuclear disarmament, arguing that "peoples have a right and even a duty to protect their existence and freedom by proportionate means against an unjust aggressor." Although his statement in no way endorsed nuclear war, it was interpreted to mean, in the context of the just-war theory, that disarmament had to be balanced against the dangers of a people's subjugation by a foreign power. Deterrence could therefore be accorded conditional acceptance.[45]

The pope's viewpoint coincided with those of the French and West German hierarchies, which were among a dozen national churches to address the nuclear question in the early 1980s. Made nervous by their proximity to Russia, the Europeans refused to question deterrence. Political goals, they said, could be achieved by brandishing nuclear weapons with no intention of launching them. "The use of a threat of mass destruction . . . is regarded as being particularly effective for the purpose of preventing war," said the German bishops, adding that naturally the threat should never be carried out. It was all very well for the U.S. bishops to take a moralistic position, argued one French critic, but if they prevailed in discrediting deterrence, what would befall the European countries that depended on the U.S. nuclear missiles aimed at Russia to compensate for the weakness of conventional forces in NATO? To the Europeans, the U.S. bishops' letter smacked of pacifism.[46]

Nor was the Vatican happy with the emphasis on active nonviolence, which might be acceptable for individuals (though even that was questionable), but certainly not as a policy for states. In a meeting with Bernardin and other members of the drafting committee, Cardinal Casaroli, the Vatican secretary of state and spokesman for the European bishops, told the Americans there could be no parity between active nonviolence and the just war. "There is only one Catholic tradition: the just-war theory." Nor did Casaroli want the bishops to make so strong a denunciation that they might "create even greater difficulties for [government authorities] in an area so enormously difficult and so full of responsibility."[47]

The French and German bishops also made it clear that, in writing about nuclear war, they did not want to cause "difficulties" for their governments. Like the Vatican, they believed that the ultimate threat was the Soviet Union, not the destruction of the world. They also differed from the American bishops on political tactics, which were perhaps more important. A majority of the German and French bishops belonged to the don't-rock-the-boat school that advocated good relations with the state, particularly if the government happened to be Christian Democratic. The German church also depended on the state for the bulk of its income through official tithing of German taxpayers, who made annual payments to the church of their choice. European governments would obviously not be pleased if a sister church in the United States helped undercut the basis of their defense strategy by condemning the Reagan government. The Vatican also had much to lose since it relied on the United States to deal with Russia.

The American bishops' view was different because they were less concerned with the East-West ideological divide than with the possibility that the world might be blown up. Increasingly distrustful of their own government, they were less than sanguine about the ability of the Reagan administration to deal constructively with the problem. Moreover, they believed that the process of wide consultation used in drafting the letter—and notably absent in the preparation of the European bishops' statements—reflected what Jesuit writer Peter Henriot called the *sensus fidelium*, the spirit that moves in ordinary believers.[48] The letter was not the narrowly based work of a small committee of bishops but involved, in the words of one historian, "almost the entire church."[49] Thus, whatever their European detractors might think, the American bishops felt they were speaking for, as well as to, a majority of American Catholics.

As a result of European and American pressures, the Vatican's suggestions were incorporated into the final draft, including a reference to the "right to lawful self-defense," although the letter retained its original vision by granting only a "strictly conditioned moral acceptance" to deterrence. Such a policy could be no more than a temporary expedient to achieve "nuclear arms control, reductions and disarmament," said the bishops, in contrast to the French and German position that the threat of nuclear destruction was acceptable. The U.S. bishops also went on record against the first use of nuclear weapons and expressed profound skepticism about any "limited" nuclear war. Nevertheless, some bishops, notably those from the liberal archdiocese of Baltimore, objected to the moral loophole on deterrence.

The controversy continued into Reagan's second term when the President decided to take his case directly to the pope by establishing diplomatic relations with the Holy See. Relations were cordial from the start, since the two power centers shared an East-West vision of the world and compatible, if not identical, goals in certain areas, including Poland and Central America.

Although John Paul's approach to the nuclear issue was infinitely more subtle than Reagan's, the urge to centralize authority in the Vatican played into the President's hands. Until Vatican II the Roman Curia had kept tight control of the church's foreign policy, but the council encouraged local bishops to take more initiative in world affairs. The peace pastoral was a logical step in that direction, but the Curia, which had never approved of power-sharing, did not like its independent tone. The U.S. bishops were already out of step with the Vatican on Nicaragua, and the pastoral added to the impression that the Americans were not following their leader. The U.S. bishops had dutifully incorporated the Vatican's suggestions into the peace pastoral, but it was still tougher—franker—than the Holy See liked.

The process of consultation used to produce the letter also caused mutterings in Rome. The reason, as moral theologian Charles Curran observed, was that the peace pastoral was a "recognition . . . that dissent in the Roman Catholic Church is possible on complex, specific issues." He thought the letter was "bound to have repercussions in other areas of moral teaching and church life," and he was right.[50]

Coincidentally or not, Cardinal Joseph Ratzinger, the powerful head of the Vatican's Congregation for the Doctrine of the Faith, began to snipe at bishops' conferences and the concept of power-sharing with Rome, and by 1986, when a crackdown on the U.S. church was in full swing, the issue had become a major source of contention. One of the first to suffer Ratzinger's wrath was Curran, who on Rome's orders was fired from his teaching position at the Catholic University of America in Washington, D.C. Archbishop Hickey, head of the church in the Capital and one of the most eloquent advocates of the peace pastoral, was ordered to enforce the ban. He did so, warning that dissent would no longer be tolerated in the church.

U.S. Capitalism

Despite the retrenchment, a second pastoral letter by the bishops, on the U.S. economy, was not affected. Although it caused even more controversy in the United States than the peace pastoral had, the subject happened to be one on which John Paul took a liberal position. Moreover, even the most determined hawks in the U.S. hierarchy, including Cardinal O'Connor, took exception to the Reagan administration's view of society's responsibility for economic democracy. Nor did the bishops have to deal with such outdated church teachings as the just-war theory. On the contrary, Catholic social teaching on economics was politically advanced, even radical. Equally important was the growing belief, in business as well as academic circles, that the divorce of economics from any value system had led to serious problems. One had only to read the daily newspaper accounts of merger mania, crooked bankers, Wall Street insider trading, widespread bribery, and countless other illegalities to realize that something was amiss.

Some religious scholars and political scientists believe that the prime cause of such immorality is the compartmentalization of political, economic, and moral-cultural systems. Each system follows its own logic, with only the most tenuous connection among religion, economics, and politics. Civil religion holds society together by providing a minimum standard for behavior: People may not kill one another, or covet their neighbor's wife, but they may deprive a neighbor of his economic due—and be called "smart operators" by a society that has made money its chief idol. The result is a system that John Maynard Keynes called "absolutely irreligious."

Although critics of the bishops' economic pastoral focused on specific recommendations, such as government welfare programs, the underlying reason for their hostility was the American church's clear intention to make a connection between the country's economic and religious systems.

Wealthy Americans, particularly well-heeled Catholics, did not want to be reminded of the rich man's problems with the eye of a needle. Nevertheless, the fact that protesting groups were unable to attract much support, even in the business community, suggested that the bishops had correctly gauged a need in society for a religious dimension to the economic debate. "For us in the United States the separation of church and state cannot be interpreted to mean that there is a separation of economic issues from religious issues, but, rather, that we must have a concern for all those socio-economic issues that touch the quality of human life," explained Milwaukee's Archbishop Weakland, chairman of the pastoral letter's drafting committee. "We are concerned by what an economic system does to people and for people and how it permits people to participate in it."[51] Archbishop Roger Mahony of Los Angeles put it vividly: "Economic institutions are not like mountains, created by forces of nature. They are like houses and cities, created by our own choices. That is why they are our responsibility."[52]

As Mahony, Weakland, and other bishops took pains to emphasize, there was nothing new in the Catholic Church's concern with the connections between religion and economics. The pastoral letter followed a long tradition of church teaching on economics and social justice, dating to the 1891 encyclical *Rerum Novarum* (*The Condition of the Working Classes*) by Pope Leo XIII in support of labor unions and the right of workers to a living wage. "When there is a question of defending the rights of individuals, the poor and badly off have a claim to especial consideration," the pope had written. "The richer class have many ways of shielding themselves, and stand less in need of help from the state; whereas the mass of the poor have no resources of their own to fall back upon, and must chiefly depend upon the resources of the state."[53]

Leo's encyclical also established the principle of "subsidiarity," meaning that higher political bodies should give help (*subsidium*) to lower ones when needed, though not replace them. Thus the state should intervene when problems were beyond the capacity of bodies that served as intermediaries between the individual citizen and the central government as, for example, to guarantee a minimum wage. Although subsidiarity provided for institutional pluralism among a multitude of citizen groups, it in no way supported the theory that the government which governs least governs best.

In a 1919 statement based on *Rerum Novarum* that foreshadowed the economic pastoral, the American bishops had urged the government to recognize labor rights, a minimum wage, progressive taxation, and controls on monopolies. Although the statement was far ahead of Catholic opinion at the time, virtually all the bishops' recommendations finally became law under Franklin D. Roosevelt.

A dozen years later, in the midst of the Depression, Pope Pius XI issued *Quadragesimo Anno* (*On Reconstructing the Social Order*), which criticized excessive concentration of wealth and encouraged greater cooperation between workers and owners. The encyclical was subsequently cited by Pope John XXIII as confirming "the right and duty of the Catholic Church to make its irreplaceable contribution to the correct solution of the pressing and grave problems that beset the entire human family."[54] John used that "right and duty" as the basis of his landmark encyclical on human rights, *Peace on Earth,* in which he gave equal weight to economic rights to food, clothing, shelter, rest, medical care, a just wage, social security, and other social benefits. Meanwhile, Vatican II published *Pastoral Constitution on the Church in the Modern World,* which attempted to show how the church could make the world more humane by promoting religious values in society's multiple institutions. An entire chapter was devoted to economic and social life. It ended with this admonition: "Christians who take an active part in present-day socioeconomic development and fight for justice and charity should be convinced that they can make a great contribution to the prosperity of humankind and to the peace of the world."[55]

Pope Paul VI continued the debate with his encyclical *On the Development of Peoples,* which examined the causes of worldwide poverty and proposed more equitable terms of trade and multilateral economic aid for the developing nations. But perhaps the most sophisticated of all the papal writings on economics was *Laborem Exercens,* or *On Human Work,* by John Paul II. Published in 1981, the encyclical decried the tendency of unregulated capitalism to reduce workers to instruments of production and insisted upon the primacy of labor as the foundation of all economic rights. The encyclical, which continued Paul's analysis of the underlying causes of poverty, displayed an understanding of the failings of both capitalism and communism in their tendency to instrumentalize labor. Human dignity, said John Paul, demanded that labor be seen as a creative experience and therefore a reflection of the creativity of God: "In the final analysis, it is always man who is *the purpose of the work,* whatever work it is that is done by man—even if the common scale of values rates it as the merest 'service,' as the most monotonous, even the most alienating work."[56] The encyclical also questioned the absolute right of ownership of property and the means of production. "Christian tradition has never upheld this right as absolute and untouchable," argued the pope. "On the contrary, it has always understood this right within the broader context of the right common to all to use the goods of the whole of creation; *the right to private property is subordinated to the right to common use,* to the fact that goods are meant for everyone."[57]

Like other papal encyclicals, particularly *Peace on Earth* and *Development of Peoples, Human Work* stressed the church's special love for the poor. That same concern was reflected throughout the Medellín Documents, issued by the Latin American bishops in 1968, which placed the region's church on a new course for social justice. A key phrase in the documents—"a preferential option for the poor"—would later set the tone for the U.S. bishops' letter on the economy. As explained by Chicago's Cardinal Bernardin, the phrase "summarizes several biblical themes: It calls the church to speak for the poor, to see the world from their perspective and to empty itself so it may experience the power of God in the midst of poverty and powerlessness." The roots of the church's role as advocate of the poor "are found in the prophets who teach us to ask questions about how we organize our life as a society," he said.[58]

John Paul took up the same theme on visits to the United States and Canada. Instead of congratulating Americans on their economic achievements, he reminded them of the gospel parable of Lazarus and the rich man and how it applied to the needs of "the poor of the United States and of the world." The poor "are your brothers and sisters in Christ," he told a crowd of 80,000 at New York's Yankee Stadium. "You must never be content to leave them just the crumbs from the feast. You must take of your substance, and not just of your abundance, in order to help them."[59] The pope was even more outspoken on a tour of Canada when he spoke of the "poor South and the rich North." In a declaration that columnist Colman McCarthy described as sounding like a *Pravda* editorial, John Paul said that the rich nations would be judged by the poor for their "imperialistic monopoly of economic and political supremacy at the expense of others."[60]

The Pauperization of America

The idea of writing a pastoral on the U.S. economy originated in 1980 at the same bishops' meeting that initiated the letter on war and peace. Bishop Peter Rosazza of Hartford, who worked with Connecticut's poor, raised the question of whether the bishops should not look at their own capitalistic system in view of an earlier statement they had made against Marxism. A majority agreed with him, particularly since the incoming administration promised to roll back many of the New Deal's achievements. A drafting committee was appointed under the leadership of Archbishop Weakland. He could speak of the dehumanization of poverty from personal experience, both as a child growing up in an impoverished family during the Depression and from his travels in Third World countries. William Weigand, also a committee member, shared a similar outlook acquired during ten years of service in a poverty-stricken *barrio* in Colombia. When appointed bishop of Salt Lake City, he elected to live in one of its poorest neighborhoods. Other committee members included Rosazza; George Speltz, the bishop of St. Cloud, Minnesota, who held a degree in economics; and Atlanta's Archbishop Thomas A. Donnellan, whose career began under New York's Cardinal Spellman, famous for his conservative financial management. Assisted by top economists from the University of Notre Dame, Harvard, and other academic centers, they undertook a five-year consultation process that ran to more than 150 hearings as well as meetings with Third World bishops.

As with the peace letter, the process was intended to achieve the broadest possible consensus and to teach Catholics that there were moral aspects to the business of getting and spending. Weakland said that one of the committee's first discoveries was that few Americans understood the positive and negative effects on other countries of the U.S. economic system. There was an urgent need, he said, "for more general understanding of the economic picture of the world."[61]

Three priorities emerged in the drafting of the letter: to define the basic needs of the poor, to give the poor priority over privileged wealth, and to use wealth and talent to fulfill human needs. The emphasis on the poor responded in part to the church's social teachings, but as consultation proceeded into Reagan's second term, it also became clear that the pauperization of the nation itself demanded attention. By the government's own definition, 33.7 million people, or almost one American in seven, were poor—an increase of 33 percent since 1980, when Reagan was elected. Structural unemployment was 7 percent, a level considered intolerable by earlier administrations. Nearly one-quarter of all American farmers had been forced off their land, many by bank foreclosures. Statistics from the Federal Reserve Board and the Internal Revenue Service showed that, in the same period, the rich had grown richer. One half of one percent of U.S. households possessed 35 percent of the nation's wealth, a rise of 10 percent from the mid-1960s. Two percent of all families held 54 percent of the country's net financial assets. Such concentration of wealth had not been seen since the Depression. Meanwhile, racial minorities, women, and children were steadily growing poorer. According to the Census Bureau, the median net worth of white households was more than eleven times that of black households and almost eight times that of Hispanic ones.

Studies by the Congressional Research Service and the Congressional Budget Office showed that the quality of life for children had declined dramatically. More than one-fifth of all children in the United States lived in poverty, in part because of the government's failure to provide sufficient money for food and health care. (Although total funding had increased, the small additions did not offset inflation or population growth. The result was a net loss to the individual child.) Another major factor was the increase in families headed by women: Nearly two-fifths of female-headed white households were below the poverty line; the figure for female-headed black families was a shocking two-thirds. The Congressional Research Service also found that 20 percent of the country's impoverished children lived in families in which at least one person was steadily employed, belying "the widespread view that a full-time job throughout the year is near-insurance against poverty."[62]

Bishops did not have to hold doctorates in economics, said Cardinal Bernardin, to see that the "disproportionate burden of poverty on women and children is appalling. The church cannot simply address the problem of the feminization of poverty through its own resources. It must also stand in the public debate for such programs as child care, food stamps, and aid to families with children. I do not contend that existing programs are without fault or should be immune from review. [But] something like them is a fundamental requirement of a just society."[63]

One reason for such statistics, the bishops would argue in their pastoral letter, was the excessive military buildup. While some of these expenditures might have been necessary, they said, elements in the defense budget were "both wasteful and dangerous for world peace." In short, defense funding had risen at the cost of social programs for the needy. As shown by the simultaneous drafting of the peace and economic pastoral letters, the bishops saw the link.

A Preferential Option for the Poor

In taking up their cause, the church tried to create for the poor a protective space in society. "The poor must be the objects of our charity but more so of our justice," explained Archbishop Weakland. "The prime purpose of [a] special commitment to the poor is to enable them to become active participants in the life of society. It is to enable all people to share in and to contribute to the common good."[64]

Such a commitment meant two things, both difficult in the context of American culture but nevertheless key issues in the final version of the pastoral letter issued at the end of 1986. One was the letter's inclusion of economic rights in the list of fundamental human rights. Securing such rights was a moral imperative, said the bishops: "That so many people are poor in a nation as rich as ours is a social and moral scandal that we cannot ignore."[65]

Economic rights had formed part of the Catholic Church's social teachings since Pope John's *Peace on Earth,* and the bishops were thus on firm ecclesiastical ground. Nevertheless, the letter's critics claimed that the American bishops wanted to turn the United States into a socialist state in which economic rights would be conferred at the cost of individual freedoms. In fact, the bishops wanted no such thing. They called for a flexible mixed economy that could be adjusted to obtain the greatest benefit for all, through fiscal, monetary, and other reforms that they spelled out.

Obviously not all economic and social claims are equal. But most people would agree that certain of them are fundamental—for example, the right to eat. The principal objection to fulfilling such rights is a practical one—whether the United States can really afford to overcome the basic causes of misery. Critics of the bishops' pastoral said it couldn't be done, but others pointed to the need for caution in dismissing certain rights because they called for major reform of the status quo. Catholic theologians asserted that "what may have to give way is not the voice of those denied their rights, but the economic and political structures which make justice 'impractical.' "[66]

That assertion led to the pastoral letter's second major challenge— a plea for conversion. Although the letter addressed the economic problems of the middle class, particularly of those on the edge of poverty, the bishops said they hoped the middle class would also be challenged. Archbishop Weakland charged that "we are all infected with the capitalist dream that there will be no end to our material wealth and prosperity, that somehow the fulfillment of that dream is owed to us, that we too should live like the characters of *Dallas* and *Falcon Crest*." Political leaders did not want to admit that there might be limits to such a dream, he said, or that "the quest for it could lead to more and more conflict on this globe." But if politicians couldn't—wouldn't—say such things, religious leaders had to. "We are being challenged today to state what our concepts of success really are, what our hopes and desires consist in, what true fulfillment in the biblical sense is all about," Weakland said. "For these reasons we are being forced again to ask the question about justice for all and, especially for us Christians, what it means to be disciples of Christ and one to whom the Beatitudes are important also for our day."[67]

One way to achieve a more communitarian vision, the bishops believed, was to encourage a more biblical people. Thus the pastoral letter on the economy made frequent reference to the Scriptures. As Archbishop Mahony observed, "Jesus did not have a naive or fanciful view of poverty. On the contrary, his concern was that everyone should have, now, what he or she needs. It was for this reason he set his face against every kind of possessiveness, and longed for a new kind of community where there would no longer be divisions into rich and poor, or powerful and helpless."[68]

But even with its biblical appeal and a carefully planned follow-up program of teaching, Weakland admitted, the economic letter would take years, perhaps generations, to be accepted, because acceptance meant conversion. Citing his own experience, he said that efforts to connect rich suburban parishes with central-city ones on more than a we'll-give-you-money basis usually failed. "That's frightening because that means people don't share ideals, hopes. They are so far apart, not just in lifestyles but in underlying values."[69] Church surveys agreed with Weakland's assessment. They showed that Catholics were not personally communitarian although they expected their parishes to be. On such close-to-home issues as food banks for the hungry or shelter for the homeless, Catholics followed their religious instinct and conscience. But on the broader economic issues that were ultimately responsible for such poverty they reacted like purely secular Americans.

Many could agree with at least some of the bishops' recommendations in the pastoral letter as, for example, measures to achieve full employment; progressive taxation; increased welfare benefits, particularly for poor families; cuts in defense spending; and a better deal for the Third

World countries, which were being asphyxiated by a $1-trillion foreign debt, much of it owed to U.S. banks. The bishops argued that the government had not developed a comprehensive employment strategy and proposed a series of measures to deal with the problem, including the expansion of job-training and apprenticeship programs, particularly in the educational and service sectors; adjustments in the minimum wage and social benefits to encourage welfare recipients to become self-sufficient; and a restructuring of federal farm programs and tax benefits to aid small- and medium-sized farmers instead of large ones. While the recommendations were broad ones, they raised questions about many areas of the economy, from the environment to stockholders and labor unions. The bishops did not pretend to offer a blueprint for specific problems but to challenge Americans to produce creative new ideas to deal with them. They also reminded corporate managers that economic decisions had a moral dimension.[70]

Although the bishops' proposals had no immediate effect, they stirred up a moral debate on economics. The pace of reform might be slow, but history showed that it did move forward. Archbishop Weakland predicted that positive results from the economic letter could not be expected before the year 2000: That was approximately the same span of time that had passed between the bishops' proposals for economic reforms in 1919 and the New Deal programs of President Roosevelt.

The "Novak Club"

Long before the third and final draft of *Economic Justice for All* was published, business and political critics began to organize the counter-attack. As with the pastoral letter on war and peace, the most common charges against the bishops were that they were playing politics and/or were idiots.

Believing it had reacted too slowly to the peace pastoral, the Reagan administration urged its friends to "be out front on this one,"[71] in the words of a top White House adviser. The cue was immediately picked up by the American Catholic Committee, which had also generated criticism of the letter on nuclear warfare. A Lay Commission of twenty-seven prominent conservative Catholics was hastily formed under the direction of William E. Simon, President Ford's treasury secretary, to debunk the economic pastoral even before the first draft was circulated. Michael Novak was asked to oversee the writing of the commission's defense of capitalism. Other committee members included Peter Grace, chairman of the chemical giant W. R. Grace; former Secretary of State Haig; Frank Shakespeare, then vice-chairman of RKO General and later U.S. ambassador to the Vatican; and the perennial Cold Warrior Clare Boothe Luce. The two token labor representatives—Edward Cleary, president of the New York State AFL-CIO, and John Henning, executive secretary-treasurer of the California Labor Federation—resigned early in the game. Cleary, who called the group the "Michael Novak Club," said that "the more I found out about the committee the more I realized it was Novak trying to slam the bishops' statement before it even appeared." Considered a comparatively conservative figure in labor politics, Cleary said he had welcomed the invitation to sit on the lay commission. Then Novak started sending members "copies of all his books," Cleary recalled, and "the more I read of his stuff, the more I realized that he represents everything I detest." The lay commission "wasn't really interested in learning labor's position," he complained. "It was like our good President: They wanted one or two labor people around so they could say that they listen to labor."[72]

Unfazed, Novak tried to make a case for "democratic capitalism," a pet theory of his, according to which democracy and capitalism were the same—a claim economists and political scientists contested. When John Paul had criticized capitalism, he had not meant the United States, said Novak, but aberrations practiced in Europe. In any case, capitalism was the last, best hope for the poor: "The aim of capitalism has been to overcome the tyranny of poverty," announced the Lay Commission's letter. That must have been news to Wall Street, where it was generally thought that the aim of capitalism was to make money. "It is not compassionate capitalism for which Novak et al. speak," countered Leon Wieseltier, literary editor of *The New Republic*. "They speak for capitalism most cruelly constructed." They wanted no controls on business, objected to government aid to the poor, and insisted that economic rights did not exist. Novak was a good spokesman for the breed, a man, said Wieseltier, who had managed to describe "the tale of the suffering servant in Isaiah as a parable of 'the modern business corporation,' which is 'a much despised incarnation of God's presence in the world.' "[73]

Although the bishops had tried to be accommodating by meeting with representatives of the Simon/Novak group and with Novak himself on several occasions, the hierarchy disliked its confrontational tactics and its refusal to recognize the church's social teachings on economics. Novak, for example, claimed that the notion of economic rights had originated at the United Nations, which everyone knew was a front for questionable Third World governments. In fact, the concept derived from *Peace on Earth*. Catholics also complained that the name of the Lay Commission was presumptuous, suggesting that it represented the entire U.S. laity when, said Bishop Francis Stafford, of Memphis, Tennessee, its members comprised a small "faction" that did not want to accept papal teachings on social questions. "What is its legitimacy?" questioned Peter Steinfels, then editor of *Commonweal*. "How does the Lay Commission speak for laity any more than *Commonweal* does, except that the Lay Commission has a lot of money to put out press releases and hold hearings?"[74]

Church sources said that by jumping the gun in publishing their letter before that of the bishops, the Lay Commission made a serious mistake. "They overreacted, and they talked about things that weren't even in the pastoral letter," said Jesuit Peter Henriot, of the Washington-based Center of Concern, who closely followed the drafting process.[75] They also put the bishops' backs up. At a meeting on the first draft of their letter, a majority of the prelates concurred with Pennsylvania's Bishop Michael Murphy, who urged Weakland's committee to stick to its guns: "Right on! Tighten up. Don't back off."[76]

While a second critique of the pastoral by the Lay Commission sank without a trace, like-minded antagonists kept up a steady barrage of insults. Yet another "alternative" pastoral letter was produced by Father Rueda, the Cuban exile priest who had helped organize the attack on Archbishop Hunthausen under Weyrich's sponsorship. According to Rueda, economic inequality was a fundamental moral virtue of capitalism, not a negative by-product. In a novel reading of Catholic social teaching, he announced that "inequality among men is not only a natural condition, but one that has been willed by God." The trouble with the church, Rueda concluded, was that it had been "infiltrated" by "radicals" and "secular humanists."[77]

Although most critics stopped short of suggesting that the bishops were communists, many were convinced that the hierarchy was playing Democratic politics by proposing economic solutions at odds with Reaganomics. Novak summed up the complaints by charging that the pastoral read "more like the platform of a political party than like a moral statement." The "tone" of the letter was "whiney"—a term frequently used by conservatives to describe those who worried about the poor—and the Democrats were "whiney," too.[78] But Archbishop Weakland had the last word. Noting that the bishops had deliberately withheld publication of the first draft of the letter until after the 1984 presidential election (as they would also withhold publication of the final version until after the 1986 congressional race), Weakland dryly observed that "Christian—and Jewish—concerns for the poor predate the election by several thousand years." The letter, he said, "is not a political instrument of either the Democratic or Republican party. It is not the church's role to come up with economic theories and solutions or take partisan positions, but the church has to be concerned about how economic issues affect the lives of people. Not to do that would be to shirk what religion is all about."[79]

Defeated on that approach, the claque tried another: The bishops were "economically illiterate." They were quacks who had no right to speak on economics because seminary training did not include the subject. They didn't know what was going on, sniped William F. Buckley, Jr., as anyone could see from their childlike innocence on economic questions. But this attack did not prosper either, because most of the critics, including Buckley, also lacked any claim to prominence in the discipline of economics. In any case, economic competence could be acquired by other means. The bishops on the drafting committee had had considerable administrative experience in meeting large payrolls and supervising sizable networks of personnel. (Weakland, for example, oversaw 500 monasteries around the globe during his ten years as head of the Benedictine order; in Milwaukee he was responsible for the administration of 268 parishes with nearly 700,000 communicants.) The bishops had interviewed dozens of experts over several years of hearings. They did not claim to be economic experts, but they felt they were competent to attempt a moral analysis of economic justice. Felix Rohatyn, a partner of Wall Street's Lazard Frères and an often visionary financier, agreed: "Their ideas may not be politically fashionable," he said, "but that doesn't take away from the moral weight of their argument. The issues are still valid."[80]

Perhaps the greatest service provided by the bishops to the American people, Catholic or otherwise, was their willingness to deal with so abstruse a subject as economics. Although it affects everyone's life, many feel incompetent to question the wisdom of the self-designated experts. But economics is not an exact science like physics—the fall of interest rates is less predictable than the fall of an apple—because it deals with an unpredictable subject, people. Human beings are at the center of economic systems, argued the bishops, and people can and should be concerned with economic justice, for the sake of themselves as well as others. The long consultation process with the laity that led up to the final draft helped spread that message in many sectors, particularly Catholic universities, which the bishops singled out for a larger role in the teaching of social and economic justice. They also recognized that while American Catholics could be "justly proud" of the vast network of churches, schools, and hospitals they had built, it was time to put more effort into the teaching of values, for without values there could be no economic justice. As a sign of their commitment, the bishops promised to respect the rights of church employees—for example, to bargain collectively; to pay just wages; and to use church property and investments for the benefit of the community, especially the poor.

A Seamless Garment

Reaction to the bishops' positions on military spending and economic reforms was mixed, not only because of the varying responses to the questions raised but also because it was impossible to place a neat ethical label on the hierarchy. Many liberals were pleased with the pastoral letters, but found themselves in opposition to the bishops' position on abortion. Similarly, pro-lifers applauded the bishops on the abortion question but disagreed with their criticism of the arms buildup and capital punishment. It was indicative of the complex pattern of dissent that the bishops were denounced by such extreme-right Catholic organs as *The Wanderer* for failing to give abortion priority over nuclear warfare while, at the other end of the spectrum, Catholics for a Free Choice, a Washington lobbying group, launched a Bishops Watch campaign to pressure the hierarchy into softening its objections to abortion.

Most of the bishops did not want to get sidetracked by the "single issue" approach, preferring Cardinal Bernardin's "seamless garment" argument, which committed the church to take action on a range of concerns affecting human dignity, from birth to death. A patient diplomat who spoke for the mainstream of the American church, Bernardin argued that moral consistency called for the defense of both the right to life and the quality of life. "The consistent ethic of life theme is based on a fundamental moral value, namely the sacredness of human life and our responsibility to protect and promote human life," he told Catholic writer Eugene Kennedy. "Take that value away and there is nothing left. The ethic shows a linkage among these issues, but it does not collapse all these issues into one, nor does it propose one solution for all these problems. While there is linkage, each of these issues is different, and each requires its own distinct moral analysis and . . . solution." Thus capital punishment could not be equated with abortion, nor abortion with nuclear war. Yet all were challenges to "a continuum of life." Moral criteria, said Bernardin, "will not lead to crystal-clear judgments on [political] candidates," who might follow the church's teachings on one issue, such as abortion, but not on another as, for example, capital punishment. Still, it was a good place to begin thinking about "a better way to engage the attention of the nation regarding the intersection of moral vision, public policy and political choices."[81]

CHAPTER 8

✠

THE ROMAN RESTORATION
IN THE UNITED STATES

THE AMERICAN BISHOPS' COMMITMENT to justice and peace gained the hierarchy unprecedented visibility as well as the respect of important sectors of opinion, if not that of the political right. This was largely due to the reasoned style of the bishops' arguments, which were based on widespread consultation with the laity and depended on persuasion rather than compulsion. In contrast, the papacy's influence steadily declined in the 1980s because John Paul refused to consider other viewpoints and because he did not follow Cardinal Bernardin's advice to explain the reasons for the Vatican's often incomprehensible decisions. Archbishop Weakland put the matter bluntly: "An authoritarian style is counterproductive," he told the pope on his trip to the United States in the fall of 1987.[1]

The visit culminated a series of set-tos between the American church and the Vatican, and the tensions showed. Although millions of believers turned out for John Paul's cross-country tour, it was "the singer they celebrated, not the song," said *Newsweek*'s religion editor, Kenneth L. Woodward.[2] As on his trips to the Third World, John Paul drew crowds wherever he went, but they either ignored his message or forgot it as soon as he left. Pickets and demonstrations, principally in San Francisco, showed that some did not like what they heard: "Curb your dogma," demanded the placards. Although bishops, religious, and lay leaders pleaded for more dialogue in the church, John Paul did not listen. Instead of responding to the questions raised in the prepared speeches, he emphasized his own agenda. The church was not Vatican II's "People of God" but "we bishops with the clergy, religious and laity." Nor was dissent legitimate. It was a "grave error," said the pope, to believe that those who selectively dissented from church teachings (i.e., on birth control) could still be "good Catholics." Although Archbishop Daniel Pilarczyk of Cincinnati hastened to reassure Catholics that those who dissented were not "out of the church," John Paul was known to say what he meant, even if his listeners did not always understand him.[3] Eight years after his first trip to the United States, it was difficult to pretend that John Paul's message was not clear: "No, no, no."

The Hunthausen Case

Unlike the pope's 1979 visit to the United States, which got rave reviews, reaction to his second trip was mixed or negative because it had finally sunk into the collective consciousness that John Paul was determined to discipline the American church. Signs of the coming storm were evident in the early 1980s, when Rome attempted to discipline American nuns, but what brought home the conflict was the punishment of Seattle's Archbishop Raymond Hunthausen, who was stripped of his powers in 1986.

Short and balding, Seattle's mild-mannered archbishop hardly seemed well cast for the leading role in a religious *cause célèbre*. But beneath the gentleness runs a maverick streak that has led Hunthausen to speak out on controversial issues in an attempt to live up to a demanding faith, whether or not he is misunderstood. Six years after taking over the archdiocese in 1975, he burst onto the national scene by urging Catholics to withhold half their federal income taxes in protest against the arms buildup.[4] Neither Hunthausen's suggestions nor a like appeal by the bishop of Amarillo, Texas, had much effect on the laity, but they were influential in encouraging the American bishops to address the subject in their controversial letter on war and peace. Hunthausen, meanwhile, put words into action by withholding that part of his taxes which he calculated would be earmarked for defense spending. The act was symbolic—the Internal Revenue Service garnisheed his salary for the amount—but it provoked the animosity of Seattle's powerful defense industry and of right-wing Catholics, who launched a campaign against him in Rome.

Hunthausen has always tempered his bold convictions with personal humility. He is well liked by his fellow bishops, many of whom follow the same collegial style of administration and uphold a respect for religious and political pluralism, even if they are not prepared to go so far as to withhold federal taxes. They shared the archbishop's fear of a nuclear war and distrust of Reagan's White House.

Unlike his peers, however, the Roman Curia was prepared to believe the worst of Seattle's archbishop, perhaps because he is so thoroughly

American in his tolerance of religious and social diversity. In 1983 the Vatican responded to Hunthausen's critics by initiating an investigation of his conduct, thereby sending a chilling message to the American church.

In the peculiarly medieval fashion whereby the Vatican undertakes such inquiries, the accused is not allowed to know the charges, has no access to the proceedings, and is not shown the results. Essentially, the accused is permitted no means of defense. Thus for two years Hunthausen was kept in the dark about interviews conducted in his own archdiocese. Documents describing his conduct were sent to Rome without his knowledge, and he was not permitted to see the final report.

Although he refused to speak about the investigation while it was in progress, the experience was obviously humiliating to a deeply spiritual man who passionately loved the church. It cost him "incalculable pain," said a fellow bishop. Hunthausen himself later acknowledged that "the long days" had been "extremely trying and agonizing ones for me." At one point, when asked if he had considered resigning, Hunthausen hesitated, then said he preferred not to answer the question. "I'm just as human as anyone else," he admitted, adding that he had gone through "the whole gamut of emotions" during the investigation.[5] In December 1984, midway through the inquiry, he suffered a heart attack.

When a summary of the results of the investigation was eventually made public at the end of 1985 by Archbishop Pio Laghi, the Vatican's representative to the United States, it only added to the confusion and distrust that had strained relations between Rome and the American church. Although Laghi praised Hunthausen for his "apostolic zeal," he listed several areas of Vatican concern—matters having to do with church teaching on sexual norms, the sacraments, and seminaries for the formation of priests. Such concerns, said Father Michael G. Ryan, then chancellor and vicar general of the Seattle archdiocese, were in effect a "list of the discussion and debate going on everywhere" in the United States.

Among the areas listed by the Vatican were the need for clear church teaching on the indissolubility of marriage and a tightening up of annulment procedures, the practice of general absolution for large groups instead of individual confession, and the participation of non-Catholics in communion at weddings and funerals. The Vatican also questioned the right of homosexuals to church services. A fifth concern was the archdiocese's seminary program, although it had been viewed as a potential model by diocesan vocation offices throughout the country. Not mentioned in Laghi's letter, but clearly to be read between the lines, was the Vatican's disapproval of Hunthausen's active support of greater participation by women in the church.

The problem with the Vatican's Seattle "concerns," as American critics were quick to point out, was that the same accusations could be leveled at many U.S. dioceses, which had taken a more understanding attitude than Rome toward broken marriages, ecumenism, and women's rights. Moreover, national polls by church and secular organizations showed that a majority of American Catholics favored such liberalization.[6] So why was Hunthausen singled out?

Many in Seattle found the answer in the archbishop's antinuclear stand. "It's very obvious that he was targeted by conservative groups nationally," said Father Marlin Connole, pastor of St. Therese's parish. "It's interesting [that] the bishops who have been investigated so far are actively involved in the nuclear issue."[7]

But the pope himself had spoken out against the nuclear threat, so there had to be more reason for the attack on Hunthausen than his aggressive peace stance. It was also possible that by singling out the archbishop, rightist Catholics had provided the Vatican with a convenient whipping boy for all the perceived ills in the American church. Such was the belief of Bishop Walter Sullivan, of Richmond, Virginia, who was also humiliated by a Vatican investigation, albeit with less spectacular repercussions. Sullivan told *Sojourners* magazine that Hunthausen's punishment "on ecclesiastical issues" made no sense unless it was related to the peace question, since many other dioceses followed similar religious practices.[8] Hunthausen did not represent a politically powerful see with millions of Catholics, nor was Seattle important to the Vatican's finances, by comparison, say, with Chicago or New York. His ecclesiastical positions made him vulnerable to Vatican discipline, and his stand on the nuclear issue assured that any moves the Roman Curia made against him would be endorsed in the United States by right-wing Catholics and powerful business interests. He was, as they say in Rome, dispensable.

After publicly revealing his alleged sins, the Vatican claimed that the case was "concluded," but in fact it was just beginning. A week after Archbishop Laghi's announcement, another was made: Hunthausen, who had for more than three years been petitioning Rome for an auxiliary bishop to help him, was to get his wish, but with a slap in the face. The newly appointed auxiliary, Bishop Donald Wuerl, turned out to be a Romanized American with ten years of Curia training who had taken part in an earlier Vatican investigation of U.S. seminaries. Hunthausen was not consulted about the appointment; on the contrary, he was told that he had no legal right to a voice in the matter.

Rumors that Wuerl had been sent to act as a "Vatican watchdog" spread fast in Seattle, but Wuerl denied them. "I report only to the archbishop," said Wuerl at his first press conference. "He is the head of the church in Seattle."[9] The archbishop thought so, too, until a dispute arose between the two men in March 1986, when Hunthausen wanted the archdiocese to support a proposed county ordinance that would protect the job rights of minorities, including homosexuals, and Wuerl dissented. When he agreed to have Wuerl as his auxiliary, the archbishop said, he had made it clear to Rome that he could not accept the imposition of an assistant with extraordinary powers, and indeed such arrangements were so rare that a Vatican spokesman, when asked to cite a precedent, could not recall a single example. Nevertheless, Wuerl had in fact received far-ranging authority over the Seattle archdiocese before his investiture as a bishop by the pope at the beginning of 1986. And when Hunthausen took his case to Archbishop Laghi, he received written confirmation of Wuerl's "complete and final decision-making power" from Rome's Congregation for Bishops.

A candid, approachable man, the archbishop found it impossible to pretend that he had not been stripped of his powers, and in September he sent a letter to Seattle's Catholics that spelled out his predicament, saying that it was "necessary for me to make the entire matter public." The reaction was overwhelming anger against Rome for its shoddy treatment of Hunthausen. A statement signed by more than 140 priests, religious, and lay leaders denounced the Vatican's "unwarranted intervention" in the archdiocese's affairs, and insisted that the archbishop was the legitimate head of the church in Seattle. A Seattle group, Concerned Catholics, collected more than 13,500 signatures to demand the "complete" restoration of Hunthausen's powers. The archdiocese's offices were flooded with telephone calls, letters, and even balloons and flowers symbolizing support for the archbishop. Protestants joined in by testifying that Hunthausen's courageous example—and not that of their own ministers—had encouraged them to return to church.

At a stormy session of the local priests' council Wuerl came under such bitter attack that he offered to resign, although most priests later recognized that he had been used as a pawn by the Vatican, a victim like Hunthausen, though to a lesser degree. Indeed, many Seattle residents thought that Wuerl's position might have been considerably worse had it not been for Hunthausen's intervention on his behalf. Feelings against the auxiliary were nonetheless bitter. Said Father David Jaeger, archdiocesan director of seminaries, "For a forty-five-year-old man, seven months a bishop, to come to this area and to do something besides offer assistance—to say that he was going to be the final authority . . . , next to a man who's been a priest forty years, bishop twenty-five years, sat in the Vatican Council—that just broke the camel's back!"[10]

"I [have been] living . . . under a cloud because I am associated with the visitation [the Vatican investigation]," Wuerl agreed. "Sometimes I get the real feeling when I read some of the articles in the press and some of the quotations, I'm not seen as me. I'm seen somehow as the incarnation of the visitation. When you live under a cloud like that, people never see you, they never see your features."[11]

Though sympathetic to Wuerl's plight, most of the leaders of the city's Catholic organizations made it clear they would have difficulty accepting the division of power, and all reaffirmed their loyalty to Hunthausen. The Seattle chancery, responsible for the archdiocese's administration, announced that it was "100 percent" behind Hunthausen. "The archbishop is our recognized leader and that will never be taken away from him," said a nun. "You can give anyone faculties and power, but if they do not have leadership, then faculties and power are to no avail."[12]

While less outspoken than priests and nuns, the American bishops made it clear, in public statements supporting Hunthausen as a "prayerful, patient, and holy man" and in private messages urging the archbishop not to succumb to the pressures by resigning, that they realized the attack was against all of them. The bishops "must face up to what is going on," said Father Richard McBrien, chairman of the theology department of the University of Notre Dame. They must "know how high the stakes are, [and] if they have any pastoral self-respect, they simply must resist."

But there was no overt organized resistance, primarily because the bishops were not sufficiently united on the matter to talk back to Rome with one voice. The Brazilians had earlier learned the importance of solidarity during their confrontation with the Curia over the punishment of Leonardo Boff and the harassment of progressive prelates. In the case of Hunthausen an outraged laity, not the bishops, took up his cause with a protest that was louder and angrier than Rome had anticipated.

"This is a great teaching moment," Hunthausen had said at the height of the crisis. But the expectation that it would teach Rome anything about

American democracy was too optimistic. John Paul had two priorities, said a high-ranking Jesuit: "doctrine and discipline." The church, the pope confirmed, was "not a democracy."[13]

A Reluctant Prophet

Whatever his detractors might think of Hunthausen, he "was doing a terrific job of evangelization," said Seattle Jesuit Jack Morris, through his stands on nuclear war, the Sanctuary movement, and other issues affecting public policy. The result, said Morris, was that "Catholics were standing straight and tall."[14] Many American priests appeared to share that opinion: In 1986 Hunthausen received the Presidents' Award of the National Federation of Priests' Councils for his inspiring commitment to gospel values.

Hunthausen himself never sought public notice in his halting search for gospel truths. In many respects his experience was similar to that of other middle-class Americans who found to their surprise that, through a seemingly small initiative—as in agreeing to hear a presentation on the Sanctuary movement at their church—they had embarked on a journey of no return.

Hunthausen grew up in a large, affectionate Catholic family, the eldest of seven children. His father ran a grocery store in the Montana mining town of Anaconda. Shy and introverted, the young "Dutch" Hunthausen found himself doing things he would rather not, such as giving welcoming speeches to visiting dignitaries at his Catholic school. He hated the ordeals, recalling how he would blush "like a scorched tomato," but he also admitted that the experience was good for him. Wanting to be an aviator, he had no intention of becoming a priest, and had it not been for the influence of his spiritual director at a small Montana college, he might have become a combat pilot in World War II.

"Ought" is a word Hunthausen frequently uses, as well as the phrase "humanly speaking." They are characteristic of a man who has always emphasized the pastoral over the intellectual in his ascent from director of a small Catholic college to bishop of Helena and archbishop of Seattle. The quintessential Vatican II bishop, Hunthausen is deeply spiritual, sensitive to social concerns, and committed to a pluralistic church organization. In the heady years after Vatican II, when local priests and nuns were able to say what they expected from leadership without fear of being slapped down by the Roman Curia, Seattle's religious community submitted such a list of qualifications for consideration. To their wonder, they received a shy, amiable Montanan who more than fulfilled their expectations.

A man of simple habits, Hunthausen saw no need to cultivate the civic and political powers in Seattle, particularly the influential defense industry. And like most American bishops, he lacked the guile and desire to play politics in the Vatican style. His administration was relaxed, and often his acts seemed naive or ill-conceived, such as allowing the homosexual group Dignity to sponsor a Mass in the Seattle cathedral. Nevertheless, the archdiocese thrived: Two-thirds of the Catholic population attended Mass (compared to 53 percent nationwide), infant baptisms were double the national average, and adult conversions triple the average. Vocations remained steady in a time of national decline, and, despite Hunthausen's controversial views, more money than ever before poured into the archdiocese's coffers. The record was the more impressive in view of the Pacific Northwest's reputation as an "unchurched" region with the lowest religious membership and attendance rates in the country. Hunthausen's emphasis on listening to his people, and being constantly present throughout the far-flung archdiocese, might have irritated Catholics accustomed to a more authoritarian style of administration, but letters and opinion polls showed that the dissenters were outnumbered eight to one. Typical of the response to the archbishop's hands-on approach was the appearance in Seattle of apple-sized, red-and-white buttons with the inscription "I love Hunthausen."[15]

As the archbishop admitted, there were many times when he was faced with "a no-win choice," as in the authorization of the Dignity Mass. Hunthausen had endorsed the church's teachings against homosexuality, yet he felt a greater need to be loyal to his heart than to use political caution. Knowing that his action might be interpreted as condoning homosexual activity, he nevertheless agreed to the Mass: "How could I deny them a church?" he asked.[16]

As in many other turning points in his life, the archbishop did not come to a sudden decision about the arms race but was carried along by events, the first of which was the bombing of Hiroshima. He was lying on the lawn outside his seminary, he recalled, when he heard the news. "From that moment on," he told the *Seattle Times'* Gary Atkins, "I could never accept the bomb; I could never accept its use again."[17]

His feelings on peace and war did not crystallize, however, until he met an antiwar Catholic writer, Jim Douglass, in Seattle. Douglass was the author of *The Non-Violent Cross* and an organizer of protests against the new Trident base near Seattle. Hunthausen had never even heard of the base until he met Douglass, but he was impressed by the writer's commitment and was forced to acknowledge that he himself had done nothing to stop the arms buildup. While it was not politic to take a stand against the defense industry, on which Seattle's economy depends, Hunthausen felt deeply that he "ought to," and in 1981 he gave a speech in which he proposed that Americans withhold taxes from a "nuclear-armed Caesar." Admitting that he had not then made a decision to withhold his own taxes, he found that in stating the challenge he had no choice but to live up to it. "The more I speak about peace and challenge people to promote peace, the more I challenge myself and find myself having to be a lot more honest and genuine," he said. "It tends to have a cleansing effect on my life."

Divisions Among American Catholics

The unexpected activism of bishops like Hunthausen shocked many American Catholics. The church, which had traditionally allied the cross with the flag, was now saying the cross should question the flag. The only explanation, many feared, was that the bishops were "meddling in politics"—and shouldn't be.

Of course the bishops had always "meddled in politics," but usually on behalf of those in power. Silence, too, is a political statement because it implies support for the status quo. During the Spellman era the American church had made that statement by failing to challenge the "American way of life" and U.S. imperialism. Spellman, for example, eagerly joined in such CIA ventures as the overthrow of an elected government in Guatemala,[18] and he strongly backed the Vietnam War. Although the cardinal supported the reckless militarism that a bishop like Hunthausen abhorred, both adhered to a tradition of ecclesiastical activism. Spellman was haughty, sometimes cruel, and some of his arm-twisting tactics were questionable at best, but the chief difference between him and the archbishop of Seattle was that Spellman backed the so-called Establishment without question while Hunthausen took a prophetic road by challenging it.

In the late 1900s neither man can be said to represent a majority of American Catholics, although it is clear, from the increasing numbers of liberal Catholic activists, that Hunthausen forms part of a growing trend, whereas the followers of the late cardinal have to depend on such small groups of hard-line traditionalists as Catholics United for the Faith. Catholic sociologists and theologians say that while many of the faithful have achieved a sense of religious maturity, the church faces an identity crisis in trying to resolve the tensions between American culture and a universal faith. Such tensions are positive in that they challenge Americans to live up to religious ideals, but they also produce constant conflicts with Rome and within the American church over social and political issues.

"Vatican II was the historical dividing point between a Eurocentric Catholicism and a world Catholicism with many different cultures," said an American prelate, who claimed that Rome "is afraid of new, more democratic models of church community developing in such areas." Agreed a representative of American women's religious orders who tried to reduce tensions with Rome, "I and others who have had experience with the Curia have felt nothing but contempt and disdain by the Vatican for anything American. They don't understand that other perspectives contain pieces of the truth, too."[19]

Archbishop Weakland said that Rome's belief that it could impose norms on all aspects of American Catholic life, including partisan politics, was unrealistic. Were American Catholics to follow such a path, he warned, "we would exclude ourselves again to the ghetto" of an earlier immigrant church. New York's Catholic governor, Mario Cuomo, made a similar point: "How, after all, has the church changed and developed through the centuries except through discussion and argument? We ought not to be afraid of that because in the long run we will be stronger for it if we manage it well."[20]

"Intelligent lay Catholics rightly do not want to look like clerical puppets," said Weakland, who argued that Rome had difficulties understanding Americans' respect for political compromise. The same was true of American Catholicism. "We need channels for being heard, especially when we are fearful or hurting," the archbishop said, in reference to the Hunthausen case. "Thus we see the consultative processes in the church today as healthy contributions to balancing the more absolutist tendencies that are almost inherent in church structure. Perhaps we have learned that people can be persuaded as much by gentle reasoning as by authoritative decrees."[21]

"Rome is afraid of the post–Vatican II renewal of U.S. Catholicism, so pressure is put on the bishops to pull things into line," argued Swiss theologian Hans Küng. They are thus left with stark options. "If they oppose Rome, they have to face both conservative Catholics' defamation and the Roman inquisition. If they go with Rome, they know that an increasing number of Catholics will ignore their orders, many seeking religious support elsewhere." As pointed out by Father Andrew Greeley, who frequently surveys Catholic attitudes, the irony is that, because of Vatican II, U.S. Catholics have become more loyal to the essentials of the faith while rejecting as irrelevant official church teachings on such questions as birth control.[22] For example, surveys show that post–Vatican II Catholics are more familiar with the Scriptures and that many use them as a measure of their lives as well as that of the institutional church, particularly in regard to the use or abuse of church authority and church law. An in-depth study of parish life sponsored by the University of Notre Dame also showed growing pressure for more pluralism in local churches. "While the [U.S.] church in recent years has tried to move from an authoritarian to a consultative model [of organization]," reported the study, "many parishioners demand of it a democratic form of responsiveness." Although parishioners were "operating with a model of democracy consistent with American cultural values," said the study, their expectations were "inconsistent with canon law."[23]

Divisions among American Catholics have arisen primarily over sexual, economic, and political issues. Or as observed by Dale Vree, editor of the religious *New Oxford Review,* the right wants to regulate the bedroom, and the left the boardroom. Sizable numbers of Catholics are out of step with the Vatican on sexual norms. A 1986 *New York Times/CBS News* poll, for instance, showed that 68 percent favored the use of artificial birth control, 73 percent supported divorce and remarriage, and 55 percent endorsed legal abortion to save the mother's life or in cases of rape or incest. Most telling, nearly 80 percent thought it was possible to disagree with the pope on such questions and still remain a good Catholic. Such findings agreed with those of other surveys, including the Notre Dame study, which also revealed support by a majority of parishioners for married priests. Another poll, carried out at the Catholic University of America, found that 47 percent of American Catholics approved of the ordination of women priests.[24]

That a significant minority of American bishops share their parishioners' attitudes toward a liberalization on celibacy was shown by a 1985–86 survey conducted by Jesuit Terrance Sweeney. Nearly one-quarter of the responding bishops said they would approve of optional celibacy for priests. While only 11 percent favored the ordination of women priests,

30 percent agreed with the idea of ordaining women deacons. One-fifth of the bishops said they would welcome the recall of married and resigned priests to active ministry.[25]

Rome did not want to hear such "heresies," and Sweeney was forced to resign from the Jesuits when he refused an order to destroy the results of the survey, a copy of which he gave to the *Los Angeles Times*. But beheading the messenger would not change the message. Attempts to restore a pre–Vatican II church are doomed to failure, warned Father Greeley, because "a new era is too far begun to be undone." "It's too late to pull back," agreed an influential American archbishop, "and so there will be more tensions with Rome. Any problem in church history that is pushed underground is going to come up again."[26]

Fundamentalist Catholics disagree with the liberal trend, but they are swimming against the tide. While polls show that increasing numbers of Americans of all political persuasions are turning to religion, they also reveal strong disapproval of politicians who attempt to force their own religious beliefs on voters. Based on such data, the Gallup organization concluded that Americans wanted their religious leaders to speak out on public issues but did not expect them to become involved in partisan politics or endorse candidates for office. Polls also show a strong resistance to laws that are perceived as an encroachment on individual liberties. According to a 1985 *Los Angeles Times* poll, for example, support for legal abortion increased from 40 to 52 percent during Reagan's presidency; only 32 percent of those who voted for Reagan endorsed his policy on abortion. Even those within the pro-life movement admitted that candidates who opposed abortion could not expect to gain much advantage at the polls; in some cases, opposition was a disadvantage.[27]

But nor did the "mushy middle," as the pro-lifers called the majority of voters, solidly support the bishops' social objectives, some of which, such as economic rights and opposition to nuclear deterrence, were highly controversial. The bishops attributed such opposition to a lack of knowledge of the church's social teachings, which, on economics at least, are fairly radical. Although many Catholics made a genuine attempt to follow the faith commitment of their leadership, surveys showed that a key element in such allegiance was the extent to which people could relate their understanding of faith to the social issues of their time.

If lifestyles often reflect the individual's position on abortion, they also define attitudes toward other members of the church. Most Catholics say they believe their church is "growing spiritually," but while an almost equal number say they look forward to the sermons, half are in disagreement with the message, either because it is too liberal or too conservative. Progressive Catholics complain that the seminaries are turning out old-fashioned clerics; conservatives say they are hotbeds of radicalism. Although liberals and conservatives have occasionally tried to sort out their differences by meeting face-to-face, a Gallup study showed that the more contact they had, the more they disliked each other. Both sides agree with the Protestant religious critic Richard John Neuhaus that American Catholicism is poised to play a larger role in the public square, but they strongly disagree about how the church should fulfill that function.[28]

Because of these divisions, conservative Catholics often find themselves more in sympathy with fundamentalist evangelicals than with members of their own faith; Pat Robertson, for example, has attracted a sizable Catholic audience. On the other side of the political spectrum liberal Catholics make common cause with like-minded Protestants and Jews. "Dogmatic differences now mean nothing," asserted Father Gilbert Padilla, a progressive Catholic pastor in Tucson, Arizona, who claimed that the real issue was how people viewed basic questions of social justice. "The separation is not just a theoretical one. It is real, and it can be deep and bitter," he said, citing his own censure by some members of his parish because he had denounced the existence of political prisoners in El Salvador. "I have been called a Marxist, a communist, a Protestant and 'no priest' by the people who accepted the eucharist from my hand." Often, Padilla said, he felt "a stronger bond of unity with the Presbyterians, Jews and Quakers with whom I gather to pray for the [Central American] refugees."[29]

Disaffection

Far from contributing to unity, the Rock of Peter added to the divisiveness through a series of disciplinary measures against prominent individuals and institutions. Archbishop Hunthausen's humiliating experience added to the disillusionment of many Catholics, not only because of his personal saintliness but also because of his high rank—if a bishop could be so treated, there was no hope for ordinary folk. Articles and letters in newspapers and magazines expressed the growing anger felt against the pope by indignant Catholics and Protestants—an unthinkable development two decades earlier. Editorial cartoonists lampooned John Paul as a hard-hearted general. One cartoon—by the *Los Angeles Times'*

Conrad—was reprinted worldwide: In the top panel John XXIII stands before an open window welcoming the sunlight; in the lower one a grumpy John Paul marches away from the window after having pulled the curtains. "No one who reads the newspapers of the past three years can be ignorant of a growing and dangerous disaffection of elements of the church in the United States from the Holy See," admitted Bishop James Malone, the then president of the bishops' conference, in the fall of 1986. Matters had reached such a pass, said Malone, that some Americans had questioned the "timeliness and utility" of the papal trip to the United States in 1987. "There are people who are angry at the actions that have been taken [by the Vatican], and others feel vindicated," observed Father Joseph O'Hare, president of the Jesuits' Fordham University. "I'm afraid the net result has been to polarize differences in the Catholic community."[30]

An indication of what became known as the "Hunthausen pain" was a meeting in San Antonio, Texas, of more than 200 priests who were vocation directors. The keynote speaker was Spokane's Bishop Lawrence Welsh, chairman of the U.S. bishops' committee on vocations. During the question-and-answer period many of the participants pointed out that Rome's actions were hurting vocational work and putting new strains on bishops and priests. But the hardest moment came when a Seattle priest asked Welsh if he could say exactly why Hunthausen had been punished, since nobody from the Vatican had ever properly explained. Clearly upset, Welsh gripped the lectern, his head down, remaining silent for so long that people began to worry. Eventually he looked up: "The archbishop is a friend of mine. I want you to know I am struggling along with you."[31]

Part of the pain was attributable to incomprehension. For Rome to have taken such a drastic action against a bishop—thereby challenging the traditional equality of bishops with the Vicar of Peter—something must have been terribly wrong in Seattle. But try as they might, American Catholics could not find a crime to fit the punishment. "Would an item-ization of specifics reveal some fundamental flaws in Archbishop Hunt-hausen?" wondered Francis T. Hurley, the archbishop of Anchorage. "Or would they appear trivial and, therefore, provide feeble basis for the extreme action taken?"[32]

In fact, the stated charges against Hunthausen were not the real issue. Vatican II had firmly restated the right of bishops to share in the government of the church in unity with Rome, but the Vatican wanted to end such collegiality, making the pope a supreme monarch and his curial court a new class of Catholic nobles. Forcing the bishops to bow to Rome's wishes—as the pope had done with the Dutch hierarchy—was one way to reassert that power. If the apparent causes were trivial, that only added to the intended humiliation, as shown by related cases in Europe.

The French bishops, for example, underwent a similar experience over their popular catechism, *Pierres Vivantes*. Cardinal Silvio Oddi, the then head of the Vatican Congregation for the Clergy, caused the French considerable anguish by denouncing the catechism without ever stating his objections. When Cardinal Ratzinger, the papal enforcer, finally entered the fray, he insisted that the catechism emphasize creation instead of liberation, although this supported his personal bias, not infallible dogma. Cardinal Jerome Hamer, Ratzinger's alter ego at the Congregation for Religious, frequently criticized religious publications for their lack of orthodoxy, yet like Oddi he refused to be specific. As a result, people became afraid to express their opinions lest they run afoul of some unnamed law. And that may well have been the point of the repression. "These Vatican officials seem unable to understand authority except as authoritarianism exercised by them to protect the bureaucratic power of the institution," complained Catholic theologian David Tracy of the University of Chicago. "Pope John XXIII exercised effective authority because he did not try to coerce the world's will but appealed to its imagination. It is because not enough church officials understand the Catholic meaning of authority as Pope John did that the church is in trouble today."[33]

Secrecy also strengthened the Curia in any power play and was one reason for the Vatican's insistence on "discretion." But Hunthausen believed that the secrecy surrounding the Vatican investigation and his subsequent disciplining "compromised my principles" because his people had a right to know what was going on. Nor did he believe it could work in such an open society. He said that the decision to investigate the archdiocese was made before he was given an opportunity to respond to complaints and that in any case many of them had already been dealt with or were based on false information, as he had previously informed the Vatican in writing. For example, one of the Vatican charges—that a Seattle Catholic hospital was providing sterilization services—was based on outdated information regarding a practice that had predated Hunthausen's arrival in Seattle and that was ended when he learned of it.[34]

A second charge against Hunthausen—that of allowing general absolution when the crowds were too large for a handful of confessors—

was an accepted practice worldwide. That many bishops in the United States endorsed its use on special occasions, such as Lent, was shown by a vote at their annual meeting in 1986 that upheld the individual bishop's right to make such judgments. Among those who supported the practice was New York's stoutly orthodox Cardinal John O'Connor. The New York archdiocese had also allowed Masses for the nationwide homosexual group Dignity, as had Chicago, Baltimore, and many other dioceses. Although Hunthausen had publicly reaffirmed church teaching at the time of the Dignity Mass in Seattle, he—and not O'Connor or any of the many other bishops who sanctioned Dignity Masses—was admonished.[35]

Then there was the matter of giving non-Catholics communion—another charge laid at Hunthausen's door. But Father Ronald F. Krisman, the associate director of the bishops' committee on the liturgy, said that most priests would choose not to embarrass a non-Catholic by refusing communion. "If you're at a wedding," explained a priest, "you can't say, 'Step aside while I examine your credentials.' "[36]

Yet a minority of Catholics did want them to step aside—along with any members of their church who disagreed with them—and the Curia shared that opinion. Cardinal Ratzinger had often spoken of a "leaner," more disciplined church, smaller in numbers, perhaps, but totally obedient to Rome. Hunthausen's opponents in Seattle upheld that narrow view. Homosexual Catholics "have no right to be there [in the church]," said William Gaffney, a retired Seattle lawyer. "I hope they get kicked the hell out of there." "If 99 percent [of the people in Seattle] back the archbishop," added Erven Park, also of Seattle, "then 99 percent would be wrong."[37]

Both men were in the habit of writing Rome to complain about Hunthausen, and Park published a newsletter called *Catholic Truth,* for which he claimed 1,600 subscribers and which he sent to the Vatican. They formed part of Paul Weyrich's coalition of "truth squads," including Catholics United for the Faith and *The Wanderer,* which published long excerpts from *Catholic Truth.* But their "truth" was extremely one-sided. *The Wanderer,* for example, suggested that the Seattle church wanted a separatist arrangement with Rome and that it was using "terrorist pressure" to achieve its objectives. *The National Review's* Joseph Sobran (who also wrote for *The Wanderer*) drew similarly provocative comparisons, suggesting that because church dissenters defended Hunthausen, he had to be guilty of lax behavior. "It's a little like the Hiss case: Why were all the Commies defending him against the charge of being a Communist?"[38]

As the Vatican admitted to *The New York Times,* the "high volume of complaints" was a factor in its actions against Hunthausen. It also conceded that American Catholics who wrote letters to the Vatican were usually angry and wanted action. But balanced against the 1,600 names that Park kept in "the card file" of *Catholic Truth* were tens of thousands of other Catholics who agreed with Hunthausen and therefore felt no need to write letters. In a self-seeking statement on the subject the Vatican tried to imply that Americans were themselves responsible for the affair because they were the ones who had demanded action in the first place. Such, too, had been the Vatican's response to complaints from the Brazilian bishops about the disciplining of Leonardo Boff and other sanctions. But as the Brazilians had forcefully pointed out, during their meeting with the pope in 1986, the Curia had a responsibility to listen to other voices and to check its information before it acted. That the Vatican was disinclined to seek other opinions indicated that it had already formed its own. Thus when Hunthausen wrote Archbishop Laghi to suggest that the complaints against him might have been unfair, he was told by the ambassador that he "enjoyed no credibility whatever in Rome."[39]

The American bishops were "unruly," in the opinion of the Curia, and Hunthausen, who symbolized the reforms of Vatican II, was a convenient scapegoat. But the archbishop had several qualities which made him an awkward target. Unlike European prelates who quietly resigned under pressure, the archbishop refused to shut up. Believing he had been treated unjustly, he said so publicly. The Vatican was aghast, but the more it tried to blame Hunthausen, the more public opinion turned against it. Vatican sources said that the Curia had "botched Seattle." "They put in place the worst possible scenario by dividing power [between Hunthausen and his auxiliary bishop]," said one expert. "They want to keep Hunthausen away [from Rome], and they won't accept responsibility for the mess." But it was hard to avoid responsibility when Hunthausen was publicly stating the obvious—that the division of power was "unworkable."[40]

Another Hunthausen attribute that undercut the Vatican was courage. Determined to stick it out despite surgery for prostate cancer, Hunthausen—with not a little urging from fellow bishops—continued to insist on the restoration of his powers. Although few were prepared to say so publicly, Bishop Thomas Gumbleton of Detroit put his finger on the matter when he said that it had "profound implications" for power-sharing with Rome because "it will keep bishops from acting with authority. It's a serious loss if every bishop is afraid to act out of his own faith commitment, but only acts on the basis of what he thinks somebody else wants him to do."[41]

Bishops from other countries agreed. The precedent was dangerous, said a Latin American cardinal, because it meant that the Vatican, and particularly the pope's local representative, could intervene in local church affairs by beheading even so important a personage as a diocese's delegated leader. He shared the opinion of European bishops who viewed the Hunthausen case as a challenge to national bishops' conferences. The equality of the bishops, acting in unity with their fellow bishop of Rome, was now under attack, despite canon laws in support of such collegiality, they said. "We all want to be able to do what we want to do," said Sacramento's Bishop Francis Quinn, noting that a restriction on one could be a restriction on all.[42]

Church lawyers also questioned the legality of the trend toward a concentration of papal power. Vatican II and earlier church teachings had established power-sharing—in a decisive vote during the Council the bishops overwhelmingly reconfirmed the status of bishops as the successors of the apostles and the principle of shared authority. (The count was: yes, 2,049; no, 104.) But both John Paul and Ratzinger had on several occasions questioned the power of the bishops' conferences. In 1985 John Paul adopted the title of "Universal Pastor of the Church."

Yet the monopoly on power—at least as regards the appointment of bishops—was relatively new. The first bishop of the United States, John Carroll, was elected by his peers in 1789—not an unusual occurrence at the time. As pointed out by biblical scholars, there was nothing in the New Testament that suggested an absolutist form of government, and even tradition denied the pope arbitrary power over local churches. Yet arbitrary was a fair description of Rome's behavior in Seattle. Whether Rome had the right to punish the bishops on such matters was another question. Some canon lawyers thought not, because the bishop's right to use his judgment was at stake.

A Decisive Meeting

When it came to a showdown, the American bishops showed themselves divided in their loyalties. On the one hand, they were proud of their American heritage and their church, among the most dynamic in the world. Membership was growing, and the laity had created a vast network of schools, hospitals, universities, publications, and other institutions. Fifty-three percent of American Catholics attended Mass, compared to only 15 percent in France, Catholicism's "eldest daughter." Many bishops also sympathized with Hunthausen, whom they respected as a caring Christian who had been punished as a warning to them all. On the other hand, public criticism of the Vatican's handling of the affair would have been equivalent to an open break with Rome, for which the bishops could not steel themselves. "We do not exist alone," emphasized Bishop Malone, the president of the bishops' conference. "We cannot exist alone. . . . We are a church."[43]

Expectation of an outright battle with Rome drew more than 200 journalists to the annual meeting of the National Conference of Catholic Bishops in Washington in November 1986. The major items on the agenda were the launching of the pastoral letter on the U.S. economy, the election of new conference officers, and the Hunthausen affair. Although the last overshadowed the others, a public fight was never in the cards because of the bishops' circumspection in dealing with Rome. Still, they made known their feelings in several ways. One was a refusal to take responsibility for a highly biased version of events in Seattle that the Vatican wanted published under the sponsorship of the bishops' conference. They also gave Hunthausen a chance to tell his side of the story in statements and in a text distributed at the bishops' meeting.[44]

"It was very quiet" when the six-hour, closed-door session on Hunthausen's problems began, said one participant. "They didn't have to gavel the bishops to order." On the tables of the bishops were thick documents containing Hunthausen's statements. Visibly tense, the archbishop was the first to speak. He described the pain he had suffered and the harm it had done to the church and how embarrassed he personally felt over the affair. He said he had no intention of challenging papal authority and that the scandal had not been the result of ill will on anyone's part. The bishops gave him a standing ovation. Twenty-seven others followed, many to speak of their anguish at the hurt spreading throughout the country. The meeting had started out "with a real feeling of division" among the bishops about how to deal with the matter, said Edward J. O'Donnell, the auxiliary bishop of St. Louis. But in the course of "hearing one another and feeling the deep anguish of all the bishops, there was a great coming together."[45]

The result was a compromise statement in which the bishops affirmed "unreservedly their loyalty to and unity with the Holy Father." But instead of agreeing that Vatican intervention in Seattle had been "just and reasonable," as had originally been proposed, they simply stated that it had been carried out "in accord with general principles of church law and procedures." They also said they were "prepared to offer any assistance judged helpful and appropriate by the parties involved"—an offer that would later be accepted by the Vatican. While the bishops were not entirely happy with the statement, they said it was the best they could do in the circumstances. "It leaves doors open," said Anchorage's Archbishop Hurley. "The process to have Hunthausen's full authority restored has not been stymied."[46]

A postscript to the statement, in the form of elections, made clear the bishops' unhappiness with Rome. Boston's Cardinal Law was defeated on eighteen different ballots, including elections for conference president and vice-president and as a delegate to the 1987 synod on the laity. Widely regarded as the pope's man in the United States, the cardinal was one of the few bishops to support publicly Rome's disciplinary actions against Hunthausen. Law, said one prelate, was "perceived by the bishops as currying favor with Rome, and the bishops don't like it." Other conservative bishops repeatedly lost to moderates or progressives; St. Louis's centrist archbishop, John May, was elected president, reconfirming the middle-of-the-road position of the majority of the hierarchy.[47]

How long that position could be held was another matter. In his statement to the bishops Archbishop Laghi mentioned how many of them had been appointed during John Paul's reign. "We have not yet reached the 'magic number' of 100, but we are not very far from it," Laghi said. The statement was not lost on the bishops: The "magic number" represented approximately one-quarter of the hierarchy, but in time it could rise to more than half. The pope also emphasized the need for loyalty to Rome in a message that church officials said was "extraordinary" for the number of times it restated the papacy's authority. John Paul identified himself as the "Vicar of Christ" for "all the particular churches," as if he were the only one when in fact all the bishops were "Vicars of Christ."[48] "There is a significant difference between the Pope's relating to the bishops of the world as sole Vicar of Christ (and therefore source of all power and authority) or as Vicar of Peter (and therefore the center of unity)," observed Bishop Kenneth E. Untener, of Saginaw, Michigan.[49]

Nevertheless, some bishops were convinced that the long debate on Hunthausen would "surely send a warning to Rome" since Laghi had been present throughout. But Laghi was a papal loyalist, and the Roman troops were more concerned with what headquarters thought than with complaints from the colonies. Such at least was the opinion of high-ranking prelates from the United States and the Third World as well as Vatican watchers in Rome. The latter said that the Curia knew little about American Catholicism and was indifferent to the opinions of most U.S. bishops. Similar complaints were voiced by American members of religious orders in Rome who said there was no understanding of the concerns of American nuns or of the U.S. church's position on Central America, because the American bishops did not have a strong presence in Rome. "The only thing they are known for is 'Little America,' " said an English journalist, referring to the manicured lawns and posh living quarters maintained in Rome for visiting American church officials.[50]

"American bishops are perceived as out on a limb, as slightly crazy people who need to be watched," he continued. "The Vatican thinks of Americans as rich, flamboyant, overly liberal. But they are also seen as indispensable for Vatican finances. The church would fall apart without American money. 'Little America' is the symbol of it all. It's like the Sicilian mentality that the streets of New York are paved with gold—and inhabited by crazies."

"Crazy" was also the description for the U.S. hierarchy used by the editor of an important Vatican publication. A prominent Roman theologian who worked with progressive church groups agreed that the Vatican thought the U.S. bishops "too far out." He said the impression may have been fostered by letters from right-wing American Catholics, who had the field to themselves because there was no representative of mainstream U.S. Catholicism in Rome to give another version of events. Nevertheless, some bishops, including Cardinal Bernardin, had tried to present that view. It was not their fault if the Curia did not want to listen.

Pope Paul VI once observed that the American Church did not realize the "great power" it possessed. The remark applies equally in John Paul's papacy. Unaccustomed to playing the Vatican's byzantine game of power politics, the U.S. bishops have not demanded a share of influence in return for the millions of dollars that the American church contributes to Rome. In contrast, the German bishops make able use of their financial leverage. Instead of sending all monies to the Vatican, they have their own international aid agencies, Adveniat and Misereor, to distribute funds, and when the German bishops feel strongly about some matter, as in the dispute with the Americans over nuclear deterrence, Rome takes their part. (See Chapter 3, pp. 43–44, and Chapter 7, pp. 189–91.)

Although the Brazilians have no money, they have numbers—the largest church in the Third World—and unity. When the chips are down, they defend one another. Nor are they afraid to talk back to Rome. The Americans have both numbers and money, which is why Brazilian bishops were surprised at their failure to stand firm on such a crucial issue as Hunthausen's disciplining. "It is a bad precedent," said a high-ranking Brazilian church leader, "because it attacks the collegiality—the principle of power-sharing—of bishops. For example, during the papacy of Paul VI we had an archbishop in Brazil, Dom Geraldo Proença Sigaud, who belonged to an extreme right-wing cult and caused a great deal of trouble for the bishops with the military regime. But even in so extreme a case, Paul refused to intervene against a bishop because it would have undermined church dogma on collegialty."[51]

Liberal European bishops, including at least one cardinal, were "astounded that the liberal block of U.S. bishops has let Archbishop Hunthausen down and failed to defend him publicly," according to an informed church source in Italy. The sentiment was apparently shared by some American bishops. Nat Hentoff reported in *The Village Voice* that a confidant of several bishops had told him they were "very embarrassed by their timidity at the November meeting of all the bishops." Some had wanted to support Hunthausen publicly but were afraid to do so because "they had done things in their dioceses quite similar to what he had been censured for. But if they were to speak out, they might be next on the hit list."[52]

While the bishops may have been afraid to speak publicly, priests, nuns, and laity were not. Some boycotted the annual Peter's Pence collection that provided funds for the pope—no small matter in view of the Vatican's growing deficit and its reliance on American Catholics for 60 percent of the collection. Even before the Hunthausen scandal, American Catholics had been protesting through their pocketbooks against "insensitive church teachings and authority," according to a 1987 study by Father Greeley. Based on surveys and polls, Greeley's work estimated that the church was losing $6 billion yearly because of the drop in American contributions, which averaged only 1.1 percent of parishioners' income, as opposed to 2.2 percent for Protestants. Many Catholics "feel that every time the Pope opens his mouth it is either to put down women or to suppress freedom or to forbid . . . sex," Greeley said.[53]

Meanwhile, in Seattle Hunthausen had become a celebrity. Everywhere he went, crowds gathered to hear and applaud him. As one elderly parishioner explained, the archbishop's political beliefs might be controversial, "but his religious beliefs are what count."[54]

Hunthausen was only one victim among many in the Roman crackdown on the U.S. church, which also took a toll of theologians, religious orders, and Catholic universities—all this in addition to a steady flow of controversial decrees from Cardinal Ratzinger's office aimed at reestablishing discipline in the bedroom. In the 1960s Paul VI had caused widespread criticism because of his ban on artificial birth control, but even at the height of the furor Americans continued to show affection for the man. In the 1980s, however, the anger was often directed at the man as well as his office because of the perception that John Paul did not understand or approve of American culture. In stirring up the Vatican because of Hunthausen's "unpatriotic" peace stand, fundamentalist Catholics had helped to make John Paul seem anti-American. The Vatican might support Reagan's White House in its confrontations with the Soviet Union, but the message received by many Catholics in the pews was that Rome did not like their open, democratic way of life. The Hunthausen dispute, warned Archbishop Hurley, had sparked a revolt that was gaining momentum. "It is no longer a question of Archbishop Hunthausen of Seattle," he said. "It's a question of the state of the church."[55]

Balancing Traditions

One reason why American Catholicism has retained its vitality while the churches in Europe have steadily declined, Catholic historians suggest, is that it never suffered from the reactions against state-imposed Catholicism that occurred in the European nations. Despite the Vatican's earlier crusades against "Americanists," the American church retained its national character, and its leaders tried for the most part to uphold a respect for the country's pluralistic traditions.

Archbishop Weakland, one of the American church's most influential leaders, warned that if the Vatican persisted in forcing its ideas on American Catholics, the U.S. church could suffer the same disaffection that beset the Dutch church after John Paul moved against the Dutch bishops in 1980. When he visited Holland four years later, Weakland found that its once lively church had become "moribund," with little attendance at Mass, a decline in religious vocations, and other indications of low morale. He worried that Americans could also drift away from the church, in the belief that "we don't have the energy to fight with that kind of thing."[56]

Weakland admitted that the American way of life had many failings, including excessive materialism and individualism, and that Rome had a point when it asserted that the U.S. church had "a tendency to assimilate the American political experience without critical judgment." On the other hand, the Vatican was nostalgic for a time when people were forced to accept church teachings as state doctrine. In its overzealous pursuit of orthodoxy, said Weakland, the church in the past had been responsible for "much cruelty, suppression of theological creativity and lack of growth. In such an atmosphere amateurs—turned theologians—easily became headhunters and leaders were picked, not for their ability to work toward a synthesis of the new knowledge and the tradition, but for the rigidity of their orthodoxy, so that often second-rate and repressive minds, riding on the waves of that fear, took over."[57]

Weakland objected to the theory that the church could know the answer to everything. "The glory of the Catholic Church, as distinct from fundamentalism, has been its willingness (at times, it is true, with much hesitation, doubt and reluctance) to accept truth wherever it comes from and to integrate it with revealed truth, but only after a long struggle to work out apparent contradiction." But just at the moment when American bishops, theologians, lay leaders, and others were tentatively moving toward a balance of culture and faith, so that the ideals of Catholicism would challenge American culture and vice versa, the word came from Rome that there could be no compromise on the Vatican's agenda. As Weakland admitted, "grappling with compromise" had been the unfinished business of Vatican II. He and like-minded bishops believed that the business should be completed, whereas John Paul's followers felt it should never have been started.[58]

Repercussions

Such was the outcry in the United States that the pope appeared to have second thoughts on the matter of Hunthausen's disciplining. Unlike Ratzinger, he was not prepared to write off an important sector of Catholics, particularly when he was about to visit their country. The decline in contributions from American Catholics was also a serious matter. In effect by refusing to talk about the matter, he admitted to reporters that he knew divisions existed between elements in the U.S. church and the Vatican: "I don't talk. I don't say," he told insistent journalists.[59] Nevertheless, he made two important gestures. One was a personal telegram of support to Hunthausen during his surgery for prostate cancer—a highly unusual action since such messages normally come from the Vatican's local representative. The second was an announcement in early 1987 of the formation of a three-man commission composed of two American cardinals, Bernardin and O'Connor, and Archbishop John Quinn of San Francisco, to reassess the situation in Seattle, with a view to restoring Hunthausen's powers.

During a visit to Rome to prepare for the papal visit, U.S. church leaders had warned John Paul of heightened tensions over the Hunthausen affair. The pope apparently took their advice because in May 1987, four months before his trip to the United States, he agreed to a solution to the "Seattle situation" proposed by the three-man commission. The compromise was actually a victory for Hunthausen, who had all his powers restored. Bishop Wuerl, who had been given extraordinary powers in the Seattle archdiocese, was replaced by a popular Irish-American, Thomas J. Murphy, who had headed a Montana diocese. Murphy was given a special position as archbishop coadjutor of Seattle, which conferred on him the right of succession when Hunthausen reached the mandatory retirement age in 1997. While the arrangement was not common, it had been used in the United States and elsewhere, and Hunthausen, Murphy, and the commission made it clear that Hunthausen was the undisputed boss. "The important point to be made," said Hunthausen, "is that *I* have the ultimate responsibility. . . . That is the change . . . from where we were to where we are."[60] Another change was consultation with Hunthausen over Wuerl's replacement. Unlike Wuerl, Murphy shares Hunthausen's Vatican II outlook, particularly regarding a larger role for the laity. He is also a strong critic of U.S. arms policies.[61]

That Hunthausen had won the long battle was conceded by A. J. Matt, Jr., editor of *The Wanderer,* who said that traditionalist Catholics had "suffered a serious setback." But the victory was not entirely one-sided because the three-man commission responsible for the compromise had orders from Rome to monitor the "Seattle situation" through 1988. According to Bernardin, Hunthausen and Murphy were "proceeding quite well" in addressing Vatican concerns, meaning that the archdiocese had tightened up on certain practices, such as ecumenical sharing of the eucharist and general absolution. But in other areas, such as the Seattle seminary program, few changes were made since it was determined that there had been little wrong in the first place. Meanwhile, Seattle's churches were full, more people were involved in archdiocesan programs, and financial contributions were running at an all-time high. Although Seattle Catholics remained suspicious of Vatican intent, it appeared that the imbroglio would be resolved through the quiet diplomacy of the three-man commission. "It shows once again that the pope is much more a political realist than some of his right-wing supporters," observed Notre Dame's McBrien. "If people and especially the bishops confront him, the pope does back off, and he has backed off." Conceded James Hitchcock, a professor of church history and a leader of the U.S. Catholic right, "The attitude of defiance of Rome has intensified."[62]

Creeping Infallibility

The Hunthausen affair was a landmark in the American church because it involved a bishop—theoretically the equal of the bishop of Rome. But the Curran uproar was as important in its own way for its challenge to American sexual mores and the academic freedom of Catholic universities.

The Reverend Charles Curran is a well-known moral theologian who taught for twenty years at the Catholic University of America (CUA) in Washington, D.C. Established by the American bishops, CUA is the only Catholic university in the country with a papal charter, which means that theologians who teach in its ecclesiastical degree programs must have a license from the church. However, under the new code of canon law a similar requirement has been extended to anyone who teaches "theological subjects" at any Catholic college. Consequently Cardinal Ratzinger's revocation of Curran's license to teach at CUA caused widespread apprehension on Catholic campuses. Such fears were not unwarranted, to judge by the draft of a Vatican decree on Catholic universities which, American educators said, would ruin the country's 235 Catholic colleges if put into effect.

As a young priest, Curran had been strongly influenced by Vatican II, and his liberal ideas caused him repeated problems with church authorities in the United States. The Irish-American fought back by doggedly sticking to his arguments. He was a popular teacher, a prolific writer (sixteen books) and much in demand on the lecture circuit. Had he not been so widely respected or so active, it is unlikely the Vatican would have pounced on him, but Curran kept waving a red flag in front of the Curia over such sexual issues as birth control, divorce, and homosexuality. In 1967, when the CUA trustees failed to renew his contract, his colleagues voted overwhelmingly to support a schoolwide strike in his support. After the university was shut down for five days, Father Curran got his contract. The following year he and twenty-one other faculty members were called on the carpet for dissenting from Pope Paul VI's encyclical, *Humanae Vitae*, which condemned artificial birth control. Despite the advice of a majority of church experts who counseled against a ban, the pope had gone ahead with the encyclical—perhaps, Curran later mused, because to have done otherwise would have been seen as a betrayal of married couples who had observed the rule despite considerable hardship.[63]

As foreseen, American Catholics simply ignored *Humanae Vitae*, and by the time of Curran's troubles in 1986, polls showed that more than four-fifths approved of artificial contraception. Curran's position on other sexual questions, such as the possibility of allowing divorce in certain circumstances, also reflected widely held opinions in the Catholic community. His writings did not offer unequivocal support for such solutions, however, but were a thoughtful attempt at compromise. While admitting that abuses could occur, he believed that contraception and sterilization were "not intrinsically evil but can be good or evil insofar as they are governed by the principles of responsible parenthood and stewardship." He also believed that abortion was justified "only for the sake of the life of the mother." Curran derived his positions from experience in counseling Catholic couples who had found it difficult to accept the church's position on sexual questions. "Everybody's family has had to deal with the issue of divorce. . . . A good number of families are increasingly having to deal with the question of a homosexual child. And in all of these things my responses are in no way in favor of any kind of promiscuity. We have to look at church teachings in light of these changes."[64]

Curran was able to do so because of a 1968 ruling on dissent by the American bishops which attempted to soften the outcry against *Humanae Vitae*. According to the bishops' "norms," theological dissent from fallible church teachings was legitimate so long as the dissenting theologian maintained respect for those with other opinions and observed "propriety" and "prudence." A "good man," as even his critics admitted, Curran could not be accused of lacking propriety, particularly since he had always been careful to uphold the church's infallible teachings—meaning those doctrines that the church claims cannot be in error. But Ratzinger's Congregation for the Doctrine of the Faith thought he had, through his widely read publications, imprudently stirred up too much discussion of questions like birth control. In any case, John Paul's Vatican was looking for an American theologian it could use as an example, so Rome later admitted, and Curran filled the bill. "There is a school of thought around that says if it weren't for Father Curran . . . , the American Catholic community would not be practicing birth control," said Father McBrien of Notre Dame. "The alternative is to admit that 85 percent of Catholic couples practicing birth control just do not abide by the papal teachings. . . . It's easier to blame him than the flock."[65]

But it was the flock at which the message was aimed. During the long process of interrogation that began in 1979, Curran had cited statistics on the sexual practices of American Catholics to show that he stood in the mainstream. "Instead of helping his case," said an official of Ratzinger's Congregation, "that only increased the determination to deal with him firmly." Anyone who opposed *Humanae Vitae,* confirmed Cardinal Silvio Oddi, then prefect of the Congregation for the Clergy, was automatically "out of the church."[66] But that meant a majority of American Catholics were "out of the church" because they shared Curran's belief that it was possible to disagree on a question that had never been declared an infallible truth, in contrast, say, to belief in the bodily assumption of the Virgin Mary into heaven. Moreover, the church's position on sexual relations had changed substantially over the centuries. In the Middle Ages it had insisted that marital relations were justifiable only for the purpose of procreation, but in 1951 Pius XII had accepted the use of the rhythm method as a way to prevent procreation. Like other matters, such as slavery and usury, the church had reversed positions that were no longer sustainable because of changing cultural perceptions, and there was no reason, said American theologians, why it could not also change its opinion on birth control. "There will always be some tension in the church," said Curran, "precisely because no one in the church—Pope or theologian—has a monopoly on the Holy Spirit."[67]

Concerned about the inevitable scandal arising from Rome's dismissal of a tenured professor, Chicago's Cardinal Bernardin tried to negotiate a compromise with Ratzinger that would enable Curran to remain at CUA in another capacity (he had not taught sexual ethics for fifteen years). But although Curran had the backing of 700 American Catholic theologians, including the Catholic Theological Society of America and many of his colleagues at CUA, Ratzinger was determined to punish him. In August 1986, the theologian was officially informed that he was "no longer . . . suitable nor eligible" to teach Catholic theology at CUA.

While the decision had not been unexpected, it was a shock none-theless because it represented the first such disciplinary action against an American theologian in recent history, and Vatican officials indicated it might not be the last. The potential fallout in the academic community was considerable, warned the Catholic Theological Society of America and the College Theology Society. "For many years, enemies of the Catholic Church in the United States have argued that Catholic colleges and universities are not independent academic institutions, but are noth-ing more than educational arms of the official church." Curran's removal, they argued, made the charge "far more difficult to rebut."[68]

It was a hard blow for Curran, who had devoted his life to CUA and was as much a fixture on campus as the student lounge and the chapel. His ouster divided students and faculty, leaving many bitter and sad. His chief opponent on the theological faculty was so upset by his firing that he burst into tears while trying to comfort Curran. Yet even his supporters admitted that Curran had been bound to lose in an open confrontation during which he publicly repeated his refusal to retract. "I keep wondering if he could have negotiated the differences," said Jesuit Robert Drinan, a former Democratic congressman, who had his own run-in with the Vatican over political activism. Like Curran's supporters in Europe, he urged that the best tactic was to delay, while avoiding a public confron-tation. But subterfuge was not in Curran's character; he believed strongly in the need for an open discussion of the matter.[69]

While many Catholics opposed Curran's punishment,* papal sup-porters said that Rome had every right to demand obedience of a theo-logian who spoke in Catholicism's name. But as Notre Dame's McBrien pointed out, theologians are not supposed to be catechists who lay out the fundamentals of Catholic belief to children and adults. "The theo-logian's job is one of critically reflecting on that tradition or raising ques-tions about it, even challenging it, and that's how doctrines evolve and move forward." While a theologian is expected to explain the church's position on birth control, the teacher also has to "face honestly and responsibly the problems in that position."[70]

Archbishop John Quinn of San Francisco blamed theology's popu-larization for Curran's troubles. Dissent might have been possible in an era when theologians engaged in speculative writing in Latin for a small

---

* Polls showed that 45 percent disagreed with the Vatican decision, 32 percent sup-ported it, and 23 percent had no opinion.

audience of other theologians and priests, he said, but "today there is wide generalized and media interest in theological issues. Consequently, like so many other issues in the church, the issue of dissent presents new dimensions which the church must weigh seriously." Yet Quinn himself had made headlines in 1980 when he had argued against *Humanae Vitae*'s ban on artificial birth control. "This problem," he had told a synod of bishops, "is not going to be solved or reduced through the simple repetition of past formulas or by ignoring dissent."[71]

Quinn's change of heart, and that of other bishops who had endorsed prudent dissent, suggested that the hierarchy either was too cowed to contradict Rome or that it no longer had confidence in the intelligence of American Catholics. Ratzinger argued the latter, by claiming that "the simple faithful need to be protected" from theologians like Curran.[72] But if the "simple faithful" were capable of discussing such complex matters as nuclear warfare and the economy, as they had done during the long consultations on the bishops' letters, why, asked American lay leaders, were they any less able to address basic questions affecting their own bodies? The U.S. bishops had for years bemoaned the failure of theologians to reach out beyond their book-lined studies to deal with issues of importance to ordinary Catholics in language they could understand. Yet when they began to do so after Vatican II, they were immediately denounced by traditionalists for confusing the people.

The crux of Curran's argument was that he had not dissented from any infallible doctrines, but Cardinal Ratzinger insisted that the "church does not build its life upon its infallible magisterium alone, but on the teaching of its authentic, ordinary magisterium as well.* The faithful must accept not only the infallible magisterium. They are to give the religious submission of intellect and will to the teaching which the Supreme Pontiff or the College of Bishops enunciates on faith or morals when they exercise the authentic magisterium, even if they do not intend to proclaim it with a definitive act."[73]

Vatican officials said that Ratzinger's response to Curran implicitly made the church's prohibition on birth control infallible doctrine. When asked how much room was left for disagreement on other sexual matters, such as divorce, a senior official replied, "Very, very little." Archbishop

---

* Magisterium refers to the church's teaching authority. "Extraordinary" magisterium describes a doctrine defined by an ecumenical council such as Vatican II; "ordinary" magisterium relates to pastoral letters, papal encyclicals, and other documents that are not "extraordinary" and have not been declared infallible.

Hickey, the CUA chancellor, stated the matter bluntly: The Vatican had said that "there is no right to public dissent." Consequently, he said, the U.S. bishops' earlier norms on dissent in regard to *Humanae Vitae* were "simply unworkable."[74]

Catholic scholars said that by abolishing any distinctions between infallible teaching and other church statements, the Vatican was bound to create more dissent and possibly havoc as well. Taken to its logical conclusion, Catholics were expected to swallow whole everything that had been said by the Vatican and the pope—and John Paul had said a great many things on his frequent travels. Indicative of the verbal acrobatics that the U.S. bishops were forced to perform because of the Ratzinger statement was Los Angeles archbishop Roger Mahony's advice that Catholics could dissent if they kept the matter to themselves or told only a few close friends. Public dissent by people who wanted to modify the church's teaching was prohibited.[75]

The hypocrisy in this position may not have been apparent to Mahony, but for theologians who were charged with seeking the truth, the idea of divorcing private and public beliefs was untenable. "Creeping infallibility," as the new order was described, called into question the possibility of teaching or writing about theology in any but a restrictive way. As pointed out by Father William Byron, CUA president, theologians were expected to observe a certain prudence in their teaching, but at the same time they needed freedom of inquiry. Without such freedom, he said, "Catholic theologians will not be able to serve to the full extent of their competence the church that commands their love and loyalty. Without theology, the church, including its dedicated Vatican authorities, will not grow in its understanding of the full implications of the Gospel of Christ." Nevertheless, Byron could not banish the fears of theologians on his own campus or elsewhere. Quite a few worried with Curran that "people are going to have to think twice about what they write."[76]

And well they might—a list of U.S. books on moral theology censored by the Vatican was growing, despite earlier approval by the U.S. bishops. For example, Cardinal Edouard Gagnon, head of the Pontifical Council for the Family, denounced as "scandalous" and a "travesty of sex education" a textbook series used by more than one-third of U.S. dioceses. According to Gagnon, the series was being used "despite repeated warnings of the Holy See." But Dubuque's Archbishop Daniel Kucera, who had approved the series, said that was news to him, since neither he nor the publisher had ever been approached by the Vatican on the matter. In any case, said Kucera, it was not Gagnon's responsibility to deal with matters of orthodoxy. While that may have been theoretically true, since such responsibility belonged to Ratzinger's office, Gagnon's conservative outlook accorded with the views of most top Curia officials, the conspicuous exception being the more liberal secretary of state, Cardinal Casaroli. Consequently Gagnon's remedy for dealing with the challenge from U.S. moral theologians could not be dismissed out of hand. But his solution seemed even more problematic than the challenge because he wanted to "change 90 percent of the teachers of moral theology and stop them from teaching."[77]

Academic Freedom

The sanctions against Curran were the more alarming because they occurred at the same time that the Congregation for Catholic Education was attempting to assert control over U.S. Catholic universities through a series of proposed norms that would make teaching theology a hazardous profession, even at colleges that were state-chartered and legally and financially independent of the local bishop. The norms also called into question the status of professors of nonreligious disciplines and jeopardized the colleges' chances to obtain government aid.

As observed by Father William F. McInnes, president of the Association of Jesuit Colleges and Universities, the proposed "Schema" was a "great" document for Poland, because it emphasized the church's right to maintain its own universities, but it did not reflect the situation in the United States, the Middle East, India, or Japan, where Catholic educators had strongly protested the proposal (of 540 responses to the Schema 67 percent were negative). Heavy on orthodoxy and legalisms, the Schema proposed that the local bishops should assert control over the universities, by having final say in the hiring and firing not just of theologians but of all personnel. Any teacher who lacked "doctrinal integrity and uprightness of life" could be dismissed, and if the local bishop did not approve of its direction, he could "declare the university to be no longer Catholic." By insisting on the proselytizing of non-Catholic students, the Schema also suggested an academic community more akin to a fundamentalist campus like Jerry Falwell's Liberty University than to such centers of intellectual diversity as Notre Dame.[78]

U.S. Catholic educators were shocked by the proposals, especially since they had been drafted by an American, Cardinal William Baum, prefect of the Congregation for Catholic Education and Hickey's predecessor as archbishop of Washington and CUA chancellor. As pointed out by the presidents of 110 American Catholic colleges, in a synthesis prepared by the Association of Catholic Colleges and Universities, the history of American higher education is quite different from that in Europe or Latin America, where the bishops run their own colleges. Most Catholic colleges in the United States were founded by religious orders, chartered by the state, and operated by independent lay boards of trustees. The shift to lay control, which occurred after Vatican II, reflected a greater sharing of responsibilities within the church. It also led to an increase in private resources—Notre Dame's assets more than doubled under lay direction—enabling the colleges to attract outstanding talent. Catholic educators did not think lay leadership had harmed the colleges' Catholic identity. Comparing Notre Dame's situation with that of twenty years earlier, Father Theodore M. Hesburgh, Notre Dame's then president, said that, "if anything, we are more professedly Catholic than ever. We have spent many more hours, at the trustees' behest, examining the true meaning of our Catholic character and really doing something about it." Notre Dame not only enjoyed a highly visible Catholic profile—90 percent of its students went to Mass compared to 3 percent at European Catholic universities—but had also become a center for the discussion of major social issues, such as the bishops' pastoral on the U.S. economy.[79]

Like other Catholic educators, Hesburgh was plainly irritated by the Vatican's failure to acknowledge the cultural factors that made the American system so successful. Without any aid from the local bishops (the exception being CUA), the colleges educate nearly 600,000 students. America's Catholic universities and colleges represent 40 percent of all such institutions in the world, compared to a handful in Europe. Germany, for instance, has only one small Catholic college, and there is only one Catholic university in Italy that teaches other than ecclesiastical subjects. "No one who understands this great and gratuitous benefit [to the church] would want to jeopardize it," said Hesburgh.[80]

But that is exactly what the Schema would do, said the presidents of Catholic colleges, who described it as "unenforceable" and with "nothing to recommend it." "Only a few of our 235 [colleges] will still be 'Catholic' " if the proposal is approved, they warned. The presidents of twenty-eight Jesuit colleges took a similar line in a letter to Cardinal Baum in which they cited the danger to "institutional autonomy, academic freedom, due process and civil constitution. If imposed, the 'Schema' would discredit the Catholic universities in the eyes of the world."[81]

The Jesuits also pointed out that attempts to interfere with academic freedom could lead to "expensive and exhausting litigation." Curran had already taken that route, by filing suit against CUA for breach of contract in a civil court.* Catholic educators said that if they were forced to fire tenured professors for something as ambiguous as "doctrinal integrity," they would have a slew of lawsuits on their hands. They also warned that Catholic universities could lose some $500 million in government aid if the Vatican insisted on using them to proselytize. Court decisions had upheld the right of religious colleges to public aid provided they were not sectarian. Thus a Catholic college could require students to attend courses in theology without losing its funding, if the courses were taught as academic disciplines and not, as the Schema proposed, for religious indoctrination. Government aid also demanded respect for academic freedom and forbade any regulation that compelled students to attend religious services. Although CUA's theological faculty did not receive such aid and therefore could not be used in a test case for public funding, Curran's suit challenged the right of an external authority (the Vatican) to break a civil contract.[82] Thus the stage was set for a confrontation between religious and civil authority in the sensitive area of academic freedom.

Catholic educators tried to head off more such suits by taking their case against the Schema to Rome, and Father Peter-Hans Kolvenbach, the Jesuits' superior general, was reported to have argued strongly against it on behalf of Jesuit colleges.[83] But the critics were undercut by a conservative lobby that agreed with the Vatican crackdown on Catholic universities and theologians. "Catholic colleges must be a source of pure Catholic teaching," insisted Monsignor Eugene Clark of St. John's University in Queens. "To present anything less would be consumer fraud."[84] His opinion was shared by a vociferous minority, including Catholics United for the Faith and the Fellowship of Catholic Scholars headed by Monsignor George Kelly, also of St. John's and a prolific cataloguer of the alleged sins of the American church.[85] Kelly, Clark, and others of their persuasion wanted to return to the "old time religion" of authori-

---

* Curran won the first round of the legal battle in April 1988, when a District of Columbia superior court upheld his argument that his status as a contracted professor was governed by civil law—not the Vatican. The ruling, and fears that the case might threaten CUA's tax exemption and fund-raising activities, contributed to a compromise in which Curran was offered an opportunity to teach in another CUA department, such as political science. But the compromise presented a difficulty: Curran's field of competence was moral theology, and to pretend otherwise, said his lawyer, would be a "sham." (*National Catholic Reporter,* April 15 and 22, 1988)

tarianism and absolutism, even though all the polls showed that a majority of American Catholics rejected a resurgence of clericalism. The traditionalists also included some important clerics, among them Boston's Cardinal Law and New York's Cardinal O'Connor, both members of CUA's board of trustees. O'Connor, as usual, was less rigid in his positions than Law. Another omen was a warning by Archbishop Pio Laghi, the Vatican's ambassador to Washington, that "to be Catholic, we have to pay a price," even if it meant the loss of federal funds for Catholic higher education.[86]

One who was forced to pay was the Reverend James Provost, who was given tenure as a canon law professor at CUA only after agreeing to Vatican demands that he alter certain of his writings on a larger role in the church for the laity, the conditions under which divorced and separated Catholics could receive communion, and church discrimination against women. The editor of CUA's canon law quarterly and among the most respected canon lawyers in the United States, Provost squeaked by after O'Connor sided with Cardinal Bernardin against Law and Archbishop Mahony of Los Angeles in supporting his application.[87]

"There's a great appetite for control of theology and theologians on the part of Rome," admitted Father Byron, CUA's president. But that appetite would have little to feed on if Rome insisted on censoring the universities' theology departments, warned Notre Dame's McBrien. Students had come of age during the reforms of Vatican II and a parallel change in American social and sexual attitudes. If forced to accept a pre–Vatican II mold, "the brightest and best of young Catholic scholars will turn to non-Catholic academic institutions," McBrien predicted. Nor was the challenge limited to theology departments, as shown by the Vatican Schema on Catholic universities. Warned Father Hesburgh: "If church or state or any power outside the university can dictate who can teach and who can learn, the university is not free and, in fact, is not a university where the truth is sought and taught. It is, rather, a place of political or religious indoctrination. The latter is perfectly fitting for a catechetical center, but not for a university." Cardinal Richard Cushing, the late archbishop of Boston and one of the country's most influential Catholic leaders, had made a similar point two decades earlier. When Curran's job was on the line in 1967, Cushing had insisted that "that fellow must teach all sides: That's scholarship."[88]

Behind the conflict over theology was a deeper one concerning the relationship of Catholicism to American culture. Catholic traditionalists feared that if orthodoxy were not restored, Catholic colleges could suffer the same fate that had befallen such Protestant universities as Harvard and Princeton, which had gradually lost their religious identity through secularization. Liberal Catholic educators said the fears were exaggerated. As at most religious colleges, key positions at Catholic universities are retained by members of the faith, usually representatives of the founding religious orders, and while the religious preference of professors is not the only qualification, it remains among the most important. Father James T. Burtchaell, professor of theology at Notre Dame and its former provost, described such hiring policies as a search for a "critical mass" of faculty members—"committed and articulate believers, who purposefully seek the comradeship of others to weave their faith into the full fabric of their intellectual life." But commitment has many expressions, argued Sister Alice Gallin, executive director of the Association of Catholic Colleges and Universities. "People tend to look only at theology," she said. "We feel that the total environment which pays attention to social justice issues and the value of the individual person is also a fruit of our religious heritage." The broader approach, she said, reflects Vatican II's mandate to reach out beyond the Catholic community, through the teaching of ecumenism, ethics, and social values, as well as theology.[89]

The tragedy, said Catholic scholars, was that just when Catholic universities were in a position to contribute to American society, their freedom was being questioned. "The Catholic university is the point at which Catholic faith and contemporary culture meet," said William J. Gould, Jr., a specialist in religion and politics. "Provided only that it has sufficient freedom to do its proper work, the Catholic university can accomplish a great deal, both in its ability to integrate secular and religious truth and in its efforts to bring the light of Christian wisdom to bear on our secular age." Some Catholic universities, most notably Notre Dame and Georgetown, had moved in that direction, by encouraging students to see that economics, science, and other disciplines were instruments for the service of people, not just ways to make money. But they had a long way to go to achieve the philosophy of the "seamless garment," in the opinion of Father Andrew Greeley. Despite enormous changes in the economic, educational, and academic condition of American Catholics, he said, many Catholic universities still failed to value research, scholarship, and service to individual professions. Those who undertook research and published it had to possess more than ordinary intellectual courage after the Curran affair. That was no accident, said social analyst

Richard N. Goodwin. "By making sexual morality or forms of worship the testing grounds of religious belief, [repressive movements] force the far more significant problems of social justice and compassionate beliefs to the margins of public concern."[90]

American Nuns

While the sanctions against Hunthausen and Curran caused an uproar in the American church, they were not the only ones to be so treated. Three years earlier, in 1983, the Vatican had moved against Agnes Mary Mansour, for thirty years a member of the Sisters of Mercy, in its first test of strength with U.S. Catholics. Like other priests and nuns, Mansour had become active in the public arena, believing that there she could best carry out her religious mission on behalf of the poor. In early 1983 Michigan's Governor James Blanchard appointed her director of the state's Department of Social Services, a job she accepted with the permission of Archbishop Edmund Szoka of Detroit. But her appointment caused outrage in conservative quarters because the department administers Medicaid funding for abortions for poor women. (Her three immediate predecessors, all Catholic lay men, had encountered no criticism.)

Although Mansour personally opposed abortion, she felt that as a matter of conscience she could not deny such funding. According to the nun and her provincial superior, who was a party to the discussions with Szoka, the archbishop simply advised her to declare that she was obliged to uphold the law and then to say as little as possible about it. Although Szoka later claimed that he gave Mansour permission to accept the job only on condition that she take a firm stand against Medicaid funding for abortion, he sounded more equivocal in an interview with the Detroit *Free Press* in which he said that he believed Mansour to be in the same position as Catholic lay men and women appointed or elected to office. "[Sister Mansour] is a Catholic, she follows the teachings of the church, but she cannot control the laws of the state, and Medicaid funding is a matter of law," he said. "To make such a big issue out of this one thing seems a bit sensational."[91]

The Vatican thought otherwise. John Paul wanted priests and nuns out of politics, elective or appointive, and Mansour's case seemed tailor-made for disciplinary action. Four months after she had taken the job, Mansour was called to an interview with Szoka and a papal delegate at which she was told that if she did not resign from her job, she would "immediately be subject to a process of dismissal." Unaware that she was entitled to due process of church law and fearful that she would be seen as "standing in defiance of the Holy Father," she accepted the Vatican's proposal that she be released from her vows rather than abandon her commitment to the poor. Mansour later said she felt railroaded into the decision because she went to the meeting unprepared for the demand that she resign her job or leave the order and thus had no legal assistance or written defense. But even if a "careful and deliberative study of all factors had been taken into account," as her religious order had requested, the outcome would probably have been the same because the Vatican was in no mood to listen to explanations. Archbishop Laghi had told the president of the Sisters of Mercy to order Mansour to resign, and that was that, as far as Rome was concerned.[92]

The Leadership Conference of Women Religious, representing the women's religious orders, said it was "grieved and shocked at the way in which the Mansour case has been concluded." But there was little the nuns could do about it. Two other Mercy sisters in public office—Elizabeth Morancy, a four-term member of the Rhode Island legislature, and Arlene Violet, Rhode Island attorney general—were also forced to resign from their order. Other nuns who chose to stay with their orders had to leave public office, while still others were left in limbo over the legality of their positions on the boards of public schools and hospitals.[93]

The Mansour case marked the beginning of a national outcry by American nuns over women's issues, the most significant of which was a full-page advertisement in *The New York Times* in 1984 that affirmed the right to a plurality of conscience among Catholics on the question of abortion. Among the ninety-seven signatories were two dozen nuns, soon to be known as the "Vatican 24."

The advertisement was a response to attacks by Cardinals Law and O'Connor on Democratic vice-presidential candidate Geraldine Ferraro's views on freedom of choice in abortion. "[The cardinals] were essentially saying that people couldn't vote for Ferraro because she had voted for Medicaid funding for abortion," explained a spokeswoman for the religious orders. "Yet the church has no teaching—much less an infallible one—on Medicaid. The sisters who signed the ad worked with the poor, and they felt that [Law and O'Connor] were taking a political position in favor of Reagan that would hurt the poor. The idea was to persuade voters to look at a range of issues, not just abortion. The Vatican came down hard on the women, but there was no public criticism of Law or

O'Connor, although privately some bishops said they had overstepped the line [between religion and politics]."[94]

A furious Vatican demanded that the nuns immediately recant or face dismissal, but having learned from Mansour's experience, the women were not about to be stampeded, and two years of negotiations ensued between the nuns' religious orders and the Congregation for Religious and Secular Institutes. The unexpected intransigence of the "Vatican 24" forced Congregation officials to resort to a variety of unedifying tactics, including threats against the nuns and their orders. At one meeting with Archbishops Laghi and Vincenzo Fagiolo, the Congregation's secretary, the former opened the interview with an announcement: "We are here for a dialogue, but I must insist that you put in writing that you adhere to the Catholic teaching on abortion." Fagiolo followed this up with the question, "How would your mommies and daddies feel if you were no longer nuns?" "We might as well have been Martians speaking to Newtonians," said one nun of the disastrous meeting. Indicative of the unreality of the situation was Fagiolo's claim that there was no diversity of opinion on abortion among American Catholics because "the bishops express the faith of the people and the bishops agree with us."[95]

The dispute was eventually resolved through a diplomatic solution in which twenty-two of the twenty-four nuns "clarified" that the advertisement had been misinterpreted as a pro-abortion statement—a far cry from the retraction the Vatican had originally demanded. Although Rome tried to claim that the women had recanted, the nuns publicly rejected the suggestion. Meanwhile, militant religious belonging to the National Coalition of American Nuns released a statement urging that contraceptives and information on their use be made available to students in junior and senior high schools as a means of reducing a rising teenage pregnancy rate.[96]

The nuns' fights on abortion and birth control were among several controversies between the religious orders and Rome, during which U.S. bishops were caught in the crossfire. "American bishops don't have the clout to protect American sisters," said Sister Margaret Traxler, one of the "Vatican 24." "They have to stand by while the sisters are maligned, slandered, buffeted and misused. It's a matter of men protecting us from other men, and they're simply not doing it."[97]

For example, the bishops made it plain that it was impossible to consider the ordination of women priests in John Paul's lifetime. The pope was vehemently opposed to the idea, so much so, according to one

U.S. church expert, that he had instructed bishops not to nominate for auxiliary bishop anyone associated with the movement for women's ordination.[98] The trouble with North American nuns, said Cardinal Ratzinger, was that they had been infected with a "feminist mentality." Only the cloistered orders had "withstood very well because they are more sheltered . . . and because they are characterized by a clear and unalterable aim: praise of God, prayer, virginity and separation from the world."[99]

American nuns saw the situation differently. Like many lay women, they felt the church treated them as second-class citizens. Although some were better educated than their bishops, they were often given routine jobs that priests did not want, while being forced to put up with lingering and often petty displays of machismo. Fagiolo and Cardinal Hamer, the Belgian prefect of the Congregation for Religious, were particularly disliked for their high-handed ways (the cardinal was known as "the Hammer"). During a three-week tour of the United States in 1985, Hamer talked about "good" nuns and "bad" nuns—the latter apparently including those who refused to wear a habit. One nun who approached Hamer about women's concerns said he "asked me if I really wanted to be a man."[100]

Nor did it help that Hamer's office refused to approve the constitutions of some women's orders because they proposed a more democratic style of internal governance. The Congregation also objected to resolutions on social priorities made at the nuns' annual assemblies because they did not reflect the Vatican's political line. For example, representatives of the orders were told that the nuns' position against U.S. policies in Central America was "inappropriate" because the religious orders should be "dedicated exclusively to spiritual matters" and not take stands on the *contra* war or Central American refugees. A spokeswoman for American nuns said that Vatican officials also condemned as "too political" a resolution against apartheid in South Africa. She said she expected further pressure from Hamer's Congregation: "We've been told that if we don't fulfill our function, they will control us."[101]

But American nuns had come too far since Vatican II to return to a cloistered community. Sister Marie Augusta Neal, a sociology professor who polled thousands of nuns, compared the change in attitudes: "If you asked what the primary mission was in 1966, most would have listed their work. If you ask the sisters that today, they would say the mission of the church is justice and peace." Equally revealing were the different replies to her question "What do you think is most needed in religious life today?"

In the 1966 survey nearly half had said, "Circumspection and patience."
In a follow-up survey in 1982 only 7 percent gave that answer. As pointed
out by Sister Margaret Cafferty, at a meeting of the Leadership Conference of Women Religious, "The times we live in may indeed have greater
need of imagination, risk and daring than of patience." But it was also
a time to beware of the "Polish temptation," said Sister Mary Jo Leddy,
provincial of the Sisters of Sion in Canada and the United States. "Be-
sieged from without, we become less self-critical within. And without
constant self-criticism, we lose our clarity of vision and lucidity in strategic
judgments." Leddy predicted that the task of religious orders would increasingly be a prophetic one—that of persuading the church that it "must
reorder itself more justly if it is to present a credible witness to the
disordered powers of this world." The struggle would not be easy, she
said, but "conflict is not merely something we cope with—it is part of
our calling."[102]

Religion and Politics

Sister Leddy's plea that the church in its internal workings reflect its
witness to the world goes to the heart of the debate about U.S. Catholicism's relations with Rome. Most American bishops, traditionalists or
liberals, feel the church has a legitimate role to play in creating spaces
in the public policy debate for questions of moral concern, whether nuclear warfare or abortion. There is little disagreement among the bishops
or with Rome on economic issues, since the Vatican supports social justice, particularly for the poor. But considerable conflict has arisen over
Rome's teachings on sexual matters and how those differences affect
Catholics who exercise political power.

For example, New York Governor Mario Cuomo obtained strong
support from Cardinal O'Connor on legislation to fund housing for the
poor, whereas the liberal Catholic and the cardinal fought publicly over
Medicaid funding for abortion. Cuomo, who personally opposes abortion,
felt that as an elected official he could not impose Catholic beliefs on the
people. O'Connor countered that this was a cop-out by an influential
Catholic who had a duty to uphold his religious beliefs in the public arena.
A loyal follower of John Paul, O'Connor did not see the political dangers
of religious militancy that other bishops perceived.[103] Integralism is a
lingering force in the European church, and John Paul has made it clear

that he wants such right-wing Catholic groups as Italy's Communion and Liberation to play a stronger role in politics.

Another danger is the injection of partisan politics into local congregations. Parishioners may not agree on U.S. policies in Central America, the arms race, or abortion, but they can submerge those differences in a common faith so long as the right to dissent is respected. In contrast, Italian parish priests complained that Communion and Liberation divided the faithful because it demanded that everyone adhere to its religious and political agenda.[104] Tensions also developed over pluralism in local church communities, many of which wanted a more democratic style of governance that accorded the laity a voice in the choice of officials and the style of rituals. But the Vatican crackdown on a liberal style of parish administration reinforced the trend toward Roman hegemony, threatening to give a clerical class the final say in everything from liturgy to guest speakers.

There are several problems in goose-step religion. One is that it conflicts with two decades of liberalization brought about by Vatican II. Another is that it cannot be applied: Taken to its logical conclusion, it would compel U.S. Catholics in public office not only to oppose abortion but also to legislate against the death penalty, change the tax system to provide for a redistribution of income, and end the arms race. While fundamentalist Catholics feel strongly about abortion, many are as opposed to the bishops' stands on social, economic, and military questions as liberals are on the issue of abortion. Few candidates can hope to represent all these viewpoints, and those who run on single-issue platforms are likely to find themselves in the same political ghetto as fundamentalist evangelicals. "Catholicism in the United States has to be with a small 'c,' " said Father Ronald Murphy, rector of the Jesuits' Georgetown University. "Our milieu does not conceive of other opinions as being the enemy and hostile."[105]

Nevertheless, he said, Rome had a point in fearing that American Catholicism could be absorbed by secularism because "Americans have a great desire to conform to American values. Let's be honest: The culture isn't Catholic or even Christian; it's materialistic." Like other Catholic educators, he felt that Catholicism's challenge should be to call Americans away from that culture by developing a theology of "responsible freedom," instead of succumbing to the temptation to religious fundamentalism. "At its best," said Murphy, "U.S. democracy enables religion to uphold a key principle—that all people are created equal. The Vatican trembles when it hears this, not understanding that Americans really mean it."[106]

"Religion and democracy will always be to some degree in tension," agreed A. James Reichley, a scholar at the Brookings Institution who specializes in religion and politics. "Religion claims to reveal universal moral truths, binding in some sense on every human will, while democracy requires compromise, serving partial interests and accommodating differences of opinion that may appear logically irreconcilable. The two, nevertheless, have crucial complementary needs. Religion, as Alexis de Tocqueville observed long ago, is nurtured by the atmosphere of social freedom promoted by republican government. Democracy, for its part, depends, now and for the foreseeable future, on values that have no reliable source outside religion."[107]

Three Bishops

The different ways in which the American church relates to U.S. democracy are illustrated by the varying styles of New York City's Cardinal O'Connor, Boston's Cardinal Law, and Archbishop Weakland of Milwaukee. All three are unusually intelligent, well educated, hardworking, and outgoing. They share a concern for the poor, like to work with people, and have little or no interest in worldly possessions. But while Weakland has sought a synthesis of culture and faith, O'Connor and Law have become known as "the sheriffs" because of their emphasis on "law and order." The more liberal Weakland is not popular at the Vatican, whereas Law and O'Connor are looked upon in curial circles as the pope's men.[108]

O'Connor is the best known of the three, not only because he heads the archdiocese of New York City but also because he has a flair for publicity and has been embroiled in several highly controversial affairs, including a showdown with City Hall over the civil rights of homosexuals and a run-in with the city's Jewish organizations following a turbulent trip to the Middle East.

Forthright and aggressive, O'Connor was educated in a no-nonsense seminary in Philadelphia and spent twenty-seven years as a Navy chaplain, retiring in 1979 with the rank of rear admiral. His highly developed sense of discipline and loyalty were apparently just what John Paul wanted: O'Connor served less than a year as bishop of Scranton before being sent to New York City in 1984. According to Notre Dame theologian Richard

McBrien, when key U.S. prelates met with the pope early that year to discuss replacements for New York and Boston, following the deaths of their moderately tolerant archbishops, John Paul flew into a rage. Recounted McBrien, "The Pope rose, took off his papal ring, laid it on the table and barked, 'No more weaklings!' "[109]

The "warrior bishop," as some of his admiring adversaries call O'Connor, is certainly no weakling. He works hard and demands action from his staff; he can be "very quick with underlings," admitted a fellow priest and friend. But, he said, O'Connor also makes time for those with complaints and encourages his priests to bring friends to talk with him at dinner. His saving virtues, all agreed, are a dry wit and an ability to admit that, like all humans, he may be guilty of arrogance and stupidity. O'Connor feels deeply that he has a duty to put forward the church's teachings, and he does so to any who will listen—and to quite a few who would as soon not. He had been on the job only a few months when he caused a national stir by questioning the abortion stand of Geraldine Ferraro, thereby breaking ranks with his fellow bishops, who opposed the singling out of individuals by name or party affiliation. O'Connor, who had not previously criticized any pro-choice candidates, was apparently prompted to announce that Ferraro "has a problem with the pope" by a statement that she had never made in the campaign, but that was part of a packet of materials prepared two years earlier by Catholics for a Free Choice (CFC). An investigation by *The Village Voice*'s Wayne Barrett suggested that Ferraro's most bitter opponents, the National Right to Life coalition, had likely sent the materials to O'Connor, even though the CFC had banned their use (the coalition's legislative director refused to comment on the charges). Cardinal Law and Scranton's Bishop James Timlin, a former aide to O'Connor, later denounced Ferraro, contributing to the belief—which was strongly encouraged by the Republicans—that the country's bishops opposed the Democratic presidential slate. As noted by Bishop Leroy Matthiesen, of Amarillo, Texas, "It's almost been said that if you vote for the Democratic ticket, you're committing a serious sin."[110]

The pope gave O'Connor his full support: At the height of the furor over the archbishop's statement on Ferraro, John Paul told reporters that the church had a duty to address political issues from "an ethical viewpoint."[111] As proof of his confidence in O'Connor, the pope made him a cardinal the following year. Rome's backing reconfirmed him in his campaign on sexual issues, which led to running battles with Governor

Cuomo, New York City mayor Ed Koch and Senator Daniel Patrick Moynihan (D.-N.Y.), among others. Koch, who knew a savvy politician when he saw one, treated the cardinal with kid gloves, although they sometimes clashed—for example, over homosexual rights.

O'Connor's assertiveness has given the New York archdiocese a new political presence after the muted era of his sickly predecessor, Cardinal Terence Cooke, who disliked the limelight and did not cultivate political connections with City Hall. But it is an influence measurably different from that exercised by Cardinal Spellman in the 1950s, when Catholic office seekers still depended on the church's political contacts to obtain votes and jobs. As Catholics became more affluent and the old patterns of ward politics disappeared, the church's power lessened. Changes of attitude have also weakened its position: A 1984 *Daily News* poll of New York City Catholics showed that they disagreed with O'Connor by wide margins on birth control, abortion for rape victims, the clergy's role in politics, and whether priests should marry. Yet the archdiocese remains an institutional power because of the services it provides. Its annual budget of $1.2 billion is larger than that of many cities. It educates 120,000 school children and operates foster homes for more than 4,000 children as well as hospitals and homes for the elderly. O'Connor is also deeply involved in a major rebuilding program in poor neighborhoods. Mayor Koch has said that the city could not possibly do without such services. They maintain O'Connor's church as a force in city life, giving the cardinal a platform from which to mobilize public opinion.[112]

Despite his energetic lobbying for church teachings on sexual practices, O'Connor has made little headway with supporting legislation. The spat with Koch over the civil rights of homosexuals, for example, was won by the mayor when the city council passed an antidiscrimination bill. A month before the vote a *News* poll of the city's Catholics had shown that 72 percent felt the church should stay out of such political battles. While O'Connor had sued the city over a law prohibiting discrimination in employment on the basis of sexual orientation, Brooklyn's Bishop Francis J. Mugavero took the more flexible attitude that the employment of a homosexual did not imply approval of homosexual behavior. An employer could not "monitor what employees do in their own family or neighborhood situations," argued Brooklyn's Auxiliary Bishop Joseph M. Sullivan. If a diocese were to fire all employees who violated church teachings, he said, "probably a hundred percent would get caught in the net."[113]

Although O'Connor's public jousts with individual politicians have nettled many bishops, he is still seen as a "conference man" who will go along with the majority of the bishops once they have made a decision—as in the case of the letter on war and peace, many sections of which O'Connor did not like but which he supported nonetheless. And while he is considered a papal loyalist, fellow bishops maintain that as a representative of the bishops he would defend their position in Rome, much as did Cardinal Spellman before him.

Cardinal Law is a different sort, a loner, in the view of his fellows, who feel that his commitment to Roman orthodoxy precludes the loyalty O'Connor expresses toward the bishops as a group.[114] That Law is suspected of currying papal favor was shown by his repeated defeat in balloting for new officers of the bishops' conference in the 1986 elections (he lost on eighteen ballots for eight different positions). One of the few bishops to support publicly Hunthausen's disciplining, he also upset his colleagues by appearing to break with the bishops' conference in its opposition to *contra* aid. His view of bishops' conferences paralleled that of Cardinal Ratzinger, who believed that they got in the way of Rome's relations with individual prelates. There was only one collegiality, said Law—"a worldwide college of bishops under Rome."[115]

Some bishops also expressed doubts about Law's plan to establish a $3.5 million think tank, the Pope John Paul II Institute, to restate church teaching in "a way that is more compelling to the contemporary mind." One of the institute's jobs, according to Law, would be to help him and eleven other cardinals appointed by the pope to write a universal catechism. But the catechism project was not popular among American bishops, who saw it as another attempt to assert Roman control over local dioceses. Suspicions were further aroused by Law's appointment of Philip Lawler, a conservative activist, to edit the archdiocesan newspaper, the *Pilot,* and to help with the institute's development. Lawler had headed the American Catholic Committee, a group of right-wing Catholics who opposed the bishops' pastoral on nuclear warfare. He had also been director of studies at the Heritage Foundation, which was set up by the New Right strategist Paul Weyrich, who had helped organize the campaign against Archbishop Hunthausen. Yet another straw in the wind was the establishment of a second Communion and Liberation outpost in Boston, the first being in New York City.

Like O'Connor, Law is more interested in sexual issues than in war and peace—children are dying daily from abortion, he said, but nobody is dying from nuclear war. Yet he had no more effect on the voters than did O'Connor: Although Law lobbied vigorously on behalf of an amendment that would have outlawed abortion, Massachusetts voters turned down the proposal by two to one.

While he has an outgoing personality and is at ease with the press, Law cannot shake a reputation for sternness that has hurt him with the voters. In contrast to O'Connor, who is often able to deflect criticism with his wit, Law sometimes allows his feelings to get the better of him, as at an unguarded moment in 1986, during graduation ceremonies at the Catholic Boston College. Wagging his finger at the audience, he lectured the amazed assembly about the need for Catholic universities to avoid the temptations of secularism. The scolding did not go down well with Massachusetts Catholics, some of whom had already been upset by the cardinal's insistence that Catholic rituals be performed by the book—lay preachers were banned, for example—and that nuns return to their traditional place.[116]

Although O'Connor has drawn the line concerning abortion and homosexual activity, the hostility that greets Law's edicts goes far deeper because he is perceived as the papal enforcer in church communities that have become more democratic through Vatican II's reforms.[117] Law's supporters think the perception unfair, but it exists among the American bishops as well. For them the American capital of orthodoxy is not New York City—many share O'Connor's theological conservativism even if they do not approve of his methods—but Boston. Law has little regard for bishops' conferences, whereas O'Connor generally plays by the conference rules. Without the protection of the conference individual bishops can be picked off by Rome, and as the more liberal bishops disappear, so, too, will the hopes of more democratic church communities. American Catholics are sufficiently self-confident and pluralistic to take an O'Connor in their stride, but Law presents a different challenge—the reassertion of Roman hegemony over the American church.

Unlike Law and O'Connor, Archbishop Weakland represents the mainstream in the American church. The former stand for the traditionalist teachings of the 1950s church; Weakland is a Vatican II bishop who wants the council's reforms to go forward. Although Weakland and O'Connor come from similar working-class backgrounds, the archbishop's outlook was formed by the Benedictine monks while O'Connor spent most of his adult life in the military. The discipline of a religious order is different from that of a diocesan priest, and it often shows in the administrative styles of bishops who come from religious orders. The Benedictines place heavy emphasis on spirituality and poverty, but they also encourage the sharing of authority: The abbot is expected to listen to his monks, particularly the youngest. "That's a different perception of authority," said Weakland, who became the head of the worldwide order at a youngish thirty-six. "You try to discern what is there, rather than always working on your own. It's the process of listening, feeling, sensing."[118]

Just as O'Connor's travels on behalf of the navy gave him the military view of the world, Weakland's decade-long experience as the Benedictines' abbot enabled him to appreciate the challenges and differences of various cultures. Living in Rome also gave him an insight possessed by few American bishops into how the Vatican works. Equally important to Weakland's worldview is his love of music, for, he said, it offers an example of how Catholicism has come to terms with and enriched art.

A gifted pianist, he was sent at the age of twenty-one to study theology in Rome. But his abbot told him he did not want Weakland to seek a degree in theology but to learn culture and get a "broad worldview of people." After Rome he studied music at New York City's Juilliard School and Columbia University (he was the first Catholic priest to get a Juilliard degree), becoming the world's leading authority on Ambrosian chant. One of his compositions, a transcription of medieval works for the *Play of Daniel*, became a critical hit when presented by the New York Pro Musica in 1958. When he was appointed archbishop of Milwaukee in 1977, he sold off his predecessor's luxurious home, preferring three small rooms in the downtown rectory. As a good Benedictine, he sorts out his belongings once a year, giving away items he no longer uses. But he keeps one luxury: a Mason & Hamlin grand piano, which he tries to play daily.[119]

Weakland is popular in Milwaukee for his low-key style of government, warm personality, and sense of humor. He prefers consultation to authoritarianism, and his reaction to human weakness is similar. Although he takes a "very strong, uncompromising, conservative point of view" on sexual matters, such as a couple living together before marriage, he admits that in his pastoral responses to such situations "I might tend to use more honey than vinegar." While upholding the church's condemnation of homosexual acts, he supports civil laws that ban discrimination against homosexuals. "I don't think people always make the distinctions," he said. "The question of housing or work rights is a different question from a legal point of view than from a moral point of view. We've always made the distinctions of how we have to act in a pluralistic society on a question and what the correct moral position is," he said.[120]

Already controversial because of his protests against police brutality toward blacks and his endorsement of the Sanctuary movement, Weakland became a nationally known figure as chairman of the bishops' committee responsible for drafting the pastoral letter on the U.S. economy. He crossed swords more than once with business critics of the letter; along the way he caught the disapproving attention of *The Wanderer* and Catholics United for the Faith. But it was not until the Hunthausen and Curran affairs that Weakland really began to feel the heat.

One of the values in Benedictine monasticism is a belief in the prophetic word, and Weakland felt strongly that someone should speak out about Rome's treatment of the U.S. church and John Paul's failure to "quite understand the American approach to pluralism." Chicago's Cardinal Bernardin, leader of the mainstream in the U.S. church, had tried to get such points across during meetings in Rome. But Bernardin, the visionary bishop who proposed the "seamless garment" philosophy and who is widely respected among his American fellows for his ability to conciliate and compromise, has often been ignored by the Curia precisely because of those gifts. His admirers among the Third World cardinals find it hard to understand why he does not demand more respect for his positions, since he represents a majority of the bishops in the world's most powerful church. But "demand" is not a word in the vocabulary of the painfully shy cardinal. Priests who knew him when he was archbishop of Cincinnati describe a deeply spiritual, often lonely man who is meticulous about details. More a diplomat than a politician, Bernardin is "too cautious," say his supporters. Nevertheless, he is not cautious enough for Rome's liking because he defends the U.S. bishops' conference in his patient, deferential way.[121]

It therefore fell to Weakland to express the unhappiness of many American Catholics over the Vatican crackdown. While other bishops also spoke out, Weakland's voice carried furthest because of his role in drafting the letter on the economy and the thoughtfulness of his criticism, which reflected his experience in Rome and respect for diverse cultures. In two columns entitled "The Price of Orthodoxy," published in the Milwaukee archdiocesan paper, he made national headlines by warning, in obvious references to the near-pillorying of Hunthausen and Curran, against fanaticism in the church. He also argued for more understanding of American Catholicism. "In a society like the United States," he said, "you're compromising constantly. I expect I'm not going to win all the time, and if I don't, I have to be satisfied with the little bit I've won and keep going on. We all struggle with how to relate one's own personal integrity and view with corporate loyalty. We do it in politics, we do it everywhere. It's fine, provided there are forums where you have a chance to put up your views."[122]

Weakland pleads for such forums for American Catholics. He believes they should be treated as adults, and as a Vatican II bishop, he feels that the best method of teaching is persuasion. "It's a whole new style of authority," explained Father Francis Eschweiler, a retired Wisconsin pastor. "It isn't a matter of power. It's a matter of how we can serve. Jesus never talked about power. He said we are ministers, servants."[123]

While other American bishops share that outlook, Weakland's contribution was his plain statement of the choices facing American Catholicism. Most Americans have never heard of integralism or of such European movements as Opus Dei and Communion and Liberation. But European Catholics, who have long memories of church involvement in politics, instantly spotted the danger. Weakland, because of his experience in Europe, saw it, too, and warned American Catholics to beware. In a carefully crafted article in *America* he laid out the stakes:

Up till Vatican II, said Weakland, the church had been strongly influenced by integralism which "sought a complete or integral Catholicism in the political realm [and] demanded the perfect coalescence of Christian morality with the legal realm of the state and, thus, the suppression of all error. No concept of separation of church and state was considered orthodox. Error has no rights, they said; and, since the Catholic Church was considered the source of all truth, its doctrine alone should dominate in political affairs."

After World War II integralism was replaced by what Weakland called a "Catholic Action" model, a reference to the militant lay movement in postwar Italy. Theoretically the model cast the clergy as teachers while the laity was to put such teaching into practice in politics and economics. It gave birth to such controversial groups as Communion and Liberation in Italy. It also spawned Catholic political parties, Catholic labor unions, organizations of Catholic industrialists, and other such associations. The advantages of the model, said Weakland, are that the groups get things done and provide a "clear identity for the clergy in political and social affairs," while supposedly saving them from soiling their hands in the "messy turmoil" of political and social issues. The disadvantages are considerable, however, because the laity often appear as puppets of the clergy—a charge frequently made against Italy's Christian Democrats. Moreover, the model has not resolved the challenge of a legitimate pluralism, because the movement's leaders insist on their political and religious agenda. Such movements also have a tendency to revert to integralism, said Weakland, pointing to Communion and Liberation's "zeal to Christianize," which he said "can soon lead members to equate their movement and its aims with the divine plan for the Kingdom." Instead of a neat division between laity and clergy, tensions soon develop between and among them, as shown by Italy's experience, where Communion and Liberation has divided the bishops and the laity.[124]

Weakland worried that John Paul wanted to use this European model for the United States, and indeed the whole world. Such fears were not unfounded, according to bishops in Europe and the Third World, who also spoke of the pope's support for such movements.[125] Meanwhile, the trend toward "no compromise" that the church demanded of the faithful, and particularly of Catholic politicians, resurrected integralism, a Catholic variation of fundamentalism. Earlier leaders in the U.S. church had fought to avoid Catholic separatism in the social and political arenas—for example, shunning the "Catholic" unions and political parties that exist in Europe and Latin America. While that idea might still seem absurd in an American setting, the "no compromise" position of bishops like Law and O'Connor undoubtedly had a polarizing effect akin to that of Communion and Liberation, which perhaps not coincidentally had subsidiaries in New York City and Boston. "The most difficult question posed to the church today by the American political process is precisely that of compromise, a solution inevitable in a pluralistic society," said Weakland. "The whole theory of integralism returns to haunt us at this point of the discussion. Vatican II rejected integralism, but it did not indicate where compromise must stop."[126]

In his criticism of the "confusion and divisions" that John Paul said had been caused by Vatican II, the pope showed that he thought compromise had gone too far. The U.S. church, which had matured through a process of dialogue and compromise, was setting a dangerous example, in the pope's view—hence the need for disciplinary measures against bishops, theologians, and other Catholic leaders who advocated a more pluralistic church. American Catholics might believe that all people were created equal, but in John Paul's church equality was frowned on as foreign to a hierarchical order in which the laity were to follow the lead of bishops and priests, even on such controversial questions as voting for particular parties and candidates. Although the Vatican denied that its outlook was integralist, the pope made it clear, through his actions and speeches, that he sought a Catholic civilization in which, as Weakland said, Roman "doctrine alone should dominate in political affairs." That a pontiff in the late twentieth century should aspire to such an ambition might seem surprising, but John Paul was simply continuing the tradition of an imperial papacy. Accustomed to the new ways of Vatican II, many Catholics tended to forget such history. John Paul, who stood for the continuity of tradition, was not exceptional—the exceptions had been his visionary predecessors, John and Paul.

CHAPTER 9

✝

SANCTUARY

SISTER MARJORIE TUITE always seemed larger than life. A tall, impressive woman with an abounding capacity for compassion, and not a little for anger, she symbolized some of the ways in which American nuns had changed in the post–Vatican II period—as well as the new directions taken by men and women of shared faith. With two master's degrees and a doctorate, the Dominican nun was typical of the highly educated religious women who moved from teaching positions (she was a teacher and principal in Harlem Catholic schools for a decade) to activism on such issues of social justice as racism, poverty, and Central America. Active in ecumenical groups and in the struggle for women's recognition in the Catholic Church, she was perhaps best known for her work with the Central American poor. She was *entregada*—completely given to the people—remembered Renny Golden, a leader in the Sanctuary movement and longtime friend.[1] A year before her sudden death in 1986, Sister Marjorie reflected on the changes in her life. As a teenager and young adult, she had not understood the theological meaning of the body of Christ. But as she grew older, the concept seemed much clearer, and it spoke of a different kind of faith. It meant that "when one person in the body is hungry or raped or oppressed or violated in whatever way, then part of me is violated and oppressed."[2] That, too, was the communitarian principle of the U.S. bishops' solidarity with their suffering brothers and sisters in Central America and of the peace and economic pastorals. The principle was as old as the Christian faith. "They love one another," Aristides had told the Roman Emperor Hadrian. It was so obvious—and so difficult in a society centered on the self. Yet within the consciences of many Americans lay a deep sense of justice that, once wakened, could lead to a new understanding of faith. Perhaps the most significant of such awakenings in the 1980s, both for the number of people it touched and the risks involved, was the ecumenical Sanctuary movement that Sister Marjorie had so strongly supported.

Sanctuary began, as conversion processes often do, with a small group of people in distress. The governments of El Salvador and Guatemala—both, in Jeane Kirkpatrick's view, "moderately repressive" dictatorships—had been systematically killing their own people. Therefore, many Salvadorans and Guatemalans fled to the United States, the majority using the time-worn land route of illegal Mexican laborers. Individual churches tried to help the Central American refugees on an ad hoc basis, but in July 1980 matters took a dramatic turn when a professional smuggler, or "coyote," abandoned twenty-six Salvadorans in the Arizona desert. Half died of dehydration and exposure before they were found. The survivors were taken to a Tucson hospital by a border patrol of the Immigration and Naturalization Service (INS), which announced that as soon as the refugees had recovered they would be arrested for deportation to El Salvador. Presbyterian pastor John Fife, who would become a co-founder of the Sanctuary movement, was one of several church people approached by immigration lawyers, who said that the Salvadorans were terrified of being sent back to their country and would the churches please help. "At that point I couldn't have put El Salvador on the map," Fife recalled. But he learned quickly enough—"about death squads, and about churches being machine-gunned, and about priests being murdered. The real driver for me was the persecution of the church," he said.[3]

Fife's initial response was to start a prayer vigil, which soon became a weekly gathering of people concerned for the refugees. Talk turned to action in large part because a retired rancher named Jim Corbett lent his van to a friend who, while driving north from the Mexican border, picked up a Salvadoran hitchhiker. At a road block north of the town of Nogales the hapless Salvadoran was arrested by the INS. Corbett, who is a Quaker with a degree in philosophy from Harvard, said that he had seen enough television coverage of El Salvador to know that the situation was bad there, but that he was no Central American activist—"at that time I probably could not have given the name of the bishop who had been murdered in El Salvador."

But Corbett couldn't get the hitchhiker out of his mind, and the following morning he decided to find out where he was and what could be done for him. Corbett said he was naive enough to believe that all he had to do was telephone the INS in order to see the man. The INS would give no information, not even the Salvadoran's name, and there was no way Corbett could talk to a refugee without legal permission. A resourceful man, Corbett called up the INS head office in Arizona and gave his name, knowing he would be mistaken for a politically prominent judge of the same name, and demanded to know who and where the Salvadoran was. Armed with that information and a G-28 form, which establishes legal representation, Corbett talked his way into seeing the refugee at the county jail. There he discovered more refugees, about fifty recently caught. He rushed out for more G-28 forms, but when he got back to the jail he was kept cooling his heels until the border patrol had removed the other Salvadorans. At closing time he was told they had gone, nobody knew where. But Corbett tracked them down, including one who was sent to a California detention center called El Centro. During one of his first visits to El Centro, Corbett was locked up by the INS when it discovered that he had taped interviews with the refugees about INS abuses. "I was starting to get an education about the border patrol and INS," he said.

A month after the hitchhiker introduced Corbett to the refugees' world, he and his wife had set up an apartment in their house for Salvadorans applying for asylum. What had started out with one man became fifty people, then hundreds of refugees, all with tales of suffering. For example, a week after the hitchhiker was seized, Corbett learned about a wounded Salvadoran woman who needed a doctor but was afraid to seek help. "She'd been shot in El Salvador just a couple of weeks before, and the bullet was still in her," said Corbett. "I just started calling doctors to see who was willing to risk license, prison and so forth in order to let us know what to do about this woman. That's how it was all along," he said of Sanctuary's origins. "We didn't ever organize by running around and asking, 'Will you become an active member of this secret organization?' When someone is in need, a lot of people respond."[4]

For two years Fife, Corbett, and other concerned individuals worked with the Tucson Ecumenical Council, representing sixty-five Catholic and Protestant churches, to raise money to bond out the refugees. The group obtained nearly $750,000 for bonds and legal expenses, some people even mortgaging their homes to contribute. But the situation was proving increasingly difficult. Bonding costs for Salvadoran refugees were gradually raised from $100 to $5,000 or more, and the hundreds of refugees had become a sea of thousands. Many were shipped out by the INS almost as soon as they were caught, but even those who went through the laborious legal process of applying for asylum were almost always turned down; of the thousands of petitions made annually by Salvadorans and Guatemalans, only 2 to 3 percent were approved.

Corbett's house was full of refugees, as were most of the homes of other Tucson church people who were trying to help the Central Americans. Nevertheless, Fife was still "doing everything very Presbyterian. Presbyterians understand legalities. We live and die by a book of order and legal procedures in our institutional life. I was doing everything possible within the bounds that had been set by government and culture to serve refugees." But as Corbett pointed out to him, it wasn't enough. Deportation was inevitable, and the most they could do for the refugees was to buy time. If they were sincere about helping the refugees, they had to meet their most critical need, to avoid capture and deportation to more suffering and possible death. Fife took the problem to the elders of his church: Should they or should they not provide sanctuary for undocumented Salvadorans in their church? "I was real clear with them: 'If the government catches us doing this, it's five years in prison for every refugee we bring in this church.' They voted to do it."

As the congregation came to know the refugees, more became involved, taking them to live in their homes and gradually joining an "underground railroad" that smuggled refugees across the border to churches in the United States, in a modern version of the nineteenth-century Underground Railroad that spirited American slaves to freedom and safety. "We were all a bunch of amateurs," Fife wryly recalled. "My training is in Bible and theology, not smuggling and covert activities. We did all the things we saw on television that we thought we were supposed to do. We had codes and code words, and it never worked out. We got a telegram in code from Corbett in Mexico one time, sat down with a whole group of us and couldn't figure out what he wanted us to do. It took us two hours."[5]

Meanwhile, the INS had figured out what was going on, and Corbett and Fife got a message to stop or face arrest. But "we couldn't stop," said Fife. "We'd already made the decision when we got involved in that whole effort that the life-and-death needs of the refugees overrode any other set of risks that we might encounter here in the United States. The conclusion we came to is the only other option we have is to give public witness to what we're doing, what the plight of the refugees is and the faith basis for our actions."

Thus was born Sanctuary, responding to the historic traditions of the Jewish and Christian churches. In March 1982, on the second anniversary of Archbishop Romero's assassination, Fife's church and four other congregations on the East and West coasts publicly declared their churches sanctuaries for undocumented Central American refugees. But as Corbett said, "Sanctuary is not a place; it's the protective community of a congregation of people with the persecuted. It has infinite dimensions."

From the beginning, the movement was open about its intentions. National and local authorities were notified of the churches' position, church meetings on the subject were public, and caravans taking refugee families to Sanctuary churches in the north were well publicized. The initiative spread quickly. Already concerned about events in El Salvador, particularly the murder of Romero and the four religious women, church people urged their congregations to study the possibility of joining Sanctuary. The movement also captured the religious imagination because it responded to deep feelings about biblical injunctions to welcome the stranger, to serve as the Good Samaritan. Americans were fascinated by normally law-abiding citizens risking jail for the sake of some Central American refugees: These were no long-haired, pot-smoking kids, so there had to be a good reason for such commitment. The reason, most congregations found, was the suffering refugee. Meeting the Central Americans in their churches, hearing of their tragedies firsthand, seeing the scars, sharing the fear—that was the way to conversion. Few saw their response as a partisan political statement, even if the Sanctuary experience later converted them into opponents of Washington's policies in Central America. "My congregation did not vote to declare public sanctuary because they determined after careful study that it was an effective political tactic to oppose the Reagan administration's policy," said Fife. "They declared sanctuary because they determined after Bible study, prayer and agonizing reflection that they could not remain faithful to the God of the Exodus and prophets and do anything less. It was for us a question of faith."[6]

Church workers confirmed that the deepest commitments were often found among staunch Republicans. In a *Wall Street Journal* article on middle America, Geraldine Brooks reported similar conclusions. In Massillon, Ohio, for example, she found four churches harboring Salvadorans and Guatemalans, though this manufacturing town was part of a congressional district that had not sent a Democrat to the House of Representatives since 1948. Church congregations were middle class; they included lawyers, retired military personnel, even a federal judge. The decision to break the law in support of Sanctuary was reached only after months of study and discussion and agonizing over the demands of conscience. Typical of such converts was an electrical contractor, William Clarke, a longtime Republican who had voted for Reagan. At first he didn't believe the claims about mass deportations, but after talking to refugees and studying the records, he decided that U.S. immigration policies were wrong. Like Fife a law-abiding Presbyterian, Clarke at first tried the legal route by attempting to persuade his Republican contacts in Washington of the importance of the refugee issue. Although he made some impression on one congressman, the message from Washington was "Refugees don't matter." That sort of bureaucratic indifference was what had so angered Corbett when he first approached the INS. Clarke, like many Americans, resented an official brush-off. Soon he was making the rounds of local churches to stir up support for Sanctuary—and succeeding. "Breaking the law is something that's not in the character of these people to do, but they're doing it for deep humanitarian reasons," a Massillon pastor told the *Journal*'s Brooks. "And when you have people out in the grassroots of Ohio saying there's something the matter, the politicians might be wise to listen."[7]

By mid-1984 nearly 150 churches and synagogues had declared for Sanctuary, which gained the support of mainline Protestant denominations, Jews, and Catholics. Several cities also joined the movement. While the numbers of people involved were still relatively small, the fuss focused attention on the administration's immigration policies and on U.S. activities in Central America, particularly El Salvador.

Although Secretary of State Haig had initially made El Salvador a major news story by announcing that the United States would hold the line against communism there, it soon became apparent to cooler heads in Washington that it was counterproductive to encourage press coverage of El Salvador: Much of the nastiness uncovered turned out to be the work of U.S. allies in the Salvadoran military.

Central America's most overpopulated country and among its poorest, tiny El Salvador has traditionally been ruled by an alliance between the military and the landowning oligarchy. Peasant uprisings have occurred regularly since the end of the nineteenth century, when large coffee growers seized the people's communal lands. Usually several thousand were slaughtered before "order" was restored, but President Maximiliano Hernández's government set a record in 1932 by killing 30,000 peasants. Democratic elections were an institutionalized farce; any attempt to establish reforms, particularly as regards land distribution, was treated as "communist subversion."[8] Such conditions provided a natural seedbed for revolutionary insurgency, and by the end of the 1970s guerrilla activities were sufficiently widespread to convince Washington that El Salvador could go the way of Nicaragua. Although the Carter administration "persuaded" the dictator of the moment, General Carlos Humberto Romero, to make way for a reformist junta, tradition proved too strong: By 1980 the reformists were gone, and it was back to killing as usual.

The ensuing bloodbath surpassed even the massacres under Hernández, and by the end of 1983 46,000 civilians had died, according to the San Salvador archdiocese.[9] Some were killed by the guerrillas, but many more were the victims of paramilitary death squads. Salvadorans in certain occupations were killed indiscriminately. They included teachers, university students, labor organizers, and Catholic catechists. Tens of thousands of Salvadorans had left the country in search of refuge in the 1970s, but the carnage in the following decade caused an unprecedented exodus. By 1985 it was calculated that at least half a million had entered the United States. Some 21,000 Salvadorans lived in refugee camps in Honduras, while 300,000 more subsisted in miserable camps in Salvadoran cities. Altogether, one-quarter of the country's 4.8 million people had been displaced by the war. Two-fifths of those who sought refuge outside the country died on the way, according to the United Nations High Commission for Refugees (UNHCR).[10]

It was the same story in Guatemala—bombings, concentration camps (euphemistically known as "model villages"), death squads, torture, massacres. The estimates of the dead were 40,000 to 100,000. The Mutual Support Group, representing families of the disappeared, reported at least 38,000 Guatemalans had been "disappeared" by the armed forces. Some 100,000 Indian peasants fled to refugee camps on the Mexican border. Guatemala, said the human rights organization, Americas Watch, "remains a nation of prisoners." Nevertheless, the Reagan administration asked Congress to provide $35.3 million in military aid to Guatemala. Things were improving in Guatemala, according to the State Department: Only ninety people a month were being "disappeared" in 1984, compared to the 1981 monthly average of 483.[11]

Red Squads

Once American churchgoers heard the testimonies of Central American refugees, they began to question government statements previously taken at face value. That, for the Reagan administration, was the worrisome thing about the movement: Its members knew that the government was lying. In pre-Irangate days that was a real shock to a sector of the public that considered itself mainstream, even conservative. And the Sanctuary movement kept growing: In addition to churches, twenty-two cities, including New York and Los Angeles, had by 1986 declared themselves sanctuaries, thereby prohibiting municipal employees from cooperating with federal agents in the apprehension of illegal aliens. Several universities and even three states—New York, New Mexico, and Wisconsin—also joined the movement. (On taking office in 1987, New Mexico's Republican governor, Garrey Carruthers, rescinded the order of his Democratic predecessor that had made the state a sanctuary.) Moreover, Sanctuary supporters were committed to changing both immigration and Central American policies. It wasn't easy to brush aside people who, like the Ohio businessman William Clarke, were the pillars of their communities and had political contacts.

At the same time, active nonviolence and civil disobedience were growing. Some 70,000 Americans signed a "Pledge of Resistance," promising to respond with peaceful sit-ins of government buildings in the event of a U.S. invasion or major military escalation anywhere in Central America. Arrests for civil disobedience jumped from 5,000 in 1984 to more than 11,000 in 1986.[12] Meanwhile, hundreds of Americans of all faiths traveled to the border regions of Nicaragua under the Witness for Peace program to protest the *contra* war.

The government's initial reaction to such agitation was to state that the dissidents in organizations like Sanctuary were allies of Central American terrorists—a charge that must not have gone down well among such conservative churchgoers as the Ohio Presbyterians. But as protest increased, the Reagan administration began to resort to dirty tricks, reviving the strategy of illegal surveillance and harassment that characterized the Nixon years.[13] In those days police intelligence units known as Red Squads had been employed to infiltrate, survey, and harass groups that engaged in ideological deviance—i.e., they opposed the Vietnam War. As governor of California, Reagan had been an enthusiastic supporter of such police work. He and his assistant, Edwin Meese, who later as attorney general became the boss of INS, set up a state agency, the California Specialized Training Institute, to teach SWAT teams how to deal with left-wing insurgents. Police and National Guard officers from across the country attended its courses at San Luis Obispo. After Reagan became President, several officials of the institute went to work for the Federal Emergency Management Agency, a little-known government office responsible for assisting the victims of natural disasters; thus control of terrorism and civil disorder was added to the agency's roster of duties. One of them later opened a law-enforcement consulting business that gave courses to local police departments on how to infiltrate and control protest movements, including Sanctuary and other groups concerned with Central America.[14]

Sanctuary churches officially came under government surveillance in April 1984 in an undercover investigation known as "Operation Sojourner," named presumably for *Sojourners* magazine, an ecumenical religious publication that supported Sanctuary and the Witness for Peace program. Government agents who infiltrated church groups were told not to tape worship services, since that would contravene First Amendment rights, but several did so despite the ban. Between 1985 and 1986 there were break-ins at churches and the offices of legal aid groups helping the refugees in eleven cities. One Sanctuary church, the Old Cambridge (Massachusetts) Baptist Church, suffered eleven break-ins in four years. In each case the local police refused to investigate. The FBI admitted to having files on the Baptist church and its members, but refused to release them under the Freedom of Information Act or explain how and why the files were compiled. Its reason: to protect an "informant source."[15]

The break-ins followed a pattern. Little or nothing of value was stolen, but files, papers, tax returns, telephone logs, and other items containing information on church members and refugee cases were removed or strewn about the premises. Often, important items like the church's membership records or tax books were carefully positioned atop a desk, opened and sometimes marked so that the message could not be missed: The intruders had gotten exactly what they were looking for.

In addition to the break-ins, Sanctuary workers were frequently harassed; some received death threats. Father Virgilio Elizondo complained that INS agents were patrolling the grounds of his San Antonio, Texas, church in order to apprehend refugees. Catholics working in the New England Sanctuary movement reported that they had been accosted in church parking lots by men claiming to be police officers. The targets, most of them women, said that they were warned against continuing their work, sometimes in threatening tones. Other Sanctuary supporters told of how they had been watched by well-dressed men with cameras and binoculars and how mail was tampered with and phone service frequently cut off. On one occasion four men, one with a camera, were caught by a *Sojourners* employee peering into the magazine's offices in Washington, D.C. When confronted, they acted embarrassed and quickly left in their car, a late-model sedan with a long CB-type antenna. *Sojourners* traced the Virginia license plate to a block of numbers assigned to the National Security Agency, a secret government office responsible for communications intelligence activities, including the monitoring of international phone traffic.[16]

Sanctuary workers were repeatedly questioned by INS agents, sometimes at 6:00 A.M. Sarah Murray, who had trouble with both her mail and her telephone, reported that a man identifying himself as a worker at a health clinic had called her roommate to ask for the location of two Salvadoran refugee children, claiming that Murray wanted him to pick them up for her. The clinic he named did not exist. Later that month a cabdriver who appeared to be waiting for her advised her to stop her work with the refugees because she was endangering her life. When she checked with the taxi company, she was told the driver was not in its employ.[17]

Three Guatemalan refugees had an equally unpleasant experience. The couple and their child were living in an apartment at a Methodist church in Pennsylvania, which began to receive visits from strangers, including a man posing as a church custodian and another as a "private teacher." The refugees later received a letter postmarked in Philadelphia and sent to a New York address known only to their family, which contained several news clippings about the kidnap, torture, and murder of the man's brother and cousin in Guatemala. Subsequently the couple found a note attached to their apartment door with one word, *muerte*—Spanish for death. In the summer of 1987 a Salvadoran woman was kidnapped and tortured in Los Angeles. Before her release, she was warned by her captors to cease her work on behalf of Central American refugees.[18]

Just who was responsible for such threats and harassment remained a mystery, but most victims were convinced that they were targeted by the FBI and/or the INS, possibly with the connivance of local police, who often proved uncommonly reluctant to investigate break-ins and threats. The government itself was quite open about its intimidation of local officials who showed any sympathy for the refugees' plight. For example, the office of New York State assemblyman Jose Serrano, sponsor of a resolution declaring the state a sanctuary for Guatemalan and Salvadoran refugees, reported a call from an immigration agency lawyer who warned that Serrano "was committing a felony" by sponsoring the resolution. While denying that a threat had been made, the New York INS office announced that it planned to investigate whether state employees were breaking the law by obeying the resolution. Meanwhile, the U.S. attorney for northeastern California sent letters to the municipal governments of Sacramento and Davis, both sanctuary cities, threatening them with the suspension of federal aid if they did not end their support for Central American refugees. The letters were written with the approval of the INS and the Justice Department.[19]

All these activities were sideshows to the main event in Arizona, where sixteen Sanctuary workers, including three nuns and two priests, were indicted in early 1985 on charges of smuggling illegal aliens into the United States. Twenty-five other church workers were named as unindicted co-conspirators. In early morning raids across the country sixty people were arrested in connection with the case. Among those indicted were Pastor Fife, Corbett, and Methodists Phil Willis-Conger and Peggy Hutchison. The three nuns—Franciscan Sister Darlene Nicgorski, and Mary Waddell and Anna Priester of the Sisters of the Blessed Virgin Mary—and Fathers Antonio Clark and Ramón Dagoberto Quiñones were selected, said Waddell, "because they [the government] thought they could separate us out fast, force us to make some kind of deal and get us out of the movement." But Waddell was having none of that. She said she had "100 percent support" from her religious order and that she had known what she was getting into. "I was just unlucky to be in the group they picked. But we are all hanging together."[20]

Although the defendants had known they might be arrested, it took considerable courage and faith to face the coming ordeal. Two Sanctuary workers, Stacey Lynn Merkt and Jack Elder, who ran a refugee center in Texas, had previously been convicted and sentenced to jail terms. Merkt, who was adopted as a "prisoner of conscience" by Amnesty International, served a 179-day sentence while pregnant. She was in prison for two and a half months and served the remainder under house arrest. Elder served 135 days at a halfway house in San Antonio before being released for good behavior.

The possible penalties for the indicted were five to twenty-five years in prison and stiff fines. Nevertheless, the defendants remained defiant. Whatever happened to them, they said, could not begin to equal the suffering and need of the Central Americans. Sister Nicgorski, for example, had worked at a Guatemalan preschool and had seen firsthand how the Indian peasants were tortured and killed by the military. She had had to leave the country after the local pastor was murdered and the nuns were warned that they would be next. When she first began work with Sanctuary, Nicgorski said, she did not know that her actions were illegal but by the time she found out, "it no longer mattered." The Gospel call to walk with the oppressed, she said, did not mention anything about the poor needing to show proper documentation. "The protection of life is a religious activity. As a School Sister of St. Francis, I am committed to giving, healing and defending life. . . . Religion is not just saying prayers and singing songs. The government can't tell us which people we can respond to and which ones we can't."[21]

But the government apparently thought it could. Using drug-bust tactics, INS agents ransacked Nicgorski's apartment while she was away on a religious retreat. They seized the Salvadoran woman who lived with her and confiscated all files and documents, including an article Nicgorski had written for a religious newsletter. Court evidence showed that an INS investigator had circled the words "poor and oppressed" in the article, writing in the margin "Marxist ideology."[22]

There were several major issues in the trial that opened in a Tucson courthouse. On the defense side was the argument that the indicted had been following their religious beliefs and that the constitutional separation of church and state forbade the government to judge actions based on religious convictions. The defense lawyers also claimed that illegal infiltration of Sanctuary churches by paid government informants was a violation of both the Fourth Amendment, protecting citizens against unreasonable search and seizure, and the First Amendment's separation of church and state. They further argued that aid to Central American refugees was sanctioned by the decisions of the Nuremberg trials, the 1948 Geneva Convention on civilians fleeing a state of war, the United Nations Convention on Refugees, and the United States 1980 Refugee Act, which required the government to admit any person who was outside his or her country "owing to a well-founded fear of being persecuted for reasons of race, religion, nationality, membership of a particular social group or political opinion." Underpinning these arguments was a larger one—that U.S. policies in Central America were violating domestic and international laws. The defense also challenged the way in which immigration laws were enforced. Citing "Defense of Necessity," the defendants said they had exhausted all legal means to protect the refugees' rights and that consequently no legal alternative existed by which they could discharge their moral responsibilities.

But Federal Court judge Earl Carroll threw out all these arguments as irrelevant, limiting the case to "illegal actions," or smuggling and harboring aliens. The government was allowed to prosecute almost entirely on the basis of tape recordings, many made by paid informants who took concealed recording equipment into Bible-study classes and prayer services in Sanctuary churches. Among the chief witnesses was informant Jesús Cruz, a Mexican in his mid-fifties whom Arizona newspaper reporters identified as a professional smuggler. Tom Fitzpatrick of the *Arizona Republic* said Cruz would have "been arrested by the government in Florida on white slavery charges. Instead of going to jail, Cruz became a paid government informer. As part of his duties, Cruz became a volunteer for the Sanctuary movement." An investigation by two other Arizona journalists, Sandy Tolan and Carol Ann Bassett, showed that Cruz and his sidekick in the Sanctuary affair, Salomón Graham, had become informants for the INS in the early 1980s and that they were paid $16,000 for their spying on the churches. The money probably was less important than protection from prosecution. Cruz was reported to have transported undocumented farm workers from Arizona to Florida in 1984, even though he was then working with the INS, and Tolan and Bassett uncovered evidence that Graham had allegedly attempted to offer prostitutes to farmworkers, a charge denied by Graham in a written affidavit. (Cruz and Graham refused to comment about the claims made against them.) A Mexican citizen who had been arrested five times—between 1970 and 1977—for illegal entry into the United States, twice while transporting illegal aliens, Graham was nevertheless considered a proper agent of the U.S. government. "Evidence of a witness's past misconduct, other than conviction of a crime, is inadmissible for the purpose of attacking the witness's credibility," argued Assistant U.S. Attorney Donald M. Reno, in charge of prosecuting the government's case against Sanctuary. (Neither Cruz nor Graham had been convicted of a crime.)[23]

Open and admittedly naive, Sanctuary workers in Arizona had taken the pair at face value after Cruz showed up one day with a truckload of fruit, saying, "This is for the refugees." "Jesús presented himself as this nice little man eager to be helpful to refugees and said he was in the roofing business, that he had free time," Fife recalled. The Bible-study meetings that formed the backbone of Sanctuary were based on trust, and the Reagan administration had tried to destroy it. As one minister told ABC News, "Everyone knows that in Nazi Germany there were Gestapo agents sitting out in the congregations of German churches. [Now] we don't know when we come to our churches and our services to worship [whether] there might be some government spy there with a tape recorder."[24]

Although many religious denominations protested the government's behavior, and the Lutherans and Presbyterians took the government to court for such snooping, their complaints had no influence on the Tucson trial because of the judge's narrow view of obedience to authority. Any prisoner who comes up against a tough judge is likely to think him cruelly severe, but Judge Carroll, by all reports, exhibited something more than that—he revealed the cultural bias of the Southwest. Such bias could not be blamed for U.S. policies in Central America that had contributed to the flood of refugees, nor was it responsible for a discriminatory attitude in Washington against Latin American migrants. But undoubtedly it contributed to the suffering undergone by Central American refugees once they crossed the U.S. border.

Although he looked on himself as a kind if stern father, Carroll had no patience with Hispanic witnesses, perhaps because he could not speak Spanish. It was not easy for refugee witnesses to recall their experiences in an intimidating courtroom setting, and they often spoke haltingly. But the prosecution was in a hurry, and when the prosecuting attorney objected to taking time to hear the translation of a statement by one Hispanic witness, Carroll upheld him because the refugee's answer had been "too long." "I think people from Latin America perhaps have a difficulty in just answering the question 'yes' or 'no' by nature of their personal attitudes," the judge explained. Although the trial produced repeated incidents of questionable proceedings, Carroll merely admonished the prosecution.[25]

In the Southwest border states Anglos had never had time for Hispanics, particularly Mexicans. As shown in Carey McWilliams's classic history of the region, *North from Mexico,* Mexicans were for a long time treated as animals, and indeed Anglos spoke of them as being not quite human.[26] Racial and cultural prejudices persisted throughout the postwar period: Studies of police brutality repeatedly showed that brown and black people were singled out for abuse. The border situation in 1980, at the start of the flood of Central American refugees, reflected the general attitude of police in the region that "bashing wets" (for wetbacks—a derogatory term for illegal Mexican laborers) was the best way to uphold law and order. That the Central Americans were fleeing institutionalized terror, and not just looking for a temporary job, made no impression on the border patrols. And since INS agents had routinely mistreated the

Mexicans, they saw no reason to change their practices when dealing with Central Americans.

Just how cruel and corrupt the INS Southwest border patrol had become was laid out in detail in 1980 in a five-part series by John M. Crewdson in *The New York Times*. Based on interviews with active and former INS agents, Crewdson recounted a long list of abuses, including bribe-taking, trafficking in narcotics and illegal aliens, selling U.S. citizens' identity cards to aliens, sexually abusing Mexican girls and women, and beating up Mexican teenagers and men. A former border patrol agent said that firing on aliens on both sides of the Rio Grande was routine. "I've seen many shootings," he said, "and these are unarmed people, people who come across just to get jobs." Another former agent who had served with the marines described how Mexicans were routinely beaten up. He was in one of the INS inspection stations, he recalled, when he heard "somebody being slammed against a wall, screaming and begging." When he went to investigate, he found two senior officers, one of whom was beating the alien. "One blocked the door so no one could see in," he said, "while the other actually did it. It went on for two or three minutes. When I tried to stop them, they told me, 'You don't belong in here—get back out there to work.'" He did not last long in the service.[27]

The INS reply to such charges was that it had a special internal enforcement system to deal with abuses, but Justice Department documents showed that the system did not work. "The only crime we didn't find [in the INS] was bank robbery," reported one Justice investigator.[28] Six years after the *Times* investigation, INS spokesman Verne Jervis repeated the official line, saying that if any abuses occurred, they were promptly dealt with by an INS office responsible for such matters.[29] But as shown in U.S. court cases, INS agents routinely ignored the law in dealing with Central American refugees. The ultimate issue in Judge Carroll's court had been not religious convictions but respect for the law. Yet the very agency responsible for seeking prosecution of the Sanctuary workers was itself flouting the law.

For example, border patrol agents frequently failed to inform detained Central American refugees of their right to apply for asylum. If they did not apply, they could immediately be shipped back to their countries—which usually occurred. In a 1982 ruling the U.S. District Court for the Southern District of Texas stated that the aliens—most of whom did not speak English or understand the INS application process—

were often not informed of their rights but encouraged to sign a "voluntary departure" agreement that many refugees thought was a permission to remain in the United States but was in fact a waiver of their rights to a formal deportation hearing as well as their right to apply for asylum. As pointed out in a complaint to the U.S. government by the United Nations High Commissioner on Refugees, such practices negated its treaty responsibilities to protect human rights and made it "fair to conclude that there is a systematic practice designed to forcibly return Salvadorans, irrespective of the merits of their asylum claims."[30]

U.S. courts also found that INS detention centers made it difficult for aliens to have access to a telephone or lawyer, that "packets of written materials explaining the legal rights of aliens are routinely confiscated," and that "INS agents routinely give incomplete, misleading and even false advice to Salvadorans regarding their legal rights." In one case reported by a Los Angeles lawyer, an INS agent grabbed a packet of information on alien rights that the lawyer had given to his Central American client. The agent refused to return the packet, claiming it was "political propaganda."[31]

The gratuitous violence that marked INS treatment of Mexicans was also directed at Central Americans. For example, in a California case that led to a severe admonishment of the INS by the court, Wilfredo Orantes Hernández related how he had fled El Salvador after he was beaten by that country's National Guard, his mother tortured, and two uncles killed. On arrival in California he was grabbed by an INS agent as he was leaving a bus. While one agent twisted his arm behind him, another pistol-whipped him. During his detention INS agents tried to get him to sign a "voluntary departure" form, even rousing him at 3:00 A.M. for the purpose. Orantes received no medical treatment for his injuries during his detention.[32]

In another case, also in California, U.S. District Court judge David Kenyon received evidence that a Salvadoran woman had been given Valium for five days while at an INS detention center, then forced to waive her rights, after which she was put on a plane for El Salvador. Kenyon ordered her flown back to the United States at government expense, saying he would not treat the worst criminal the way the INS had treated the woman.[33]

Yet many of the INS detention centers seemed worse than prisons for convicted criminals. Often located in areas remote from legal aid, they usually consisted of barracks and some solitary confinement cells for rebellious refugees. Food was poor, medical treatment frequently non-existent. During the summer detainees were forced to stand, sit, or lie in treeless yards under a blazing sun that regularly pushed temperatures to between 100 and 120 degrees. During the winter they froze in the unheated barracks. They had less possibility of obtaining the most minimal rights than prisoners serving time for major crimes.[34]

The Reagan administration did not want refugees from El Salvador and Guatemala to gain asylum because that would draw public attention to the failure of its policies there. Although court cases, on-site investigations, and documentation by countless refugees showed that many Central Americans had fled in fear for their lives, their applications for asylum were routinely turned down as lacking such sufficient proof of persecution as, say, pictures of torture sessions. According to the State Department, the Central Americans were just looking for jobs. Violence had fallen off under President José Napoleón Duarte, claimed the government, and there was no reason why Salvadorans could not return to their country. But when asked why an agrarian reform program didn't seem to be working in El Salvador, the State Department's response was "What can you expect when the country is in a civil war?" "With U.S. aid going to the government of José Napoleón Duarte, the administration wants to portray the Duarte government as legitimate and in control, so the administration has pursued a policy both heartless and disingenuous," editorialized the San Jose, California, *Mercury*. "The INS required those who claimed their lives were in danger to provide some documentation—a letter from a death squad, presumably."[35]

The statistics spoke for themselves. According to the INS, 17,066 Salvadorans were detained in 1985; of these, 4,740 were deported to El Salvador and 129 granted asylum.[36] The rest presumably bought time through applying for an asylum they were unlikely to get. In contrast, aliens fleeing countries with leftist governments usually had no trouble gaining entry—for example, Poles, Nicaraguans, and Iranians. In 1984, when only 328 Salvadoran applications out of 5,455 were approved, one-quarter of all Nicaraguan requests went through. More than three-fifths of the Iranian and seven-eighths of the Polish applications were granted.[37]

The Booby Prize

By the time the verdict was brought in at the Tucson trial, the government had spent $2 million of taxpayers' money to achieve exactly the opposite of its original intent: Not only had the trial not frightened off Sanctuary workers; the publicity generated by it attracted many more recruits. In the interim the number of churches and synagogues belonging to Sanctuary climbed to 307, and the INS found itself slapped with a flurry of suits by angry religious denominations that would keep it occupied for years to come. "On the scale of bad judgment," editorialized the San Francisco *Examiner,* "the federal Justice Department outdid everyone else, . . . winning the booby prize hands-down" for bringing religious people to trial. Pointing out that Sanctuary dealt with only a tiny fraction of the millions of illegal aliens in the United States, the *Examiner* said that "for this the Justice Department would raise a hurricane of church-state furies, while the gigantic bulk of illegal immigration goes untended. This crackdown is preposterous also in view of other illegal inflows that are far worse, and to which adequate enforcement power has not been assigned. Let us see some gains against the tidal wave of cocaine before we start assigning federal detectives to poke around in churches for a few scared immigrants."[38]

As Jim Corbett observed, the Reagan administration had "completely misjudged what this movement is about." When it came to a choice between conscience and the law, many American churchgoers would choose the former. To stop Sanctuary, predicted Corbett, Washington would "have to put the church in prison."[39]

Certainly those who had been put on trial remained unrepentant. Of the original sixteen, eight were found guilty of eighteen of seventy-one charges. Cases against two defendants, the Blessed Virgin Mary nuns, were dropped "out of compassion" for Sister Anna Priester's illness (Hodgkin's disease) despite the nuns' protests that they wanted to remain with the indicted. Two Salvadoran women unknown to the Sanctuary workers pleaded guilty to misdemeanors (Sanctuary activists speculated that they had been planted by the government). Four of the remaining defendants, including Corbett, were acquitted. Fife, Sister Nicgorski, the two priests, and Methodists Willis-Conger and Hutchison were found guilty, as well as a Catholic lay worker, Maria Socorro Pardo de Aguilar, and Wendy LeWin, a Unitarian Universalist. The sentencing was less severe than expected. Judge Carroll, who placed the defendants on three to five years' probation, said that he had been encouraged to be lenient by forty-seven members of Congress, who asked him to "consider the underlying circumstances in Central America and the humanitarian motives of the defendants." Carroll also received a letter urging leniency from Arizona's Democratic senator, Dennis DeConcini, who had nominated him for the federal bench. Although Carroll originally forbade the defendants to associate with Sanctuary while on probation, he rescinded the order after several of them refused to sign such an agreement.

The sentencing process, which took place three days before centennial celebrations for the Statue of Liberty, provided the Sanctuary workers with their only opportunity to talk about Central America and the religious motivation for their work on behalf of refugees. Hutchison spoke for them all when she told a packed courtroom that "many of the refugees, material witnesses in this case, believed that the torch of liberty still burned when they fled to the United States." She compared the government's policy of deporting Central American refugees to their war-torn countries with the refusal of the United States to admit thousands of Jewish refugees from Nazi Germany before World War II. Like Jews today, Hutchison said, "I stand before this court to proclaim, 'Never again.' "[40]

Hutchison's prediction that Washington's refugee policy would face continuing challenges was fulfilled to a large extent in March 1987 when the Supreme Court rejected the administration's claim that to qualify for asylum refugees had to prove "clear probability" that they would be killed, tortured, or otherwise persecuted for their beliefs if they returned to their countries. The court said that refugees need only show a "reasonable possibility." Although the case was not related to Sanctuary, it had a significant impact on Central American refugees, many of whom were able to gain asylum, and on Sanctuary, which changed its emphasis to legal and economic aid. Meanwhile, the movement continued to grow: By the fall of 1987 more than 400 churches and synagogues belonged, the largest being Catholic and Unitarian Universalist. "In terms of influence, it is perhaps the single most successful effort to help people become aware of our policies in foreign countries," William R. Farmer, a religion professor at Southern Methodist University, told The New York Times. "It's a powerful movement. When people see and listen to the refugees, they are transformed. It's not mainstream, but it's having an effect on the mainstream."[41]

Covenant Communities

"So now here I am with four small children dependent on me, and Jack facing a fifteen-year jail sentence if convicted," said Jack Elder's wife, Diane, at the time of his trial in Texas for aiding Central American refugees. "Some days I look at what is going on around me, and I think I must be crazy to be doing what I'm doing. But I have no choice, not really. Life is so simple for me now—things really *are* white and black. It is only our frail human egos which fill in the shades of gray. God calls us to two things really—divine obedience and love. We can serve the cause of truth or untruth, justice, the cause of right or wrong, morality or immorality."[42]

Diane Elder did not speak lightly. Others might decry the unfair treatment meted out to refugees, but words alone would not change government policy—or values. Only personal witness could. That was the reason Sanctuary workers risked imprisonment. As the early Christians had shown, behavior was the basis of conversion. Challenging the established authorities had never been easy, but, said Elder's co-worker Stacy Merkt, "If we don't take that small step and act regardless of our fears and regardless of whether or not we have courage, we'll never know what courage is. It is step by step and inch by inch that we struggle in our process to live out our faith."[43]

Along the road, explained Corbett, people discovered that individual criticism of or resistance to unjust policies was not enough. "Only in community," he said, "can we do justice."[44] Although the Sanctuary movement is perhaps the clearest expression of the covenant communities that began to emerge in the United States in the 1980s, many others exist, an example being the ecumenical groups that work with the urban poor. The important thing is not religious denomination but an attitude toward faith, as the Latin Americans soon discovered in the development of their base communities. Their covenant is to love, serve, and witness; to uphold it is to experience a rebirth of faith. Pastor Fife spoke similarly of a "conversion" to the Christian faith—a return to the basic principles of the early church. "The refugees have clearly become the bearers of the new reformation taking place in the churches of Latin America," he said. "Call it liberation theology or the Holy Spirit or whatever term you like, they have evangelized Sanctuary congregations and renewed them in spirit and in truth."[45]

The desire for covenant community lay at the root of the U.S. Catholic bishops' pastorals on nuclear warfare and economics, and their repeated denunciations of the *contra* war and U.S. military aid to El Salvador. In different ways and with different voices mainline Protestant churches and the Catholic leadership were saying the same thing—that there could be no community in the United States unless its citizens began to address the key questions of peace and justice, particularly the plight of the poor. Church leaders said they did not expect a mass conversion, but then mass movements had never occurred without the dedication of small groups of individuals. In Latin America the base community movement began in a remote Brazilian village. Despite persecution and poverty the seed flourished, until it became a forest extending from the Rio Grande to Patagonia. It grew not by word but by example—the commitment of people who gave their lives for the poor. As Fife said, that was what Christianity was really about. Over the centuries it had been subverted by power and wealth, but the religious awakening in Latin America had jolted First World churches into a reexamination of faith. The charge that the church was becoming "political" instead of remaining strictly "religious" was made primarily because of "the decision of the institutional church and of congregations to enter into protective community with the poor and persecuted," argued Corbett. "As it joins the violated in the face of organized violence, the church is ceasing to be the nominally apolitical pillar of the established powers."[46]

The Long Haul

As Sanctuary shows, the more faith communities are persecuted, the more they prosper. The Reagan administration made a "booby prize hands-down" political blunder by persecuting church workers in the Sanctuary movement. Similarly, it can be—and was—argued that the Vatican made a mistake in its crackdown on the U.S. church, particularly the disciplining of Archbishop Hunthausen, which caused such widespread dissent among American Catholics that the pope was compelled to send a letter to the U.S. bishops pleading for "unity and universality" under the "successor of Peter." These two authoritarian actions had similar results. The first was a deeper understanding among the covenant communities of just how difficult it was to achieve change. The communities didn't mind being different—in fact, that was the whole point—but they also spoke of the "long haul," recognizing that it would take years, perhaps decades, to make any impact on U.S. policies in Central America or the authoritarian ways of Rome. The second was the acknowledgment by both Catholics and Protestants that while the U.S. Catholic Church had made enormous progress in its communitarian commitment since Vatican II, the bishops' conference lacked the will and the way to move beyond a certain stage of dissent.

Although religious orders and individual bishops took a strong stand in support of Central American refugees, including many of the Southwest's bishops, as a body the bishops could not bring themselves to join other religious denominations in publicly endorsing Sanctuary. Divided on the issue and warned by legal counsel that Sanctuary was illegal, the bishops' conference remained silent despite the efforts of some prelates to persuade its members of the need to appreciate the religious implications. As Father Elizondo observed after INS agents pursued two refugees into the driveway of his Texas church, "We're not questioning the legality [of their pursuit], but the morality of it. Something can be perfectly legal and totally immoral, but this country is not used to those distinctions."[47] Archbishop Weakland, who had harbored eight Salvadorans in his home, made the same point. There were civil laws and church laws, he said, but the highest law was what was right—what was moral.[48]

PART IV

THE WORLD

CHAPTER 10
✠
THE RELIGIOUS
INTERNATIONAL

WHILE SANCTUARY and the Latin American base communities show how religion can become a vehicle for change, other, perhaps more powerful, organizations on the religious right have sought to restore a hierarchical order of social and economic privilege. Unlike the progressive church movements, which see religion as a means to democracy, their opponents on the right use religion to further the political and economic goals of a small group of powerful individuals, including corporate chieftains and cardinals. Yet most who join these organizations do not perceive the manipulation and believe they are doing God's work.

The international Catholic right shares certain beliefs with U.S. Protestant fundamentalists, including a strident anticommunism and reverence for authority. Nevertheless, the internationalists are different in several important respects. One is a penchant for secrecy that has spawned a multitude of conspiracy theories. Another is a tendency to become involved in political intrigue, sometimes with the CIA or other intelligence agencies. These groups also uphold inherited privilege, and some of their rites make the antics of Jim and Tammy Faye Bakker seem like child's play.

Students of the subject disagree as to which group is the most powerful or dangerous, but undoubtedly the most venerable is the Sovereign Military and Hospitaller Order of St. John of Jerusalem of Rhodes and Malta, better known as the Knights of Malta, or SMOM. One of Catholicism's oldest chivalric orders, SMOM is unique in several ways. Although it has no territory outside its headquarters in a Roman palazzo, it enjoys the status of a sovereign state, maintaining relations with forty-nine countries and issuing its own passports and stamps. Its 13,000 members include some of the world's most powerful figures, among them heads of state. It pledges allegiance to the pope, but neither he nor the order's grand master in Rome has real control over SMOM's various national associations, some of whose members have been involved in fascist plots and CIA covert wars. And while dedicated to charitable work, such as funding leprosariums and contributing medical supplies to the Third World, it also serves as an old-boys' club for the European aristocracy and the political right in the United States and Latin America. The men and women who are chosen to become knights and dames generally share a reactionary Catholic worldview, but they must also be rich and/or titled. Some are attracted to the order by the benefits implicit in hobnobbing with the wealthy and powerful, but there is also a snob appeal in belonging to so ancient a chivalric order.

Unlike the plebeian Knights of Columbus, the Knights of Malta is the most elite of Catholic lay orders. It was founded in the eleventh century to provide medical aid and military protection for pilgrims to the holy city of Jerusalem. The order's knights participated in several important crusades, and gifts it received soon gave it control over extensive estates throughout Europe. The wealth of the knights' grand priories greatly increased in the fourteenth century when they absorbed the estates belonging to the Knights Templar, whom they helped to destroy, and for a time they maintained control of the island of Rhodes. Forced from Rhodes by Sultan Muhammad II in the fifteenth century, they eventually settled on the island of Malta, which gave the order its name. The Knights remained a major military presence in the Mediterranean until 1789, when Napoleon occupied Malta. After a brief sojourn in Russia, the order in 1834 established headquarters in Rome under papal protection. By the end of the century, it had become a charitable organization of the aristocracy devoted to the care of the sick and the wounded. It maintained its exclusivity by refusing to accept members from Europe and Latin America who were not of the nobility or heads of state. In recent years the ruling has been relaxed for Latin America, but even as late as the 1940s the order refused to admit Eva Perón as a dame because of her proletarian background.[1]

An exception was made for the United States because of its rising political, economic, and military power, and in 1927 a branch of SMOM was established on the East Coast. Most of the founding members were tycoons of industry and finance who would strongly oppose Roosevelt's New Deal (one, John J. Raskob, the chairman of the board of General Motors, even became involved in a plot to seize the White House). They were soon joined by such titans as John Farrell, president of U.S. Steel; Joseph P. Grace, of W. R. Grace & Co.; Joseph Kennedy, the Boston entrepreneur and father of the future President of the United States; and George MacDonald of Pennsylvania, who made a fortune in oil and utilities. MacDonald was typical of those who joined SMOM for the sheer fun of it. In recognition of generous contributions to the church, he was made a papal marquis as well as a grand master of the Knights of Malta. MacDonald loved to dress up in the splashy Knights costume, with its ostrich-plumed hat, gold spurs, and a uniform with gold epaulets, sashes, and the medal with the Knights' eight-pointed Maltese cross. Many of the approximately 1,500 Americans who subsequently joined the knighthood also enjoyed the rituals of induction at the local cathedral and the ceremonies in honor of the order's patron, St. John.[2] But for others, SMOM was more than pomp and circumstance—it was a source of money and power.

Among the latter was New York's Cardinal Spellman, at one time the most powerful Catholic churchman in the United States. He became involved with the American branch of SMOM almost from its founding, and was the order's official church patron in the United States when he was auxiliary bishop of Boston. After he became archbishop of New York in 1939, he changed his title to "Grand Protector" (apparently to distinguish it from that of King Leopold and Queen Wilhelmina, who were mere "protectors" of the Belgian and Dutch branches of the Knights). Spellman enjoyed the support of the right wing of the Curia, particularly Cardinal Nicola Canali, who dominated Vatican finances, and Canali authorized his monopoly over Knight appointments in the United States. The quid pro quo was that instead of sending the American Knights' contributions to SMOM headquarters in Rome, Spellman funneled the money into Canali's coffers. When SMOM's grand master demanded an accounting from Spellman, he got no answer. No action was taken against Spellman, however, because at the time the order was fighting for its life against Canali, who wanted to gain control of its wealth.[3]

Spellman's financial contributions to the Vatican, his friendship with Pius XII, and his access to U.S. economic and political elites, some of them Knights, gave him immense power, and by World War II he had become the Vatican's go-between with the White House and its proconsul in Latin America. When Spruille Braden, U.S. ambassador to Colombia during the early 1940s, complained about the anti-American tone of a pastoral letter issued by Colombian archbishop Ismael Perdomo, Spellman sent a personal emissary to Bogotá to lecture Perdomo on the need for cooperation in the war effort. At this meeting, which took place in

Braden's presence, the archbishop was instructed to show Braden anything he wrote about the United States before releasing it. Braden was impressed. "It was good theater," he said.[4]

Spellman also played an important role as emissary between the White House and Rome as, for example, in relaying the pope's concern about Allied bombings of Italy. And he encouraged Vatican cooperation with the Office of Strategic Services (OSS), the wartime forerunner of the CIA that was headed by his old friend General William ("Wild Bill") Donovan.[5]

Much of the European aristocracy that provided SMOM with its membership was allied with the Falangist groups in Spain, the Catholic integralist–Vichy French, the Italian fascists, and the German-Austrian supporters of Hitler. While they objected to Hitler's attempts to create a Nordic system of belief in competition with the teachings of the Catholic Church, some agreed with the Nazis on the "Jewish question." For example, Franz von Papen, a Catholic aristocrat from the Westphalian nobility and Knight Magistral Grand Cross of SMOM, paved the way for Hitler's assumption of power after von Papen became chancellor with the support of the Nazis.[6]

During the war the Vatican's position was ambivalent, not because Pius XII approved of Nazism—on the contrary, he abhorred it—but because he feared communism more than fascism and because he was afraid to risk the loss of the church's power by taking an uncompromising stand against the self-declared masters of Europe. Or as the British Foreign Office put it, the pope, "for worldly rather than spiritual reasons, has allowed himself, like others, to be bullied." Although the Vatican undertook many private initiatives to help Jewish and other refugees, Pius remained silent through most of the war. He refused to condemn the German invasion of Poland in the belief that the Poles were at fault, and despite repeated pleas from the Polish government in exile he failed to condemn Nazi genocide. "We cannot forget that there are 40 million Catholics in the Reich," he said at the time of the invasion of Poland. "What would they be exposed to after such an act by the Holy See?" When he did speak out, as in his 1942 Christmas message about the deaths of "hundreds of thousands of people . . . merely because of their race or their descent," the appeal was lost in the opacity of Vaticanese language. Similarly, the Vatican said nothing about the massacre of hundreds of thousands of Serbs belonging to the Serbian Orthodox Church during the Nazi Catholic puppet dictatorship of Croatia, apparently because its leader, Ante Pavelić, and his Ustashi thugs had the support of the local Catholic clergy. The only important Catholic voice to speak out against the slaughter was that of the French cardinal Eugene Tisserant, who said that at least 350,000 people had been killed by Pavelić's forces. The Holy See, said Tisserant, had accommodated itself "for its own exclusive advantage—and very little else."[7]

Much the same might have been said of some American members of the Knights of Malta. For example, W. R. Grace & Co. was on the U.S. government's "watch list" of companies known or suspected to be trading with the enemy during World War II. State Department documents showed that some Grace personnel in Latin America were kept under surveillance because of their ties to Nazi agents, particularly those in the company's shipping lines and in the Panagra airline, which Grace owned jointly with Pan American Airways. (J. Peter Grace, who took over the company at the end of the war and became SMOM's leading American Knight, later employed a Nazi war criminal and chemist, aiding him to enter the United States under the U.S. government recruitment program of Nazi scientists known as "Project Paperclip.") Joseph Kennedy, another prominent American Knight, was forced in 1940 to leave his post as U.S. ambassador to Great Britain because of his noninterventionist stance.[8]

After the war, the Vatican, the OSS, the SS (Schutzstaffel, the elite guard of Nazi intelligence), and the various branches of SMOM joined to do battle against the common Soviet enemy—and to help Nazi war criminals escape. In 1945, when the outcome of the war was no longer in doubt, the OSS approached Reinhard Gehlen, who was Hitler's chief of intelligence on the Eastern Front. The aim was to revamp the Gehlen Organization into an OSS-controlled operation. The plan was so successful that "Gehlen Org" was transformed into West Germany's postwar intelligence agency, the BND, with help and money from the OSS's successor, the CIA. Paralleling the OSS-Gehlen plan was "Project Paperclip," which smuggled more than 900 German scientists into the United States. Gehlen's brother was secretary to one of the chief officials in SMOM's Rome headquarters, and the Knights were active as gobetweens. Baron Luigi Parrilli, an Italian aristocrat who was a Knight of Malta, papal chamberlain, and fascist sympathizer, took part in the negotiations between SS leaders and the CIA's future director, Allen Dulles. Meanwhile, James Jesus Angleton, who would later become the CIA's controversial director of counterintelligence, was dispatched by Admiral

Ellery Stone, U.S. proconsul in occupied Italy, to rescue Prince Valerio Borghese from possible arrest by the Italian Resistance, which had sentenced him to death for war crimes. Borghese, who survived to be a leader in Italy's postwar fascist politics, was a Bailiff Grand Cross of Honor and Devotion of SMOM, and in gratitude for U.S. services to him and other Knights, SMOM gave Stone, Angleton, and Angleton's deputy its Grand Cross award. Other recipients of the coveted award were Reinhard Gehlen and Truman's Vatican envoy, Myron C. Taylor.[9]

SMOM provided more than medals. One of its directors arranged for the printing of 2,000 SMOM passports for political refugees, many of them Nazis. A branch of the Knights in southern Germany ran a large refugee camp, and the leading Bavarian Knight of Malta was reported to have arranged travel "for no small number of ex-Nazis."[10] That the Vatican, the OSS, and the U.S. Army's Counter Intelligence Corps (CIC) were a party to such arrangements is shown by files that Justice Department investigators discovered in the 1980s.[11] Catholic monasteries and convents were used as safe houses for war criminals on their way to Latin America. Sometimes the CIC supplied false documents, while church organizations provided the means of escape—a famous case being the flight to Bolivia of Klaus Barbie, the "butcher of Lyon." A key contact in the underground railway, known as the "Rat Line," was a Croatian priest, Krunoslav Draganović, who had been an adviser to Ante Pavelić and a member of his Ustashi terrorists and who ran the Croatian Committee for Pontifical Assistance, an aid and resettlement agency of the Holy See. Draganović passed along upwards of 30,000 Croatians, including most of the Pavelić government and Pavelić himself, who escaped to Argentina. The priest also helped SS officers escape, according to Barbie, who said that Draganović described his work as "purely humanitarian."[12]

CIC reports to Washington gave detailed descriptions of Pavelić's stay in Rome under church protection "disguised as a priest within Vatican City" and predicted his escape to Argentina, then ruled by the dictator Juan Perón, a Bailiff Grand Cross of Honor and Devotion of the Knights of Malta. They also reported Pavelić's contacts with Monsignor Giovanni Battista Montini, the Vatican's under secretary of state and the future Pope Paul VI. Montini, a close friend of SMOM and the OSS's principal contact in the Vatican during the war, supervised the Vatican bureau that issued refugee travel documents. CIC reports and other documentation show that he was privy to the activities of the Croatian Committee for Pontifical Assistance. He apparently shared Pius XII's conviction that

Pavelić and his Ustashi troops might overthrow Marshal Tito's government and reestablish a Catholic state in Yugoslavia. Ivo Omrcanin, a close friend of Draganović who was working at the Vatican when the priest was smuggling Croatians abroad, said that "the Pope would never have considered anybody who was fighting communism . . . a war criminal."[13]

The relationship of the Vatican, SMOM, and the OSS/CIA was also important in the crucial 1948 Italian elections. Baron Parrilli again served as a go-between, this time with the CIA, in planning Vatican strategy to prevent a Communist victory by backing the Christian Democrats. A key figure in the plan was Luigi Gedda, a Turin doctor, Knight of Malta, and Catholic integralist who wanted to restore Europe to an age before Protestantism and the French Revolution. Gedda was head of Italy's Catholic Action, a militant lay movement of young people who served as papal shock troops—C. L. Sulzberger, of *The New York Times,* reported from Rome that Catholic Action "is armed, active and tough." Gedda organized a network of 18,000 "civic committees" to get out the vote. James Angleton, then the CIA's Vatican connection, strongly recommended CIA funding for Gedda's political machine. (The CIA pumped $65 million into Italian centrist and right-wing movements between 1946 and 1972, according to hearings by the House of Representatives.) Other important players were Montini and Spellman, the latter funneling huge amounts of New York money into clandestine church activities in Italy. Spellman encouraged a letter-writing campaign whereby Italian Americans urged their relatives to vote against the Italian Communists, and he joined such famous Americans as Frank Sinatra, Bing Crosby, and Gary Cooper in a radio blitz of Italy at election time. Meanwhile, Catholic Action's papal troops prepared for battle with U.S. jeeps, guns, and other supplies. The Christian Democrats won the election and Washington, under pressure from Spellman, agreed to repay the Vatican's election expenditures through Italy's black currency market.[14]

High-ranking Knights of Malta were involved in Italian politics during the following decades, and on two occasions, in 1964 and 1970, they attempted unsuccessful right-wing coups. The second attempt was led by Angleton's Prince Borghese and the prince's neo-Nazi protégé, Stefano Delle Chiaie, one of the period's most dangerous terrorists. Borghese and Delle Chiaie were connected to the notorious P-2 Masonic Lodge, an organization with ties to the Mafia and the Vatican that schemed to take over the Italian state and was responsible for a string of terrorist acts. P-2 was unmasked in 1981 during police investigations into the Mafia contacts and financial crimes of Italian banker Michele Sindona, who for many years was the chief influence in the Vatican Bank, thanks to his contacts with Paul VI and Prince Massimo Spada, a Vatican nobleman, top financial adviser to the Holy See, and a Knight of Malta. Numerous members of the P-2 also turned out to be Knights of Malta, including several military and police intelligence chiefs and bankers. The most sinister was Count Umberto Ortolani, SMOM's ambassador to Uruguay and the brains behind the P-2. Ortolani had extensive bank and real estate holdings in Uruguay and was at one time the head of Uruguay's second largest private bank, Banco Financiero Sudamericano. He had also established a P-2 branch in Montevideo, with some 500 members, including prominent military hard-liners. When the P-2 scandal broke, Ortolani fled to São Paulo, Brazil, whence the Italian police were unable to extradite him because of Brazil's resistant extradition laws.[15]

The membership overlap of P-2 and SMOM is not surprising in view of the conspiratorial, right-wing outlook of some factions of the European Knights. For example, SMOM members also belong to the European Freedom Council, a spin-off of the Anti-Bolshevik Bloc of Nations. The Bloc is itself a regional federation of ex-Nazis, including the Croatian Ustashi, that came into being with U.S. financial aid in another variation of Project Paperclip and the rehabilitation of "Gehlen Org" by the OSS/CIA.[16] These groups form the core of the ultraright World Anti-Communist League (WACL), which in the 1980s oversaw the private funding network for the Nicaraguan *contras* in cooperation with the New York branch of SMOM and a cabal of American Knights, including former CIA director William Casey and J. Peter Grace (see p. 295).

The Knights as a group are primarily attracted by the cachet of membership in an ancient and romantic religious order and by the *noblesse oblige* of a charity sponsored by aristocrats. Or as one specialist put it, "Humberto Ortolani is quite a different case from a vice-president of a Midwest corporation in the United States."[17] On the other hand, the process of selection guarantees that those recommended for membership by the national associations and their "protectors" (either the local cardinal or king or queen) share a political outlook and exercise political and economic influence. Prospective members cannot apply to join but are recommended by the existing membership for what is usually pro forma approval by headquarters in Rome. As in any aristocratic organization, children have hereditary rights of membership, which they do not always exercise (Kennedy children failed to join). Members of local SMOM associations tend to frequent the same clubs and boardrooms. Often they have gone to the same schools and followed parallel careers in government and business. In the United States they are virtually a Catholic establishment.

Contrary to conspiracy theories that SMOM is running a secret world government, its dubious character arises from the actions of individual Knights or groups of Knights who support political projects that "would be good for our side," in the words of a knowledgeable church source.[18] SMOM is more useful for such projects than a private club or foundation because its sovereign status provides diplomatic immunity—valuable in sending shipments through foreign customs, for example—and it maintains a network of contacts around the world. A SMOM seal on a Knight's project also gives it the appearance of church support, although the Vatican may have no control over the venture or even know of its existence. This is particularly true of the activities of Knights outside Europe, most of whom are not personally known to headquarters in Rome. In any case, headquarters is hardly equipped to run a world conspiracy. Housed in a small palace on a narrow, crowded Roman street, SMOM's offices are more suitable to a museum than a military command post. The order's grand master, Sir Andrew Bertie, a Scottish friar and a cousin of England's Queen Elizabeth, and his court are primarily concerned with protocol, knightly honors, and the Vatican intrigue that inevitably infects church institutions in Rome. Church sources familiar with SMOM's workings dismiss the idea that the grand master is "privy to all the schemes of Knights in other countries," and they cite the case of J. Peter Grace, Jr., the best-known American Knight and the most controversial.[19]

Knight Grace

Scion of the W. R. Grace fortune in Latin America, Grace is high-handed, ambitious, and frenetically busy. Such qualities helped him build the family business from annual sales of $12 million when he took control in 1945 to $7.1 billion by the mid-1980s, but they have not always endeared him to the church. Although Grace is admired for his fund-raising on behalf of Catholic institutions, he evokes mixed reactions in New York church circles, where he is seen as a second power center in competition with the archdiocese through his position as president of the U.S. eastern Knights. Spellman, who was tough as nails and shared Grace's right-wing philosophy, knew how to handle the Knight, but later cardinals, who fell heir to the role of "Grand Protector," found the relationship more vexing. According to a source intimate with Terence Cooke, Spellman's successor, the cardinal had difficulty controlling Grace. "He would call up five and six times a month with some idea, and Cooke would tell him, 'Peter, you can't do that,' because Grace was involving the Knights of Malta in a political scheme. Ordinary Knights out in the Middle West aren't into that sort of thing, but Peter, who is a crusader and really believes he is a religious knight, would use them for his political schemes. And he was all over the place. One minute we would get a message that he was flying to Brazil, the next to Japan. You never knew what he would get into next. Cooke was always afraid he would drag the Knights and the church into some political mess involving the government. He wanted to send a complaint to Rome about Grace's activities, but who do you complain to in Rome? Some old gentleman in a marble palace [SMOM headquarters]?

"Grace got the Knights involved in *contra* funding when Cooke was dying, and Cooke's chief concern, even though he was so ill, was Grace. 'What's Peter doing?' he would ask. Grace can never get enough power, and he can cause the church embarrassment. He's a very important Catholic layman who speaks to Republican corporate leaders who are Catholics and who is identified with Reaganism. He has done some good things for the church, such as his charitable foundation, but he is dangerous."[20]

An expert on the Knights of Malta came to similar conclusions: "When Grace puts pressure on the archdiocese, he is saying, I am an important Catholic layman. But he is doing it for political reasons. Nor should one forget that W. R. Grace is a major corporate power."[21]

Blunt and often outrageous, Grace has been accustomed to flaunting his power since he was a young executive in his father's empire. In those days, W. R. Grace was chiefly involved in shipping, airlines, sugar plantations, and mining in Latin America, and some chemicals. But Grace, soured by the loss of company properties in Cuba after the 1959 revolution and by rising nationalism in Peru (originally the pillar of the empire), gradually abandoned Latin America to concentrate on agricultural chemicals, oil, and, later, retailing and restaurants. Grace describes his hobbies as "economics and anticommunism," and he pursued both in his public activities. For example, he was a trustee of the American Committee for Liberation from Bolshevism, which was founded in 1950 and later became Radio Liberty. Under the guiding hand of the CIA, the committee funded various "research institutes," which were "little more than front groups for ex-Nazi intelligence officers," according to John Loftus, who had access to secret documents on the subject as a prosecutor in the Office of Special Investigations, the Justice Department's Nazi-hunting unit.[22]

A year after the committee was established, Grace hired a Nazi scientist, Otto Ambros, following his release from prison, where he had served three years for war crimes because of his work with I. G. Farben, the multinational chemical giant that fueled Hitler's war machine. Ambros subsequently became a director of a subsidiary of the giant Flick conglomerate, another German dynasty that played a role similar to that of Farben during the war. While Friedrich Flick, Sr., was being tried for war crimes, his son and heir Friedrich Karl was sent to the United States to work in a small New York bank controlled by the Grace family. Grace later claimed that the younger Flick "is like a member of the family." Flick purchased 26 percent of W. R. Grace stock, but the deal came under strong attack in Germany when it was revealed that Flick had paid off German politicians to hush up the illegal use of a tax loophole to make the Grace investment. Grace got little sympathy from Wall Street when he had to buy back the Flick stock since he has treated the Street much as he has the New York archdiocese, by thumbing his nose at its advice and warnings.[23]

Grace feels strongly about the "communist threat" in Latin America, and since the sixties has actively promoted the American corporate way of life in the region. For many years he was board chairman of the American Institute for Free Labor Development (AIFLD), a Trojan Horse for the multinationals and the State Department that was involved in a string of U.S.-supported coups, including the overthrow of elected governments in Brazil and the Dominican Republic. He also chaired a businessmen's committee charged with evaluating President Kennedy's Alliance for Progress that recommended less aid to the Latin Americans and more tax breaks and subsidies for U.S. corporations. He expressed his feelings about Latin Americans and government aid when he told a meeting of the American Feed and Grain Manufacturers Association that the number-one cause of government waste was "Puerto Rican food stamps," Puerto Ricans being the biggest recipient of such aid—a claim that was factually untrue and a racial slur.[24]

His statement caused a furor in Puerto Rico, where his company has investments, forcing him to fly to the island to make an official apology. Nevertheless, Grace continued to air his controversial opinions, as in a

$400,000 newspaper and TV advertising campaign in support of Reagan-omics. He nagged so much about government waste that Reagan finally appointed him to head a task force on ways to reduce government spending. The task force produced some 2,500 recommendations, including those by representatives of oil, plastics, and chemical corporations, among them W. R. Grace, who were charged with advising the government on how to prune spending by the Environmental Protection Agency. Congressional committees raised the question of conflict of interest, since W. R. Grace was embroiled in a major lawsuit in Massachusetts over W. R. Grace's alleged contamination of well water. In any case, the Congressional Budget Office and the General Accounting Office, which reviewed the task force's work, found that few of the recommendations were of practical use.[25]

In addition to running the task force and his company, Grace found time to support the Novak-Simon attack on the U.S. bishops' economic pastoral (see Chapter 7); the Reagan-backed, anti-Castro radio station, Radio Martí; and various schemes against the Sandinistas, including a *contra* lobby headed by Lewis Lehrman, the drugstore tycoon, former candidate against Mario Cuomo for governor of New York, and a Knight of Malta. In May 1984, when Managua's Cardinal Obando y Bravo was visiting Cardinal O'Connor in New York, a Grace representative was dispatched to meet with the Nicaraguan to discuss his request for money for his archdiocese's leadership formation programs. No friend of the Sandinistas, the cardinal painted the situation in Nicaragua in the blackest terms, according to a memorandum of the conversation sent to Grace. The memo recommended that funds from the Sarita Kenedy East Foundation, of which Grace had partial control, be used to support the cardinal's programs since they "represent the best organized opposition in Nicaragua." Some $30,000 were reportedly earmarked for the Managua archdiocese, but the plan was ruined by public revelation of the memo and Obando's meeting with a Grace representative. In the end, the aid was limited to a shipment of rosaries that was confiscated by Nicaraguan customs. Although Obando later claimed that he had never solicited money from W. R. Grace, the memorandum from Peter Grace's representative, John Meehan, clearly showed that Obando had hoped to obtain substantial financial support from the Catholic millionaire.[26]

O'Connor, who is SMOM's current "Grand Protector," strongly supported Obando and saw nothing untoward in making the archdiocese's offices available for the ninety-minute interview with Meehan. As a close associate of the cardinal explained, O'Connor believed in respect for the hierarchy, and he "implicitly trusted" Obando, whereas he felt "total repugnance" for the so-called "popular church" that supported the Sandinista government. On the other hand, said his associate, O'Connor was not unaware "of the horror stories about the *contras*," and he supported the policy of the U.S. bishops' conference in opposing aid to the *contras*.[27]

Grace, in contrast, was gung ho for the *contra* cause and used SMOM's network to help provide private funding. Millions of dollars in supplies were channeled through the Knights to the *contra* camps in Honduras; distribution was facilitated by SMOM's diplomatic privileges and its Central American membership. Among the largest shipments handled by the Knights were those from the Americares Foundation, directed, among others, by Grace; former Treasury Secretary William Simon, also a Knight; and Prescott Bush, Jr., brother of Vice President George Bush. Founded during the Vietnam War to raise money for Saigon children, Americares later focused its attention on Poland, Lebanon, Afghanistan, and Central America. Most of its supplies are donated by U.S. pharmaceutical companies and AID, but it also received contributions from Pat Robertson's Christian Broadcasting Network. Another important contributor was the Nicaraguan Freedom Fund, established by the Reverend Sun Myung Moon's Unification Church. Simon was a board member of the fund, as was Cold Warrior Clare Boothe Luce, SMOM's leading American Dame and a board member of Moon's *Washington Times*. Logistics in Central America were handled by Roberto Alejos, a wealthy Guatemalan sugar and coffee grower who was SMOM's ambassador to Honduras and had had a relationship with the CIA since 1960 when the agency used his estates to train Cubans for the Bay of Pigs invasion. Grace's explanation of why the Knights of Malta were running the supply network instead of such established aid groups as the Red Cross was that "the Knights have been doing this for 900 years. They have their own cross [the Maltese cross]. . . . They'd consider themselves way beyond the Red Cross."[28]

Although Grace told fellow Knights that their good deeds in Central America "reflect glory on the Order of Malta," on-the-spot investigations showed just the contrary. Supplies sent to Guatemala, for example, were used by the military in its "model village" program, which forcibly relocated Indian peasants to controlled settlements that were little better than concentration camps. A report by a Canadian government aid mission to El Salvador stated that the Knights' supplies were also going to

military-controlled relocation camps of displaced Salvadorans. Santa Te-
cla, the camp the mission visited with the Knights of Malta ambassador,
"left an awful impression on us," according to the Canadian report. "In
some ways, it reminded us more of a squalid prison camp than a social
rehabilitation or reintegration experiment." Yet another settlement, near
San Juan de Opico, adjoined a heavy artillery training camp for the
military and "caused some trepidation to those installed there."[29]

The Canadians questioned the "neutrality of relocation schemes undertaken by a government at war with part of its own population," and
drew a sharp distinction between groups like AID, the Knights of Malta,
and Project Hope, which were working with the government, and independent charitable organizations that served the people's needs. The
mission recommended that the Canadian government not participate in
any of the government-associated projects. It was clear to the Canadians
that the U.S. and Salvadoran governments were attempting to destroy
any possible peasant support for the guerrillas by bombing the peasants
out of the countryside and forcing them into relocation camps similar to
the "model villages" in Guatemala. Unlike the Knights of Malta, the
Canadians wanted nothing to do with a plan that they said was "ethically
questionable."[30]

In contrast to Grace's Knights, SMOM members in other parts of
the country are more circumspect (the U.S. membership is divided into
three associations—eastern, southern, and western). In California, for
example, most of the Knights' charity goes to traditional good works,
such as hospitals and clinics. But of course the western Knights do not
have such a determined crusader to lead them.[31] Grace, who often works
sixteen to eighteen hours a day, is a driven man. He always wears two
watches, one with the local time wherever he happens to be, the other
with the time back at New York headquarters. He is in such a hurry that,
on occasion, he dictates to two secretaries at the same time. He wears a
gun in his belt which he will display when showing off a thirty-four-inch
waist—one of his many vanities. Another is his refusal to wear a hearing
aid, forcing people to shout to make themselves heard. Although he is
famous for telling off his executives and for demanding yards-long "spread
sheets" with infinitesimal operating detail, a former executive gave him
high marks for building W. R. Grace into a corporate giant. As to the
"spread sheets," he said, Grace "feels about numbers as other men do
about women or alcohol. It's a passion."[32]

Passionate is also a good description of Grace's feelings about peace activists, affirmative action, environmental programs, government bureaucracy, and the media, all of which he loathes. Described by one biographer as "a living example of the roots of Reaganism," Grace hates the New Deal and passionately yearns for a time when business was unfettered.[33] But he also stands in the older SMOM tradition of kings and crusading knights. His stamp on the eastern chapter of SMOM, which he has led for many years, is clearly reflected in the choice of members, eight of whom are on the board of W. R. Grace, including the order's chancellor, John D. J. Moore, former U.S. ambassador to Ireland.

Other influential Knights and Dames include(d):

• William Casey, director of the CIA from 1981 until his death in 1987. Casey, who began his government career as chief of the OSS covert intelligence branch in Western Europe, symbolized SMOM's links to the U.S. and European intelligence services. (Another example is former CIA director John McCone, also a Knight.)

Casey was a good example of the cynicism of some Catholics in government—a man who could divorce public morality from private morality without seeing the connection. According to *The Washington Post*, he had intended to lie to a Senate commission about the sale of U.S. arms to Iran by saying that government authorities knew nothing about the delivery of U.S. antitank missiles. Casey changed his testimony, said the *Post,* only after Secretary of State George Shultz raised hell. The *Post*'s Bob Woodward confirmed—as did Lt. Colonel Oliver North—that Casey was aware of the illegal transfer of money to the *contras* from U.S. arms sales to Iran. Nevertheless, he mumble-bumbled through congressional questioning about the CIA's role in the scandal, asserting in public that "I don't know anything about [a] diversion of funds." (An Intelligence Committee report found that Casey had been "less than candid" in his testimony to Congress.)[34]

An aggressive businessman and master of deception, Casey was a vain man who made a fortune as a New York City lawyer. He skirted the law on several occasions, as in his controversial dealings with fugitive financier Robert Vesco when Casey was head of the Securities and Exchange Commission. But this did not hurt his standing in Republican circles, and in 1980 he became Reagan's campaign manager. He received the CIA directorship as a reward for his services.[35]

Both before and after Reagan nominated him to head the CIA, he was part of a small inner circle that chose cabinet appointees, and he continued to influence policy through "The Group," a select gathering of influential conservatives that also included James L. Buckley, the brother of William Buckley and a former New York senator, and Frank Shakespeare, chairman of the New Right's Heritage Foundation. Both Buckley and Shakespeare are Knights.[36]

• General Alexander Haig (Ret.). Best known for his role in Watergate, Haig was also involved in White House plotting to overthrow Chilean president Salvador Allende. (Another party to the plot was McCone, who, on leaving the CIA, joined the board of ITT, which offered the CIA $1 million for its anti-Allende activities.) Commander of NATO under Carter and Reagan's first secretary of state, Haig set the tone for the Reagan administration by announcing that international terrorism would replace human rights as Washington's key concern.[37] The mercurial secretary frequently fought with other members of Reagan's cabinet, including Jeane Kirkpatrick, then U.S. ambassador to the United Nations and also a right-wing Catholic.

• William and James Buckley. A protégé of Cardinal Spellman, William Buckley, Jr., gained the cardinal's support in launching his conservative Christian journal of opinion, *National Review*. William Casey was the lawyer who incorporated the publication in 1955. The sixth of ten children born to an Irish-American oil tycoon, Buckley grew from a precocious child into a precocious adult—a man who gloried in being a "professional and recreational snob," in the words of one critic. But the *enfant terrible* of the *National Review* and the television talk show "Firing Line" is more than an amusing gadfly. He was an apologist for Senator Joseph R. McCarthy (a position that endeared him to Cardinal Spellman), and in the 1950s he worked as a CIA covert agent in Mexico City under E. Howard Hunt of Watergate fame. (Buckley, who became Hunt's life-long friend, solicited funds to pay for his legal defense.) Like Haig and McCone, he supported the CIA's destabilization campaign against Allende's government, chiefly through disinformation.[38]

One of the most influential men in the back corridors of Republican power, Buckley served as a political consultant to the National Security Council during the Reagan administration. His brother James, a former New York senator, was under secretary of state for security affairs and president of Radio Free Europe and Radio Liberty, both with a history of employing Nazi collaborators. Under Buckley they were accused of broadcasting anti-Semitic material and of providing positive descriptions of a Nazi unit involved in the murder of thousands of Jews in the western Ukraine.[39]

• Clare Boothe Luce. The grande dame of the Cold War and a Dame of Malta, Luce was a popular playwright and the wife of the publishing tycoon Henry R. Luce, who co-founded *Time* magazine. Although she originally supported Franklin Roosevelt, she switched to the Republicans, serving two terms in Congress, and in the 1950s became ambassador to Italy. She was prominent in the notorious China Lobby, the intellectual force behind Senator McCarthy's witch-hunts. The lobby was so named because of its strong support for Chiang Kai-shek's regime, loyalty to which became a test of loyalty to the United States. Not only did the lobby succeed in smearing State Department dissenters as "Reds," including some of its leading China experts; it also set the stage for U.S. involvement in Vietnam by persuading the American public that the fall of any Asian territory to the communists was a sellout to communism. Fear of the domestic repercussions of such a charge was so great that both Democratic and Republican governments allowed themselves to be sucked into the quagmire of Southeast Asia.[40]

Luce, who converted to Catholicism in mid-life, became a symbol of conservatism, giving her support to a multitude of right-wing causes. These included the *contras'* Nicaraguan Freedom Fund and the American Catholic Committee in which William Simon was active. (See Chapter 7, pp. 200–201.) She also served on Reagan's Foreign Intelligence Advisory Board. Luce died in 1987 at the age of eighty-four.

• William Simon, treasury secretary under Nixon and Ford and a Republican millionaire. He became a deal maker on leaving government, using his privately held Wesray Corp. to buy up undervalued companies. Tense and impatient with subordinates, he was nevertheless regarded as a "smooth" operator by his peers in the boardroom.[41]

Simon was a lavish contributor to Catholic institutions, particularly the Paterson, New Jersey, diocese, where he grew up in a middle-class family, and to his alma mater, Lafayette College in Pennsylvania. He also gave considerable support to conservative causes and institutions as head of the board of trustees of the John M. Olin Foundation set up by the chemical and weapons manufacturer Olin Corp. Under Simon's tutelage, and with the help of three other conservative foundations—Sarah Scaife, Smith Richardson, and J.M.—the Olin Foundation in 1978 established a "clearinghouse" for corporate donations called the Institute for Educational Affairs (IEA). The idea was to provide business with a stable of intellectuals financed by the corporations. IEA grantees were soon churning out books on subjects dear to the heart of corporate America, and some fifty conservative and neoconservative publications, including student newspapers, also received substantial funding. But the major emphasis of the foundations, which increasingly worked together, was to establish university chairs in economics, law, and other social sciences and to provide grants to colleges and think tanks to support the corporate agenda. Simon himself wrote two books in praise of private enterprise. He also found time to head the lay commission of the American Catholic Committee that attacked the bishops' letter on the economy, and was prominent in the *contra* private aid network.

• Frank Shakespeare. A broadcasting executive and personal friend of Reagan, Shakespeare served as executive vice-president of CBS-TV, vice-chairman of RKO General Inc., director of the U.S. Information Agency, and—what seemed a requisite position for American Knights— director of Radio Free Europe and Radio Liberty. He was also chairman of the New Right's Heritage Foundation, which played an important role in setting policy for Reagan's administration. He was ambassador to Portugal from 1985 to 1987, when he replaced William Wilson, also a Knight of Malta, as ambassador to the Vatican following Wilson's fall from favor. (See Chapter 3, pp. 73–74.) Like Luce and Grace, he belonged to the Simon-Novak commission of the American Catholic Committee that tried to undercut the U.S. bishops' pastoral on the economy.

• Cardinal Bernard Law, one of the highest-ranking conservatives in the American Church and widely regarded as the pope's man in the United States. (See Chapter 8, pp. 251–52.)

• Thomas Bolan, a partner in Saxe, Bacon and Bolan, the law firm of Senator McCarthy's deceased aide Roy Cohn. Among the firm's clients is the New York archdiocese. Bolan was chosen by Reagan to greet the pope on behalf of the U.S. government when John Paul stopped in Alaska en route from the Philippines.

• Patrick J. Frawley, Jr. Heir to the Schick razor fortune, Frawley is a well-known funder of right-wing Catholic causes, such as the Christian Anti-Communist Crusade. His wife, Geraldine, is publisher of the conservative *National Catholic Register* and a Dame of Malta.

• Lewis E. Lehrman, a convert. Lehrman's $60-million drugstore-chain fortune made him the moneybag of the New York Republican party after Nelson Rockefeller's death. In 1982 he made a bid for the governor's seat against Mario Cuomo in which he was unsuccessful, though supported by a cabal of Knights, including William Buckley, Grace, and Bolan. Lehrman served the necessary time at Radio Free Europe and was also on the board of the Heritage Foundation. His Citizens for America lobbied extensively for the Nicaraguan *contras*.

Other prominent American Knights include:

• Former senator Jeremiah Denton (R.-Ala.), who lost his seat in the 1986 election. Denton gained notoriety during his hearings on terrorism when prominent Catholic religious orders were attacked for preaching "violent Marxist revolution."

• Senator Pete Domenici, Republican senator from New Mexico since 1972.

• Walter J. Hickel, former governor of Alaska and former secretary of the interior.

• Admiral James D. Watkins, Reagan's hard-line chief of naval operations.

• Frank V. Ortiz, U.S. ambassador to Argentina. He was removed from his post as ambassador to Guatemala by President Carter because he was considered "too conciliatory" to the military regime, according to *The Washington Post*.

• Chrysler chief Lee Iacocca.

• Robert Abplanalp, the aerosol magnate.

• Baron Hilton of the hotel chain.

• William S. Schreyer, chairman of Merrill Lynch.

• Francis X. Stankard, chief executive officer of the international division of Chase Manhattan.

• Martin F. Shea, executive vice-president of Morgan Guaranty Trust.

• Joseph Brennan, former chairman of the executive committee of the Emigrant Savings Bank of New York. Brennan was a member of an independent commission appointed by the pope to study the relationship between the Vatican Bank and Italy's P-2 Masonic lodge.

• Richard R. Shinn, chairman of the Metropolitan Life Insurance Company.

The international membership list also reads like a *Who's Who* of wealth and power; it includes King Juan Carlos of Spain; Spiros S. Skouras, president of Prudential Lines; and Paul-Louis Weiller, a close friend of Richard Nixon, a member of the board of directors of Renault, and the former head of Air France.

Opus Dei

Like the Knights of Malta, the international Catholic movement
Opus Dei has damaged its reputation by secretiveness and the sometimes
scandalous behavior of its members. But unlike SMOM, which never
lacks for members because of its prestige, Opus Dei, by its own admission,
has had to work hard to attract a relatively small following. This is due
also to the sacrifices it demands of its members. The movement suffered
a further blow when its charismatic leader, the Spanish priest Monsignor
Josemaría Escrivá de Balaguer y Albás, died in 1975. Escrivá, who
founded Opus Dei in Madrid in 1928, had a magnetic personality, and
his fundamentalist message of salvation appealed to Spaniards searching
for a spiritual anchor in the aftermath of the civil war. But Opus Dei—
Latin for "Work of God"—is not everyone's idea of a religious community
because it is based on a hierarchical model of society (Spain in the 1920s)
and practices a form of thought control. It also displays the characteristics
of a cult, including worship of the founder, known as the "Father," and
violent self-mortification by its followers. While members speak enthusiastically of how the "Work" has given their lives spiritual meaning and
discipline, critics, including former high-ranking Opus officials, question
its recruitment methods among the young. Moreover, the political and
economic connections of Opus Dei members have on occasion embarrassed the church, although the movement's leadership insists that it is
concerned solely with personal salvation.

While SMOM represents the elites, Opus Dei draws from the rising
middle classes, particularly professionals in teaching, engineering, law,
journalism, government, and business. It has some 73,000 members in
eighty-seven countries, the largest number being in Spain and Latin America. A branch founded in the United States in 1949 has not grown as fast
as expected because of the cultural difficulties involved in a Spanish trans-
plant. Nor is the country's open, egalitarian society well suited to a secretive, elitist religious movement. Nevertheless, the "Work" has gained
standing from John Paul's support, one sign of which was Cardinal O'Connor's decision in 1987 to welcome Opus Dei priests to the New York
archdiocese.

The Father

Born in 1902 in a small town at the foot of the Spanish Pyrenees,
Escrivá was the son of a modest tradesman. In those days the priesthood

was one of the few openings to higher education for Spain's poorer classes, and when Escrivá entered a seminary he also began to work for a law degree. By 1925 he was both lawyer and priest. In 1928, while celebrating Mass, he had a celestial vision telling him to form Opus Dei. The vision was colored by Spanish asceticism and Escrivá's longing to change the world. Physical mortification—one of the more controversial Opus Dei practices—was not uncommon at the time among traditional Spanish Catholics, but Escrivá tended to overdo it. He frequently flagellated himself so violently that his bathroom walls were spattered with blood. For most of his life he wore a cilice, a metal chain with sharp tips that prick the skin.[42]

Escrivá was also influenced by the Spanish Civil War (1936–39), which interrupted his plans for the movement and unleashed massive persecution of the church. At one point, so the story goes, he was attacked by an anticlerical worker who called him a donkey, to which Escrivá responded, "Donkey, yes, but a donkey of God." The episode supplied Escrivá with a trademark—a small statue of a donkey is on display in most Opus Dei houses and centers, a gift from the "Father" and symbol of humility. Escrivá fled to Burgos, which was controlled by Franco's forces, and it was there that he wrote his most famous work, *The Way,* a compendium of 999 "maxims" that became Opus Dei's spiritual handbook. The civil war intensified Escrivá's militant anticommunism, but he was also impelled toward the political right by the longing of a petit bourgeois to be accepted by the aristocracy. In 1968 he successfully petitioned the government for a title that had belonged to an eighteenth-century nobleman. The same elitism was reflected in Opus Dei's early emphasis on recruiting from the "intellectual" class (i.e., those with university degrees) and a rigid hierarchy that kept people in their social rank. Escrivá saw himself as a latter-day knight, leading the faithful into battle against godless communism and the "rottenness" in the Catholic Church. It was for this war that he needed educated men—but not women—who would influence and change society, "intellectuals" who would assume command of government, industry, and finance. The idea, explained Opus Dei ideologist Rafael Calvo Serer, was to create an "International of Elites" to challenge International Communism and the International of the Dollar. Escrivá used money and an aristocratic title as means to persuade people to adopt his conservative brand of Catholicism. Those not persuaded, who did not understand the need to be saved, would learn through "holy coercion" and "holy forcefulness."[43]

Asceticism, anticommunism, a rigid hierarchy, and religious militancy thus became the distinguishing marks of Opus Dei. But secrecy—another characteristic of the "Work"—has earned it considerable disrepute. Opus Dei's internal documents and the testimony of former members show that it has followed a deliberate policy of keeping secret its membership, hierarchy, rituals, and rules. Many former members say that if they had known what they were getting into they would not have joined. (Most religious orders are open about how they operate and what is expected of their membership.) Until 1982 the recruiting age for Opus was fifteen; it has since been raised to seventeen, but one former official said that Opus recruiters continued to lure children of eight and ten into its clubs. Escrivá's mania for secrecy reflected his conviction that in a society like Spain, with strong strains of anticlericalism, recruiting would be easier if performed by lay people who did not identify themselves with a priestly caste or religious organization. But what began as a clever tactic developed into an elaborate facade for a Catholic fundamentalist dictatorship, as shown by the secret 479-article *Constitutions* that governed the membership between 1950 and 1982 and still apparently governs it. Former and active members said they knew nothing of the articles, which were the blueprint of an Orwellian society ruled by the "Father" and his priests. Indicative of the strong feelings in some church circles against Opus Dei's activities was a directive issued in 1981 by England's Cardinal Basil Hume that forbade the movement to recruit anyone under the age of eighteen or without consultation with his or her parents. Hume acted after complaints from parents, some of whom said that the "Work" had alienated their children.[44]

Many devout people are members of Opus Dei. Those who experienced Escrivá's warmth, spirituality, and determination speak of him as a father in the fullest sense of the word. Dozens of the faithful around the world are convinced that by praying to him they have received miraculous help, to cure an illness or get a job. They believe they are misunderstood in an age that ignores the need for sanctity in everyday life. But balanced against such sincerity is an efficient machine run to achieve world power. Opus Dei boasts that in various countries it influences 487 universities and high schools, 52 radio and television stations, 694 publications, 38 news and publicity agencies, and 12 film and distribution companies. Its effectiveness is alleged to be purely spiritual, since it is expressed through Opus Dei's religious counseling of members who own or work at universities, newspapers, and other institutions. Opus insists that its members are free to make their own professional and political decisions, its task being to guide them toward the correct moral choices. But there is a fatal duality in the scheme. While Opus pushes its members to succeed as adults in the secular world, it treats them as children in religious matters. "You need a director [a priest] in order to offer yourself, to surrender yourself . . . by obedience," Escrivá told his followers. (He spoke of his recruits as the "nursery.") Through weekly confession, "heart-to-heart" talks, known as "confidences," and other contacts, members of Opus Dei receive instruction on every aspect of their lives. On the one hand, they are told, "Obey and you will be saved," said Father Pedro Miguel Lamet, former director of the Spanish religious weekly *Vida Nueva*. On the other, they are urged to succeed in a competitive world in order to attract new members and contribute to Opus Dei's considerable financial needs. The conflict between child and adult often ends in rebellion against a "religious prison," as one recruit described it, and explains why Opus Dei has produced so many disillusioned former members. Detailed supervision of members' lives also makes it difficult for Opus to distance itself from scandals in which its followers become involved.[45]

The outlines of this peculiarly Spanish edifice were already present in Escrivá's *The Way*, but it was not until after World War II, when Opus Dei began to expand in Spain and elsewhere, that it erected a formal structure with Vatican approval. As pointed out by Father Giancarlo Rocca, a scholar of the Pauline Fathers, the "Work" presents itself as a re-creation of the early church through its emphasis on a "family" consisting of equal but diverse members. In fact, the "family" has little or nothing in common with the early church but is a variation of the traditional Spanish religious society dominated by a clerical class. Contrary to Opus Dei's claims that it has created a unique lay movement of saintly people, few of its followers are considered members under canon law, and this is evident from Opus Dei's listing in the *Annuario Pontificio*, the Vatican's directory, which states that it has a membership of 1,273 priests and 352 seminarians but no laity. The *Annuario* also gives the full title of the movement, Holy Cross and Opus Dei, the former referring to the Priestly Society of the Holy Cross, which runs Opus Dei. The movement's internal structure accords with its juridical reality: Most of the important posts are held by priests, many of them Spaniards. Nor are they ordinary priests from a diocese or religious order, whom Opus will accept only on an associative basis. Opus priests are recruited, usually in their teens and before they have had any sexual experience, for careful grooming in Opus

Dei doctrine and practice before taking orders. Thus they are shielded from any outside contamination, particularly from liberal church influence. Completing the closed circle is a strict rule that all the laity in the movement must go to confession to Opus Dei priests at least once a week; confession to other priests is forbidden. This monopoly on confession is particularly important because it can be used for psychological control, particularly in societies like Spain, where many Catholics still associate the sacrament with fear and guilt.[46]

Whether deliberately, or because his followers idolized him, Escrivá established an organization that has strong cultist overtones. Opus Dei priests claim that the movement's doctrine is perfect and "undebatable" because it came from Escrivá, who had "concrete knowledge of God's will." But some of the doctrine is highly questionable, such as the belief that God directly appointed Escrivá to be the earthly father of all Opus Dei members. *Crónica,* the movement's internal confidential journal, claimed that at the Last Supper Christ prayed "to seal this strong indestructible unity of Opus Dei with a spirit of filiation to the Father [Escrivá]. . . ." The Father's "Work" was described in the words of the Song of Songs: "All is beautiful, my love, and there is no fault in thee." In contrast to this perfect work, according to Escrivá, the church was a "stinking corpse." His successor and lifelong friend, Monsignor Alvaro del Portillo y Díez de Sollano, did not deny the cultist aspects of Opus Dei in an interview with *The New York Times.* "We are his children," he said of Escrivá. "We cannot criticize our father."[47]

Former high-ranking officials of Opus Dei confirmed that the "Father" was more important in their lives than the pope or even God. "Mortification for the Father, prayer for the Father, work offered for the Father's intentions; everything from one corner to the other had to do with the 'Father,' " said Maria del Carmen Tapia. A member for nineteen years and at one time the highest-ranking woman in Opus Dei, Tapia said that life at central headquarters in Rome centered almost exclusively on the "Father"—his wants, his rages (known by those who suffered them as "blessed"), his tastes. "The music he liked was the music everybody was supposed to like," she said. Similarly, men, especially priests, and women were (and still are) expected to dress smartly because the "Father" liked good-looking, well-groomed people. Opus Dei residences and centers, whether in South America, Europe, or the United States, also reflect a standardized taste—that of the provincial tradesman who has made good in the capital. Furnishings inevitably include pictures of Escrivá and his symbolic donkey, as well as overstuffed furniture; marble floors; plastic and paper flowers; and bric-a-brac galore, some of it awful, some of it priceless.[48]

Tapia, who joined the Madrid branch when she was twenty-two, said that it was only years later, when she was the director of the Opus Dei women's division in Venezuela, that she was allowed to read the society's secret *Constitutions*. The experience in Venezuela, away from the rigid rituals in Spain and Rome, changed her outlook, helping her to clarify her feelings about Escrivá and freedom of worship. "God was again number one in my spiritual life. I understood that no superior, not even the Father, had the right to abrogate my conscience." That understanding led to her recall to Rome, where she said the "Father" had her placed under virtual house arrest for eight months, then expelled her from Opus Dei in what Tapia described as a "screaming" scene. She was told that she was leaving in mortal sin and that "in spite of a life of penance it was unlikely I would be saved."[49]

Tapia's story parallels that of other former Opus Dei members, who discovered that they were not children and could be good Catholics without belonging to the "Work" or praying to the "Father." Some described being threatened, not with physical violence but with the loss of their souls. Opus was not above using stronger means of pressure, however, as shown by its attempts to suppress Father Rocca's book on the movement, through the offices of Archbishop Vincenzo Fagiolo, secretary of the Congregation for Religious and an Opus Dei sympathizer. Fagiolo, who was also the scourge of American nuns (see Chapter 8, p. 244), tried to persuade Rocca's religious order to stop publication of the book, but the order upheld Rocca. In another case, involving the Spanish Catholic weekly, *Vida Nueva*, pressure by the Curia prevented the magazine from publishing Opus Dei's application for Vatican recognition of its worldwide status and independence. But *Vida Nueva* won that duel by running as blank pages the space in which the article would have appeared, with the announcement that its publication had been banned. When the Spanish newspaper *El País* then published the censored story, the readership was far larger than it would have been in *Vida Nueva*.[50]

Suppression also characterizes Opus Dei's internal regulations. The movement's 1950 *Constitutions* was kept secret for a good reason—anyone who was not an Opus Dei adept would likely be shocked by its demands. Under a Vatican ruling Opus was allowed to give only a shortened, sanitized version of the *Constitutions* to local bishops if they asked for it;

few did. Opus Dei's new *Codex,* or constitution, which was promulgated in 1982, is an updated, broader version of the summaries previously available to bishops, differing primarily in the age limits for recruitment and an order to its members to avoid secretiveness. The key to the *Codex* appears in a concluding article which states that the 1950 *Constitutions* will continue in effect for all the obligations not covered in the *Codex.* Those obligations, described in detail in the *Constitutions* but not in the *Codex,* are the underpinnings of Opus Dei's religious dictatorship.[51]

Opus Dei is organized like a pyramid, with "numeraries" at the top. Numeraries must belong to the middle or upper classes, hold a university degree (which can be obtained while with Opus), have a good appearance (physical disfigurements, such as a limp or stutter, are unacceptable), and show loyalty and zeal in recruiting new members. They must be unmarried and, following a period of initiation, are expected to pledge the three traditional religious vows of poverty, chastity, and obedience. Both women and men can be numeraries, but the sexes are strictly separated, living in different communities and usually forbidden to speak to each other. Escrivá's view of women was that they "need not be scholars; it's enough for them to be prudent." Hence the women's job, in addition to recruiting young women, is primarily housework. Young men, on the other hand, are encouraged to obtain university degrees and to develop a priestly vocation in order to expand the Society of the Holy Cross, which is composed of the elite of the male numeraries. All male numeraries, regardless of whether they become priests, are expected to have a profession, such as law or accounting, all income from which goes to support the "Work." (Any income earned by women numeraries also goes to Opus.) Money, while important, is secondary to recruiting. Professionals successful in the business world, who bear no religious insigne, such as a priest's cassock, often have access to social groups that would be wary of or hostile to a priest. Moreover, they can impress younger people who admire their professional abilities. The emphasis in Opus Dei on prosperous careers, well-dressed members, and comfortably furnished houses and centers (which are spotlessly clean, thanks to the Opus Dei women) is part of the "bait," to use Escrivá's word, that attracts new members. On the surface, at least, the message is persuasive: Follow me, and you, too, will have material success and spiritual salvation.[52]

The life of a numerary is onerous. He is expected to leap out of bed the moment the alarm clock goes off (the "heroic minute," according to Escrivá), kiss the floor, and exclaim, *"Serviam! Serviam!"* ("I serve! I serve!") This is followed by a cold shower to mortify the body and a maximum of a half hour to dress; then prayers, Mass, and communion in the house's oratory. On the way to work the numerary says the rosary, at noon the Angelus. In the afternoon he maintains a "minor silence," speaking as little as possible. After tea there is a half-hour meditation in the oratory. The numerary must then find time for required spiritual reading—only those books and pamphlets authorized by Opus—and five minutes of reading a pre–Vatican II Bible. After dinner members of the house discuss how their day of recruiting has gone. They then return to the oratory to fill in their daily "life plan"—a card containing twenty-six categories which must be checked to show whether they have performed "personal mortification" (the use of a cilice for two hours a day and weekly whippings), gone to confession, made an accounting of personal expenses, and other obligations. The cards must be up to date because the house director may ask for them at any time. Afterwards, special Opus Dei prayers are said in Latin. The numerary then retires to bed, first sprinkling holy water over the sheets and saying three Hail Marys while kneeling.[53]

A schedule that rigorous would be difficult in a monastery, but the numeraries are also expected to be out in the world, making recruits. (On average, the numerary is supposed to cultivate fifteen "friends" at a time for possible recruitment.) According to former Opus Dei members, prestige within the order depends primarily on this numbers game. The competition and taxing "life plan" sometimes produce severe nervous tensions, they said. Although women numeraries also live a highly structured life of prayer, the pressures on them for recruitment are less severe and they do not have to endure the same physical mortifications as the men, although they are expected to sleep on wooden boards, which supposedly cool their sexual appetites.[54]

Below the numeraries in the pyramid are the associates, who basically have the same obligations as the numeraries but come from the working class, do not have a university degree, and are not expected to live in Opus Dei houses, in part because of the expense. Class divisions are rigorously enforced: A businessman, for example, would not attend a religious retreat with a laborer. Similarly, women associates often are maids at Opus Dei houses, centers, and schools, while the housekeeper is a numerary (the associates can always be identified by their starched maids' uniforms). The associates are not expected to sleep on boards, presumably because, being of a lower class, they are not as sexually highstrung as the numeraries.[55]

Beneath the associates are the supernumeraries, married people who devote only part of their time to the "Work," but are expected to contribute up to 10 percent of their incomes and to follow a vigorous schedule of confession, "confidences," discussion circles, and retreats with Opus Dei priests. Neither Escrivá nor his successor, Monsignor Portillo, admired the married state. "Marriage," said Escrivá, "is for the rank and file, not for the officers of Christ's army. For, unlike food, which is necessary for every individual, procreation is necessary only for the species, and individuals can dispense with it." Portillo thought that self-flagellation was a "little" matter compared to the "much worse [things] the husband does to the wife, and the wife to the husband."[56]

A final category consists of "co-operators," or sympathizers, who can be Catholics or non-Catholics and who usually make financial donations. Sargent Shriver, George McGovern's running mate in the 1972 presidential election, was a co-operator, but he gave up the association because, he said, "I didn't feel a need for discipline or control over me." Shriver, while supporting the Opus Dei theory of sanctification of lay life, said the organization was too "structured" for most Americans. "There are people in Opus Dei who are so engulfed in the structure, so enraptured by the system, that anything different is seen as un-Christian and threatening. There is a certain obliqueness about it, too. They don't speak to you directly, but to left and right. If you ask them about the number of people in the United States who belong [approximately 3,000], they act like you are asking for the secret of the atom bomb."[57]

Opus Dei's secretiveness is but one reason why it is controversial. Another is its financial arrangements with the numeraries and associates. Internal regulations specify that they must cede the administration of their goods and properties to "whoever seems best" and that they must make out a will, which Opus Dei keeps. In addition, Opus Dei receives their earnings while they are members. Given the strong pressures to "give all" to Opus Dei, some students of the subject are convinced that Opus is the end recipient. Such was the charge of a Spanish woman, Covadonga Carcedo García, who was a member of the "Work" for five years until she revolted against serving as "cheap labor." She took Opus to court to obtain the return of a will she said she had signed in its favor as well as the will of her father, of which she was the beneficiary. She also claimed that she had signed "at least twenty papers that theoretically made me the owner of real estate, companies, and businesses." Opus Dei denies that it owns any of the expensive houses, centers, schools, and other installations that exist in dozens of countries and that operate under its supervision but not its legal control. But investigations by Father Rocca and *Tiempo,* one of the largest-circulation weeklies in Spain, suggest that control is exercised through boards of directors dominated by Opus members, many of them numeraries—a supposition confirmed by a former Opus Dei member in Colombia, where the "Work" has an extensive network of facilities, including a university. *Tiempo*'s investigations also alleged that the "Work" used its members in finance and business to ferret out the financial resources of potential donors, who were then approached for contributions. The magazine, which obtained its information from an Opus director of one such campaign, said that if the donor proved reluctant, the Opus representative would remind him of how much money he had on deposit in certain banks, name the properties he owned, and give him to understand that Opus knew exactly how much he was worth. Most of those approached in this way made donations. Maria del Carmen Tapia made similar charges. Citing her own case, she asserted that one reason why the "Work" focused on well-to-do youth was to "use" them to obtain donations from their relatives.[58]

Another Opus practice that disturbs critics is censorship. Escrivá said, "Don't buy [books] without advice from a Catholic who has real knowledge and discernment. It's so easy to buy something useless or harmful." To ensure good reading habits, a division, euphemistically called the Department of Bibliographical Studies, categorizes books, newspapers, magazines, and films. One circle means that members should exercise care when reading or seeing the work. Only Opus directors or specially trained members may read or see material with two circles; three circles means the work is prohibited to all. In the third category are Marxist theory and liberation theology. Also on the prohibited or controlled list are works by Jean-Paul Sartre, Kierkegaard, Schopenhauer, John Stuart Mill, Dumas, Molière, Balzac, and Boris Pasternak. Members are discouraged from reading the works of twentieth-century writers unless they are by an Opus Dei member or sympathizer. Opus is particularly insular about theology, sending its seminarians to study at its own institute in Rome and discouraging any theological innovation. "Intellectual control is so complete," said a Spanish priest and former Opus Dei member, "that members accept a life without discussion of anything." A former Colombian member agreed that the lack of intellectual freedom contributed to a tendency among members to be imperceptive about themselves and to attribute all criticism to ignorance.[59]

Censorship not only produces a certain way of thinking but can also cause difficulties for young members who attend public high schools and universities. One former member said that an Opus Dei priest censored the books he was assigned in high school and that consequently he often read only one or two books of an average school assignment of ten. He admitted that he "lied a lot," particularly to avoid "home visits" by Opus superiors. He said he never lacked employment, thanks to the Opus Dei network of connections, but that, because so much of his earnings went to Opus Dei, he eventually left. The jobs and recommendations immediately ceased.[60]

Like everything else, mail sent to Opus Dei houses is carefully monitored. Dr. John Roche, an Oxford University scientist and for many years an Opus Dei member, cited the case of a young woman in London who had recently joined the movement. A letter had been sent to her offering a scholarship, he said, but she did not receive it because it was concealed from her by Opus Dei, which had other plans for her future.[61] Roche, who was a local director of Opus Dei, left the movement because of the rigid controls, but he was also deeply disturbed by the elaborate deceptions used to make young people "whistle," or join Opus Dei. As Roche described it, teenage members of Opus Dei, working under the supervision of older numeraries, would invite their friends or schoolmates to a local Opus Dei center for a game of basketball, a film, or a lecture on some topic of interest. "They are advised not to reveal at first that they are members or that the center is run by Opus Dei." The potential recruit may then be invited to an Opus Dei house, where the "right atmosphere" (expensive furnishings, excellent food, and plenty of good cheer) encourages the young man or woman to join an Opus Dei activity, such as a weekly meditation, an outing, or a program to visit the poor, always in the company of the numerary who is working on him or her. Impressionable and idealistic, the young man or woman does not realize that all is meticulously planned, including visits to the poor, which, according to Roche, are aimed not at helping the poor but at giving the numerary an opportunity, en route and back, for more proselytism. When Roche complained that such tactics were used by notorious sects and political groups, an Opus Dei priest responded, "But it works!"[62]

The pressures on the potential recruit are enormous. Roche described the case of a young woman who was attending one of Opus Dei's catering schools. One day the girl telephoned her mother in tears, saying how unhappy she was and that she wanted to leave the school. The mother called the school's directress, who claimed the girl was merely worried about school examinations and persuaded the mother that she should continue at the school. The mother bitterly regretted her decision because her daughter joined Opus Dei shortly afterwards and became completely estranged from her.[63]

Maria del Carmen Tapia, the eldest and the only girl in her family, was engaged to be married when she was recruited. She broke the engagement, gave up her job, and left her family. She was not allowed to give any explanation to her parents. When they eventually found out the reason for their daughter's behavior, they were upset, and Tapia's relationship with her parents became "cold and distant." She was convinced at the time that, in joining Opus Dei, she had become a member of a saintly family. "Brotherhood is more important than the linkages of blood relatives. Father is the main figure. That's a typical thing of the sects."[64]

Opus Dei spokesmen said such stories were the tales of embittered failures, but there were too many former Opus Dei members with similar experiences to dismiss such charges as unfounded. In a book on his experience, Klaus Steigleder, a member for five years, told how, at fourteen, he was coaxed into a theater group at a Cologne youth club without knowing it was related to Opus and that it took him years to discover what he had gotten himself into. Father Vladimir Felzmann, the movement's first Czech member, said that Opus Dei warned young people not to tell their parents that they intended to join, and membership therefore began with a lie. Felzmann, who was with Opus for twenty-two years, said that "as I know Opus Dei's history and the pain its members have suffered, I do not condemn the individuals. But how can a priest in love with the open God of life encourage young people—or anyone for that matter—to a life whose characteristics are of martial law in a country under siege?"[65]

A Prelature

Those who knew Escrivá in the days before Opus Dei became an international movement spoke of him as a "very compassionate man with an open heart." But things began to change after he moved to Rome in 1946 with the aim of expanding the "Work" beyond Spain. Tapia, who at the time was head of the women's division and worked closely with Escrivá, said that he told her that "when he went to Rome he lost his innocence"—a common occurrence, according to priests and bishops who have worked at the Vatican. "He learned the rules of the game," said

Tapia. "He became entangled with complicated things, like new buildings, new houses, and with power." Other former high-ranking Opus Dei members made similar observations, complaining that the spirituality that had originally attracted them to the "Work" was gradually replaced by a rigid, power-hungry bureaucracy.[66]

But it was not only the inevitable intrigue in Rome that left its mark. Back in Spain, Opus Dei members were making rapid advances in the Franco government under Admiral Luis Carrero Blanco, an Opus Dei sympathizer who, as premier, virtually ran the country. Until Carrero's assassination in 1973, Opus Dei leaders were arguably the strongest conservative political influence in Spain. As cabinet members, the "two Lópezes" (Gregorio López Bravo and Laureano López Rodó) modernized the economy and encouraged trade with Europe and the United States. Both men were Opus Dei members, as were Jorge Brosa, director of Banco Español de Crédito, Spain's biggest bank, and Luis Valls Taberner, president of Banco Popular. López Rodó, Brosa, and Valls were celibate numeraries. Known as "technocrats," to distinguish them from Franco's old-fashioned Falange, the Opus Dei group at one time controlled four ministries as well as numerous lesser government posts. "When members of Opus Dei became ministers of governments," said Tapia, "it was a kind of glory for [Escrivá], a kind of triumph. He would minimize the person on the one hand, but at the same time he was using that person."[67]

Although Opus members ceased to dominate the government after Franco's death in 1975, they retained a strong influence on Spain's banking system and industry. Meanwhile, the society expanded to other countries in Europe, and to the United States and Latin America, gaining political influence in the latter, particularly in Pinochet's Chile.

Opus Dei had received juridical recognition from the Vatican as a secular institute in 1950, but by the 1960s Escrivá had become dissatisfied with the status. Other secular institutes had appeared, ending Opus Dei's claim to be the only one. Moreover, the institutes were under the jurisdiction of the Congregation for Religious, which Opus Dei believed was confusing to the public since religious orders were associated with vows and a structured religious life, whereas Opus Dei wanted to present itself as a lay society. Escrivá's goal was to change the movement's jurisdiction to the Congregation for Bishops, the idea being that the head of Opus Dei and his successors would become bishops of a personal prelature. Most prelatures are geographically defined territories that have not yet become dioceses, whereas a personal prelature has a worldwide jurisdiction similar to that of a major religious order, such as the Jesuits. Although Vatican II provided the groundwork for the creation of such prelatures, the only juridical precedents were the military vicariate, composed of priests who served in the armed forces around the world, and the Mission of France, an association of priests and workers.[68]

The lack of such precedent was one reason why it took Opus Dei two decades to become a prelature. Another was that both John XXIII and Paul VI were cool to the idea—John because of Opus Dei's reactionary reputation, Paul because of its ambitions to become a church within the church. For what Escrivá and Portillo wanted was freedom from the jurisdiction of local bishops in order to build their own religious edifice. As pointed out by Vatican expert Giancarlo Zízola, the proposed prelature would have led to parallel seminaries, clergy, pastoral programs, and lay groups, with those under Opus Dei's control answerable only to Escrivá or his successor. The bishops didn't like it. Neither did Cardinal Pericle Felici, in charge of the Vatican's commission on canon law. The Spanish bishops, who were trying to distance the church from Franco and did not approve of Opus Dei's pretensions, also lobbied against the prelature. They were particularly upset by a document written in 1972 under the auspices of Cardinal Pietro Palazzini, an Opus Dei supporter and the then head of the Congregation for the Clergy, that denounced members of the Spanish episcopacy because of their anti-Franco policy. The document, which was reportedly written with the aid of Portillo, then Opus Dei secretary general, caused such an uproar that Palazzini was booted upstairs by Paul VI (Paul made him a cardinal but took away his job at the congregation).[69]

Matters changed radically when John Paul became pope. Opus Dei had courted the pope since his days as archbishop of Krakow. He had been invited to speak at various Opus Dei centers in Europe and at headquarters in Rome. The speeches were later made into a book, copies of which were sent by Wojtyla to the Vatican Secretariat of State. In 1978, when he was in Rome for the funeral of John Paul I, Wojtyla visited Opus Dei's mansion to pray at the black marble crypt of "El Padre," who had died three years earlier. Monsignor Portillo, his successor and, by some accounts, the brains of Opus Dei, was welcomed at the Vatican by the new pope, who in turn was invited to visit Opus Dei's house and centers. Portillo had by then marshaled a formidable group of supporters in the Curia, and in February 1979 the long-delayed prelature project was again set in motion. Cardinal Sebastiano Baggio, an Opus Dei sympathizer and then head of the Congregation for Bishops, was given the job of shepherding the project through the Vatican's commissions and congregations. Meanwhile, Cardinal Palazzini was recalled to head the Vatican office in charge of the beatification of saints. One of his first cases was Escrivá. Palazzini named Portillo the chief adviser in the beatification process.[70]

An aristocratic Spaniard with degrees in engineering and canon law, Portillo achieved what Escrivá could not. Although some bishops, including the Spaniards and the Italians, protested the prelature, it was approved in 1982 because John Paul wanted it that way. But the prelature, while enhancing Opus Dei's status, did not take the form that Escrivá and Portillo had hoped because Opus Dei remained subject to the jurisdiction of the local bishop. Although John Paul approves of Opus Dei's anticommunism and religious fervor, his chief concern is hierarchical authority. Opus Dei would have had the juridical standing of a parallel church had the original proposal been approved. Under the current structure its only hope of achieving jurisdictional independence is through Rome's appointment of Opus Dei priests as bishops (which has occurred in Latin America). Portillo himself has not been made a bishop.[71]

Nevertheless, the pope has shown his favor in numerous ways. He often praises Opus Dei's dedication, and personally ordains Opus Dei priests. He has also appointed Opus Dei members to important positions. Joaquín Navarro-Valls, a Spanish numerary, was named Vatican press spokesman, and Father Fernando Ocariz, an Opus Dei priest, became a top adviser to Cardinal Ratzinger's Congregation for the Doctrine of the Faith. Opus Dei priests and sympathizers were appointed bishops in Latin America and Europe through the good offices of Cardinal Bernardin Gantin, Baggio's successor as head of the Congregation for Bishops and an Opus Dei sympathizer. The congregation's secretary, Archbishop Lucas Moreira Neves, who was later named archbishop of Salvador, Brazil, is also an Opus Dei sympathizer, as is the Spanish cardinal, Eduardo Martínez Somalo, for many years the second highest official at the Secretariat of State (a sister and nephew of Martínez are Opus Dei members).

"Opus responds in part to Pope Wojtyla's idea of creating an army of lay people who are both consecrated and at the same time capable of being active in the temporal world under Rome's control," explained Juan Arias, Vatican correspondent for the Spanish newspaper *El País*. "He likes their activism, their anticommunism, their internal compactness where no plurality of ideas exist."[72] But as pointed out by *The New York*

Times's Henry Kamm, open manifestations of papal favor do not necessarily translate into influence. "What causes Opus Dei to be regarded as a greater power than under previous popes is the sense that an era has come to a close. It is a sense that Pope John Paul II has put a stop to interpreting liberally the documents of the Second Vatican Council and that a new era of conservativism has begun."[73]

The "Holy Mafia"

Called the "Holy Mafia" by its critics, Opus Dei has frequently been involved in scandals, causing some Vatican observers to believe that it no longer enjoys unqualified papal favor. In 1986 charges that Opus Dei was running a secret organization led the Italian parliament to demand a government investigation. (The Italian constitution prohibits secret societies.) Although the government absolved Opus Dei of illegal conduct, the affair caused the Vatican considerable embarrassment. It is not normal, an official of the Curia admitted, for religious societies to keep their constitutions secret. "Opus was granted permission to do so, but their secrecy is an exaggeration," he said. As a result of the investigation, the Vatican made it clear that it expected Opus Dei to comport itself in a more open manner.[74]

While the inquiry reflected the animosity felt against the Vatican by Italian leftist and left-of-center politicians, it also responded to fears of political machinations by secret societies that had carried over from the scandal of the P-2 lodge that was unmasked in 1981. Opus Dei was drawn into that imbroglio by assertions that it had been negotiating with Roberto Calvi, head of Milan's Ambrosiano Bank and a key figure in P-2, regarding a possible bailout for Ambrosiano that would save the Vatican Bank financial losses and embarrassment arising from its dealings with Calvi. The banker's body, either murdered or a suicide, was later found hanging from Blackfriars Bridge in London. His widow maintained that he had been in touch with Cardinal Palazzini, the Opus Dei sympathizer in charge of Escrivá's beatification process, about the rescue operation, presumably to be carried out with the help of Opus Dei members who owned or controlled banks in Spain. The trade-off, according to Vatican observers, was to have been a takeover by Opus Dei members of the Vatican Bank and the Vatican Radio controlled by the more progressive Jesuits. Letters were found on Calvi from Francesco Pazienza, a Calvi aide with links to Italian and U.S. intelligence, in which Pazienza referred to contacts between Palazzini and Calvi. Although three Milan judges questioned Palazzini on the subject as part of an investigation into the Vatican Bank's illegal financial dealings, allegations of an Opus Dei conspiracy remained unproven.[75]

At the start of 1983, Opus seemed poised for a major expansion based on papal favor and its new status as a prelature. Its main base remained in Spain, where it raised the largest contributions and enjoyed the most substantial political and economic influence, but the movement also gained members and influence in Italy. The popular television journalist Alberto Michelini led Opus Dei's invasion of the Italian parliament. It was also strong in Latin America, particularly in Mexico, Colombia, Peru, and Chile. Opus Dei members and sympathizers supported the CIA-backed coup that overthrew Chilean president Allende, and one of them, Hernán Cubillos, became General Pinochet's foreign minister. Cubillos, who founded *Qué Pasa,* a magazine under Opus Dei influence, was later identified as an "important" CIA agent by the *Los Angeles Times.*[76]

Opus Dei's influence in Chile derives from its strong presence in education and the media, and from sympathetic priests and bishops. Its members teach in various departments of the Catholic University in Santiago, and it has a university residence and student center, Alborada, where government officials often speak to and meet with the students. South of Santiago Opus Dei maintains an agricultural school for 100 needy students that is typical of its "good works." In addition to a network of schools, centers, and clubs for the middle class, Opus supports vocational centers for lower-class youth who can be recruited as associate members. (Critics charge that these schools perpetuate Opus Dei's rigid social system by discouraging the young from aspiring to a higher class.)[77]

However, most of Opus Dei's income and energies are spent on high schools for the middle class and on its universities in Spain, Mexico, Colombia, and Peru. In Colombia Opus Dei oversees the Universidad de la Sabana in Bogotá, with more than 5,000 students. University courses emphasize education, journalism, business, and law, reflecting Opus Dei priorities for penetrating lay society. The "best and brightest" of the students, in the words of a former member, are invited to join the Club Delta, an Opus Dei recreational and religious center, and to visit its luxurious country house outside Bogotá. The purpose of these facilities is recruitment, according to the former member. It also helps to have a friendly bishop or cardinal—in Colombia's case, Cardinal Alfonso López Trujillo.[78]

Opus Dei's deepest penetration is in Peru, where, in addition to a university, it has six bishops of its own, one-ninth of the total. Opus Dei bishops or sympathizers have also been appointed in Argentina, Brazil, Central America, and Mexico. The most controversial appointments were those of the Spaniard Fernando Saenz as auxiliary bishop of Santa Ana in El Salvador, followed by the installation of a conservative Italian, Jose Carmen Di Pietro, as bishop of the diocese of Sonsonate. These appointments broke with a tradition of naming Salvadorans as bishops and, according to the Salvadoran Jesuit magazine, *Estudios Centroamérica,* showed the Vatican's determination to control socially activist sectors in the church. The magazine said that the Vatican wanted to reduce tensions between the Salvadoran church and the pro-U.S. Christian Democratic government (as, for example, over human rights violations), in the belief that the right-of-center regime would serve the church's institutional interests (i.e., that it would prevent a Marxist guerrilla victory). One result of this policy was the neutralization of the Salvadoran hierarchy, which was unable to formulate a pastoral plan to deal with the problems created by the civil war.[79]

In Chile, Peru, and El Salvador, Opus Dei provides invaluable support to right-wing political groups through its religious courses and schools, and through newspapers, magazines, and television outlets influenced or owned by members. "It serves a function for the political right and power holders," said a student of Opus Dei activities in Latin America. "Its strong endorsement of a class society can also be used as a rationale by the middle and upper classes to justify their lifestyles, even though they may not be members. And because it serves the purpose of the upper classes, it is able to exert an influence on the political and economic situation." A Spanish priest made a similar observation about the influence of Opus Dei bankers and industrialists in Europe: "They want to stop the growth of socialism and pacify the labor movement through religion."[80]

Because class lines are less rigid in the United States and Americans rebel against thought control, U.S. Opus Dei membership remains small, approximately 3,000. Founded in Chicago by a Spanish priest in 1949, it has since established thirty student centers in Chicago, Boston, New York City, St. Louis, Milwaukee, San Francisco, South Bend and Valparaiso, Indiana, and Washington, D.C. Local church officials are often unaware that these are Opus Dei operations. "You don't even hear talk about them," said Father William Barry, assistant to the New England Jesuit provincial. Some in the American church thought there should be more talk. Opus Dei, said the priest-author Andrew Greeley, is a "devious, antidemocratic, reactionary, semi-fascist institution, desperately hungry for absolute power in the church. It ought to be forced either to come out into the open or be suppressed."[81]

Spain

Spain, the birthplace of Opus Dei, has the largest membership— 24,000; some 5,000 are numeraries. The Spanish branch has the biggest network of centers and schools, including Pamplona's University of Navarra, which specializes in journalism, medicine, and architecture, and a business school in Barcelona with ties to Harvard University. The imposing religious sanctuary at Torreciudad was constructed with funds from Opus Dei members to honor Escrivá, who believed he was cured of a serious childhood illness through the intercession of the Virgin of Torreciudad. The Spanish branch also helps finance the "Work" in countries with small memberships, including some Western European countries and reportedly Poland.[82]

Church sources estimate that one-third of the Spanish hierarchy sympathizes with Opus Dei, possibly because of the "way the wind is blowing in Rome," as a Spanish journalist said. But other bishops strongly oppose the movement, because the political and financial activities of its members have frequently embarrassed them. Opus Dei followers are strategically placed in the Spanish press, and Spanish sources claim that members control more than 1,500 companies and financial entities. The "Work" also has followers in the police and military; center-right parties, particularly the Alianza Popular; and the court of King Juan Carlos. But familiarity has bred contempt, particularly among the educated classes. "I know dozens of journalists who were Opus Dei members when they were studying at the University of Navarra but have since left and are very bitter against it," said a prominent Spanish journalist. Spanish church sources confirmed that approximately one-quarter of those recruited subsequently left the movement. Although Opus Dei connections can be useful to a person's career, they may "also be negative in Spain," said the journalist. "Just as there is more militancy in Spain by Opus Dei than anywhere else, so, too, there is more hatred against it."[83]

The movement's tightly controlled circles in Spain led to the formation of a powerful club, known as the "Holy Octopus," through which Opus Dei's coreligionists frequently consulted with one another and provided mutual support, as in the financial sector. There is no evidence that the Opus Dei directorate itself was running such activities. Nevertheless, many Spaniards concluded that because so many Opus Dei people were involved at one time in the government and are still heavily involved in banking, Opus Dei was running the government and continues to dominate the banks. As Maria Carmen del Tapia pointed out, this impression was fostered by Escrivá's pride in the political and economic success of his "children," who were publicly identified as Opus Dei members. But when the "children" got out of hand, miring themselves in scandal, the movement's leaders no longer wanted Opus Dei's name associated with them.

Such was the case in the Matesa scandal, which erupted in 1969. Matesa was a holding company for the export of textile machinery that was owned by Opus Dei members. It defrauded the government of hundreds of thousands of dollars in subsidies and loans through a fake export scheme, including two large credits obtained from the finance ministry a month before the roof fell in. The ministers of finance and trade, who had strongly backed Matesa's expansion, were members of Opus Dei. The ensuing scandal not only damaged the government but also caused Opus embarrassing publicity. And no sooner had the Matesa affair died down than Opus was hit by another scandal, when a numerary, who had been sent to Portugal to found an Opus Dei branch and open a subsidiary of a Spanish bank controlled by an Opus Dei banker, absconded with $225,000.[84]

But these were minor affairs compared to the scandal in 1983 over the expropriation and collapse of Rumasa, Spain's largest conglomerate. Its onetime owner, the sherry baron José María Ruíz Mateos, publicly blamed Rumasa's demise on the machinations of Opus Dei, of which he had been a member since the early 1960s. However, the evidence shows that Ruíz Mateos had only himself to blame for the fall of his empire. Nor is there any proof to support his claim that Opus Dei made a deal with the socialist government when it came to power in 1982 by agreeing to sacrifice Rumasa in order to protect other Opus Dei interests in the financial sector. Nevertheless, Opus Dei was deeply involved with Ruíz Mateos, who was one of its principal contributors in Spain. His rise and fall is a cautionary tale about the dangers awaiting religious movements that form close associations with secular power.

Like Felipe González, the socialist prime minister, Ruíz Mateos is a bootstrap Andalusian who made it to the top by challenging the grandees who traditionally dominated Spain's political and economic life. Ruíz built a small family sherry business into a conglomerate with eighteen banks and 647 companies that marketed wines and sherries, including the Dry Sack brand; controlled the country's largest hotel chain, department stores, real estate companies, and construction firms; and maintained a foreign network of financial entities in Europe and Latin America. Investigations by the Spanish banking authorities showed that many of the companies were paper fronts for a financially overextended pyramid in danger of collapse. For years Spain's central bank had tried to persuade Ruíz Mateos to put his house in order, but Ruíz ignored their pleas and warnings. Rumasa's assets were inflated by up to 500 percent, and most of the companies' credit came from the Rumasa banks, which on average had 62 percent of their capital on loan to Rumasa companies. The conglomerate's debt was growing at an exponential rate—seventeen of the eighteen banks were in deficit—and when the González government came to power, it had no choice but to deal with the threat. Lacking adequate legislation to control a holding company and fearing that Rumasa's failure could bring down Spain's wobbly banking system, it chose to expropriate the sprawling enterprise. Most of the pyramid turned out to be a pile of ashes: The rescue operation cost Spanish taxpayers more than $346 million.[85]

The Spanish Association of Private Banks, headed by Rafael Termes, also an Opus Dei member, applauded the expropriation as necessary to safeguard the banking system. But while true, the statement was seen by Ruíz Mateos as a betrayal by an Opus Dei brother and, by extension, as an Opus Dei conspiracy to destroy him. Accustomed to fixing things, through political influence or "tips," Ruíz also convinced himself that he had been betrayed by Luis Valls Taberner, an Opus numerary and president of the Banco Popular Español, the seventh largest bank in Spain. Ruíz depended on Valls to save him from a showdown with the banking authorities, but Valls could not work miracles and refused to take responsibility for Ruíz's financial difficulties. He did advise Ruíz to leave Spain after the expropriation, possibly to avoid more scandal for Opus Dei. Ruíz went to London in the belief that Valls could somehow fix matters, but a Madrid court indicted him in absentia on charges of currency smuggling, false bookkeeping, and defrauding the social security system. He was arrested at the Frankfurt airport in 1984 and subsequently extradited to Spain. After a spate in prison, various legal battles, and the payment of a whopping bail, he regained his freedom, vowing to take vengeance on all who had "wronged" him, starting with Opus Dei.[86]

Ruíz believed, as Opus Dei had taught him, that his work at Rumasa was sanctified. He followed the Opus Dei formula scrupulously—daily attendance at Mass, the construction of a chapel in his home, enormous donations to Opus Dei, and a large family. That his business methods were questionable apparently never bothered him. When he and his family learned of Rumasa's expropriation on the late evening news, they immediately went to pray to the Virgin to ask if it was God's will. "José María's reaction was, 'Why didn't God protect us from this?' " said a close friend. "He had done everything Opus Dei had said: He had thirteen kids, didn't fool around with women, didn't live extravagantly. Religiously he couldn't understand why this had happened."[87]

While Ruíz's charges against Valls and other Opus members were self-serving, he had other arguments that were difficult to refute. One was his contribution of more than $11 million to the Institute of Education and Investigation, which had been established by López Bravo to provide student scholarships and other aid, apparently for Opus Dei's University of Navarra. The institute was co-owned by a British organization linked to Opus, and Ruíz said he made the donation to the institute on Opus Dei's orders. (The donation appeared on the institute's books as an interest-free, seventy-five-year loan; in Rumasa's books it appeared as a donation.) Opus denied that it owned the institute that had received the money—which was technically true. López Bravo also denied that the money had been used as a loan for Opus Dei, which was also technically true. But neither denied Ruíz's claim that he had given Opus $11 million.[88]

"I have been a member of Opus Dei for twenty-three years," said Ruíz. "Why did my brothers in the faith abandon me?" (Ruíz was unilaterally "retired" from membership by the Opus Dei directorate in 1986.) "I gave them all this money, and then they threw me to the wolves."[89] A slight, fiery Spaniard who can be both arrogant and ingratiating, Ruíz is not above twisting the truth—for years he refused to admit his membership in Opus Dei. His conviction that he would have been treated differently had Escrivá been alive was probably wishful thinking, but informed Spaniards, including those who mistrusted him, agreed that he was used by Opus Dei—as he used it—and then disowned when he became an embarrassment. "Opus Dei knew perfectly well that Rumasa was in bad shape because Valls ran the Banco Popular and knew what was going on," said a prominent journalist. "But Opus was making money out of Ruíz Mateos. That was important, too. Maybe it explains why they didn't throw him out sooner."[90] Opus Dei's official explanation for expelling Ruíz was that he had ceased to be a member because he had failed to attend required spiritual sessions.

Wheeler-dealers exist in other Catholic organizations, as in most religious denominations. But when they are exposed, their religious affiliation normally does not tar the institution. That has repeatedly occurred with Opus Dei, perhaps because it puts so much emphasis on the temporal success of its members and because it demands a portion, if not all, of the monetary rewards of that success. But undoubtedly the biggest problem is secretiveness—the inability, as Sargent Shriver put it, to address an issue directly and openly. Secret groups inevitably give the impression that they have something to hide; they also encourage rumors and conspiracy theories. A former employee of Ruíz said that she was convinced that Rumasa belonged to Opus Dei until she went to work for Ruíz and found it was untrue.[91] Yet many Spaniards to this day believe that Rumasa was a tentacle of the "Holy Octopus."

Communion and Liberation

"He has an Opus air about him," said a Spanish photographer of Monsignor Luigi Giussani after an interview with the founder of Communion and Liberation (CL).[92] That "air" of religious intransigence is undoubtedly present in Giussani's lay movement, which is "pushy," "noisy," and "obnoxious," according to its critics. But though politically and theologically conservative, CL differs from Opus Dei in several important respects, including its Italian origin. A younger, less structured movement than Opus Dei, CL is as controversial in Italy as Opus Dei is in Spain, but it has one great advantage: It is not secretive. On the contrary, CL openly proclaims its intention to change Italian society, frequently taking the Italian bishops and the Christian Democrats to task. While it targets the same age group as Opus Dei, it does not favor an elaborate recruitment process or severe controls. No one in CL uses whips or cilices or sleeps on boards.

CL is also more open about its political intentions. Like Opus Dei, it displays a tendency toward integralism, or the imposition of Catholic doctrine on society through control of the government. In Spain Opus Dei works through right-wing parties, but its methods are less direct than those of CL in Italy, where a CL spinoff, Movimento Popolare (MP), has established itself as the Roman Catholic wing of the Christian Democrats, with the express intention of taking over the latter or establishing a Catholic party. Its religio-political ambitions are not limited to Italy: The movement has branches in a dozen countries, including the United States, where, however, the spread of its doctrine has been limited by cultural differences. That its small communities in New York City, Boston, and Washington, D.C., will seed a Catholic Party of the United States seems farfetched, just as MP's goal to take control of the Christian Democrats is unlikely, though it commands some two million votes. Italian political and religious observers see MP more as a nuisance than a political threat—a pressure group that lobbies strenuously for the pope's agenda, in contrast to the nominally Catholic Christian Democrats, who have grown flabby and corrupt from years in power. CL's militancy disturbs Italian church leaders because it is a divisive factor in the parishes, yet many say they could deal with the "childish noisiness" were it not for papal favor. John Paul's open support of CL as a universal model for the laity frightens bishops around the world, who see it as an attempt to resurrect an integralist model of society. Church leaders do not believe that a provincial Italian movement like CL can be transplanted successfully to other countries. Quite another thing is Vatican pressure on bishops abroad to force Catholic politicians to adhere to Catholic doctrine. Out of personal conviction or because Rome expects such commitment, or both, New York's Cardinal O'Connor and Boston's Cardinal Law have insisted that Catholic politicians uphold such doctrine. Their sponsorship of CL branches is of small consequence compared to their role as the "pope's men" in the United States. Even in Italy, CL is less important as a movement than as an indication of Rome's determination to assert its voice in local politics.[93]

A Catholic View

CL began in Milan in 1954 when Giussani, a theologian and teacher active in student work, sought a way to challenge Marxism's appeal to youth. Catholicism was having little effect on his students' lives, being reserved primarily for the rituals of birth, marriage, and death, but Giussani was convinced that Christ's vision embodied an exciting message that could compete with the left. Giussani at the time was working with the youth division of Catholic Action, Italy's principal lay movement. Its youth cadres had done much to prevent a communist victory in the 1948 election (see p. 289 of this chapter), but by the 1950s it had lost its fire and was a poor match for the energetic left. Giussani gradually built up his own following among Catholic Action youth, called Gioventù Studentesca, through his teaching that religion should not be restricted to private worship but play a key role in civil life, particularly in high schools and universities, factories, the media, and political parties—what CL later called the "strategy of presence."[94]

Like other Catholic organizations, Giussani's movement lost many members during the student uprisings that swept Europe in the late 1960s—an experience that former members said permanently marked it. In 1969 Gioventù broke with Catholic Action, taking most of what remained of the Milan youth division with it and reforming as Communion and Liberation. Four years later it gained official church recognition. The seventies were a period of rapid growth for CL because of the backlash in Italy against the left. While Giussani's message offered no theological innovation—his followers boast of its "simplicity"—the stress on pride in one's religion and its importance in daily life attracted those seeking religious certitude in the midst of Italy's continuing political crises. By 1986 the movement had 70,000 followers, one-third in their teens or early twenties. Like most religious movements, CL became more structured with the passage of time, and in the 1980s a hard-core membership, known as the "Fraternity" and composed of some 6,000 men and women, was formed to provide the leadership. It received official recognition from the Pontifical Council for the Laity in 1982. In addition, CL counts 500 priests in its membership and approximately 500 "Memores Domini," men and women who belong to the "Fraternity" and who live in community, taking the traditional vows of poverty, chastity, and obedience.[95]

CL is active in fifty-four Italian cities, but its strength is concentrated in the northern belt between Milan and Rimini on the Adriatic. Like Opus Dei, it is a top-down organization with strong emphasis on obedience. Giussani, the president for life, is constantly quoted by his followers, but the cultist aspects of CL are minor compared to Opus Dei's devotion to the "Father." Giussani governs through a central committee of thirty people responsible for different sectors of CL, such as university students and workers. Much of its organizational success stems from cooperatives founded by CL members to fill social needs—job bureaus or cheap restaurants for students, for example—that also enable them to proselytize. Some of the cooperatives have also become businesses: Jaca Book is a CL publishing house, and there are various publications, including the weekly tabloid, *Il Sabato,* and its monthly magazine, *30*

Giorni. Like Opus Dei, CL does not own these businesses; they belong to individual members who use the cooperative, publication, or other business to attract new members and promote CL's right-wing, anticommunist views. For example, CL members run *Avvenire,* a weekly church paper that previously belonged to the Italian bishops; until 1987 a CL member was responsible for the Vatican's television programming. Neither venture prospered, however: *Avvenire* is deeply in debt, and CL was replaced by Opus Dei at Vatican television because of CL's dull programming—a feature also of its publications. But financial backers—primarily bankers and industrialists in northern Italy—appear less interested in profits than in CL's conservative influence on students and workers. Government agencies also donate substantial sums for CL activities, among them an annual youth festival at Rimini, thanks to the influence of some 1,000 CL-backed municipal officials elected on the MP ticket.[96]

The chief objections to CL's presence in Italy are its politicized message, the means used to deliver it, and the connection between CL and MP. CL spokesmen bridle at the charge of integralism—or that a true Catholic must uphold a Catholic ideology with only one political and social outlook, that of the Vatican. But the movement's own literature admits to integralist yearnings despite its rejection of the word. It demands in the social and political arenas the presence of Catholics who will reaffirm their Catholic heritage. It does not want "anonymous Christians" who take a certain position because it seems the right thing to do but Catholics who vote according to Catholic teaching. Giussani said it clearly in his writings: "The greatness of human liberty makes it impossible to find satisfaction except in a community in which all are Catholics."[97]

"CL does not distinguish between religion and politics," said a prominent Jesuit in Milan. "On the one hand, it says that politics must be redeemed to achieve a better society; on the other, it insists that only Catholics can redeem politics." "Where many of us part company with CL," agreed a Milan priest active in youth work, "is in its desire to use politics to announce the Gospel. We think there is another way that does not involve the church directly in partisan politics, and that is through education and the formation of morals. People must be able to choose freely based on their conscience. Just because a political party has a Catholic label doesn't make it moral, as is clear from the Christian Democrats' behavior."[98]

CL spokesmen counter that "we don't want to impose our Christian ideals on anyone, but we want an equal hearing." But many Italian Catholics, including a majority of the bishops, are put off by the way CL demands a hearing. In a variation on Escrivá's "holy coercion," CL theoretician Rocco Buttiglione said that CL members should impress the truth on their misguided brothers and sisters. Dialogue does not mean compromise, he said. Young or middle-aged, "Giussani's Musketeers," as the Italians call them, projected the same know-it-all arrogance as the zealots in the Reagan administration. Said a Milan priest who worked for ten years with high school and university students, "The CL kids are so convinced they are right that they take on everyone in a very aggressive way, even the teachers. It got to the point where we priests who were teachers found ourselves opposing the 'Catholic list' in school elections because it was controlled by CL. Some of the students suffered a severe crisis of faith and career when they eventually rejected CL authority. Afterwards, they didn't want to have anything to do with the church or school."[99]

"Most of the students shun the CL kids," said a Milan high school student, who estimated that no more than 100 of the 3,000 students in her school belonged to the movement. "They are convinced they are absolutely right, but they can't explain why. They act like troops—you either belong, or you're the enemy. Quite a few students voted for the Communist Party in the last school election, even though they are Catholic, as a way of protesting against CL." Milan priests complained of similar confrontations. "The CL people don't want to work with parishioners who belong to other organizations such as Catholic Action. They are very aggressive—they can always get out lots of people for a demonstration or a prayer meeting, for example—but if a pastor accepts them, all the other groups have to take orders from CL or leave. There is no dialogue." Agreed Giovanni Saldarini, the conservative auxiliary bishop of Milan, "CL has its positive aspects, as, for example, in being able to turn out crowds, but it causes pastoral problems by dividing the parishes."[100]

According to a parish priest who was a follower of Giussani in his youth, "In the early years there was a greater feeling of community and spirituality, but after the student upheavals in the late 1960s, the movement changed. The sense of community was replaced by an authoritarian structure, and spirituality was reduced to a hard choice between Catholicism and a corrupt world. The CL leadership thought that the only way to keep young people away from Marxism was to make the authoritarian, anticommunist aspect of the movement stronger. They may really believe this is the solution, but I don't think it is a good instrument for the formation of youth."[101]

Church leaders in Milan also worried about the political fallout from CL's close identification with a political movement. "The MP is the political expression of CL," said Bishop Saldarini. "It could cause the church problems because CL is a church organization. The MP takes aggressive positions—for example, it has accused the Christian Democrats of not being true to Catholicism—and this leads to difficulties for the church with other parties. The MP movement is young and sometimes imprudent, and if it takes a mistaken position, the church could be blamed." Even CL supporters admitted that the divisions between CL and MP were artificial. "CL as a religious institution does not take an official position on partisan politics," asserted Father Angelo Macchi, a CL supporter and director of the Jesuits' Milan publication, *Aggiornamenti sociali*. "Although CL members founded MP to support Christian teaching in politics, they are supposed to be separate," he said. "A person who belongs to CL and MP and votes for an MP candidate on the Christian Democratic ticket assumes a personal responsibility. Of course," he added, "voters who uphold Christian principles cannot support a leftist party or one that is pro-abortion [which excludes all but the Christian Democrats]."[102]

Although MP made its political debut in 1975, it did not hit its stride until the 1980s when it became an important force in northern Italy, particularly the region of Lombardy, of which Milan is the capital. Roberto Formigoni, its dynamic leader, was elected to the European Parliament in 1984 with heavy CL support and voted president of the parliament's political affairs committee. Some 1,000 MP candidates also won office on the Christian Democratic ticket in Italy's 1985 municipal elections, including the deputy mayor of Milan. Formigoni's attempts to portray himself and the MP as the sole political option for Lombardy's Catholics was refuted by Milan's Cardinal Carlo Maria Martini, who is wary of CL's political ambitions. Martini, who is also at odds with John Paul over the pope's political agenda, said that the church could not support a particular candidate or political party, although it did expect Catholics to apply Christian ethics when voting.[103]

Relations with the Christian Democratic leadership proved equally discordant. As admitted by Maurizio Vitali, director of the CL magazine, *Litterae Communionis*, "There is a strong strain in the Christian Democrats that objects to mixing politics and religion." The Christian Democrats also objected to frequent attacks by MP on their "secular" attitudes, particularly their alleged failure to take a stronger position in legislative battles over divorce, abortion, and other social issues of concern to the church. Scarred veterans of Italy's political wars, the Christian Democrats viewed MP with jaundiced eyes: For all its talk of Catholic idealism, MP showed itself as cynical as other parties in its quest for power. Determined to play a role in Italy's coalition governments, it began in 1986 to court the Christian Democrats' traditional rival, the anticlerical Italian Socialist Party, which received substantial coverage in the CL press and was frequently invited to CL conferences. "Undoubtedly there is a great respect for our position among the Socialists," announced Formigoni, though he failed to add that the respect was based solely on political calculation. Nor was MP above using its political influence to further the business interests of CL enterprises. For example, Jaca Book, the CL publishing house, received hundreds of millions of lire from the MP-dominated Lombardy regional council for the purchase of such books as *Biblical Message* and an expensive tome in commemoration of John Paul's visit to Milan. "Jaca has to be subsidized," explained a Milan bookseller, "because its books are too expensive and esoteric for the ordinary reader. I might sell one of their books in a year."[104]

Foreign Interests

As in Italy, where CL constantly boasts of papal support, it has tried to parlay its Vatican connections into a substantial presence in Latin America. It has vigorously supported the campaign of Colombian Cardinal Alfonso López Trujillo against progressive elements in the Latin American church, particularly liberation theologians and the Christian base communities. It also backs López's theory of a "third way," which ostensibly means church support for a middle way between capitalism and communism but in fact is an endorsement of the Christian Democratic parties in Latin America. To aid López's cause at the Vatican, CL members in 1981 launched a magazine, *Incontri,* which attacked liberation theology, the base communities, and other such "aberrations." Its contributors included López's close collaborator, Alberto Methol Ferré, an influential Uruguayan layman, and Guzmán Carriquiry, a high-ranking official of the Pontifical Council for the Laity, which played a major role in furthering the political agenda of CL and John Paul. *Incontri* did its best to cause trouble in Europe for liberals in the Latin American church, but its excessive intellectualism prevented it from attracting a large audience. It was therefore revamped as *30 Giorni,* a slick magazine with a more popular approach and broader subject matter. Thanks to Vatican support, including exclusive interviews with Cardinal Ratzinger, *30 Giorni* gradually emerged as an international platform for the Catholic right. In addition to the original *Incontri* contributors, writers for *30 Giorni* included José Napoleón Duarte, El Salvador's Christian Democratic president; Emilio Maspero, head of the Christian Democrats' Latin American labor confederation; Humberto Belli, a member of the U.S. State Department's anti-Sandinista lobby and a close associate of Managua's Cardinal Obando y Bravo, himself a Christian Democratic sympathizer; the U.S. religious neoconservatives Richard John Neuhaus and Michael Novak; and New York's Cardinal O'Connor. Although the magazine's chief targets were liberation theology and liberalization in the Latin American Catholic Church, it also criticized liberals in other countries, such as U.S. theologian Charles Curran. Similar viewpoints were reinforced by frequent visits and international conferences; among the most popular speakers were López Trujillo and CL theoretician Rocco Buttiglione.[105]

Opposition to the *30 Giorni* circle comes from Milan's more liberal Cardinal Martini and like-minded prelates in the United States and Latin America. Fireworks are likely when the two groups meet, as occurred when Martini invited Milwaukee's Archbishop Weakland to Milan to give a series of talks on the U.S. bishops' economic pastoral. Martini had come under sharp attack by European industrialists because of a similar pastoral letter he had written on the Italian economy, and he brought Weakland to Milan to show that the Italian bishops were not the only church leaders concerned with such issues. The visit was preceded by a critical article on the U.S. economic pastoral written by Novak and published in *Avvenire,* controlled by CL. In an ill-starred attempt to broaden the dialogue the Milan archdiocese invited not only CL economists but also industrialists from other European countries for a discussion with Weakland. The organizers of the visit said the German businessmen were particularly hard on Weakland, claiming, as they had in Martini's case, that bishops were incompetent to speak on economic matters—the same line taken by Novak and other business critics of the American bishops. Weakland, in later describing the confrontation, said he became so upset that he ended by retorting in German.[106]

The same crowd that attacked Weakland was represented at a symposium, "The Church and Economics," co-sponsored by the German

Christian Democrats and the Pontifical Council for the Laity and addressed by Cologne's late Cardinal Höffner, also a member of the *30 Giorni* circle. A follow-up meeting was held in Washington, where the original sponsor, the Pontifical Council, was replaced by the Employers Association of Germany, a major business group. Buttiglione was listed as a key speaker at the meeting. While there was nothing conspiratorial about these meetings, they showed the similarity of interests among CL, its sympathizers in the Pontifical Council for the Laity, the Christian Democrats, and industrial leaders in Italy, Germany, and Switzerland, including heads of multinationals with investments in Latin America. The Christian Democrats—López Trujillo's "third way"—hold out the best hope for such business interests in European countries with a strong left, such as Italy, and in Latin America, where it is hoped that the Christian Democrats can keep the lid on rising nationalism and popular discontent. Like Opus Dei, CL offers a religious answer to the challenge of liberation theology and base communities, which are nationalistic and popular. But CL's message is more attractive because of its more modern packaging. It also has historical ties with Latin America's political center: Just as CL was an outgrowth of Catholic Action, Latin America's Christian Democratic parties evolved from local Catholic Action groups. More important, John Paul has shown a preference for CL over Opus Dei, possibly because of the latter's secretiveness and/or its involvement in repeated scandals.[107]

While CL has established branches in seven Latin American countries, they are too new to have a significant following. In Brazil, its primary target, CL has not been welcomed by liberal bishops. Plans to establish a major center in São Paulo were thwarted by Cardinal Arns, who, like his friend, Cardinal Martini, views CL with deep suspicion. CL delegations to São Paulo only deepened the hostility, according to São Paulo church sources. At one such meeting, the Italians announced that they intended to hold a conference to reunite the liberal bishops in the Brazilian church (the majority) with their conservative colleagues—with the pope's blessing, of course. They also warned Arns against having any dealings with Cardinal Martini or any other church leader who did not toe the Vatican line. When Arns resisted a demand that CL be allowed to take over the São Paulo base communities, he was told that Milan headquarters had sent a message: "That means war." Church sources in Milan said that such behavior was typical. "The CL people think that, because they have papal support, they're running the church and that the cardinals have to do what they say," said one source. Agreed a São Paulo theologian: "They're European know-it-alls. Giussani is a good, holy man, but some of his assistants act as if they were John Paul's *éminences grises.*"[108]

Two Souls

John Paul first became interested in CL when he was archbishop of Krakow. CL priests often took Italian university students on pilgrimages to Poland, and through those visits a friendship developed between CL and Wojtyla and his followers. After he became pope, John Paul encouraged a closer relationship between CL and Light-Life, a similar Polish movement. In 1981 the two movements sponsored an international conference in Rome attended by twenty-one such groups from around the world. Among the speakers was Stanislaw Grygiel, a Polish professor of philosophy who was brought to Rome by John Paul and who formed part of his Polish court. Grygiel's talk was illuminating because it explained why the pope was so keen on groups like CL. Light-Life, CL, and similar movements were to play a special role in renewing the church from within, said Grygiel. Only with such dedicated troops could the pope lead the church into the third millennium.[109]

Like Catholic Poles, CL is totally loyal to the leader and determined to make its presence felt in society. It is also anticommunist and theologically orthodox, and its young people radiate a joyful conviction. "Looking at your faces, so open, so happy . . . , I experience a deep feeling of joy and the desire to show you my affection for your decision of faith and to help you to be ever more mature in Christ," the pope told a gathering of CL youth.[110]

Other church leaders took a different view. "John Paul," said an official of the U.S. bishops' conference, "wants a laity that is totally orthodox and obedient to the political designs of the Vatican." "I can't emphasize how dangerous CL is because it has papal support," warned a Latin American cardinal. "Whenever the Pope talks about the laity, he speaks of a group of young, aggressive, singing people that everybody knows is CL."[111]

John Paul's affection for CL is shared by the Pontifical Council for the Laity, which is heavily weighted with CL supporters, including West German bishop Paul Cordes, vice president of the council, and Guzmán Carriquiry, the highest-placed layman in the Curia. On a visit to the New

York archdiocese in 1986, Cordes made a point of praising CL. "You should trust Communion and Liberation," he said. "They are splendid young people. They have the Pope's approval. The Holy Father hopes they will take charge of the whole university apostolate in the United States." O'Connor, who attended CL's youth festival in Rimini, agreed that CL was marvelous, although it remained unclear how successful its young Italian missionaries would be in New York City.[112]

Cordes also tried to promote CL as a universal model for the laity in the working papers for the 1987 synod on the laity. According to Cordes, CL and Opus Dei had "anticipated" Vatican II by forming lay movements to carry on the church's work. Moreover, CL had the "theological and practical support" of the pope. Cardinal Ratzinger joined the cheerleading. "What is hopeful at the level of the universal church . . . is the rise of new movements," he said, singling out CL as an example. Other church leaders were less enthusiastic. "The vast majority of laypeople are not members of Catholic organizations and play little or no part in the voluntary activities of their parishes," said Britain's Cardinal Hume. "It is very important to make clear to them that the vocation and role of the laity is to be found in the conscientious discharge of their family responsibilities, in the conduct of their daily lives, at work and in society." In other words, they did not have to join a Catholic party to be saved.[113]

Most of the Italian bishops shared Hume's reservations. Under Popes John XXIII and Paul VI the Italian church disengaged itself from partisan politics. Vatican II's emphasis on religious renewal encouraged a new generation of Italian bishops to take greater interest in liturgical reforms and religious formation, in contrast to their predecessors' deep involvement in political intrigue. Italian politicians said that as an Italian Paul would never have pinned all the church's hopes on the Christian Democrats as the political guarantor of its survival. "Most of the bishops feel that it isn't good for the church or the Christian Democrats for the church to be so closely associated with it," said an Italian religious historian. But John Paul, lacking an Italian's grasp of local culture and politics, showed no hesitation in identifying the church with the party and demanding that the Italian bishops follow suit.[114]

The battle within the Italian church has centered on control of Catholic Action, which, with some 565,000 members, is the largest lay movement in Italy. It has followed post–Vatican II policy by distancing itself from the Christian Democrats and sanctioning political pluralism. Like the bishops, it has shifted its emphasis from political militancy to the formation of values. Instead of CL's hard-line tactics, it prefers persuasion and a respect for different opinions. "We have an obligation, in the formation of Italian youth and lay leaders, to foster brother- and sisterhood among all persons of goodwill and not impose our values upon others," said a Catholic Action leader.[115]

CL leaders think such attitudes a sign of weakness. They blamed Catholic Action's pluralism for the legalization of divorce and abortion. They also criticized the bishops for not taking a direct role in the management of Italian politics. Viewed from outside—and John Paul is an outsider—CL's allegations appeared to have substance, since the "spiritual option," as Paul VI called it, failed to prevent the secularization of broad sectors of society. But Italian church sources called that view superficial. "The problem facing the church is the reevangelization of Italy, and that is something that cannot be legislated by a government," said Milan Jesuit Gaston Brambilasca, who works with an Italian version of the Latin American base communities. "Italians go to church to baptize their children, but after the children's first communion, that's the end of it. What is lacking is evangelization, not more politicization, and the key to evangelization is community—people working together for the common good. After Vatican II quite a few of the bishops began to move in the direction of a new, more communal church, but the base has not assimilated Vatican II. Maybe the reason for Italy's slowness in achieving a spiritual renewal is because the Vatican is headquartered here."[116]

Italians refer to Catholic Action and CL as the "two souls of Italian Catholicism." The struggle for power between the "two souls" has several dimensions. One is control over the Italian laity. Another is the growing conflict between the Pope and a majority of the Italian bishops, who support Catholic Action because they do not want to be dragged back to the narrow political confines of the 1950s. The battle has also landed the Vatican in the middle of Italy's political arena—political leaders, including Socialist Bettino Craxi, a former prime minister, have accused the pope of playing partisan politics. As a result of such noisy goings-on, the rest of the world's bishops have been alerted to John Paul's political model; until 1986, when the fight between Catholic Action and CL became public, few had even heard of Communion and Liberation.

In April of that year Catholic Action held a meeting to elect a new leadership and establish policy for the next decade. The organization had been headed by Professor Alberto Monticone, who followed Paul VI's policy of disengagement, and a majority of the Catholic Action regional representatives wanted to elect a leadership that would continue the Monticone line. They were supported by a majority of the Italian bishops, including Milan's Cardinal Martini, the leader of the Italian church's liberal wing and head of the largest archdiocese in Italy. Ranged against them were a minority of CL sympathizers who hoped to seize the leadership with the support of John Paul and Cardinal Ugo Poletti, the president of the Italian Episcopal Conference and a papal yes-man. Poletti opened the meeting with an attack on Catholic Action policies, which was followed by a harsh lecture from John Paul, who criticized Catholic Action for not taking a stronger stand on the Catholic option in political debate, giving the delegates to understand that he wanted it to emulate CL. (Some delegates were so upset that they walked out in the middle of the pope's speech.) To make sure that there was no doubt of what he expected, John Paul summoned Catholic Action delegates to the Vatican for a lecture on the future leadership of the movement. But the delegates, refusing to bow to papal pressure, chose a new leadership that reflected the Monticone line. Not one CL sympathizer was elected.[117]

Poletti was furious. The vicar of Rome, Poletti had been chosen president of the bishops' conference by John Paul in the expectation that he would whip the Italian church into line. After the Catholic Action election, Poletti berated Monticone. He also refused to authorize publication of the meeting's conclusions until he had corrected "certain doctrinal imprecisions." He then sacked Bishop Fiorino Tagliaferri, Catholic Action's popular spiritual adviser, despite a strong appeal from the aging Cardinal Anastasio Ballestrero, former president of the bishops' conference and one of the most respected men in the Italian church. Monsignor Antonio Bianchi, a CL supporter, was named in his place. "Pray for your bishops who have much need of help," Ballestrero entreated Italian journalists after learning of the appointment.[118]

Upset by the bullying tactics, the bishops made their feelings known to the pope by electing Catholic Action supporters to represent them at the 1987 synod on the laity (Cardinal Martini received the largest number of votes). Poletti was not elected, but it was a foregone conclusion that the pope would appoint him as his representative. The bishops had worked hard to establish unity among themselves (which had not existed prior to Vatican II), and they were dismayed by the divisions that Poletti and the pope were creating. Just as John Paul took a different position on religious involvement in politics, depending on the country (no involvement in Latin America; active involvement in Italy and Poland), so he contradicted himself in regard to the bishops' authority. Although he spoke constantly about the need for obedience to and unity with the local bishop, his support for CL had the effect of undermining the bishops. Supporters of Milan's Cardinal Martini said that CL had declared a de facto war on the cardinal. "When a dispute arises with CL," said a Milan priest and Martini loyalist, "the CL people say, 'You may have Martini, but we have the Pope.'" Bishop Cordes, CL's sponsor at the Pontifical Council for the Laity, was quite blunt about the matter. As long as CL has the pope's support, he said, it doesn't matter what the local bishops think. But such an attitude was bound to revive "the old tensions between the papacy and the episcopacy," warned Italian theologian Severino Dianich. "We have the impression," commented a bishop, "that the bishops no longer count but only the orders of the Curia."[119]

The Vatican's concept of an army on the march under a single general and banner was reinforced by papal orders to the bishops to get out on the hustings in the weeks leading up to Italy's mid-1987 general election. Citing the 1948 election as an example of how Italian Catholics had "saved democracy," John Paul insisted that "no one should be surprised if Catholics, when making decisions, are inspired by their deep convictions and docilely follow the guidance of their pastors." Catholics must uphold a "unified commitment in public life," said the pope, in order to resist a "culture of death" symbolized by the legalization of abortion and divorce. The bishops took up the same theme of a "unified commitment" in an unusual pastoral letter that directed Catholics not to abstain from voting and to support the party that upheld Catholic ideals, meaning the Christian Democrats.

Their statement broke with a twenty-five-year tradition of refraining from comment on elections and was greeted with outrage by all the parties—except, needless to say, the Christian Democrats. The Socialists, Republicans, Liberals, and Social Democrats argued that "the defense of Christian values is not the prerogative of a single party." They also accused the pope of "regression to earlier centuries" and of "partisan support for the Christian Democrats." Former prime minister Craxi charged the church with "denying the political freedom of Catholics," reminding the pope of a concordat (or treaty) which he had signed with the Vatican which reaffirmed the "separation of church and state." But John Paul was unimpressed, urging Catholics to the polls in "this moment of danger," as Pius XII had done forty years earlier.[120]

Tradition, Family and Property

However threatening SMOM, Opus Dei, or CL may seem to their critics, they are benign compared to Tradition, Family and Property (TFP). Unlike those other movements, which have an official relationship with the Catholic Church, TFP is opposed by the Catholic leadership because of its beliefs and recruiting procedures. While it presents itself as an orthodox Catholic group that is strongly anticommunist, its doctrine is a brew of medievalism and mysticism. It practices cult worship of its aging Brazilian founder, Plinio Correa de Oliveira, and his mother, Lucilia ("Saint Monica"), and has established a fraternity of underlings, known as the "Holy Slavery," who swear undying allegiance to "Dominus Plinio." Although TFP has branches in fifteen countries, including the United States, its membership is small, an estimated 2,000 youths and men. It could be dismissed as a fragment of a lunatic fringe were it not for its political machinations on behalf of the extreme right and its devious methods in recruiting fourteen- to sixteen-year-old boys. Testimony by former members and relatives in several countries describes a brainwashing process, including brutal self-mortification, that is aimed at weaning the youth from his family by replacing his own parents with a worship of Plinio and his mother. Instead of promoting family unity, Tradition, Family and Property destroys it. Because of such practices, it was banned by the Venezuelan government in 1984; it has also had problems with the authorities in France. The Catholic churches in Venezuela, Brazil, and Chile have denounced it, and even the cult's former protector, Brazilian Archbishop Antonio de Castro Mayer, broke with it because of its "blasphemous" and "heretical" worship of Oliveira's mother. Nevertheless, President Reagan in 1984 told the U.S. branch of TFP that he hoped for the movement's "continued growth and prosperity." "With your help and the help of all patriotic Americans," said the President, "I know our nation can surmount all the challenges which lie ahead."[121]

"Dominus Plinio"

A retired professor of history, prolific writer, and onetime leader of the São Paulo division of Catholic Action, Oliveira was influenced by the Brazilian government's neofascist integralist policies in the 1930s and early 1940s. He also has leanings toward the European aristocracy, as shown by TFP's medieval rituals and dress, and by his relationship with the

Braganças, the royal family of Portugal (two of the Braganças, one of them the pretender to the Brazilian throne, are TFP members).

Oliveira was fifty-two when he founded TFP in São Paulo in 1960. By then, he had accumulated a considerable number of hates, including the French Revolution, Protestantism, liberal Catholicism, and Marxism. With the support of Archbishop Castro Mayer and Archbishop Geraldo de Proença Sigaud, both large landowners, he organized TFP to combat the land redistribution initiatives of the Brazilian church and government. Agrarian reform has remained a prime TFP target as much on economic as on ideological grounds. A major part of TFP income comes from the landed proprietors of South America who, as might be expected, associate agrarian reform with Marxism. Hostility toward the redistribution of land also fits into Oliveira's peculiar view of history. As he sees it, the West has been in a decline ever since the Middle Ages, its civilization having been infected by the Renaissance, the French Revolution, Protestantism, and other plagues, including democracy. "From the hatred of monarchy and aristocracy are born the demagogic democracies which fight tradition, persecute the elites, degrade the general tone of life and breed an environment of vulgarity," he wrote. "The mass production of republics everywhere in the world is . . . a typical product of the [French] Revolution." In contrast, the "Inquisition was the most beautiful page in the history of the church, because, while it went on, Catholicism managed to cleanse itself of heretics."[122]

Oliveira's nostalgia for the Middle Ages is evident in the rituals, clothes, furniture, and paraphernalia of TFP. Its young militants, who can occasionally be seen on city streets handing out TFP tracts, wear scarlet capes and black berets and carry medieval banners with a lion rampant. (According to Oliveira, "the lion elevates the soul to a higher plane, it speaks of battle, makes one feel the nobility and beauty of the fight and communicates a sense of the battle to all those who contemplate it.") TFP houses, usually located in wealthy residential areas, are furnished in a Spanish colonial style, with heavy wooden chairs and benches, banners, tapestries, shields, swords, and an obligatory picture of the founder. The Bogotá house displays large portraits of "Dominus Plinio" in six of its rooms. São Paulo headquarters, known as the "Palace," has, in addition to the usual colonial bric-a-brac, a gilded chamber called the "Hall of Knights." According to Reuters correspondent Uli Schmetzer, one of the few outsiders permitted to see it, the hall is dominated by a throne, with a panel depicting Saint George slaying a dragon whose three heads represent the three scourges of Catholicism—the Protestants, the French Revolution, and communism. Former TFP members say that Oliveira uses the throne during induction ceremonies into the "Holy Slavery."[123]

The "Hermits of San Bento," Oliveira's commandos for the coming world revolution, wear a monk's habit, with a chain at the waist, an oversized scapular with an image of Saint James, and jackboots. Young recruits are impressed by this mummery, which continues into athletic training and competitions that include single combat with spears and crossbows. Some of the "games" are deliberately rough, as in contests between youths who use maces to belabor each other. One former member said his arm was broken three times in such fights. "Our leaders said that this training was necessary because Catholics had the image of being saintly, and we had to show we weren't sissies," he said. Judo and karate are also included in the training for "self-defense," as is an antiguerrilla course that features long marches through forests or jungle without rest, food, or water, and much crawling through swamps. In a complicated series of vigorously enforced rituals members learn such knightly procedures as how to march correctly, to maintain silence, and to avoid looking at one another. Failure to observe the niceties of behavior imposes severe penance, including self-flagellation or whipping by another member. Members wear cilices, the instrument of self-torture favored by Opus Dei. Other punishments include long periods of reciting the rosary with arms outstretched in the shape of a cross, walking six miles while praying, staying up all night to study the works of Dr. Plinio, fasting for up to forty-eight hours, and, in the most serious cases, confinement in monks' cells on a TFP farm 100 miles from São Paulo. According to the Brazilian magazine *Istoé*, one recruit was interned in a pigpen for twelve hours while being forced to shout, "I am a pig; I am an imbecile."[124]

One result of such training is absolute obedience to Oliveira. Another is a bullying attitude toward critics, particularly the parents of members and former members. Venezuelan parents who lost their sons to the TFP branch in Caracas said that, when they tried to regain them, they were told by Brazilian members not to interfere or they would never see their boys again. The mother of a former Venezuelan member who testified against TFP in the Venezuelan congress received threats, and the man himself had his car windows broken. "Red crosses were written on the seats," he said, "and they had written in red, 'Reprobate Judas, your end is near.' "[125]

After hearing from former members that TFP considered the Venezuelan liberator Simón Bolivar a "traitor" because he had led the revolution for independence from Spain, and that TFP members had for ten minutes applauded the news of the death of John Paul I, the Venezuelan government outlawed the organization. John Paul II was about to visit the country, and a story (never proven) was going the rounds that TFP members were using his picture for target practice. Although TFP was forced to leave Venezuela, it had enough influence to survive in other nations, particularly in Brazil and Chile, where it had helped promote military coups. Its "Rosary Marches" in São Paulo and Belo Horizonte, which attracted thousands of like-minded protestors, particularly conservative women's groups, were a key factor in the military's decision in 1964 to overthrow President Goulart's reformist government. Oliveira was proud of TFP's part in the demise of a government that had sponsored agrarian reform and encouraged "agitations." Dictatorships, he wrote, should be supported in order to protect order. In 1968 TFP led an attack on the liberal wing of the Brazilian church, including Dom Helder Cámara, the prophetic archbishop of Recife. It demanded that the military regime arrest Cámara and other church leaders because they supported land reform and peasant federations. This was followed by a sustained campaign against Dom Pedro Casaldáliga, the popular bishop of São Felix in the Amazon, who was accused by TFP of being a "guerrilla" because he defended landless peasants. TFP also supported the Rural Democratic Union, composed of large landowners, in its ongoing war on the peasantry. (See Chapter 5, pp. 125–27.) The Brazilian bishops countered the TFP attack by warning Catholics against collaborating with the movement, which they said was a heretical cult.[126]

In his writings Oliveira urged his followers to be "willing and able to meet the enemy in self-defense [with] head-on physical confrontations," but some went beyond self-defense, according to Colonel Dickson M. Grael, a right-wing Brazilian military official. In 1971, Grael was in charge of preparations for a Brazilian invasion of Uruguay, to be launched in the event of an election victory by a left-wing coalition known as the Broad Front; the invasion was called off when the Front lost the election. According to Grael's book on the subject, *The Shadow of Impunity*, the TFP branch in Uruguay received through the Brazilian air force attaché in Montevideo explosives that were used to bomb the installations of the Uruguayan Communist Party, one of the participants in the Broad Front. TFP has paid for its activities in Uruguay and elsewhere: The TFP "Palace" in São Paulo was bombed, and its Colombian installations have been repeatedly bombed, most recently on the eve of the pope's visit there in 1986. Oliveira is always accompanied by armed guards.[127]

In a replay of its Brazilian aggressions, TFP supported demonstrations against President Allende in Chile and churned out antigovernment propaganda, including books and articles in the Chilean TFP publication, *Fiducia.* Its partners in the anti-Allende campaign included the equally militant Fatherland and Liberty, with CIA connections, and members of the *gremios,* or business and professional organizations. After the coup Jaime Guzmán, who ran *Fiducia,* became the military junta's principal ideologist, and TFP gained control of several important national organizations, including the National Secretariat of Youth. As in Brazil, TFP repeatedly attacked the bishops, including Santiago's Cardinal Raul Silva. Among its better-known works was a hatchet job called *The Church of Silence,* which called on the Chilean laity to "show their love for the Church by refusing obedience to their pastors" and was widely publicized in the government press. The hierarchy responded by announcing that those responsible for the book had "placed themselves outside the body of the Catholic Church," which was interpreted as a de facto excommunication of Guzmán and his followers. "The nearly universal view within the church of Latin America," said Thomas Quigley, Latin America adviser to the U.S. Catholic Conference, "is that TFP represents a fanatical fringe minority of the privileged sectors that is at variance with the authentic tradition of the Catholic Church."[128]

Possibly because of its notoriety in countries like Brazil and Chile, TFP's national associations and publications are known elsewhere by other names. In Spain TFP is called the Sociedad Cultural Covadonga; in Italy, Alleanza Cattolica; Canada, Young Canadians for a Christian Civilization; and France, Lecture et Tradition. But its recruiting methods have sometimes ended in scandal and an unmasking, as occurred in France, where the TFP director ran afoul of the French authorities when irate parents denounced his recruiting as a criminal "abuse of confidence." TFP was also forced to close its school for boys, Saint-Benoit, when angry parents discovered that TFP was a Brazilian cult and complained to the police. But Oliveira, who reportedly believes himself immortal, refused to give up, turning out long diatribes on the French socialists, agrarian reform, and other hates that were published as TFP advertisements in some of the world's leading newspapers, including *The New York Times, The Washington Post,* and the London *Observer,* at more than $100,000 per ad. Funding was reported to have come from industrialists and large landowners in Latin America, some of whom, unaware of the cultist aspects of TFP, thought it a bona fide Catholic organization.[129]

In the United States the American branch goes under the TFP name but also works through the Foundation for a Christian Civilization. (John R. Spann, the president of the American TFP, is a board member of the foundation; other board members are also connected to TFP.) The American TFP has headquarters in Pleasantville, New York, with branches in Washington, D.C., and California, and an estate in Bedford, New York, called "Our Lady of Good Success," that was donated by a wealthy Texan family. Although the American TFP has had some bad publicity, notably during a fight with fearful Bedford residents over its acquisition of the $2.4-million estate for a conference center and boys' school, it is little known in the United States. Its youthful militants occasionally organize protests, as in demonstrations against homosexual rights. TFP also belongs to an extreme right coalition known as RAMBO that sponsors rightist protests, such as a demonstration against Chevron Oil for its business dealings with the leftist Angolan regime. RAMBO works with the New Right's Conservative Caucus, and it was through this connection that its leadership became friendly with Paul Weyrich, the ubiquitous crusader of the American right. Weyrich helped TFP organize a press conference in Washington to denounce agrarian reform in Brazil and the "trained and armed bandits coming out of the basic Christian communities." In recognition of his role "as a friend who has defended the TFP movement on several occasions and has offered sound advice on the battle terrain," TFP in 1986 gave a banquet to honor Weyrich at its Bedford estate. Other influential American friends claimed by TFP included North Carolina's ultraconservative senator, Jesse Helms, Republican minority leader of the Senate Foreign Relations Committee; Morton Blackwell, president of the Leadership Foundation and a former Reagan administration adviser on Central America (Blackwell was also present at the Washington press conference on agrarian reform); and Roger Fontaine, one of the authors of the "Santa Fe Document" that attacked liberation theology (see Chapter 4, pp. 89–90) and Reagan's first Central America adviser on the National Security Council.[130]

A Cult

The testimony of former TFP members and the families of TFP recruits shows that the organization seeks to enlist those whose families are politically conservative and strongly anticommunist. "It makes it easier to recruit the boy that way," explained the parents of a TFP member who was thirteen years old when approached by a TFP "apostle," or older boy who is a TFP recruiter. Their story was the same as those of other parents in Venezuela and Brazil who lost their children to TFP. "In the beginning the parents think it's a good thing," said Ricardo Pochat, an executive whose fifteen-year-old son was recruited at one of six exclusive private schools in Caracas frequented by "apostles." "My son's new friends were well dressed and seemingly well educated young men. They said they were against drugs and supported the family, and because TFP has a reputation for anticommunism and strict Catholicism, we thought with relief, well, here are some friends of whom we can approve."[131]

Meanwhile, unbeknown to the parents, the youth is being indoctrinated in Oliveira's peculiar cult at the local TFP residence. Through films, games, and talks he is taught to despise the "filth" of the world, as exemplified by excursions to the beach or pool where temptation lurks in a bikini. He learns of the coming "*baggare*," or punishment that will be inflicted on the world because of the sins of the flesh, which are responsible for the French Revolution and other political horrors. Only Plinio, who has a direct mandate from God, and his followers will be saved. Attracted by the religious fanaticism and the medieval pomp, the youth begins to see himself as a knight who will save the world. At this point, he signs a pledge in blood at the TFP house and learns a secret TFP code to communicate with his new brothers in order to avoid interference from his parents.[132]

"A year after my fourteen-year-old son was recruited by TFP, we began to notice changes," said Franz Dozsa, the father of another Venezuelan youth who joined the movement. Like other families, the Dozsas became concerned about their son's falling grades; his reluctance to join family social events, particularly with women; and his more aggressive personality. At first, Dozsa and the others attributed these changes to the inevitable problems of teenage adjustment. When his son proposed a "tourist excursion" to São Paulo with his new friends, Dozsa, like the other parents, approved, and paid for it, in the belief that the experience of another country and culture might be good for the boy. But the trip to São Paulo, according to parents and former members, is the turning point in recruitment. Subjected to intensive indoctrination, medieval rituals, and cult worship of Plinio and his mother, and encouraged in their aggressiveness ("I ended up enjoying it when I whipped or beat my

companions," said a former member), they return home as changed people. They have learned that everything wicked in them has come from
their families and that such sinfulness has produced the plagues of the
French Revolution, Protestantism, and communism. Women are especially maligned, particularly the recruit's mother, sisters, and girlfriends;
the lone exception to this universe of Jezebels is Oliveira's mother.
("Woman," according to TFP, "is a creature of God whose faculties
fluctuate between the state of a human and an animal.") "Everyone who
disagrees with TFP is identified as a communist," reported one mother,
who said her son had accused her of being a paid Russian agent.[133]

Family relations rapidly disintegrate. Studies, sports, and social life
cease to have meaning, and the youth refuses to attend Mass or other
Catholic ceremonies because they are conducted by "communist priests."
The only thing that counts is the approval of his TFP directors and especially Plinio, to whom he obsessively prays. Relics from Plinio are
particularly treasured—Pochat's son, for example, kept a case of them,
including a bar of soap once used by Plinio, stray hairs said to have come
from his head, and even used Kleenex. When a boy comes of age, he
abandons his family, perhaps never to see them again. José Luis Salas,
a former Venezuelan member, said that even when members of the family
begged to speak to a youth because of the serious illness of a parent,
their call was refused. "There was a particularly pathetic case of one
member who refused to have anything to do with his family even when
his sister died," said Salas. "When his mother attempted to rescue him
from TFP, he insulted her. Shortly afterwards, he suffered a car accident
that left him seriously incapacitated. That was when TFP returned the
son to his parents, practically dead, because he was no longer useful to
the cause."[134]

A round-faced, frail-looking man with a practiced smile and genteel
manners, Oliveira still mesmerizes young recruits on their visits to the
"Palace" in São Paulo. How long he can continue to spin his web is
questionable, given his age, nor is it clear who or what will follow him.
According to former TFP members, the movement is so organized that
only Oliveira has complete knowledge and control of its affairs. Since he
thinks himself immortal, no successor has been designated. That such a
cult should enjoy the respect of influential conservative circles in the New
and Old Worlds is due primarily to its rabid anticommunism. But TFP
also responds to a longing among such groups for a hierarchical society
that recalls the Middle Ages, with its clear divisions between rich and

poor and a belief in the God-given right of a small minority to rule the majority.

Although TFP is among the most extremist groups in the Religious International, it shares with Opus Dei and Communion and Liberation a sense of crusading righteousness. Members of these "movements," as they are known in the Vatican, look upon themselves as the chosen few who will cleanse society and restore a pre–Vatican II Catholicism. Introspective and authoritarian, they promise salvation in the next world in return for spiritual and physical sacrifice in this one—much as do Protestant fundamentalists. The chief objection to such groups is not their political conservatism or even their rites, strange though they may seem by modern standards, but their impact on teenagers, who are easy targets because of their idealism and lack of experience. As pointed out by Father Felzmann, Opus Dei's first Czech member, young people need an "open God of life" to encourage them to work for a better future. The key to that future is not a religious dictatorship by one group but "people working together for the common good," in the words of Milan Jesuit Brambilasca.

CHAPTER 11
✠
THE BANNER CARRIERS

THE NEW "ECCLESIAL MOVEMENTS," as Communion and Liberation's founder, Luigi Giussani, called them, were at the center of the debate at the synod on the laity in the fall of 1987. Although many of the 230 assembled bishops wanted to discuss other matters, such as a larger role for the laity in the church and an end to discrimination against women, Communion and Liberation (CL), Opus Dei, and other such groups (TFP excluded) dominated the agenda with the support of their Curia mentors. Not only did the "movements" take up much of the synod discussion; they also set the tone for the meeting, which, unlike previous synods, was shrouded in secrecy. Fearful of any public discussion of the laity with the laity, the Curia forbade the bishops from sharing their proposals with the media, warning that photocopying such documents would be a "grave sin." The fifty-six observers representing the laity were not even allowed to see the proposals—which were in Latin—though the meeting was about them. Nevertheless, the synod documents soon leaked out, copies of which were sold on streets near the Vatican. "Instead of listening to the voice of grass-roots Catholics as articulated by national bishops," complained Canadian Archbishop Donat Chiasson, "the church bureaucracy chose rather to lecture synod bishops."[1]

Synod watchers speculated that the reason for the blackout was the fierce debate over the "movements" between European and Latin American supporters and critics. The latter, including Milan's Cardinal Martini and Brazil's Cardinal Lorscheider, claimed that the movements were divisive and undercut the authority of the local bishop. But Bishop Cordes, vice-president of the Pontifical Council for the Laity, and other movement supporters insisted that the final arbiter was the pope, and John Paul had given the movements his unqualified approval by calling them "absolutely irreplaceable." As recognized by Chicago's Cardinal Bernardin, papal authority was the real issue in the controversy, the movements symbolizing the larger struggle between "local church and universal church." Neither CL nor Opus Dei posed a challenge to the church in the United States, but the power struggle with Rome was "indeed a U.S. problem," said Bernardin.[2]

The movements were hierarchical, authoritarian, politically right-wing, blindly obedient to the pope, and committed to a narrow Catholicism in the Ratzinger style that excluded any who dissented. In contrast, church leaders like Martini, Lorscheider, and Bernardin wanted a more open and pluralistic model of church in which all joined together for the common good and in which there were no exclusions. During the first days of the synod, when the bishops spoke of their hopes and concerns, it was clear that a majority supported a more liberal model, while the Vatican was trying to pull the church back into a pre–Vatican II mold. Like previous battles over the same question, the bottom line was, Who was in charge? Rome or the bishops? If the pope could impose such international movements as CL and Opus Dei on local bishops, he would be able to yank the cord tighter. He would also further an integralist agenda by demanding that bishops command the faithful to vote for political candidates who upheld Vatican teachings, as he had done in Italy during the 1987 election. Bishops who publicly oppose right-wing groups supported by the pope run the risk of being accused of disloyalty to him, worried Archbishop Chiasson.[3]

That such was the plan was shown by the delegates John Paul appointed to the synod, many of whom were directors of right-wing groups, including CL's Giussani and Opus Dei's Portillo. While it was forbidden to circulate outside materials during the meeting, CL's magazine, *30 Giorni*, was nevertheless distributed in the synod hall to all the delegates. The issue contained an interview with Jean Dherse, former head of the Channel tunnel project between Britain and France, in which he attacked the U.S. bishops' pastoral on the economy, claiming that the bishops were a minority of zealots who wanted to impose their ideas on a reluctant majority. Dherse also happened to be one of two lay "special secretaries" charged with drafting synod texts. One of the two assistants to the special secretaries was a member of Opus Dei's German branch. The recording secretary for the synod, Cardinal Hyacinthe Thiandoum, was a friend and defender of the reactionary French Archbishop Marcel Lefebvre, who had broken with Rome over Vatican II and whom John Paul was trying to coax back into the church. Bishops complained that they were stuck with a prearranged agenda that did not allow them to advance the cause of lay people. For example, proposals that women be admitted to all nonordained ministries were dropped from the vague and platitudinous final text. "The synod was not ready to work out the differences between men and women, their specific tasks and implementation according to local culture," said Milwaukee's Archbishop Weakland, one of the synod's strongest spokesmen for women's rights. Nor was it able to tackle anything else that might anger the pope. As Weakland and other U.S. delegates to the meeting later told the annual conference of U.S. bishops, attempts to advance or discuss important issues facing the church were rebuffed by the Vatican. "Nothing" came out of the meeting, agreed Canada's Chiasson, who said that the carefully edited final proposals were so bland that the pope had nothing to challenge him.[4]

Many lay people were bitter about the lost opportunities. In the United States, where the bishops had undertaken a two-year process of consultation with some 200,000 people, lay leaders complained of the waste of time, money, and personnel on a pointless exercise. CL and the other "movements," on the other hand, were delighted with the outcome because the synod confirmed their power as papal favorites. The resurgence of clericalism, so evident in the manipulation of the synod, also accorded with the movements' philosophy—as did the Vatican's refusal to contemplate dissent. "At every stage, our remarks were narrowed and refined until almost nothing remained," said one frustrated bishop of the supposed "dialogue."[5]

If the synod failed to fulfill the expectations of many Catholics, it did show them what they were up against. As on John Paul's trip to the United States in the weeks before the synod, the carefully staged drama reflected the closed mentality of a fortress church. Dialogue was not possible, said Chiasson, because "they are afraid" of losing control. Of course, synods had never served as a parliament of the church. When they were established by Vatican II, they were viewed as a means of keeping alive the collegial spirit that had prevailed during the council through regular consultation among the bishops and the pope. But the pope always had the last word because the synod documents were merely advisory, and he could reject or change them. In the first synods after Vatican II the bishops made a genuine contribution—for example, the document on justice in the world that emerged from the 1971 synod. But that was due in large part to Pope Paul's support for the process. Under John Paul consultation was reduced to rubber-stamp assemblies from which the bishops emerged angry and disappointed. "The worst mistake we could make is to attach too much importance to these synods," said one bishop. Yet bishops, as well as ordinary Catholics, did attach importance to them because there was no other mechanism of communication between the local churches and Rome. The message from the 1987 synod was that communications would continue but in one direction only—from Rome to the colonies.[6]

A Multinational Corporation

A clear sign of the New Order was the appointment of papal yes-men as bishops. In earlier times local churches had been responsible for selecting their own prelates, but after Vatican I in the nineteenth century Rome claimed a worldwide monopoly on such appointments, a practice that was later legalized in canon law. Vatican II changed matters somewhat by encouraging the papacy to consult with local bishops and cardinals about their successors and the appointment of auxiliary bishops, although the pope retained final authority. Since John Paul's election, however, the advice of liberal church leaders has been ignored in the selection of prelates. Austria's Cardinal Franz-Josef König, for example, had been told by the pope that he would make no decision about König's successor without consulting him. The moderate König had played a key role in gaining support for John Paul's papacy at the 1978 conclave, and presumably on that basis the aging cardinal was owed the courtesy of being allowed to comment on the pope's preferences. But John Paul did not bother to speak to König, who learned about the appointment of his successor, Hans Groer, after the fact.

The Austrians were not pleased with the little-known monk, who seemed a poor replacement for the brilliant König, one of the stars of Vatican II. But they took a philosophical attitude toward the change, until the Vatican announced the appointment of three other conservative bishops. The appointments caused an uproar in the liberal Austrian church because they were clearly a warning to the bishops about their "lax" views on birth control and divorce. One of the appointments was to a newly created vicariate for the armed forces, notwithstanding the bishops' arguments against a special category for the military in a small country with no overseas commitments. A second was the naming of Austria's Opus Dei leader, Klaus Kung, to a diocese in western Austria despite warnings from the retiring bishop and other local Catholic leaders that he would polarize the community. The "final straw," in the words of one church leader, was the appointment of Kurt Krenn, a Romanized theologian also associated with Opus Dei, as auxiliary bishop of Vienna.

Krenn's principal credentials appeared to be his friendship with John Paul, with whom he frequently breakfasted, and his opposition to birth control. The Austrian church has a tradition dating to the thirteenth century of consultation in the selection of bishops, but John Paul ignored it. "The Austrian bishops' conference is being run over from abroad," complained Monsignor Florian Kutner, echoing the protests of major lay groups, priests and nuns, 120 Catholic journalists, and Archbishop Karl Berg, president of the bishops' conference. Such was the hostility that Krenn had to have a police escort during ceremonies for his consecration as bishop and Cardinal König was forced to go on Austrian television to plead for calm. Although John Paul had felt the anger of Dutch Catholics on his visit to Holland after a similar reorganization of the hierarchy, he appeared unmoved by Austrian complaints that the Vatican was wrecking their church as well. "You should have no doubt," he warned the Austrian bishops on their visit to Rome in mid-1987, "of the right of the Pope to appoint bishops."[7]

Similarly, Brazil's popular archbishop Helder Cámara had no say in the selection of his successor, the conservative archbishop José Cardoso Sobrinho. How much such appointments could affect local churches was shown when Cardoso withdrew church support from programs with the poor that had been organized under Cámara and forbade him from speaking in the archdiocese.[8]

The process of selection depends on the papal nuncios, or the Curia's ambassadors, who act as the pope's representatives in foreign countries and are often political reactionaries (in Latin America, for example, they are frequently aligned with local dictators). Some were rude and domineering, as was the case of the papal nuncio to Brazil, Archbishop Carlo Furno, who, according to Brazilian sources, so upset local bishops by his tongue-lashings that some threatened to resign.[9] Archbishop Laghi, the Vatican's ambassador to the United States, was a more polished diplomat, but his recommendations also reflected the papal line. As far as John Paul was concerned, that was how it should be: He was a "centipede," he said, whose legs were the papal nuncios.

The Vatican's argument for the system is that, in the choice of bishops, it has to be guided by universal, not local, concerns. In fact Rome can maintain control over its far-flung empire only through the appointment of like-minded administrators, recommended by the papal nuncios or by influential cardinals and archbishops within the pope's inner circle. As in a multinational corporation, the branch managers are promoted on the basis of their unquestioning obedience to corporate policy, even if the policy runs contrary to the real interests of the institution.

Bishops who do not toe the line receive a "friendly" visit from a fellow prelate who is in the Vatican's confidence. Those who persist in their independence are deliberately isolated. While there is considerable opposition among the bishops to the idea that "everything has to be validated in Rome," in the words of one church leader, the only way they can deal with the problem is as a group. Individual bishops can be picked off at Rome's leisure, but that it is much more difficult to coerce a bishops' conference was shown by Ratzinger's defeats in confrontations with the Peruvian and Brazilian bishops. The strength and independence of some of the conferences, particularly those in Brazil and the United States, are also seen as a threat to centralized rule. Consequently one of the first items on the Restoration's agenda was to destroy the authority of the conferences.

Ratzinger led the attack, reversing his earlier position in support of collegial bodies that represented the consensus of a group of bishops. Although Vatican II had recognized the importance of bishops' conferences, Ratzinger claimed they had no basis in theology or tradition, an argument that could have been made as well against many other church structures. According to the cardinal, the conferences got in the way of individual bishops, who should deal directly with Rome. He did not like the idea of a "group spirit" because he was convinced that a "passive majority [would] accept the position of the enterprising minorities." Much the same criticism had been leveled at the U.S. bishops' conference by conservative Americans, who objected to its pastoral letters on peace and the economy, although both documents were the result of consultation with all the bishops. Ratzinger's disparaging comments were made in the same month that the U.S. bishops released their draft letter on the economy, suggesting that criticism by influential American Catholic businessmen and politicians had made an impact on the Vatican.[10] The cardinal also claimed that a new code of canon law severely proscribed the authority of the conferences when in fact the code merely restated the obvious—that the conferences did not replace individual bishops.

Revision of the code had been mandated by John XXIII twenty-four years earlier as the second part of a pincer operation to revive an outdated church, the other being Vatican II. But despite the work of nearly 100 cardinals and 200 legal experts, John Paul was not satisfied with the results until he and a hand-chosen commission of conservative jurists had gone over the code. Several key passages were changed, including a section that had originally guaranteed the laity full participation in church government. John Paul's censors downgraded the laity's role to "cooperation" with church authorities. Equally significant, a liberal law on the laity's relationship to politics and government was changed to reflect the papacy's integralist thinking. In its original wording the law had stated that "in the exercise of temporal activity [the laity] is not subject to canon laws but to civil laws like other citizens." The revised law said, "The laity is obliged to give testimony to Christ in the conduct of temporal affairs and the exercise of secular responsibilities." In other words, Catholic government officials were obliged to uphold Catholic teaching in all spheres of life, regardless of whether it was counter to the civil law, as in the case of legal abortion in the United States.[11]

As with the laity, the new code expressed distrust of the bishops, stating that the synods were merely consultative bodies with no deliberative powers and that, if such were bestowed, they could be given only by the pope. The pontiff was also empowered to "conclude, transfer, suspend or dissolve the synod." Nevertheless, John Paul's supporters insisted that he was an "enthusiastic supporter" of the synod system, which was true to the extent that synods offered the pope an opportunity to build a consensus behind policies he had already chosen. His motto for government was "with Peter and under Peter," meaning that the bishops were to support his decisions, not challenge them. But some prelates questioned whether there was any point in such meetings if John Paul was not prepared to listen to their opinions. At the 1980 synod, for example, a realistic church policy on birth control and divorce was urged by numerous bishops, including those from the Third World. But the pope's response was, "They must be silenced!"[12]

The Guardians

In the years after the Latin American bishops' historic meeting in Medellín, when the region's church had made a preferential option for the poor, the Roman Curia succeeded in changing the nature of the bishops' regional conference, CELAM, by replacing progressives with conservatives. A decade later the institution that had sponsored Medellín wanted to disown it. But the new CELAM leadership failed to persuade the Latin American bishops, who reconfirmed their commitment to Medellín at a hemisphere meeting in Puebla, Mexico, in 1979. One reason for that reconfirmation was that the religious orders remained steadfast to Medellín, many of their members dying for its commitment to the poor. When CELAM would no longer carry the banner, the Latin American Confederation of Religious (CLAR) took up the cause despite dire threats from CELAM's then secretary general, the Colombian López Trujillo. The hope of Medellín was nourished by countless priests and nuns and by powerful church leaders who were themselves religious, such as the Brazilian cardinals Arns and Lorscheider, both Franciscans.

Something similar has happened during the Restoration of John Paul. While the bishops have been out front in the battle over Vatican II, the religious orders have been fighting parallel but more successful skirmishes on the sidelines. An individual bishop can be monitored and isolated, since he is physically stationary in a diocese. A bishops' conference, though more unwieldly, can also be kept under observation by the papal nuncio. And of course Rome holds the ultimate weapon in its power to appoint bishops. In contrast, the religious orders are scattered all over the world and are not subject to the same controls as diocesan priests, who work under the bishops in the hierarchical chain of command. The religious have their own constitutions and elect their own leaders, and are self-financed and to a large extent self-motivated. While Rome can cause the religious orders a good deal of distress—and did so—it has not been able to get a hold on them because their memberships are too numerous and diffuse, and their leaders too intelligent.

John Paul's intervention into the affairs of the Jesuits is a good example. Historically the best educated and most combative of the religious orders, the Jesuits are known for their confrontations with the papacy, despite a special vow of obedience to the pope. Their founder, Ignatius of Loyola, was imprisoned by the Inquisition on charges of heresy in 1526 but managed to escape with his head, although he and his followers remained suspect by Rome. Despite, or in some cases because of, their successful evangelization campaigns in the New World, the Jesuits aroused considerable controversy, and in the 1700s were expelled from the colonies of France, Spain, and Portugal. In 1773 Clement XIV dissolved the order, but the Catholic world found it impossible to do without the energetic Jesuits, who were soon restored to their earlier position. Not without reason is the Jesuit superior general known as the "Black Pope" (so named because Jesuit dress is black while the pope's robes are white), for the order educated the aristocracy of Europe as well as the princes of the church. The Jesuits also played a major role in Catholicism's renewal, providing some of the most important theologians at Vatican II, including the German Jesuit Karl Rahner and the American John Courtney Murray.

Like every other sector in the church, the religious orders were in trouble during the post–Vatican II years, when many priests and nuns left because of a desire to return to a lay status or because they could not cope with the changes in the church. Much experimentation occurred in liturgy, theology, and other fields, but by the mid-1970s the upheaval became less noticeable as people began to settle into new patterns. The Jesuits lost more than 7,000 members in the period, but they also began to sort out their priorities, thanks largely to the growing influence of priests from the Third World. In 1974 the order made a historic decision to identify evangelization with social justice.

Fearful that the Jesuits would be "deformed" through partisan political struggles, Paul VI called them to order, warning that any engagement in political and social struggles had to be subordinated to the Jesuits' spiritual mission and sanctioned by local bishops. Nevertheless, some Jesuits ran for office, while others became known for their social activism. The "Society," as it is called, has often been on the cutting edge of the church, and the activists naturally cause controversy, not only in Rome but within the order itself. John Paul I apparently shared his predecessor's concern because he wrote a message to the Jesuits in which he warned against involvement in politics. The seven-page statement was found on his desk after his sudden death.[13]

The conservatives laid the blame for the Jesuits' unruly state on the order's gentle superior general, Father Pedro Arrupe. A U.S.-trained doctor, the Spaniard was serving in Hiroshima at the time of the atomic bomb explosion, and that experience focused his concern on peace and justice. He was chosen to lead the Jesuits in 1965 at the start of the postconciliar period and tried to steer the order through the stormy years by being open to dialogue and encouraging a greater sensitivity toward Third World cultures. Had he been less flexible, it is probable that even more priests would have abandoned the Jesuits, but Rome did not see it that way, blaming Arrupe for all the real and perceived ills in the order.

Upon becoming pope, John Paul II sent his predecessor's message to Arrupe with the warning "It is as if I had written it." Relations between Arrupe and the pope continued to worsen until the Spaniard, by then seventy-three, became convinced that the only way to solve the impasse was to resign, using the excuse of advancing age although he was physically active and mentally alert. John Paul, who had repeatedly refused to receive the Jesuit, eventually conceded him ten minutes in May 1980. Arrupe's proposed resignation startled the pope, who told him to postpone any call for an election until a more "opportune" time, apparently with a view to controlling the selection of the Jesuit's successor. A year later, with the succession still undecided, Arrupe suffered a cerebral hemorrhage that left him permanently incapacitated. Consequently his deputy, the American Jesuit Vincent O'Keefe, wrote to the order's regional superiors inquiring whether they thought the order should not accept Arrupe's resignation and elect a successor. A good-humored, easygoing American, O'Keefe had been groomed by Arrupe as his replacement and was popular throughout the order. His election was a foregone conclusion until the pope stepped in to suspend the order's internal regulations and impose his own man, an eighty-year-old Italian Jesuit, Father Paolo Dezza, as temporary head. The letter announcing the papal takeover was sent to Arrupe on his sickbed. It shunted O'Keefe aside and made clear that the pope would not tolerate any more superiors general in the Arrupe style.[14]

Arrupe, who had been publicly humiliated by the pope on more than one occasion, humbly accepted John Paul's decision. But many Jesuits were angry at the way matters had been handled by the pope and were convinced that Dezza and his younger aide, Father Giuseppe Pittau, were intent on taking over the order. In fact both men were loyal Jesuits dedicated to the Society's survival. Through patient diplomacy they managed to convince the pope that the situation was more positive than it had seemed, to the point that John Paul gave the Jesuits a pep talk in early 1982, praising them for their obedience and telling them that "the quest for justice is an integral part of your vocation."[15]

Arrupe and O'Keefe having served as sacrificial offerings, the way was cleared for a general congregation, or assembly, to elect a new superior general. Much was at stake because a shift in or confirmation of the order's direction would have a major impact throughout the church. Supporters of the Restoration hoped for a more conservative leader, but there was little the Curia could do to influence the outcome because the congregation was a sovereign body and two-thirds of its delegates were elected by the Jesuits themselves. The order has a long history of counseling princes and kings, and their successors are no less skilled at palace intrigue. Reasoning that a well-known priest would likely be controversial and thus liable to suffer the same opposition that had plagued Arrupe, they sought out an unknown man who stood for the Arrupe tradition but who was so discreet that it would be difficult to attack him with the charges of liberalism, pseudo-Marxism, and the other epithets that had been hurled at Arrupe.

Much to Rome's surprise—but apparently not to most Jesuits'—a shy Dutch linguist who had worked in Lebanon was chosen superior general by a majority on the first ballot. With his owlish look, oversize glasses, and trim, gray goatee, Father Peter-Hans Kolvenbach had the appearance of a harmless scholar. Since he rarely spoke in public, and was extremely prudent when he did, it was some time before the Vatican realized that he was just as committed to liberation theology and an option for the poor as Arrupe had been. He also followed his predecessor's style of dialogue, encouraging the order's 25,000 Jesuits to be actively involved in serving their societies by helping people to deepen their faith and at the same time seek a better society. He spoke often of the work of the Jesuits in Latin America as an example of how spirituality could be joined to living the option for the poor. "Our order would never have made a preferential option for the poor if it had not been for the Jesuits in Central and South America," he said. "They opened our eyes to the need for liberation."[16]

Most Jesuits found Kolvenbach a worthy successor to Arrupe. But unlike the Spaniard, he did not have to shepherd the order through a period of crisis. Because the Jesuits were thriving in the Third World, where vocations were on the rise, the order's membership had stabilized, and therefore Kolvenbach did not have to suffer constant criticisms about an identity crisis. He had also entered the arena with the advantage of hindsight, knowing that if the Jesuits were to help safeguard the reformist spirit of Vatican II, he would have to play the Romans' game with extreme care. In this he was supported by the heads of the Franciscans and Dominicans in a religious triumvirate that carried the banner for Vatican II while the bishops were fighting in the center of the field—much as the Latin American Confederation of Religious had been the guardian of Medellín.

If anything, the Dominicans are more radical than the Jesuits, insisting on greater pluralism in the church and upholding the Third World's right to choose its own political and economic solutions. In a replay of the Jesuits' troubles, the order elected the South African theologian Albert Nolan as its head, only to have the pope veto him because of his outspoken opposition to the white government in Pretoria. The Irishman

Damian Aloysius Byrne was elected in his place, but Byrne was also committed to the struggle for justice and peace, which the Dominicans believe is a "constitutive element of evangelization."

The Franciscans also suffered from—and survived—papal intervention. With two other branches, the Capuchins and Conventuals, they total the world's largest order—40,000 members. Like the Jesuits, they include outstanding theologians, such as Leonardo Boff, and uphold the reformist spirit of Vatican II. But true to form, John Paul believed the order had become too activist and should spend more time in contemplation, as he told the Franciscans in a sternly worded letter in 1985. To make sure they obeyed orders, he sent his own delegate, an Italian archbishop from the Curia, to preside over a meeting convened by the Franciscans to elect their new minister general. Although the archbishop did his best to get a conservative chosen, the Franciscans overwhelmingly reelected their liberal, California-born leader, Father John Vaughn. Cardinal Ratzinger continued to snipe at the Franciscans, insisting they should cease their "critical" questioning of church authority, but Vaughn held firm with Byrne and Kolvenbach.

Like other sectors of the church, the religious orders are split. Among the conservative minority are doctrinal hard-liners, such as the Dominican Cardinal Jerome Hamer, head of the Vatican Congregation for Religious and Ratzinger's former secretary in the Congregation for the Doctrine of the Faith. Most of the divisions reflect the individual's cultural experience. For example, the Poles have tried to pull the Franciscans to the right, while the Brazilians tug to the left. Polish Franciscans are convinced that liberation theology is a front for communism, whereas the Brazilians believe it a means to popular democracy. Similarly, some Jesuits in the United States supported Washington's policies in Central America, unable to understand the reality of oppression and poverty that their brother Jesuits daily experienced in, for example, El Salvador. Nevertheless, the splits among the male religious orders have not prevented them from moving forward under the banner of Vatican II.

The situation facing women's religious orders, which are also divided because of cultural differences, is more difficult, yet they, too, march behind the banner. Rome tends to treat the nuns in an offhand manner, reflecting the Curia's attitude that their job is to keep house. Many nuns have accepted that role, particularly the older women from Eastern Europe, Italy, Spain, and parts of Latin America, who cannot understand their sisters' concern for justice and peace. Although the leadership of the large international orders is progressive, there are differences even among these women, the European and Latin American nuns failing to see why the American and Canadian sisters are so stirred up about women's rights in the church.

Indicative of how divisions within an order can play into the Curia's hands is the sorry case of the cloistered Carmelite nuns. Like other religious orders, the Carmelites undertook to revise their constitution in accordance with the changes brought about by Vatican II. The updating took a decade and reflected consultation with all of the order's 826 convents. A survey by the Carmelites' then superior general showed that 80 percent of the 11,000 nuns supported the new constitution, which would permit them to be more involved in helping society. But the remaining one-fifth, mostly in Spain, opposed the changes. Paul VI, who viewed the Carmelite minority as a holdover from the Franco period, supported the majority, but the dispute simmered on into John Paul's papacy. As a young man in Poland, John Paul had toyed with the idea of becoming a Carmelite priest, and he had maintained a special interest in the order throughout his career. Seeing a potential ally in the pope, the conservatives, led by the prioress of Madrid, appealed to him for help. John Paul answered their call by throwing out the constitution that the majority of the nuns had approved and ordering the Congregation for Religious, headed by Ratzinger's former secretary, Cardinal Hamer, to write a new one reflecting the position of the conservative minority, including detailed instructions on daily life, even the making of beds.[17]

The pope's action shocked the religious world because the constitution of a religious order is like the internal discipline of a family. The rules reflect the experience of the priests and nuns who observe them. Thus the very basis of religious life is challenged when outsiders who do not live by those rules attempt to impose their will on the community. As all religious admit, differences are normal in their communities since no human being is like another. But usually an effort is made to respect different religious gifts, those who prefer a more contemplative life not being expected to join the activists on the barricades, and vice versa. Since the point of departure is in the community itself, there has to be respect for the views of both the minority and the majority. "I live in a community with ninety other sisters, and most of them do not understand my work in the slums," explained a Latin American nun who helped the poor in a working-class neighborhood of Madrid, Spain. "They long for the past because they don't know anything else." Yet while they did not understand her motivation, a few occasionally came to the slums to see what she was doing, and none tried to force her to change her commitment. In contrast, the pope's intervention in the Carmelites was a coercive measure against the majority that created even more divisions among the sisters, many of whom objected to the reestablishment of practices that had gone out with the last century. It was also seen as a worrisome precedent since other women's orders, particularly those in the United States, had had their constitutions rejected by Hamer's office with the warning that if they did not rewrite them in accordance with Rome's wishes, they might suffer the same fate as the Carmelites.[18]

Many nuns, outraged by such treatment, have refused to bow to Rome's dictates. Religious constitutions have therefore became one more area of tension in a long-running guerrilla war between the religious orders and the Curia. Another major battle has developed over censorship. The tactic used by the orders' superiors has been to throw up a shield between their people and the Curia and to give a bit here and there in order to safeguard their independence. As the Europeans pointed out, most Americans are not good at the game because it requires subterfuge. "You go into one of the curial offices, where you are told you have to do such and such," explained a Spanish religious. "You carefully write down such and such, nod your head and go away and do nothing, just like the Asians. The Americans are too open. If they say they are going to do something, they do it. Or they argue and get into trouble. Lesson one in Rome is, Always avoid frontal attack."[19]

To protect their own people, religious superiors frequently seek out members of the Curia to inform them about problems, thereby helping to discredit distorted versions from other sources. They have also gained strength by working as a group. While agreeing to monitor their religious publications, for example, they refused to accept censorship by the Curia. They also insisted that the Vatican thoroughly investigate the truth of complaints against the magazines before demanding disciplinary action. But while large international orders were generally successful in holding off the Curia, smaller ones, particularly those based in Italy, proved more vulnerable. For example, the Curia took strong exception to an issue of *Missione Oggi,* a publication affiliated with the Italian Saverian missionaries, that was favorable to the Sandinista government. Although the issue included an interview with Cardinal Obando y Bravo, it was generally supportive of the Nicaraguan revolution. To make matters worse, *Missione* had backed Leonardo Boff in his battles with Rome, and Boff was among those interviewed in the offending issue. Its publication led to irate letters and phone calls from the Curia, which claimed that the magazine was opposed to the church because it contained positive articles on the Sandinistas. The Curia wanted the magazine's editor, Eugenio Melandri, dismissed for his temerity, and in 1987 Melandri was sent to Spain for a "vacation" in the hope that the controversy would subside.[20]

The Comboni missionaries gave in to similar pressures to sack the editor of their Italian magazine, *Nigrizia*, which covers developments in Africa. The Italian government was angered by the magazine's exposés of Italian arms sales to South Africa, and sought the Vatican's help in silencing the magazine. In 1987 Father Alessandro Zanotelli, who had been the magazine's editor for nine years, was forced to resign on orders of Cardinal Josef Tomko, head of the Congregation for the Propagation of the Faith, which coordinates missionary work. Zanotelli, who was reassigned to Nairobi as a missionary, said that the then Italian foreign minister, Giulio Andreotti, had known about his dismissal before he himself found out. He blamed his dismissal on *Nigrizia*'s stories on Italian arms sales and its criticism of the ineffectiveness of Italian development aid to Africa. "We simply couldn't keep quiet about business interests manipulating foreign aid or about [the] arms traffic," he said. Agreed Father Carmine Curci, a fellow staff member, "If we were to . . . keep silent, what kind of magazine would we be putting out? When our missionaries come across villages that have been destroyed with Italian weapons, for example in Chad, are we supposed to keep quiet?"[21]

But the axe continue to fall. In late 1987, Jesuit Pedro Lamet was fired from his post as director of the Spanish Catholic weekly *Vida Nueva* under pressure from Rome and conservative members of the Spanish hierarchy. The magazine's editorial staff resigned in protest. Lamet, who had run the liberal magazine for a decade, was accused of publishing articles critical of the conservative trend in the church. He had been warned of Vatican displeasure by the papal nuncio and had also earned the enmity of Opus Dei. Under Lamet the magazine followed a Vatican II philosophy and became one of the most influential Catholic publications in the Spanish-speaking world. His successor, a layman picked by the hierarchy, promised a publication that would be loyal to "the only possible church, that represented by the seat of Peter."[22]

It was apparent from the experience of *Missione*, *Nigrizia*, and other publications that were taken to task that the Vatican was primarily concerned with orthodoxy, as, for example, regarding the Sandinista revolution, although no church doctrine stated that it was a sin to support the Nicaraguans, any more than it was to question arms sales to South Africa. Religious superiors thought it ridiculous to expect total adherence to all the church's stands, particularly on such controversial political questions, but as shown by the dismissal of Zanotelli and Lamet, the Curia held the upper hand.

The situation is even more delicate for religious publishing houses, since by canon law the local bishop has to approve a book, and it is easier for Rome to control a bishop than a religious order. Paulist Press, the multinational publishing house of the Society of St. Paul, for example, was called on the carpet by John Paul, who demanded that it show more "pastoral vigilance" over the material it published. Among its books were works by the Belgian theologian Edward Schillebeeckx, who had been criticized by the Congregation for the Doctrine of the Faith; an interview with Fidel Castro on his religious sentiments by a Brazilian Dominican; and an adult catechism, *Christ Among Us*, that had proved enormously popular in the United States. When Cardinal Ratzinger wrote to tell Peter Gerety, then archbishop of Newark, New Jersey, that his imprimatur had to be withdrawn from *Christ Among Us,* Paulist Press was forced to cease publication of the work. The decision was a blow to the press because the book was its best-seller, and to the author, Anthony Wilhelm, who depended on its royalties for most of his income. Written in a warm, down-to-earth style, *Christ Among Us* was widely used in educational work until Ratzinger objected, among other reasons because it questioned the existence of devils. Paulist Press also had to discontinue a sex-education booklet for parents because of Vatican objections (its treatment of homosexuality, contraception, and masturbation was judged troublesome). Another book, on divorced Catholics, published by Harper and Row, was questioned by Ratzinger because it suggested that divorced and remarried Catholics might be able to return to the sacraments from which they had been barred.

That Rome wanted Catholics to think correctly, and uniformly, was illustrated by the announcement that a universal catechism would be written under Ratzinger's direction, in order to end "deviations" by local churches in the teaching of the faith. Ratzinger's idea of a universal catechism had been proposed by Boston's conservative Cardinal Law at the 1985 synod and accepted by the Vatican, even though the bishops' conferences had not asked for it—did not in fact want it. Bishops have traditionally developed their own catechism materials based on church teachings, and Vatican II upheld·that practice by ruling that a common catechism for vastly different peoples and cultures was impractical. After the council local churches began to train catechists in pedagogy and Scripture so that teaching might be extended to adults, instead of being limited, as in the past, to catechism recitations by children. The new approach brought a richer spiritual life to the community, and many lay people as well as bishops were loath to accept a universal catechism written by a conservative German intellectual. Ratzinger had already indicated that he would take a narrow interpretation of church teachings by forcing the French bishops to rewrite their popular catechism, *Pierres Vivantes*. The cardinal objected to the book because it opened with a description of God as the liberator who had led His people out of Egypt—the same God of the Exodus so popular in Latin America. Ratzinger insisted that the catechism start with the creation in Genesis because it was the "first book," although some scholars argued that the idea of creation was developed later in the Bible. In any case, the change in emphasis was significant because it made liberation a lesser theme.[23]

Meanwhile, Cardinal Silvio Oddi, the then head of the Vatican Congregation for the Clergy, announced that all bishops' conferences should replace their catechisms with one that he had approved—which happened to be 400 years old! While other bishops ignored Oddi, his recommended book, *Roman Catechism,* duly appeared under Cardinal Law's sponsorship. As an example of past practices, some of them highly dubious, the book had historical interest, but as a catechism of current church teachings it was a disaster. Laws and traditions that had changed were not mentioned except in footnotes referring to unexplained canon laws and making many passages unintelligible, ridiculous, or insulting. One norm, for instance, insisted that married couples "abstain from marital relations for some days previous to their receiving communion." Another asserted that only the baptized would be saved by God, though this was contrary to Vatican II teaching. Yet another denigrated Jews. Nevertheless, Oddi insisted that *Roman Catechism* be used for teaching families the norms of their faith.[24]

Although some dismissed Oddi as an eccentric, he represented a trend in the Vatican toward "Romespeak," in which only certain ideas and interpretations would be tolerated. Symptomatic of the sickness, a major speech given by Pope John XXIII at the opening of Vatican II did not appear in its original form in the collection of papal statements published by the Vatican during John Paul's papacy. In the original Italian

John had told the bishops that they should distinguish between "the substance of the ancient doctrine [of the church] that is the deposit of faith" and the historical formulations of dogma, which could produce varying interpretations and structures in different periods (i.e., people in the Middle Ages believed in witches; those in the twentieth century did not). This distinction was important because it cut the ground from under the traditionalists in the Curia, who insisted on the immutability of dogmatic formulations, denying the possibility of new ideas that changed perceptions and threatened Rome's monopoly on truth. On two occasions after his first reading of the speech, Pope John had cited the same passage in the same terms, so there could be no doubt of his meaning. But when translated into a new official version in Latin, the speech said nothing about the possibilities of changing doctrinal formulations but, on the contrary, confirmed their immutability.[25]

CHAPTER 12

✛

THE NICARAGUAN CHURCH

THE BOTTOM LINE in disputes between the Vatican and churches in Brazil, Italy, the United States, and elsewhere was autonomy: Local churches wanted more; Rome insisted they have less. Right-wing groups, including the "movements," sided with the Vatican, while progressive Catholics, as well as a majority of bishops, opposed Roman encroachment. These religious struggles frequently spilled over into the political arena because conservative Catholics demanded that Catholic office seekers concentrate exclusively on the Vatican's agenda, including anticommunism and legislation against divorce and abortion. In contrast, more liberal Catholics lobbied for issues of justice and peace, particularly a better deal for the poor. While the disputes stemmed from different causes—sexual morals in the United States, popular empowerment in Brazil—they were variations on the same theme that had divided the church since Vatican II: to go forward or backward.

Matters became more complicated when Washington's political ambitions were injected into the struggle, as occurred in revolutionary Nicaragua. As we have seen, neither Rome nor Washington approved of the Sandinistas because the left-wing government challenged their rule. Often, the two power centers gave the appearance of working together, though their motives for opposing the Sandinistas were different. Unlike the United States and Brazil, where Catholics rallied behind bishops and theologians under attack by Rome, the Catholic Church in Nicaragua split, as did the Protestants. The split was not just between political conservatives and progressives, or rich and poor, but cut across ideological and class lines. Churches that opposed the Sandinistas were often as poor as those who supported them, even though the government stood for justice for the poor. So bitter was the political-religious struggle that priests publicly disowned their bishops, and bishops disowned priests. Religious orders divided, as did foreign and Nicaraguan priests and nuns.

Many families also split. Instead of providing solace during a time of war and great suffering, religion proved another source of division. Drawn into the ideological battles of the *contra* war, the church became a political instrument, and politics distorted Catholicism's religious message—as it had often done before.

Opposing Sides

As *contra* leader Alfonso Robelo admitted in the spring of 1987, the *contras* were a lost cause. Despite the money lavished on them by the U.S. government and private sources, despite CIA training and organizational support, they were unable to gain even a foothold in Nicaragua. They could continue to harass the borders, but by themselves they would never take Managua. Similarly, Washington could keep turning the screws by leveling economic sanctions against Nicaragua and by vetoing loans to the Sandinista government from such multilateral agencies as the Inter-American Development Bank, but these measures could not dislodge the Sandinistas and would only cause more suffering among the poor. However great the discontent against the Sandinista government, the overwhelming majority of Nicaraguans agreed that they would never willingly countenance a government by Anastasio Somoza's former henchmen in the *contras*. More than 40,000 Nicaraguans had died to rid the country of the Somoza dictatorship, and many more were prepared to die to prevent the restoration of such a government.

What the Reagan administration could not understand was the deep resentment of the Nicaraguan people against U.S.-imposed tyrants. The Somoza dynasty was thrust on them by the United States, which had occupied the country for more than two decades, and in the previous century a U.S. carpetbagger, William Walker, had run the country for two years. The legacy of this past is an ultranationalism directed not against individual Americans or their culture but against the imperial power in Washington. While many Nicaraguans do not belong to the Sandinista party, most endorse Sandinismo, named for the national hero, Augusto César Sandino, who fought against an occupying U.S. Marine force in the late 1920s and early 1930s. Sandinismo is not an ideology but a gut feeling about Nicaragua. In the United States it's called patriotism.

While the *contras* were (and will be) a lost cause, the outcome of the religious conflict was less certain. Some high-ranking Sandinista officials believed it could cause the government more damage than the *contras* ever inflicted, because it involved churches that affected Nicaraguan attitudes toward the Sandinistas and the government's image abroad.[1] On one side were the government and its supporters in the Catholic and Protestant churches, on the other the Catholic hierarchy and the fundamentalist evangelical churches. Both sides had strong backing in the United States, Latin America, and Europe. Because of the deep religiosity of the Nicaraguan people, the issue outweighed many others, including freedom of the press. The average Nicaraguan does not read a newspaper, whereas the majority feel a need for God. Christianity is as deeply embedded in the culture as Sandinismo; consequently God's approval is crucial to the revolution, at least in this first stage. Fear that such approval would not be needed in the future was at the root of the conflict between the government and the churches. Convinced that Nicaragua was headed toward a Marxist dictatorship, the Sandinistas' religious opponents, led by Managua's Cardinal Obando y Bravo, fought the government and its religious supporters at every turn, even to the point of supporting the *contras*. The government retaliated by severely harassing these churches and, in some cases, persecuting their pastors. On one level the conflict was over politics—for example, whether the Sandinistas should negotiate with the *contras*. But the political questions were part of a larger religious controversy as to how faith should be interpreted and who should run the churches.

The most important religious players in the dispute were Catholic, since 80 percent of the 3 million Nicaraguans belong to that faith. Catholics were also a major force in the 1979 revolution; among the rank and file they far outnumbered Sandinista militants. The hierarchy blessed the revolution only when the outcome was no longer in doubt, but even so the Sandinista leaders praised Obando for his opposition to Somoza and promised respect for religious freedom. They also appointed four priests to important government positions and encouraged priests and nuns to assume leadership of such government projects as literacy programs, health centers, and agricultural cooperatives. This recognition of the importance of Catholicism gave the revolution a unique cast: Unlike leftist revolutions in other countries, the Sandinista government welcomed the church's participation.

Contrary to later claims by the Sandinistas that the bishops were political reactionaries, the hierarchy, including Obando, encouraged the formation of base communities. As early as 1970, when Obando was appointed archbishop of Managua, they also began to distance themselves from the Somoza regime, becoming increasingly outspoken against government corruption and repression. Obando and other bishops also gave tentative support to student activism against the dictatorship, such as marches and occupation of the Managua cathedral, and it was through such resistance that student leaders and some priests came in contact with the Sandinista Front of National Liberation (FSLN). The escalation of violence, including the wholesale massacre of civilians by Somoza's National Guard, pushed the hierarchy into open opposition to Somoza, while many members of the base communities joined the guerrillas or provided a support network. Although the bishops attempted to negotiate a settlement, Somoza's refusal to step down prevented a peaceful solution, and by 1979 even moderate political sectors were working with the guerrillas to overthrow the dictator. In June of that year the bishops published an extraordinary statement justifying the revolution as the only means to end an "evident and prolonged tyranny, which seriously threatens the fundamental rights of the individual and undermines the common good of the country."[2]

The Nicaraguan bishops did not publish the statement because they supported the FSLN. Like a majority of the Latin American bishops, they belonged to the political center, wanting reforms but not revolution. As in Chile, the hierarchy had hoped for a moderate government run by the Christian Democrats or another party in the political center. But by mid-1979 it was clear that the only group that could beat Somoza was the FSLN and that a majority of the population supported the guerrillas. And indeed the Sandinistas triumphed a month later. The Nicaraguan bishops did not intend to repeat the experience of the Cuban hierarchy, which by opposition to the revolution removed itself from the process. They recognized the necessity of working with the Sandinistas, and that is why they issued their unusual statement in support of armed rebellion. Five months later they appeared to formalize that association in a pastoral letter that gave qualified endorsement to socialism and, by extension, to the new Sandinista government. But within months of the letter relations with the government began to deteriorate, eventually leading to an open break.

The bishops were under a variety of pressures. One was the growing concern in Rome, where John Paul took a dim view of priests in government and particularly a leftist one. Another was the influence of Colombian cardinal Alfonso López Trujillo and his fellow conservatives in the Latin American Episcopal Conference (CELAM), the bishops' regional service organization. CELAM delegations regularly visited Obando to caution him against the dangers of a "parallel" popular church as represented by the priests in government and Sandinista supporters in the base communities. Yet another reason for the change was the eventual recognition by upper- and middle-class sectors closely allied to Obando and other bishops that the uprising had not been simply a changing of the guard but a genuine class revolution intent on overturning the country's economic and social structures. In the heat of battle against Somoza, the wealthy businessmen and ranchers who joined forces with the guerrillas had assumed that the FSLN would share power with them. But while willing to accept friendly criticism, the Sandinistas had no intention of dividing the pie. They had the army and the backing of a majority of the people and therefore saw no reason to give up what they had achieved with their own blood. Moreover, Chile's experience was a vivid lesson in the dangers of political compromise. President Allende had believed he could achieve structural change through a pluralistic democracy, only to be overthrown by the military with the connivance of the CIA and the middle-class Christian Democrats. The Sandinistas wanted no bourgeois presence that could become a Trojan horse.

The controversy over political models divided the church between those who wanted a moderately reformist government and those who believed that radical structural changes were the only way to overcome the poverty in which a majority of the people lived. But the dispute was not only political because it also involved different interpretations of religious faith. On the one side a traditional church was concerned primarily with personal piety and a hierarchical chain of command; on the other, a radical community of Catholics supported the revolution because it was committed to the poor and because they believed they could help humanize it from within. From the viewpoint of the institutional church the latter were a danger to church unity and authority. Sandinista supporters in the church refused to take orders from the bishops, insisting that the church did not depend solely on the hierarchy but belonged to everyone. Since many worked with the government, ideological differences with traditional Catholics were exacerbated, pitching the church into the middle of a major political battle. The Vatican also worried that the marriage of Sandinista nationalism with Catholic religiosity could set a dangerous precedent for the rest of Latin America, particularly in countries where Christian base communities were the vanguard of the struggle for democracy, in the church itself as well as in secular society.

Both sides in the struggle suffered serious reverses. Although the traditional church maintained the loyalties of a majority of the native-born clergy, the hierarchy's opposition to the revolution weakened the church's influence among the idealistic young. At the same time, many of the most dedicated members of the base communities were absorbed into the revolutionary process, depriving it of its most important source of independent criticism. The mass of the people were confused by the bitter struggle between antigovernment bishops and clergy and pro-government priests and nuns. "People don't know to whom to give their loyalties anymore," said an American Capuchin missionary with many years of experience in Nicaragua.[3]

The War

Had the *contra* war not occurred, tensions between the government and the traditional church would still have existed, but they might have been dealt with in a different manner. The war brought out the worst in both sides—which many of Reagan's critics contended was the point of the exercise. Although the bishops were not unanimously hostile to the government, and some privately disagreed with Obando's confrontational tactics, their position hardened because of the tit-for-tat reaction of the Sandinistas to Obando and his fellow bishop, Pablo Antonio Vega. Convinced that anything had to be better than communism, and unwilling to examine the shadings in a revolution that was more nationalistic than Marxist, Obando and Vega encouraged the *contras,* not only by refusing to condemn their atrocities but also by attending events in the United States sponsored by *contra* leaders or their U.S. supporters. Although the hierarchy in 1986 condemned both the United States and the Soviet Union for providing military aid for the war, Obando and Vega left no doubt about where their sympathies lay. In reprisal, the government closed the church's radio station and a Managua archdiocesan newspaper, threatened and briefly jailed Obando supporters, and expelled eighteen priests, including Vega himself. By 1986, when Vega was expelled, neither side was able to hear the other. The bishops could not admit that anything good had been achieved by the revolution, and the Sandinistas made it clear they would not tolerate a critical church. Relations between the traditional church and the pro-Sandinista popular church were equally bad, raising the specter of an irrevocable schism.

While conceding that there was no institutionalized persecution of the church, human rights groups, including Americas Watch and Amnesty International, protested that the sanctions against the church were disproportionate to the offense. Church supporters of the Sandinistas in the United States and Europe also complained that such actions gave ammunition to the revolution's enemies. But these were the views of outsiders. People in Nicaragua continued to believe that the United States might invade, and invasion rumors were taken seriously by the government and the populace. Under such a threat Nicaraguans were prepared to believe the worst of anyone who did not support the revolution, including the unfounded charge that Obando was a CIA agent. Neither the government press nor the opposition daily, *La Prensa,* provided a balanced picture of events, and after *La Prensa*'s closure in 1986, Nicaraguans heard only one side of the story. Spokesmen for the traditional church gave their version to their friends at home and abroad; proponents of the popular church did the same. As Aryeh Neier, Americas Watch vice-chairman, observed, the situation was "like a *Rashomon* story in which it ultimately becomes impossible to establish the truth."[4]

The Sandinistas might have followed a hard-line policy had there been no war, but the war made it inevitable. Nicaraguans had had no experience of democracy before the revolution, and just when they were beginning to achieve some social and economic breakthroughs, the *contra* war began. Although consultation remained an important aspect of the revolution, as shown by discussions held throughout the country for a new constitution, "the idea of independent initiative, of a genuinely popular democracy, is gradually being lost because of the inevitable militarism produced by the *contra* war," said a high-ranking government official.[5] Half the budget was earmarked for the military, and most of the country's young people passed through the war machine, which taught them the only skills they were likely to learn. (In contrast to more industrialized El Salvador, for example, two-thirds of the Nicaraguan work force had no factory experience.) Under emergency war powers, the government established production goals and job classifications for all workers, who needed official approval to change categories. A high percentage of the country's university-trained technicians and professionals left the country, less for political than economic reasons, because there were few jobs for their talents unless they worked for the government. As in other Latin American countries, such a situation produced a burgeoning bureaucracy of unmotivated, inefficient people who were not trained to think and instead barricaded themselves behind mountains of paperwork.

"The nature of an army is to obey," continued the government official, "and Nicaraguans' long experience of dictatorship reinforces that
tendency." He said these factors—more than any ideological "project"—
posed the greatest threat to the revolution. "Marxism-Leninism was/is
the project," agreed a European socialist. "But I don't think the ideology
is as important as the reality of a country which has no democratic traditions. The *contra* war is producing a bureaucratic elite." (One of the
most frequently cited examples of such elitism was a government-run
emporium in Managua where diplomats, foreign journalists, and high-
ranking Sandinista officials with access to dollar accounts could buy a
large selection of imported goods unavailable to most Nicaraguans, ranging from toilet paper to smoked salmon and stereo sets.)[6]

"I don't believe the opposition's claims that Tomás Borge [the tough-
talking minister of the interior] plotted all along to make Nicaragua a
communist state," declared a Sandinista official. "The original idea in
the first year after the revolution was not to indoctrinate, a case in point
being the literacy campaign, which was genuinely concerned with social
justice. But the *contra* war changed things. A pyramid is forming in which
the bottom is composed of a mass of women and children and the top of
technocrats and military people formed in the army tradition. It is a top-
down model all too familiar in Latin America, only in this case it is leftist,
not rightist."[7]

Neier of Americas Watch agreed that a long military siege tended
to produce a conformist mentality, no matter what the government's
ideology. "Look at our own experience in the United States," he said.
"During World War I, for example, there were 1,900 federal prosecutions
for [free] speech. The effects of militarism lingered on for a long time,
into the 1920s and 1930s. The door is still open in Nicaragua, but the
longer the war drags on, the more set will become hard-line responses
from the Nicaraguan government. The Sandinistas want to stay in power,
and unfortunately the situation is so polarized that there are very few
people who could provide leadership for a genuine dialogue and a more
democratic model of government."[8]

Had Nicaragua not been so polarized, the bishops, the base communities, and/or the country's opposition parties might have played such
a role, but the bishops and most of the parties were so biased in their
hatred of the revolution that they sounded like mouthpieces for President
Reagan. Most of the surviving base communities were equally biased, on
behalf of the government. But even had government critics been less

abrasive, the Sandinistas would not have countenanced a serious challenge to their power. Nor was this intransigence unusual in Latin America. Much the same situation prevailed in Colombia, a "formal democracy" controlled by the political right, which beat back all attempts by left-wing groups to weaken its monopoly on power. The major difference was that in Colombia outspoken opponents of the government were likely to be killed, whereas in Nicaragua they were usually jailed for a few hours or days, with the warning to shut up or face worse consequences, such as expulsion from the country.

Conor Cruise O'Brien, the Irish writer on international relations, described the Sandinista government as "elitist and authoritarian but not totalitarian and not physically oppressive, although it can be held—and is held by the opposition—that rule by an elite and press censorship in themselves constitute repression. That may be so, but if so, it is a milder form of oppression than the word generally conjures up or than prevails in most of Latin America. The security forces are more restrained, and less likely to throw their weight around, than in other Latin American countries. This is no Gulag state."[9]

Proof of the Sandinistas' popularity was the 1984 election in which they received 65 percent of the votes. By Latin American standards the contest was relatively clean and at least as fair as (many would say fairer than) elections the same year in El Salvador and Uruguay, which were hailed by Washington as triumphs for democracy. But because of the suffering caused by the *contra* war and bureaucratic incompetence, the government's popularity subsequently declined, although most Nicaraguans continued to oppose the *contras*. Contrary to Washington's hopes, the war did not split the Sandinista leadership but rather rallied it to the flag. Washington also had to have known that, however great the pressures, the Sandinistas would not allow themselves to be pushed out of office. Nor was there any large armed underground in Nicaragua to challenge them. The *contras* were supposed to provide that alternative, but their butchery, corruption, and disorganization showed them to be little better than bandits. Since it was clear by the mid-eighties that the *contras* were going nowhere, why did Washington continue to support a war in which the chief victims were the poor? Richard John Neuhaus, the neoconservative Lutheran pastor who strongly supported Reagan's policy in Central America, gave an answer that was probably close to the truth. "Washington believes," he said, "that Nicaragua must serve as a warning to the rest of Central America to never again challenge U.S. hegemony because of the enormous economic and political costs. It's too bad that the [Nicaraguan] poor must suffer, but historically the poor have always suffered. Nicaragua must be a lesson to the others."[10]

Casualties from the *contra* war totaled 16,939 Nicaraguans between 1981 and 1986. Most of the dead were civilians; more than 400 were children. More than a quarter million people were displaced by the war, and the economy was in ruins. Shortages of basic items such as milk became common, and Nicaraguans spent hours standing in line to obtain rationed goods. Even water was rationed. "People are exhausted by the war," said a U.S. nun.[11]

According to Interior Minister Borge, total economic losses arising from the war, including material damages and the loss of aid and trade because of the U.S. economic embargo, were $2.8 billion by May 1987. "Without this problem," he said, "we could have had growth rates in the gross national product of nearly 6 percent. We succeeded in reducing illiteracy by more than 50 percent to only 11 percent, but it has increased again to 20 percent. The economic situation does not allow us to provide the solution we would like. Social programs have been cut back by nearly 50 percent because our resources must go to the war. We are near to real hunger."[12]

Describing the situation, Borge grew increasingly angry. "Why in hell do they [Washington] have to tell us what to do? Who gives the North Americans the right to tell us that we should be more or less democratic? Or that we have to have a democracy like that of Costa Rica, or that of Mr. Reagan? If that's the model for democracy, we don't want to be democrats!"[13]

Evangelizing the Sandinistas

While Borge might scorn Costa Rica's democracy, neither he nor the other *comandantes* who ran the government were prepared to write off the Catholic Church, despite Obando, Vega, and other church critics. The revolution needed a Catholic presence for pragmatic as well as philosophical reasons. Believers or not, government leaders recognized the intense religiosity of a majority of the people: To deny them religion, particularly during such a time of suffering, would be politically unwise. The Sandinistas were also aware that the Vatican could do the revolution considerable damage by leaning on churches in other countries. U.S. political and church sources unanimously agreed that a major reason for

periodic Congressional cutoffs of *contra* aid and for the Reagan administration's failure to invade Nicaragua was massive lobbying by religious
groups opposed to the *contra* war. The U.S. bishops' opposition to such
aid was particularly important, but after Bishop Vega and other Nicaraguan priests were expelled by the Sandinistas, some bishops, including
New York's Cardinal O'Connor and Cardinal Law of Boston, began to
insist that the U.S. hierarchy take a stronger line with the Sandinistas.
"The Vatican's position on Nicaragua has hardened over the past four
years," said a spokesman for the U.S. bishops' conference in the spring
of 1986. "Rome wants the bishops to pay more attention to human rights
violations. They have told us not to deal with *contra* aid."[14]

    Another consideration shaping the Nicaraguan government's rela-
tions with Catholicism was the image it projected abroad. At least in the
early years of the revolution, the presence of priests in the government
helped persuade some European governments that the Sandinistas were
sincere in their promises to respect a mixed economy and political pluralism. While considerable disenchantment later set in, particularly
among the Social Democrats, the religious element remained an important ingredient in Sandinista public relations. Progressive churches in
other Latin American countries saw Sandinista cooperation with the popular church as a sign of hope for a Christian-Marxist dialogue, although
some were at the same time disturbed by government harassment of
Nicaragua's traditional church. The Peruvian priest Gustavo Gutiérrez,
regarded as the father of liberation theology, appeared to be among those
who were distancing themselves from Nicaragua's popular church. It was
not, he said, necessarily a good expression of liberation theology. While
the glamour gradually wore off the Nicaraguan experiment because it no
longer was new and a bureaucratic elite had emerged, revolutionary Nicaragua was still widely admired in Latin America, particularly among the
young, as a David fighting Goliath.[15]

    In the long run the most important element in church-state relations
may be the extent to which Catholic supporters can hold the Sandinistas
to their promises. This is a major reason given for the popular church's
close association with the government and the presence of priests in high
official positions. Jesuit César Jerez, president of the University of Central
America in Managua, argued eloquently for a "critical presence" within
the revolution that would enable Christians to criticize abuses and prevent
it from becoming antireligious. "If we refuse to be present, what credibility will we have later if we are criticizing things?" he asked. Like other

church supporters of the revolution, Jerez had made a "leap of faith" in the conviction that it was "worth the risks involved in order to evangelize the new Nicaragua." The popular church did not "overlook the Marxist elements involved in building the new Nicaragua," he said. "Such elements, however, do not mean that the Sandinistas are pursuing a rigid Marxist strategy to establish a socialist regime. The Sandinistas pay much more attention to national history than to doctrinal Marxism. If the church reacts in a strong, somehow blind way, it could be a big mistake for Nicaragua and for other nations in the Third World. All over Latin America, where Christianity has a lot to do with social changes happening there, [we ask], Is it possible to evangelize those new areas? I have the hope that is possible, although 'evangelize' sounds like a big word."[16]

Jerez contended that the Sandinistas were not opposed to religion but to political actions by certain bishops, such as Obando's support for the *contras*. He also believed that the church "should be mature enough" to engage in an internal dialogue. But dialogue presupposed a certain equality among the participants, and a claim to equality was one of the things the hierarchical church most disliked about the popular church. Moreover, the bishops contended that the popular church was itself guilty of political actions by giving religious approbation to the government. Latin America's bishops had traditionally done just that, but the governments were always centrist or right-wing. The Sandinistas made quite clear what they wanted from the institutional church—legitimation of the revolution—but that, said Vatican sources, was something they were unlikely to get from John Paul. Jerez might see nuances in the Nicaraguan situation, but for a Polish churchman, it was just another Marxist dictatorship. The Vatican view was that accommodations could be made with the Sandinistas, as they had been made in Poland, but it would have been uncharacteristic, to say the least, for the pope to embrace the revolution.[17]

One of the difficulties in church-state relations in Nicaragua was the constant interference by the state in religious matters and the frequent interjection of the bishops' personal opinions into the political process. Until late 1986, when the Vatican took a hand in the matter, Cardinal Obando and other anti-Sandinista clergy frequently gave sermons that were highly charged with political overtones. Consequently the sermons were censored by the government-controlled media; priests were also warned that they could be expelled from the country if they did not temper their words. When Obando expelled pro-Sandinista priests and nuns from their parishes or demanded that their religious orders recall them, the government responded by expelling pro-Obando priests. Partisan politics and religion became so confused that it was, admitted Jerez, as "if the times of the Councils of Nicaea and Ephesus were among us again," with warring factions that anathematized each other. "This of course demonstrates the relevance of religion in Latin America today," he said. "But the other side of the coin is the frequency with which people of very diverse political interests try to manipulate or ideologize religion."[18]

As Jerez admitted, some Sandinista supporters were guilty of manipulation through "blind submission to political plans or directives and dubious identifications between revolutionary processes and the Kingdom of God." He also conceded that it was not so easy for religious leaders to maintain a critical presence, "especially when critical support must be given from inside the very structures of power." But Jerez nevertheless believed—as did many U.S. religious and political supporters of the Sandinistas—that criticism could be made only within Nicaragua, not outside, and then only in private dialogue. "Writing or criticizing from outside somehow doesn't have credibility inside the country," he said. Other concerned observers, including progressive Catholic and Protestant leaders in the United States, argued that they were not helping the revolutionary process by withholding all criticism. "The prospect that the *contra* war might wind down should focus attention on how Nicaragua would develop if it were at peace," wrote Aryeh Neier, Americas Watch vice-chairman. "Will it become a hard totalitarian state, another Cuba? Or will it evolve politically along the lines of Mexico, dominated by one party but not practicing severe repression? Or will it follow some other model, or create its own?" While admitting that internal forces would be the most significant determining factor, Neier maintained that the United States would be a continuing influence, for good or bad—and he strongly argued for a positive role, including genuine humanitarian assistance. Neier also underlined the important future role of critics of the *contras,* citing the failure of U.S. opponents of the Vietnam War to criticize Hanoi's human rights violations. The failure was "a great disservice to the tens of thousands of Vietnamese who were incarcerated in re-education camps and to the hundreds of thousands who fled as 'boat people,' " he said. "If the postwar Nicaraguan government behaves oppressively, it should be those who were most outspoken in denouncing our government's sponsorship of the *contras* who should speak loudest in criticizing Sandinista repression."[19]

Religious Harassment

The delicate issue of criticism was raised in the spring of 1986 not only by Americas Watch and Amnesty International but also by such stout defenders of the revolution as *Sojourners* magazine, a prime mover in the Witness for Peace program that sent church people to Nicaragua to serve as peaceful witnesses against the *contra* war. The reason for concern was a clampdown on dissent following the imposition in October 1985 of a sweeping state of emergency decree that gave the government powers to restrict freedom of movement, expression, and association; suspend the right to strike; and intrude on personal privacy. The groups most affected were labor unions, political parties, the media, and the churches. Several hundred Nicaraguans were arrested, most of whom were released within a few hours, according to Amnesty International. The human rights organization said it was concerned about "prolonged pretrial incommunicado detention of political prisoners and restrictions on their right to a fair trial; and poor prison conditions for political prisoners." Amnesty said it had received some reports of torture and arbitrary killings, but that the Nicaraguan government had stated that military personnel responsible for these abuses had been tried, sentenced, and imprisoned. (Borge reported that 400 Sandinista soldiers were serving time for such acts.) While abuses appeared to have declined by the end of 1986, the conflict with the Catholic Church remained hot, as did the confrontation with fundamentalist Protestant churches, in part because of temporary detention or expulsion of church people. Church groups were also at odds with the government because of the conflict with the Miskito Indians in northeastern Nicaragua, where the Protestant Moravian Church dominates (American-born Capuchin missionaries are also active in the area).[20] In addition to the Indians, the main conflicts between the state and the traditional Catholic Church centered on the military draft and priests in government posts.

The four priests in government were Foreign Minister Miguel D'Escoto, a Maryknoll missionary; Jesuit Fernando Cardenal, minister of education; Father Ernesto Cardenal, an internationally known poet and minister of culture; and Father Edgard Parrales, minister of social welfare and later Nicaragua's ambassador to the Organization of American States. The bishops repeatedly demanded that they resign from office; all refused. Fernando Cardenal was subsequently forced to resign from the Jesuits; his brother Ernesto was personally upbraided by the pope on his visit to

Nicaragua. (See Chapter 3, pp. 60–61.) Parrales quit the priesthood. D'Escoto, though treated as an outlaw by Cardinal Obando, was protected by Maryknoll, and the case was left in limbo in Rome. The Dominicans and Franciscans also blocked Obando's attempts to expel their people from the Managua archdiocese, demanding that the cardinal follow canon law procedures by putting his complaints in writing—which he allegedly failed to do. Nevertheless, Obando succeeded in expelling or transferring forty priests and nuns because of their support for the revolution. The government, in turn, expelled eighteen pro-Obando priests, some in retaliation for the cardinal's treatment of religious who supported the Sandinistas.[21]

The traditional church strongly opposed the draft, the first in Nicaraguan history, even though the country was at war. In a 1983 statement on the subject the bishops held that "no one should be punished, persecuted or discriminated against for adopting a position [of] conscientious objection" to military conscription. They based their position on the grounds that an "absolute dictatorship of a political party" was not a legitimate government and that no Nicaraguan should be required to take up arms for a party. "It is not correct to mix, confuse or identify the concepts of fatherland, state, revolution and Sandinismo," they said.[22]

While the bishops had a point about confusing patriotism with partisan politics, their argument about legitimacy ceased to apply after 1984, when the majority voted for the Sandinista government in an election that international observers testified had been relatively clean. To deny an elected government the right to impose a draft during wartime was ridiculous. However, the longer the war went on, the more unpopular the draft became, since it affected all men between the ages of twenty-five and forty, and the Nicaraguans were exhausted by war. In mid-1987 the first large demonstration against the draft occurred in a town northeast of Managua after a local recruit was accidentally shot during military exercises.[23]

In response to the bishops' statement on the draft, Sandinista mobs, known as *turbas,* prevented Masses in eight churches, and Managua's auxiliary bishop, Bosco Vivas, was attacked when he tried to enter a local church. He was told that he "would be a dead man" if he actually entered. That night the doors were torn off several churches run by pro-Obando priests. According to Obando, his car was attacked twice (but with no injuries) by *turbas,* who broke the glass, once when Obando was inside.[24]

These incidents hardened the attitude of the hierarchy, which was already upset by the treatment meted out to Bishop Salvador Schlaefer the previous year. Schlaefer, an American-born Capuchin missionary who runs the Bluefields diocese on the east coast, was caught up in the conflict between the rebellious Miskito Indians, to whom the Capuchins have traditionally ministered, and the government in Managua, which saw the Indians as a fifth column in a strategic area near the Honduran border. Nor was the English-speaking Creole population in Bluefields keen on the revolution—an estrangement that led to further tensions with the Sandinistas. Although the Capuchins had been the first religious group to denounce the repression by Somoza's National Guard, they were regarded with distrust in certain Sandinista circles because of their defense of the Miskitos and the Creoles. On three different occasions in 1982 Schlaefer was "taken out" of his diocese by Sandinista authorities, meaning that he was expelled from the area. On the third occasion he was taken to a local airport and flown to Managua, where he was set free. The Sandinistas' explanation was that such actions were necessary to guarantee the bishop's safety.[25]

In December 1983, following the Sandinistas' forcible relocation of thousands of Indians from the border area, the Indians persuaded Schlaefer to accompany an exodus of more than 3,000 Miskitos from Nicaragua to Honduras, presumably as a protective measure against Sandinista attack. The bishop, who was visiting the Indians at the time, said that "the idea, as I see it, is that the Miskitos had the exodus planned for some time, and took advantage of my visit to leave." Contrary to Sandinista reports that Schlaefer had been kidnapped by the *contras,* the bishop said that he and another American priest, Wendelin Shafer, were not forced to make the journey but decided to go because the Indians were their "longtime friends" and they could not abandon them. At the time both priests were in their early sixties, and the trek through the rain forest was no picnic, particularly with Sandinista aircraft circling overhead. Schlaefer said the planes did not bomb or strafe them but that they could hear the Miskitos being attacked by Sandinista mortar fire. A large, affable Wisconsinite, Schlaefer normally maintains a discreet silence on church-state relations, avoiding the confrontational tactics of Obando. But the needs of the Miskitos overrode political prudence. "They can throw me out if they are not in agreement with my attitude, or they can kill me," Schlaefer said of the Nicaraguan government. "The pope sent me to Nicaragua to serve the church, not to serve any government but the people."[26]

Relations between the government and the traditional church continued to worsen in 1984 following the arrest of Father Amado Peña, a pro-Obando priest and outspoken critic of the revolution who was charged with counterrevolutionary activities. Peña's story, as reported by Amnesty International, was that after celebrating Mass in Managua he had accepted a lift from a man who had attended the service. Along the road, the driver pulled up behind a parked car and asked Peña to pass a bag to a man in the other car. The State Security Service, who were conveniently on hand, made a videotape of the scene, which showed the priest stepping from the car with the bag in his hand, followed by the appearance of police officers who seized and opened the bag, to reveal a "terrorist kit" of several hand grenades, dynamite, and a white-and-yellow Vatican flag on which the letters FDN (the *contra* insignia) had been stitched. The flag seemed a suspect addition. Even more suspect, in Amnesty International's opinion, was that "the drivers of the two cars were apparently neither questioned, detained nor publicly identified by the State Security Service." Peña was told to go home when the filming was completed. Four days later, after the government news media had denounced him as a terrorist accomplice, he was seized and placed under house arrest in a Managua seminary. The furious Obando then led a protest march of thirty priests to the seminary despite government warnings of dire consequences. Within hours of the march ten foreign priests who had been critical of the government were expelled from the country. Several had been resident in Nicaragua for more than thirty years. Amnesty International adopted Father Peña as a prisoner of conscience, stating that he had been "falsely implicated in criminal activity by the State Security Service because of his expression of his political views." Although charges were brought against the priest, the case never went to trial and the charges were dropped a few months later.[27]

Obando claimed that such acts were evidence of religious persecution, but in a Latin American context a better description—one that was used by the pope in an angry letter to the Nicaraguan government—was harassment. As the Sandinistas pointed out, no priests or nuns had been murdered in Nicaragua, in contrast to the killings in neighboring Central American nations; and many Latin American governments, including so-called democracies, had expelled priests and nuns for political reasons. On the other hand, the government's tactics were crude and clearly violated international norms against arbitrary detention and freedom of expression. The aim, as Amnesty International pointed out, was "to intimidate," but the effect was to give *contra* supporters in the United States more ammunition for their campaign.

Although the Sandinistas justified such actions on the ground that the country was at war, they ignored the fact that the shooting war was subject to political actions that could shift for or against them, according to perceptions of the U.S. public, or at least of politically active groups. Dependence on U.S. public opinion understandably galled the nationalists, who had to divert scarce human and material resources to fight a war that had been started by the United States. Even when the Sandinistas bent over backward to explain their position in the United States, they were often rebuffed by a Congress beholden to the White House. As the war ground on, and the Sandinistas became increasingly dependent on the communist bloc for military and economic aid, some adopted the attitude "To hell with the Americans"—and their churches, too. "The government's attitude," said a U.S. missionary close to Foreign Minister D'Escoto, "is that, after the $100 million in aid voted [for the *contras* in 1986], there is nothing to be done about the United States. Forget it, they say. Their priority is to win the war, and the solidarity and support of the U.S. church groups are no longer a priority, since they can't deliver." Foreign Minister D'Escoto, a Nicaraguan priest born and educated in the United States, underlined the point in an interview with the Jesuit magazine *America*. "We don't want the American bishops to defend Nicaragua," D'Escoto told the magazine. "We don't need the American bishops or anyone to defend us. We are more than able to defend ourselves. I would ask the American bishops to defend themselves and their own souls. The hands of every American are bloodied with the blood of innocent Nicaraguan people. The American Catholic Church . . . is an accomplice, unless it protests. These are crimes in which every American citizen is implicated because this is—or isn't it?—a democracy. Is not everyone co-responsible?"[28]

Such outspoken language was typical of D'Escoto—and many others involved in the church-state confrontation, including Obando, who regularly traded insults with the foreign minister. The same impassioned rhetoric was normal at political meetings conducted by the Sandinistas or the opposition. It roared over the radio and turned the newspapers into propaganda sheets. It divided people who lived on the same block or came from the same village, even from the same family. Father Jerez might plead for dialogue, but Nicaraguans were angry. They were fed up with the war and the Sandinistas' bureaucratic bumbling, and many were hungry. "People talk about dialogue, but it's a meaningless word after so many decades of dictatorship," said a U.S. priest who had worked in Nicaragua for several decades. "It's not something that just materializes out of the air. Yet dialogue is what the church and society needs—not more rhetoric." "The most difficult thing is to try to discover the truth," agreed a Spanish Christian Brother, "because you are attacked by both sides." Disillusioned with the revolution, he was equally scathing in his denunciation of Obando and his followers. Religious hymns had been written in Obando's honor, he said, and those who did not know the words were "automatically considered Obando's enemy. In this country there is no middle ground. People say, 'You're either with us or against us.' Even reconciliation is a loaded word because it's automatically understood to mean support for the *contras*."[29]

So the religious wars rolled on. In the fall of 1985 the bishops caused a scandal by claiming the government had failed to honor a promise that it would not draft seminarians. Two cases were cited involving eleven youths who had been drafted in the Granada and Juigalpa dioceses. In fact, none of the young men had been attending an official seminary but had been living in a house and on a ranch owned by two priests. Although the incident could not be described as religious persecution, even in the broadest sense, Sunday Masses in Granada were suspended as a protest. When Obando showed up in Juigalpa for a protest Mass, the army intervened, prohibiting the service and forcing more than 2,000 people who had been trucked in for the occasion to return home. The government also ordered thirty foreign priests identified with the hierarchy to report to security headquarters in Managua (twenty-three showed up). The priests were told they would be expelled from the country if they continued their criticisms of the government, even if they used biblical quotations for the purpose. A few days later, Nicaraguan clergy were also told to report to security headquarters, where they were photographed and had their fingerprints taken. They were warned that continuing opposition could lead to their arrest for counterrevolutionary activities.[30]

The government also confiscated a new church newspaper, *Iglesia,* claiming that Obando's press office had failed to complete legal registration requirements, a charge the archdiocese denied. The government occupied the offices of the archdiocesan Commission of Social Promotion, where *Iglesia* was printed. (The premises were later returned to the church, but not the confiscated equipment, including the printing press.) A journalist who worked for *Iglesia* was held incommunicado for four days, while others associated with the Commission were called in to give statements. Apparently, the chief cause of the government's harsh action was a series of articles critical of the military draft.[31]

When the bishops wanted to transmit a critical letter from the pope over their radio station, *Radio Católica,* they were denied permission by the authorities. In January 1986, the government closed the station because of its failure to broadcast President Ortega's year-end speech, which all Nicaraguan stations were supposed to transmit live. (The archdiocese claimed the failure was due to a technical difficulty.) Meanwhile, official permits were required for outdoor meetings, including those by churches; in some cases local *comandantes* demanded the names and addresses of participants at indoor religious meetings, such as retreats. Obando's column in the opposition newspaper *La Prensa* was censored, as was the rest of the paper. In a widely publicized article in *The Washington Post,* the cardinal charged that the Sandinistas had "gagged and bound" the church. He repeated the bishops' condemnation of "any outside interference, whether by the United States or the Soviet Union," arguing that "the Sandinistas are just as much the tools of Soviet interests as the insurgent forces are of the United States." The same theme was taken up by Bishop Julián Barni of León, generally considered a moderate, who said the superpowers should stay out of Nicaragua. "I wish that the Russians would also suspend the $100 million in arms and all [that the Sandinistas are receiving]." (The Soviets had provided approximately $500 million in military aid by 1986; they also supplied most of Nicaragua's oil.)[32]

While the bishops were battling Sandinistas, other church people were being abducted by the *contra* forces. A group from Witness for Peace was briefly held hostage, and Maryknoll nun Nancy Donovan was abducted with eight others after the *contras* slaughtered thirteen civilians near San Juan de Limay in the northern department of Estelí. Donovan, who taught literacy and Bible classes, was held eight hours before being released, apparently because of her pointed warning that her kidnapping "could cause repercussions." On returning to Limay she "spent that night and the next day washing the bodies of the dead, comforting families and praying with them and burying the dead from Limay."[33]

In mid-1987 Franciscan friar Tomás Zavaleta was killed when his car hit a land mine reportedly set by the *contras.* Also killed in the explosion was the secretary of a local agricultural project sponsored by Oxfam. Another passenger, Franciscan Father Ignacio Urbina, was seriously injured. In October Father Enrique Blandón, a pro-Sandinista priest, and the Reverend Gustavo Adolfo Tiffer, a Seventh-Day Adventist minister, were kidnapped by the *contras* and held for eleven days. Blandón said the *contras* had threatened to kill him.[34]

Such incidents were all too common in the northern border area. Nuns bringing medical supplies to the Miskito Indian regions reported being threatened with death, and lay church workers were prime targets for killing. Some were brutally tortured. Eleuterio Matute, for example, was dragged from his house with his sixteen-year-old son. The *contras* killed the youth with three bullets, but they tortured the father. They slit his abdomen to the chest bone, repeatedly stabbed him in the chest, and cut out his tongue. The examiner who inspected the body said that the heart had been taken out. Matute had been widely respected in the hamlet of Cruz de Piedra for his health and catechism work.[35]

What infuriated many Nicaraguans was that the bishops rarely, if ever, said a word in condemnation of such *contra* atrocities. True, lay leaders from the traditional church had been hauled off to jail for questioning by the Sandinistas, but they did not have their abdomens split open or their tongues and hearts cut out. Bishop Vega, who was even less diplomatic than Obando, summed up the hierarchy's indifference. When asked why he had not denounced the *contras*' murder of a nine-year-old girl, he shrugged. "It is worse to kill the soul than the body," he said.[36]

Like Obando, Vega repeatedly overstepped the line by giving aid and comfort to the *contras*' backers—for example, attending meetings in the United States in March and June of 1986, sponsored, respectively, by the right-wing Heritage Foundation and the neoconservatives' openly pro-*contra* Prodemca, which received U.S. government funding. During a Heritage seminar he said the Sandinistas had killed three priests—a statement he must have known was untrue. His claims of religious persecution were later used by President Reagan to help justify the administration's request for $100 million in *contra* aid. ("Reverend Father, we've heard you," announced the President.) Vega not only failed to denounce the *contras* or their U.S. backers; he also challenged a ruling by the International World Court that had condemned Washington for mining Nicaraguan harbors. In July, immediately after the congressional vote in favor of *contra* aid, Vega was expelled from Nicaragua. The Sandinistas also expelled Monsignor Bismarck Carballo, official spokesman for Cardinal Obando, and they made it clear that Obando might be next. The cardinal was outraged, the pope no less so. "In my eighteen years as a bishop, I've never seen a situation as grave as this," said Obando. John Paul described the bishop's expulsion as an act of the "Dark Ages." "I would very much like to hope," he said, "that those responsible for this decision rethink the seriousness of such an act, which also contradicts repeated claims of a desire for a peaceful and respectful coexistence with the church."[37]

Vega's expulsion had a sobering effect on several players in the drama. Obando became uncharacteristically prudent, toning down his sermons and refusing to talk with the press, saying only that the future was "in the hands of God." Some pro-Obando priests expressed genuine fear for their physical safety. That the Sandinistas could get rough was attested to by an Associated Press reporter covering a religious procession in honor of Managua's patron saint. "Several agents surrounded an unsuspecting young marcher and beat him up, then tried to seize an AP photographer's film of what had happened," he said. "The incident was described on state television that night as a brawl between drunken revelers." Expulsions continued. In September 1986, Montfort missionary Everett Brown was refused reentry into Nicaragua although he had worked in the country for twelve years. Father Gregorio Landaverde, the vicar of Bishop Vega's diocese, was expelled in December. The following month Cardinal Obando was beaten up in Florida by assailants who entered the Miami residence of the family of his secretary. Obando, who was staying with the family, was the only one to suffer physical abuse. If a robbery, the attack was a strange one, because the assailants took only the cardinal's wallet, watch, eyeglasses, and some of his personal documents.[38]

Whether ordinary thieves or Sandinista or *contra* agents were responsible for the Miami assault, events in Nicaragua, particularly Vega's expulsion, had a dampening effect on the Sandinistas' church supporters in the United States and Europe. Previously enthusiastic backers of the Sandinistas within the U.S. bishops' conference spoke darkly of how there "might not be any space left for the institutional church in Nicaragua." Europeans also admitted to being worried. "Throwing out Vega and Carballo and closing down the church's radio station and newspaper were signs of weakness," said the liberal Italian Bishop Dante Bernini. "These acts didn't go down well in Europe, even among Sandinista church supporters. They were a mistake."[39]

While Vega's expulsion cost the Sandinistas international support, it also helped to open the way for negotiations between the Vatican and Managua. The bishop's public complaints over his mistreatment were so loud and so political that even the Vatican was forced to admit that the Sandinistas might have had a reason to dislike him. The failure of the *contras* to overthrow the Sandinistas and the approaching end of Reagan's term were also factors in Rome's decision to attempt a new tack. Vatican and Latin American church sources said that Vega was told by Rome to stop holding press conferences. The Vatican foreign office began to have second thoughts about Obando's hard-line tactics in the fall of 1986. A new papal nuncio and experienced troubleshooter, Archbishop Paolo Gilio, was dispatched to Managua to do "everything possible" to improve church-state relations, and in September Cardinal Obando and President Ortega held talks for the first time in two years. The result was the establishment of a mixed government-episcopal commission charged with "normalizing" relations. Indicative of the new atmosphere was the government's attitude toward a Catholic congress sponsored by the traditional church the following November. The government provided security for church events, which received favorable coverage in the government-controlled press. Ortega abandoned his customary olive-green fatigues for civilian dress for a meeting with Cardinal Law of Boston. He also met with Nobel Peace Prize laureate Mother Teresa of Calcutta, giving her permission to open a branch of her Sisters of Charity in Nicaragua. John Paul sent a message calling on the Nicaraguans to make peace among themselves at this "decisive moment."[40]

Both sides had pragmatic reasons to support a thaw. On the one hand, the contest with the traditional church was damaging the Sandinistas' popularity with Nicaraguan Catholics. On the other, it was pushing the contestants toward an irreversible break that could destroy any space for the traditional church. Religious and diplomatic informants also said that the Vatican Secretariat of State disapproved of the *contra* war as counterproductive. "They know Nicaragua isn't the same as Grenada," said a Latin American ambassador to the Vatican. "U.S. policy has not produced any results and Reagan is at the end of his term. The Vatican cannot wait any longer, which is the reason it has embarked on a new policy."[41] Vatican sources said the pope wanted a "mediating church" in the style of San Salvador's Archbishop Arturo Rivera y Damas, who served as the chief go-between for the Salvadoran government and the guerrillas.[42]

The church-state negotiations were long and difficult, because each side demanded that the other be the first to make concessions. The church wanted the Sandinistas to show their goodwill by allowing it to reopen Radio Católica and by authorizing Vega and the others to return. The government claimed it was necessary to achieve a broad accord on all aspects of church-state relations before dealing with specifics. At issue was how much autonomy the church could expect and the price for that freedom. The *contra* war intruded into the negotiations because the government insisted that the condition for the return of Vega and the others was that they repent of their support for the rebels. While some who had been expelled upheld the episcopal line that all foreign military aid should cease, Vega clung stubbornly to the *contras.* Nor could the church realistically expect that, as long as the war continued, the Sandinistas would meet all its demands. These included complete freedom to evangelize, the right to promote reconciliation among the Nicaraguan people, and guarantees for its right to all means of mass communication—radio, television, and the written word.[43]

In other words, the church wanted the right to be critical. But criticism, particularly criticism that appeared to support the *contras,* had been the root of the problem in the first place. According to President Daniel Ortega, difficulties with the church would cease when U.S. pressures on Nicaragua stopped. But that was probably wishful thinking on both counts. Even if such pressures were to end—a big if—tensions between church and state were bound to continue because of ideological differences. On the other hand, recognition by both sides that each occupied its own proper space would make dialogue easier. The challenge to the Vatican was to bargain down the price for Sandinista recognition of such space.

Diplomatic and religious sources said that Rome was prepared to promise neutrality by the church in return for a guaranteed base within Nicaraguan society. Although the Sandinistas wanted Rome to recognize, and therefore legitimate, the revolution, Vatican sources warned that any concessions by the Vatican should be seen as "purely tactical" to avoid further division in the Nicaraguan church and the loss of any influence on the Sandinista experiment. "John Paul opposes the Nicaraguan revolution because he believes it a Central American variation of Poland, and therefore Rome will never publicly recognize the revolution's legitimacy," predicted a church informant. "At the same time, the Vatican doesn't want to give away too many cards, because it needs to maintain good relations with the United States as its chief ally in the East-West conflict."[44]

Although negotiations between the government and the hierarchy dragged on for months, with no solution seemingly in sight, they had the merit of giving both sides a breathing space—the Sandinistas in order to recoup lost prestige in Europe and Latin America, the church to continue its religious work. And it was in the area of religion, not politics, that the traditional church had the edge. While Cardinal Obando was not everyone's ideal of the "good pastor," being autocratic, vain, and hot-tempered, there could be no doubt that the prelate had the courage of his convictions. Although few Nicaraguans shared Obando's enthusiasm for the *contras*, many held to his traditional religious beliefs, and they honored him for refusing to compromise with the state over religious freedoms. Consequently, when the Sandinistas needed a mediator to enable them to fulfill their part of a five-nation Central American peace accord, signed in August 1987, they turned to their avowed enemy, the cardinal.

The peace plan, which was promoted by Costa Rican president Oscar Arias—and for which he received the 1987 Nobel Peace Prize—took the Reagan administration by surprise. Aimed at ending hostilities between left and right, it cut the ground from under the White House, which was still vigorously pursuing the *contra* war, by providing a framework for a cease-fire in Nicaragua. As an indication of its good intentions, the Sandinistas authorized the reopening of the opposition newspaper *La Prensa* and Radio Católica. It also agreed to end the exile of the radio station's director, Monsignor Carballo, as well as Bishop Vega and an Italian priest. Although Carballo returned to Nicaragua, Vega remained in Miami, saying that he did not "wish to lend myself to the deceit that the situation is improving." Meanwhile, President Ortega appointed Obando to head the National Reconciliation Commission to oversee the surrender and return to civilian life of *contras* (few took advantage of the amnesty). In November the government asked Obando to become the mediator in talks with the *contras* about a cease-fire. According to Ortega, Obando was the "ideal" person to serve as go-between. Indicative of the thaw in church-state relations, government officials took to calling the cardinal "His Eminence" and the "illustrious bishop."[45]

Nevertheless, the bishops did not change their critical stance, insisting that the government end the military draft and hold direct talks with the *contras*, a proposal initially rejected but later accepted by Ortega. Obando's intervention should "not be interpreted as a political dialogue with the counterrevolutionary leadership to negotiate power," he warned. Ortega also told Sandinista cadres that concessions to the Arias peace plan in no way jeopardized Sandinista control of the country. One of the concessions—free elections—would be tested in 1989. But Ortega said that even if the Sandinistas lost the elections, they would still retain real power. He also warned opposition groups not to allow the *contras* to use them, a reference to dissident political parties as well as the bishops, who refused to urge the *contras* to accept an amnesty. Church sources said that while tensions with the government had decreased because of the peace plan, the hierarchy and the Sandinistas were still miles apart on many issues.[46]

In spite of everything—or perhaps because of it—religion flourished in Nicaragua, primarily among traditional Catholic and fundamentalist Protestant churches. According to government statistics, Catholic parishes increased from 167 to 178 between 1979 and 1986, the number of priests from 293 to 430, religious congregations from 54 to 82, and seminaries from 2 to 8. In addition, there were 85 Protestant denominations with 2,000 pastors compared to 46 denominations with 1,500 pastors before the revolution. These statistics showed that government harassment had not prevented the growth of churches but, on the contrary, probably encouraged it. A breakdown of the figures suggested that the religious institutions that most benefited were traditional churches that promised religious certitudes in a time of political and social upheaval. Religious surveys and sociological studies in Latin America and other Third World countries confirmed that people turned to religion in periods of national stress not only for comfort but also as a substitute for political impotence. Father Uriel Molina, pastor of a pro-government church in Managua famous for its Sandinista Masses, put his finger on the challenge. "The churches of priests who are against the revolution are full," he said, "because they offer a space for protest, just as our churches did in the time of Somoza. Now, churches like mine have few people, not because they reject the church but because they are too busy carrying out the tasks of the revolution. This is another way of achieving Christian identity." "Many Catholic revolutionaries have put formal religion aside," agreed the Sandinista leader of a Managuan base community. "We realize God is not up in the sky, light-years away. God is health, literacy, production. We can find Him by working for those things."[47]

That may well be true, but it did not answer the spiritual yearning of the Nicaraguan people. Even the most generous estimates by supporters of the popular church claimed no more than one-quarter of the country's priests and nuns. The number of committed followers was perhaps 50,000. But many of the committed were so busy carrying out the tasks of the revolution, to use Molina's words, that they had no time for pastoral work. A sizable number of the priests were engaged in intellectual activities to justify the revolution or in organizational skirmishes with Obando's church. As noted by a Nicaraguan theologian involved in a long battle against Obando's attempts to expel Molina, so much energy was dedicated to such issues that "there never seems to be time to work with the base groups." The nuns tried to fill the gap by living and working with the poor, but there were not enough of them. Meanwhile, the formerly thriving movement of Christian base communities stagnated in many parts of the country, partly because of opposition from the bishops, but also because the communities were absorbed by the Sandinista political machine. A good example of the dilemma facing those in the popular church was Foreign Minister D'Escoto, who had the charisma and vision to provide a strong religious leadership but who was too occupied with the demands of foreign policy to devote much energy to spiritual ministry. As admitted by some in the popular church, the price of political power was a secular erosion of spirituality. For many Nicaraguans, particularly the urban young, the revolution provided all that was necessary in a faith, but for many more, it was not enough.[48]

The Protestants

Like the Catholics, the Protestants were split between churches that supported the revolution and those that opposed it, and for much the same reasons. They also suffered deep internal schisms, some churches actually expelling pastors who expressed pro-Sandinista sentiments. Progressive Protestants, or what would be called the Protestant wing of the popular church, were in the minority, and, like their Catholic counterparts, were losing membership. While few Protestant churches suffered outright persecution—the principal exception being the Moravian Church because of its involvement in the Miskito conflict—they were subjected to the same unpleasantries experienced by Obando's church, including temporary detention of pastors. In one case an evangelical minister was killed by Sandinista soldiers (the culprits were punished by the government). In another a Pentecostal preacher, Prudencio Baltodano, was brutally treated by Sandinista soldiers, who cut off one of his ears. In 1982, after Tomás Borge denounced an "invasion by the sects," thirty church buildings belonging to the Jehovah's Witnesses, Mormons, and

Seventh-Day Adventists were seized by Sandinista *turbas*. Some were returned (though not those of the Jehovah's Witnesses) through the intervention of the Evangelical Committee for Aid and Development (CEPAD), an umbrella group for the evangelical churches that supported the revolution and that acted as go-between for the Sandinistas and the dissident churches. Unlike Catholicism, which is embedded in Nicaraguan culture, many of the Protestant churches, particularly the evangelicals, suffered from their association with U.S. churches and pastors, raising Sandinista suspicions of a CIA connection. Despite such problems the fundamentalist Protestant churches rapidly multiplied, accounting for approximately 15 percent of the population by the mid-eighties. The most successful denominations were the Pentecostals, who made up 85 percent of the evangelicals. The largest of these were the Assemblies of God with more than 60,000 members.[49]

Like traditional Catholics, the strongly anticommunist fundamentalists believed that support for the revolution represented an unacceptable mixing of religion and politics, whereas opposition to the regime was condoned on the ground that Marxism was the work of the devil. The mainline Protestant churches—the Methodists, Presbyterians, and Baptists—tended to take the opposite position. Baptist ministers, for example, said that while their church had been harassed under the Somoza government, it had been able to operate freely under the Sandinistas (a dissenting wing took issue with that opinion). Some evangelical pastors were also supportive, particularly those identified with CEPAD, and on occasion foreign evangelicals also provided help as, for instance, a religious crusade and food relief effort in Managua sponsored by the Reverend Larry Jones, president of the Oklahoma-based Feed the Children. But the majority of the evangelicals remained neutral toward or resistant to the revolution.[50]

Like the Catholics, the progressive and conservative wings—as represented by CEPAD and the National Council of Evangelical Pastors (CNPEN), respectively—wasted enormous amounts of energy fighting each other. CEPAD, which was founded as a church relief agency after the devastating earthquake in 1972, was the older and better financed of the two. Though not originally envisioned as a council of churches, it gradually evolved into an umbrella group for forty-six denominations and another twenty on a cooperative basis, including the Assemblies of God. It also became the principal funnel for foreign donations from sister churches in other countries. Generally supportive of the revolution, it worked with the government on social projects, such as the construction of low-cost housing and medical aid. It also defended the evangelicals, explaining their religious beliefs to the government and getting dissident pastors out of trouble. As a goodwill gesture to the conservatives, it helped launch CNPEN. Unlike many Catholics in the popular church, who simply wrote off Obando's church, CEPAD tried to placate its conservative critics and to serve as a bridge between the fundamentalists and the Sandinistas. But the fundamentalists didn't see it that way. They complained that CEPAD misrepresented the evangelical position by seeming to endorse the government. CEPAD hogged all the foreign aid, they said, and the government made CEPAD approval necessary for everything they did. Though the criticism was exaggerated, it was true that the Sandinistas preferred to deal with CEPAD while refusing to recognize CNPEN after it broke away from its parent organization. CNPEN director Felix Rosales complained bitterly of the government's refusal to recognize the council and of restrictions on public worship, such as government permits to hold outdoor services.[51]

Differences between CEPAD and CNPEN also reflected different interpretations of faith. CEPAD was ecumenical, democratic, and concerned with social justice as well as saving souls. CNPEN wanted nothing to do with Catholics; upheld a hierarchical structure in which the pastor, not the congregation, represented the church; and dismissed good works as useless or, if they were co-sponsored by the government, as Sandinista propaganda. Backbiting—a common characteristic of the fiercely independent evangelical communities—also set the pastors against CEPAD, particularly since it controlled a near-monopoly on funding for the churches. But as with the Catholics, the principal issue dividing CEPAD and CNPEN was the relationship between the churches and the revolution. CNPEN spokesmen charged CEPAD with being too forgiving of the Sandinistas' failures, while CEPAD countered that the CNPEN pastors refused to see anything good in the revolution.

The Miskitos

The most tragic situation involving the churches in Nicaragua was the conflict between the Miskito Indians and the Sandinista government. Churches, communities, the entire region of Moskitia were ravaged by the conflict between the *contras* and the Sandinistas. At stake were the lives of some 110,000 Miskito, Sumu, and Rama Indians—the largest

surviving lowland Indian population in Latin America. Fiercely independent, the Indians traditionally roamed the huge but undeveloped province
of Zelaya in the eastern half of the country and north across the River
Coco that marks the boundary with Honduras. Whites often find life in
the humid backlands tedious and primitive, but to the Indians the region
is a cornucopia of natural beauty, with abundant wildlife for fishing and
hunting. Travel is difficult, though. Many parts of the tropical rain forests
can be reached only by river transport. Even in the larger towns the roads
often peter out in the bush. From the Miskito viewpoint, the lack of roads
has been an advantage: Until recently, it discouraged whites from penetrating Indian territories.

Long ago, the Miskitos learned the importance of playing off the
whites against one another. In the seventeenth century the Indians were
courted by the British. In return for dominance in the region and protection from the marauding Spaniards, they agreed to operate in Britain's
interest. To consolidate their control over the region, the British created
a Miskito kingdom. The Indian monarch, however, was never more than
a symbolic go-between with the village chieftains, who wished to trade
local produce for manufactured goods, particularly muskets—hence the
Miskito name. Although the Miskitos, the largest of the Nicaraguan Indian tribes, maintained contact with market economies and powerful
nation-states, they retained considerable independence, unlike the peasants and Indians on the Pacific coast. Contrary to the Sandinistas' claims
that the Miskitos had no experience of autonomy, they enjoyed a higher
degree of self-government during their alliance with the British than
did other indigenous populations. That right was incorporated into a
nineteenth-century treaty in which the Crown recognized Nicaragua's
sovereignty over Moskitia.

The only lasting cultural imprint left by the British was a Creolized
English. More important was the influence of missionaries from the Moravian Church of Czechoslovakia, who established a foothold in the area
in the mid-nineteenth century (the Catholic Church had made little attempt to proselytize among the Indians). By the 1900s most of the Miskitos
were converted, and Indian pastors gradually replaced those of German
and North American origin. The Miskitos' historical distrust of "Spaniards," as they call Nicaraguans from the Pacific coast, was thus reinforced
by religious and linguistic differences. The cultural and racial subtleties
inherent in this estrangement are evident even today. For example, to
promote its literacy campaign among the brown and black populations

of the Atlantic coast, the Sandinistas used pictures of white students on billboards. And when Borge said the Indians were "marginated" because "they don't speak Spanish there but Miskito or English," he was voicing a common attitude among Nicaraguans. President Ortega, for example, made much the same observation in 1987 during a meeting with CEPAD and foreign visitors, including church representatives from Canada. The Miskito language, he said, was "deformed [because] the English language is combined with the Miskito language. Their ways, their cultural expressions are not pure."[52]

Rule by prerevolutionary Managua was exploitive. The Somoza dynasty gave rich concessions to foreign, mostly U.S., companies that fattened on Moskitia's abundant gold, timber, and fishing resources. Pay and working conditions were poor, and the Indians saw little of the profits. At the same time, their communal life remained relatively untouched. Because of the remoteness of the Atlantic territories, the Miskitos and other Indians participated hardly at all in the revolution. But the Miskitos welcomed the Sandinista takeover as putting an end to traditional exploitation of indigenous groups by right-wing military regimes. Nevertheless, the majority's distrust—based on a Spanish educational system that spends as much time studying the Atlantic coast as U.S. schools do Central America, that is to say, hardly at all—was evident from the start in the way the Sandinistas reacted to the establishment of an Indian organization, Misurasata. Their initial misgivings did not arise from overt racial or ideological prejudices but from the fear common among Latin American revolutionaries that foreigners, which is how they regarded the English-speaking Indians, might undermine the hard-won victory, as they had in Guatemala and Chile. Nor does Marxist ideology offer much guidance for dealing with indigenous peoples. Even the hard-liners in the Nicaraguan government considered the Soviet Union's treatment of its minority groups to be inappropriate. Cuba had no Indian population at the time of its 1959 revolution, and alliances between Indians and Marxist guerrillas elsewhere in Latin America were primarily tactical, not ideological, even in Peru and Guatemala.

Nevertheless, the Sandinistas gave Misurasata a voice in the Council of State, and when the organization complained that the literacy campaign on the Atlantic coast was conducted entirely in Spanish, Indians were hired to teach the natives to read and write in their own tongue. But two obstacles arose to doom this promising start. One was the Indians' increasing self-confidence, expressed primarily in demands for government recognition of their land rights. The other was the Sandinistas' discovery that they could not mold Misurasata into a government-controlled mass organization, as they had Nicaraguan youth and labor groups. Officials often encountered passive resistance to their programs among the Indian population unless the Misurasata leadership approved the project. The idea that the Indians were merely responding to age-old tribal loyalties escaped the Sandinistas, who believed, in Daniel Ortega's words, that the revolution had to "rescue them and incorporate them into the process." But no Indian group in Latin America has willingly allowed itself to be integrated into government development plans—regardless of the government's ideology—because integration has always meant the extinction of Indian culture.[53]

Mutual distrust led to the arrest in 1981 of thirty-three Indians representing the Misurasata leadership and a skirmish in the village of Prinzapolka, in which four Indians and four Nicaraguan soldiers were killed. Things came to a head in December of that year with the so-called Red Christmas plot, the Sandinistas' name for an alleged plan by the *contras* to seize the Miskito territories. Twenty-eight *contras*, including two Miskitos, attacked the Indian border town of San Carlos and captured, mutilated, and killed six Sandinista soldiers. According to a team from the Inter-American Commission on Human Rights (IACHR), an agency of the Organization of American States which investigated the incident, Sandinista soldiers at the border post of Leimus retaliated by capturing thirty-five unarmed Miskitos who were passing through the town on their way from work to their villages to celebrate Christmas. Some were taken to the river and shot; others were buried alive. (According to Americas Watch, seventeen were killed.) The Defense Ministry insisted that the Miskitos died while trying to escape and that the list of those who had been detained at Leimus had been lost, a story the IACHR found "unsatisfactory." In January 1982, the government forced 8,500 Miskitos to leave their villages along the Coco River and settle in government camps to the south known as Tasba Pri.[54]

The government thought it had reason to suspect the Indian leadership, particularly Steadman Fagoth, who, on escaping across the border to Honduras, immediately went to work for the CIA. The Sandinistas also felt justified in moving the Indian population from the war zone along the border—and were upheld in their decision by such human rights groups as the IACHR and Americas Watch. But human rights groups did not approve of the way the Indians were forcibly relocated to government camps. The Sandinistas razed Indian villages and farms, and forty-four Moravian church buildings were closed or destroyed. The churches were also used to quarter Sandinista troops. Nor did Americas Watch, the IACHR, or Amnesty International accept Sandinista explanations for the Leimus killings, the killing of seven Miskitos at Walpa Siksa in 1982, and the disappearance of some seventy civilian Miskito detainees between July and September 1982. Among the "disappeared" were three Moravian Indian pastors; two others were killed during clashes with the Sandinistas. In addition, eighteen Moravian Indian pastors were imprisoned by government forces, and some were maltreated before being released.[55]

After the Indians were relocated and their villages were destroyed, it was open war between the Miskitos and the Sandinistas. For a while the Miskito military leadership split between Fagoth's Misura in the north and Brooklyn Rivera's Misurasata in the south, the latter insisting that its aim was not to overthrow the Sandinistas but to obtain government recognition of Indian rights. Fagoth, who boasted openly of his CIA links and used brutal recruitment methods, was eventually replaced by the less bloodthirsty Wycliffe Diego, a Miskito pastor, but Diego, Fagoth, and Rivera reunited in a common front in mid-1987. Meanwhile, the government allowed the Indians to return to the Coco River and initiated discussions on limited autonomy for the Miskito region. The latter led in September 1987 to approval by the Nicaraguan National Assembly of an autonomy law for the Atlantic Coast that recognizes the Indians' communal land rights, establishes Miskito as the first language in Indian schools, and guarantees that municipal governments will be locally elected. The Sandinistas also developed a pro-Sandinista Indian organization, Misatan, while opening negotiations with local Miskito military commanders to achieve a truce in certain areas. These initiatives were accompanied by apologies from the government for the mistakes it had committed in Indian territories. Nevertheless, many Indians remained skeptical about Sandinista intentions.

Throughout the Miskito tragedy the Moravian Church tried to play a mediating role while remaining steadfast to its people. Pastors who were jailed turned the other cheek, reminding their people of the perfidies of the *contras* and their CIA masters—which even Fagoth, of all people, admitted. Had traditional Catholics or the fundamentalists been in the Moravians' place, the shooting war would undoubtedly have become a holy crusade—certainly, the Moravians suffered sufficiently at the Sandinistas' hands to be angry. But the Moravian Church strongly believes in tolerance: "In essentials unity, in nonessentials freedom, in all things charity." The survival of an Indian culture is obviously not a "nonessential," yet the Moravians were prepared to give the Sandinistas the benefit of the doubt that, if the *contra* war ceased, an autonomy based on tolerance could be achieved for the Miskito territories. More than any other church in Nicaragua, the Moravians followed the prophetic path of genuine reconciliation. Although the Moravians agreed that it was a risky enterprise, they believed that "particular commitments . . . must not keep us from talking to one another." The first talking point was peace. "We have heard the whole cry of our people," declared the Moravian Church in Nicaragua, "from laborers, professionals, young people, children and the parties to violent conflicts: 'We want peace, we are tired of war.' "[56]

The Moravian Church could speak with one voice in Nicaragua, even though different Miskito leaders appeared to side, now with the *contras*, now with the Sandinistas, because it understood a basic principle in the Indians' ethnicity (one that Bishop Schlaefer also recognized): The Indians were not loyal to any white man's agenda but only to their own culture and history. Despite squabbles among such different Indian groups as Misurasata, Misura, Kisan-war, Kisan-peace, and Misatan, they were all "our boys" to the Indian villagers. No *comandante* spoke for all the Miskitos because the Indians traditionally followed a communal lifestyle without a hierarchy, even in the days of the Miskito kings. The Sandinistas thought that if they dealt with Kisan-peace and Misatan, they could control the Indians—the very mistake made by the CIA in believing that it could manipulate Misura, Misurasata, and Kisan-war. Unfortunately the Sandinistas clung to the belief that it was only because the Indians were "confused and backward," to use Ortega's expression, that they insisted on including people like Fagoth and Rivera in autonomy discussions. But as one Moravian missionary pointed out, the Miskitos "do not divide trust so easily. Westerners want to know which side each individual or community is on—a Western construct which facilitates a strategy of divide and rule. On the basis of 500 years of experience with Westerners, [the Indians] are generally inclined to trust other Indians first; non-Spanish-speaking Westerners, second; Spanish-speaking Nicaraguans, least of all."[57]

Although much was made by the Sandinistas of exaggerated land claims by the Miskitos, both the Indians and government leaders privately recognized that such questions were negotiable, as were military and economic issues. The sticking point in the conflict was that the Indians wanted freedom to do things their own way without being bossed around by Spanish-speaking revolutionaries from the western side of the country. Members of the Moravian Church believed it possible to overcome the deep distrust between Pacific and Atlantic coasts, and perhaps, without the tensions of the *contra* war, they may be proved right. Meanwhile, said a Moravian missionary, "the question is not whether the church is being harassed, but whether it is being faithful—whether it *can* be faithful in this situation."[58]

Blood Sports

Jesuit peace activist Daniel Berrigan found the Nicaraguan situation troubling. He was upset by the bishops' failure to condemn the *contra* atrocities, and equally unhappy with the Sandinistas' lack of "sensitivity toward the truth," since, he said, the fortunes of the revolution depended on truthfulness. After Ernesto Cardenal, the poet-priest and minister of culture, refused to admit any errors in the government's policy toward the Miskitos, Berrigan found himself wondering about a revolution that assumed an "absolute platonic form, beyond question or critique." What Cardenal did not realize, said Berrigan, was that he had become the "surrogate and victim" of a romantic ideal of revolution that did not admit human fallibility. Cardenal was acclaimed and feted in Europe and North America as "a kind of substitute for the unresolved violence of perthe affluent (even of affluent Christians) who love blood sports, but perhaps no sport so well as the distancing and projecting on another of the violent vision of revolution. A revolutionary fantasy, need it be added; an upheaval that will bring change in every direction—except their own."[59]

Though the judgment was harsh, Berrigan had a valid point in charging that many foreigners, particularly Americans, projected their hopes and hates onto the revolution, dismissing reality when it conflicted with their expectations. They didn't see—as Berrigan did—that the victims of such exaggerations were the Nicaraguans themselves. For example, some U.S. church supporters of the revolution followed Cardenal's line by denying any mistakes in the government's dealings with the Indians. Look at all the wonderful things the Sandinistas have done for the Indians, they said. What other government would even discuss autonomy? Similarly, right-wing religious groups described the Indians as martyrs to communism, failing to recognize that the Indians had also made mistakes. The extent to which either side really cared about the people involved could be questioned—often they seemed no more than propaganda fodder in the "war of ideas."

An example of how the Americans harmed the people they were supposedly trying to help was provided by the neoconservative Institute on Religion and Democracy (IRD). Formed to push the Reagan agenda among church groups, the IRD strongly backed the White House's position on El Salvador and Nicaragua. Its briefing papers and newsletter loyally reflected the party line and were sometimes used by the White House in briefings for religious leaders. Most of the material on Nicaragua was venomously anti-Sandinista and made no attempt to present another viewpoint. The IRD specialized in the smear, particularly against liberal churches that supported the Nicaraguan revolution, and it caused considerable consternation in 1984 by circulating a petition to end financial contributions from the National Council of Churches to CEPAD and other pro-Sandinista church groups in Nicaragua. The petition obtained only 2,000 signatures and did nothing to stem the flow of aid, although it did stir up controversy within the U.S. churches, which presumably was the point of the exercise.[60]

The IRD had already made a name for itself in Nicaragua by giving Obando y Bravo a religious freedom award in 1982, and the petition campaign made it even more suspect in the eyes of the Nicaraguan government. Not only was the institute closely identified with the Reagan administration's Central American policies; several of its associates were directly involved in the *contra* support effort, including Michael Novak, one of the directors of the Moonies' Nicaraguan Freedom Fund. Penn Kemble, who helped found the IRD, also ran the Washington-based organization Friends of the Democratic Center in Central America (Prodemca) that funneled U.S. government funds to the Nicaraguan opposition daily, *La Prensa*, and Nicaragua's Permanent Human Rights Commission. Prodemca took out full-page advertisements in the U.S. press calling for military assistance to the *contras*. Humberto Belli, also associated with the institute, frequently spoke against the Sandinistas in the United States and published *Nicaragua: Christians Under Fire* and *Breaking Faith*, highly biased books on the churches' situation in Nicaragua. An ex–*La Prensa* editor and friend of Obando, Belli was accused of working with the CIA by Edgar Chamorro, a former high-ranking *contra* leader. Chamorro said that the CIA helped Belli produce *Nica-*

ragua. "There are a lot of appendixes that the CIA gave to Belli or Belli got from Nicaragua with the CIA because they were working together," Chamorro told *The Nation*'s Alexander Cockburn. According to Chamorro, Belli decided that an institute would be a better vehicle than the *contras* for a book's publication. *Nicaragua* was therefore published under the sponsorship of the Puebla Institute, a newly created outfit headed by Belli and co-sponsored by Lutheran pastor Richard John Neuhaus, also a founder of the IRD.[61]

While Belli denied Chamorro's account of CIA ties, his Puebla Institute soon joined the constellation of support groups for White House propaganda. Nina Shea, the program director of the controversial International League for Human Rights and part author of a slanted report on Nicaragua, became director of the Puebla Institute, with Belli as president, and the institute began to churn out more anti-Sandinista material. It paralleled the work of the League, which depended for its findings on Nicaragua's Permanent Human Rights Commission, which had received funding from Prodemca and which, by its own director's admission, did not investigate the accusations it reported. Meanwhile, Belli, who had undergone a conversion to charismatic (fundamentalist) Catholicism while still in Latin America, hooked up with the University of Steubenville, Ohio, a center of Catholic charismatics. The Steubenville group was part of a larger body of Catholic charismatics known as the Word of God, located in Ann Arbor, Michigan, that sometimes cooperated with the Protestant Pentecostals. The Catholic charismatics caused considerable problems for liberal U.S. bishops, such as Newark's then archbishop Peter Gerety, while also providing support through their international organization, Sword of the Spirit, for Obando's archdiocese in Managua. After Belli became active with Hispanic charismatics, the archdiocese was invaded by charismatic preachers who began organizing Christian base communities for the traditional church as a counterbalance to the pro-Sandinista communities.[62]

Such activities made the Nicaraguan government highly suspicious of anyone connected to the IRD, which it considered a CIA front. Although the IRD had received a grant from the U.S. Information Agency for an international religious conference co-sponsored with the State Department, there was no evidence of CIA funding. In Managua, however, government officials were convinced that the IRD was the center of an international religious conspiracy, especially since the opposition *La Prensa* repeated IRD accusations against the Sandinistas' church supporters. Consequently any Nicaraguan associated with the Institute had to expect trouble. Obando, for example, was not allowed to forget that he had gone to the United States to accept an award from the Institute. ("A person does not make a long trip to get a medal without having investigated previously why they are giving him such an honor, and who it is that is giving him the honor," Foreign Minister D'Escoto hinted darkly.) Yet Obando was a powerful churchman who knew how to take care of himself. If he chose to take a risk in accepting the IRD award, it was a calculated decision in the high-stakes poker game with the government. That was not true of the poor evangelical pastors who suffered severe harassment because the IRD decided to use them in the propaganda war.[63]

That the conservative evangelical pastors in the CNPEN did not get on with the more liberal CEPAD was no secret in Nicaragua, but the IRD did not help CNPEN by supposedly championing its cause. In 1985 the Institute published an interview with Kate Rafferty, a journalist who worked with the California-based fundamentalist group Open Doors. She cited a long list of grievances against CEPAD, based on her interviews in Nicaragua, and including the charge that CEPAD was diverting humanitarian aid provided by U.S. churches to political work for the regime. The interview, published as a briefing paper by IRD, was skillfully interwoven with accusations against the National Council of Churches and gave the impression that Rafferty was speaking for CNPEN. CEPAD, the National Council of Churches, and the Sandinista government were furious at the insinuations, but it was not the IRD or Rafferty who paid for the consequences but the evangelical pastors in CNPEN who already had enough trouble with the government. In a letter to the IRD, Guillermo Osorno, secretary general of CNPEN, complained that Rafferty "has no legal right to make such statements without realizing the great harm which they are causing us." While some evangelical pastors probably griped to Rafferty—as they did to other journalists—it did not help CNPEN to be described as a victim of CEPAD, particularly since the situation was a great deal more complex than the picture Rafferty painted. Nor did CNPEN want to be associated with the IRD. "CNPEN has never had any ties with the IRD," insisted Osorno, in a plea to be left alone.[64]

Similarly, the IRD caused considerable unpleasantness for Gustavo Parajón, a highly respected Baptist pastor and medical doctor who founded CEPAD, by insinuating that he was promoting Marxism in the churches because "he's a Sandinista supporter." As proof of Parajón's sins, the IRD published an interview with Miguel Bolaños Hunter, a defector from Nicaragua's state security who made sweeping, unproven allegations that were challenged by respected human rights organizations. Bolaños claimed that Parajón was a state informer, reporting "everything that CEPAD talked about" to state security. Although an IRD representative later admitted to *Sojourners* magazine that "I don't know if it's true [about Parajón], and I don't know how to find out," the institute had no qualms about the interview, which, said IRD militant David Jessup, reflected "usual operating procedures." Yet such "procedures" did not help the Nicaraguans but, on the contrary, hurt both CNPEN and CEPAD. The IRD was so intent on justifying hatred of the Nicaraguan revolution that it never considered the damage it was inflicting on the evangelical pastors in CNPEN, most of whom served the poor, or CEPAD, which was a major source of food and medicine for the poor. As candidly admitted by Pastor Neuhaus, an IRD founder, the suffering of the poor was a regrettable side effect of the great campaign against a leftist government.[65]

A similar mindlessness was evident in alleged covert aid from Lieutenant Colonel Oliver North's network to Cardinal Obando, whose church, according to *Newsweek,* may have received $125,000 through a *contra* account in a Cayman Islands bank. Obando said the allegation was "a tremendous slander" and "a falsehood," although Father Frederico Arguello, a conservative Nicaraguan priest described by *Newsweek* as "close to Obando," admitted to receiving $31,000 from North accounts "to help the church and the poor." Obando may not have known about the ultimate source of the money—the CIA has often injected money into political and labor organizations without their leaders' knowledge. As one U.S. intelligence source told *Newsweek,* the cardinal may have "thought it was just another rich North American or West German." (The West German Catholic Church provides substantial support for churches throughout Latin America.) The Nicaraguan government, which at the time was more concerned about Vatican-sponsored church-state negotiations, did not make an issue of the revelations. Nevertheless, they hurt Obando's credibility, just as the IRD had hurt CNPEN, and Prodemca's money had proved the kiss of death for *La Prensa.*[66]

As Father Berrigan observed, it was easy to enjoy the "blood sports" from afar. No matter what happened in Nicaragua, it would have no effect on the lifestyle of the average American, who could afford to be righteous, for or against the revolution. Much harder was the path chosen by the

Moravian Church, which, as one of its missionaries wryly admitted, was misunderstood by both right and left. The Moravians kept their counsel, quietly succored their suffering people, sought reconciliation, and tried to be faithful. They also tried to live up to their code, by sorting out the essential from the nonessential. The most essential thing, they agreed, was peace. It was what the Miskitos wanted; it was what the overwhelming majority of Nicaraguans wanted. But the Nicaraguans, it seemed, could not be trusted to settle matters by themselves: hence the *contra* war, the interjection of East-West politics by both Washington and the Vatican, and the subsequent entrance of the communist bloc, which provided the Sandinistas with the military and economic aid that the United States would not. The cycle was familiar—much the same had happened twenty years earlier when the Cubans had toppled a corrupt dictator. Yet history never quite repeats itself. Nicaragua is not another Cuba, not only because its history and people are different but also because religion plays such a determining role in post-revolutionary society.

Steadfastness

Although the *contras'* supporters constantly invoked God's blessing, the claim was cynical and self-serving. As New York's Cardinal O'Connor told Congress, "Direct military aid to any force attempting to overthrow a government with which we are not at war and with which we maintain diplomatic relations is illegal, and, in our judgment, immoral and therefore cannot merit our support." Nor, believed thoughtful Christians like Berrigan, did God identify with the Sandinista government or the political opposition led by Cardinal Obando. The early Christians converted the masters of the Roman world not through political lobbies but by their religious example—their steadfastness to the community of faith. As pointed out by Methodist writer Deborah Huntington, "The Christian vision must remain distinct from politics. The beauty of the vision that our churches can give is a theology of life, as witnesses to values that must survive." Berrigan described it in biblical terms as "the one necessary thing." "One works, plans, dedicates a lifetime to tasks that favor the human condition; indeed, one is enjoined to do so. But the work must fall continually under close scrutiny. The carnal ties that bind one's spirit, like a strangling umbilical, to jargon of effectiveness, media hype, goals, quotas, guaranteed results—all forms and visions and expectations of nirvana—these must be discarded, placed to one side in favor of what the Gospel calls 'the one necessary thing' "—the values that must survive.[67]

The popular church discerned such values in the Sandinista revolution. Its leaders also believed it was necessary to maintain a "critical presence" from within in order to prevent antireligious attitudes and to remind the Sandinistas of their promises. From a tactical viewpoint it could be argued that such presence made sense. Quite a few Nicaraguan Christians also believed that they were living their faith by doing the work of the revolution, as, for example, in health and literacy programs. Yet a problem arose. As Huntington observed, "The danger to those who follow a leftist position is the loss of faith." Faith in the revolution remained strong among the Sandinista cadres, but many no longer felt the need for the "close scrutiny" of spiritual discipline. The urban young increasingly rejected religion, partly because the traditional church opposed the revolution, but also because of indoctrination by the Sandinista army and police. Even popular church leaders recognized that the Christian base communities had been absorbed by the process. "The most educated people went off to the government ministries, while the kids joined the army," a base community leader admitted.[68] The price of this loss was inestimable because base communities of ordinary people could have provided an independent but loyal opposition to keep the Sandinistas honest. Instead, Nicaragua had a hierarchical church run by the traditionalists and a hierarchical state apparatus but no independent group of Christians able to stand outside the political disputes between the two.

Obando's church, though just as sincere as the popular church, made similar mistakes by making ideology more important than religion, thus forfeiting the goodwill of many Nicaraguan Christians. The support of Obando, Vega, and other church leaders for the *contras* could be explained on ideological grounds, but not on religious ones, for as Cardinal O'Connor had pointed out, the war was immoral. Had Obando and Vega consistently opposed all foreign military interference, as Archbishop Rivera y Dama did in El Salvador, they would have been in a stronger position to criticize the Soviet buildup in Nicaragua. But they lost any claim to neutrality by showing their preference for one side. Their politicking also confused the issue of religious freedom, giving ammunition to the Sandinistas, who claimed that harassment of the churches was in response to political, not religious, actions. Common sense should have made the bishops realize that the revolution was irrevocable, but it was only in the fall of 1986, after much damage had been done to church-state relations, that the Vatican faced that reality.

CHAPTER 13

✠

THE PEOPLE OF GOD

IN THE MEDIEVAL DETECTIVE STORY *The Name of the Rose,* Umberto Eco captured the atmosphere of a period when dissidents were put to death for urging a reversion to an earlier church, uncorrupted by power and wealth. The papacy correctly interpreted such reformist calls as treasonous because they challenged the greedy ambitions of the princes of the church. Worse, such "heretics" often inflamed the peasantry to revolt against their impoverished condition. Theological and cultural deviation offered a convenient excuse to rid the church of dangerous thinking.

Eco's book is a religious whodunit that can be read as a parable about the modern church, because the points he makes apply as well to John Paul's Vatican. As in the Middle Ages, Rome uses theology as a weapon of cultural and political domination against the "simple," as Eco called the poor. In today's context the largest number of Catholics are "simple" people living in the Third World, particularly Latin America, where 90 percent of the inhabitants are baptized Catholics, and two-thirds of them are poor. As observed by a Latin American cardinal, this reality not only challenges Rome on the issue of numbers but also calls into question a whole series of European assumptions about religious practices. Or, as *The Rose*'s hero remarked, in what could be a definition of liberation theology, "Many of these 'heresies' . . . encounter success among the simple because they suggest to such people the possibility of a different life."[1]

Throughout the Third World the "simple" have begun to make a connection between religion and politics that is radically different from colonialist Catholicism's support for elitist governments. Although the latter promised equality in heaven, on earth it encouraged cultural inferiority and religious fatalism—the belief that "I'm a nothing," heard so often in Third World slums. The internal structures of the church reinforced those of secular society through a top-down hierarchy run by white men in a foreign capital. But Vatican II, which convened in the period when many colonies became independent nations, changed perceptions by stating unequivocally that everyone—black, brown, yellow, or white, cardinal or peasant, Latin American or Roman—was an equal in the sight of God. The concept of the "People of God"—of many different peoples with complementary responsibilities and charisms within the church—carried a message of empowerment that broke with the colonial past. It suggested, for example, that a theologian did not have to be a European in order to propose new directions for the church. It meant that statues and paintings of the Holy Family and the Apostles no longer had to depict white people with golden curls. The stifling ceremonies of old, with Masses in an unintelligible Latin, were replaced by lively local rituals in which pent-up cultural energies burst forth in new forms of liturgy, particularly dancing and singing. Most important, religious empowerment provided the training tools for political democratization.

These changes have not been limited to one country or region but reflect a worldwide phenomenon in which the "simple" have become the majority in the church. With 900 million members Catholicism now ranks as the world's largest religion. At home in every continent, it is culturally and ethnically more diverse than at any time in its history. But if it were given a face, its color would not be white: More than half the Catholic population lives in the Third World. By the end of the century the figure will rise to 70 percent, with Latin America accounting for the largest number. Such a far-reaching change has occurred only once before in Christianity, wrote the late Jesuit theologian Karl Rahner—in the first century, when the primitive church, under the Apostle Paul, opened itself to the diverse cultures of the ancient world.[2]

The importance of the "simple" does not lie in numbers alone, for they have begun to challenge First World Catholics on two important questions. One is the kind of church best suited to deal with the needs of the third millennium. The other is the mission of the church—its reason for being. Unencumbered by vast quantities of material goods, and forced to struggle for their daily bread, the poor constantly contend with life-and-death issues that make the "values that must survive" stand out in stark relief. Chief among them are service, solidarity, justice, and charity. "Poor nations undoubtedly need aid from the First World for their own development," said Bishop Luís Fernandes, an advocate of Brazil's base community movement. "On the other hand, rich nations really need poor nations in order to breathe in the human, Christian, and evangelical values that flourish more naturally in poor countries. Rich people need poor people to call into question the false happiness that they cling to and that leaves only the bitter taste of frustration."[3]

Although the Third World is as much a prey as the First to greedy exploiters and political demagogues, its communal traditions have never-theless survived, in contrast to the highly individualistic societies in the industrialized nations. Such traditions have encouraged the development of decentralized churches whose structure is more horizontal than vertical. Deeply rooted in the local culture, these faith communities promote co-responsibility—each member has a different talent, and all, including the pastor, view their gifts as a service. The communities have also developed their own liturgies and theologies to correspond to their reality. These are not intellectual exercises, devised in a university or theological faculty, but the living expression of a people seeking a more Christ-centered faith as well as a way to cope with life's problems. Gradually the people grad-uate from a "cared-for community" to a "caring community," reaching out to other groups, sometimes of different faiths, in a common endeavor, as in Africa and Latin America, where many church communities have joined together to protest repression. As observed by Ivan Vallier, a U.S. pioneer in the sociological study of religion in Latin America, the linkage between religion and human welfare "enhances the charisma of both, helping to bring sacred meaning to the latter and secular legitimacy to the former."[4]

The supportive structure of these communal churches gives the peo-ple a courage they might otherwise lack, and indeed many Third World churches have thrived because of the blood of martyrs, particularly in Latin America. These churches also give their people a needed sense of empowerment to deal with the temporal authorities. The more they are repressed, the more they grow, as shown by the "church of the catacombs" in El Quiché, Guatemala, which flourished despite military persecution of catechists, priests, and nuns. (See Chapter 1, pp. 5–7.) But the faith communities that endure do not see political power as an end. Though they seek justice and peace, their fundamental concern is religion. Car-dinal Paulo Evaristo Arns, the archbishop of São Paulo, underscored the point in his description of local Christian base communities: "People do not come to the base communities when there is no praying or singing. They may come four or five times to organize practical things, but nothing further will come of it. When, however, people pray and sing, when they feel themselves together, when the Gospel is read and, on this basis, actions are taken and the national situation is analyzed, then the groups remain united. Along with the Gospels, this religiosity is the most valuable element in the base communities."[5]

In other words, first things first. While the Brazilian base communities have spawned politically active groups, particularly at the local level, they have managed to retain the distinction between religion and partisan politics. Although some members identify with the left-of-center Workers Party, base community leaders believe it would not be good for the communities or the party to amalgamate. The base communities have something different to offer, providing a light—a challenge—to an imperfect secular society. The experience of Nicaragua's base communities, which were largely absorbed by the revolutionary government, has also been a cautionary lesson to churches in other countries and may help explain the increased emphasis on spiritual and biblical themes by liberation theologians.

As elsewhere in the Third World, the Latin Americans' new faith communities could not survive without the encouragement and protection of the institutional church. Such ties represent a continuum with existing traditions, but at the same time the communities have reached back to the roots of Christianity in the early church. They also pose a challenge to postindustrial society by demanding that the state be at the service of the people, not vice versa. All this might seem pie-in-the-sky—most prophetic groups are so viewed—were it not for the amazing changes that have occurred in the Latin American church in only two decades. If such a hierarchical, reactionary church could renew itself in so short a time, said the Swiss Catholic writer Walbert Buhlmann, then there is hope for churches in other parts of the world. While admitting that the base communities represented no more than 5 percent of the Latin American population and that they faced many dangers, from the Vatican as well as the state, Buhlmann found it a sign of hope that a seed should have been planted at all.[6] Twenty years of watering have produced approximately 300,000 communities in Latin America—not much perhaps for the effort and blood expended, but change has often come about through such small groups of committed people.

The communitarian model of church emerging in the Third World is based on service, and its challenge lies in its radicalness—in the dual knowledge that while the Kingdom of God lies not in this world, the community's witness on behalf of love and peace makes its membership more worthy of God's promise, and also makes the earthly kingdom a more habitable place. Throughout history churches and synagogues have claimed to stand for peace and justice; hence, their frequent involvement in politics as a means to achieve such ends. But more often than not, they have been an instrument of partisan politics instead of assuming a prophetic religious role in challenging the political system itself. Third World churches have begun to take the latter path. Michel Azcueta, a radical Catholic and the mayor of the sprawling Lima slum of El Salvador, told of how the first inhabitants arriving in the early 1970s built their homes in the desert. "Since we had nothing, we made everything." They did it through self-organization and the help of Catholic religious and lay leaders, including Azcueta, a teacher who has lived in El Salvador since its founding. From nothing emerged schools, health clinics, churches, popular libraries, even a radio station. The experience deepened the people's faith commitment; it also made El Salvador one of the most politically effective neighborhoods in Lima. (See Chapter 5, pp. 116–20.) But, as Azcueta said, it was politics with a difference, because religion challenged the system. "I think one begins to change," he said, "when one goes back to the Gospels and discovers a small but very important difference. When one says that it is necessary to help the poor, I think everybody accepts that. But often we hide the causes of poverty—it's easy to say that someone is poor because he is lazy or a drunkard or squanders his money. But when one decides to serve the exploited, that's when it becomes clear that poverty just doesn't happen and that there are reasons for it. That's when a political commitment arises, but it's a commitment that originates in faith itself."[7]

Two Churches

The Third World model of the Catholic Church responds to Vatican II. In countries where the process is more advanced, such as Brazil, the glimmer of a third-millennium church can be seen in a pluralistic institution that is responsive to the religious and social needs of its people and strongly challenges a materialistic and often unjust secular society. The bishops do not view their role as worldly princes of a European church but as servants of the Brazilians, particularly the poor. Such was the role sought by Vatican II, which throughout its documents urged church leaders to set examples to the faithful through community service and witness. Or as Dom Helder Cámara observed, "We who are charged with announcing the message of Christ need to learn the incomparable lesson that he taught us by his own example. He taught first of all with his life, and only then did he preach."[8]

Like Christ, the Third World's Catholic leaders have taught through example, often putting their lives on the line to defend the religious principle of the sanctity of life. When, during the military regime, Cardinal Arns called on the people to attend a Mass to protest the murder of a young student by the security forces, tens of thousands of Brazilians showed up. Arns's power did not derive from hierarchical church structures but from his courageous defense of human rights. Unlike the military, the church is a voluntary association, and for that reason it depends for its authority on the people's willingness to accept its guidance and leadership. Before Vatican II most Catholics faced an either-or choice. They either blindly accepted the institution's authority or they were not Catholics. But since then the concept of authority has shifted from the institution to the community of believers—the People of God. The power of Arns and other great church leaders comes from the people, and it grows in proportion to its use for the common good. Therein lies the division between the Third World churches and Rome: While the Vatican sees power as a way to strengthen the entrenched interests of the bureaucracy, Third World bishops, priests, nuns, and laity look on it as an instrument to enable the mass of the poor to take history into their own hands.

As Canadian archbishop Donat Chiasson pointed out following the secretive synod on the laity in 1987, John Paul's Vatican is "afraid of the dialogue" taken for granted by Vatican II churches in Canada, the United States, and the Third World. Dialogue has strengthened these churches, making them a more vital presence in their societies. But Rome is unable to "recognize that the Spirit is alive in the world. . . . What do we have to hide from people with whom we feel communion? It was very evident at the synod that there was nothing to hide except the nothingness."[9]

In contrast to Popes John and Paul, John Paul does not trust the world. Like the pre–Vatican II popes, he sees the church's mission as one of resistance to the modern world and its evils. Although he has ample reason to condemn the lack of respect for human rights in communist countries and the excessive consumerism of Western ones, he has forfeited the opportunity to make any real impact by denying the possibility of dialogue, with the world and within his own institution. Pope John recognized that a church that holds itself in "holy isolation" cannot hope to influence the ways of the world. Moreover, the scandals within the church, such as those that have plagued the Vatican Bank, suggest a hypocrisy in such holiness. As the bishops admitted at their 1971 synod, those who speak to people about justice "must first be just in their eyes."

As during the Reformation and other periods of dissent, John Paul's church has built a wall around itself and only one commander is allowed to speak for the rest. Those who criticize the papal line are subjected to Vatican investigations, interrogations, censorship, and dismissal. John Paul is marching backwards, and those who will not follow his direction have been told to leave the church. But while honestly believing that his is the only path to unity, the pope has caused widespread dissension in the church, raising the specter of schism. In Poland Catholics do not dissent publicly, although privately they ignore the church's teachings, as shown by the high rates of divorce and abortion. The appearance of unity has been crucial to the Polish church's survival, and John Paul is convinced that dissent is a sign of weakness. But what serves the Polish church does not necessarily respond to the needs of a worldwide institution with many different cultures. As the French theologian Marie-Dominique Chenu pointed out, uniformity is a caricature of genuine unity, which depends on a respect for diversity.

The key issue in the struggle is the relationship of local churches to Rome. Contrary to Vatican claims, there is no God-given reason for Rome to exercise absolute authority. Prior to Vatican I, when authority was centralized, bishops often were nominated by the local churches and the pope was expected to confirm the appointments. Earlier church councils, such as those at Constance and Basel in the fifteenth century, established the authority of the bishops as a body over that of the pope, although their rulings were later reversed. Church historians and theologians argue that papal centralization is of relatively recent origin and corresponds to secular historical developments rather than church dogma. If church structures have changed in accordance with the times, they say, there is no reason they cannot alter again, particularly since papal centralization runs counter to the pastoral directions of Vatican II. Moreover, a sharing of power would better reflect the original Christian vision: Peter's role was not to dominate the other Apostles but to serve as a sign of unity by helping them.

While bishops' appointments remain a major source of tension between local churches and the Vatican, they form part of the larger controversy over the model of church. Many of the bishops attending the 1987 synod on the laity spoke strongly of the need to support Vatican II's vision of the People of God by emphasizing service instead of the artificial divisions between clergy and laity that characterized the pre–Vatican II church and that are again apparent in John Paul's papacy. Carried to its conclusion, the vision suggests a model of church in which priests, religious, and lay people also have a say in the appointment of bishops and in the direction of local churches.

Although the Vatican may "shudder" at the mention of democracy, as one U.S. Catholic educator put it, Rome's fear of pluralism is not grounded in Scripture but reflects the traditional belief that the church structure has to be protected from outside influences in order to pursue its religious mission. But so much effort has gone into protecting the structure that the mission—spreading Christ's message—has often been ignored or relegated to a secondary role. Third World churches have challenged Rome on this crucial omission, by giving more importance to the message than the structure. In the Lima slum of El Salvador, for example, faith is lived out through service to the community, such service being an expression of deep spirituality. Or as the slum's mayor said, commitment "originates in faith itself." As in similar communities elsewhere in the Third World, religious commitment strengthens and is strengthened by such democratic practices as participation, representation, and consent. Church historians argue that Roman Catholicism would also be strengthened by democratic procedures that enable all to participate in spreading the message. The most commonly cited is a synod of bishops that would meet periodically to make laws with the consent of the pope; the pope, however, could not make laws without the consent of the synod. Moreover, the synod would be truly representative by including delegates of the clergy, religious orders, and lay men and women as well as bishops. It would control its own agenda, follow parliamentary procedures, and keep a public record of debates. The pope would continue to run the church government as its executive head, but the synod would serve as a check on authoritarian tendencies.

While the proposal may sound reasonable enough to Catholics accustomed to democratic traditions, there is no possibility of such an opening in John Paul's lifetime. On the contrary, said Archbishop Chiasson, "The door is being closed on the openness that was promoted by the Second Vatican Council." Chiasson believes that the real church "is lived at home" and that this church will safeguard the promise of Vatican II. Such, too, is the belief of many church leaders in the Third World and the United States. Although they admit that the Vatican can cause them trouble, they contend that the changes brought about by Vatican II are too far advanced to be undone. As Milwaukee's Archbishop Weakland told the pope on his 1987 visit to the United States, the faithful want to contribute to the formulation of teachings and to collaborate fully in the life of the church—they want to be treated not as children but as thoughtful adults. Church leaders also agree with Notre Dame theologian Richard McBrien, who said that the pope is enough of a political realist to back away from controversial issues when the outcry from the faithful is loud enough, as occurred in Archbishop Hunthausen's case. The principal problem, according to the bishops, is not an individual case that might be resolved through "better communications" with the pope, but that John Paul—like President Reagan—has succeeded in setting the agenda. Instead of concentrating on how to spread the Christian message, the bishops have constantly been on the defensive in meeting challenges from Rome. For example, the message of the U.S. bishops' economic pastoral, which should have been the highlight of their annual meeting in 1986, was overshadowed by the media's focus on the battles with Rome over Archbishop Hunthausen. Yet as Vatican II recognized, the most important challenge facing modern Catholicism is not internal church organization but the conversion of hearts and minds to religious values.[10]

As Brazilian Bishop Fernandes said, such values have a better chance of survival in poorer cultures not yet contaminated by the "therapeutic ideology of self-absorption," in the words of one U.S. Catholic critic.[11] Surveys of American attitudes do not paint a promising future: According to a 1986 *Washington Post*–ABC News poll of eighteen- to twenty-five-year-olds, only 43 percent listed "developing a meaningful philosophy of life" as an important goal, whereas 83 percent of those surveyed in 1967 believed such a philosophy important. While less than half of those in the 1967 survey regarded "being very well off financially" as essential, 71 percent in the 1986 poll said it was. The shift from spiritual and intellectual to materialistic values has paralleled a decline in ethics in the secular arena, which even hard-nosed business leaders admit is distressing. On the other hand, the *Post*-ABC poll reflected a liberal attitude toward social mores and government, confirming the results of numerous other surveys that showed a strong respect for freedom and tolerance. Yet religious analysts question the reliability of liberal attitudes under stress, such as a sharp economic downturn, without a "meaningful philosophy of life" to back them up.[12]

Polls show that Americans want their churches to pay more attention to their religious needs, but at the same time they want their society to become more ethical. Yet if the churches do not address the moral questions of public policy, who will? The answer, according to pastors and priests, is that the people will—or could—if the churches stop dictating to them and encourage them to take responsibility for their own decisions. As shown by the backlash against fundamentalist politicians in the 1986 election and the unfavorable publicity generated by the insistence of Cardinals Law and O'Connor that Catholic politicians uphold Catholic doctrine, the majority of Americans do not want to be told whom to vote for. They will listen to arguments about the religious issues in public debate but will not be persuaded by religious absolutism. No church, not even the Catholic, the largest, is in a position to dictate the choice of values, and quite a few religious leaders believe they should not try to dictate at all.

Three sides have emerged in the debate—those, such as Protestant and Catholic fundamentalists, who believe that partisan politics is the means to achieve a particular set of values; progressive church people who want to establish a coalition with secular movements to change foreign and domestic policies; and centrists and progressives who contend that too much time is being spent on social activism and not enough on the formation of religious values. The third group believes that churches must regain the crucial "apart-ness" of the early Christian church in its religious witness. That witness was a demanding one that did not preach the lowest common denominator in order to be accepted but followed a radical way of community life faithful to the Galilean vision. Nor did it flee the world, as the pre–Vatican II church did. Instead, it confronted it on its own religious terms—as has the Sanctuary movement in the United States. Law-abiding citizens who have joined Sanctuary do not defy the law for political reasons but for religious ones, to succor their suffering brothers and sisters. Their example may not change the politics of immigration, but it certainly has tested it where it most needs challenging—on religious and moral grounds.

Although the U.S. bishops have taken a prophetic role in issuing such pastorals as the letters on peace and the economy, the majority of Catholics lag behind, in part because they are unaware of Catholic social teaching but also because they lack the community formation to "let go." It is "so difficult to bring ourselves to let go of what is familiar, secure and comfortable" to take on a new perspective, said Archbishop Hunthausen. "One can learn of new ways of living only when one is open to letting go of the old." But Catholics will not be open to different perspectives until they take more responsibility for their church communities. This may be the "Catholic moment," said layman John A. McDermott, but the community as a whole has less effect on public issues than the

Jews or the Quakers. "Despite the Second Vatican Council's call for reforms in terms of collegiality in governance and the concept of the 'People of God,' little has actually changed in the experience of most lay people. For most of us, we are *in* the church but not *of* it. Few pastoral councils or parish councils have emerged to become stable institutions of collegial participation and shared governance. Much of what is offered lay people by way of participation has been rudely but tellingly described as 'Catholic Sandbox.' " Consequently many Catholics lack the sense that the church can be "an organizing principle for their whole lives."[13]

Monsignor George G. Higgins, who for years worked in the cause of justice and peace as the U.S. Catholic Church's spokesman on labor-management issues, also worried about a "churchy" trend that places more emphasis on the role of church professionals in promoting justice and defending human rights than in the participation of the People of God—or ordinary Catholics. "We must be prepared to listen to those members of the laity who think that . . . the church in the United States is devoting a lot of time, energy and money to training and feeding church professionals, both clerical and lay, and insufficient time, energy and money to programs aimed at helping lay people prepare themselves to play their own autonomous role as Christians in the temporal order."[14]

Higgins's and McDermott's point is that if American society is to become more concerned with values, the churches must give more time to developing those values and less to social activism, for without values social and political change is meaningless. Chilean liberation theologian Pablo Richard made a similar observation in a different context—a meeting with an old friend in Caracas who is a priest and a biblical expert. The man told Richard that he had stopped doing interpretive studies of the Bible in order to work full-time in a poor neighborhood with a group of young people. " 'But that's the function of the local minister!' I retorted. 'You're doing what they should be doing!' We have to start believing in local people," insisted Richard. Priests and other religious professionals have an important role to play as teachers, said the theologian, but lay people must also become ministers to the community and the rest of the world. "That was basically the structure of the primitive church."[15]

Richard was speaking about base communities in Latin America, and, as the Latin American liberation theologians have pointed out, it is improbable that the same community structures or theology can be transferred to a society as different as that of the United States. More likely are small faith communities that grow within local church structures, such as the parish. That the seeds are there is shown by the increasing number of Catholics who have rediscovered Jesus, the growth of parishes run by lay people in areas without priests, and the development of a nationwide network of lay groups dedicated to peace and greater opportunities for the poor.

Catholics are also resisting the Vatican's attempted rollback, believing, as U.S. theologian Charles Curran said, that "it's my church, too." The People of God will continue their march, despite the power plays and intrigue in Rome. And the Third World will continue to beckon to the First, reminding it of the Galilean vision of Christian solidarity. As a young Guatemalan said, a few months before she was killed by the military, " 'What good is life unless you give it away?' [Mark 8:35]— unless you can give it for a better world, even if you never see that world but have only carried your grain of sand to the building site. Then you're fulfilled as a person."[16]

Central America's "martyrs do not die for mystical ideals," said Father Fernando Bermúdez, who worked with the Guatemalan poor in the war-ravaged region of El Quiché. "Nor do they die just to get themselves to heaven. They die because they want life in this world for everyone, because they want a new society."[17]

NOTES

Chapter 1:
The Way of the Cross

1. Fernando Bermúdez, *Death and Resurrection in Guatemala* (Maryknoll: Orbis Books, 1986). Bermúdez's small book is among the most moving accounts of the persecution of the Guatemalan church. See also Penny Lernoux, "Revolution and Counterrevolution in the Central American Church," *Revolution and Counterrevolution in Central America and the Caribbean* (Boulder: Westview Press, 1984), pp. 117–52; Phillip Berryman, *The Religious Roots of Rebellion* (Maryknoll: Orbis Books, 1984), pp. 35–46, 163–23.

2. Bermúdez, ibid., p. 63.

3. Jim Wallis, *The Call to Conversion* (San Francisco: Harper & Row, 1981), p. 174.

4. Aristides, "Apology 15," *The Ante-Nicene Fathers*, ed. Allan Menzies (New York: Charles Scribner's Sons, 1926), pp. 263–79.

5. The Rev. D. I. Lanslots, OSB, *The Primitive Church* (Rockford: Tan Books, reprint of Herder Book Co., 1926), p. 42.

6. The Rev. Matthew L. Lamb, "Liberation Theology and Social Justice," *Process Studies*, Summer 1985, p. 119.

7. Conference of Major Superiors of Men and the Leadership Conference of Women Religious, "The Role of U.S. Religious in Human Promotion," Washington, D.C., 1984, p. 7.

8. Author's interview with Giancarlo Zízola, Rome, October 1986.

9. Walter Russell Mead, *Mortal Splendor* (Boston: Houghton Mifflin, 1987), p. 38.

10. See Chapter 3, page 00.

11. *Latinamerica Press*, July 16, 1987; "Justice in the World," Part III (Synod of Bishops, Rome, 1971).

12. Giancarlo Zízola, *La Restauración del Papa Wojtyla* (Madrid: Ediciones Cristiandad, 1985), p. 318.

13. *National Catholic Reporter*, May 8, 1987.

14. *National Catholic Reporter*, May 15, 1987; *Sojourners*, January 1987.

15. Author's interviews, United States, Europe, and Latin America, 1985–86; *Latinamerica Press*, July 16, 1987.

16. *Latinamerica Press*, ibid.; Zízola, *La Restauración del Papa Wojtyla*, p. 320.

17. John A. McDermott, "Weakness Amid Strength: The Roman Catholic Paradox," *New Oxford Review*, July/August 1986.

Chapter 2:
The Reawakening

1. The Rev. Hans Küng, *On Being a Christian* (New York: Doubleday, 1976), p. 497.

2. Paul Johnson, *A History of Christianity* (New York: Atheneum, 1977), p. 275.

3. Ibid., p. 356.

4. Richard Gilman, *Faith, Sex, Mystery* (New York: Simon and Schuster, 1986), p. 211.

5. The Rev. Avery Dulles, S.J., "The Church," *The Documents of Vatican II* (London: Geoffrey Chapman, 1972), p. 11.

Chapter 3:
The Catholic Counterreformation

1. Penny Lernoux, *Cry of the People* (New York: Penguin, 1982), p. 427.
2. Interview with Father Marie-Dominique Chenu in *Il Regno* (Bologna), August 1983; Giancarlo Zízola, *La Restauración del Papa Wojtyla* (Madrid: *Ediciones Cristiandad*, 1985), p. 65; interviews with author, Rome and Bologna, October 1986.
3. Trevor Hall and Kathryn Spink, *Pope John Paul II: A Man & His People* (New York: Exeter, 1985), p. 26.
4. Janine Wedel, "The Myth of the 'Mother Church' in Poland," Pacific News Service, September 22, 1986.
5. T. M. Pasca, "The Three Churches of Catholicism," *The Nation*, February 1, 1986.
6. *National Catholic Reporter*, October 16, 1981.
7. Ibid.
8. See, for example, John Paul's encyclicals, *Redemptor Hominis* and *Laborem Exercens*.
9. Zízola, *La Restauración del Papa Wojtyla*; Hall and Spink, *Pope John Paul II: A Man & His People*; George Huntston Williams, *The Mind of John Paul II* (New York: Seabury, 1981); Mieczyslaw Malinski, *Pope John Paul II* (New York: Seabury, 1979); interviews with author, Rome, October 1986.
10. Hall and Spink, *Pope John Paul II: A Man & His People*, p. 37.
11. Peter Hebblethwaite, "Understanding Pope Wojtyla" and "The Popes and Politics," *IDOC Bulletin* (Rome), No. 11–12, 1982.
12. Author's interview, September 1986.
13. Frei Leonardo Boff, *Church: Charism & Power* (New York: Crossroad, 1986), p. 46 (translation of *Igreja: Carisma e poder*, published by Editora Vozes, Petrópolis, Brazil, 1981).
14. Author's interview, Rome, October 1986.

15. Author's interview, Rome, October 1986.
16. Author's interview, Rome, October 1986.
17. Author's interview, Rome, October 1986.
18. Author's interview, Rome, October 1986.
19. Author's interview, Bogotá, September 1986.
20. Johann Baptist Metz, *The Emergent Church* (New York: Crossroad, 1981), pp. 121–23; Zízola, *La Restauración del Papa Wojtyla*, pp. 82, 244–245; author's interview with Metz, Massachusetts, July 1986.
21. Zízola, *La Restauración del Papa Wojtyla*, pp. 184–86; Pasca, "The Three Churches of Catholicism."
22. Zízola, ibid.
23. Zízola, ibid., p. 220; *O São Paulo* (newspaper of archdiocese of São Paulo), June 1, 8, and 22, 1984; *Folha de São Paulo*, June 1, 1984; *Istoé*, June 6, 1984; *Manchete*, June 16, 1984; author's interviews, June/July, 1984.
24. Author's interview, Italy, October 1986.
25. Johnson, *A History of Christianity*, p. 172.
26. Author's interviews, Rome, 1986.
27. Zízola, *La Restauración del Papa Wojtyla*, p. 79.
28. Author's interview, Rome, 1986.
29. *National Catholic Reporter*, September 12 and 19 and November 21, 1986; *Newsweek*, December 15, 1986; *Vida Nueva* (Madrid), October 11, 1986; Zízola, *La Restauración del Papa Wojtyla*, p. 277; author's interviews, Rome, 1986.
30. *New York Times*, June 25, 1984; Associated Press, March 18, 1986; A. Roy Megarry, "Church in Politics: a Puzzling Stand," *Globe and Mail* (Toronto), August 28, 1986; author's interview, Rome, October, 1986.
31. ANSA news agency, February 7, 1986; *National Catholic Reporter*,

March 7, 1986; *Newsweek*, April 14, 1986; "Marcos' Legacy," *IDOC Bulletin* 86/5, September/October, 1986; author's interview, Rome, October 1986.

32. *Mustard Seed* (monthly publication of the Franciscans), September 1986; *Time*, February 24, 1986; *Newsweek*, April 14, 1986; *New York Times* feature service, March 8, 1986; *National Catholic Reporter*, March 28, 1986; author's interviews, Rome, October 1986.

33. Ibid.; *National Catholic Reporter*, February 21, 1986.

34. *National Catholic Reporter*, January 30 and February 6 and 13, 1987; *Vida Nueva* April 16, 1987.

35. Ibid.; author's interviews, Rome, October 1986; *Cape Times*, August 29, 1986; South Africa Crisis Information Group, August 28, 1986; *Vida Nueva*, October 11, 1986, and April 16, 1987; *L'Osservatore Romano*, August 31, 1986.

36. *National Catholic Reporter*, April 4, 1986; "tombstones" (or legally required advertisements about bond issues and government loans) relating to participation in the South African bond issues by the Banco di Roma per la Svizzera published in *Frankfurter Allgemeine*, June 11, 1985; *Financial Times*, September 28, 1982; *International Herald Tribune*, June 1, 1983; *Handelsblatt*, December 2, 1982, and November 16–17, 1984; letter from board of directors, Banco di Roma per la Svizzera, n.d., part of enclosure with Vatican correspondence, November 11, 1985.

37. Pope John Paul II, *Redemptor Hominis*, Rome, March 4, 1979; Associated Press, May 18, 1985.

38. Gianni Baget Bozzo, "The Conservative Pope and the Innovator Karol Wojtyla," *IDOC Bulletin* No. 11–12.

39. Hebblethwaite, "The Popes and Politics"; *Time*, September 28, 1981.

40. Hebblethwaite, ibid.; Pope John Paul II, *Laborem Exercens*, Rome, September 14, 1981.

41. Ibid; Zízola, *La Restauración del Papa Wojtyla*, pp. 200–201; Paul

Lakeland, "Economics as a Religious Issue," *Cross Currents*, Winter 1985–86.

42. *Laborem Exercens*, op. cit.

43. Lakeland, "Economics as a Religious Issue"; Boff, *Church: Charism & Power*, pp. 55–56.

44. Author's interview, Rome, October 1986.

45. Author's interview, Rome, October 1986.

46. *National Catholic Reporter*, September 6, 1985; Zízola, *La Restauración del Papa Wojtyla*, pp. 43–49.

47. *National Catholic Reporter*, October 16, 1981; *Vida Nueva*, February 14, 1987.

48. *National Catholic Reporter*, February 15, 1980; *Vida Nueva*, ibid.; collected speeches of John Paul II on his trip to the United States in 1979 in *U.S.A.: The Message of Justice, Peace and Love* (Boston: St. Paul Editions, 1979).

49. *New York Times*, December 23, 1986.

50. *National Catholic Reporter*, January 25, 1980; Zízola, *La Restauración del Papa Wojtyla*, pp. 121–22.

51. Zízola, ibid., pp. 122–26; Johnson, *A History of Christianity*, pp. 163–164; *National Catholic Reporter*, February 1, 1980.

52. Zízola, *La Restauración del Papa Wojtyla*, p. 125; *National Catholic Reporter*, January 25, 1980.

53. Zízola, ibid.

54. United Press International, May 12, 1985; Agence France Presse, May 12, 1985; Zízola, *La Restauración del Papa Wojtyla*, p. 128.

55. Conor Cruise O'Brien, "God and Man in Nicaragua," *Atlantic Monthly*, August 1986.

56. Ibid.; *El Salvador Bulletin* (Berkeley), April 1983; Zízola, *La Restauración del Papa Wojtyla*, p. 93.

57. O'Brien, "God and Man in Nicaragua"; Hall and Spink, *Pope John Paul II: A Man & His People*, pp. 62–63; Phillip Berryman, *The Religious Roots of Rebellion* (Maryknoll: Orbis, 1984), p. 274.

58. *Semana* (Bogotá), February 5, 1985.

59. *Semana*, August 26, 1986.

60. *Catholic New York*, December 18, 1986.

61. Zízola, *La Restauración del Papa Wojtyla*, pp. 86–87, 111; author's interview with Zízola, Rome, October 1986; *Time*, May 19, 1980; *National Catholic Reporter*, May 16, 1980.

62. Author's interview, Bologna, October 1986.

63. *El Tiempo* (Bogotá), June 27, 1986.

64. Author's interview, Bogotá, June 1986.

65. Zízola, *La Restauración del Papa Wojtyla*, pp. 278–80.

66. *National Catholic Reporter*, May 2, 1986; *New York Times*, January 14, 1987; Agence France Presse, February 19, 1987.

67. *MIZ* (Berlin), March 15, 1986.

68. Author's interviews, February and September, 1986.

69. Author's interviews, Rome, October 1986; Religious News Service, April 17, 1986.

70. Author's interviews, Rome, October 1986.

71. Thomas F. Troy, *Donovan and the CIA: A History of the Establishment of the Central Intelligence Agency* (Maryland: Aletheia Books, 1981); Hearings before the Committee on Standards of Official Conduct, House of Representatives, 1976, p. 662, from report as printed in *The Village Voice*, February 16, 1976, and addended to transcript of the hearings; *National Catholic Reporter*, February 27, 1981.

72. Author's interview, Rome, October 1986.

73. *National Catholic Reporter*, February 20 and 27 and April 3, 1987.

74. *National Catholic Reporter*, May 15, 1987.

75. Penny Lernoux, "Blood Taints Church in Argentina," *National Catholic Reporter*, April 12, 1985; Emilio F. Mignone, *Iglesia y Dictadura* (Buenos Aires: Ediciones del Pensamiento Nacional, 1986), pp. 85–93; author's interviews, Rome, October 1986.

76. *New York Times*, January 30, 1987.

77. *Business Week*, July 28, 1980; *National Catholic Reporter*, October 2, 1981.

78. Author's interview, New York, May 1986; *New York Times*, July 10, 1984.

79. The Rev. Thomas J. Reese, S.J., "U.S. Relations with the Holy See," *America*, January 17, 1987.

80. *National Catholic Reporter*, October 2, 1981.

81. Author's interview, Rome, October 1986; *New York Times*, May 21 and 22, 1986; Associated Press, May 21, 1986; *National Catholic Reporter*, April 4, 1986.

82. Author's interviews, Rome, October 1986.

83. Colman McCarthy, "Pope 'Weak-Hearted' Where Heart Counts," *National Catholic Reporter*, October 9, 1987.

**Chapter 4:
Liberation Theology:
Rome versus Latin America**

1. The book *The Ratzinger Report* (San Francisco: Ignatius Press, 1985) was based on an exclusive interview with Cardinal Ratzinger by Italian journalist Vittorio Messorio. It was a sellout in Italy, the United States, and other countries.

2. Author's interview, Rome, October 1986.

3. E. J. Dionne, Jr., "The Pope's Guardian of Orthodoxy," *New York Times Magazine*, November 24, 1985; Hans Küng, "Speaking Out After a Long Silence," *National Catholic Reporter*, October 11, 1985; Peter Hebblethwaite, "Ratzinger: Young Turk to Grand Inquisitor," *National Catholic Reporter*, May 24, 1985.

4. Giancarlo Zízola, *La Restaura-*

ción del Papa Wojtyla (Madrid: *Edi-ciones Cristiandad*, 1985), p. 134; *National Catholic Reporter*, January 31 and March 7, 1986.

5. Hebblethwaite, "Ratzinger: Young Turk"; *The Ratzinger Report*, pp. 141–42.

6. Dionne, "The Pope's Guardian of Orthodoxy."

7. Ibid.

8. *The Ratzinger Report*, pp. 141–142.

9. Adista religious news agency (Rome), November 25, 1985; *National Catholic Reporter*, June 21, 1985; Küng, "Speaking Out After a Long Silence."

10. *The Ratzinger Report*, p. 43; Daniel C. Maguire, "The Power and the Prole," *National Catholic Reporter*, May 2, 1986.

11. *The Ratzinger Report*, p. 36; interviews with author, Germany, 1976, and Rome, 1986; James Fallows, "Vatican City," *National Geographic*, December 1985.

12. *Washington Post*, November 14, 1986.

13. *National Catholic Reporter*, November 23, 1979.

14. *The Ratzinger Report*, p. 147.

15. Küng, "Speaking Out After a Long Silence."

16. Dionne, "The Pope's Guardian of Orthodoxy."

17. *National Catholic Reporter*, November 26, 1986.

18. Interview with author, Rome, October 1986; *Newsweek*, October 20, 1986.

19. Penny Lernoux, *Cry of the People* (New York: Penguin, 1982), p. xix.

20. *National Catholic Reporter*, quoting Major Gen. Robert L. Schweitzer, October 30, 1981.

21. The Committee of Santa Fe, *A New Inter-American Policy for the Eighties* (Santa Fe, N.M., 1980).

22. *National Catholic Reporter*, April 6, 1984.

23. Phillip Berryman, *Liberation*

Theology (New York, Pantheon, 1986), p. 215.

24. Zízola, *La Restauración del Papa Wojtyla*, pp. 25–26.

25. Interview with author, Bogotá, March 1984.

26. *Newsweek*, April 14, 1986.

27. *National Catholic Reporter*, December 6, 1985.

28. Luis Pásara, *Radicalización y conflicto en la Iglesia peruana* (Lima: Ediciones El Virrey, 1986), p. 139; *Latinamerica Press* (Lima), May 10, 1984; Zízola, *La Restauración del Papa Wojtyla*, p. 237.

29. Interviews with author, Bogotá, March 1984.

30. Zízola, *La Restauración del Papa Wojtyla*, p. 264; *National Catholic Reporter*, October 19, 1984; author's interviews, Lima, January/February, 1985.

31. John Paul's speech to the Peruvian bishops, Rome, October 4, 1984.

32. Peruvian Episcopal Conference, "A Challenge to the Faith," Lima, November 26, 1984.

33. Giancarlo Zízola, "Parla il teologo Gutiérrez, *Il Giorno*, October 5, 1984.

34. Berryman, *Liberation Theology*, p. 210; *The Ratzinger Report*, p. 170.

35. Author's interview with Bishop Ivo Lorscheiter, Santo Domingo, Dominican Republic, October 1984.

36. Alfred T. Hennelly, S.J., "The Red-Hot Issue: Liberation Theology," *America*, May 24, 1986.

37. Berryman, *Liberation Theology*, p. 199.

38. *National Catholic Reporter*, August 16, 1985.

39. Author's interview with Archbishop Arturo Rivera y Damas, Santo Domingo, October 1984.

40. Congregation for the Doctrine of the Faith, "Instruction on Christian Freedom and Liberation," Vatican City, March 22, 1986.

41. *Newsweek*, April 14, 1986.

42. "Instruction on Christian Free-

dom and Liberation"; *Latinamerica Press*, May 1, 1986; *National Catholic Reporter*, April 18 and May 9, 1986.

43. "Instruction on Christian Freedom and Liberation."

44. Author's interviews, Puebla, January 1979; Bogotá, February 1979 and March 1984; Brazil, 1980 and 1984.

45. *Latinamerica Press*, June 7, 1984; *National Catholic Reporter*, April 20, 1984.

46. Interview with Leonardo Boff, *Latinamerica Press*, September 1, 1983; *National Catholic Reporter*, October 12, 1984; correspondence with author, October 1, 1984.

47. *Latinamerica Press*, September 27, 1984.

48. Author's interview, South America, 1984.

49. *Semana* (Bogotá), October 8, 1984.

50. Ibid.; Zízola, *La Restauración del Papa Wojtyla*, p. 262.

51. *National Catholic Reporter*, March 7, 1986.

52. *Newsweek*, April 4, 1986.

53. *Movimento Nacional dos Direitos Humanos, Roma Locuta* (Petrópolis: Editora Vozes, 1985).

54. *National Catholic Reporter*, April 11, 1986.

55. Author's interviews, Bogotá, September 1986.

56. Ibid.

57. Ibid.

58. *Latinamerica Press*, May 1, 1986.

59. *National Catholic Reporter*, April 25, 1986.

60. *Latinamerica Press*, August 28, 1986.

61. Ibid.; author's interviews, Bogotá, September 1986; Adista news agency, March 2, 1987.

Chapter 5:
Religious Empowerment:
The Rise of Popular Movements

1. Author's interview, Lima, February 1985.

2. The Rev. Edward L. Cleary, O.P., *Crisis and Change* (Maryknoll: Orbis, 1985), p. 124.

3. Daniel Levine, "Religion and Politics: Drawing Lines, Understanding Change," *Latin American Research Review*, Vol. XX, No. 1, 1985, pp. 185–200.

4. *National Catholic Reporter*, March 6, 1987; *Latin America Update*, July/August 1986; *Latinamerica Press*, October 9, 1986; *Latin American Weekly Report* (London), March 19, 1987.

5. *Latin American Regional Reports Brazil* (London), November 27, 1986; *Latin American Weekly Report*, October 9, 1986.

6. *Sem Terra* (São Paulo), August 1986; author's interview with Bishop Tomás Balduino, Bogotá, September 1986.

7. *Brasil* (São Paulo), July 1986; *National Catholic Reporter*, July 18 and November 14, 1986; *Sem Terra*, July 1986.

8. *Brasil*, ibid.; *Latin American Regional Reports Brazil*, July 10, 1986; *World Press Review*, September 1986.

9. *Latin American Regional Reports Brazil*, July 10, 1986.

10. Interview, Bogotá, February 1986; *National Catholic Reporter*, April 10, 1987; *Vida Nueva*, March 7, 1987; *Latinamerica Press*, July 3, 1986; *Latin American Weekly Report*, Sept. 4, 1986; *News Notes* (Maryknoll Justice and Peace Office), July 1986.

11. *Wall Street Journal*, August 28, 1986; *New York Times*, July 7, 1986; *Latin American Weekly Report*, June 26, 1986; *Brasil*, September 1986; author's interview, Bishop Balduino.

12. *Latinamerica Press*, July 31, 1986; author's interview, Bishop Balduino; *Latin America Update*, July/August 1986; *Latin American Weekly*

Report, June 26, 1986; *Latin American Regional Reports Brazil*, September 18, 1986; interview with Cardinal Paulo Evaristo Arns, *Report on the Americas*, September/December 1986.

13. *Latin American Regional Reports Brazil*, September 18, 1986; *New York Times*, July 7, 1986; *El Espectador* (Bogotá), July 4, 1986; *Latinamerica Press*, October 9, 1986.

14. *Brasil*, June and July, 1986; *Latin American Weekly Report*, June 26, 1986; *Latinamerica Press*, October 9, 1986; *National Catholic Reporter*, October 25, 1985.

15. *Latinamerica Press*, July 3, 1986; *News Notes*, July 1986.

16. *Latinamerica Press*, July 3, 1986; *Brasil*, June 1986.

17. *Latinamerica Press*, October 9, 1986.

18. *Report on the Americas*, September/December 1986; *Latinamerica Press*, October 16, 1986.

19. Maria Helena Moreira Alves, "Grassroots Organizations, Trade Unions, and the Church," *IDOC Bulletin*, vol. 16, no. 4, August 1985.

20. *Newsweek*, December 9, 1985.

21. *Brasil: Nunca Mais* with preface by Cardinal Paulo Evaristo Arns (Petrópolis: Editora Vozes, 1985).

22. Author's interview with Bishop Balduino; author's interview with Frei Gilberto Gorgulho, Bogotá, September 1986; Jane Kramer, "Letter from the Elysian Fields," *The New Yorker*, March 2, 1987.

23. Tarcisio Beal, "Brazil's New Church: Revolution and Reaction," n.d.

24. Scott Mainwaring, "Brazil: The Catholic Church and the Popular Movement in Nova Iguaçu, 1974–1985," *Religion and Political Conflict in Latin America* (Chapel Hill: University of North Carolina Press, 1986); author's interviews, São Paulo, November 1984.

25. *O São Paulo*, July 18, 1986; Beal, "Brazil's New Church"; author's interview, Bogotá, February 26, 1987.

26. Kramer, "Letter from the Ely-sian Fields"; author's interview, Bogotá, October 1, 1986.

27. *Latinamerica Press*, October 16, 1986.

28. Kramer, "Letter from the Elysian Fields"; *Veja* (Brazil), March 26, 1986; author's interviews, Bogotá, September 1985 and February 26, 1987.

29. Author's interviews, Brazil, November 1984, and Rome, October 1986; *Latinamerica Press*, March 21, 1985; *Wall Street Journal*, August 28, 1986.

30. Author's interviews, Conceição do Araguaia, July 1980.

31. *El Mercurio* (Santiago), March 2, 1987; Agence France-Presse, March 14, 1987.

32. Ibid.; *Cauce* (Santiago), March 9, 1987; *New York Times*, March 14, 1987.

33. "Chile Briefing," Amnesty International, September 1986.

34. *El Mercurio*, March 2, 1987; *El Tiempo* (Bogotá), April 4, 1987; *National Catholic Reporter*, April 17, 1987; author's interview, Bogotá, April 1987; *Latinamerica Press*, April 16, 1987.

35. *New York Times*, April 1, 1987; *Washington Post*, April 1, 1987.

36. Ibid.

37. *Newsweek*, September 15, 1986; Amnesty International *Annual Report*, 1986, p. 135; "Chile Briefing"; *Time*, September 22, 1986; *Latin American Weekly Report*, September 25, 1986.

38. Ibid.

39. *Latin American Regional Reports Southern Cone*, July 3, 1986.

40. *El Mercurio*, March 30, 1987.

41. *Newsweek*, September 15, 1986; *Time*, September 22, 1986; Associated Press, December 28, 1986.

42. Interviews, Santiago, October 1972.

43. *El Mercurio*, March 30, 1987; *Latin American Regional Reports Southern Cone*, September 6, 1985; author's interviews, Rome, October 1986.

44. The Rev. Robert F. Drinan, S.J., "Church Leaders Blowing the Winds of Change in Chile," *National*

Catholic Reporter, May 2, 1986; *Latinamerica Press*, July 11, 1985; Reuters, April 7, 1986; *Latin American Weekly Report*, March 26, 1987; *Latin American Regional Reports Southern Cone*, December 25, 1986; "Selected Statements of the Chilean Catholic Church," Washington Office on Latin America, July 1985.

45. "Chile Briefing"; Amnesty International *Bulletin*, February 1987; *Latin American Weekly Report*, March 26, 1987; Brian H. Smith, "Chile: Deepening the Allegiance of Working-Class Sectors to the Church in the 1970s," *Religion and Political Conflict in Latin America*, p. 185; *Sojourners*, April 1986; *Washington Post*, September 6, 1986.

46. *National Catholic Reporter*, November 23, 1984, and October 3, 1986; *Time*, September 22, 1986; *Catholic New York*, September 25, 1986; report from Chilean Bishops Conference, March 1987.

47. Agence France-Presse, June 1, 1985; *Latinamerica Press*, May 22 and August 21, 1986; Associated Press, August 6, 1986; *National Catholic Reporter*, September 5, 1986; *El Espectador*, March 10, 1987.

48. *National Catholic Reporter*, September 2, 1983.

49. *National Catholic Reporter*, September 14, 1984, and May 24, 1985; Barbara Erickson, "Martyred Curé Is Resistance Symbol in Chile," *National Catholic Reporter*, August 29, 1986.

50. Ibid.

51. *Maryknoll Magazine*, May 1987; *National Catholic Reporter*, September 14, 1986; *Vida Nueva*, September 27, 1986; *Latinamerica Press*, September 25, 1986.

52. Smith, "Chile: Deepening the Allegiance," p. 169; *El Mercurio*, March 2, 1987.

53. *National Catholic Reporter*, April 17, 1987.

54. Smith, "Chile: Deepening the Allegiance," p. 181.

55. Ibid., p. 171.

56. *Latinamerica Press*, November 20 and December 11, 1986; *O São Paulo*, January 30, 1987.

57. Associated Press, September 29, 1986; *National Catholic Reporter*, December 23, 1983; *Latinamerica Press*, February 13, 1986.

58. *Sojourners*, April 1986; *Latinamerica Press*, October 30, 1986; *Informativo* (Lima), September 26, 1986; *Vida Nueva*, September 27, 1986.

59. *Latinamerica Press*, October 30, 1986; *National Catholic Reporter*, April 17, 1987; author's interview, Bogotá, April 1987.

60. *El Mercurio*, March 30, 1987.

61. *Latinamerica Press*, citing studies by Chilean sociologists Arturo Chacón and Humberto Lagos, March 6, 1986.

62. Ibid.

63. Patricia Politzer, *Miedo en Chile* (Santiago: Centro de Estudios Sociales, 1985), pp. 243–44.

64. *Newsweek*, April 13, 1987; *Latin American Regional Reports Southern Cone*, April 16, 1987; Associated Press, April 9, 1987; Agence France-Presse, April 9, 1987; Reuters, April 9, 1987.

65. *Time*, April 13, 1987; *New York Times*, April 12, 1987.

66. *Washington Post*, April 1, 1987; *Vida Nueva*, April 11 and 16, 1987.

Chapter 6:
Religious Wars in Latin America:
The "Sects"

1. *El Tiempo*, September 29, 1985; *O São Paulo*, April 4, 1986.

2. Ibid.; *Las sectas en Centroamérica*, Pro Mundi Vita, Bulletin 100, Brussels, 1985; *Informativo Popular Latinoaméricano*, Instituto de Estudos Especiais de Pontifícia Universidade Católica de São Paulo, Brazil, June 1985; *Latin American Regional Reports Brazil*, August 9, 1985; *New York Times*, October 25, 1987.

3. *National Catholic Reporter*, May 16, 1986; *New York Times*, May 4, 1986; *America*, May 24 and September 27, 1986.

4. *El Tiempo*, June 12, 1986; interview, Bogotá, June 1986.

5. *Latinamerica Press*, November 14, 1985; *Las sectas en Centroamérica*.

6. Deborah Huntington, "The Prophet Motive," *NACLA Report on the Americas*, January/February 1984, p. 9; *Newsweek*, September 1, 1986.

7. *Newsweek*, September 1, 1986.

8. *Latinamerica Press*, March 6, 1986, and March 5, 1987; *Latin American Regional Reports Southern Cone*, February 5, 1987.

9. Michael D'Antonio, "The Christian Right Abroad," Alicia Patterson Foundation *Reporter*, Fall 1987.

10. Associated Press, November 24, 1987.

11. Sara Diamond, "God's Far-Right Arm," *Mediafile*, July/August 1984; Edward S. Herman and Frank Brodhead, *Demonstration Elections* (Boston: South End Press, 1984), pp. 103, 111, 117, 141; Associated Press, May 9, 1985.

12. Jim Castelli, "Robertson—Extremist with a Baby Face," People for the American Way, n.d., p. 15; Flo Conway and Jim Siegelman, *Holy Terror* (New York; Delta, 1982), p. 424; Donna Eberwine, "To Ríos Montt with Love Lift," *The Nation*, February 26, 1983.

13. Pat Robertson, "700 Club," October 26, 1982.

14. Conway and Siegelman, *Holy Terror*, p. 424; Eberwine, "To Ríos Montt with Love Lift."

15. For detailed documentation of the CIA's involvement, see Stephen Schlesinger and Stephen Kinzer, *Bitter Fruit* (Garden City: Doubleday, 1982).

16. Castelli, "Robertson—Extremist with a Baby Face," p. 15; Eberwine, "To Ríos Montt with Love Lift"; Penny Lernoux, "Revolution and Counterrevolution in the Central American Church," *Revolution and Counterrevo-lution in Central America and the Caribbean* (Boulder: Westview Press, 1984), pp. 141–51; Fernando Bermúdez, *Death and Resurrection in Guatemala* (Maryknoll: Orbis, 1985), p. 46; *Covert Action*, Spring 1987; author's interviews, Guatemala, and Campeche, Mexico, July 1988.

17. Eberwine, Lernoux, and Bermúdez, ibid.; Conway and Siegleman, *Holy Terror*, p. 426; *New York Times*, March 28, 1985; *Covert Action*, Spring 1987; D'Antonio, "The Christian Right Abroad."

18. *National Catholic Reporter*, April 26, 1985; *Latinamerica Press*, April 3, 1986; Tom Barry, Deb Preusch, and Beth Sims, *The New Right Humanitarians* (Albuquerque: Inter-Hemispheric Education Resource Center, 1986), pp. 23, 49; author's interviews with Miskito Indian leaders, Bogotá, January 1985, and March, April, and May, 1986; Vicki Kemper, "In the Name of Relief," *Sojourners*, October 1985.

19. Barry, Preusch, and Sims, ibid.; *Sojourners*, January 1986; Pat Robertson, "700 Club," April 23, 1985; Associated Press, July 3, 1985; National Catholic News Service, July 10, 1985.

20. Kemper, "In the Name of Relief"; *Latinamerica Press*, April 3, 1986.

21. *Sojourners*, April 1986; author's interview with Jim Wallis, Washington, D.C., May 1986; Jim Wallis, "Christians and *Contras*," *Sojourners*, October 1985.

22. Letter from Averill N. Allen, director, Inter-American School, Quezaltenango, Guatemala, February 28, 1983.

23. Marlise Simons, "Latin America's New Gospel," *New York Times Magazine*, November 7, 1982.

24. In Guatemala, for example, evangelical converts sharply increased after the 1976 earthquake that devastated the country. The sects' U.S. sponsors provided millions of dollars in aid as well as missionaries to spread the word that the disaster had been a sign from God that the Guatemalans should repent

of their sins. Membership in the new churches jumped by 14 percent that year, some said because of a swap of food, medicine, and construction materials, in what was called *ánima por lámina*, meaning "soul for tin roof," the latter used in the reconstruction of villages (Huntington, "The Prophet Motive," "God's Saving Plan," *NACLA Report on the Americas*, January/February 1984, p. 26). The author's interviews with converts in urban slums in Latin America also revealed the importance of material aid as an inducement to join the sects.

25. D'Antonio, "The Christian Right Abroad."

26. Pablo Richard, "Central America: Sects Use Marketing Techniques, Dollars to 'Sell' Gospel," *Latinamerica Press*, May 9, 1985; *New York Times*, October 25, 1987.

27. D'Antonio, "The Christian Right Abroad."

28. *Las sectas en Centroamerica*.

Chapter 7:
The "Americanists"

1. Author's interviews, Europe and United States, 1986.

2. Jay P. Dolan, *The American Catholic Experience* (New York: Doubleday, 1985), p. 303.

3. The Rev. James Hennesey, S.J., *American Catholics* (Oxford: Oxford University Press, 1981), p. 200.

4. Ibid., pp. 289–93; John Cooney, *The American Pope* (New York: Times Books, 1984).

5. Penny Lernoux, *Cry of the People* (New York: Penguin, 1982), pp. 281–310.

6. Author's interview, Washington, D.C., May 1986.

7. *National Catholic Reporter*, August 3, 1984; John J. Fialka, "Atom-Weapons Issue Stirs Divisive Debate in the Catholic Church," *Wall Street Journal*, June 9, 1982.

8. *Latinamerica Press*, October 10, 1985.

9. *National Catholic Reporter*, August 3, 1984.

10. Ibid.

11. Ibid.

12. Author's interviews, Washington, D.C., May 1986.

13. Michael Novak, "Who Are the Real Progressives?" *IDOC Bulletin*, No. 8–9, 1982, Rome.

14. Author's interview, New York City, May 1986.

15. Program for "Conference on Religious Liberty," Loy Henderson Conference Room, State Department, Washington, D.C., April 15–16, 1985; *Washington Post*, April 20, 1985; *Washington Times*, July 18, 1985.

16. Letter from Bishop Leroy C. Hodapp, United Methodist Church, Indiana Area, to Ed Robb, IRD, April 16, 1985.

17. Wayne Barrett, "Holier Than Thou: The Backroom Politics of Archbishop O'Connor," in *The Vatican & the Reagan Administration* by Ana Maria Ezcurra (New York: Circus Publications, 1986), p. 1.

18. Tommie Sue Montgomery, "The Crisis in El Salvador," *Florida Times-Union*, February 7, 1982.

19. Advertisement by *New Oxford Review*, September 5, 1986; author's interview with Jim Wallis, *Sojourners*, December 1988.

20. *"La Iglesia y Centroamérica,"* *Revista* (Caracas), February 1982, pp. 92–94.

21. Bishop James Malone, speech to National Conference of Catholic Bishops, Washington, D.C., November 10, 1986.

22. *National Catholic Reporter*, September 11, 1981.

23. *Wall Street Journal*, December 8, 1983.

24. Richard E. Feinberg, *The Intemperate Zone* (New York: W. W. Norton, 1983), p. 186.

25. Richard Barnet, "Losing Moral Ground," *Sojourners*, March 1985.

26. *Wall Street Journal*, December 8, 1983.

27. *National Catholic Reporter*, April 20, 1984.

28. James LeMoyne, "U.S. Said to Plan a Long Presence in Honduras Bases," *New York Times*, July 13, 1986.

29. Ibid.

30. *Washington Post*, July 25, 1986.

31. Colman McCarthy, "Motley's Crew and the Church," *Washington Post*, July 14, 1985.

32. The Rev. Leo J. Sommer, M. M., "Missioners' View of Central America," *Maryknoll Magazine*, April 1986.

33. Ibid.

34. EFE news agency, November 28 and December 1, 1987; Associated Press, December 16, 1987; *Time*, December 28, 1987.

35. Cardinal John Krol, "Salt II: A Statement of Support," *Origins*, September 13, 1979.

36. A. James Reichley, *Religion in American Public Life* (Washington, D.C.: Brookings Institution, 1985), p. 296.

37. The Rev. Peter J. Henriot, S.J., "Peace Pastoral: Ecclesiological Implications," Center of Concern, Washington, D.C., March 15, 1984.

38. *National Catholic Reporter*, August 3, 1984; Fialka, "Atom-Weapons Issue."

39. *National Catholic Reporter*, September 26, 1986.

40. *Seattle Post-Intelligencer*, July 25, 1982; *National Catholic Reporter*, August 3, 1984.

41. *Justice and War in the Nuclear Age*, American Catholic Committee (Lanham: University Press of America, 1983).

42. Fialka, "Atom-Weapons Issue."

43. Barrett, "Holier Than Thou," p. lxxv.

44. Ibid., pp. lxxv–lxxvii.

45. Henriot, "Peace Pastoral," p. 2; the Rev. James V. Schall, S.J., "Intellectual Origins of the Peace Movement," *Justice and War in the Nuclear Age*, pp. 49–51.

46. *Out of Justice, Peace* (Joint Pastoral Letter of the West German Bishops) and *Winning the Peace* (Joint Pastoral Letter of the French Bishops), ed. and introd. by the Rev. James V. Schall (San Francisco: Ignatius Press, 1984), pp. 17–27.

47. Reichley, *Religion in American Public Life*, p. 297.

48. Henriot, "Peace Pastoral," p. 6.

49. Reichley, *Religion in American Public Life*, p. 298.

50. Charles E. Curran, "The Moral Theology of the Bishops' Pastoral," in *Catholics and Nuclear War*, edited by Philip J. Murnion (New York: Crossroads, 1983), p. 55.

51. Archbishop Rembert G. Weakland, "How to Read the Economic Pastoral," *Catholicism in Crisis*, March 1986.

52. Archbishop Roger Mahony, "There Your Heart Will Be," *Catholicism in Crisis*, July 1984.

53. Pope Leo XIII, *The Condition of Labor* (*Rerum Novarum*), 1891.

54. Cited in *Mater et Magistra*, encyclical letter of Pope John XXIII, 1961.

55. *A Pastoral Constitution on the Church in the Modern World*, document of the Second Vatican Council, 1965.

56. Pope John Paul II, *On Human Work*, 1981.

57. Ibid.

58. Cardinal Joseph Bernardin, "The Fact of Poverty Today: A Challenge for the Church," speech at Catholic University, reprinted in *Congressional Record*, February 22, 1985.

59. Pope John Paul II, "Open Wide the Doors for Christ," speech delivered at New York's Yankee Stadium, October 2, 1979.

60. Colman McCarthy, "The Bishops Get Radical," *Washington Post*, November 17, 1984.

61. Weakland, "How to Read the Economic Pastoral."

62. *Sojourners*, August/September 1985.

63. Bernardin, "The Fact of Poverty Today."

64. Archbishop Rembert Weakland, "Peace Through Economic Justice," speech to Interfaith Peace and Justice Conference, Appleton, Wisconsin, May 9, 1986.

65. National Conference of Catholic Bishops, *Economic Justice for All: Catholic Social Teaching and the U.S. Economy*, Washington, D.C., November 1986.

66. See, for example, the argument of theologians Michael J. Himes and Kenneth R. Himes, "Rights, Economics & the Trinity," *Commonweal*, March 14, 1986.

67. Weakland, "Peace Through Economic Justice."

68. Mahony, "There Your Heart Will Be."

69. *Milwaukee Journal*, November 10, 1986.

70. *Economic Justice for All*, pp. 113–59.

71. Eugene Kennedy, *Re-Imagining American Catholicism* (New York: Vintage, 1985), p. 7.

72. *The Christian Century*, October 24, 1984; *National Catholic Reporter*, November 20, 1984.

73. Lay Commission on Catholic Social Teaching and the U.S. Economy, *Toward the Future: Catholic Social Thought and the U.S. Economy, a Lay Letter*, November 1984; Leon Wieseltier, "Conservatives Must End the Charade, Face Responsibility," *Los Angeles Times*, January 13, 1985.

74. *Business Week*, November 12, 1984.

75. Author's interview, Washington, D.C., May 1986.

76. *National Catholic Reporter*, July 5, 1985.

77. *National Catholic Reporter*, November 20, 1984; Peter Steinfels, "The Bishops and Their Critics," *Dissent*, Spring 1985.

78. Michael Novak, "The Bishops and the Poor," *Washington Post*, November 13, 1984; *Washington Post* editorial, November 13, 1984.

79. *Business Week*, November 12, 1984.

80. *Time*, November 26, 1984.

81. Kennedy, *Re-Imagining American Catholicism*, pp. 136–37.

Chapter 8:
The Roman Restoration in the United States

1. *Newsweek*, September 28, 1987.

2. Ibid.

3. *National Catholic Reporter*, October 2 and 9, 1987.

4. Archbishop Raymond Hunthausen, "Faith and Disarmament," speech delivered at the Pacific Lutheran University, Tacoma, Washington, June 12, 1981.

5. *The Progress* (newspaper of the archdiocese of Seattle), September 11, 1986; *Catholic New York*, September 11, 1986.

6. See, for example, the findings of the Notre Dame "Study of Catholic Parish Life" published in 1986.

7. *National Catholic Reporter*, September 12, 1986.

8. *Sojourners*, November 1986.

9. *National Catholic Reporter*, September 12, 1986.

10. *National Catholic Reporter*, October 3, 1986.

11. *The Progress*, September 11, 1986.

12. Tim McCarthy, "Rome Opposition Among Seattle Catholics Deep," *National Catholic Reporter*, October 3, 1986.

13. Author's interview, New York, May 1986; *Catholic New York*, July 3, 1986.

14. *National Catholic Reporter*, December 13, 1985.

15. *Washington Post*, February 2, 1987; Gary Atkins, "Archbishop Hunthausen," *Seattle Times*, June 20, 1982.

16. Cynthia H. Wilson, "Peace on Earth," *The Weekly* (Seattle), December 21, 1983.

17. Atkins, "Archbishop Hunthausen."

18. Stephen Schlesinger and Stephen Kinzer, *Bitter Fruit* (Garden City: Doubleday, 1982), p. 155.

19. Author's interviews, Washington, D.C., May 1986.

20. *Milwaukee Sentinel*, October 21, 1986; *New York Times*, October 3, 1986.

21. *Milwaukee Sentinel*, October 21, 1986.

22. *National Catholic Reporter*, September 6, 1985.

23. *National Catholic Reporter*, February 6, 1987.

24. *National Catholic Reporter*, March 28 and June 20, 1986, and February 20, 1987; *New York Times*, August 24, 1986; *Washington Post*, January 3, 1987.

25. *National Catholic Reporter*, August 29, 1986.

26. *National Catholic Reporter*, September 6, 1985; author's interview, United States, May 1986.

27. *Sojourners*, February 1986; Thomas Ferguson and Joel Rogers, "The Myth of America's Turn to the Right," *Atlantic Monthly*, May 7, 1986; James J. Kelly, "Tracking the Intractable," *Cross Currents*, Summer/Fall 1985, p. 217, citing *To Rescue the Future: The Pro-Life Movement in the 80's* (Toronto: Life Cycle Books, 1983).

28. Sister Dolores Liptak, RSM, with the Center for applied Research in the Apostolate and the Center of Concern, *"La Iglesia Católica de los Estados Unidos en la Encrucijada,"* Pro Mundi Vita (Brussels), Bulletin No. 94, p. 38; Hennesey, *American Catholics*, p. 331.

29. Ibid.; *Los Angeles Times*, August 16, 1986; Gilbert Padilla, "New Religion Wields Two-Edged Sword,"

National Catholic Reporter, August 15, 1986.

30. *New York Times*, October 12 and November 11, 1986; *Washington Post*, November 11, 1986.

31. Tom Fox, "Inside NCR," *National Catholic Reporter*, October 17, 1986.

32. *National Catholic Reporter*, October 3, 1986.

33. Author's interviews, Rome, October 1986; Eugene Kennedy, "A Dissenting Voice," *New York Times Magazine*, November 9, 1986.

34. Text of speech by Archbishop Raymond Hunthausen presented to fellow bishops at the executive session of the bishops' conference, Washington, D.C., November 11, 1986; *America*, September 20, 1986.

35. Ibid.; *New York Times*, November 10 and 13, 1986; *Washington Post*, November 16, 1986; *Catholic New York*, November 6, 1986.

36. *New York Times*, November 10, 1986.

37. *Washington Post*, February 2, 1987.

38. *The Wanderer*, October 2, 1986; *National Review*, December 19, 1986.

39. E. J. Dionne, Jr., *New York Times*, December 24, 1986; *Washington Post*, February 2, 1987; Hunthausen, "Faith and Disarmament"; "Chronology of Recent Events in the Archdiocese of Seattle" prepared by Archbishop Pro Nuncio Pio Laghi, Washington, D.C., October 27, 1986.

40. Peter Hebblethwaite, "Bishops as an Endangered Species," *National Catholic Reporter*, November 7, 1986; author's interviews, Rome, October 1986.

41. *National Catholic Reporter*, October 3 and November 7, 1986.

42. Interviews with author, Italy, October 1986, and Latin America, November 1986; *Washington Post*, November 11, 1986.

43. *Catholic New York*, November 13, 1986.

44. Ibid.

45. *Washington Post*, November 13, 1986; *New York Times*, December 1, 1986; *National Catholic Reporter*, November 21, 1986.

46. Ibid.; *New York Times*, November 14, 1986.

47. *National Catholic Reporter*, November 21, 1986; *Washington Post*, November 16, 1986; *New York Times*, December 1, 1986; *Catholic New York*, November 6, 1986.

48. Text of talk by Archbishop Pio Laghi to the National Conference of Catholic Bishops, Washington, D.C., November 10, 1986; message from John Paul to the Catholic bishops of the United States, in Laghi text; *New York Times*, November 13, 1986.

49. Bishop Kenneth E. Untener, "Local Church and Universal Church," *America*, October 13, 1984.

50. *Catholic New York*, December 11, 1986; interviews with author, the United States, May 1986; Rome, October 1986; Bogotá, November 1986.

51. Interview with author, South America, September 1986.

52. Correspondence with author, February 23, 1984; Nat Hentoff, "Reporting the Wars of the Catholics," *Village Voice*, February 10, 1987.

53. *Washington Post*, June 13, 1987; *New York Times*, June 10, 1987; *Newsweek*, June 15, 1987.

54. *New York Times*, November 17, 1986.

55. *New York Times*, October 30, 1986.

56. *New York Times*, October 9, 1986.

57. Ibid.; Archbishop Rembert G. Weakland, "The price of orthodoxy—1," *Catholic Herald* (Milwaukee archdiocesan paper), September 11, 1986.

58. Archbishop Rembert G. Weakland, "The Church in Worldly Affairs," *America*, October 18, 1986; *Washington Post*, September 27, 1986.

59. *New York Times*, November 20,

1986; *Catholic New York*, November 27, 1986.

60. *New York Times*, April 25 and May 27 and 31, 1987; Washington *Post*, May 27 and 28, 1987; *Catholic New York*, March 26, May 28, and June 4, 1987; *National Catholic Reporter*, April 24, May 1 and 15, and June 5 and 19, 1987.

61. Ibid.

62. Ibid.

63. Joan Barthel, "The Silent Spring of Father Curran," *Washington Post Magazine*, March 22, 1987; *National Catholic Reporter*, September 5, 1986.

64. *Washington Post*, September 4, 1986.

65. Ibid.

66. *National Catholic Reporter*, February 8, 1985; *New York Times*, July 20, 1986.

67. *New York Times*, October 18, 1986.

68. *The Chronicle of Higher Education*, March 19, 1986.

69. Barthel, "The Silent Spring of Father Curran"; author's interviews, Washington, D.C., May 1986, and Rome, October 1986.

70. *New York Times*, August 21, 1986.

71. Associated Press, September 29, 1980; *New York Times* news service, October 10, 1980; *Time*, October 13, 1980.

72. *Catholic New York*, September 11, 1986; *National Catholic Reporter*, September 5, 1986.

73. Letter from Cardinal Joseph Ratzinger to Father Charles Curran, September 17, 1985, Rome; *National Catholic Reporter*, March 21 and August 29, 1986; *New York Times*, August 19, 1986.

74. *New York Times*, July 20, 1986; *National Catholic Reporter*, September 5, 1986; *Time*, September 1, 1986.

75. *National Catholic Reporter*, October 24, 1986.

76. *Time*, October 13, 1986; the Rev. William J. Byron, S.J., "Credentialed, Commissioned and Free," *America*, August 23, 1986.

77. *Origins* (documentary service of the National Catholic News Service), August 28, 1986; *National Catholic Reporter*, August 16, 1985, and April 4, 1986; *New York Times*, September 27, 1986.

78. Author's interview with Father McInnes, Washington, D.C., May 1986; Congregation for Catholic Education, "Proposed Schema for a Pontifical Document on Catholic Universities," published in *Chronicle of Higher Education*, March 26, 1986; *Vida Nueva*, April 23, 1988.

79. The Rev. Theodore M. Hesburgh, C.S.C., "Catholic Education in America," *America*, October 4, 1986.

80. Ibid.

81. *Chronicle of Higher Education*, March 26, 1986; letter to Cardinal William Baum from the presidents of twenty-eight U.S. Jesuit colleges, February 15, 1986.

82. *National Catholic Reporter*, March 13, 1987; *New York Times*, March 3, 1987.

83. Author's interview, Washington, D.C., May 1986.

84. *New York Times*, October 8, 1986.

85. See, for example, Kelly's *The Battle for the American Church* (New York: Doubleday, 1979) and *The Crisis of Authority* (Chicago: Regnery Gateway, 1982).

86. *Boston Globe*, May 20, 1986; *National Catholic Reporter*, October 10, 1986, and February 27, 1987.

87. *Washington Post*, August 21 and 29, 1986; *Catholic New York*, September 4, 1986; *National Catholic Reporter*, August 1 and September 5, 1986.

88. Barthel, "The Silent Spring of Father Curran"; Jonathan Yardley, "The Vatican's Setback for Catholic Colleges," *Washington Post*, August 25, 1986; *National Catholic Reporter*, January 23, 1987; *New York Times*, August 29, 1986.

89. *Chronicle of Higher Education*, November 23, 1985; *New York Times*, October 8, 1986.

90. William J. Gould, Jr., "Rome vs. American Catholicism," *Washington Post*, October 19, 1986; Paul A. Lister, "Scholarship in the Doldrums," *National Catholic Reporter*, October 3, 1986; *National Catholic Reporter*, quoting Richard N. Goodwin of the *Los Angeles Times–Washington Post* News Service, October 10, 1984.

91. Sister Madonna Kolbenschlag, H.M. "Analysis and Commentary on the Documents of the Mansour Case," October 1983.

92. Ibid.

93. *National Catholic Reporter*, May 27, 1983, and August 15, 1986.

94. Author's interview, Washington, D.C., May 1986.

95. *New York Times*, July 22 and 27, 1986; *Washington Post*, July 4, 1986; *Time*, October 13, 1986; *National Catholic Reporter*, July 4 and August 15, 1986.

96. *National Catholic Reporter*, December 12, 1985; *Catholic New York*, June 26, 1986; *Washington Post*, July 25, 1986.

97. *National Catholic Reporter*, August 15, 1986.

98. Nat Hentoff citing Eugene Kennedy in "Profiles," *The New Yorker*, March 23, 1987.

99. Cardinal Joseph Ratzinger with Vittorio Messori, *The Ratzinger Report* (San Francisco: Ignatius Press, 1985), p. 99.

100. *National Catholic Reporter*, September 6, 1985.

101. Author's interviews, Washington, D.C., May 1986, and Rome, October 1986.

102. *Time*, February 4, 1985; Sister Margaret Cafferty, P.B.V.M., "The Woman's Word of Testimony," speech delivered at national assembly of Leadership Conference of Women Religious, Washington, D.C., September 5, 1985; Sister Mary Jo Leddy, N.D.S., "Mighty

Spirit Stirs Religious Life in Americas," *National Catholic Reporter*, December 20, 1985.

103. Author's interviews, United States, May 1986.

104. Author's interviews, Rome and Milan, October 1986.

105. Author's interview, Washington, D.C., May 1986.

106. Ibid.

107. David S. Broder, "The Vital Contribution Religion Has Made," *Washington Post*, December 24, 1986.

108. Author's interviews, United States, May 1986; Rome, October 1986.

109. *USA Today*, September 30, 1986.

110. Nat Hentoff, "Profiles," March 23 and 30, 1987, *The New Yorker*; *Catholic New York*, October 16, 1986; Wayne Barrett, "Holier Than Thou: The Backroom Politics of Archbishop O'Connor," reprint of *Village Voice* article, December 24, 1984, in Ana Maria Ezcurra, *The Vatican & The Reagan Administration* (New York: Circus Publications, 1986), pp. l–lxxxii.

111. United Press International, September 21, 1984.

112. *National Catholic Reporter*, May 3, 1985; *New York Times*, February 17, 1986.

113. Hentoff, "Profiles," *The New Yorker*, March 23 and 30, 1987.

114. Author's interviews, United States, May 1986.

115. Tim McCarthy, "Law Rises to Boston Challenge," *National Catholic Reporter*, March 13, 1987.

116. Ibid; *National Catholic Reporter*, June 20, 1986.

117. Author's interviews, Massachusetts, May, and July, 1986.

118. Dick Jones and Marie Rohde, "Tempting the Vatican?," *Milwaukee Journal Magazine*, November 9, 1986.

119. Ibid; Marjorie Hyer, "The Strength That Comes from Learning Poverty Firsthand," *Washington Post*, November 18, 1984; *Catholic Herald* (Milwaukee archdiocese), November 5,

1977; author's interview with Archbishop Weakland, Appleton, Wisconsin, May 1986.

120. Author's interviews, Wisconsin, May 1986; Jones and Rohde, "Tempting the Vatican?"

121. Author's interviews, Washington, D.C., May 1986, and Rome, October 1986.

122. Jones and Rohde, "Tempting the Vatican?"

123. Ibid.

124. Archbishop Rembert G. Weakland, "The Church in Worldly Affairs," *America*, October 18, 1986.

125. Author's interviews, Latin America, Europe, and the United States, 1986.

126. Weakland, "The Church in Worldly Affairs."

Chapter 9:
Sanctuary

1. *National Catholic Reporter*, July 18, 1986.

2. *Sojourners*, April 1985.

3. *Sojourners*, March 1985.

4. Ibid.

5. Ibid.

6. The Rev. John M. Fife, "The Sanctuary Movement: Where Have We Been? Where Are We Going?" *Church & Society*, March/April 1985.

7. Author's interviews, New York, May 1986; Geraldine Brooks, "Scores of U.S. Churches Take In Illegal Aliens Fleeing Latin America," *Wall Street Journal*, June 21, 1984.

8. For a capsule survey of Salvadoran conditions, see Penny Lernoux, *Cry of the People* (New York: Penguin, 1982), Chapter 3.

9. *National Catholic Reporter*, November 11, 1983.

10. *Draining the Sea . . . Sixth Supplement to the Report on Human Rights in El Salvador*, Americas Watch, March 1985; Mercedes de Uriarte, "No Sense of Place," Alicia Patterson Foundation *Reporter*, Fall 1982.

11. *Little Hope: Human Rights in Guatemala*, Americas Watch, February 1985, pp. 1–5.

12. Gary MacEoin, "Gospel of Change," *The Progressive*, December 1985; *National Catholic Reporter*, September 12, 1986.

13. For a summary of the Red Squads in the 1960s and 1970s and their similarity to illegal government activities in the 1980s, see Frank Donner, "The Return of the Red Squads," *The Nation*, October 12, 1985.

14. *Sojourners*, February 1986; Bruce Shapiro, "Teaching Cops About Terrorism," *The Nation*, October 12, 1985.

15. Letter from staff of Old Cambridge Baptist Church outlining break-ins, Cambridge, Massachusetts, February 7, 1986; letter from Congressman Don Edwards, chairman, House Subcommittee on Civil and Constitutional Rights, to William H. Webster, director, FBI, inquiring about complaints of break-ins of Sanctuary churches, January 29, 1986.

16. Author's interviews, May 1986, Washington, D.C.; *National Catholic Reporter*, January 10, 1986; *Sojourners*, February 1984.

17. Alfie Kohn, "The Return of Cointelpro?" *The Nation*, January 25, 1986.

18. *National Catholic Reporter*, August 16, 1985.

19. *New York Times*, July 13, 1986; *National Catholic Reporter*, October 3, 986.

20. *National Catholic Reporter*, February 1, 1985.

21. *Mustard Seed*, March 1986.

22. Ibid.; *Washington Post*, April 18, 1986.

23. Net Hentoff, "Snoops in the Pews," *The Progressive*, August 1985; Sandy Tolan and Carol Ann Bassett, "Informers in the Sanctuary Movement," *The Nation*, July 20 and 27, 1985.

24. Hentoff, ibid.

25. *Mustard Seed*, March 1986; *Sojourners*, April 1986.

26. Carey McWilliams, *North from Mexico: The Spanish-Speaking People of the United States* (New York: Monthly Review Press, 1948).

27. John M. Crewdson, five-part series on INS, *New York Times*, January 13–17, 1980.

28. Ibid.

29. Author's interview, Washington, D.C., May 1986.

30. Ignatius Bau, *This Ground Is Holy* (New York: Paulist Press, 1985), pp. 60–74.

31. Gary MacEoin, "The Constitutional and Legal Aspects of the Refugee Crisis," *Sanctuary* (New York: Harper & Row, 1985), Chapter 13.

32. Ibid.

33. Bill Girdner, "Little-Noted Trial Could Extend New Rights to Salvadoran Refugees," Pacific News Service, July 14, 1986.

34. MacEoin, "The Constitutional and Legal Aspects of the Refugee Crisis"; Martha Boerthel, "INS Creates Hopelessness for Refugees, *Texas Observer*, August 17, 1984.

35. *San Jose Mercury*, January 21, 1985.

36. Author's interview with INS spokesman Verne Jervis, Washington, D.C., May 1986.

37. *Chicago Sun-Times*, February 5, 1985.

38. *San Francisco Examiner*, January 20, 1985.

39. *National Catholic Reporter*, January 25, 1985.

40. *Sojourners*, October 1986.

41. *New York Times*, October 27, 1987; *Basta*, June 1987.

42. Diane Elder, Casa Oscar Romero, San Benito, Texas, June 1984.

43. *Sojourners*, March 1985.

44. Fife, "The Sanctuary Movement."

45. Jim Corbett, "The Covenant as Sanctuary," *Sanctuary*, p. 186.

46. Ibid., pp. 183–84.

47. Arthur Jones, "Bishops' Silence over Sanctuary Cries Out," *National Catholic Reporter*, August 1, 1986.

48. Dick Jones and Marie Rohde, *Milwaukee Journal Magazine*, November 9, 1986.

Chrapter 10:
The Religious International

1. For two factual histories of the Knights of Malta, see Alexander Sutherland, *The Knights of Malta* (Philadelphia: Carey & Hart, 1846), vols. I and II, and Edgar Erskine Hume, *Medical Work of the Knights Hospitallers of Saint John of Jerusalem* (Baltimore: Johns Hopkins Press, 1940); for a thinly fictionalized and often amusing account of the power struggles within the order, see Roger Peyrefitte, *Knights of Malta* (New York: Criterion, 1959).

2. Martin A. Lee, "Who Are the Knights of Malta?" *National Catholic Reporter*, October 14, 1983; Stephen Birmingham, *Real Lace: America's Irish Rich* (New York: Harper & Row, 1973), pp. 280–81.

3. The Rev. Robert I. Gannon, S.J., *The Cardinal Spellman Story* (New York: Doubleday, 1962), p. 58; John Cooney, *The American Pope* (New York: Times Books, 1984), pp. 62–63; Peyrefitte, pp. 113–17; Kevin Coogan, "The Friends of Michele Sindona," *Parapolitics*, August 15, 1982.

4. Cooney, *The American Pope*, pp. 123–24.

5. Ibid., p. 139; Frederic Laurent, *L'Orchestre Noir* (Paris: Editions Stock, 1978), p. 29.

6. Coogan, "The Friends of Michele Sindona"; Françoise Hervet, "The Sovereign Military Order of Malta," *Covert Action*, Winter 1986.

7. Carlo Falconi, *Los Hombres de la Historia: Pio XII* (Buenos Aires: Centro Editor de America Latina, 1969), pp. 69–73; J. N. D. Kelly, *The Oxford*

Dictionary of Popes (Oxford: Oxford University, 1986); Scott Anderson and Jon Lee Anderson, *Inside the League* (New York: Dodd, Mead, 1986), pp. 26–29; Cooney, *The American Pope*, p. 138; *National Catholic Reporter*, January 16, 1987.

8. Charles Higham, *Trading With the Enemy: An Exploration of the Nazi-American Money Plot, 1933–1949* (New York: Delacorte, 1983), pp. 20–31; Joe Conason with Martin A. Rosenblatt, "The Corporate State of Grace," *Village Voice*, April 12, 1983; Clarence G. Lasby, *Project Paperclip* (New York: Atheneum, 1971); Hervet, "The Sovereign Military Order of Malta"; *The New Columbia Encyclopedia*, ed. William H. Harris and Judith S. Levey (New York: Columbia University Press, 1975), p. 1465.

9. Martin A. Lee, "Their Will Be Done," *Mother Jones*, July 1983; Hervet, "The Sovereign Military Order of Malta"; Peter Dale Scott, "How Allen Dulles and the SS Preserved Each Other," *Covert Action*, Winter 1986.

10. Ibid.; Guenther Reinhardt, *Crime Without Punishment* (New York: New American Library, 1953), p. 280.

11. See, for example, the results of an investigation by John Loftus, a former prosecutor in the Office of Special Investigations, the Justice Department's Nazi-hunting unit, in *The Belarus Secret* (New York: Knopf, 1982), and a summary of documents on Vatican involvement retrieved from the National Archives in Washington and Fort Meade, Maryland, by William Bole of the Religious News Service, published in *National Catholic Reporter*, May 16, 1986.

12. Ibid.; Anderson and Anderson, *Inside the League*, p. 39; Scott, "How Allen Dulles and the SS Preserved Each Other."

13. Ibid.; Peyrefitte, *Knights of Malta*, p. 44; Coogan, "The Friends of Michele Sindona."

14. *Parapolitics*, March 1982; Scott,

"How Allen Dulles and the SS Preserved Each Other"; Hervet, "The Sovereign Military Order of Malta"; Hearings before the Committee on Standards of Official Conduct, House of Representatives, 1976, from report as printed in *The Village Voice*, February 16, 1976, and addended to transcript of hearings; Cooney, *The American Pope*, pp. 157–61; Lee, "Their Will Be Done."

15. Jonathan Marshall, "Brief Notes on the Political Importance of Secret Societies," *Parapolitics*, March 1983; Hervet, "The Sovereign Military Order of Malta"; Penny Lernoux, *In Banks We Trust* (New York: Penguin, 1986), chapters 9 and 10; author's interviews, São Paulo, 1984.

16. Author's interview, New York City, May 1986; Anderson and Anderson, *Inside the League*, p. 36.

17. Author's interview, New York City, May 1986.

18. Author's interview, Washington, D.C., May 1986.

19. Authors' interviews, New York City, May 1986, and Rome, October 1986.

20. Author's interview, New York City, May 1986.

21. Author's interview, New York City, May 1986.

22. Loftus, *The Belarus Secret*, pp. 106–107, 178.

23. Conason and Rosenblatt, "The Corporate State of Grace"; Hervet, "The Sovereign Military Order of Malta"; *Business Week*, October 5, 1981, and January 27, 1986; *Newsweek*, January 16, 1984.

24. Penny Lernoux, *Cry of the People* (New York: Penguin, 1982), Chapter 7; Conason and Rosenblatt, ibid.; *Newsweek*, ibid.

25. *Wall Street Journal*, March 1, 1984; *U.S. News & World Report*, July 25, 1983; Conason and Rosenblatt, ibid; *New York Times*, July 29, 1986.

26. *Wall Street Journal*, May 8, 1987; memo from John Meehan to J. Peter Grace, May 9, 1984; *National Cath-*

olic Reporter, August 31, 1984; *Amanecer* (Managua), July/August 1984.

27. Author's interview, New York City, May 1986.

28. *Washington Post*, December 27, 1984; *Wall Street Journal*, May 8, 1987; Anderson and Anderson, *Inside the League*, p. 183; Hervet, "The Sovereign Military Order of Malta."

29. *Washington Post*, May 3, 1985; *Manchester Guardian*, March 13, 1985; *National Catholic Reporter*, January 11, 1985; *Covert Action*, Winter 1986; *Wall Street Journal*, May 8, 1987; letter from Louis Chiurato, counsellor, Knights of Malta embassy in San Salvador, January 28, 1985; report by observer mission of Canadian Council for International Cooperation on visit to El Salvador and Honduras, Ottawa, June 14, 1985.

30. Ibid.

31. *Annuaire, 1981* of the Ordre Souverain Militaire Hospitalier de Saint Jean de Jerusalem de Rhodes et de Malte (Rome: Bureau de Presse du Grand Magistère, 1981).

32. *Business Week*, October 5, 1981; *Wall Street Journal*, May 8, 1987; *Newsweek*, January 16, 1984; Osborn Elliott, *Men at the Top* (New York: Harper & Row, 1959), p. 28; author's interview, New York City, May 1986.

33. Conason and Rosenblatt, "The Corporate State of Grace."

34. *Time*, December 22, 1986, and February 16, 1987; *National Catholic Reporter*, March 27, 1987; Agence France Presse, September 26, 1987.

35. News release, U.S. Information Agency, December 15, 1980; *Covert Action*, April 1981; *National Catholic Reporter*, February 6, 1981; *Newsweek*, April 2, 1984; *Time*, December 22, 1986, and February 16 and May 18, 1987; Associated Press, February 2, 1987.

36. *Covert Action*, April 1981; *Washington Post*, September 23, 1985; *New York Times Book Review*, July 13, 1986.

37. Lernoux, *Cry of the People*, p. 204; Seymour M. Hersh, *The Price of*

Power (New York: Summit, 1983), pp. 275, 277, 281, 286–88, 318; United Press International, January 10, 1981.

38. Cooney, *The American Pope*, p. 225; *Washington Post*, September 23, 1985; *The Nation*, October 22, 1983; E. Howard Hunt, *Undercover* (New York: Berkley, 1974), pp. 69–70, 322; Taylor Branch and Eugene M. Propper, *Labyrinth* (New York: Viking, 1982), p. 228; John Dinges and Saul Landau, *Assassination on Embassy Row* (New York: Pantheon, 1980), pp. 21–22.

39. Loftus, *The Belarus Secret*, pp. 118, 133, 137, 143, 178; Anderson and Anderson, *Inside the League*, p. 38; *The Nation*, June 22, 1985.

40. For a history of the lobby, see Ross Y. Koen, *The China Lobby in American Politics* (New York: Harper & Row, 1974).

41. Arthur Jones, "Simon Says," *National Catholic Reporter*, June 21, 1985.

42. Andrés Vázquez de Prada, *El Fundador del Opus Dei* (Madrid: Ediciones Rialp, 1983), p. 161; Jesús Ynfante, *La prodigiosa aventura del Opus Dei* (Madrid: Ruedo Ibérico, 1970), p. 16.

43. Ynfante, ibid., pp. 3, 17, 30–32; *New Statesman*, March 1985; author's interview, Bogotá, 1986; Marshall, "Brief Notes"; Josemaría Escrivá, *The Way* (Chicago: Scepter, 1965), pp. 21, 29, 100; Jean-Jacques Thierry, *Opus Dei* (New York: Courtland Press, 1975), pp. 13–14; *The Times* (London), January 12, 1981.

44. Opus Dei *Constituciones* (translation from the Latin to Spanish), Rome, 1950, Articles 36, 188–89 (Madrid: Ediciones Tiempo, July 1986); *Código de Derecho Particular de la Obra de Dios* (translation from the Latin to Spanish), Rome, 1982, Article 20 and *"Disposiciones Finales,"* no. 2 (Madrid: Ediciones Tiempo, July 1986); Klaus Steigleder, *L'Opus Dei* (Torino: Claudiana, 1986), pp. 95–253; Thierry, ibid., pp. 51–52; John J. Roche, "Winning Recruits in Opus Dei: A Personal Experience," and letter from John Horrigan, Opus Dei Information Office, London, *The Clergy Review*, No. 70, 1985; Maria del Carmen Tapia, "Good Housekeepers for Opus Dei," *National Catholic Reporter*, May 27, 1983; Giancarlo Zízola, *La Restauración del Papa Wojtyla* (Madrid: Ediciones Cristiandad, 1985), pp. 164–65; Henry Kamm, "The Secret World of Opus Dei," *New York Times Magazine*, January 8, 1984; *New Statesman*, ibid.; Giancarlo Rocca, *L' "Opus Dei"* (Rome: Edizioni Paoline, 1985), pp. 78–79.

45. Ibid.; Escrivá, *The Way*, p. 33; *Church & State*, September 1985; Ana Maria Ezcurra, *The Vatican & The Reagan Administration* (New York: Circus Publications, 1986), p. 94; *The Times* (London), January 12, 1981; author's interview with the Rev. Pedro Miguel Lamet, S. J., Madrid, October 1986; *Tiempo* (Madrid), July 28, 1986.

46. Rocca, *L' "Opus Dei,"* pp. 18, 30–32, 40, 68, 111, 125; *Annuario Pontificio* (Vatican City: Libreria Editrice Vaticana, 1986), p. 1029; Kamm, "The Secret World of Opus Dei"; Tapia, "Good Housekeepers for Opus Dei"; Ynfante, *La prodigiosa aventura*, pp. 125 and 139; *Tiempo*, July 28, 1986; *20 Questions to Msgr. Alvaro del Portillo* (New York: Scepter, 1985), p. 21; author's interviews, South America, 1985–86; Escrivá, *The Way*, pp. 60–66; Francisco Luna Luca de Tena, *Cómo Confesarse Bién* (Medellín: Servicio de Documentación, 1982).

47. Kamm, ibid.; *Time*, June 11, 1984; *The Times*, January 12, 1981.

48. Tapia, "Good Housekeepers for Opus Dei"; author's interviews, South America, 1985–86; New York City, May 1986; and Rome and Madrid, October 1986.

49. Tapia, ibid.

50. Ibid.; author's interviews with the Rev. Giancarlo Rocca, Rome, October 1986, and Lamet, Madrid, October 1986.

51. *Constituciones*, Articles 36, 188–89; *Código de Derecho*, Article 20, "Disposiciones Finales," no. 2.

52. Ibid.; Escrivá, *The Way*, pp. 94, 219; Thierry, *Opus Dei*, pp. 33–36, 53–54; Ynfante, *La prodigiosa aventura*, pp. 114–30.

53. Ibid.; Escrivá, ibid., p. 59; *Tiempo*, July 28, 1986.

54. Ynfante, *La prodigiosa aventura*; Roche, "Winning Recruits"; Steigleder, *L'Opus Dei*, pp. 95–253; *Constituciones*, Article 447.

55. Ibid.; Thierry, *Opus Dei*, pp. 53–64; *Tiempo*, July 28, 1986.

56. Ibid.; Escrivá, *The Way*, p. 26; Kamm, "The Secret World of Opus Dei"; Tapia, "Good Housekeepers for Opus Dei."

57. Author's interview with Sargent Shriver, Washington, D.C., May 1986.

58. *Constituciones*, Articles 55 and 59; Sandro Magister, *"Santa Facciatosta," L'Espresso* (Rome), March 2, 1986; author's interview with Magister, Rome, October 1986; *Tiempo*, July 7, 14, and 28, 1986; author's interview with Rocca, October 1986; Tapia, "Good Housekeepers for Opus Dei"; author's interview, Bogotá, September 1985; author's interview with Luis Gordon Beguer, Opus Dei spokesman, Madrid, October 1986.

59. Escrivá, *The Way*, p. 87; *Tiempo*, June 30, 1986; Kamm, "The Secret World of Opus Dei"; author's interview, Bogotá, ibid.; flyer describing Opus Dei's Roman Academic Center of the Holy Cross; author's interview with Magister, October 1986; author's interviews with Father Malcolm Kennedy, Opus Dei chaplain at the Heights School for Boys in Potomac, Maryland, in New York City, May 1986.

60. Author's interview, Bogotá, ibid.

61. Ibid.; *The Times*, January 12, 1981; Roche, "Winning Recruits."

62. Roche, ibid.

63. Ibid.

64. Tapia, "Good Housekeepers for Opus Dei."

65. Steigleder, *L'Opus Dei*, pp. 95–253; *Newsweek*, March 24, 1986.

66. Tapia, "Good Housekeepers for Opus Dei"; author's interviews, Rome and Madrid, October 1986.

67. Tapia, ibid.

68. Rocca, *L' "Opus Dei,"* pp. 78–79; *Vida Nueva*, November 3, 1979; author's interview with Maurizio Di Giacomo, an Italian journalist and specialist on Opus Dei, Rome, October 1986.

69. Ibid.; Tapia, "Good Housekeepers for Opus Dei"; Zízola, *La Restauración del Papa Wojtyla*, pp. 160–61; *National Catholic Reporter*, April 18, 1980; *El País* (Madrid), October 23, 1986; *The Times*, January 12, 1981.

70. Ibid.; Rocca, *L' "Opus Dei,"* pp. 78–79; *Vida Nueva*, November 3, 1979; author's interview with Di Giacomo, October 1986; author's interview, South America, 1984.

71. Zízola, *La Restauración del Papa Wojtyla*, pp. 159–66; Rocca, ibid.; author's interviews with Rocca, Di Giacomo, Magister, and Lamet, October 1986; *Vida Nueva*, November 3, 1979; *Tiempo*, April 8, 1986; *National Catholic Reporter*, April 18, 1980; Magister, *"Santa Facciatosta."*

72. *MIZ* (West Berlin), March 15, 1986; Associated Press, January 15, 1984; *Columbia* (Knights of Columbus publication), March 1985; *National Catholic Reporter*, April 18, 1980, and December 14, 1984; *Time*, June 11, 1984; Adista religious news agency, April 21, 1986; *Tiempo*, April 8, 1986; author's interviews, Rome and Madrid, October 1986, and Bogotá, June 1986 and February 1987; Zízola, *La Restauración del Papa Wojtyla*, p. 176; *Church & State*, September 1985.

73. Kamm, "The Secret World of Opus Dei."

74. Adista religious news service, December 11, 1986; *Newsweek*, March 24, 1986; *National Catholic Reporter*, March 28, 1986; *L'Espresso*, December

7, 1986; *O São Paulo*, January 15, 1987; *Church & State*, September 1985.

75. *El País*, October 23, 1986; Zízola, *La Restauración del Papa Wojtyla*, pp. 166–77; *Church & State*, ibid.; Lernoux, *In Banks We Trust*, pp. 215–18.

76. *Semana* (Bogotá), April 23, 1985; author's interview with Giuseppe Corigliano, Opus Dei spokesman, Rome, October 1986; *Time*, June 11, 1984; Lee, "Who Are the Knights of Malta?"; United Press International, October 8, 1978; Associated Press, November 14, 1978.

77. Promotional literature on Alborada and the Opus Dei agricultural school, Las Garzas; author's interviews, Bogotá, August 1985, and Rome, October 1986.

78. Author's interviews, Bogotá, 1986; promotional literature on Universidad de la Sabana.

79. Adista religious news service, November 10, 1986, and April 16 and 21, 1987; *National Catholic Reporter*, December 19, 1986; Brooklyn *Tablet*, September 13, 1986; *Latinamerica Press*, November 11 and 27, 1986.

80. Author's interviews, Bogotá, August 1985, and Madrid, October 1986.

81. *National Catholic Reporter*, January 23, 1981; *Church & State*, September 1985.

82. José A. Vidal-Quadras, "Torreciudad, a Shrine to Our Lady," 1978; *Tiempo*, July 14, 1986.

83. *The Times*, January 12, 1981; *Vida Nueva*, August 16, 1986; *Tiempo*, ibid., and July 21, 1986; author's interviews, Madrid, October 1986.

84. Ernesto Ekaizer, *José Maria Ruíz Mateos, El Ultimo Magnate* (Madrid: Plaza & Janes, 1985), pp. 93–94; R. T. Naylor, *Hot Money and the Politics of Debt* (New York: Linden Press, 1987), p. 128; *Wall Street Journal*, December 30, 1982; *Tiempo*, July 14, 1986.

85. Ekaizer, ibid., pp. 7, 19, 403–40, 630, 714; Naylor, ibid., p. 129; *Business Week*, March 14, 1983; *The Economist*, March 5, 1983.

86. Ekaizer, ibid., pp. 327–41, 351–56, 403–40; 621, 711–18; author's interviews, Madrid, October 1986; author's interview with José María Ruíz Mateos, Madrid, October 1986.

87. Ekaizer, ibid., p. 712; author's interviews, Madrid, October 1986; author's interview, Ruíz Mateos, ibid.

88. Ekaizer, ibid., pp. 351–65, 509–528, 616–23; author's interviews, ibid.; *The Economist*, April 16, 1983; press release, Opus Dei, April 30, 1986.

89. Author's interview with Ruíz Mateos, October 1986.

90. Ibid.; author's interviews, Madrid, October 1986; author's interview with Beguer, October 1986.

91. Author's interview, Madrid, October 1986.

92. Pedro Miguel Lamet, " 'Comunión y Liberación,' en España," *Vida Nueva*, November 9, 1985.

93. Author's interviews, New York City and Washington, D.C., May 1986, and Rome, Bologna, Milan, and Madrid, October 1986; Franco Ottaviano, *Gli Estremisti Bianchi* (Rome: Datanews, 1986), pp. 73–176.

94. Ottaviano, ibid., pp. 9–42; Rocca Buttiglione, "Comunione e Liberazione," paper, October 1985; Michael Waldstein and Kevin Flannery, S.J., "Why Communion and Liberation Attracted Two in Boston," *National Catholic Reporter*, February 20, 1987; *Semana*, February 5, 1985; author's interviews, Milan, October 1986.

95. Ottaviano, ibid.; Buttiglione, ibid.; author's interview with Maurizio Vitali, director of CL magazine, *Litterae Communionis*, Milan, October 1986; *Jesus* (Rome), August 1985; Fausto Perrenchio, "La Fraternita di Comunione e Liberazione," *Aggiornamenti Sociali* (Milan), April 1983; decree recognizing the "Fraternita di Comunione e Liberazione" by the Pontificum Consilium Pro Laicis, February 11, 1982. For a sample of Guissani's writings, see *Huellas de experiencia cristiana* and *El sentido religioso* (Madrid: Ediciones Encuentro,

1978); *Moralidad: memoria y deseo* (Ediciones Encuentro, 1983); and *En busca del rostro humano* (Ediciones Encuentro, 1985).

96. Author's interviews, Rome and Milan, October 1986; author's interview with Vitali, ibid.; Ottaviano, ibid., pp. 56–169; *Vida Nueva*, February 14, 1987; Adista religious news service, January 7, 1987; *Time*, September 8, 1986.

97. Ottaviano, ibid., p. 111, citing *Litterae Communionis*, January 1986; Giussani, *Huellas* . . . , ibid., p. 166; Adista religious news service, November 3, 1986.

98. Author's interviews, Milan, October 1986.

99. Ibid.; Buttiglione, "Comunione e Liberazione"; *Time*, September 8, 1986.

100. Author's interviews, Milan, October 1986; author's interview with Auxiliary Bishop Giovanni Saldarini, Milan, October 1986.

101. Author's interview, Milan, October 1986.

102. Author's interview with Saldarini, October 1986; author's interview with Father Angelo Macchi, Milan, October 1986.

103. Ottaviano, *Gli Estremisti Bianche*, pp. 73–169; author's interviews with Vitali and Macchi, October 1986; *Time*, September 8, 1986; Alfredo Giannantonio, untitled paper on CL, Milan, December 1986.

104. Ibid.; author's interviews, Milan, October 1986; Adista religious news service, December 5, 1985, and January 7, March 26, and May 4, 1987.

105. Author's interviews, Rome and Milan, October 1986; *Cristiani a Genova* (Genoa), December 10, 1983; *30 Giorni*, April 1986; Adista religious news service, December 5, 1985.

106. Author's interviews, Milan, October 1987; author's interview with Archbishop Rembert Weakland, Appleton, Wisconsin, May 1987.

107. Author's interviews, Rome and Milan, October 1987; copy of program for U.S. conference on "The Christian Between the Demands of Faith and the Duties of a Career," sponsored by the Pontifical Council for the Laity, 1986; Adista religious news service, November 14, 1986.

108. Author's interviews, Rome and Milan, October 1986; correspondence with author, October 1984.

109. Ottaviano, *Gli Estremisti Bianche*, pp. 146–47.

110. Pope John Paul, "Build the Civilization of Truth and Love," speech at CL annual youth festival in Rimini, August 29, 1982, and "Go into All the World," speech by John Paul on the occasion of the thirtieth anniversary of Communion and Liberation, in "Communion and Liberation," *Litterae Communionis*, Document No. 7, Milan, n.d.

111. Author's interviews, Washington, D.C., May 1986, and Rome, October 1986.

112. Adista religious news service, February 10, 1986; *National Catholic Reporter*, March 28, 1986; author's interviews, New York City, May 1986, and Milan, October 1986.

113. Adista religious news service, April 27, 1987; Cardinal Joseph Ratzinger with Vittorio Messori, *The Ratzinger Report* (San Francisco: Ignatius Press, 1985), p. 43; *National Catholic Reporter*, May 29, 1987.

114. *National Catholic Reporter*, March 28, 1986; Ottaviano, *Gli Estremisti Bianche*, pp. 104–105, 140; author's interview, Bologna, October 1986.

115. Paolo Danuvola, "L'Azione Cattolica nella Chiesa Italiana," *Aggiornamenti Sociali*, September/October, 1986; Giannantonio, untitled paper on CL, December 1986; author's interviews, Milan, October 1986.

116. Ottaviano, *Gli Estremisti Bianche*, p. 90; Adista religious news service, May 4, 1987; *National Catholic Reporter*, May 16, 1986; author's interview with Father Gaston Brambilasca, Milan, October 1986.

117. *National Catholic Reporter*,

ibid.; Giannantonio, untitled paper on CL, December 1986; author's interviews, Rome and Milan, October 1986.
118. *O São Paulo*, May 16, 1986; *National Catholic Reporter*, ibid.; Adista religious news agency, March 23, 1987; *Vida Nueva*, April 4, 1987.
119. Author's interviews, Rome, Bologna, and Milan, October 1986; Adista religious news service, April 9 and 27, 1987.
120. *Vida Nueva*, May 30, 1987; Associated Press, May 25, 1987; *Catholic New York*, May 28, 1987.
121. *Manchete* (Brazil), May 13, 1978, and January 27, 1979; *The Providence Visitor*, April 1, 1976; *Veja* (Brazil), August 22, 1979; *Folha de São Paulo* (São Paulo), March 15, 1985; *Latinamerica Press*, December 6, 1984; Agence France-Presse, November 13, 1984; *El Diario de Caracas* (Caracas), October 11 and 21 and November 3, 1984; *El Nacional* (Caracas), October 10, 19, and 20, 1984; *El Universal* (Caracas), October 9 and 24, 1984; *El Mundo* (Caracas), November 14, 1984; *Semana* (Bogotá), November 20 and December 3 and 20, 1984; *El Espectador* (Bogotá), November 9, 1984; *The Daily Journal* (Caracas), January 26, 1985; *El Periodista* (Buenos Aires), November 24, 1984; criminal complaint filed with the Fiscalia General de la República de Venezuela, August 16, 1984; *Resumen* (Caracas), October 21, 1984; author's interviews, Caracas, 1984, and Bogotá, 1986; San Diego *Union*, February 22, 1985; letter from President Ronald Reagan to John R. Spann, American TFP president, February 13, 1984.
122. *Tradición, Familia Propiedad Informa*, Bogotá, May 1982; *Folha de São Paulo*, ibid.; *El Universal*, October 9, 1984; interview, Bogotá, 1986; Bruce Frankel, "Foundation Shrouded in Mystery Here," *Reporter Dispatch*, March 13, 1979, and "A Return to the Middle Ages," *Reporter Dispatch*, March 12, 1979; Plinio Correa de Oliveira, *Revolución y Contra-Revolucion* (Santiago:

Ediciones Paulinas, 1959); Tradición, Familia Propiedad, *Medio Siglo de epopeya anticomunista* (Madrid: Editorial Fernando III El Santo, 1983).
123. "Inconformidad," No. 18 (TFP Bogotá publication), n.d.; interview, Bogotá, 1986; Frankel, "A return . . ."; *El Mundo*, November 14, 1984; *Folha de São Paulo*, March 15, 1985.
124. Frankel, ibid.; *El Periodista*, November 24, 1984; *Manchete*, May 13, 1978; *El Diario de Caracas*, October 21, 1984; criminal complaint . . . , August 16, 1984; author's interviews, Caracas, 1984; Daniel Samper, "Los motivos del león," *El Tiempo*, January 13, 1985; *El Universal*, October 9, 1984; San Diego *Union*, February 22, 1985; *Istoé* (Brazil), September 5, 1984; letter from Joseph Becelia, first secretary of the U.S. Embassy, Brasilia, March 14, 1979; Frankel, "Foundation shrouded . . . ."
125. *El Universal*, October 9 and 24, 1984; author's interviews, Caracas, 1984; correspondence, March 16, 1979, and March 29, 1985; *El Espectador*, December 8, 1984.
126. *Latin America Weekly Report*, October 19, 1984; Lernoux, *Cry of the People*, pp. 161, 283, 294–304; Audrey Stone, "On Behalf of Tradition: A Study of Opus Dei and Tradition, Family and Property" (unpublished thesis), April 14, 1986; Thomas Niehaus and Brady Tysen, "The Catholic Right in Contemporary Brazil: The Case of the Society for the Defense of Tradition, Family and Property (TFP)," *Religion in Latin American Life and Literature* (Waco: Marrkham Press fund, 1980), p. 399; Frederick C. Turner, *Catholicism and Political Development in Latin America* (Chapel Hill: University of North Carolina Press, 1971), p. 99; Walter Sampson, "Fatima," *Covert Action*, Spring 1987; Council on Hemispheric Affairs, *Washington Report on the Hemisphere*, January 12, 1982; Frankel, "Foundation shrouded . . ."; "La Izquierda 'Católica' incita a la guerrilla en Iberoamérica, *Tra-*

dición, *Familia Propiedad Informa,* n.d.;
Latin America (London), June 6, 1975;
Latinamerica Press, September 4, 1986.

127. *El Nacional,* May 22, 1985;
Lernoux, *Cry of the People,* p. 192;
Frankel, ibid.; Sociedad Colombiana de
Defensa de la Tradición, Familia y Pro-
piedad, "Elenco de actividades de la TFP
colombiana, 1969–83," n.d.; Merrill
Collett, "Tradition, Family and Property
Fights Sex and Socialism" (paper), Ca-
racas, 1985; *Solidaridad* (Bogotá), July
1986.

128. Lernoux, ibid., pp. 295–300;
Thomas G. Sanders and Brian H. Smith,
"The Catholic Church under a Military
Regime," *Military Government and the
Movement Toward Democracy in South
America* (Bloomington: Indiana Univer-
sity Press, 1981), p. 338; *Washington Re-
port on the Hemisphere,* January 12,
1982; letter from Thomas Quigley,
March 21, 1979; *The Providence Visitor,*
April 1, 1976.

129. See Note 121; also, *Cristianità,*
April 1983; *Alleanza Cattolica* (Italy),
November 1984 and February 1985;
Catholic New Times (Canada); *Tradición
Familia Propiedad Informa,* No. 22, May
1982; *Washington Post,* December 9 and
10, 1981; *Semana,* December 3, 1984;
Latinamerica Press, December 6, 1984;
Collett, "Tradition, Family . . ." (paper).

130. *El Universal,* October 9, 1984;
subscription application to *The American*
TFP; IRS Form 990 for private founda-
tion tax exemption filed by the Foundation for a Christian Civilization, Inc.;
Frankel, "Foundation Shrouded . . .";
The Reporter Dispatch, March 12 and 14,
1979; *Patent Trader,* April 5, 1979;
Church & State, July/August, 1979; letter
from Beth D. Randall, director, New
York State Regional Office, Anti-Defa-
mation League of B'nai B'rith, New
York City, March 22, 1979; *New York
Times,* December 17, 1978; *Covert Ac-
tion,* Summer 1986; *TFP Newsletter,* vol.
IV, nos. 19 and 20, 1986; interview, Bo-
gotá, 1986; *National Catholic Reporter,*

October 17, 1986; author's interviews,
Washington, D.C., May 1986.

131. Author's interviews, Caracas,
1984; Collett, "Tradition, Family . . ."
(paper); *El Nacional,* May 22, 1985;
Samper, "Los motivos del león"; *El Periodista,* November 24, 1984; criminal
complaint, August 16, 1984.

132. Ibid.

133. Ibid.; *El Portero* (Buenos
Aires), May 1985.

134. Ibid.; *El Universal* (statement
by José L. Salas Abad), October 24,
1984; *Manchete,* May 13, 1978.

Chapter 11:
The Banner Carriers

1. *Vida Nueva,* October 31 and November 7, 1987; *National Catholic Reporter,* November 6 and 13, 1987.

2. Adista religious news service,
October 22, 1987; *Vida Nueva,* October
24 and November 7, 1987; *National Catholic Reporter,* October 23, 1987.

3. Ibid.; *L'Osservatore Romano,*
October 26 and November 2, 1987; *National Catholic Reporter,* November 6
and 13, 1987.

4. *Vida Nueva,* November 21, 1987;
National Catholic Reporter, October 23
and November 6, 20, and 27, 1987; *Time,*
November 9, 1987.

5. *National Catholic Reporter,* November 6 and 27, 1987.

6. *Vida Nueva,* November 7, 1987;
National Catholic Reporter, November 6,
1987.

7. *Newsweek,* October 20, 1986;
National Catholic Reporter, September
26, 1986, and May 15, 1987; *Vida Nueva,*
May 16 and July 11, 1987; author's interview, Milan, October 1986.

8. Author's interview, Latin America, 1984.

9. Author's interviews, Bogotá,
September 1986.

10. *The Ratzinger Report* (San
Francisco: Ignatius Press, 1985), pp.
59–61; Peter Hebblethwaite, "Bishops'

Groups Draw Fire from Ratzinger," *National Catholic Reporter*, December 14, 1984.

11. Giancarlo Zízola, *La Restauración del Papa Wojtyla* (Madrid: Ediciones Cristiandad, 1985), pp. 211–24.

12. Ibid., pp. 215–16; Paul Johnson, *Pope John Paul II and the Catholic Restoration* (Ann Arbor: Servant Books, 1981), p. 129; *National Catholic Reporter*, November 22, 1985.

13. Zízola, *La Restauración del Papa Wojtyla*, p. 149.

14. Ibid., p. 153; author's interviews, New York, May 1986, and Rome, October 1986; EFE Spanish news agency, August 10, 1980.

15. *National Catholic Reporter*, November 6, 1981, and March 12, 1982.

16. United Press International, September 13, 1983; *National Catholic Reporter*, November 9, 1984; author's interviews, Rome, October 1986; *Vida Neuva*, January 31, 1987.

17. Zízola, *La Restauración del Papa Wojtyla*, pp. 230–31; *National Catholic Reporter*, March 13, 1987; *Vida Nueva*, January 10 and April 18, 1987.

18. Ibid.; author's interviews, Washington, D.C., May 1986, and Rome and Madrid, October 1986.

19. Author's interviews, Rome, October 1986.

20. Author's interviews, including interview with Eugenio Melandri, Rome, October 1986; "Nicaragua: La Poesia Difficile," *Missione Oggi*, December 1985; "Il nostro mercato di morte," *Nigrizia*, October 1985; Adista religious news agency, February 23, 1987; *National Catholic Reporter*, May 22, 1987.

21. *National Catholic Reporter*, ibid; *Vida Nueva*, May 30, 1987.

22. *Vida Nueva*, December 5, 1987; author's interview with the Rev. Pedro Lamet, S.J. Madrid, October 1986.

23. Peter Hebblethwaite, "Getting Back from the Brink with One Ultimate Catechism," *National Catholic Reporter*, February 27, 1987; author's interview, Rome, October 1986.

24. Adista news agency, December 5, 1985; *National Catholic Reporter*, January 24, 1986.

25. *Vida Nueva*, October 25, 1986.

Chapter 12:
The Nicaraguan Church

1. Author's interviews, Managua, March 1986, and Rome, October 1986.

2. Philip J. Williams, "The Catholic Hierarchy in the Nicaraguan Revolution," *Latin American Studies*, vol. 17, pp. 341–69; Michael Dodson, "Nicaragua," *Religion and Political Conflict in Latin America* (Chapel Hill: University of North Carolina Press, 1986), pp. 79–105; Nicaraguan Episcopal Conference, "Mensaje al Pueblo Nicaraguense: Momento Insurreccional," Managua, 1979.

3. Author's interviews, Managua, March 1986 and July 1988.

4. "Human Rights in Nicaragua," Americas Watch, March 1986, pp. 1–56; "Nicaragua: The Human Rights Record," Amnesty International, March 1986, pp. 20–21; author's interviews, Managua and Bogotá, March 1986; United States, May 1986; and Europe, October 1986; Agence France-Presse, July 6, 1987.

5. Author's interview, Managua, March 1986.

6. Author's interviews, Managua, March 1986.

7. Author's interview, Managua, March 1986.

8. Author's interview, Bogotá, March 1986.

9. Conor Cruise O'Brien, "God and Man in Nicaragua," *Atlantic Monthly*, August 1986.

10. Author's interview with the Rev. Richard John Neuhaus, New York City, May 1986.

11. *America*, November 29, 1986; "Letter," Ecumenical Committee of U.S. Citizens in Mexico, March 9, 1987; press release, Nicaraguan Embassy, Bo-

gotá, 1987; author's interview, Managua, March 1986.

12. Camilo Cano Busquets and María Jimena Duzán, "Borge 'contra' Galvin," *El Espectador* (Bogotá), May 31, 1987.

13. Ibid.

14. Author's interview, Washington, May 1986.

15. Author's interviews, Latin America, the United States, and Europe, 1986; *National Catholic Reporter*, February 21, 1986.

16. *National Jesuit News*, January 1987; the Rev. César Jerez, S.J., "The Church and the Nicaraguan Revolution" (London: Catholic Institute for International Relations, 1984); author's interview with Father Jerez, Managua, March 1986.

17. Ibid.; author's interviews, Bogotá, September 1986, and Rome, October 1986; *Washington Post*, November 29, 1986.

18. Author's interviews, Managua, March 1986 and July 1988; Jerez, "The Church and the Nicaraguan Revolution."

19. *National Jesuit News*, January 1987; Jerez, "The Church and the Nicaraguan Revolution"; author's interviews, United States, May and July 1986; Aryeh Neier, "After the Contras Are Gone," *New York Times*, January 13, 1987.

20. "Human Rights in Nicaragua," Americas Watch, March 1986; "Nicaragua: The Human Rights Record," Amnesty International, March 1986, pp. 1–36; author's interview with *Sojourners*, Washington, D.C., May 1986; *Semana* (Bogotá), June 9, 1987.

21. Dodson, "Nicaragua," pp. 98–99; "Update," Central American Historical Institute (Washington, D.C.), August 30 and December 19, 1984; United Press International, January 21, 1985; author's interviews, Managua, March 1986, and Rome, October 1986; Phillip Berryman, *The Religious Roots of Rebellion* (Maryknoll: Orbis, 1984), pp.

242–43; Associated Press, December 10, 1984, and October 27, 1985; *Latinamerica Press*, February 19, 1987; Episcopal Conference of Nicaragua, "Letter from the Conference of Bishops of Nicaragua to Bishops' Conferences Around the World," Managua, July 7, 1986; *Catholic New York*, July 17, 1986.

22. O'Brien, "God and Man in Nicaragua"; author's interviews, Managua, March 1986; Ansa Italian news agency, June 20, 1987.

23. Ibid.

24. Associated Press, October 31 and November 3, 1983; Patricia Hynds, "The Ideological Struggle Within the Catholic Church in Nicaragua," *Covert Action*, Winter 1983; "Interview with Archbishop of Managua," *Congressional Record*, April 18, 1985, pp. H2218–19.

25. Penny Lernoux, *Cry of the People* (New York: Penguin, 1982), pp. 81–89; correspondence with author, September 4 and October 9, 1986.

26. United Press International, December 23, 1983; *Washington Post*, December 23 and 24, 1983.

27. "Nicaragua: The Human Rights Record," Amnesty International, March 1986, p. 21; Agence France-Presse, July 9, 1984; *El Tiempo* (Bogotá), July 26, 1984; author's interviews, Managua, March 1986.

28. *Catholic New York*, June 26, 1986; "Nicaragua: The Human Rights Record," ibid., pp. 21–22; author's interviews, Managua, March 1986, and Bogotá, September 1986; interview by Father Thomas H. Stahel, S.J., of Foreign Minister Miguel D'Escoto, *America*, November 16, 1985.

29. Author's interviews, Managua, March 1986 and July 1988.

30. Ibid.; United Press International, October 26, 1985; "Human Rights in Nicaragua," Americas Watch, March 1986, p. 54.

31. Author's interviews, Managua, March 1986; "Human Rights in Nicaragua," ibid., pp. 48–49; *Latin American Weekly Report*, October 25, 1985; "Update," November 5, 1985; *New York Times*, June 20, 1986.

32. Associated Press, December 10, 1985; United Press International, January 2, 1986; *National Catholic Reporter*, February 14, 1986; author's interviews, Managua, March 1986; "Human Rights in Nicaragua," ibid., pp. 7, 50–51; *Catholic New York*, June 26, 1986; Cardinal Miguel Obando y Bravo, "Nicaragua: The Sandinistas Have 'Gagged and Bound' Us," *Washington Post*, May 12, 1986; *Time*, May 12, 1986; "Letter from the Conference of Bishops . . . ."

33. *National Catholic Reporter*, January 18, 1985; United Press International, January 9, 1985; author's interview with Sister Nancy Donovan, Managua, July 1988.

34. *Latin American Weekly Report*, July 16, 1987; *National Catholic Reporter*, July 17 and October 30, 1987.

35. Author's interviews, Managua March 1986; "Human Rights in Nicaragua," Americas Watch, March 1986, p. 87.

36. "Update," August 12, 1985; *Latinamerica Press*, September 10, 1987.

37. *New York Times*, July 6 and 17 and September 4, 1986; *Washington Post*, July 5 and 16, 1986; *National Catholic Reporter*, July 18 and August 15, 1986; the Rev. Joseph Mulligan, S.J., "Nicaraguan Bishops Continue Opposition Role," Instituto Histórico Centroamericano (Managua), March 1986; *Newsweek*, August 4, 1986; *Lucha* (New York), July/August, 1986; *Catholic New York*, July 31, August 7, and September 18, 1986; Associated Press, July 4, 1986.

38. *Newsweek*, ibid.; Richard Boudreaux, Associated Press series on the Catholic Church in Latin America, September 29, 1986; *National Catholic Reporter*, September 19, 1986, and January 30, 1987; EFE Spanish news agency, January 18, 1987; *New York Times*, January 19, 1987.

39. *National Catholic Reporter*, July 18, 1986; author's interviews, United States, July 1986; Bogotá, September 1986; and Rome, October 1986.

40. Interview with Bishop Pablo Antonio Vega, Bogotá, July 1986; *O São Paulo* (São Paulo), August 29 and September 12, 1986; author's interviews, Bogotá, September 1986, and Rome, October 1986; Ansa news service, September 16, 1986; *Catholic New York*, August 21, 1986; *New York Times*, September 28, 1986; *El Tiempo*, September 22, 1986; *Latinamerica Press*, October 23, 1986; *Latin American Regional Reports Mexico & Central America* (London), October 30, 1986; *Washington Post*, November 28, 1986; *National Catholic Reporter*, December 5, 1986; *Latin American Weekly Report*, April 16, 1987.

41. Author's interviews, Rome, October 1986.

42. Ibid.

43. Author's interviews, Rome, October 1986; *Catholic New York*, May 7, 1987.

44. *Washington Post*, November 29, 1986; *National Catholic Reporter*, August 29 and December 26, 1986; *Vida Nueva* (Madrid), January 2, March 14, and May 23, 1987; *Latinamerica Press*, February 26, 1987; *Latin American Regional Reports Mexico & Central America*, June 11, 1987; *The Nation*, April 18, 1987.

45. *National Catholic Reporter*, September 4, 1987; Associated Press, August 28 and November 7 and 14, 1987; *New York Times*, November 25, 1987; *Vida Nueva*, September 26, 1987.

46. *Latinamerica Press*, November 5, 1987; EFE news agency, November 7, 1987; *The Nation*, November 21, 1987; Reuters, December 14, 1987.

47. Author's interviews, Managua, March 1986; *Newsweek*, August 4, 1986; *Latinamerica Press*, December 4, 1986; "Letter" from the Ecumenical Committee . . . ; Boudreaux, Associated Press series, September 29, 1986.

48. Author's interviews, ibid.; Boudreaux, ibid.; Williams, "The Catholic Hierarchy . . ."; *El Tiempo*, May 1,

1985; *National Catholic Reporter*, March 14, 1986; *Time*, May 12, 1986; *Amanecer* (Managua), January/May, 1986; Berryman, *Religious Roots of Rebellion*, pp. 265–66.

49. "Update," January 21, 1986, and March 10, 1987; "Human Rights in Nicaragua: Reagan, Rhetoric and Reality," Americas Watch, July 1985, p. 39; *Crucible of Hope* (Washington: Sojourners, 1984), p. 31.

50. *Washington Times*, April 11, 1985; Jeanne Pugh, "Revolution Makes Religions Take Sides," *St. Petersburg Times*, January 18, 1986; *Barricada* (Managua), March 23, 1987; "Update," March 10, 1987.

51. "Update," ibid.; author's interview with Deborah Huntington, New York City, May 1986; *Crucible of Hope*, p. 31.; *Christianity Today*, February 6, 1987; author's interviews, Managua, March 1986.

52. Penny Lernoux, "Strangers in a Familiar Land," *The Nation*, September 14, 1985; interview with Tomás Borge by Tatiana Coll in *Por Esto*, No. 8, August 20, 1981, reprinted in *National Revolution and Indigenous Identity*, ed. Klaudine Ohland and Robin Schneider (Copenhagen: International Work Group for Indigenous Affairs, 1983), p. 192; "Ortega Speaks at CEPAD Meeting in Managua," Foreign Broadcast Information Service, November 19, 1986.

53. Ibid.

54. Ibid.; Penny Lernoux, "The Indians and the *Comandantes*," *The Nation*, September 28, 1985; Inter-American Commission on Human Rights, "Report on the Situation of Human Rights of a Segment of the Nicaraguan Population of Miskito Origin," Inter-American Commission on Human Rights, Organization of American States, 1984; *National Revolution and Indigenous Identity*, p. 192; "The Miskitos in Nicaragua," Americas Watch, November 1984; "Nicaragua: The Human Rights Record," Amnesty International, March 1986, pp. 7–10; "Annual Report of the Inter-American Commission on Human Rights, 1985–1986," Inter-American Commission on Human Rights, Organization of American States, 1986.

55. Ibid.; "Human Rights in Nicaragua: Reagan, Rhetoric and Reality," Americas Watch, July 1985, pp. 14 and 53; "Violations of the Laws of War by Both Sides in Nicaragua," Americas Watch, March 1985, p. 4; *Maryknoll*, March 1986.

56. *Wall Street Journal*, March 2, 1987; Margaret D. Wilde, "Christian Presence in Nicaragua: Separation and Hope," *The Saal*, Summer 1984; "Declaration of the VII Triennial Synod," Moravian Church in Nicaragua, Puerto Cabezas, Zelaya, February 20, 1986, published in *The North American Moravian*, May 1986; correspondence with author, March 5, 1987.

57. Correspondence, ibid.; Foreign Broadcasts, November 19, 1986; Gabriela Battaglia, "Nicaragua's Indians: Pariahs of the Revolution," *Swiss Review of World Affairs*, January 1987; *National Revolution and Indigenous Identity*, p. 192; author's interviews, Bogotá, 1985 and 1986, and Managua, March 1986 and July 1988.

58. Ibid.

59. The Rev. Daniel Berrigan, S.J., *Steadfastness of the Saints* (Maryknoll: Orbis, 1985), pp. 79–82.

60. *Religion & Democracy* (IRD), January 1983 and September 1984; news release from IRD, July 6, 1984; letter from IRD board members, the Revs. Richard J. Neuhaus and Edmund W. Robb, Jr., and Michael Novak, July 1984; *National Catholic Reporter*, March 30 and July 20, 1984; *The Christian Century*, November 28, 1984; *Sequoia*, August 1985.

61. *Religion and Democracy*, July 1984; *Amanecer*, May/July, 1986; Alexander Cockburn, "Beat the Devil," *The Nation*, June 13, 1987; "Letters," *The Nation*, November 7, 1987; Puebla In-

stitute promotional literature, Garden
City, Mich., n.d.

62. Cockburn, ibid., and "Beat the
Devil," *The Nation*, December 6, 1986;
Humberto Belli, *Breaking Faith* (West-
chester, Ill.: Crossway Books, 1985); author's interview with Lino Hernández,
director of the Permanent Human Rights
Commission in Nicaragua, Managua,
March 1986; author's interviews, Managua, March 1986; New York City and
Washington, D.C., May 1986; and Bogotá, September 1986; *America*, August
23, 1986; *National Catholic Reporter*,
May 23, 1986, and January 9, 1987; *Covert Action*, Spring 1987.

63. Author's interviews, Managua,
March 1986; Stahel interview, *America*,
November 16, 1985.

64. "Who Speaks for Nicaragua's
Evangelicals? An Interview with Kate
Rafferty of Open Doors," Briefing Pa-
per, Institute on Religion and Democ-
racy, Washington, D.C., January 1985;
Religion & Democracy, May/June, 1985;
Sojourners, March 1987.

65. *Sojourners*, ibid.; author's interview with Huntington, May 1986;
Christianity and Crisis, October 1, 1984;
author's interview with Neuhaus, May
1986.

66. *Newsweek*, June 15, 1987; Reuters, June 13, 1987; *National Catholic Reporter*, June 19 and July 3, 1987;
Latinamerica Press, July 9, 1987.

67. *Maryknoll*, April, 1986; author's interview with Huntington, May
1986; Berrigan, *Steadfastness of the
Saints*, p. 90.

68. *Latinamerica Press*, August 21,
1986.

Chapter 13:
The People of God

1. Umberto Eco, *The Name of the
Rose* (New York: Harcourt Brace Jo-
vanovich, 1983), p. 152.

2. *Newsweek*, December 9, 1985;
America, June 13, 1987.

3. *Sojourners*, December 1987.

4. Quoted in John A. Coleman, *An
American Strategic Theology* (New
York: Paulist Press, 1982), p. 126.

5. Richard Schaull, *Heralds of a
New Reformation* (Maryknoll: Orbis,
1984), p. 122.

6. The Rev. Walbert Buhlmann,
The Church of the Future (Maryknoll:
Orbis, 1986), pp. 26, 97.

7. *Vida Nueva*, November 7, 1987.

8. *Sojourners*, December 1987.

9. *National Catholic Reporter*, November 13, 1987.

10. Ibid.; author's interviews, Europe, Latin America, and the United
States, 1985, 1986, 1987, and 1988.

11. Richard Wightman Fox, book
review of *Caesar's Coin*, *National Catholic Reporter*, November 27, 1987.

12. *National Catholic Reporter*,
June 20, 1986; Herbert McClosky and
John Zaller, *The American Ethos* (Cambridge: Harvard University Press, 1984),
pp. 62–233.

13. *National Catholic Reporter*, Oc-
tober 24, 1986; John A. McDermott,
"Weakness Amid Strength: The Roman
Catholic Paradox," *New Oxford Review*,
July/August, 1986.

14. Msgr. George G. Higgins, "The
Social Mission of the Church After Vatican II," *America*, July 26, 1986.

15. *Latinamerica Press*, July 16,
1987.

16. The Rev. Fernando Bermúdez,
Death and Resurrection in Guatemala
(Maryknoll: Orbis, 1986), p. 67.

17. Ibid.

INDEX